THE LIVES OF AGNES SMEDLEY

The Lives of
AGNES SMEDLEY

RUTH PRICE

OXFORD
UNIVERSITY PRESS

2005

OXFORD
UNIVERSITY PRESS

Oxford   New York

Auckland   Bangkok   Buenos Aires   Cape Town   Chennai
Dar es Salaam   Delhi   Hong Kong   Istanbul   Karachi   Kolkata
Kuala Lumpur   Madrid   Melbourne   Mexico City   Mumbai   Nairobi
São Paulo   Shanghai   Taipei   Tokyo   Toronto

Published by Oxford University Press, Inc.
198 Madison Avenue, New York, NY 10016

www.oup.com

Library of Congress Cataloging-in-Publication Data
Price, Ruth, 1951–
The lives of Agnes Smedley / Ruth Price.
p. cm.
Includes bibliographical references and index.
ISBN-13: 978-0-19-514189-4
ISBN-10: 0-19-514189-X
1. Smedley, Agnes, 1892–1950.
2. Authors, American — 20th century — Biography.
3. Journalists — United States — Biography.
4. Feminists — United States — Biography.
5. Radicals — United States — Biography.
6. Espionage, Soviet — United States. I. Title.
PS3537.M16Z85   2004
818'.5209 — dc22   2004014874

Book design and composition by Mark McGarry, Texas Type & Book Works
Set in Electra

9 8 7 6 5 4 3 2 1
Printed in the United States of America
on acid-free paper

To David
For letting me speak

I will be as harsh as truth, and as uncompromising as justice. On this subject I do not wish to think, or speak, or write with moderation. No! No! Tell a man whose house is on fire to give him a moderate alarm; tell him to moderately rescue his wife from the hands of the ravisher . . . but tell me not to use moderation in a cause like the present! I am in earnest. I will not equivocate—I will not retreat a single inch—AND I WILL BE HEARD.

WILLIAM LLOYD GARRISON

CONTENTS

ACKNOWLEDGMENTS

First and foremost, I would like to thank the Library of Congress, my home away from home throughout the many years of this project. Without its extraordinary holdings, this book might well have been completed sooner, but it would have lacked the same depth. I am particularly grateful there to Thomas Mann for his unparalleled reference skills, and to Bruce Martin for ensuring that I always had a room in which to work. Thanks also to Sarah Prichard, George Caldwell, Carol Armbruster, Beverly Brannon, Jacqueline Goggin, John Earl Haynes, Virginia Wood, Chris Wright, Judy Lu, Allen Thrasher, Sam Andrusco, and the late Louis Jacob, whose reference assistance went well beyond the call of duty. At the National Archives, John Taylor and David Keppley were an invaluable resource, as was Henry Guzda at the Department of Labor. The National Endowment for the Humanities, the American Institute of Indian Studies, the International Research and Exchanges Board, and the D.C. Commission on the Arts and Humanities provided critical support at an early stage. Tappan Mukherjee, Elliot Porter, Krishna Bose, Jane Singh, Barbara Ramusack, Nirode Barooah, and Kathleen Suneja made the India sections of this book more possible. E. Grey Diamond, Robert Farnsworth, Lynn Lubkeman, Ruth Weiss Yeh, Jack Hamilton, Tom Grunfeld, Hugh Deane, Huang Hua, Luo Ying, Zhou Peiyun, Liu Liqun, Jiang Feng, An Wei, Li Shoubao, Lu Fu-Jia, and the Smedley-Strong-Snow Society rendered able assistance on the China chapters. Todd Weinberg, Kate Watters, Stephen Koch, and Harvey Klehr greatly facilitated my Moscow research. I am forever grateful to Tillie Olsen, Sharon Negri, Louise de Salvo, Robert Gottlieb, Arnold Rampersad, Carter McKenzie, Claudia LeMarquand, Rachel Gorlin, Chia-kun Chu, Joyce Seltzer, Sheri Holman, Ida Zakula, Sheila Keifetz, Anne Colcord, Judy Gregory, Donald Sheckler, Billy Privett, George Humphries, John Rojas, Martin Rosenblatt, Jonathan House, Judith Schwarz, Lee Anderson, Donna Sicklesmith, Lynn Goldfarb, Ken Locker, Robert Soloman, Birgit Schafer, Liva Baker and the late Erwin Glickes, Elizabeth Smedley, Florence Becker Lennon, Toni Willison, and Betty Barnes; to my agent, Elizabeth Sheinkman; to my editor, Peter Ginna, and, also at Oxford, Furaha Norton, Joellyn Ausanka, and India Cooper; to my dear friends Douglas and Tonette Jacob, Annie Ross, Lexie Freeman, Michael Mannion, Kira Ferrand, Frank Clemente, Bristow Hardin, Mark Splain, and Barbara Bowen; and to my son, Ethan, who has never known me without Agnes.

A NOTE ON SPELLING

Because this book is about the life and times of Agnes Smedley, I have decided to use the Wade-Giles rather than the Pinyin system in the spelling of Chinese names and places, since it was the one in use during her lifetime and allows more name recognition for the general reader.

LIST OF ABBREVIATIONS

ABMAC	American Bureau for Medical Aid to China
ACLU	American Civil Liberties Union
BIC	Berlin India Committee
CCP	Chinese Communist Party
CCCP	Russian Communist Party
CFCFEP	Committee for a Democratic Far Eastern Policy
CF&I	Colorado Fuel and Iron Company
CIA	Central Intelligence Agency
CPUSA	American Communist Party
FBI	Federal Bureau of Investigation
FEB	Far East Bureau of the Comintern
FEC	Far East Command
FFFI	Friends of Freedom for India
GRU	Soviet Military Intelligence
HUAC	House Un-American Activities Committee
IAH	Workers International Aid
IPR	Institute of Pacific Relations
IURW	International Union of Revolutionary Writers
IWW	Industrial Workers of the World
KMT	Kuomintang Party
KPD	German Communist Party

LAI	League Against Imperialism
LLWW	League of Left Wing Writers
OMS	Comintern Department of International Liaison
PPTUS	Pan Pacific Trade Union Secretariat
SCAP	Supreme Commander of the Allied Powers
SMP	Shanghai Municipal Police
UMW	United Mine Workers of America
WFM	Western Federation of Miners

THE LIVES OF AGNES SMEDLEY

Introduction

I may not be innocent, but I'm right.

AGNES SMEDLEY, 1932

THE PUBLICATION of this book represents the culmination of a personal and intellectual odyssey that has consumed me for over a decade and a half. My acquaintance with Agnes Smedley began as a graduate student in literature at the City College of New York in 1976. At a particularly low point in that city's now forgotten fiscal crisis, I arrived at the Harlem campus one morning to find my path barred by police cars. Until the budget situation was resolved, all classes were canceled. Approaching the grim matter as a brief vacation, I headed for a bookstore, where my search for a good read led me to a reprint of Smedley's 1929 novel, *Daughter of Earth*, which was then enjoying a rebirth in women's studies circles. I spent the following days on a friend's couch, mesmerized by the dark, raw power of Smedley's book. It was one of those stories that, when read at the right time, permanently alters one's sensibility.

"What I have written is not a work of beauty," she begins.

It is the story of a life, written in desperation, in unhappiness... To die would have been beautiful. But I belong to those who do not die for the sake of beauty. I belong to those who die from other causes—exhausted by poverty, victims of wealth and power, fighters in a great cause. A few of us die, desperate from the pain or disillusionment of love, but for most of us "the earthquake but discloseth new foundations." For we are of the earth and our struggle is the struggle of earth.[1]

Like many first novels, *Daughter of Earth* was a coming-of-age tale. But this was about a young woman from a family like mine—a working-class family—that lacked the emotional and financial resources to nurture its gifted daughter. Smedley's bitter exploration of the psychic damage sustained by her heroine, which no adult fame or glory ever fully redressed, spoke a truth I had not previously encountered in fiction. So did her heroine's instinctive embrace of radical politics as an expression of personal pain. If this book had made such an impression on me, I wondered, why was its author so unknown?

Over the next several years, as I struggled to find my own way as a writer, I had neither the time nor the means to indulge my curiosity. It was not until the mid-1980s that I took up my sojourn with Smedley. Soon enough, I discovered that Agnes Smedley (1892–1950) was one of the most significant American women of the twentieth century—a flamboyant journalist, feminist, and political activist who made historic contributions to letters and politics on three continents. Indeed, it seemed she had crammed enough experience, and enough controversy, into her fifty-eight years to fill the lifetimes of several lesser women.

One measure of the size of Smedley's life, and the magnetism of her personality, was the extraordinary roster of her friends, who included Margaret Sanger, Emma Goldman, Roger Baldwin, Upton Sinclair, Kaethe Kollwitz, Madame Sun Yat-sen, Mao Tse-tung, Jawaharlal Nehru, Langston Hughes, Carson McCullers, General Joseph Stilwell, Harold Ickes, Edgar Snow, Theodore White, and Katherine Anne Porter. The roster of her enemies was no less noteworthy, from J. Edgar Hoover to Chiang Kai-shek, Douglas MacArthur, Elizabeth Hardwick, and Robert Lowell.

A highly abbreviated summary of Smedley's life, mentioning only some of its most prominent episodes decade by decade, might run as follows:

—In the first years of the 1900s, Agnes came of age in the Colorado labor wars that culminated in the Ludlow Massacre.

—In the 1910s, she became a radical activist in California, threw herself into India's fight for freedom from British rule, and then moved to Greenwich Village, where she became Margaret Sanger's right hand in the fledgling birth control movement and was accused of being a German agent.

—In the 1930s, she fell in love with China and filed groundbreaking articles as the first Western journalist to cover the Chinese Communists after Chiang Kai-shek turned on them, faced death alongside Chinese soldiers in the Sino-Japanese War, and wrote three acclaimed books about the Chinese Revolution.

—In the 1940s, she published a best-selling memoir, joined a circle of prominent American writers at Yaddo, the celebrated writers' colony, and generated a political firestorm as she fought off accusations by General MacArthur's staff and U.S. cold warriors that she had run a Soviet spy ring in Shanghai.

—In 1950, Smedley died while under investigation by the House Un-American Activities Committee and was buried in the People's Cemetery for Revolutionary Martyrs in Beijing—leaving behind a still-boiling debate over her alleged conspiracy with Communist agents.

Newspaper headlines regularly marked the swath Agnes cut through history:

—From 1918: HOLD AMERICAN GIRL AS INDIA PLOTTER; AGNES SMEDLEY ACCUSED OF TRYING TO CAUSE UPRISINGS AGAINST THE BRITISH.

—From 1937: AMERICAN WOMAN AIDS CHINESE RISING: AGNES SMEDLEY, AUTHOR, TAKES LEADING ROLE AS 250,000 MEN PLOT NORTHWEST RED REGIME.

—From 1950: AGNES SMEDLEY'S DEATH LINKED TO RED SPY RING: AUTHORESS WAS READY TO TESTIFY.

More than the headlines, it was Smedley's own writing that drew me to her. In addition to her novel, I discovered scores of articles, literary and political, that she had written for the *Nation*, the *Manchester Guardian*, the *New Republic*, and other publications across the globe. In these pieces, and in her three books of China reportage, one biography, and a memoir, Smedley's ear for dialogue and gift for physical description, along with considerable narrative skill, turned otherwise obscure tales of political upheaval into epic adventures in which decent, uneducated people, tried beyond their limits, found the fire and courage to rise up against oppression.

Most engaging of all was Agnes's correspondence, in which her outsized personality fairly leapt off the page.

"Of course you curse because you get such little information from here," read one letter from the Chinese Communists' base in Yenan, where Agnes was the first Western journalist in residence. "Well ... I'll give you gossip." She then related how she had outraged some Red Army leaders—and especially their wives—by teaching others among the leaders Western dances.

Chu Teh's wife laid down the law against our dancing here. First I taught Ho Lung to foxtrot one afternoon, and he can foxtrot, boy! He's filled with rhythm and music ... I suppose [it was considered] a kind of public sexual intercourse ... and ... a fine story got about ... I've got a reputation for corrupting the Army. It does not worry me at all ... I haven't "corrupted" Mao yet, but I shall do so soon. He said that if he ever goes abroad, he will study dancing and singing—that he wishes to learn the latest foxtrots! I think he should leave his wife here if he does.[2]

The note was vintage Agnes. So was the following, penned some years earlier during her stay in Weimar Berlin and full of the anguish that was the obverse of her brassy self-confidence.

> I am writing this in the middle of the night.
>   I cannot hold out. All my sleeplessness and my "insane" spells . . . have returned to torture me. How long I can last I do not know. I prefer death to these spells . . . The nights approach with their burden of dread . . . My subconscious . . . seems to be a nest of fear.[3]

What biographer could resist a subject who revealed her feelings with such candor? No aspect of Agnes's life seemed too private to reveal to friends. Exposure to Margaret Sanger and Greenwich Village bohemia had taught Smedley the pursuit, if not always the fulfillment, of an active sex life, and her correspondence teemed with intimate details, often related with wry humor. "Out here," Smedley wrote soon after her arrival in China in 1929, "I've had chances to sleep with all colors and shapes. One French gun-runner, short and round and bumpy; one fifty year old monarchist German who believes in the dominating role of the penis in influencing women; one high Chinese official whose actions I'm ashamed to describe; one round left-wing Kuomintang man who was soft and slobbery."[4]

It was her defiance, though, that cemented my attachment. If Mao's wife didn't like Smedley's behavior—which she distinctly did not—then she could kiss Smedley's rear end. If American officials objected to Smedley's political agitation against the government of Chiang Kai-shek, too bad for them. "Why should I do anything to please the gangsters, money changers, slave dealers, opium traffickers, and salesmen of China?" she snarled. "For the sake of the American people who read my writings, for the sake of the Chinese masses whom I defend, I have not the least intention of taking any action that could please the counter-revolution or its paymasters, Japanese and other imperialists."[5] She was a virago who challenged the world.

Smedley sparked intense and divergent emotional responses in a tremendous range of people. Political conservatives saw her as either a dizzy camp follower of the Chinese Communists or a dangerous revolutionary to be suppressed at all costs. Most of her radical contemporaries thought her intellectually and temperamentally unfit to be a serious revolutionary at all. Fellow journalists dismissed her fervent brand of reportage as wildly slanted; others were offended by what they considered her unfeminine and immoral personal conduct. Among those who actually knew her, the majority tended to see either a troubled, unstable eccentric or an impossibly soft-hearted dreamer. Yet she earned the lifelong affection and staunch loyalty of such friends as Edgar Snow and Katherine Anne Porter.

The debate surrounding Agnes Smedley's character and actions is still taking place. Depending on their personal politics, contemporary scholars see her either as a selfless activist devoted to the Chinese people or another 1930s-style American radical deluded by her love for Moscow. Modern feminists have reclaimed her as a prototype for today's emancipated woman, hailing the very behavior that was formerly reviled. Others still cannot see past Smedley's anger to glimpse the woman beneath. Only Agnes Smedley's closest personal friends, and the enduring admirers of her autobiographical novel, *Daughter of Earth,* have gotten beyond black-and-white judgments based on Smedley's political activities or unorthodox personal life to perceive the deeper significance of who she was: a rebel in the largest and finest sense of the word.[6]

Agnes Smedley worked for many of the same political causes as her leftist peers and shared their hunger to extend justice, freedom, and equality to all. But she was never a 1930s-style American radical. Smedley's radicalism came out of a different—rebellious—tradition. Unlike many of the more cynical revolutionaries with whom she was often confused in later years, Smedley's rebellion, however anguished, was always an attempt to serve life, not deny it. Nowhere was this conflict of traditions more evident than in Smedley's split from her contemporaries on that crucial issue for all radicals during the first half of the twentieth century: whether the Soviet Union was in fact the Promised Land.

Like every radical's of her era, Agnes Smedley's political views were markedly influenced by the Bolshevik Revolution. However, unlike most of her peers, Smedley quickly withdrew her unqualified support when the new Soviet government sacrificed individual freedom in order to consolidate power in the state. Although Smedley valued Russia's dramatic efforts to equalize opportunity for its people and enthusiastically supported the Third International's utopian promise of one harmonious world society, she did not link her beliefs to the theoretical shifting sands of Soviet Communism during her lifetime; her grasp of Marxism was rudimentary at best. Instead, what Smedley accepted was what she could verify from her own personal experience, and that did not include postponing the relief of mankind's suffering while something could be done. As a result, during a period when few of her more doctrinaire colleagues questioned Stalin's wisdom in determining their attitudes and actions, Smedley obstinately pursued her own course. Or so I thought.

Soon enough, my exploration of the controversial issues surrounding Smedley's relationship to Communism, to various Communist parties, and to the

Communist International, and—the $64,000 question—whether she engaged in espionage on behalf of the Soviet Union during her years in China proved unsettling.

For more than half a century, the right has promoted the view that whether or not it can actually prove that Smedley was a Communist or belonged to a Communist Party, she was, and in that capacity she worked for the Comintern in China and spied for the Soviet Union—and was an evil hussy to boot. No less adamantly, the left has maintained that Smedley was an unblemished heroine, the tragic victim of a McCarthyite smear who was neither a Communist, a member of any Communist Party, an agent of the Comintern, nor a Soviet spy. As a self-identified leftist, I, too, initially dismissed the accusations against Smedley. *My* Smedley was an uncompromising rebel, and I was certain that the charges against her had been triggered by people as frightened by her unbroken, independent spirit as her supposed "Communism." I hoped in my research to exonerate Agnes once and for all of the cold war accusations against her. But there were some problems.

Relatively early in my inquiry, I discovered a cache of materials written by Agnes that had been preserved in Moscow, making her the only American besides John Reed with a collection of papers in a Soviet literary archive. No one could explain to me why the papers had been saved. There were also FBI interviews with Agnes's contemporaries who insisted that Agnes had, like them, been "an agent of Moscow"; they had heard this while in the USSR or from higher-ups in the CPUSA. Some even said they had actually worked with her, but I was suspicious of their accounts: Such "ex-Communist witnesses" are often considered partisan, unreliable sources by leftist historians. Then, in the summer of 1988, I was invited to China to conduct research on Smedley.

In those months before the tragic events of Tiananmen Square, several elderly Chinese and foreign expatriates who had known Smedley spoke quite openly with me about her work for the Communist International during her years in China. One woman broke down and wept retelling—for the first time, she said—her own role in the CPUSA's destruction of Smedley's reputation in China more than forty years before. But I did not know what to do with this material. Then, halfway through my first draft, while composing the chapter that dealt with Agnes's activities in Berlin during 1927, I made a discovery that shook my assumptions.

Some time earlier, I had read a political biography of the German Communist Willi Muenzenberg. Written by his wife, it stressed Muenzenberg's unusual independence from the Comintern in the 1920s when he established the publishing empire and Communist "front" organizations that he ran from Berlin in service to the world revolution in which Smedley and her radical peers placed their hopes. On rereading it, what stood out for me was the author's description of Muenzenberg's close friendship with a Russian Jew named Jakob Mirov-Abramov, who worked next door to Muenzenberg at that time. Ostensibly third secretary at the Soviet Embassy in Berlin, in reality Mirov-Abramov was the chief assistant of Iosef Piatnitsky, head of the Otdel Mezhdunarodnoi Svyazi (Department of International Liaison), or OMS: the important albeit unpublicized section of the Comintern's central committee that handled intelligence.

I now remembered an FBI interview with a man the agency referred to as "Confidential Informant T-1," who identified himself as secretary of the League Against Imperialism, one of the front organizations Muenzenberg ran in Berlin, and for which Agnes was accused of working. In the report, "T-1" said that he had received reports from Smedley in Shanghai "by medium of Moscow" on the terroristic rule of Chiang Kai-shek. Moreover, "T-1" noted, Agnes had "a very high standing in the Secret Department of the Comintern" and with "Mironov, a big man of the Russian intelligence and also of the Secret Department of the Comintern."[7] I had earlier dismissed "T-1's" claims after a search for Mironov in several encyclopedias of the Comintern failed to turn up the name. Now, though, I realized that "T-1" was in fact Louis Gibarti, described in the Muenzenberg biography as well as in the FBI report as secretary of the League Against Imperialism. He was also one of Muenzenberg's top deputies, and his point man on China in 1927, when Agnes first became interested in that country. Having uncovered "T-1's" identity, I realized he might actually know something.

Armed with this new knowledge, I decided to look up Mironov again—this time under the names Abramov-Mirov and Mirov-Abramov, as he was called in the Muenzenberg book. Sure enough, under those appellations I turned up detailed descriptions of the man and his OMS responsibilities in Berlin. These involved overseeing important technical issues for the Comintern including the creation of Communist front organizations, the establishment and maintenance of secret telegraphic links between Moscow and other major cities, and the smuggling of propaganda, people, money, and arms from one country into another—as well as the operation of various espionage and covert action programs run separately from mainstream Comintern activities. Every task dovetailed neatly with accusations the British Shanghai Municipal Police had leveled against Agnes in the 1930s, which I had also previously dismissed.

Either the FBI, in transcribing the interview with Gibarti, had spelled Mirov's name incorrectly or Gibarti had known Mirov as Mironov—as had, I now remembered, Max Klausen, one of the principals in the Soviet spy ring of Dr. Richard Sorge, in which Agnes was accused of working. Under interrogation in Tokyo in the early 1940s, Klausen had stated that when he was in Moscow with Agnes in 1934, "Mironov" of the Secret Department of the

Comintern (by then promoted and living in Moscow) had arranged for Smedley to obtain special ration coupons for food at the store for foreigners.[8]

By this time I recognized that I had made a vital connection in unraveling Smedley's covert life, but this was the *last* thing I wanted to establish. *My* Agnes—the invincible rebel of my romantic imaginings—was gone. Against my wishes, I had succeeded in proving what her worst enemies failed to accomplish in half a century of trying. But the times were swiftly changing. Although the possibility of further research in China abruptly ended with the Tiananmen Massacre of June 1989, I now had several articles I was given in China the previous year translated into English. Like my interviews, they corroborated Agnes's connection to the Comintern, and the invaluable assistance that relationship had rendered to underground Chinese Communists and other Comintern operatives during Agnes's years in Shanghai.

Then the Soviet empire crumbled and some of Agnes's Comintern files became available in Moscow. Conservative scholars, delighted that someone like myself had finally "seen the light," provided me with additional Soviet documents, and informed me of newly released material from Great Britain's Government Code and Cypher School, whose Project MASK had decoded OMS radio messages in the 1930s. Almost everything I found referred to the end of Smedley's relationship to the Comintern rather than its beginning, but it was a spectacular ending nonetheless.

Having failed to discover the truth of Smedley's covert life until more than halfway through my first draft, I returned to chapter one armed with my new understanding of Agnes and made several further discoveries. Like Smedley's descriptions of her years in China, it turned out, her recollections of her early involvement in the Indian independence movement concealed as much as they revealed. Beginning in the summer of 1912, I now discovered, Smedley, barely twenty, had aligned herself with Indian revolutionaries in the San Francisco Bay Area who were receiving money from the German imperial government to foment armed revolution in India—both before America's entrance into World War I and after. When Smedley was finally arrested in March of 1918 for her alleged complicity in one of the Indians' myriad plots to secure India's freedom, her accusers did not know the half of her involvement.

The real Agnes, I came to realize, was a master of deception, a skillful poseur who had prevailed on powerful friends like Roger Baldwin and Margaret Sanger to defend her as an innocent victim of wartime hysteria while she remained on our wartime enemy's payroll, actively participating in the Indians' activities even as her case made its way to the Supreme Court! Even the propaganda operation she established in the late teens in New York City to influence public opinion on Indian deportations from the United States now appeared the very model of

a front organization, controlled and manipulated behind the scenes by Virendranath Chattopadhyaya, the Indian revolutionary in Berlin who would become
a key lieutenant of Muenzenberg's—and the love of Agnes's life. From the time
Agnes lived in California to the end of her life, I now saw, she exploited her relationships with influential liberals ranging from Sanger and Baldwin to Secretary
of the Interior Harold Ickes and Senator Claude Pepper, as well as progressive
institutions like Baldwin's American Civil Liberties Union and Sanger's birth
control movement, to shield her clandestine activities.

In revisiting Smedley's Berlin years, allusions in British intelligence reports,
German Foreign Office documents, and articles by Indian scholars to "certain
influential German Communists" as major backers of Smedley and Chattopadhyaya's Indian nationalist activities in Berlin in the 1920s now spoke loudly to
me of the influence of Willi Muenzenberg. During her years in Berlin and
later, when she left for China in the service of the Comintern's OMS, his
impact on Smedley both as a writer and a covert operative seemed profound and
inescapable.

My colleagues on the left have wanted nothing to do with my discovery. As
in the case of Alger Hiss, it appears that no document can be sufficiently damning or exist as something other than "disinformation" if it proves that a martyr of
the McCarthy era has actually engaged in espionage on behalf of the Soviet
Union. The taboo against anyone on the left admitting such a thing has survived
the end of the cold war virtually intact. For a progressive to admit that cold war
accusations of Soviet espionage involving American leftists of an earlier generation can now be verified requires moving beyond discussions of historical con-
text and addressing the deeper moral issues that until this time have made such
acknowledgments the exclusive province of the right.

I no longer think of Smedley as the tragic victim of a McCarthyite smear. In
truth, I consider her as cunning and crafty an operator as her detractors on the
right ever alleged. However, I refuse to concede the moral high ground to them.
Although Smedley led a covert life for more than a quarter of a century, and was
guilty of at least as much as what she was accused of by Japanese, Chinese,
American, British, French, and German officials over the course of her lifetime,
I do *not* see her as the vice-ridden villainess in the conservative, black-and-white
portrait.

That Smedley did damage, there is no question. Her path was littered with
people she hurt personally, people whose goodwill she exploited and whose reputations suffered on her behalf because they believed her lies. Moreover, while
it does not appear that Agnes's espionage activities visited direct harm on anyone, the beneficiaries of her services—the Soviets, the Chinese Communists,
and, indirectly, the German imperial government—were entities with many

crimes on their hands. Still, having come full circle in my journey with Smedley, I believe that the principles by which she lived and died ultimately tran-
scend the realm of ideology to embrace humanity's more universal struggles.

In her finest moments (and even in some of her worst) Agnes Smedley acted
from a truly generous heart. Inspired by an abiding love and faith in ordinary
people, she resisted with all the force of her being the misery and evil she saw
around her and did what she could—in her own headstrong, often damaging
fashion—to move humanity forward. More than fifty years have passed since
Smedley's death. The cold war is over. Maybe we can begin to see her as someone larger than the sum of her actions. In rediscovering Agnes Smedley, perhaps
we can find our own roots in our shared humanity.

CHAPTER 1

Beginnings

Law! What do I care about law? Hain't I got the power?

CORNELIUS VANDERBILT

OVER THE COURSE of her lifetime, Agnes Smedley had a great deal to say about her family of origin, only some of which was true, but there is no disputing her claim that she hailed from an old and distinguished American family. Like the Rallses—Agnes's mother's side of the family—the Quaker Smedleys arrived in America from England in the seventeenth century. Members of both the Smedley and Ralls clans fought in the American Revolution.[1] While the Rallses were content to live a simple agricultural life on the land their forebears wrested from virgin forest in a remote corner of northern Missouri, the Smedleys were a disparate collection of "rebels, wanderers, tellers of tall tales, singers of songs," Agnes later wrote, who disliked the toil and poor remuneration of a farmer's life.[2] It also appears to be the case that from the time Samuel Smedley fled Williamstown, Massachusetts, for upstate New York in the first years of the nineteenth century and "did not leave behind him there a savory reputation," the Smedleys' nonconforming behavior had exposed them to gossip.[3]

In 1879, when a Civil War veteran named Jacob Armstrong and his wife, the former Mary Smedley, arrived on the outskirts of Osgood, Missouri, and built a farm alongside John Clark Ralls's, the rumbling about the Smedleys grew louder. One of Mary's forebears was Cherokee,[4] and according to Agnes's later account, Mary's Native American heritage could still be discerned in her tall, large-boned frame and broad face lit by eyes "as black as the night when there is no moon."[5] In this community, as in others at the time, "mixed bloods" like

Mary Smedley were viewed not merely as descendants of an inferior race but as "faulty stock" who suffered the vices of both races and the virtues of neither.[6] Mary added fuel to the fire by behaving in a manner her neighbors considered distinctly unfeminine.

By the latter part of the nineteenth century, most women had retreated from their pioneer roles into their homes, venturing into the larger world only in pursuit of culture or a more genteel atmosphere. Mary—a woman Agnes would recall as being of "unusual capacity and determination"—insisted on doing everything "from curing diseases with herbs to managing a big farm and rearing more than a dozen children."[7] With their newly acquired sense of propriety, the good women of Osgood feared and shunned her.

Not long after Mary's arrival, a rumor spread from farm to farm that she had tired of the husband sixteen years her senior and found solace in the arms of her neighbor John Ralls. Later versions questioned the paternity of Mary's youngest, whose voice, the neighbors whispered, bore an uncanny resemblance to Ralls's.[8] A more troubling tale would surface a few years hence, when Ralls's wife, the former Rausey Privett, came down with an undetermined illness she could not seem to shake.

Mary, whose Indian blood gave her particular credibility in the matter of health-giving remedies, offered to treat Rausey with herbs. Under Mary's care, the soft-spoken, well-regarded schoolteacher grew progressively worse. The story that Mary Smedley was poisoning Rausey to win John Ralls for her own, and that John Ralls, who stood to inherit the rich farmland that had belonged to Rausey's parents, was a willing accomplice, circulated in the community.[9] Near the end of her life, according to a relative, Rausey suspected what was going on and asked her brother-in-law to intervene, but the effort reportedly accomplished little beyond provoking John Ralls, an otherwise gentle man, into an explosive fit of temper.[10]

On March 16, 1888, Rausey died at the age of forty-six. Even those who did not consider her demise outright murder believed that Mary's ministrations had contributed to her death. The haste with which she was laid to rest fueled the speculation. Less than ten months later, Mary's husband, who had always enjoyed excellent health, was also dead. Mary Smedley Armstrong married John Ralls just three months afterward, cementing her role as a pariah in the community. Agnes would claim many years later that her grandfather Ralls attempted to confess his role in the crime on his deathbed, but her aunt/grandmother Mary smothered his admission with a well-placed hand.

Probably no one was more affected by the unusual chain of events than John Ralls's eldest daughter, Sarah Lydia. Near the start of Rausey's illness, the moon-faced Sara Liddie (as she was known) had fallen in love with Mary's younger brother Charles, who had joined his sister in Missouri. A handsome twenty-two-year-old with long lean legs, a dashing mustache, and "the soul and imagination of a vagabond," as Agnes recalled him, Charles worked as a cattle broker for local stock raisers, riding the rails between Osgood and notorious cow towns like Kansas City.[11] The charismatic Charles had little more than a third-grade education and could read and write only with difficulty, but he shared the pioneers' faith in their ability to shape their own destiny, and their belief that life's rewards went to those whose eyes were the quickest and whose grasp was the strongest. Among the brawling, hard-drinking cowboys and dissolute populace of saloon keepers, gamblers, prostitutes, and con men who sought to part the cattle hands from their earnings at the end of the trail, Charles was a natural fit.

Sara Liddie was dazzled. Her father was aghast. John Ralls's own interest in Charles' sister notwithstanding, Ralls considered Charles too much beneath him socially to be a suitable partner for his daughter. Ralls tried his utmost, according to Agnes's later account, to dissuade her mother from keeping company with the smooth-talking Charles. Like the other farmers, she would write, Ralls considered Charles "unsteady, unreliable . . . shiftless; that was the Indian blood in [his] veins . . . you could never trust foreigners or Indians."[12] Agnes

Charles and Sarah Smedley around the time of their marriage, 1887. *Courtesy Ruth Ralls Fisher.*

either did not know or preferred not to mention the mental illness that also ran on the Smedley side of the family.[13] Yet despite John Ralls's advice — or perhaps because of it — on April 13, 1887, the seventeen-year-old Sara Liddie ran off and married her good-looking beau.

Charles's work was never regular and his earnings were always uncertain, but during the cattle boom of the 1880s he prospered. In the last decade of the nineteenth century, however, the bottom fell out of the business, and as beef prices plummeted Charles and his neighbors experienced the most profound economic depression they had known. Agnes, the second surviving child of Charles and Sara Liddie (now Sarah Ralls Smedley), was born in the midst of this difficult period, on February 23, 1892, in a two-room cabin without plumbing or electricity, which the Smedleys rented from a local farmer.

For the first few years of Agnes's life financial necessity compelled Charles to work the soil in order to feed his growing family, but the Smedleys were no worse off than others in the area. For a time, Agnes later wrote, she experienced no greater terror than a "great, roaring" cyclone that she and her sisters, Nellie and Myrtle, overheard from their perch on a featherbed in the family's cellar cave.[14]

Agnes's father was the major figure in her early life. The stolid farmers might look down on Charles, tainted as he was by blood and family scandal. In Agnes's young eyes, he was the "living, articulate expression" of everything their neigh-

Missouri birthplace of Agnes Smedley, with childhood friend Mamie McCullough. *Courtesy Mamie McCullough.*

bors dreamed about but were too scared to act on.[15] Garbed like a cowboy in a ten-gallon hat dipped over one eye and a multihued silver-buckled belt, Charles was so handsome, Agnes would claim, she could always spot him in a crowd. He was also a star performer at harvest dances. This "colorful man who dared what no one else dared," as Agnes later recalled him, regaled his doting daughter with spirited yarns, cowboy songs, and mournful ballads that recounted the mythic exploits of local hero Jesse James.

In the years since Reconstruction, James had been resurrected by his Missouri brethren as a kind of western Robin Hood—a "good" badman who broke the law in order to serve a stronger personal morality.[16] According to these tales (which had any number of variations) James had killed and robbed banks and trains, but he had stolen from the rich to give to the poor and never allowed anyone to experience pain.[17] An impressionable Agnes swallowed these stories whole.

Sarah gave birth to one son and then another in rapid succession, Agnes later recounted, and Charles, like most men in their world, preferred boys to girls. But of the five children in the Smedley family, Agnes was most akin to her father temperamentally, and she would write that to be like Charles, "to drive horses as he drove them, to pitch hay as he pitched it, to make him as proud of me as he was of my new baby brother," was her youthful goal.[18] Before she even entered school, Agnes, who had been blessed with precocious verbal ability,

Smedley family portrait circa 1898. Front left to right: Myrtle, John, Sam; back: Charles, Agnes, Nellie, Sarah. *Courtesy Elizabeth Smedley.*

could best her father at storytelling. Charles might speak of the recent cyclone as having lifted "cattle an' horses...an' men an'...sucked up a smokehouse in one place an' left the house, ten feet away, standin' clean as a whistle," she would write. In her version the house that remained was their own![19]

Although the community had written off Agnes's aunt/grandmother Mary as beyond the pale of social acceptability, she was still an imposing presence in Agnes's girlhood. "She was like an invading army in a foreign country," Agnes recalled. "And like all invaders, she was a tyrant. On Sundays we were always at her home—no one thought of it as other than her home—for dinner...One day I found a fly in the piece of blackberry cobbler she had carved and put on my plate. I pushed it aside. She turned her black eyes on me and laid down a law I have never forgotten:

"'Flies won't hurt you if they're well cooked!' The table was silent; no one dared speak. All looked at me as if I had sinned. I hesitated, then ate the fly and the blackberry cobbler together."[20]

By the time Agnes turned five, Charles had wearied of what Agnes later described as the "endless pettiness" of their agricultural life.[21] Like other ambitious men of his era, he cast an eye toward the growing cities. On a trip to nearby St. Joseph, he met up with a flamboyant hustler who ran a traveling medicine show and joined his act.[22] Part circus, part carnival, the popular shows employed any number of "pitch doctors" like Charles's new boss to sell a worthless assortment of tonics, salves, pills, and liniments to unsophisticated rural folk who preferred such remedies to the advice of professional physicians. It was a vastly profitable industry that was bilking naive consumers out of more than eighty million dollars a year at the dawn of the twentieth century. With his magnetic presence and gift of gab, Charles proved extremely adept, no doubt exploiting his Native American heritage to bolster his credibility as an herbalist.

Agnes later wrote that when Charles returned home for a visit in the spring of 1898, he arrived in a carriage drawn by two white horses, wearing "store clothes...and...a black tie that flew in the wind."[23] Sarah was not impressed, but Agnes would recall that after several attempts to persuade Charles to abandon his dubious calling, her mother accepted his decision meekly. She was, however, losing faith in her husband's judgment and considered his behavior a betrayal. Feeling helpless and victimized, Sarah succumbed to a bout of the clinical depression that ran in the Ralls family.[24]

John Ralls supported his daughter and her children through the winter of 1898–99, but the weight of Sarah's sadness left her with scant reserves for nurturing. Myrtle, Agnes's hoyden of a little sister, and her younger brothers, John and

Sam, believed that no harm was ever done them by their mother's lack of involvement.[25] But Agnes's needs were different, and so was her role in the family.

From the outset, it appears, Agnes was at odds with her taciturn mother. Agnes was Sarah's problem child—the only one of her siblings, Agnes later wrote, whom Sarah considered "stubborn and a liar."[26] By the time she turned five, Agnes would recall, Sarah often hit her with a "tough little switch that cut like a knife into the flesh" to discourage her unfortunate tendencies.[27] Agnes's resemblance to her absent father aggravated the tensions between her and her mother. According to Agnes's later account, Sarah increasingly singled out her second eldest during this time for ritualized physical abuse.

Agnes's sensitivity made her mother's ill-treatment that much more difficult to endure. Searching for ways to win the warmth and attention she craved, she found solace setting "beautiful . . . glorious" fires, as she would describe them.[28] Then she broke her arm. When her mother nursed her through it, Agnes discovered the advantages of physical infirmity in procuring the maternal sustenance that was otherwise not forthcoming. Long after her arm healed, Agnes would write, she continued to complain of pain. The idea that people only loved her when she was ill or injured, that she could find love through suffering, would remain with her for life.

Sarah relied on her daughter for support in Charles's absence, Agnes wrote years later, and she often imagined winning her mother's elusive love through elaborate acts of kindness. But Sarah refused any responsibility for the marital discord, defining herself solely as Charles's victim. How could Agnes rescue her mother without betraying the father she adored? Even as she strove to win Sarah's heart, how could she put aside her anger at the abuse? Agnes was still too young to do without her mother's affection, but the relationship was too fraught with ambivalence, tension, and lack of understanding for Agnes to find it. Her affection for Sarah was hopelessly tangled with feelings of anger, fear, and disgust.

According to Agnes's subsequent retelling, when Charles surfaced once again in the autumn of 1899, he returned "shorn of all his former glory. His fine clothes had been replaced by a soiled shirt and a pair of blue overalls."[29] The team of beautiful white horses was also gone. Evidently her father had been run out of town by a posse of irate citizens. Sarah's shame can only be guessed. Still, Charles was never one to lack a plan. In St. Joseph, he had heard about people who had made considerable money in the Colorado mines. Like the hunters, trappers, prospectors, lumberjacks, and cowboys before him who had rejected a life of grinding routine and limited prospects to pioneer a wild frontier, Charles planned to do the same—armed, like his spiritual predecessors, with little beyond his own quick wits and a weapon. Sometime between the fall of 1900 and early 1901, Agnes's father departed Missouri in search of the happiness and prosperity he always believed lay just past wherever he was, as his daughter later explained.

By this time, Sarah had grown weary of her husband's inability "to stick to anything for more than a year . . . Always wanting to change, always complaining, always telling stories that weren't true and singing songs instead of working; and thinking hard-working people couldn't see through him," Agnes recalled.[30] Under different circumstances, perhaps Sarah might have considered abandoning her feckless husband to his fate, but the events of the next few months would give her pause.

More than a decade after Rausey Ralls's death, her siblings remained in the area. One brother, a timid, defiant fellow named Newton Jasper Privett, had married a local beauty, and around the time of Charles's departure she took up with a widower named John W. Wolf.[31] Gossip about the reputed adulterers was so thick that Agnes later purported to know, even as an eight-year-old, about the unused shed at the foot of a wheat field where the couple "had their love."[32] It was months, though, before Privett learned he was a cuckold. When he did, he took after Wolf with a loaded shotgun and scattered his brains across the road in full view of his family.

The community's sympathies were solidly on the side of Privett, the wronged husband. Still, the murder rocked the small town. Wolf's remains were taken to the center of Osgood and displayed so people could see for themselves the wages of sin. Classes at Agnes's school were dismissed to let students view the body—a sight so distressing one of Agnes's young cousins reportedly fainted.

The homicide, however justified, was apparently the last straw for Sarah. Tied as she was to Osgood, she might well have felt as if her family would always be a magnet for unsavory gossip. As the murder trial of Jasper Privett entered its final stage, Sarah arranged for her family to rendezvous with Charles in southern Colorado.

In 1901 the Smedleys became city people. They lived in the town of Trinidad, Colorado, nestled between two mountain peaks in the foothills of the Rockies. A booming commercial center of ten thousand, Trinidad was the third largest city in the state and the seat of Las Animas County. Three railroad lines passed daily through this picturesque site on the line of the old Santa Fe Trail. A gas and electric power plant, telephone and telegraph lines, and recently installed sewer and water systems served those who could afford to use them. Modern banks, markets, and other urban services were also available to the city's more fortunate residents.

The reason for Trinidad's success was coal. Within the last ten years, the most extensive deposits of coking coal in the West had been discovered under the lush hills of pine, piñon and cedar that ringed the metropolis. The Colorado Fuel and Iron Company, part of John D. Rockefeller's Standard Oil Trust and the area's largest employer, used the town as a hub of operations for its scattered enterprises, which encompassed oil fields and refineries, copper mining and smelting, a steel complex, and transcontinental railroads.

The Smedleys' home was on the outskirts of town, near the yards and shops of the Colorado and Southern Railroad and across the tracks from more prosperous residents. It was no more than a canvas platform tent and lacked plumbing and electricity, but Sarah had wedged the three beds that slept the seven Smedleys along one side and arranged the other like a parlor, Agnes later wrote, with a rocking chair, a clock, and the sewing machine her mother had transported from Missouri. From the board shed Charles had built out front, which served as the family's kitchen, the Smedleys enjoyed a view of the Purgatory River, which flowed through the center of town.

Charles had yet to make his fortune and was struggling along as a teamster, performing small jobs for the CF&I. As a native-born American, though, he worked aboveground, unlike the thousands of newly arrived European immigrants who labored in the mines. In the coalfields outside town, where nine-tenths of the industry's workforce was deployed, these men had reached three thousand feet below the surface of the earth: a depth where the potential for instant destruction or a lingering death from respiratory troubles caused by the heat, moisture, toxic gases, and coal dust was frightening. Yet the companies observed few health or safety precautions. In 1901 and 1902 alone, 128 fatal accidents and another 186 mishaps that caused crippling injuries ranging from severed and broken limbs to fractured skulls and broken backs had occurred, but coroners' juries rarely found the companies guilty, and the companies violated with apparent impunity state laws regarding proper ventilation in the mines.[33] Additional legislation protecting the miners' health and welfare on and off the job also existed on the books, but it, too, was routinely ignored, and the men smoldered with resentment at being treated like so many "machines to grind out profits."[34] Anyone who complained openly about the weigh boss, long hours, bad pay, or dangerous conditions faced immediate dismissal. Still, conditions were so dismal that more than twenty-five hundred wildcat strikes over living and working conditions had erupted in the last twenty years.

Agnes later wrote that everything was "new and wonderful" with her family during the first months of their reunion, but that was not exactly the case.[35] The

town was sharply stratified, which came as a shock to her. American-born laborers like Charles looked down on the immigrant miners; those higher up in
Trinidad's social hierarchy looked down in their turn on the blue-collar Smedleys, and that made her ashamed. In Missouri, she would write, her family had
been poor—but so was everyone around her. She had not known the ways that
poverty hurt. At the city school she now attended, Agnes had met the sons and
daughters of Trinidad's elite, and though their world of comfort and beauty fired
her imagination, she could no more easily penetrate their magic circle than she
could obtain the advantages she craved.

Unable to alter her family's status, Agnes recognized by the age of nine the
cultural, economic, and racial differences that separated her from privileged
children. That awareness left her acutely self-conscious and damaged an already
fragile sense of self-worth. Photographs of Agnes from this period reveal a wistfully attractive child with soft, sandy curls and piercingly clear gray-blue eyes,
but Agnes later wrote that she felt she was homely.

Her self-doubt did not extend to her intellectual ability, though. Agnes
would later observe that she had inherited from Charles an ability "to do and
learn things" others could not, and she acted out her resentment in academic
revenge. "I, for all my faded dresses and stringy, ugly hair, who had never seen
a toothbrush or a bathtub, who had never slept between sheets or in a nightgown," she would write of her stellar performance in her class's "seat of honor,"
"stood with my hands glued to my sides and replied without one falter or one
mistake!" Meanwhile the girl whose father was a doctor had to listen.[36]

Although the atmosphere of hostility, suspicion, and racism that prevailed in
and around the coalfields—fostered by coal companies to discourage employees from identifying common concerns—had thwarted previous attempts by
the United Mine Workers of America to organize southern Colorado's coal
men into a union, in the early autumn of 1903 the UMW dispatched veteran
organizer Mary "Mother" Jones to Trinidad and the situation changed.[37] The
UMW sent Jones specifically to prevent a premature strike from erupting, but
she was poorly cast in the role of peacemaker. Her view that UMW goals like
better wages and working conditions were the very least to which the men were
entitled rendered Jones incapable of evaluating the situation impartially. After
conferring with officials in the Western Federation of Miners, a far more radical labor organization whose economic and political actions were wreaking
havoc in the northern part of the state, Jones determined that the miners were
"in practical slavery to the company" and the time was ripe for revolt.[38] On
November 9, 1903, while Agnes and her family were living in Trinidad, all but

613 of the 8,000 coal mine workers in Las Animas County walked off their jobs.[39]

Unfortunately for the men, neither the coal companies nor their close ally Colorado governor James H. Peabody chose to distinguish between the reformist UMW and the militant WFM in their handling of the dispute. Seizing on the strike as an excuse to sweep the former union into their ongoing campaign against the latter, Peabody and the coal companies at whose behest he served determined that the time had come to annihilate organized labor in Colorado once and for all. Immediately, CF&I and Victor Fuel, another Rockefeller subsidiary, hired more than one hundred American-born thugs and had them deputized by the county sheriff, to intimidate foreign miners.[40] The companies then posted notice that anyone who did not return to work at once would be evicted from his home without further warning.

The first incidents of violence flared soon after. Incensed over their evictions, a group of immigrant women struck a marshal with a cleaver and nearly severed his ear.[41] Deputy sheriffs guarding the coke ovens at a CF&I camp fired a volley of more than one hundred gunshots that left two men dead and two others wounded. Governor Peabody's offer to protect company-hired strikebreakers only further inflamed striking workers.

The mines themselves were located outside town, but Trinidad played a crucial role as the site of local UMW headquarters and numerous fiery union gatherings. No one who lived in the city during this turbulent period remained neutral, and though in light of her subsequent political convictions Agnes dearly wished it were otherwise, neither her mother nor her father evinced any solidarity with the immigrant miners during the conflict.

Agnes would later insist that she remember her mother's "instinctive and unhesitating sympathy" for the striking miners; Sarah "hated rich or powerful people or institutions," Agnes maintained.[42] In truth (as Agnes herself acknowledged elsewhere), Sarah shared her American-born neighbors' hostility toward the miners—as foreigners and as Catholics. She simply could not see how the fortunes of these lice-ridden men who "forced her to hang a lump of asafoetide in a little bag" around her children's necks were in any way tied to her own.[43] Charles, Agnes would claim, was "less clear" in his views.[44] In fact, as befitted someone who viewed the world solely in terms of his self-interest, her father stood squarely on the side of the coal companies and scabbed for CF&I throughout the strike.[45] Very likely Charles also joined hundreds of other quick-fisted nativists in one of several vigilante groups the companies funded to menace striking miners, for if Charles were still to become the employer he intended to be, it was critical that he remain in the company's good graces. The town of Trinidad was theoretically free from corporation control. In reality, though, the coal companies monitored residents' actions as closely here as they did in other company towns, and while they did not tolerate union activism, they rewarded demonstrations of loyalty.

Near the start of 1904, CF&I hired the Reno gang—a band of former train robbers, murderers, counterfeiters, and safecrackers—to harass union leaders. Their assault and pistol-whipping of three UMW officials on a Trinidad train ratcheted the conflict to another level. Miners reacted to the increasing violence by stockpiling weapons themselves.[46] Mother Jones, who was under orders to discourage the miners from any act that could be construed as a reason for calling out state troops, instead urged the miners on, exhorting them at union rallies to spend their money on guns and ammunition to use against scabbing miners.

Nearly four months into the strike, with no sign that the miners were relenting, Governor Peabody declared Las Animas County in a state of insurrection and rebellion and placed it under martial law. On March 23, 1904, Major Zeph Hill arrived in Trinidad with four hundred members of the Colorado National Guard. In between skirmishes, the troops camped on a hill directly across the Purgatory River from the Smedleys' home. Agnes, who had recently turned twelve, would maintain that she was forbidden from playing outdoors because the bullets with which the troops settled their quarrels made it too risky.[47]

Habeas corpus was suspended under martial law, and a nine o'clock curfew and press censorship were imposed; all assemblies were forbidden. Men, women, and children found themselves roused from their beds in the middle of the night, dragged to the isolated prairie, and interrogated about hidden weapons. By the time authorities turned their attention to deportation, conditions in Agnes's girlhood town less resembled a strike than a civil war. Nearly eight hundred people suspected of union sympathies were forced to leave the district and ordered never to return even though no formal charges were ever brought against them. Mother Jones, who defiantly addressed striking miners the day after the National Guard arrived, was given five minutes to pack before being led at gunpoint to a train bound for New Mexico.

Helpless before the overwhelming efforts of the coal companies, the governor, and the antiunion vigilantes, most of the strikers returned to work. The effort continued in a desultory fashion throughout the spring and summer of 1904. However, by mid-October even local UMW leaders reluctantly conceded that the coal companies, aided by the governor, had won a complete victory in the southern coalfields.[48] Almost a year after the strike began, the union surrendered the area less organized than before, shattered, along with the radical Western Federation of Miners, in the struggle. More than forty people had been killed. Another hundred had been wounded. Fifteen hundred more had been arrested or imprisoned in bullpens or military concentration camps. What remained was a festering bitterness that would simmer in the coalfields and coal camps of Las Animas County for another decade before it erupted in the infamous Ludlow Massacre.[49]

As a child living through the event, Agnes shared her parents' biases. Italians were still "Dagos" to her; she referred to Mexican Indians as "trifling."[50] It would take another ten years for Agnes to amend her views. But the 1903-4 coal strike was a seminal influence nonetheless. The crude class conflict was Agnes's first exposure to the quintessentially western form of American radicalism she would later make her own. Watching workers hit a boss hard while remaining tough in an underdog battle, employing violence to make their voices heard just as bosses used it to discourage workers from joining together, instructed Agnes in what would become critical elements of her political strategy. So would the men's unspoken message—that in the face of hardship and oppression, success was ultimately less significant than the act of standing up for oneself. And in UMW organizer Mother Jones, the fearsome agitator whose presence was ubiquitous throughout the strike's most tumultuous phase, Agnes found a female role model who was as different from the passive Sarah as a woman could be.

Whether Agnes encountered Jones at union rallies, in the local paper, or through wagging adult tongues, merely living in Trinidad at the time ensured there was no escaping this woman doubtful of all institutions and theory, suspicious of the powerful, and skeptical of any goodwill unaccompanied by swift action. For Agnes, Jones was the first female to suggest an alternative image of womanhood in which it was acceptable and even admirable to resist with all the force of one's being the unjust circumstances that robbed people of freedom and opportunity.

That fall Governor Peabody stood for reelection, and his controversial handling of Colorado's labor unrest was the key issue in the fiercely contested race. The strike, however, had wrought no change in Charles. Not only did he vote for Peabody; according to a later account by Agnes, he electioneered for Trinidad's political bosses, purchasing votes for the Colorado governor. Every pro-Peabody voter he delivered to the polls received one dollar; Charles was paid a percentage.[51] Sarah's antiforeign prejudice also survived the strike intact. However, it apparently instilled in her sufficient class consciousness to support Peabody's opponent: a rare act of open defiance, which precipitated a major domestic conflict in the Smedley household.[52] When the final ballots were tallied, Peabody lost the election by ten thousand votes, but the Colorado legislature reinstalled him as governor anyway.[53] These lessons on the limits of the ballot box in effecting social change were not lost on Agnes.

Shortly after the strike concluded, Charles determined that the time was ripe for him to strike it rich in the coalfields. Unaware that the era in Colorado's history when a lone individual could make his fortune in the coal mines had ended twenty years previously, he leased a mine in the nearby town of Forbes for a single season, which was all he could afford. Lacking access to the railroads, the sophisticated technology used to discover and process coal, or the start-up capital that had become essential, Charles struck out on his own. Agnes and her older sister, Nellie, were removed from school to help Sarah care for the family and Charles's crew of foreign miners, who boarded in their adobe home. At the end of the season the mine operator arrived to settle the account, and Charles learned for the first time that usurious terms in the contract he had signed but could not read left him inexplicably in arrears.[54]

Sarah and the children returned to Trinidad while Charles moved to a mining camp near Ludlow in order to work off his debt. In exchange for his loyalty, the coal companies had arranged for him to become one of the detested deputy sheriffs who enforced the poststrike clampdown in the camps.[55] The mood was ugly. Companies had already blacklisted any miners who had been active in the strike. Those who remained had their pay and services frozen at prestrike levels. Though Agnes never acknowledged her father's position, she later wrote know-

Charles Smedley's mining crew, Forbes, Colorado. *Courtesy Steve Finney.*

ingly of the men like Charles, armed with Colt .45s, who let every miner know that "for less than a nickel [they] would fill a damned furriner full of lead."[56] Agnes always maintained that Charles never understood exactly how or why the mine had failed, but that he knew he had been beaten; while he was away, she would say, whatever money her father did not spend on alcohol, his new mistress, or repayment of the debt he gambled away at poker.

It was at this juncture that Sarah's younger sister, Tillie, who had left a beau and job behind in Osgood to share in the Smedleys' good fortune, stepped in. This "flaming and vital" beauty, as Agnes later described her, gave most of her earnings at a Trinidad laundry to Sarah, providing Agnes and her siblings with most of the clothing they had during the winter of 1905–6 and enabling Sarah to open a boardinghouse for railroad workers near the family's old location across the tracks.[57] To satisfy her own needs, Tillie turned to part time prostitution in Trinidad's flourishing red light district.[58]

Unburdened by social conventions, Tillie threatened to scratch out the eyes of anyone who challenged her behavior, Agnes later wrote. She need not have worried about Sarah. Although her mother still clung to her own respectability as a married woman, secretly, according to Agnes's later account, her mother admired Tillie's freedom and lived vicariously through the woman who had not yet been "broke in to the bridle."[59]

The boardinghouse venture quickly proved unprofitable, and Sarah began to

Trinidad, Colorado, after the Purgatory River flooded, destroying the Smedleys' tent home. *Courtesy Elizabeth Smedley.*

take in laundry to keep the family going. Besides the drop in social status, Agnes's mother found herself working thirteen hours a day for little more than ten dollars a week. Too meek to confront her husband about not sending home his wages and too dependent to leave him, Sarah sank instead into a depression Agnes would describe as so severe that her mother did not care whether she lived or died.

Financial necessity compelled Sarah to place the thirteen-year-old Agnes in a series of after-school jobs she despised. At her first position, washing dishes and babysitting for the wife of a railway fireman, the arm Agnes had broken five years previously (and which Sarah had tenderly nursed) ached mysteriously until she was discharged. At her next post, as a sleep-in maid at an upscale boardinghouse, she was fired for drinking her employer's milk. Later she worked as a tobacco stripper for the King Coal Cigar Company, but she would say that she could concentrate only when her employer spoke nicely to her and sat nearby. Eventually she was dismissed for dawdling.

While Sarah labored by the side of a washtub, remote and withdrawn, the schoolwork Agnes had once loved became a burden. Angry and ashamed among her privileged peers, she sought comfort in adolescent rebellion. Agnes later wrote that she would slip a "box of macaroni here, a can of peas there, and at all times any fruit within reach" into her pockets or under her coat when the clerk at the store turned his back.[60] She would say she procured warm stockings and shirts for her younger brothers in the same way, and Sarah had neither the time nor inclination to inquire how her daughter obtained them.

Years later, Agnes wrote that she was learning that if she behaved aggressively enough, "nothing hurt...no reprimand of my teacher, no look or word."[61] She befriended some of the rougher kids in her part of town and became one of their leaders, she would recall, organizing assaults on boys and girls in the alleys behind her home. But she was not without softer feelings. In the years to come Agnes would also write about three handsome young Canadian ministers whom she followed to a Presbyterian church after hearing them sing at her school. Under their influence, she would say, she tearfully agreed to become a practicing Christian. Once they departed, though, she would claim she found the whole exercise "too dull" to continue.[62]

Agnes had never been close to her mother while the family lived in Missouri. Now the rage and pain the two women nursed against the absent Charles created a bond between them that would never be broken. In her new role as Sarah's champion, Agnes became convinced that Charles had left the family not for compelling financial reasons but because he was an outright villain who knew her mother was too frail to support them. When Sarah developed rheumatism and neuralgia, it was Agnes who nursed her mother back to health, and she

Victor Fuel mining camp, Delagua, Colorado, 1907 home of the Smedleys.
Courtesy Steve Finney.

continued to help Sarah even after she recovered, wringing and hanging laundry and ferrying water from the hydrant outside their home. Small wonder, then, that when Agnes's older sister, Nellie, wed and left Trinidad in November 1906, Agnes could not imagine, given the price their mother paid to be a married lady, why her sister wished to do the same.

Charles returned to Trinidad at the close of the year, the debt on the mine repaid. Near the start of 1907, Victor Fuel hired him to do some hauling and excavating work at Delagua, a mining camp nineteen miles to the north, and he took off again, this time accompanied by his family.[63] The stony, barren town was owned lock, stock, and barrel by the company. Signs posted on its front gates warned visitors to stay away. The air there was "still thick with hostility," Agnes recalled, and she never forgot "the black mouths of [the] mines, with tipples thrust far out over slag dumps, and the long, low row of coal ovens, glowing dull red at night" that destroyed all the surrounding vegetation.[64]

Charles arrived in Delagua as a day laborer, but after a few months a local mine owner intervened on his behalf and Charles became an independent contractor, hiring nearly two dozen former cowboys from beyond the Divide to prepare the earth for the construction of several new buildings.[65] As the era of the great cattle drives drew to a close, the men often worked as manual laborers, and

Agnes, now the eldest daughter at home, was forced to leave school a second time in order to help her mother board Charles's crew. But she enjoyed the cowboys, and in later years she credited them, "with all their virtues and their faults," with playing a major role in shaping her worldview.[66] Their determined individualism suggested to her a way of meeting life on one's own terms, however eccentric, and being accountable only to oneself in one's actions. Their songs and jokes and stories also became standards in her adult repertoire.

Big Buck, a closemouthed, proud-spirited cowboy "colossal in height and bearing," as Agnes described him, was particularly precious to her. In the years to come, she would recall him as the embodiment of the western cowboy: "a strain of ironic humor in all he did; generous in all material things he possessed or earned; very remote in thought and spirit; [and] stubbornly convinced of the inferiority of Mexicans, Indians, Mormons and men frail of body."[67] Buck taught Agnes and her tomboy sister Myrtle to ride, shoot, use a lasso and perform jack-knife tricks. He also discouraged Agnes from using feminine wiles to get her way. Buck, she later wrote, expected her to "face the consequences of my acts

Charles Smedley and "Big Buck," Charles's employee
and Agnes's first suitor. *Courtesy Steve Finney.*

every bit as much as a man," and if, in a fit of pique, she hit him or threw something at him, the speed with which he sent her "twirling with a thud from the
paw he called his hand" encouraged her to rethink her views.[68]

With limited access to women, the cowboys rarely married; as Agnes saw it,
that, too, was a blessing. Already, at the age of fifteen, Agnes could not envision
an intimate relationship without disastrous consequences, and the men's solitary
life seemed to skirt the treacherous emotional dependence she believed had
destroyed her mother and feared would ruin her if she let someone in. Here in
Delagua, it was Charles who leaned on his wife rather than vice versa. After the
fiasco at Forbes, he counted on Sarah, with her superior schooling, to help him
with his accounting. But Charles's need, expressed to Agnes in the way he looked
at her mother "with the unwavering faith and confidence of a child," terrified
her, she later wrote.[69] Certain that betrayal swiftly followed such guileless trust,
all she could see in her father's gaze was a lost man "dangerously submerged" in
another.

Agnes often suggested in later years that in Delagua the immigrant miners,
still tied hand and foot to the company whose behavior had been the most rep-
rehensible during the strike, regarded the Smedleys as no different from themselves. On occasion she even went so far as to pass herself off as a coal miner's
daughter.[70] But if Agnes actually met some of the "rough, unhappy" men, as she
later described them, who worked inside the mines, the virulent prejudice and
antiunion stance that lay behind her family's current good fortune would have
alienated the miners as effectively as the Smedleys' earlier poverty and backwardness had isolated them from Trinidad's elite.[71]

Like other American-born laborers in the area, Charles never worked underground; he lived in fear of the dangerous mines. His job, which placed him only
below Victor officials in terms of social respectability, afforded the Smedleys
freedoms and privileges well beyond the ones accorded to foreign miners. When
the fifteen-year-old Agnes ventured into Trinidad to shop in the spring of 1907,
her dress was white and lacy; the outing was reported in the society column of
the local paper.[72]

Now that they were financially secure, Sarah implored her daughter to have
Charles buy her a piano to advance her genteel upbringing, Agnes would write,
but she was no longer interested in the refined pleasures that had preoccupied
her a few years previously. The Smedleys' prosperity had come too late for her to
trust it, and unlike her younger siblings Agnes was too scarred to bounce back
once the family was again secure. "A young tree cannot grow tall and straight
and beautiful if its roots are always watered with acid," she later wrote.[73] All she
wanted was to leave.

In order to distance herself from her family's grip, Agnes invented what

would prove to be the first of several aliases, along with a new persona. "Marie,"
as Agnes began to refer to herself, was that happy, successful person she hoped
to become.[74] While she awaited her transformation, the family's circumstances
took a turn for the worse. Near the close of 1907, Charles's drinking problem
careened out of control and he lost his job. The Smedleys returned to Trinidad,
penniless once again.

Charles mortgaged his team of horses so that they could get by, but Agnes
later wrote that their home was a "nest of daily quarrels," her father screaming
and her mother weeping.[75] More ominously, she would write, Charles began to
speak favorably of men who hit their wives. One day during this low period, she
returned home to find her father approaching her mother with a short, doubled-
up rope. Rueful only that she had not grabbed her revolver first, she would
recall, she inserted herself between her parents and challenged her father to
strike her instead of Sarah; she would then go for his throat with her teeth. She
waited a moment for Charles to back off, then hit him.[76]

The experience was a terrible shock, for it meant that she had wrested control of the family from her father. After the incident, the colorful man who had
once "dared what no one else dared" vanished forever in her eyes, replaced in
her later accounts by a ragged, stoop-shouldered fellow who reeked of liquor
and drooled.

In 1908, the peripatetic Smedleys moved again—this time to the CF&I mining camp of Tercio, where Charles found work transporting houses for the company. By this time, Myrtle was old enough to help out, and Agnes was able to sit
in on classes at Tercio's well-equipped school.[77] Decades later, a classmate
recalled her as a dreamer who passed her days "gazing at the hills to the south
and west from the school house windows."[78] She was. Although Agnes had yet to
complete the eighth grade, she had begun to nurse ferocious intellectual ambitions that burned all the brighter, she would write, because she was "ugly and
poor."[79] While her brothers shot marbles and her sister practiced trick-riding
skills, Agnes struggled with tomes that ranged "from trashy romance to a ghastly
book on school law and one called Behaviorist Psychology," under the misguided impression, she later wrote, that an education consisted of reading great
quantities of books.[80]

One young teacher, a graduate of the state's new normal school, pierced
Agnes's resentful exterior and encouraged her to take the county teacher's exam.
With opportunities for a job outside the home that offered good wages and
improved social status still rare for working-class women, primary school teaching represented the summit of ambition at this time. Las Animas County was in
such desperate need of teachers for its mushrooming rural population that it was
accepting strong scores and a statement attesting to good moral character in

Agnes Smedley (third from left) circa 1908 as a student at
Tercio, the Colorado Fuel and Iron Company mining camp
where the Smedleys lived. *Courtesy Elizabeth Smedley.*

place of an eighth-grade diploma.[81] Agnes was still a year under the minimum
age of eighteen, but she leapt at the suggestion.

On March 18, 1909, she borrowed a horse and a skirt and blouse from her
teacher friend and rode across the Divide to the town where the exam was being
held. "In fear and trembling," she later wrote, Agnes (now "Marie" again for the
exam) took her seat among the older, better-educated women.[82] Fifteen years
later, she could still recall her poor scores in arithmetic, grammar, and school
law, but her outstanding results in other subjects won her the equivalent of
lower secondary school certification and a job in the Barela Mesa Rural School
District that paid forty dollars a month.[83]

The climate on the purple mesa where she taught was so harsh that the school
year ran only from May through September, but Agnes was accustomed to physical hardship, and she settled in quickly. After her school day ended, she continued her crash course in self-improvement, plowing through the cast-off high
school texts of a pen pal she acquired in a magazine for housewives, she would
recall. On the weekends, she later said, she sought companionship among the

"hearty...hairy chested" cowboys who lived in the area.[84] Although Agnes was the only woman among them, the men perceived her as beyond their reach and dared not approach her sexually. Roaming freely with them on horseback and dancing late into the evenings, she felt as safe in their company as "girls within convent walls," Agnes would recall.[85]

The following semester, Agnes was assigned to a school in nearby Burro Canyon, but her experience here was less fortunate. A few days after she started, she learned that her sister Nellie had died in childbirth, untended by a doctor, on the Kansas homestead where she lived. She was only twenty. Weeks later, Agnes learned that her mother was seriously ill. Since Charles was away hauling freight in Vermejo Park, a millionaire sportsman's paradise just over the New Mexico border, Agnes was left to tend her mother on her own.

The gravity of her illness loosened Sarah's tongue, and Agnes would write that her mother confided to her daughter "those things touching the emotions" Sarah had not previously expressed.[86] It was too late to save her. On January 31, 1910, Sarah died of gastritis at the age of forty. Decades afterward, Agnes still vividly recalled those first grief-stricken moments "as I stood by the body of the woman who had given me life...a brilliant light ran in circles, then contracted until it was a tiny black spot, then became lost in nothingness, and nothingness throbbed in beats like the waves of a sea against a cliff."[87] Agnes signed the death certificate, and she would recall that she did not cry, that day or ever, over the death of her mother. However, soon after Sarah died, Agnes began to experience symptoms of an undiagnosable, disabling heart ailment that would plague her for the rest of her life.[88]

Toward Charles, who Agnes felt had deliberately left her to deal with her mother alone, she nursed a "hard, inarticulate hatred and resentment."[89] Judging her father's absence as further proof of his villainy, Agnes later maintained, perhaps apocryphally, that when Charles learned of his wife's death, "he fell to his knees and wept dramatically, then rifled her old tin trunk. With the forty dollars he found hidden between the quilt patches, he went to the saloon and got drunk with the boys."[90]

Sarah's body was taken to Liberal, Kansas, where she was buried alongside her oldest daughter, and Agnes resigned from her teaching position to care for her siblings and infant nephew, whom Sarah had brought to Tercio after Nellie's funeral. For the next few months, Agnes gave herself over to full-time homemaking. Like her mother's and Nellie's before her, Agnes's days were an endless round of cooking, cleaning, washing, and ironing. Had she been more like them, Agnes later wrote, perhaps she would have accepted the burden until she married and raised a family of her own, "remain[ing] in the mining towns all my life ...and d[ying] in my early thirties."[91] But Agnes was neither as pliant nor as yield-

The Smedley siblings shortly before the family disbanded, 1910. *Courtesy Elizabeth Smedley.*

ing as the other two Smedley women. She was too needy herself to give herself over altogether to caring for others. In time, the housework and worry oppressed her. As she grew restless, angry, and resentful, a desire to flee took hold.

Agnes's teaching license was due to expire in September 1910. Faced with a premature end to the better life she had only fleetingly known, Agnes did not hesitate. That August, she dispatched the sixteen-year-old Myrtle to a ranch in Gunnison, Colorado. Johnnie, her favorite, who had just turned fourteen, and Sammie, who was not quite twelve, she entrusted to Charles's uncertain care. Grabbing her infant nephew in her arms, Agnes took off, the "clatter of the hoofs of the horse of Jesse James," she later wrote, echoing in her ears.[92]

CHAPTER 2

Emergence as a Radical

O brave men, how long will you remain slaves?
Arise and sacrifice yourselves.

GHADR, PUBLICATION OF
THE GHADR PARTY

T HE NEXT TWELVE MONTHS of Agnes's life were committed to her
search for what she then believed were "better, nobler things," she later
wrote.[1] In Greeley, a kind of western Brook Farm founded along the principles
of the French social theorist Charles Fourier, Agnes enrolled in business school,
bankrolled by her aunt Tillie, who lived in nearby Denver with various gentle-
man "friends." At the start of 1911, her course work completed, Agnes moved in
with her aunt.

Agnes had expressed an interest in journalism, a not unreasonable aspiration
for a trained secretary at the time, and two of Tillie's clients helped her find stenography work on local publications, but she soon grew disaffected with the
tenor of office life, unwilling to accept a gender role she saw as passive and
impotent. She preferred to meet the men on their own ground, single-mindedly
pursuing money and doing as she pleased. After considerable wrangling, she
secured a position selling magazine subscriptions on the road.

The life of a traveling salesperson was considered highly disreputable for
women at that time, but Agnes enjoyed it immensely. As a way of distancing herself from the female sex, Agnes had begun rejecting dainty blouses and corseted
garb for shirts and string ties while she still taught school. Now that she was the
one wielding power, advancing an agenda she herself had determined, she wore
a dress without complaint, but she referred to herself by the male appellation
"Georgie."[2]

Agnes did not attempt to see her family again until the summer of 1911. Although their circumstances had not changed in the year since she departed, Agnes felt so guilty she thought her father had developed delirium tremens, and the boys looked dirty and disheveled. Still, she found it easier to buy them warm clothing than acknowledge her love for them, she recalled. Haunted by her mother's choices, Agnes feared that succumbing to her gentler feelings would defeat her plans for a better future, and she fled after a day. "I would not be a woman," she would write. "I would not."[3]

Years later, she observed that after leaving Tercio, "a black curtain descended softly and erased from my memory the faces of those I loved," but she had yet to acknowledge, she would confess, that "one builds fortifications only where there is weakness."[4] To deny her inner turmoil, Agnes picked up the pace of her travels, sprinting through Texas and a succession of western states. However, the work that had only recently seemed thrilling now seemed fatiguing, and the practical difficulties and loneliness inherent in a life without friends or family upset her. When men inevitably harassed her with unsolicited sexual advances, Agnes felt vulnerable, and the rebuffs of conventional homemakers "cut like a knife."[5] Soon the heart trouble she first experienced after her mother's death recurred. Not long after, she began dissolving into uncontrollable fits of weeping. Within weeks, Agnes said, she became so physically exhausted she could not lift herself from her bed.

Perhaps the following story, which she penned at the time, offers another clue.

Georgie Wesley worked . . . taking subscriptions . . .

Her work was hard. It required grit that many did not possess. When she thought of leaving Dallas, the memory of Mr. Boster's kindness brought a sense of regret.

One evening Mr. Boster met her and insisted that she should go to dinner with him. After some hesitation, she accepted...

Mr. Boster . . . was thoughtful and jolly, and Georgie seemed unusually happy.

. . . Georgie caught herself saying:

"I believe I'll leave Dallas soon, Mr. Boster."

"Why? Surely not! You have been here only a short time . . . you have no business following this work . . . it's too hard . . . I admire your pluck, but . . . Won't you stay in this city if I secure you a good position?" . . .

Next day . . . the "key-puncher" [Miss Ray] . . . informed [Georgie], in a haughty manner, of her . . . engagement to Mr. Boster . . . and her desire that a "travelling woman" not impose herself upon her future husband . . . Georgie was at first indignant . . . but the . . . phrase, hurled at her in such sneering manner . . . brought back the pain she thought had been dulled . . .

"Oh, I know he won't marry that Miss Ray," [Georgie] told herself over and over again . . . "But—I guess it is better . . . that I leave, anyhow. He has everything—everything . . . He will marry someone in his own sphere."[6]

Less than a month after visiting her family, "Georgie" checked into a sanitarium with symptoms of what she took to be altitude sickness.[7] The physician who examined her, however, was less concerned with Agnes's heart trouble (which he did not consider very serious, she wrote) than her emotional well-being. Noting that she had been under a nervous strain for some time, he prescribed the regimen of tonics and drugs, exercise, high-protein diet, isolation, good climate, and bed rest then in use to treat neurasthenia.

Although a contemporary diagnosis would more likely be a depressive episode or anxiety disorder, neurasthenia had become an increasingly common disorder in the decades before Freud's theories took hold in the United States. The malady, which manifested as a catalog of vague and various mental and physical ailments, including the lassitude, angina-like palpitations, and throat constrictions that affected Agnes, was viewed as a hereditary weakness of the nerve force that could be triggered by sudden shocks, including young women leaving the sphere of home and family to function in a larger world.[8] While neurasthenia lacked the stigma of mental illness, in a patient like Agnes with a family history of depression, doctors expected only a certain degree of recovery. In the future she would need to vigilantly shield herself from stress if she wished to avoid a relapse.

After a few weeks of treatment, Agnes's nerve force was considered sufficiently rebuilt for her to return to the world, but by then she had lost interest in her life on the road. Buck, one of the cowboys who had worked for her father, had written during Agnes's illness and invited her to recuperate with him in Clifton, Arizona, and she accepted his approach. The emotional deprivation that fueled Agnes's opportunism made it easy for her to deny the sentiments that lay behind Buck's offer to pay for her hotel room and meals and then profess astonishment, as she later confessed, when the forty-two-year-old proposed. Agnes had no intention of marrying at this time, let alone someone like Buck who came from a world she wished to forget. But he was willing to cover her tuition at a school near Phoenix if she wished to attend, and she agreed to accept his assistance while she pondered his overture.

Agnes's months at the Tempe Normal School were a time of intellectual and creative growth. In addition to taking courses in natural science and literature,

Agnes wrote poetry, joined the campus literary society, and drafted several auto-biographical stories for the school paper. She also began to read on contemporary social issues. The Progressive movement was then at its height, and muckraking authors like Upton Sinclair, Ida Tarbell, and Lincoln Steffens were providing some of its most significant contributions to reform. Agnes still blamed Charles and being born female, rather than the excesses of industrial capitalism, for her adverse circumstances, but she sympathized with the writers' attempts to expose the evils of a system grown fat and corrupt at the expense of those who could not help themselves.[9]

On solitary desert walks, Agnes also studied the history of the Navajo and Apache tribes to whom the land around Tempe had once belonged. While she did so, she revisited the matter of her own Native American heritage. During her Trinidad girlhood, she would write, her awareness that she was different from the "perfect" little white children had made her so acutely self-conscious she developed psychosomatic throat constrictions in response.[10] Here in Tempe, she made peace with her racial background, going so far as to christen herself with a Navajo name: Ayahoo.[11] The word did not exist in the Cherokee language of her father's forebears, but Agnes would later contend it was a childhood name Charles had bequeathed her.[12] By the time she left Arizona, it was the darker skinned races who would always be *us* to her; Caucasians had become the other.

Agnes was still uncertain of her physical attractiveness and embarrassed by the rough manners that betrayed her working-class origins. By playing up her image as a hard western character, she shielded her vulnerability from her classmates, boasting of her earlier hand-to-mouth existence and the male "friend" who was financing her studies.[13] A woman, Agnes later wrote, could either "be beautiful, or she could command respect by intellectual ability, a show of power, a victory."[14] She chose the latter. However, by the spring of 1912, she had not responded to Buck's proposal, and while Agnes dallied another suitor arrived.

She was a twenty-six-year-old Barnard graduate named Thorberg Brundin. Tall and stately, with blond hair, blue eyes, and a slight Swedish accent, she would oversee Agnes's political and intellectual awakening. Thorberg was part of a rising generation of women who thumbed their noses at the tradition of self-sacrifice and submergence in the family that had formerly confined women to their homes. A proponent of self-expression, equality of the sexes, and the extension in every direction of the power and freedom of women, she had abandoned her life in Greenwich Village to see a bit of the world before entering graduate school.

After attending a campus debate in which Agnes spoke in favor of women's suffrage (a subject in which she was well versed, Colorado having been one of the earliest states to grant women the vote), Thorberg—who considered the vote merely a starting point in a revolution that would affect all relations between the sexes—followed Agnes back to her room. As she later recalled the encounter, Thorberg launched headlong into an animated monologue on the "antiquated, reactionary...uncreative—static..." nature of educational institutions, her eyes flitting from the riding paraphernalia on Agnes's wall to the revolver and holster on her bedpost and the dagger she used as a paper knife.[15] Thorberg was the first intellectual, the first bohemian, and the first socialist Agnes had ever met; she was also the most educated, cultured, and sophisticated. Agnes would write that she was overcome by this "goddess," but Thorberg's irreverence made it easier for Agnes to avoid the bristly resentment she might otherwise have felt.[16]

By playing up her image as a dirt-poor daughter of earth, Agnes found a persona in which she felt comfortable and could appeal to Thorberg, an eastern intellectual, as a cause as well as a person. And in Agnes (or rather "Ayahoo," as she now preferred to be known), Thorberg believed she had discovered an exotic: a symbol of life not lived at a remove. That spring the two women attended an Easter dance performed by local Yacqui Indians and the first drama of ideas Agnes had ever seen. Since she was not yet able to "understand anything on a stage that did not have a lot going on: clog dancing, loud music and

Thorberg Brundin, Agnes's friend and future sister-in-law. *Courtesy Agnes Smedley Collection, University Archives, Arizona State University.*

laughter, rough jokes, gaudy clothing, and very extravagant acting," Agnes later explained, the experience was dreadfully boring [17]

As the women became acquainted, Thor—as her friends called her—pointed out to Agnes the limitations of the Progressive movement with which she was flirting. Why settle for mere reform, Thorberg pressed, when one could build a more just and egalitarian society altogether?[18] Under her tutelage, Agnes took her first tentative steps beyond her family in apportioning blame for being hindered from achieving her full potential, but she was still a ways from the moral generosity that prompted Thor to stake her hopes on a goal beyond personal success.

There was a definite romantic flavor to Agnes's attraction to Thorberg, but in its emotional primitivism it appeared to lack a sexual component. That Agnes's first love interest was a woman seemed largely a safe way for her to explore her more delicate feelings; at twenty, as Agnes later wrote, her horror of sex was rivaled only by her ignorance.[19] Still, the relationship prompted Agnes to advise Buck that she would not be returning. Having terminated the understanding that had subsidized her education, she fled Tempe a month before school let out to be nearer her female friend.

Agnes found secretarial work in Phoenix, where Thorberg was staying, but she did not get to spend much time with her friend, who soon left town to spend the summer in San Francisco. The blow of Thor's departure, however, was cushioned by a visit from her younger brother, Ernest, a sensitive, introspective man who was then working as a hydrographer. Ernest lacked his sister's charisma, but he compensated for it with blond good looks, a lively intellect, and a belief that women were men's equals. Gentle, kind, and musical, Ernest saw in Agnes's emotional intensity the perfect foil for his Scandinavian reserve, and Agnes would write that his affection for her led him to hope that if she became his partner, she might grow more comfortable with "the desire for love, tenderness and companionship that existed beneath [her] rough and defiant manner."[20]

Ernest, too, was heading for San Francisco, and he encouraged Agnes to accompany him there. Agnes questioned whether she loved him, she later admitted, but she was flattered by his interest and tantalized by his talk. Besides, in San Francisco there would also be Thor. However, before Agnes made up her mind, a scorching message arrived from the Kansas homestead where her brothers now lived. It was Johnnie who wrote, and he complained bitterly of their treatment by Nellie's widower, who had taken over their care. Instead of sending her brothers to school, she would recall that he told her, their uncle (whom an acquaintance described as a gambler and "a mean son of a gun") had worked them like beasts on his farm.[21] Recently, according to Agnes's account, he had

beaten Sammie, the youngest, "until the skin had been broken on his body and
the blood had run down his back."[22]

The image of her brother with "his shirt torn off and his back a bleeding
wound," as she later wrote, so disturbed her that she had another neurasthenic
episode, but she still refused to sacrifice her future for theirs by taking over their
care.[23] Instead, as she would write, she penned a furious diatribe to her father
demanding that he care for the boys himself and another to her brother-in-law
in which she unleashed "a torrent of murderous hatred."[24] In a third note to her
brothers she included money. Then she packed her few belongings and followed Ernest west.

By the time Agnes reached Thorberg's apartment in San Francisco, Ernest
was already ensconced there. So, too, was Thorberg's lover Robert Haberman, a
fiercely intelligent Romanian Jew whose presence had not figured in her plans.[25]
Belatedly, Agnes realized that if she shared a house with the three of them, she
would be expected to practice the same bohemian morality as her friends, who
approved of premarital sex and believed that women as well as men were meant
to explore their physical desires.[26] Agnes had successfully rebelled against other
areas of her upbringing, but the idea that sex was a degrading activity, particularly
for women, was one aspect of her childhood training she found hard to shake.

Agnes's husband, Ernest Brundin, at the time of
their marriage. *Courtesy Eleanor Brundin.*

She was not immune to the unfocused sexual desire that had led her at the age of sixteen to explore Trinidad's dance halls. Once she had even briefly succumbed to a "high class" city man, as she later described him, whose kisses tasted "like liquid silver" on her lips.[27] But the encounter turned to disaster. Running together her pleasurable sensations with the image of "one child a year that riveted women into slavery," she would write, Agnes panicked as the embrace became more intimate, and her date molested her.[28] Since then, her discomfort with her sexuality and fear of becoming pregnant had, if anything, increased, wreaking havoc on those rare moments when her desire overcame her resistance. Ernest's second wife would attest that Agnes was initially responsive and capable of being a provocative tease, but if Ernest pressured her to go further, she froze and became physically repelled.[29] To forestall an awkward situation, Agnes prevailed on him to underwrite her financially while she attended classes at nearby Berkeley. She passed the summer of 1912 in virginal peace, visiting San Francisco only on weekends.[30]

Both the Brundins were active in the Socialist Party, but Haberman was already a respected Marxist theoretician, and under his influence Agnes was soon comfortable enough with Socialist jargon to evince disdain for America's worship of the same "almighty dollar" she had recently courted.[31] Eager to please her friends, she later claimed that she joined the Socialist Party at this time.[32] But life in a company town had made Agnes dubious about the ballot as an agent of social change, and her ambition to rise above her class made her too ambivalent to make common cause with others from backgrounds like hers.

When Haberman invited her to a Socialist Party picnic, Agnes was revolted by the merry-go-round, shooting gallery, cheap geegaws, and crude dance floor brought in for the event. The people, she would write, "were so unbeautiful, so dull and dreary looking, so cheaply dressed — just like the things I had always known and hated."[33] She could not understand why he had brought her. Politically, she was more attracted to the drama unfolding at Berkeley, which revolved around an upper-caste Hindu nationalist named Har Dayal.

Though the history of Indian resistance to British rule in India can be dated almost to the time of British conquest, it was not until the second half of the nineteenth century that a wave of newly educated Indians began to agitate for the creation of institutions that gave them a voice in India's political and economic life. When the Indian National Congress was established in 1885, it passed several resolutions demanding a larger share in the governing and administration of the country. However, at the close of the nineteenth century, the British government still refused to take them seriously.

British arrogance and unresponsiveness, along with the drain of India's wealth, lay behind the Indians' initial impulse for freedom from Great Britain. In the first years of the twentieth century, the viceroyalty of Lord Curzon brought further indignities. Indian disaffection with British rule intensified, and the growth of patriotic impulses bred a spirit of revolt. As India's political and national consciousness reached unprecedented levels, a generation of political leaders stopped inquiring whether India should free itself of British domination and began asking how. Indian moderates (including many Congress leaders) believed in some form of self-government under the British, to be achieved through constitutional means. Indian extremists, however, longed for total independence, which they saw as attainable only through armed revolt. The latter had a loyal following, particularly among young male students in Bengal, epicenter of the rising nationalist movement.

A surge in revolutionary activities during the first decade of the twentieth century had triggered a rigorous government repression, but British authorities failed to eradicate the movement. Outside India—in England, France, Germany, Japan, and the United States—Indian revolutionaries formed new bases, from which they distributed anti-British propaganda and addressed Indian students and other Indian audiences. They also developed several elaborate plots to purchase and ship sufficient arms and ammunition to wrest India from British rule. By 1910, Indian revolutionaries abroad had established close and active contact with their counterparts in the secret societies of India. So when the twenty-seven-year-old Har Dayal, who had associated with radical nationalists during his student days at Oxford and in Paris, arrived in the United States in 1911, it was hardly surprising that the British police detectives stationed in America to observe the activities of Indian extremists placed him under surveillance.

At Harvard, where he spent his first winter, Dayal quickly earned a reputation as a gifted student of Buddhism. During the summer of 1912, he lectured on Indian philosophy at Stanford and Berkeley, but he was also hard at work on his own "philosophical synthesis" for the perfection of man: a heady brew that combined the traditional Indian holy man's practice of renunciation and asceticism with a disparate collection of rebellious Western ideas ranging from the anarcho-syndicalism of the Industrial Workers of the World to aspects of Communism, socialism, free love, and labor reform.[34]

Still, British authorities were skeptical that Dayal's current passion expressed the true scope of his interests. Cognizant of his view that the British Raj was a despotic, predatory government, which was crushing his people spiritually and economically, spying on them, apprehending them, undermining their character,

Indian nationalist Har Dayal, founder of the Hindustan Ghadr Party.

and robbing India outright of an estimated two hundred million dollars a year, they suspected that his commitment to India's freedom remained undiminished.

Dayal's fascination with American radicalism was perhaps sincere. However, there seems little doubt that it also conveniently masked his primary calling as an organizer of Indian rebellion. Van Wyck Brooks, a Stanford literary critic who had befriended Dayal, posited that "whether as an Indian nationalist or an anarchist internationalist, he was a revolutionist at every moment with a shrewd psychological knowledge of the value of the martyr's role for attracting and retaining disciples to carry out his work...India was always on his mind... nationalism was his ruling passion."[35]

Of paramount importance to Dayal during the summer of 1912 was his search for American supporters. In addition to Brooks, Dayal had become acquainted with other respected Bay Area figures including Jack London, *San Francisco Bulletin* publisher Fremont Older, social crusader Charles Erskine Scott Wood, and poet-suffragist Sara Bard Field. On the campuses of Stanford and Berkeley, Dayal's enthusiasm for American radicalism, and particularly women's emancipation, also put him in contact with female undergraduates— who were even less likely than his famous U.S. acquaintances to attract the notice of authorities and therefore of great value in covert work.

At the political gatherings Dayal attended, he would identify potential recruits and invite them to a subsequent private meeting. At this time subjects closer to his heart would be discussed. Then, at a suitable future date, a young woman might be approached to join Dayal's inner circle.[36] It appears that Agnes was one of the Berkeley coeds who attracted Dayal's notice that summer. At restricted meetings in the home of Gertrude Baldwin Woods, renegade wife of a noted Harvard Sanskritist, Agnes began to hear about the situation in India from a radical nationalist perspective—a fact that did not go unnoticed by British agents in the United States, who opened a file on her.[37]

Agnes also gave some attention that summer to the more local issue of anti-Asian prejudice.[38] In California, where the majority of America's two hundred thousand unskilled Asian immigrants lived, the nation's racist xenophobia was most extreme, and legislation was currently under consideration that would eliminate already tightly restricted Asian immigration entirely. Working-class laborers, middle-class progressive reformers, and even the Socialist Party looked down on California's Asian community as racially inferior, unassimilable, and a threat to wages. Of all the state's detested Asian populations, none was more reviled than the "ragheads"—the derisive term by which the Sikhs, who comprised the overwhelming majority of California's Indian immigrant population, were known.

Agnes in repose, California, circa 1912. *Courtesy Steve Finney.*

Stigmatized, ridiculed, and bullied for maintaining their customs in America, discriminated against in theaters, restaurants, and hotels, charged higher rents than Caucasians for substandard housing in undesirable sections of town, they faced the most limited opportunities for work and the lowest wages of all Asian immigrant groups.[39] Having made greater peace with her racial identity than with the working-class background she still battled to escape, Agnes found it easier to identify with California's beleaguered Asian community than with Bay Area Socialists who wore buttons urging workers of the world to unite while simultaneously advocating Asian exclusion.

As the summer drew to a close, Ernest pressed her for a decision. Unable to find work in San Francisco, he had accepted a job in southern California, and he wanted her to accompany him there. Agnes preferred to cast their relationship in platonic terms, but Ernest thought there was room for more. Although he did not demand sex and romance as a quid pro quo for his continued support, he was attracted to Agnes and, after waiting for months, frustrated that their affair remained unconsummated.[40]

Agnes, however, did not appear similarly drawn to Ernest. In the years to come, she would acknowledge his indispensable role in drawing her out of what she described as a "lower standard of thought, life and culture" and helping her reconsider the negative view of men she had formed from her father. At the time, however, Agnes's discomfort with what she had been raised to think of as feminine qualities led her to scorn Ernest as weak.[41] Unable to grasp how love might motivate his attempts to accommodate her, she thought he enjoyed the pain she caused.[42] Her exploitation of him extended into every area of their life.

Ernest did not believe in the institution of marriage for people who did not plan to have children—a possibility Agnes flatly refused to entertain. But she was not yet free of the desire for the social respectability it conferred, her protestations notwithstanding, and it was she who pursued the ceremony that turned the twenty-year-old "Ayahoo" Smedley into Mrs. Ernest Brundin that August 24.[43] Her awareness of the autonomy her mother had sacrificed at the altar, however, inclined her to concede nothing in this marriage. In the same misplaced, vengeful spirit that governed all her relations with her spouse, Agnes refused to follow Ernest south, claiming she could earn more money in San Francisco and be nearer to schools. For the next eight months, Agnes remained in the Bay Area alone, working as a stenographer on a local paper, living in an apartment of her own, and enjoying the status and financial security of a traditional wife without performing any wifely functions. Indeed, the marriage seemingly meant so little to her that when she wrote her father two weeks after the ceremony, the fact that she had gotten married did not even come up.[44]

Early in 1913, California stepped up the harassment of its Asian population. The state legislature was considering the Anti-Alien Land Act, which forbade all aliens (and therefore all Asians) from leasing or owning land unless they were eligible for citizenship. Though the bill eventually passed with an overwhelming majority, Agnes's first act of political resistance was lobbying to block it.[45] Many Indian immigrants, as citizens under the British Crown, considered appealing their right to own property in the United States through British constitutional channels. Har Dayal, for one, believed such efforts were futile. Other Asian aliens who fought discriminatory American measures might win their battles, he argued, but they had the backing of their governments. British officials were wholly indifferent to the requests and complaints of Indian nationals. If the British government of India treated the Indians like slaves in their own country, why, he asked, should they expect British help to end their humiliation in America?

Seizing the opportunity provided by the anti-Asian immigration and land legislation, Dayal returned to the open nationalist agitation that had made him a blood enemy of the British. Throughout the spring of 1913 he traveled the length of the Pacific Coast, organizing Sikh immigrants who had left their native Punjab to work the farms and orchards of the Pacific West into what became known as the Hindustan Ghadr Party (*Ghadr* meaning rebellion in Dayal's native tongue of Urdu), which had its headquarters in San Francisco.[46]

Its goal was armed mutiny against the British Raj in India, but the most potent weapon in the Ghadr Party arsenal was the fiery propaganda campaign it waged at meetings and in its weekly newspaper. Widely distributed to American audiences in translation, the paper was filled with impassioned speeches by George Washington, Abraham Lincoln, and Patrick Henry. Articles emphasized members' willingness to lay down their lives for the cause of India's freedom.[47] A number of sympathetic Bay Area American progressives, prosperous Indian immigrants and veteran Indian revolutionaries, were among the party's first supporters.

The uneducated, mostly illiterate Sikhs whom Dayal sought as foot soldiers in his revolution had originally been chary of joining forces with an upper-caste Hindu. Geography, class, and religion had separated one from the other in their native land; so they preferred it here. Now, however, the Sikh émigrés embraced Dayal's vision, at a loss as to how else to end the oppression to which they were subjected in India and the abuse they experienced in the United States. So did Agnes.[48] Her early life and experience as a female, she later wrote, had already taught her a great deal about the resentment bred of unjust suffering, making it easy for her to identify with the Indians' poverty and enslavement.[49] But Dayal's belief that asceticism and personal sacrifice were as necessary as arms in liberating his people from poverty, disease, inequality, and ignorance was equally vital to Agnes's embrace of the Indian independence movement. Through his own example, Dayal appealed to her most idealistic impulses and won her heart as well as her mind.

Agnes would claim in the years to come that the Indian nationalist movement as exemplified by the Ghadr Party appealed to her because it was "just about as distant from American life and thought as any movement can be," but the Ghadr Party was not nearly so foreign as it might have seemed.[50] Dayal's interest in things American had led him to model his organization on the IWW, the Western labor movement born out of the labor conflict Agnes witnessed in her youth. Its plan to overwhelm the British with all-out, violent resistance was not so different from the class war Colorado miners had waged—with one significant distinction. Unlike the immigrant miners, for whom she had evinced no sympathy, or the "dull and dreary looking" American workers Agnes met through the Socialist Party, rank-and-file members of the Ghadr Party were drawn exclusively from the Indian lower classes rather than her own.[51]

In the Ghadr movement, Agnes had identified an outlet for her anger that could be expressed in radical political activity but allowed her to sidestep her conflicted emotions about her own class background. No American movement could offer that. A later statement by Agnes suggests that she approached Dayal about participating in his fledgling revolutionary movement around this time, but it would be another year before there was a need for someone like herself.[52] So when Ernest returned to San Francisco in May 1913 and urged her again to come with him to the town of El Centro, near the Mexican border, Agnes reluctantly agreed.

The economic miracle that was transforming life in the Imperial Valley depended almost entirely on a narrow stream of water channeled from the nearby Colorado River. This irrigation system, fed through a series of ditches, made it possible to cultivate what had formerly been arid desert land. The cost of the improvements was high, and the climate remained blazing hot, but the valley's newfound agricultural viability held the promise of enormous future gain. In the process, it had turned El Centro, the major city in this area east of San Diego, into a boom town.

Agnes found work in the lobby of the Barbara Worth Hotel typing the business correspondence of the land speculators flooding into the region. One such fellow worked for the *Los Angeles Examiner*, and Agnes would say that she asked him if she could contribute articles to the paper. He was willing to make her a correspondent for a consideration he preferred to be sexual, but she claimed that she persuaded him instead to accept a 20 percent commission on any work she sold.[53] In the evenings, Agnes returned to Ernest's apartment to confront the reality of her married life.

It was an unmitigated disaster. Agnes was not without the need or desire for love. "The hunger for love, for tenderness and affection, was one of the deepest and most tyrannical urges within me. And I was lonely," she would write.[54] Had the early years of her life left her less damaged, perhaps Ernest could have been a more suitable companion. Over time, he might have helped her recover her trust in men. But Agnes could not keep from looking down on him for not being more aggressive, and the inner war she fought to be reasonable often made her irrationally angry. Her violent mood swings left them both exhausted, and the additional pressure of their newly sexual relationship occasionally pushed her beyond her limits.

"I was so ashamed of myself because I was called 'Mrs.' that I could hardly look people in the face," she later wrote. Moments before marriage, a woman was "supposed to think that the sex act is a degrading, debasing, shameful act; then she is married with a few words, and society tells her that now she may have sex relations every hour of the day if she wishes. Of course, an attitude formulated during the early years of her life cannot be changed in two minutes by the words of an official or a priest . . . If the woman is sensitive, she becomes actually psychically ill, if not physically."[55]

The newlyweds shared domestic tasks. *Courtesy Steve Finney.*

Agnes not only considered sex an unseemly activity for a decent woman like herself; she lived in dread of becoming pregnant. Determined never to bring a child into life to hurt as she had, she also feared that having a child ensured a premature end to her upward mobility. Apparently neither she nor Ernest had access to birth control, and the shameful atmosphere with which she surrounded the subject of sex placed any discussion off limits. The outcome she so desperately feared was perhaps inevitable. Weeks into their physical relationship, Agnes discovered she was pregnant.

Plunging into despair, she held Ernest entirely responsible for the unwanted circumstance. "Fear, bitterness, hatred . . . swept through me like a hurricane. Everything that was hopeful vanished," Agnes recalled.[56] Her distress so consumed her that she said she tried to drown herself in her bathtub, but her landlady heard her splashing and choking and intervened. In acknowledgment of the threat Agnes's pregnancy appeared to pose to her mental health, a physician performed an illegal abortion.

Agnes survived this first crisis of her married life, but it left her resolutely opposed to shouldering any further burdens a traditional marriage might impose. This included sharing a home with her husband. In the future, Ernest would need to come to her if he wished to see her. In June 1913 she moved by herself to San Diego and assumed a position as faculty secretary at the San Diego Normal School. That fall, she enrolled for classes.

Agnes quickly distinguished herself as a student. In her off-hours, she founded a student newspaper, on which she served as business manager, and acquired a camera and began taking photographs. Older, more worldly, and more confident than she had been in Tempe, she became the charismatic center of a campus literary clique, people who, according to one admirer, appreciated the "unusual amount of cleverness . . . originality . . . and laughter" she brought to their lives.[57] Agnes's friends saw an antic singer and dancer whose gifts as a raconteur and zest for parlor tricks like telling fortunes with apple seeds were in great demand at parties. Her theatrical ability was also showcased in several campus productions including a vaudeville interpretation of *The Merchant of Venice*. But if Agnes was increasingly comfortable courting the limelight, she remained uncomfortable with herself.

When Myrtle joined her sister in 1914, she was taken aback by what a friend described as Agnes's attempts to play the proper young matron. Her affection for hosting "delightful" theater parties, the disdain Agnes professed for lowbrow habits like gum chewing, and her attempts to lose her accent and dialect struck Myrtle as affected and pretentious.[58] The scared, defiant girl who had once led the toughest kids beyond the tracks was barely recognizable beneath Agnes's modish clothes, elaborate hairdo, and attempts to reduce her full-figured form,

Agnes enjoyed dressing in costume. *Courtesy Steve Finney.*

At the beach, circa 1914, with a classmate from the San Diego Normal School. *Courtesy Steve Finney.*

Agnes (left) and her sister Myrtle on a jaunt in Tijuana, Mexico. *Courtesy Steve Finney.*

and Myrtle was determined to do something about it. [59] If the high-spirited former cowgirl went off to shoot pool or ride her motorcycle to Tijuana, she would urge her older sister to join her. Agnes often found the temptation impossible to resist.

The sight of the two Smedley sisters dancing the "Dippy," wearing costumes or form-fitting bathing suits, or imbibing quantities of alcohol at beach parties and wienie roasts became a familiar one to their classmates. [60] Egged on by her daredevil sibling, Agnes purchased a Ford she named Wiggles, in which she executed stunts "that would never be attempted by many veterans," the student paper reported. [61] At least one classmates confessed to being befuddled by what she described as Agnes's "erratic" persona. [62]

In March 1914, Har Dayal was arrested as an undesirable alien and fled the United States for Europe. The political movement he had created continued to grow in his absence. When war broke out that August, Ghadrites rejoiced. With England preoccupied by a war with Germany, the men believed all they needed was the return of a few thousand zealous revolutionaries for India to burst into flames. Thousands of poor, uneducated Sikh immigrants heeded the Ghadr Party's call for volunteers. Unrealistic, impatient, intransigent—the Ghadrites may well have been everything their critics later alleged, but their readiness to die as martyrs in armed combat for the freedom and dignity they felt were denied them by British rule had a profound impact on Agnes's emerging political consciousness. With the empathy of shared experience, she understood their shame, their inclination to act rather than talk to avenge a wrong. The propaganda that was a highlight and focal point of their movement influenced her as well.

As the spring semester of 1914 drew to a close, Agnes needed only a few more classes to graduate. However, by August 29, when the first batch of Ghadrites departed from San Francisco, she had abandoned her studies and become an active worker in the Ghadr movement. [63] After making contact, most likely, with Bhagwan Singh, one of a trio of Indian revolutionaries who ran the Ghadr Party following Dayal's departure, Agnes had embarked on the covert life she would pursue, off and on, for the next two and a half decades. [64] That fall, when she began to teach typing and stenography in the school's commercial department, her work was little more than a day job that kept her in food and shelter while providing cover for her other activities.

In February 1915, British authorities crushed the first attempt by Ghadr revolutionaries to carry off an armed uprising in their native Punjab. However, by

spring the Ghadr Party was no longer the only organization fomenting revolution in India from American shores. Hoping to distract British troops from the
war front while England protected its interests in India, the German Foreign
Office had helped Har Dayal and other prominent Indian exiles establish
another group. The Berlin India Committee would offer leadership to Indian
revolutionaries and oversee a quarter-million-dollar war chest provided by the
Germans for their activities. Under its direction, a number of young Bengali
extremists had begun to assemble men and ships to carry weapons and ammunition to India, and neutral America became the major base of operations against
the British Raj.

The San Francisco Bay Area was the center of Indian revolutionaries' clandestine activities, but San Diego also played a critical role. When this second
group of extremist Indian nationalists embarked on the implementation of their
plans, American coeds like Agnes who had earlier garnered Dayal's attention
were pressed into service, along with the often unruly Ghadrites. In short order,
the women were serving as couriers and letter carriers, renting safe deposit boxes
in which the Indians stored sensitive documents, and performing other delicate
services in the name of India's freedom. A select few were also entrusted to
become organizers, propagandists, American agents for Dayal, and launderers of
German funds.[65]

In the late spring of 1915, when the two largest arms-running schemes were at
their peak, Agnes announced that she and Myrtle would be attending the summer session at the University of California, Berkeley. The sisters left for the Bay
Area at the end of the spring semester, but Agnes never enrolled for classes.[66]
Berkeley was then a white-hot center of Indo-German arms-smuggling efforts,
with a private factory that prepared arms and ammunition for shipment, and privately Agnes later confessed to being acquainted with Eckhart Von Schack, the
German vice-consul in San Francisco who was then the chief dispenser of funds
to West Coast Indian revolutionaries.[67] Publicly, though, she would maintain
that she had not "the least connection, directly or indirectly, with the acts of certain . . . East Indians in connection with a shipment of arms to India in 1915."[68]
Her participation in the Indian independence movement that summer, she contended, was confined to reading up on the situation in India and attending lectures and meetings conducted by Indian nationalist leaders—even though it was
common knowledge by this time that all such meetings were of a highly covert
nature.[69]

Ernest, too, spent the summer of 1915 in the Bay Area, anticipating some
improvement in their relationship, but Agnes later wrote that her terror of having children hovered "like a bird of prey" over her head.[70] When she unexpect-
edly found herself pregnant a second time, it became yet another stone in the

mountain of evidence she was accumulating against the marriage. She resorted to another illegal abortion, she would recall, and on the streetcar ride home she lay on her seat sweating and moaning and clutching Ernest's hand. Mortified by her public display, Ernest ordered her to sit up. A moment later, he apologized for his angry outburst but the damage was done. Agnes, who had mistreated him on so many occasions, later confessed that she could not forgive the one cruel thing he did to her.

At the beginning of 1916, Ernest made a final effort to preserve their foundering marriage. Cutting short his own plans for further schooling, he moved into Agnes's home in San Diego. Even so, she could not keep the trauma of her parents' relationship from visiting her own. When the muckraking novelist Upton Sinclair arrived in the city for a six-month stay, she discovered that by immersing herself in political work, she could keep difficult personal issues at bay. It was a latent talent she would call on repeatedly in the years to come.

By this time Sinclair's *The Jungle* had achieved a striking success in reaching a mass audience with a Socialist message, and Agnes, impressed, attended sev-

After Agnes left the family, Charles Smedley worked as a sheriff in the Oklahoma Panhandle. *Courtesy Elizabeth Smedley.*

eral of his lectures. Afterward she introduced herself to the famous author. As she had with Thor, she recast her childhood years as the mythic tale of a coal miner's daughter who escaped direst poverty on the fields near Ludlow. On this second telling, she performed better, highlighting those elements that made for a good story and overlooking those that muddied her effect (like the fact that her father had never been a miner but rather had been one of the detested deputy sheriffs who brutalized them). Sinclair would declare himself delighted at having made the acquaintance of so true a daughter of the working class.[71]

Agnes urged him to address her students, then worked with them to establish a chapter of the Intercollegiate Socialist Society. She also began to participate in the organization of liberal San Diegans that had sponsored Sinclair's talks.[72] In the years since 1912, when the IWW Free Speech Fights had rocked the town, the Open Forum had become the venue for prominent leftists including Emma Goldman and Eugene Debs to air their views. It was here that Agnes first encountered rank-and-file members of the now notorious organization. Later she said she felt a real affinity with these western men of action who "did not talk of the working class as if it were some far and distant wonder," but she was in no hurry to join them.[73]

By the summer of 1916, Agnes had concluded that she could no longer endure her marriage. "I take the blame," she would write that she told Ernest. "I do not want to be married; marriage is too terrible and I should never have entered it. I was wrong—for you loved me and I do not know what love means. I want my name back, also."[74] Like a number of Ghadr Party supporters, both Indian and American, she traveled to San Francisco that August to attend what she described as a lecture by Ram Chandra, the Hindu revolutionary who had assumed command of the organization.[75] The Berlin India Committee, however, which appeared to be hosting the event, referred to it as a conference at which they would determine Chandra's fate.[76]

On the advice of the BIC, a veritable stream of silver had flowed from the German Consulate at San Francisco into Ghadr Party coffers since the beginning of the European war. However, Ram Chandra refused to account for it, and his behavior fanned existing tensions between the German Foreign Office and the Indian revolutionaries, and among Hindu, Sikh, and Muslim elements within the Indian revolutionary movement. Hundreds of thousands of German dollars had been expended on numerous efforts to spark an armed uprising in India, but not a single one had succeeded.

The charges of embezzlement were splintering the Ghadr Party. Upper-caste Hindus from Bengal, who were favored by the BIC, blamed the Ghadrites' inability to keep their mouths closed rather than any shortcomings of their own for inhibiting the secret implementation of their plans.[77] They scorned the Sikh

Ghadrites as ignorant fanatics whom they could advise and order around. Ghadr Party rank and file, in their turn, cursed the "English-knowing babus" (as they referred to the party's anglicized Hindu leaders) and accused Ram Chandra of ruining their movement.

Agnes said that after the lecture she met privately with the embattled Ghadr chief but made no further effort to contact him.[78] Her admission, however, concealed as much as it revealed, for by the time the conference ended, the Sikh faction—led by Bhagwan Singh and supported by BIC leaders, the German foreign minister, the German Consulate, the German ambassador, and the party's American supporters—had wrested control of the movement from Chandra.

By summer's end, Agnes had struck up a worshipful acquaintance with Singh, a poet and former priest. Unlike the "little dried up fellows" at San Diego's Socialist local, she later wrote, whose rantings on technical aspects of Marxism bored her silly, Singh's militant faith was grounded in experience rather than theory.[79] Throughout that fall, the new Ghadr leader visited Agnes at the ranch in Dulzura where Agnes spent weekends with her sister, scandalizing its conservative owners, who supported the taboo on interracial relationships.[80] They prevailed on Myrtle to cut off contact with her sister, but Agnes appeared

Ghadr Party leader Bhagwan Singh. *National Archives of India.*

In San Diego, shortly before Agnes departed for New York City. *Courtesy Steve Finney.*

less interested in a romantic partner than in a continuing role in the Indian struggle for freedom.

Over the course of 1916, the BIC had established a base on the East Coast, three thousand miles away from the obstreperous Ghadr Party, and as the center of the Indian movement shifted from the West Coast to New York City, Agnes grew increasingly interested in relocating there. That December, as the holidays approached and German foreign minister Alfred Zimmerman prepared to approve an additional fifty thousand dollars for BIC plans, she got her wish. Singh, one of a few Ghadr Party figures who remained close to the BIC, apparently asked Agnes to transport some documents relating to the matter to New York City. On December 31, she headed east.

CHAPTER 3

Indian Activism in Greenwich Village

There is no room for the hyphen in our citizenship... He who is not with us is against us and should be treated as an enemy alien... We have room in this country for but one flag... We have room for but one language... The German-American alliance, the Sinn Feiners, the East Side Russian revolutionary organizations... and the IWW are anti-American to the core... Our bitter experience should teach us for a generation to crush under our heel any movement that smacks in the slightest of the German game.

THEODORE ROOSEVELT

A GNES REACHED New York City near the start of 1917. Thor, who had herself only just returned east, met her sister-in-law's train at Grand Central Station. Agnes's treatment of Ernest disturbed Thor, but she remained a friend, and she and Haberman (they had recently married) had invited Agnes to stay with them in Greenwich Village.

In the years before America entered the war, an extraordinary collection of artists, writers, radicals, and free spirits had converged on this part of Manhattan, transforming a neighborhood of low-rise buildings, leafy squares, and cobbled streets into America's bohemia. The youthful participants in this vibrant, indecorous experiment had rejected materialistic bourgeois life for a funky Chautauqua of art exhibitions and plays, all-night poetic orgies, evenings at Mabel Dodge's salon, and festivals and costume balls where admiring crowds watched Isadora Duncan perform ancient Greek dances. If Agnes had been looking for a place to expand her horizons, she could not have found a more congenial spot.

Beyond a joint commitment to flouting convention and contempt for the powers that be, these refugees from middle-class philistinism embraced no overarching worldview, but political tastes inclined more toward the anarchism and syndicalism of Emma Goldman and "Big" Bill Haywood than more staid Marxist theory. The broadly conceived socialism they envisioned was distinguished by a conviction that it would be accomplished through art as well as political and economic action, and accompanied by a cultural transformation as well.[1]

Thorberg was a popular member of the community, and she introduced Agnes to a number of local characters, among them her good friend and colleague Henrietta Rodman. Rodman, the doyenne of Village female radicals, was the guiding force behind the famous Liberal Club and a charter member of Heterodoxy, a picturesque luncheon club for self-declared unorthodox women.[2] With her androgynously close-cropped hair, shapeless sacks, and sandals worn with queer brown socks, she epitomized the lifestyle radicalism that was a hallmark of Village life.

In the 1930s Agnes was embarrassed by suggestions that she had been unduly affected by her years in Greenwich Village. By then, Agnes would recall, the "mere bohemianism" of the community's individualistic rebels was considered a negative influence on a sober revolutionary like herself. There is little question, though, that Villagers' emphasis on personal fulfillment and self-expression influenced Agnes's style. Within months after moving to New York City, Agnes had abandoned her pose as a sober young matron and woven her taste for cowboy tunes and country dances, gift for mimicry, and earthy sense of humor into a more beguiling persona as an outsized western character. "Naughty Mrs. Brundin," as Henrietta's brother, Bayard, described Agnes, could be the life of the party.[3] Still, in the beginning she struggled mightily.

It was "so easy to be drawn beyond your depth in New York City," Agnes later wrote. Watching Thor's friends sprawl on her couch, smoking cigarettes while they discussed the theater, politics, art, philosophy, and Freud, Agnes felt as alienated and ill at ease as she had among the little white girls in Trinidad. It would be years before she felt comfortable in the realm of abstract thought, exchanging ideas with people who "used books critically, skeptically, comparatively," as she later wrote.[4]

After a childhood and youth that were one long Calvary, a female friend later observed, Agnes had thirsted after knowledge in the belief that its magic "would lead her into the shining land of happiness." Having acquired it at great cost, her discovery "that the little bit of knowledge she had gathered . . . was still nothing . . . that besides knowledge there was also . . . something called culture," rattled her confidence.[5] Thor's friends' laughter at Agnes's faux pas and their romantic idealization of the working class exacerbated her tormenting sense of difference.

Agnes, like so many other escapees from small-town life, had come to New York harboring ambitions of leadership. "Success, written on the heart of America, was also written on" hers, she later wrote.[6] But when Agnes accompanied Thor and Robert Haberman to the Village's celebrated Socialist local, the "rich and noted men and women who lectured on poverty, injustice and the suppression of the masses took no more notice of her than the chairs they gripped in passing," she would resentfully observe.[7] It was only the pro-India struggle, far smaller and less popular than the organized Socialist movement, that valued her contributions and sought her out.

Radical acquaintances asked Agnes what place she thought a purely nationalist battle had in the workers' international movement for freedom, she later recalled. What made her think India's landed classes would do a better job than the British in responding to the country's working people? Such debates were beyond her. Unlike most Village intellectuals, who shared America's general indifference toward a subject so far from their lives and self-interest, Agnes understood on a visceral level the injustice of British policy in India, and it fueled her wrath.

While living on the West Coast, Robert Haberman, like Agnes, had gotten involved in the Indian revolutionaries' activities; recently he had helped them smuggle a cache of machine guns into India.[8] Through him and her own connections, Agnes was soon in contact with Indian extremists in the city. Introductions took place either at the Habermans' or the nearby Civic Club, whose low membership fees and lack of racial discrimination made it a favored spot for Indians to interact with responsive Americans. Sponsored by the Habermans, Agnes soon joined the club herself.[9]

None of the Indians Agnes met during her first weeks in New York made a deeper impression on her than the fifty-two-year-old Lajpat Rai, the most renowned Indian nationalist leader then living in the United States and a popular speaker at the club's Saturday afternoon lectures.[10] Since being deported from India for his involvement in the Arya Samaj, India's leading social reform movement, Rai, a former professor, resided mostly in New York, where his moderate views and accessible style had won a number of American liberals to his cause.[11] Agnes later wrote that she was struck by his courage and singleness of purpose and sought him out as her guru. She became secretary of the India study group that Rai conducted at the Civic Club and agreed to type a manuscript on his experience in America in exchange for private tutoring in Indian history.[12] Soon she was seeing him nearly every day. Her attachment to Rai, she later wrote, enabled her to learn more from him than from any other source.

Like an Indian holy man, Rai scorned the Western preoccupation with power and money. He devoted himself entirely to advancing the cause of India's freedom without focusing on rewards or results, Agnes would recall. His instruction, which was as much about the way to live one's life as it was about Indian history, offered her a model of character and integrity. Agnes later wrote that she worried Rai looked down on her because she was still as "primitive as a weed," but she longed for the warmth of a father figure in her life.[13] And it seems that

Rai, a lonely but decent man, allowed Agnes to be close to him without imposing the sexual involvement she found so problematic. He liked her fire and
enthusiasm, Agnes later confessed, and encouraged her to become a teacher in
India.[14]

Much as Agnes admired Rai, however, she did not share his reformist views.
Convinced "that India could not advance until it was freed from British rule—
as America had been freed—by revolution," as she wrote years later, Agnes was
more closely aligned politically with the young Indian extremists in the city.[15] Of
them, she was personally fondest of a twenty-three-year-old Bengali named
Sailendra Nath Ghose, who had recently been dispatched to New York City
with an updated cipher system for the conspirators and instructions to improve
communication between Indian revolutionaries in the United States and their
associates in Bengal.[16]

Ill at ease among Village intellectuals, Agnes sank easily into friendship with
Ghose. His puppy-dog crush was soon the stuff of gossip in Village circles, but
Agnes, who had rebuffed her own brothers' repeated entreaties for assistance,
appeared grateful for the opportunity to nurture a surrogate sibling. Dismissing
Ghose's attraction to her as part of his "voluptuary nature," Agnes showered him
with affection; later she recalled good-humoredly how his mischievous antics
used to make her long to take "take down his pants and give him a hell of a
spanking!"[17]

Fresh from India and unfamiliar with the mores of bohemian radicals, Ghose
appeared content to worship Agnes from afar.[18] Agnes's involvement was not
strictly platonic with every Indian she met. Ghose's mentor, M. N. Roy, a der-
ring-doer for the Indian Revolutionary Party in Bengal and a comrade-in-arms of
Haberman, attracted her intensely.[19] Tall, lean, and handsome, with a thick
mustache and glittering eyes, Roy had worked on several German-financed
schemes to import arms into India since the outbreak of World War I, most
notably on an abortive effort to smuggle thirty thousand rifles and twelve million
rounds of ammunition into Bengal aboard the tanker SS *Maverick*, which had
sailed under an American flag during the hectic summer of 1915.

After attending the 1916 Indian revolutionaries' conference in San Francisco,
Roy was supposed to have traveled to Berlin to meet with BIC leaders, but he
had fallen in love with a Stanford coed while visiting the Bay Area and literally
missed his ship. Outraged by his lack of discipline, German authorities had cut
off his funding, but Roy remained confident that he would, in the not too distant future, assume a position of leadership in the movement, on his terms,
without subordinating himself to the dictates of the BIC or the Germans who
paid their bills.

Roy was "arrogant, self important, and ill tempered in discussion ... often

M. N. Roy, Indian revolutionary and Agnes's bête noir.

vehement in seeking to impose his opinion on others," according to one contemporary.[20] Aside from his desire for Indian independence, another recalled,
the well-bred Brahmin was in no way a radical, and he retained a firm belief in
child marriage, the caste system, and other institutions that held India back.[21]
Agnes sneered at Roy's cynicism, his failure to extend his revolutionary ideas to
women, and his tendency to "regard me and my ideas as a standing insult to
himself," as she described it,[22] but his resemblance to the cowboys who had
formed her tastes overrode her judgment.

By 1917, Roy had married his American sweetheart, but that did not preclude
his being attracted to Agnes, too.[23] Mistaking her for a practitioner of free love,
he slid his hands down Agnes's arm one evening, "caught my hands in a warm,
trembling grip [and] with a quick, impulsive movement," drew her close and
kissed her.[24] Agnes recalled that at first she responded with ardor. Once she lay
beneath him, however, she froze, convinced that no decent woman experienced
sexual desire or accepted responsibility for such feelings. Then, she would write,
she allowed Roy to physically overpower her as she had permitted others in the
past, humiliated by the need that led her to comply.

While she lay in bed, weeping and furious with herself, he let himself out
the door, smiling "faintly" at his conquest, she would write.[25] A few years later
they encountered one another again, and Roy claimed he could not understand
why Agnes seemed to have a grudge against him.[26] She had neither forgotten
nor forgiven what occurred.

The encounter was traumatic, but it marked a turning point in Agnes's life. Her distress moved her to confront the fears that poisoned her intimate encounters. Through fellow Villager Margaret Sanger, who was then in the midst of a public campaign over women's right to detailed information about contraception, Agnes acquired a basic knowledge of birth control. Sanger's advocacy of women's need to accept their sexual activity as biologically appropriate behavior, whether with their marital partner or an evening's acquaintance, also effected a fundamental shift in Agnes's attitude. In fact, the older woman's awareness that improved access to birth control was vital in eliminating the backward thinking that kept poor and working-class women from enjoying sex touched Agnes so deeply that she became an acolyte in Sanger's fledgling movement.

Thorberg described her sister-in-law as "very able, exceedingly earnest, and a hard worker"—qualities that were much in evidence as Agnes began to assist Sanger in the office of the *Birth Control Review*.[27] After Sanger heard her proselytize on Manhattan street corners, she recognized something more valuable in Agnes: a gifted organizer in the making. Like her father the snake oil salesman, Agnes knew how to mine the force of her personality in order to make a sale. Sanger did not necessarily understand the "extraordinarily shy and mysterious"

Birth control pioneer Margaret Sanger. *From the collections of the Library of Congress.*

woman, as she later described her youthful volunteer, and she was so taken in
by Agnes's stories that she literally believed Agnes had been born in a covered
wagon, but Sanger appreciated Agnes's efforts to remember her roots as she
searched for a better life, and how that made her a natural champion of the
underdog.[28]

Back as a "traveling woman," Agnes had successfully traded on her charisma
for purely personal gain. Now that she was pitching the greater good, she was
even more effective. However, as the spring of 1917 approached, America's looming entrance into the European conflict would propel her in another direction.

Although U.S. diplomatic officials had shown little interest in India during
the first years of the European war, Great Britain was pressing American officials
to adopt a more aggressive policy regarding Indian nationalist activity in the
United States. Amid a growing clamor for tightened national security and an
end to German intrigues in America, the U.S. Department of Justice identified
the ideological and legal means by which they could appease their British allies.
If they branded the Indian revolutionaries' actions a conspiracy, they could
charge the Indians with violating U.S. neutrality laws by plotting against the
Allies on American soil. That did not bode well for Agnes.

Federal officials began closing in on the Indians and their associates.[29] The
discovery of a large store of German-bought rifles, swords, revolvers, and cannon
parts in a Houston Street warehouse led New York City police to the Manhattan
home of Chandra Chakravarty, the thin-faced, falsetto-voiced leader of the
BIC in America. Shortly after midnight on March 6, 1917, officers arrested
Chakravarty along with his Prussian companion. Within days, the men admitted
receiving more than sixty thousand dollars from the German military attaché in
New York for their Berlin-directed conspiracy and promised to tell all they knew.
On March 10, a front-page story in the *New York Times* reported the unearthing
of a "worldwide German plot to instigate rebellions and uprisings against British
rule in India."[30] Federal officials warned that a thorough investigation had only
just begun.

Working closely with the British, the State Department began calling in
many of the Indian revolutionaries Agnes had known on both coasts to discuss
their involvement with various arms shipments, the BIC, and the Ghadr Party.
That April, days after America entered the war, nearly one hundred Indian revolutionaries, including disgraced former Ghadr chief Ram Chandra and fifteen
other Ghadr Party leaders, were taken into custody in New York, Chicago, and
San Francisco, along with dozens of high-ranking German diplomatic officials.

The American public, long suspicious of the presumed split loyalties of its
immigrants, harbored little affection for the Indian revolutionaries' foreignness,
their radicalism, or their apparent pro-German sympathies. With newspapers

from coast to coast running front-page stories on the "Hindu-German Conspiracy" ("Hindu" being their generic term for all Indians, regardless of religion), the period of the United States as the center of Indo-German efforts against the British Raj came to a close. America's involvement in the war did not, however, put an end to the collaboration between the Germans and the Indian revolutionaries; BIC leaders and their German paymasters simply shifted their base of operations from the United States to Mexico. The costly failure of the Indians' numerous arms-running ventures convinced the Germans, though, to limit their future commitment only to underwriting propagandistic activities.[31]

Late that May, with most of the Indian revolutionaries in the United States either under surveillance, indicted, under arrest, or awaiting trial, Roy decided that his moment to seize leadership of the exile movement had come. Fleeing New York for Mexico, he met with local German agents and promoted himself as the most significant Indian conspirator in Mexico and therefore the best suited to maintain contact with his American-based counterparts and manage German funds. The German legation anointed Roy to oversee all Indian revolutionary activity in Mexico and gave him fifty thousand dollars to dispense as he saw fit.[32]

In Mexico City, Roy (using the nom de guerre Manuel Mendez) established himself in a sumptuous house on the wealthy Colonia Roma. By the time his protégé, Sailendra Nath Ghose, joined him, Roy was passing himself off as an Indian prince and mingling in the upper echelons of local society.

Agnes later wrote that because British political detectives were closely tracking the Indians' activities in the United States, before he left Ghose had asked her, as a favor, to act as a "kind of communication center" for the Indian revolutionaries abroad.[33] His request, she said, had frightened her. President Wilson's prediction—that once the United States became involved in World War I, Americans would forget such a thing as tolerance ever existed—was proving true. If she were caught, Agnes knew, she was likely to be sentenced less harshly than an Indian for collaborating in their German-financed plans. But she was also aware that her countrymen, engaged in the fight to preserve democracy, would view her political activity as equivalent to sympathizing with the Central Powers. Still, she agreed. Having turned her back on her own family, she later wrote, she felt a sense of "duty and responsibility" toward the Indians.[34]

Agnes's loyalty was somewhat misplaced. In her desire to be of service, she failed to distinguish between the party of uneducated Sikhs from the Punjab that had won her heart and the upper-caste Hindus from Bengal to whom she pledged her aid. Both shared a common goal, but there were significant differences between the two groups. By involving herself as intimately as she had in the Bengalis' labyrinthine schemes, Agnes opened herself up to the deception, betrayal, and internecine warfare endemic among them. Soon she would be consumed.

Lajpat Rai, who had come to mistrust the Bengali revolutionaries, was concerned about Agnes's welfare. Repeatedly he tried to discourage her from further involvement and threatened to have nothing more to do with Agnes if she persisted in her relationships with them.[35] His entreaties left her unmoved. In the years to come, Agnes would exploit her brief attachment to the esteemed Indian moderate to disguise her more radical associations and activities, but her insistence on maintaining those connections at this time essentially killed her friendship with Rai.

Pledged to secrecy, Agnes did not explain even to Thor why she suddenly left her sister-in-law's house that May and moved into the Bank Street apartment of Henrietta Rodman's brother, Bayard. That summer, while every Indian revolutionary who could escaped the United States and made his way to Mexico, Agnes wrote daily to Ghose, apprising him of the goings-on and rerouting correspondence between Indian revolutionary leaders in Mexico, on the West Coast, and in Berlin.[36]

Agnes had also agreed, in Ghose's absence, to oversee the publication and distribution of several thousand copies of *The Isolation of Japan in World Politics,* a virulently anti-Allied manuscript. The project was of particular importance to the BIC and the Germans, so Agnes was amply recompensed for the task—so well, in fact, that she quit her day job to devote herself to her clandestine activities. To justify her unexpected leisure, Agnes, like other Indian operatives receiving German funds from the BIC at this time, circulated a fanciful tale about having inherited money from a relative with considerable real estate holdings.[37]

To avoid detection by the British secret service agents Agnes correctly suspected of opening her mail and surveilling her, she began moving from apartment to apartment. From her room at 2 Bank Street, Agnes went to 156 Waverly Place. Then she shifted to 16 East Ninth Street. By mid-March of 1918, she would move seven more times. However, the next phase of the Indo-German propaganda campaign required more than a change of apartments. For this venture, Agnes and her fellow conspirators Bhagwan Singh and Tarak Nath Das (author of the manuscript in Agnes's care) needed Ghose to return to the United States. Disenchanted with Roy's tendency to value his personal advancement above India's revolution, Ghose was happy to oblige.

As Das envisioned the plan, the three men would pose as members of a special commission of the "Indian Nationalist Party," a fictitious political party purportedly based in Calcutta, which sought India's independence and the establishment of a federated republic there.[38] In letters to President Wilson and foreign diplomats, the Indians would seek official recognition as diplomatic representatives. The enterprise was an outright fraud, but if they managed to pull it off, the revolutionaries would gain incredible entrée and diplomatic privileges in the countries where they were credentialed.

Because mail between the United States and Mexico was being censored as a wartime measure, Ghose would pick up drafts of the men's so-called diplomatic correspondence in person in San Francisco, where Das and Singh awaited trial. (Ghose would also be the Indian Nationalist Party's sole agent in the flesh until the latter two were free to travel.) Once he delivered the materials to New York, Agnes would retype them on official stationery, sign them, attach a cover letter, and mail them off.[39] In the same way that Das had another young American woman storing a quantity of bomb-making manuals for the Indians in Oakland, Agnes would keep the men's codes and foreign addresses at her home. She would also handle any correspondence as the responses came in.

All the conspirators needed from Roy was a portion of the German currency allotted for such activities, but Roy, who seemed jealous of Agnes's relationship with Ghose, was reluctant to underwrite the venture. Convinced that their bond was sexual, Roy later wrote, he tried to discourage Ghose from becoming further involved with Agnes, warning him that the infatuation of a young man for a woman "much older" than himself (Agnes was two years Ghose's senior) was dangerous.[40] He would recall urging Ghose to remain in Mexico, doing something that would give him some revolutionary experience instead of returning to the United States, as Agnes proposed.

Roy's advice was perhaps self-serving, but it was not wrong. Ghose was a fugitive from justice in the United States, under indictment in the Hindu-German Conspiracy case, and the climate for the work he would undertake was inhospitable. Ghose chose to ignore him. That November—as seventeen Indian revolutionaries, including the discredited former Ghadr leader Ram Chandra, the equally discredited BIC agent Chandra Chakravarty, and the former German consul general and vice-consul went on trial in San Francisco for conspiring in neutral America from August 1914 to August 1915 to launch a military expedition to India and foment revolt—Ghose arrived with a bundle of Roy's German money and several vials of a deadly East Indian poison with which he intended to punish Chakravarty and his Prussian companion for their confessions.[41]

Ghose was not alone in his rage. Inside the courtroom, tensions among the Indians over the failed intrigues and betrayals ran so high that Justice Department officials had assigned a special military guard just to protect Chakravarty. The place seethed with animosity. Legally, the subject at hand was whether the defendants had entered into a conspiracy on what was then neutral American soil, but the real issues were California's history of anti-Asian prejudice, the threat the Indian revolutionaries posed to the British Crown, and the matter of their German financing. Throughout the proceedings, the British secret service would offer the U.S. prosecutor every assistance—securing evidence, breaking the Indians' codes and messages, and explaining the inner workings of the German government during the period on which the trial focused.[42]

Within a month, Ghose had returned to San Francisco and the diplomatic correspondence venture was humming along. In her capacity as secretary for the fictitious Pulin Behari Bose, Agnes signed the letters "Marie Rogers."[43] Marie was the name Agnes had invented for herself years earlier and associated with auspicious times; Marie Rogers would later reappear as the heroine of her autobiographical novel, *Daughter of Earth*.

Across the ocean, the world was convulsing. As the trial advanced in San Francisco, the Russian Bolshevik Party overthrew the liberal provisional government created after the fall of the tsar several months earlier. In the name of the local "soviets," or councils, that had represented Russia's workers, peasants, and soldiers since that time, they established a workers' state in its place. Like Marx and his followers, the revolutionary socialists who led the coup d'état known as the Bolshevik Revolution had not given much thought to the government they would establish after they assumed power, but party leader V. I. Lenin had spoken often of his desire for a far more democratic republic than the parliamentary system his minority party toppled—one with a universally armed people and a universal militia to replace the country's detested police force, a standing army, and elected officials who could be recalled by a majority of voters.[44]

At the moment, the Bolsheviks were engaged in a ruthless utopian campaign whose goal was the abolition of all vestiges of private property and the creation of a centralized communist economy, which they were certain would quickly turn Russia into the most productive country in the world. Agnes, like other radicals of substance and integrity, viewed the unexpected triumph of their revolution as one of the great events in world history. If a working-class state had been formed in the most regressive country in Europe, she assumed, the final victory of socialism was close at hand.[45] The paucity of genuine information coming out of Russia and the malicious coverage provided by a shaken mainstream press made it hard for someone like her to question the glowing accounts by John Reed in the *Liberator*, or to differentiate between the revolution as she idealistically envisioned it and the Bolsheviki who, she read, had led the country's most exploited citizens to power. A dictatorship of the proletariat and a dictatorship of the Bolshevik Party were one and the same to her. The word *soviet* was a bewitching term.

The Indian revolutionaries, on the other hand, were more nationalist than socialist in their sympathies. However, as phrases like *class struggle, interna-*

tional solidarity, and *dictatorship of the proletariat*—until now spoken only with foreign-accents at the Socialist Party's Rand School—gained more common acceptance, BIC chief Virendranath Chattopadhyaya seized on the events in Russia to further the Indians' aims. Near the close of 1917, after the Bolsheviks had liberated Muslims in the Asian part of the Russian Empire and proclaimed the right of all nations to self-determination, Chattopadhyaya, or Chatto, as he was known, established contact with the soviet government.[46] From his new base in neutral Sweden (where he still received German money but was freer from the exigencies of German foreign policy) he announced his refusal to allow Germany to use Indian revolutionaries as pawns any longer. He declared his independence from the German Foreign Office and his blanket opposition to all imperialism, whether German or English. Other Indians followed suit.

Acting, it would appear, on Chatto's instructions, on December 12, 1917, the German-financed Indian Nationalist Party (whose entire membership consisted of Agnes, Das, Ghose, Singh, and the fictitious Pulin Behari Bose) drafted a letter to Leon Trotsky, the Bolsheviks' commissioner of foreign affairs, in which they requested Russian support for the Indian revolutionists standing trial in San Francisco.[47] But Das believed it would be better for Ghose to plead the Indians' case in person. Since the United States, like the Allied powers and virtually every other nation in the world, did not officially recognize the Bolshevik regime, Agnes met with *Masses* cartoonist Robert Minor about the clandestine maneuvers necessary for such a trip.[48]

Agnes passed on Minor's suggestions to Ghose in a letter dated February 27, 1918. However, he never received her missive. Cut off by Roy for disparaging him in San Francisco, Ghose was already headed east when Army Intelligence agents in San Francisco intercepted Agnes's correspondence. Immediately, they opened an inquiry into the matter of Das's manuscript and the Indian Nationalist Party.[49]

Ghose arrived in New York City on March 11, unaware of what was transpiring. Incomprehensibly, he elected to stay at the home of Chakravarty and his Prussian companion, but he spent most of his time with Agnes in her latest furnished room. Ghose would ring three times to let her know it was him; then the charlady would let him in.[50] Agnes was growing weary. She had transported the boxes of books and documents in her care several times over the last few weeks. But there would be no more moves. At 8:00 A.M. on the morning of March 15, 1918, a U.S. Naval Intelligence agent entered Agnes's apartment on a ruse and brought her in for questioning.

While she was being interrogated, other agents searched her apartment—without a warrant—and seized a mass of the diplomatic correspondence, including a carbon of the letter to Trotsky, appeals to the Brazilian Embassy and the governments of Paraguay, Panama, Denmark, and Chile, one of two wax seals Ghose had purchased in San Francisco, several copies of Das's book, and correspondence that investigating officers claimed signaled Agnes's intention to travel to Japan in the interests of the Indian Nationalist Party.[51]

The catechism was brutal, Agnes later wrote. Her examiners probed her, taunted her, and accused her of sleeping with Rai for money. She had never been questioned by the police before and would recall being terrified, but she soon discovered the satisfaction of suffering for a principle, and the righteousness of her cause emboldened her. Under questioning, Agnes denied having written Ghose, knowing any of the other Indians, or receiving German money. Unclear as to what extent her interrogators understood her involvement with the Indians, or of what exactly she was accused, she refused to answer further questions.

After Agnes failed to show up at her job or at New York University, where she had enrolled for courses in journalism and Spanish (in preparation, evidently, to join the Indian revolutionaries in Mexico) her friend Bayard Rodman stopped by her apartment to check on her.[52] Not finding her at home, he joked with Agnes's charlady that perhaps his spirited acquaintance was out cavorting with her bohemian set.[53] When Ghose stopped by later and saw that Agnes was still missing, he had darker, more accurate forebodings.

Agnes was detained overnight at the Delancey Street Jail. Then she was remanded to the Naval Intelligence Bureau for further questioning. While she was gone, the War Department, already suspicious of the Habermans, interrogated Thorberg and searched her home.[54] Agnes—who later wrote that she observed the Indian conspirators' code that "no man knows what another man is doing and no one asks"—had never discussed her activities with her sister-in-law, and Thor could provide no information.[55] Immediately after her grilling, though, Thorberg wired Haberman in Mexico, where he was in contact with Roy, that "that young fool, Agnes" had been implicated in the plot.[56]

Under questioning, Agnes continued to deny knowing Das (whom she had indeed never met), as well as Singh and Ghose, with whom she was acquainted. That Saturday, two detectives brought her back to her room to gather her necessities, then returned her to Delancey Street, where she remained incommunicado for the next two days. On the afternoon of March 18, Agnes was arrested and charged with violating the Espionage Act for conspiring to falsely represent herself as an official of the Indian Nationalist Party.

Ghose was apprehended the following day, at the request of the U.S. attorney in San Francisco, while trying to visit Agnes. By this time, Chakravarty and other government witnesses had received telegrams threatening them with fatal poisoning for betraying the Indian revolutionaries, but the toxic vials remained among Ghose's effects at the time of his arrest. Justice Department officials now confiscated them, along with the rest of Ghose's possessions. A few days later, Das was arrested in San Francisco.

Federal authorities neither knew nor claimed that Agnes was involved in the Indian-German intrigues on trial in that city, but news reports like the account in the *New York Times* asserting that "the arrest of this American radical worker was one of the most important developments in months in the worldwide German directed plot to cause trouble in India and weaken America's ally, Great Britain" further incited the wartime hysteria.[57] Moreover, being charged under the Espionage Act, while a merciless campaign was under way to suppress all forms of progressive dissent, practically guaranteed that Agnes and Ghose's activities on behalf of the Indian Nationalist Party would be interpreted as traitorous.

Under questioning Ghose proclaimed his love for Agnes, but he refused to discuss his political activities; both of them denied the charges against them at their arraignment. Unable to make bail, which was set at twenty-five thousand dollars for Ghose and ten thousand dollars for Agnes, the two were taken to New York City's House of Detention, otherwise known as the Tombs: a cold, dirty, vermin ridden place where, it was said, "the wealthy could still procure the privileges always attendant on money and the poor suffered even more indignities for lack of it."[58]

The Indian revolutionaries in Mexico followed their case closely. Some, like Herambalal Gupta, were concerned about Agnes's well-being, but Roy, who Ghose strongly suspected was responsible for their arrest, dismissed the pair's predicament as a "frivolous adventure" and later wrote that he refused to "waste" his money bailing them out of jail.[59] He was, however, concerned about what they might disclose under pressure. To maintain control and discourage the release of damaging information, he asked Purendra Narayan Sinha, a loyal lieutenant on Roy's New York payroll, to retain an attorney for Agnes and Ghose. Sinha and Roy then created a code, which discussed the prisoners' case as a medical situation, to prevent the correspondence from alerting wartime censors.[60]

Jointly, Agnes and Ghose would be referred to as *the invalids* or *the patients*. Individually, Agnes was *Ma*, and *the young man* was Ghose. *The hospital* was the Tombs; *taking them out* meant getting them released on bail. Their *medical bill* was their bail; *patent medicine* was money. *Physicians* meant lawyers; *doctors* meant the district attorney or federal authorities; their *health* referred to their case. Being *well* meant free; *collapsed* meant arrested. Postal censors delivered copies of the correspondence to Army Intelligence officials almost as soon as the letters were written; British intelligence agents in the United States decoded them nearly as quickly. The "Willie" letters, as they came to be known, may have failed in their intended purpose, but they illuminate the intense, rancorous connection between Agnes and Roy at this time and shed light on the Indian revolutionaries' battle for Comintern sponsorship three years hence.

On April 1, 1918, the U.S. District Court for the Southern District of New York returned indictments against Agnes and Ghose (along with the fictitious Bose, Tarak Nath Das, and Bhagwan Singh) for attempting to stir up rebellion against British rule in India and for passing themselves off as diplomats. Uncomfortable with their financial dependence on Roy for legal counsel she did not trust, Agnes believed she and Ghose would fare better with an attorney of their choosing. Since no one would be likely to assist her if it were known she already had a lawyer—never mind one that was paid for with German funds—when Agnes approached her classmate Truda Weil for help in raising a thousand dollars for a trial attorney, she never mentioned that fact. The "Agnes Smedley Defense Fund," whose officers included Agnes's former boss, A. Lyle de Jarnette; her journalism professor, James Melvin Lee; Henrietta Rodman's husband, Herman DeFrem; New York Post reporter Royal Davis; and Elizabeth Freeman of the People's Council, was soon cranking out fund-raising letters on Agnes's behalf.[61]

The final day of the San Francisco trial was April 24, 1918. Ghadr Party rank and file understood that a prison term was a certainty for most of the defendants, but that knowledge did not quell their ire. As two hundred spectators, attorneys, and defendants filed out of the courtroom at the noon recess, the strains among the Indians that had threatened to erupt throughout the trial finally exploded. Ram Singh, a defendant identified with Bhagwan Singh's faction of the Ghadr Party, had somehow managed to smuggle a weapon past the guard. Quietly, he approached Ram Chandra and fired four bullets into his body. Chandra staggered back and fell dead in front of the witness stand. Although it was never proven, Bhagwan Singh was thought to be behind it. When the jurors returned that afternoon, twenty-nine of the remaining thirty defendants were found guilty. Fifteen were Ghadr Party members. Bhagwan Singh was sentenced to eighteen months in prison. Tarak Nath Das received twenty-two months—the longest sentence passed. By the time the trial ended, the tab for the assistance the British government provided to U.S. prosecutors had reached more than two million dollars.

For chief U.S. attorney John Preston, the trial was an unqualified triumph. His ambitions stoked by the widespread publicity, he was already plotting a second action against Smedley and Ghose. In Soviet Russia, the Bolsheviks were furiously repudiating foreign loans and nationalizing foreign assets, conceding enormous material and territorial gains to imperial Germany, exporting a fearsome tide of revolutionary propaganda—and swiftly replacing the Germans as the most malignant enemy of panicky American leaders. While a federal campaign prepared the country for an intervention intended to destroy the fledgling Bolshevik government, Preston exploited swelling negative sentiments by recasting the former Hindu-German conspiracy as the present Hindu-Bolshevik danger, relying on the Indian Nationalist Party letter to Trotsky and Agnes's advice to Ghose on sneaking into Russia as his proof.

On May 7, 1918, eight weeks after Agnes entered the Tombs, Dr. Percy Stickney Grant raised her bail. On her release, Agnes moved into Henrietta Rodman's apartment, where she resumed her search for another attorney. Sinha was furious. Despite his best efforts to rein in the pair, he wrote Roy,

> even now the patients will have their own way—a way which, of course, leads right to hell. Even at this stage something could be done towards their recovery through the physician engaged by me, but the patients, at the suggestion of their equally idiotic friends [the BIC], want to change him. The physician has already done some good work for one of the invalids, and was willing to treat them at a nominal fee, but he has not been treated well, and has consequently changed his attitude somewhat . . . I feel I cannot do all I can for them simply for the obstinacy of the invalids. I am deeply grieved for that patient who has lost all his senses and has become a mere puppet; but what can you do with an insane? I have been insulted too—a thing which I do not for a moment stand—but as long as they are sick I shall continue doing whatever I can.[62]

"Of course," he added, knowing Roy's aversion to Agnes, "you understand all."

In the personal appeals she drafted to potential donors throughout the country, Agnes portrayed herself as the picture of injured innocence. The city was in turmoil, she wrote Charles Erskine Scott Wood, a Ghadr Party founding member,

> and everyone with money feels that my fight is not their fight . . . I am an American woman, twenty-six years of age, a student at New York University. Over one year ago I came to New York to attend school . . . My affairs [are] in a desperate and hopeless condition. I have no attorney, and my defense fund amounts to less than two hundred dollars . . . Newspapers called me a German spy and [so] inflamed the public mind that I have found it almost impossible to overcome the prejudice . . . I have no family and have lived a secluded life, devoting myself to my work and my studies . . .
>
> Let me tell you I am an American, and my ancestry goes back to the Revolutionary War. And that I am not in the least bit pro-German. I have merely believed in the independence of India, as well as for other countries.[63]

By the following month, she had raised enough money to retain the noted constitutional lawyer Gilbert Roe and his associate, Charles Recht. The pair met every one of Agnes's exacting requirements. They were liberal minded, "American in every respect...with American sympathies" in the war, she said, and willing to defend her on moral as well as technical grounds.[64] The men, both Civic Club members, appeared to know nothing beyond what Agnes chose to tell them, and Roe advised a colleague that she would receive "as good a defense as if she had been a real criminal, and a rich one at that," regardless of her ability to pay.[65]

Days after Roe and Recht took up their case, Agnes and Ghose were indicted in San Francisco on much the same lines as in New York, along with Tarak Nath Das and several Caucasian associates of the Indians who lived on the West Coast. Under section three of the Espionage Act, the section under which radicals were most commonly prosecuted, Agnes was also charged with distributing Das's pamphlet. As would often prove the case, authorities were correct in suspecting her covert activities. The problem, now and in the future, was the questionable legality and doubtful accuracy of what they accused her of doing.

Had the federal officials responsible for prosecuting Agnes known of her early activities with the Ghadr Party or her receipt of German funds, had they simply obtained a warrant before searching her apartment or detained her legally in the Tombs, they might have stood a better chance of conviction. The particular charges they brought against Agnes merely caught her up in the broader, more suspect wartime prosecution of American radicals and allowed her to deny the accusations with self-righteous indignation. So effectively did she do this that several contributors to her defense fund urged her to tell her whole story "frankly" so she could clear her name. To them, Agnes, who knew better than to do so, responded that such an action on her part would likely cause Ghose to be handed over to the British and shot.[66]

Distrustful of Roy's motives, she had instructed Ghose not to speak to Sinha while she attempted to shoulder Roy aside. Her refusal to cooperate with him meant that Ghose remained in prison, but he dutifully complied. Late that June, a frustrated Sinha advised Roy that "the other one who is out is not letting me do all I can for him. I don't understand what it means. Still I am trying to do something."[67] Two weeks later, Sinha reported that since the "patients" did not wish any further aid, he no longer knew was happening, but he was worried.

Their new "physician," he wrote, had advised them to admit their faults to the "doctor"—that is, plead guilty to federal officials —which could only spell trouble for Roy. Had they remained with the "physician" Sinha had retained for them, such a situation could have been avoided. But Agnes and Ghose had not only "deserted" the lawyer; they had abandoned Roy.[68] Ghose was having a difficult time in the Tombs, Sinha noted, and there were things Sinha could do that would "to a certain extent relieve [Ghose's] sufferings," but Agnes had ordered Ghose to decline, and the pair seemed to have sufficient funds without Roy's assistance. Sinha cursed the irony of fate that had put him and Roy in this position.[69] Still, he wrote, he planned to visit their new attorney and see if he could learn anything useful.

Agnes finally consented to a meeting with Sinha in August. Since he could not comprehend how literally the altruistic young woman had absorbed the instruction of her Indian mentors, he misconstrued her willingness to suffer as a desire to pose as a martyr. Like Roy, who later expressed outrage that Agnes had dared to "play high politics" with him, Sinha perceived her challenge to their authority as an affront to their masculinity.[70] Despite Agnes's repeated assurances that Roy's secrets were safe with her, her lawyers' advice notwithstanding, Sinha eventually snapped at her that "in Indian affairs, you cannot and do not understand a thing, you simply make trouble," he told Roy.[71]

Neither knew it at the moment, but their relationship was at an end. British secret service agents had identified Sinha as the man known to American military intelligence as "Willie," and he was brought in for questioning. Soon he, too, was under indictment. Furious, he blamed Agnes alone for his prosecution by American authorities. That same month, a warrant was issued for the removal of Ghose and Agnes to California. Roe and Recht fought valiantly to keep the two out of jail and have the San Francisco indictment dismissed. However, with the war on, the courts had little compassion for the conspirators. Unable to post bail on her second indictment, Agnes returned to the Tombs October 29.

CHAPTER 4

Moscow Beckons

I thought your fire was crimson, but you burn blue in the dark.

JOHN REED

AGNES WAS MARKEDLY more cavalier about her second incarceration, swaggeringly describing it as a gift that freed her from the need to earn a living. Like Bhagwan Singh, who was using his period of enforced idleness to draft revolutionary poetry, Agnes passed her days composing stories about the prostitutes, alcoholics, lunatics, and thieves who surrounded her. Her deft portraits of these people for whom the class struggle was not an abstract concept but a reality made clear in what direction Agnes's literary talent lay.

> May sat near the barred gate smoking a cigarette and resting her fat hands on her fatter knees. If convicted of forgery this time it meant eight fingerprints — one for each year she had been in the business. She was no amateur; one isn't an amateur at 45, after passing from the factory and the stage into private business.
>
> May's complaint wasn't so much that she had been caught, but that she had been caught on such a trifle. She had sent cigars to a fictitious son in Camp Upton and given a check to the cigar store, receiving only $10 in change.
>
> Her bail was $500, but her man, Vic, was too cowardly to furnish it. It meant trouble for him if he did . . .
>
> "How can you worry about $500 bail?" I exclaimed. "Mine is $10,000."
>
> "Well," May retorted, "I didn't try to swing the world by the tail. All I wanted was a little change."[1]

Unaware that her mail was being opened, Agnes corresponded with Singh and Das and arranged for friends she said were only "too glad" to help to send her Indian colleagues money, gifts, and other forms of assistance. Kitty Marion, a British suffragist Agnes knew from the birth control movement, and Molly Steimer, a Russian anarchist, were also being held in the Tombs; whenever they could, the women led meetings on birth control and socialism. "Every protest against the present system is worthwhile," Steimer instructed. "Someone must start."[2]

By the fall of 1918, Agnes and Ghose's case had snaked its way up to the Supreme Court. That November, four days after the Armistice was declared, Justice Augustus Hand ruled that neither Agnes nor Ghose could be removed to San Francisco until the Court decided on the writ of habeas corpus Roe had filed; he ordered their bail reduced.[3] Henrietta Rodman raised the funds to free Agnes this time, and Village acquaintances celebrated her release at a small reception hosted by Sanger.

Cognizant of Agnes's potential as an organizer, Sanger wished to wean Agnes from her Indian activities so she could devote more attention to the birth control movement, but even now, at the height of her involvement, Agnes never made more than a partial commitment to Sanger's work. It was not that she rejected women's right to the same freedom and privileges as men. It was more that no issue in the women's movement—be it birth control, suffrage, or companionate marriage—ever fully engaged her. According to Agnes, the day of feminism was waning.[4] She preferred to devote her energies to the freedom of India's subject peoples.

The New York indictment against Agnes and Ghose was dismissed that December, based on the government's failure to proceed with a speedy trial, and Ghose was finally released.[5] However, the San Francisco indictment against them still stood, and the U.S. attorney there was avid to try the pair alongside Das and Singh. By this time, Roger Baldwin's National Civil Liberties Bureau had agreed to subsidize Agnes's legal expenses, but the three Indians indicted along with her had fewer resources and no sponsor. So while Roe labored to prevent their extradition to the West Coast, Agnes borrowed space in a corner of Baldwin's bureau and began to raise money for the Indians' legal fees.

The Hindu Defense Fund, which Agnes created in consultation with Das during the first days of 1919, boasted Village notables Margaret Sanger and Norman Thomas on its steering committee and hosted concerts, balls, and a Carnegie Hall forum for fifteen hundred that brought in a considerable sum. Still, Agnes was in a bleak frame of mind. "I am pretty much disillusioned now," she wrote Das. "This past year has taught me, for instance, that governments cannot be trusted, save to serve the interests of special groups, special interests. It has taught me that the arm of Great Britain is strong enough to reach into the heart of America and have American citizens arrested and imprisoned because we dared believe in the freedom of India. All our efforts to defend ourselves seem tragically humorous at times—so few of us against a World Empire!"[6]

She was nearly twenty-seven: an age, she later wrote, "when serious-minded middle-class men and women were completing their schooling and embarking on careers. They had homes, protection, and guidance."[7] Agnes did not—by her own choosing—but she was confused and unhappy. After stridently rejecting a life that embraced such traditional female goals as marriage and family, she had yet to come up with anything to replace them. When her divorce came through, Agnes experienced it not as the joyous opportunity to reclaim her maiden name she had anticipated but rather as a stinging rejection.[8] And though she indulged in casual affairs with a number of men including the journalist Albert Rhys Williams, a handsome rogue whose aura of romance and adventure made him a local Lothario, they did not work for her either sexually or emotionally.[9]

Fortified by her knowledge of birth control and a still somewhat shaky belief in her right to pursue her own sexual pleasure, Agnes perhaps hoped that in promiscuity she could satisfy her need for companionship while still retaining her freedom. Instead the loveless encounters left her lonely, dissatisfied, and resentful that she succumbed to sex at all. A pessary might allow Agnes to be as sexually predatory as any man. Her inability to trust anyone sufficiently to permit real intimacy, though, denied her the happiness she sought. If she were to feel, as she wished, that her life had meaning, she needed more meaningful work. So far, it was only through her involvement in the Indian independence movement that she maintained some sense of dignity and could feel that she "was not just living, just reacting to life," she recalled.[10] Shortly thereafter, Agnes identified a larger role for herself in the Indians' struggle .

For more than two years, the Berlin India Committee had hoped to establish a propaganda organization in the United States that would build on the Ghadr Party's achievement in fostering American support for India's independence. Aided by BIC leader Virendranath Chattopadhyaya and Ghose, who would act as her silent partner, Agnes agreed to create one. Chatto never had anything overtly to do with the Friends of Freedom for India, which Agnes launched in March 1919 from an office inside the Rand School of Social Science, but his influence was present in everything from the news on India he sent them for publication to the hiring of staff and the organization's relationship to the West Coast Ghadr Party.[11]

From the start, the FFFI bore a strong resemblance to the Communist front organizations with which Agnes would later be associated. Agnes, who served as its secretary, was the only radical in a position of leadership. Its president, Robert Morss Lovett, was a well-regarded civil libertarian who taught at the University of Chicago; vice presidents Dudley Field Malone and Frank Walsh were accomplished liberal attorneys in the Wilson administration. Agnes pointedly spoke of the FFFI as a "purely American organization, standing upon American ideals, and appealing to Americans to support us."[12] Indian efforts at propaganda, she argued, could only make an intellectual appeal to American audiences, whereas she instinctively knew how to draw on American principles, traditions, and ideas. But while Agnes charted the organization's course, true control of the FFFI reposed in Chatto's hands.

That same March, an ocean away, the beleaguered Soviet state launched a militant international organization, the Comintern, to provide organization and leadership for the world revolution the Soviet rulers saw as imminent. Although they were besieged by hostile armies supported by the Allied powers, and virtually cut off from the outside world, Bolshevik leaders remained confident that their proletarian revolution would triumph over Europe and spread across the globe sometime soon. The facts appeared to bear them out. During a fevered period in 1918 and 1919, revolution had broken out in Hungary, Austria, Bul-

Virendranath Chattopadhyaya, Indian revolutionary and the love of Agnes's life. *Courtesy Nirode Barooah.*

garia, and Germany. Mutinies ravaged the French army, workers seized factories in several major Italian cities, and a radical shop steward movement sprouted in England.

Unlike its predecessor, the Second (Socialist) International, the Third (Communist) International was pledged to do everything in its power to assure the speedy final victory of Communism. Bolshevik leaders had endowed the Comintern with ample funds to encourage the world's working classes to overthrow capitalism and usher in a more equitable Communist society, and the "golden rain of Moscow," as the anarchist Emma Goldman wrote, was bankrolling any number of activities that promoted Communism—or encouraged the appearance of Communist strength and numbers.[13] Chatto did not think India was ready for Bolshevism and was not looking for it to follow too closely in Russia's footsteps, but he was amenable to some elements of the Soviet system in his vision of a free India. At this time, when men as august as Trotsky were declaring that the hour of proletarian dictatorship in Europe was the harbinger of liberation for Asia's colonial slaves, Chatto presented himself to the Comintern as chief of the Indian independence movement abroad and began to maneuver for Soviet funding.

Although he still enjoyed the support of most prominent Indian seditionists in Europe, the failure of the arms-running ventures had made Chatto vulnerable to attack, and the backing of American organizations like the FFFI and the Ghadr Party was vital in establishing his bona fides with the Soviets.[14] According to Louis Budenz, who was then director of publicity at the Civil Liberties Bureau, Agnes was a willing accomplice in this. Years later, he would say that when Roger Baldwin introduced him to Agnes around this time, she spoke not only of her public function at the FFFI but of her "secret work" for India, which involved the Soviet state.[15]

By 1919, her "inheritance" from the BIC exhausted, Agnes had become a cub reporter for the *New York Call*, the Socialist Party paper, and office manager at the *Birth Control Review*.[16] In her off-hours, she coordinated the FFFI response to the pending deportation of several Indian extremists convicted in the San Francisco conspiracy case. As the nation's first Red Scare heated up, deporting aliens convicted of a crime was an increasingly common method of handling the "problem" of foreign radicals. By June 1919, Tarak Nath Das, Bhagwan Singh, and seven other Ghadr Party members had been slated for deportation, and a bill awaiting passage in Congress suggested several more were in imminent danger.

Employing her hustler's charm, Agnes persuaded Roger Baldwin, Norman Thomas, and Margaret Sanger to join the FFFI board and roped scores of respected liberals into similar commitments. She organized a mass meeting at the Central Opera House, put together a fund-raising dinner for five hundred, and kept up a prodigious correspondence—warning thousands of Irish Americans, anarchists, Bolsheviks, Wobblies, radical socialists, professionals, and society women of the danger deportation posed to the Indians' lives, mailing the organization's newsletter to more than three thousand publications throughout America, Europe, and Asia, and distributing close to a quarter of a million FFFI pamphlets (written largely by Tarak Nath Das from behind prison walls). Her tireless efforts paid off in the articles and photographs that appeared in Upton Sinclair's *Appeal to Reason*, the *Nation*, the *Dial*, *Survey*, *Gale's Magazine*, the *New York Call*, the *Hartford Daily Courant*, and the *Gaelic American*.

Suren Karr, one of the Indians with whom Agnes worked, urged the West Coast Ghadr leaders to formally "acknowledge her services" on their behalf. She was, he wrote, one of the most "noble, self-sacrificing" people he had ever encountered: a splendid writer who worked with no personal stake in the outcome, generously volunteering her time and money after working a full day to support herself.[17] Robert Morss Lovett, president of the FFFI, recalled Agnes as the "mainspring" of their movement. "Indefatigable, resourceful, magnetic, she met every crisis with intelligence and courage," he later wrote.[18] Of course, none of the prominent American progressives with whom she worked at the FFFI had any idea of Chatto's existence, let alone his influence on the organization, or its attempts to ally with the Comintern.

The skill with which the FFFI influenced public opinion on the deportations made Agnes a nationally ranked figure in the Indian nationalist struggle and a player in Village radical circles, but her attention was more focused on the escalating crisis in British India, about which she learned from Chatto.[19] Tempers were at a flashpoint. Hundreds of thousands of Indians who had fought overseas or served as noncombatants behind Allied lines had grown accustomed during the war to being viewed as Britain's allies. They resented being treated again as "natives" at home. The recently passed Rowlatt Bill, which extended emergency wartime measures and ushered in a new wave of repression instead of promised reforms, further provoked long-smoldering hostilities.

In April 1919, Mohandas Karamchand Gandhi, back in India after years abroad, was arrested at a rally opposing the bill. When British troops shot and killed several demonstrators demanding his release, their actions touched off a riot. Three days later, the soldiers retaliated. Without a word of warning, they opened fire on ten thousand unarmed and terrified men, women, and children at a subsequent protest, killing four hundred civilians and wounding twelve hundred others. Almost overnight, the Amritsar Massacre, as it came to be known, transformed millions of moderate Indians from steadfast backers of the Raj into nationalist revolutionaries who doubted all future British claims of fair play.

Like other behind-the-scenes figures at the FFFI, Agnes endeavored to influence public opinion, providing graphic photos Chatto sent her from Sweden to more than a thousand American and European papers. The War Department suspected the Bolsheviks were underwriting Chatto's propaganda and delivering it through their courier system.[20] Was the material Agnes received, or the act of receiving it, illegal? It was not. But in New York City, where the crackdown on radicals was most severe, where police routinely dispersed all unauthorized assemblages and reported them to their superiors, where foreign-language meetings were banned and mob actions against radicals were either ignored or actively encouraged, where printing firms were under pressure not to print radical literature and any display of the red flag (international symbol of the radical left) was against the law, it was treated as if it were.

Agnes's attorneys tried to discourage their client from being linked with "Bolshevist" Indians like Chattopadhyaya by emphasizing her connection to the moderate Rai.[21] In January 1919, however, American military intelligence agents had broken into Roe's office to conduct what they termed a "discreet investigation" of their own and found a statement by Agnes that they believed tied her directly to the West Coast Indian revolutionaries.[22] Obviously, they noted in passing the document to their superiors, it was to "be distinctly understood that the source of any information contained in this statement must never be disclosed, and that fact impressed upon any person into whose hands the material may be placed." Nevertheless, the agents instructed "that a copy be placed in the hands of the District Attorney in San Francisco, duly informing him of the necessity to keep the source of his information absolutely confidential."[23]

Agnes's experience during America's first Red Scare confirmed for her the correctness of her decision to become a radical. These days, when she discussed her upcoming trial in San Francisco, she vaunted that she had "nothing but contempt" for U.S. Attorney John Preston.[24] He had prostituted American courts by turning them over to the British Empire, and for that he was "too mean to live." Even if she were sent to prison again, she told Das, it no longer mattered that much to her; imprisonment had never crushed an ideal. Many who went in "a spark," she wrote, "come out a living flame."[25]

When the revolutionary wing of the Socialist Party birthed America's first two Communist parties, Agnes sympathized "as a matter of course" with their decision. Only a fool would do otherwise after living her life, she tartly observed. Still, she joined neither, preferring to sign on instead with what she called the "American Bolsheviks" of the IWW.[26] Agnes never took much part in the by then moribund organization, but her membership was a tacit acknowledgment of the western radical tradition out of which she had sprung and which would always distinguish her from her more theoretical East Coast peers.

On November 7, 1919, while radicals throughout the city celebrated the second anniversary of the Bolshevik Revolution with parties, dancing, and meetings, the nation's first Red Scare approached its zenith. Justice Department agents, acting on the instructions of Attorney General A. Mitchell Palmer, swept into homes across New York City, smashing mirrors, breaking furniture and fixtures and arresting 650 people. A few days later, seven hundred uniformed police and plainclothesmen, acting at the behest of the statewide Lusk Committee, accompanied federal narcotics, bomb squad, Justice Department, and Immigration Service agents on a raid of several dozen branches of the new Communist parties and the offices of fifty radical publications. One thousand people were arrested on that Saturday night alone, although in the end police had sufficient evidence to hold only thirty-five. The notorious Palmer raids, as they came to be known, concluded on November 25 with a second attack on the New York City headquarters of the Union of Russian Workers.

The next day, Attorney General Palmer tersely informed Roe that the San Francisco indictments against Agnes and Ghose had been dismissed. On the basis of that decision, the Supreme Court dismissed Roe's appeal.[27] The legal battle was over; the pair had won on a technicality. The agency had known for some time that the San Francisco indictments against Agnes and Ghose were too weak to pursue, the Justice Department official in charge of the case noted in an internal memo, but he had not dismissed them earlier out of deference to Preston.

"It would seem that the case probably sprang out of the close relations between this Government and the English Government," the solicitor general had advised Palmer, "and the supposed connection of these defendants with some effort to raise disturbances in India under German instigation. But proof of this hardly appeared admissible under the allegations of the indictment," even if evidence conclusively proving Agnes and Ghose's involvement could be produced, he observed.[28]

Agnes had in fact been guilty as hell, but the government had bungled the case and she was once again a free woman. The British intelligence agents who had played such a hand in the matter, however, refused to let it rest. They kept her under surveillance, filing reports with American officials on everything from Agnes's actions at the FFFI to her insulting references to British soldiers, the British flag, and that "dirty little English pup" the Prince of Wales and harassed the landladies of the rooming houses in which she stayed until she was evicted.[29] At the time of the Palmer raids, Agnes found herself homeless. Florence Tenenbaum, a Civic Club acquaintance from a wealthy Jewish family, agreed to take her in, and for the rest of her sojourn in New York City, Agnes made her home on an army cot in the hallway of Florence's West Fourth Street apartment.

Almost as soon as they had met, Florence declared herself in love.[30] Agnes was not the first woman to whom Florence was attracted—while she was attending Smith College, she later wrote, there had been others—but she found Agnes in possession of a greater charm and force than any other woman she had known. Vital, wildly funny, full of songs and stories and practical jokes, Agnes had a "picturesqueness," as Florence described it, that set her apart. The Tenenbaums' dislike of their daughter's roommate added to her appeal.

Florence had been rather aimless until now, but in ministering to Agnes's needs she discovered an outlet for her own considerable energies. When Agnes returned at the end of a long day, Florence would get up and make her breakfast so she could sleep late the next morning. Afterward, she would stroke Agnes's forehead with gentle hands and offer what Florence later recalled as "a sort of massage to take the kinks out." Her massages were not erotic, she wrote, but Agnes "did not care either way—it was my choice."[31] In later years Agnes alluded to a period of homosexuality that probably referred to her relationship with Florence.[32] However, at this time, when there was still no hard and fast line separating the different kinds of attachments that existed between women, neither identified herself as a lesbian.[33]

Life with Agnes always had a dramatic tone, Florence later recounted. A superb actress, Agnes found it challenging to assume other personalities and could so alter her body language and facial expressions that people did not recognize her. She also had a penchant for dressing in costume—whether it was Indian saris or the shabby garb of a Polish peasant she donned to cover a story. On the previous St. Patrick's Day, Agnes had joined a contingent of fifty turban-clad Indians marching under the flag of the Indian republic: the first non-Irishmen ever to participate in the parade. "Watch for the movies," she wrote her Ghadr Party friends, "and you'll see us big as life . . . I'll be there all dressed up with no place to go, hair blackened and all."[34] Given a chance, though, Agnes expressed herself best in action.

Ostensibly, the two hundred radicals who assembled at the Church of the Ascension one sunny morning that December sought amnesty for the fifteen hundred men and women still in prison for their opposition to World War I. In reality, however, their planned "Liberty Walk" up Fifth Avenue was a protest against the Red Scare. According to Florence, Agnes arrived spoiling for a fight. As long as police allowed placard-wielding marchers to walk, she said, Agnes maintained control, but when they started to disrupt the procession, tearing a placard from the hands of Socialist Party activist Samuel Friedman and beating him to the ground, she flung herself at the offending cop "like a fury unleashed," pounding him full force in the chest.[35] For better or worse, Florence would recall, no incident better captured her friend's intransigent spirit.

Florence knew, she later wrote, that Agnes was "full of flaws."[36] She was. Haunted by the sense that her education, culture, and class marked her as somehow inferior, Agnes accepted the refuge female friendship offered from her conflicts with men, but there was always the trace of a con in her relationships. Along with Thorberg and other Village chums including Ellen Kennan, Gertrude Nafe, Josephine Bennett, Mary Knoblauch, and Margaret Sanger, Florence would demonstrate her loyalty again and again through the many crises that rocked Agnes's adult life, but in the end Agnes never entirely trusted the connection. Fond as she was of her women friends, she could not see what these people of the upper classes had in common with someone like herself.[37] To hide her discomfort, Agnes would exaggerate the differences between them, plying the women with tales of being born in a covered wagon, the child of squatting farmers, or the daughter of a miner. Then, fearful that they would exploit her if she let them, she made sure that in her dealings with them it was she who did the taking. But the depth of her heart and personal magnetism were such that she never lacked for admirers.

At the *New York Call*, Agnes was initially restricted to short pieces and features on women and India, but in 1920 the focus of the Red Scare shifted from the raids to the courts and she got a break. Her assignment, covering the trials of Communist Party founders Benjamin Gitlow and James Larkin, was front-page news. Agnes's pieces on Larkin, a fiery Irish nationalist whose divine gospel of discontent had injected the revolutionary syndicalism of the IWW into the American Communist Party, were particularly effective.

> The courtroom was silent. Larkin stood, towering above the marshals at his back, his hands folded and his chin held high ... He gazed unwaveringly into the eyes of the judge ...
> By two o'clock Larkin's pedigree had been taken ...
> He was still smoking his pipe, his huge, slightly stooped shoulders and his head, touched with gray, looming far above the marshals.[38]

When the self-taught agitator, as defiant and uncompromising in the courtroom as he was on the streets, was sentenced to hard labor at Sing Sing, Agnes accompanied his train to prison.[39] Later, when he was transferred to Dannemora, a maximum security facility near the Canadian border, she used her Irish political connections to gain entrance there.

The resulting exposé on the ill-treatment of Dannemora's political prisoners was as much a product of Agnes's imagination as truth, Larkin's fellow inmate

Benjamin Gitlow later wrote, and it cost her the friendship of her Irish political associates and her fellow activist Elizabeth Gurley Flynn, who arrived at the prison the day Agnes's article appeared and was denied entrance as a result.[40] In Agnes's zeal to combat evil, she could be remarkably insensitive to the personal toll her behavior exacted. Since the outcry that ensued from her piece led officials to return Larkin and Gitlow to Sing Sing, the fact that she had stepped on some toes to make it happen did not particularly concern her.

Agnes worked with the FFFI throughout the spring of 1920, honing her skills as an organizer and propagandist. Doing battle under the repressive conditions of the Red Scare was wearing her down. The political climate was not conducive to the more active work she had wanted from the outset of her involvement with the Indians—an opportunity to engage directly with the Sikh farmers and laborers agitating for independence. She toyed with the idea of going to India, but her stature in the independence movement made it unlikely British India officials would let her in.

That June, the bill allowing the Department of Labor to deport any alien convicted of violating or conspiring to violate American neutrality laws slipped through a nearly empty Congress, without an exemption for the Indians as had been promised. Agnes took the defeat quite personally. All her efforts to protect the men from deportation, she wrote, had amounted "to nothing, practically. It was a treacherous piece of work."[41] Weeks later, thirty-nine Indian laborers were brought to Ellis Island for deportation; a nationwide roundup was rumored to be imminent. Agnes notified her colleagues in the Ghadr Party that she would be resigning from the FFFI before the month was out. She was distressed at her inability to halt the deportations and desirous of a less tangential connection to the Indian nationalist struggle. She would remain as nominal secretary of the organization a bit longer, but not much.

Having absorbed her father's dictum that success and happiness lay where he was not, she began to entertain flight fantasies. She was not alone in this. As the corrosive effects of the Red Scare eroded Greenwich Village's unique blend of lifestyle and political radicalism, a mass exodus was under way. During the latter half of 1920, droves of artists, intellectuals and activists were fleeing the community for the country, for Paris—and for Moscow. When Das approached Agnes with a proposal that required foreign travel, she was predisposed to accept.

In Mexico, it appeared, Roy had befriended the veteran Bolshevik Michael Borodin, who introduced him to the study of Marxian dialectics. Since then,

Roy had become a Communist and founded a Mexican Communist Party. Detractors jeered that the institution consisted of "six members and a calico cat," but with Borodin's support it had won affiliation with the Communist International.[42] More significant, from the perspective of the Indian revolutionaries, was the fact that Roy's thesis on how the Comintern should deal with colonialism in the East had been accepted as a supplement to the one advanced by the chairman of the Soviet Republic, Vladimir Lenin, at the second Comintern congress in Moscow, for this raised the question of which Indian leader—Roy or Chatto—would advise the Comintern on India and receive its coveted funds.

Lenin, who knew there was no Communist Party inside India nor any real organization of Indian Communists abroad, appeared to share Chatto's assessment of Indian conditions. He had asked the Comintern to support bourgeois nationalist movements for independence until such time as genuine Communist parties could be established.[43] However, Roy had argued for a policy that backed the creation of Communist parties, revolution, and the establishment of new soviet republics. Until the theoretical dispute was resolved at the next congress, the Comintern could offer neither Indian practical support.

British intelligence agents dismissed what they termed Roy's "ultraleft" stance as an opportunistic ploy intended to curry favor with the Bolsheviks, but the acceptance of his thesis made him an international figure who had to be reckoned with.[44] In response to this implicit challenge to his own leadership, Chatto had sent the Russians a detailed description of a plan that would unite all the organizations agitating for India's liberation, nationalist and Communist, under his control. At an upcoming meeting of his key lieutenants in Berlin, he intended to develop a counterthesis to Roy's, which his group would present to Moscow. It was this meeting Das had asked Agnes to attend on behalf of the FFFI.[45]

Implicit in his question was whether she wanted a career as a professional revolutionary. By the fall of 1920, Agnes's articles were appearing regularly under her byline in the *Call*, the *Birth Control Review*, and (under the nom de guerre Alice Bird) the *Modern Review*, a respected Indian liberal journal. If she left for Russia at this time, she would have to do so in a clandestine manner, without a passport—forcing her into an underground existence and making it impossible for her to reenter the United States legally. It was not an easy decision, and to better think the matter over she spent a solitary week in rural upstate New York. In the end, the bitter, confused struggles of her own family convinced her that she belonged "on the barricades for freedom and equality," a friend later recalled.[46] Agnes agreed to go.

On her return to the city, the news that nearly one hundred Indian laborers had been deported during her absence dispelled any lingering doubts she might have nursed. She entered into correspondence with Maksim Litvinoff, a Soviet diplomat who was one of Chatto's strongest allies, regarding preparations for her trip.[47]

December 17 was the day of Agnes's departure, and Florence would say that she wept more piteously that morning than she ever did before or after. Even so, she accompanied Thorberg and Das to the Polish-American freighter on which Agnes would travel to Europe as a stewardess. Das had asked her to deliver a briefcase filled with documents to Chatto in Berlin, and he carried the precious cargo himself until the last moment.[48] Agnes did not know it at the time, but it would be thirteen years before she saw the United States again.

As she had planned, Agnes jumped ship in Danzig, escaping by the skin of her teeth, she wrote. The ship's captain had intercepted a telegram from a friend she left unnamed that welcomed her to Europe. By the time he had ordered that she be brought before him, Agnes explained, she was already ashore.[49] From Danzig, Agnes wired a colleague of Chattopadhyaya's as she had been instructed, requesting that the German Foreign Office have her stewardess papers visaed and authorize her to proceed to Berlin.[50] By the second week of January 1921, Agnes (or rather "Alice" now, for she had traveled to Europe as Alice Bird) had caught up with the Indian revolutionaries, who maintained a small office in the city.

American and British authorities were only a few steps behind. On January 10, 1921, a young J. Edgar Hoover ordered the post office to forward copies of all Agnes's mail to his Bureau of Investigation. The State Department also opened a file on her, and a military intelligence agent disguised as a reporter stopped by the FFFI office in the hope of learning Agnes's whereabouts. (He was told that she was out.) By the time the Justice Department confirmed that Agnes had indeed violated U.S. passport regulations in her flight, she had established herself in Berlin, albeit illegally.

If Agnes had thought that in coming to Germany she was abandoning materialistic, machine-made America for the rich, dense culture of Europe, she was naive. Berlin in the opening days of 1921 was not at all like the Paris in which disillusioned young American writers found comfort and asylum. Berlin was tense. The bitter mood of defeat and despair that had begotten the Weimar Republic two years previously hung like a cloud over the German populace. The exacting terms of the Versailles Treaty and the Reich's own disorganized finances were creating hunger, unemployment, and inflation. The fledgling democracy had already survived attempts at revolution from the left and right, but its fate remained uncertain.

"I think you are the only person whom I have ever known who tolerated my many faults and eccentricities," Agnes wrote tenderly to Florence in January 1921. "You are the only one who really understood. And I have marked Kabir's poem with you in mind, in which he says: 'Listen to me friend: he understands who loves.'... This is no silly sentimentality when I speak so. I think of few in America today. But I see your short silly hair very often and think with laughter of your barnyard [pets] in the morning and of your intellectual abandonment turned loose on noble folk."[51] Still, even in the midst of her loving words, she could not refrain from adding a list of publications to which she wished Florence would subscribe for her.

Agnes shrank from declaring outright what she knew would hurt Florence deeply, but she wrote because she also had something important to convey. Almost immediately on her arrival in Berlin, Agnes had fallen in love with Virendranath Chattopadhyaya, the Indian revolutionary leader in exile whose worldwide network of revolutionary activity was the reason for her presence abroad, and she had plunged into a life with him.

Not even Agnes's wildest romantic reckonings could fashion the forty-one-year-old Chatto into a handsome man. Short and thin, with piercing black eyes set in a pockmarked face framed by a mass of graying hair, Chatto was downright homely. But he was cultured, musical, charming, and witty, and though his only suit was much the worse for wear and he had very little money, Agnes admired his holy man's disdain for worldly goods in pursuit of a higher truth. What she saw was a man who personified her social and political views—a man with a mind "as sharp and ruthless as a saber," she later wrote, and a boundless hatred for the people who had subjugated the land of his birth.[52]

By 1921, Gandhi had emerged as the dominant figure on the Indian political stage, but Chatto, an unrelenting advocate of armed struggle, urged Agnes not to be taken in by the pacifist leader. Gandhi was of more importance to the world at large than to the Indians, Agnes would write that Chatto advised her; he lacked political acuity and might waver at a decisive moment. Like Jesus Christ's, she later recalled Chatto as saying, Gandhi's philosophy was one of despair. He preached personal perfection because he was appalled by "the terrifying political difficulties. He was trying to combine the two, but...is unclear socially and knows nothing of economics. He was trained in British constitutional law, and that is always a poison that works in the system of Indian leaders ...causing them to betray our people time and again for the sake of British phrases."[53]

Agnes and Chatto were an unlikely match. She was American, working class, spottily educated, and emotionally deprived. Chatto was the scion of a distinguished Brahmin family, a multilingual Cambridge graduate raised in a luxuri-

Agnes during her years in Berlin. *Courtesy Florence Becker Lennon.*

ous home with devoted parents and a phalanx of servants to attend to his needs. Agnes's efforts to live a meaningful life had come at considerable personal cost. Chatto had been encouraged and expected to achieve great things. Even as a revolutionary, he was so shrouded in mystique that the British writer and intelligence agent Somerset Maugham had written a story based on his exploits.[54]

The Chattopadhyayas were a celebrated clan. Chatto's older sister, Sarojini Naidu, would become a leading figure in the Indian National Congress and Gandhi's chief aide-de-camp. His younger brother, Harindranath, would become one of India's best-known poets and playwrights. Many of Chatto's contemporaries in the movement considered him India's most brilliant leader.[55] Agnes would write that she found him as primal a force as thunder or lightning and worshiped him both as an individual and a political principle. Chatto appeared less besotted, but after two decades wandering the globe he seemed grateful for her companionship, and Agnes basked in his reflected glory.

As a precondition to Comintern support, Lenin had instructed Chatto to submit a signed statement from the organizations with which he worked affirming his leadership of the émigré Indian nationalists. By late January 1921, most of the Indians with whom Chatto associated had agreed to support him.[56] However, he was still attempting to bring the Ghadr Party under his control when the Soviet Foreign Office ordered him to assemble all his representatives in Moscow at once.[57] Reluctant to move forward without the Ghadrites, he requested a two-month postponement, and the couple took off for Austria and Sweden.

While Agnes drafted articles for the *Modern Review*, Chatto attempted to raise sufficient funds to rally the Sikhs to his cause. In Stockholm, he also arranged for the Bolsheviks to provide Agnes with a fake German passport under the name Violet Ali Khan Hussain. Over the years, the Russian revolutionaries had mastered a variety of clandestine-action techniques to escape the watchful eyes of the tsar's secret political police, of which forging passports was but one. But when the lovers left Sweden that March, Chatto had failed to procure enough money to buy the Ghadrites outright.

From Berlin, he directed his colleague Tarak Nath Das (now president-elect of the FFFI) to offer the party forty thousand dollars the Soviets had already earmarked for Indian propaganda in the United States.[58] But in his absence, Roy had persuaded Comintern leaders to fund the Ghadrites directly through an émigré *Indian* Communist Party he had founded in Tashkent the previous year while on assignment for the Comintern. The move, which bypassed Chatto entirely, effectively committed the Sikh revolutionaries to Roy. Soon enough, Chatto's group received word from Moscow that since an Indian Communist Party already existed, it ran contrary to Communist principles to support a nationalist movement like his.[59]

Chatto's supporters were still considering how to appeal the decision when a Soviet agent arrived in Berlin with instructions from Georgi Chicherin, the people's commissar of foreign affairs, and an invitation for the group to visit Moscow. Roy sent his American wife, Evelyn, to negotiate with Chatto and his colleagues while he stayed behind in Moscow to lobby Comintern officials. The various factions in Berlin struggled to hammer out a position vis-à-vis Russia and plan a united program for revolution in India with Comintern support, but they could not reach consensus.

Chicherin had sent word that he wished Communist propagandizing to start in India at once and requested that Chatto limit the size of the delegation he brought to Moscow. Evelyn Roy demanded strict adherence to communism and recognition of her husband as the group's leader before she pledged Roy's cooperation. The Ghadr Party, now controlled by Roy, declared itself in favor of Roy's Communism rather than Chatto's revolutionary nationalism. Agnes, no doubt jealous of the Stanford-educated woman with impeccable radical credentials (Evelyn's uncle was Eamon de Valera, the American-born Irish leader), legally married to the better-connected Indian leader, argued that while the FFFI was in favor of Russian help for political revolution in India, she did not want Communist propaganda to begin there immediately as the Soviets wished, nor did she wish to see Chatto's group declared either Bolshevik or Communist, as that would limit who might assist them.[60] The discussion at an impasse, Chatto threatened to break off negotiations entirely if Moscow insisted on setting terms for the debate. Chicherin agreed to drop his demands and assured Chatto that he could bring whomever he wished with him to Moscow.[61] In deference to Lenin's view that a good nationalist was better than a bad Communist, Chicherin also promised to support the entire range of political opinions expressed by the nationalist revolutionaries under Chatto's command. Unfortunately, Chatto did not realize that the man on whom he counted as a major ally had relinquished his Comintern responsibilities and no longer wielded much influence on the organization.

A meeting at which Chatto's group would present a statement on their impression of conditions in India was scheduled for May 25, a month before the third Comintern congress convened. Money for the delegates' expenses was dispatched to the Comintern's western headquarters in Berlin, and a Soviet representative began arranging the false visas, papers, and identity cards needed to travel the "underground railway" to Moscow. Early that May, Chatto's entourage of fourteen (Agnes being the only Caucasian and the only woman among them) set out via Sweden for the mecca of the socialist world.[62]

The Russia in which Agnes found herself was in a state of flux. The brutal civil war that the Allied powers had supported for the last three years had only recently concluded in a victory for the Russian revolutionaries, and Agnes later wrote that she could still see the "grim Red soldiers, clad in captured British clothing and carrying captured British and French guns," pouring into Moscow from the southern front.[63] But the years of war, revolution, and civil struggle had exhausted the country, and the close of the heady, uncompromising phase of the Russian Revolution, when huge personal sacrifices had been made to build a new society, found the people hovering on the brink of despair.

Typhus was decimating the Volga region; thousands of refugees were homeless. Most citizens still lacked adequate clothing, and "almost no telephone worked, no lock locked, and no train ran on time," Agnes later reported.[64] However, Lenin's New Economic Policy, introduced two months previously to rescue the foundering regime, had made significant concessions to peasants and private capital, and by the spring of 1921 the Bolsheviks' strategic retreat from their earlier, more militant policies was creating the first measure of economic prosperity the workers' state had known. Privately, party idealists questioned the point of their self-denial, but, as food reappeared in shops, mills and factories reopened, and the standard of living improved, the general public breathed more easily—a relief Agnes would misread as proof that they remained "filled with hope and enthusiasm."[65]

Soviet leaders, who were looking for improved international relations and foreign investment in the altered economic climate, viewed visitors like Agnes as valuable emissaries in amending perceptions abroad, and they wooed her with visits to model factories, show schools, and state homes where they trained the country's *bezprizorni* (orphans of the revolution). She also received free tickets to concerts and to theatrical performances that introduced her, to great effect, to the didactic power of drama in reaching the illiterate.[66]

The influence of the proletcult literary movement, with its extravagant praise of the masses and grandiose, utopian depictions of the future of the revolution, was evident in Agnes's first articles from Moscow. Her tales for the American *Liberator* and the Indian press, delivered to their destinations by Bolshevik couriers, were rife with depictions of illiterate Ukrainian and Azerbaijan women who had thrown off their veils and taken up rifles against the counterrevolution, ready "to fight to the very last battle until victory is won," and of the "international bandits" who had tried to destroy Soviet Russia.[67] The "most intelligent, the most conscious, and the most clear thinking" men and women of every language and race, she wrote, were streaming into Moscow for the congress. They were living at "perhaps the most critical moment in the history of the working class... when a world proletariat, more conscious than ever before throughout the ages, is starting... the uncompromising conflict which can end only in victory."[68]

Agnes and Chatto were staying at the Lux Hotel, along with the rest of the foreign guests including Roy and his wife, and the foursome clashed immediately. Still furious with Agnes for "playing high politics" with him in New York, Roy took her relationship with Chatto as a personal affront to himself.[69] A "fanatical hero worshipper... she seemed to believe that to fall in love with famous Indian revolutionaries would be the expression of her loyalty to India," he still fumed years later.[70] Beyond the bad blood and political rivalry was the dissonance in their styles. Agnes and Chatto were ascetics, both by temperament and necessity, who took pride in living simply. The Roys were sybarites who preferred a lifestyle that was hardly proletarian; their social climbing aroused Chatto and Agnes's scorn. Roy, in his turn, looked with aristocratic disdain on the lowborn Agnes and derided the couple for buttonholing visitors in the hotel corridors to discuss the iniquities of British rule in India. "It was like carrying coals to Newcastle," Roy would sneer. "All members of the Communist International, whether Russian or non-Russian, were against imperialism and sympathized with the struggle of the colonial peoples for freedom. The question...

was how the liberation . . . was to be brought about, and what sort of a regime would replace the colonial rule."[71] Since the answer for Roy and other Communist delegates was to be found only in the Russian model, Roy later wrote that his companions fled to their rooms whenever the "dark cloud" (as Roy's friend Borodin referred to Agnes and Chatto) appeared.[72]

Enraged by Roy's attempts to speak for the Indians and skeptical of his proposal to bring the Communist Revolution to India, Chatto's delegation frantically attempted in the weeks before the congress to convince Comintern and government officials that the Indian Communist Party Roy had founded in Tashkent was merely his personal affair. Lenin's own analysis of Indian conditions, they argued, made Chatto a more logical choice as the Comintern's representative on India, but they swayed no one.[73] Chicherin was kind but did little.[74] Karl Radek, the Comintern's general secretary and a member of the executive committee's governing "Little Bureau," had already committed to Chatto's rival. After consulting with Roy, Radek informed Chatto's group that unless they could get the congress to pass another thesis more to their liking, he was bound to honor Roy's.[75]

In the interest, ostensibly, of exploring a working agreement with Chatto, the Comintern executive committee formed a commission to hear the group out, but it was stacked with Roy allies including Michael Borodin and August Thalheimer, the German Communist leader. Sebald Rutgers, the Dutch Communist who chaired the commission, refused to deal with them collectively and instead interrogated them one by one on their resistance to Communism as the only organization appropriate for the new India, or to pledging themselves to further its cause worldwide, as Roy had done.[76] Their response—that it was more important for all classes and organizations committed to overthrowing the British government to join forces before they committed to anything else—fell on deaf ears. Infuriated by the rigged proceedings, Chatto ordered his delegation to boycott the commission.

It was around this time, as it became increasingly unlikely her lover would prevail, that Agnes met the anarchists Emma Goldman and Alexander Berkman, who had already heard "a great deal about Agnes in connection with her Hindu activities," Goldman would write, during their sojourn in the United States.[77] Unlike some "automatons," as Goldman called them, who lived only for revolution and disdained emotions as bourgeois sentimentality, Goldman cared enormously about people and feelings.[78] For her part, Agnes, who could be as warm and funny in her personal relations as she was driven in her political ones, did her utmost to beguile the celebrated radical twenty-three years her senior.

In 1912, Goldman's participation in the San Diego Free Speech Fights had helped bring the IWW national fame. Perhaps Agnes, who had not arrived in

the city until after the din died down, regaled Goldman with this fanciful
account that later appeared in her novel.

> A woman named Emma Goldman was announced to speak on the social
> drama. The business men of the city refused to permit the lecture. Who was
> she, I asked. A very terrible sort, I learned, a free-for-all public character with
> a long and dangerous tongue . . .
>
> For days after the suppression of her lectures, the public fight raged . . . I
> knew little of theory of any kind, but I listened. The opponents of free speech
> were like the land speculators I had known. The things the working men and
> the Socialists said expressed my own feelings and convictions. Then, when
> the police and the businessmen were turned loose upon them, I also was
> moved to action, and I helped break their shock . . . I heard my friends called
> unspeakable names, saw them imprisoned and beaten, and streams of water
> from fire hoses turned upon their street meetings."[79]

The "dear girl" was "a real personality," Goldman informed stateside
friends.[80] In the striking Agnes, Goldman believed she had found a kindred
spirit: an "earnest and true rebel," much like herself, who fused emotion with
thought in her political commitments and approached social problems in a
more individualistic than collective spirit.[81] Perceiving Agnes's radicalism to be

Friend and mentor Emma Goldman. *From the collections of the Library of Congress.*

not simply the result of childhood poverty but a spiritual hunger with which Goldman identified, she pursued the friendship.

When Goldman and Berkman had moved to Russia in 1919, they initially championed the revolution and cooperated with the Bolsheviks in cultural if not political endeavors. However, their support for the regime waned when the one-party dictatorship that the Bolshevik (now the Russian Communist) Party established in the name of Soviet democracy began to eliminate all organs of self-government, competing political parties and presses, the armed forces, and the country's judiciary system—Lenin's good intentions notwithstanding.

If Goldman and Berkman disliked the centralized authority, the abuse and injustice masquerading under the guise of a new and higher ethic repelled them. They placed a higher value on individual life than the Bolsheviks did, and their recent participation in the Kronstadt uprising had completed their disenchantment. After watching the Communist leaders brutally massacre revolutionary workers, soldiers, and sailors for demanding that freely elected soviets, rather than political parties, represent the Russian people, the two anarchists had stopped believing that Soviet authorities represented the revolutionary ideals for which the Russian people had fought. By the time that Agnes met the couple, their two-room apartment was functioning as a kind of salon for the disaffected in Moscow.

In the days she spent with Goldman and Berkman, Agnes heard troubling stories about the revolution's dark side: of the persecution of honest revolutionaries who tore the mask from Russia's "lying face," as Goldman put it, and of mass executions by the Cheka, the country's secret police.[82] Originally established to seize property and help with issues of resettlement, ration cards, and the publication of lists of enemies of the people, the Cheka had gained authority to arrest and execute suspected opponents of the regime, and the massive intimidation campaign it was currently conducting relied on summary justice and random punishment unrelated to individual guilt. The Red Terror would eventually claim the lives of as many as a quarter of a million "class enemies" along with scores of ordinary criminals guilty of such lesser evils as food speculation.[83]

"When I first went to Russia," Agnes wrote her friend Ellen Kennan after learning of the problem, "I did not know of the persecution and imprisonment of all anarchists or anarchist Communists. Only after I had been there a few weeks, and after I had talked with Emma, Sasha [Berkman] and many others did I learn the truth. Had I known it, I should have written the truth . . . in the *Liberator*, and not what I wrote."[84] The truth, as she told Florence, was that "Much we read of Russia is imagination and desire only. . . No person is safe from intrigues and the danger of prison. The prisons are jammed with anarchists and syndicalists *who fought for the revolution*. Emma Goldman and Berkman are out only because of their international reputations. And they are under house arrest; they expect to go to prison any day, and may be there now for all I know. Any Communist who excuses such things is a scoundrel and a blackguard. Yet they do excuse it—and *defend* it. Lord, but I was ready to fight."[85]

In addition to the Cheka's official function of ferreting out suspected counterrevolutionaries, underground Cheka agents and a newly established foreign department conducted extensive espionage and counterespionage operations, often utilizing agent provocateurs to unmask suspected spies and double agents. Nothing was more terrible in these days of the Terror than being suspected of espionage, Roy later observed; even Lenin could not save someone from the fatal consequences of being arrested on that charge.[86] Foreign nationals came under particular scrutiny, and the constant suspicion under which the Indians lived fostered a degree of paranoia in which, as Agnes wrote, "everybody calls everybody else a spy, secretly . . . and everybody is under surveillance. You never feel safe." [87]

Under the circumstances, it was perhaps inevitable that as Roy and Chatto's delegation jockeyed for support in the weeks before the congress, an epidemic of "spy mania," as Agnes put it, ran through both camps. "The Indians opposing our plan," she told Florence, "did such dirty work as to call me a *British* spy— not even an *American* spy—but a *British* one!!! So I was under investigation! *Anyone* can do such a thing. If I had not been a member of a large delegation I suppose I would have been locked up. Just wait until *some* skunks come to western Europe. If I'm not expelled or locked up or something, I'll raise a small-sized hell."[88] Roy would complain about Chatto's group, which he said lodged a formal complaint with the Cheka office claiming that *Roy* was sheltering a supporter who was a British agent.[89]

By the time the third Comintern congress convened late that June in the royal halls of the Kremlin, many of Chatto's Indian supporters had already left Moscow in disgust. Those like Agnes who stayed attended as nonvoting delegates.[90] Her faith in the Soviet regime had flagged, and the group's outsider status made it difficult to be heard, but Agnes's trust in the Comintern as an independent organ of world revolution survived, and its support of a free India remained alluring.

The mood at the congress was somber. The unanticipated defeat of the earlier revolutionary outbursts and labor agitation in western Europe, and the failure of other resistance to materialize, had caused even Comintern chairman Grigori Zinoviev to admit that the world proletarian revolution was not just around the corner; it might in fact take years. Still, the institution's Russian leaders held firm that it would come, and their experience encouraged them to look more closely to Asia for the revolution's next wave.

On the faint chance that he might, even at this late date, influence Comintern policy on India, Chatto had drafted a thesis in opposition to Roy's and delivered copies to Zinoviev and Lenin with notes requesting meetings with them at which he might discuss it in more detail.[91] Zinoviev ignored him, and while Lenin wrote back that he had read it "with great interest" and planned to speak with Chatto about it soon, in mid-July, when the Congress closed, Lenin left Moscow without having granted Chatto and Agnes an audience.[92] Chatto blamed the Comintern's Little Bureau, and particularly Karl Radek and Bela Kun (its only non-Russian member) for ostracizing his delegation,[93] but the couple were also aware of Roy's role in turning Radek, Trotsky, Zinoviev, and Bukharin against them.

Roy categorically denied any foul play and attributed whatever suspicions or ill will Chatto's supporters harbored to the pernicious influence of Agnes, whom he later described as "the driving force" of the group. Reluctant to confront the personal history that lay at the root of their tension, Roy would contend that he had no idea why Agnes "seemed to have a grudge against" him.[94] His discomfort in her presence manifested itself in an irrational dislike that ascribed base motives to her actions and transformed even her dedication to a free India into "her pretension to be a more passionate Indian patriot than the Indians themselves."[95]

Blaming Agnes rather than political rivalry for poisoning Chatto against him, Roy still referred to her nearly half a century later as "the evil genius of the Indian revolutionary group which came to Moscow." Without Agnes's influence, Roy posited, Chatto was an intelligent and practical man who would have behaved differently; he went so far as to argue that Chatto had wanted to cultivate Roy's acquaintance, "but Smedley stood in the way. She was hysterical—a pathological case, a fit subject for psycho-analysis."[96]

The months in Moscow took a toll on Agnes. She was impatient with visiting radicals who wrote glowingly of how Russian workers controlled the nation's industries, or directed its affairs, while the Party dictatorship tightened, or spoke of not needing money when they received everything free, and saw how many Russians lived in want. Agnes knew that the privileges foreigners enjoyed came on the backs of ordinary citizens. When the American organizer Ella Reeves Bloor arrived to attend the founding conference of Profintern, the organization that would deal with trade union issues, Agnes took umbrage that amidst great poverty Bloor chose to wear "lace dressed over silk colored slips . . . long strings of colored beads, rings, etc."[97] Bloor's lover, a young American Communist named Earl Browder, Agnes dismissed out of hand as "an idiot."[98]

Agnes had always looked down on what she considered "female" men. The idea that this "dainty" fellow, as she described Browder, who bought baby blue silk Russian smocks in the market and wore them with long black silk ribbons, posed, "with his baby white skin and fair toothbrush mustache . . . as the delegate from the Kansas *miners!*" repelled her. Listening to the two of them speak of representing the miners, when Agnes was certain neither Browder nor Bloor had been within a thousand miles of a mine, she felt she was hearing a personal insult to the working class from which she had sprung. "So help me gawd!" she wrote Florence. "It was awful. I was so disgusted I couldn't even protest."[99]

That August, the Comintern commission established three months earlier to hear out the Indians reconvened for two days of meetings. At this time Chatto laid before them a final plan that would allow him to maintain some control over future revolutionary work in India. Essentially, he sought the dissolution of Roy's Communist Party of India and its replacement by a broad revolutionary board on which Chatto played a key role. With all the Russian leaders supporting Roy, Roy did not need to compromise. He refused unconditionally to work with non-Communist nationalist revolutionaries, meaning Chatto, his most formidable rival. The few remaining Indians in Chatto's delegation saw the handwriting on the wall and jumped ship.

At the same time the Comintern elected to pursue a "united front" policy in which it would work with exactly the sort of reformist organizations and parties Chatto urged, it quixotically elected to pursue Roy's ultraleft policy in India. In September 1921, Agnes and Chatto were informed that the Indian revolutionaries should not count on any Comintern support. Evelyn Roy could not refrain from gloating. Although Chatto and his friends had spent months trying to "discredit Roy and to usurp his place," she crowed, it was her husband who had been recognized as the Comintern's sole agent for India.[100] Since the Indian nationalists refused to use Roy's Communist Party as its intermediary, she wrote, the Comintern had advised them to seek help elsewhere. Henceforth, she and her husband would be directing all work on India from Moscow. Not long after, Agnes and Chatto departed in defeat.

Roger Baldwin, who had also attended the congress, summed up for Agnes his impression of the challenges that beset the Indian independence movement abroad. "India will need all the patience she can command to put up with the narrowness and petty spirit of some of her apostles of freedom, who forget their first and highest obligations."[101]

Traveling under the alias "Mrs. Petroikas," Agnes stopped briefly in Stockholm, then continued on to Geneva, where she received five thousand marks toward

her expenses from the Soviet Legation.[102] Shortly thereafter she returned to
Berlin, where she availed herself of her freedom to discuss the plight of Berkman and Goldman, who remained under house arrest in Moscow, with their
mutual friend Ellen Kennan. Agnes was monitoring their situation closely, she
informed Kennan. Both were forbidden from receiving visitors or going out
without a guard, and they were desperate to leave. Berkman was bearing things
bravely, she wrote, but Goldman was "bitter to the bottom of her soul, suffering
terribly, [and] selling her books, clothes, and other possessions in order to live."
Fearful for their physical safety, Agnes said she had contacted Goldman's attorney in the States. Never would she forgive the Russian Communist Party for its
actions, she vowed, "however revolutionary it pretends to be."[103]

CHAPTER 5

Love and Pain in Berlin

Man reaches scarce a hundred; yet his tears
Would fill a lifetime of a thousand years.

ANCIENT CHINESE COUPLET

T HE COMINTERN had decided to support Roy, but neither Agnes nor Chatto intended to cease agitating for nationalist revolution in India. Indeed, it seemed to Agnes that with Germany economically helpless and Russia still too weak to mount an effective challenge to British imperialism, a triumphant revolution in India would solve not only India's problems but all Europe's as well. Aware, now, of the challenges in promulgating independence from abroad, she was galled to be in Berlin, but sources Agnes left unnamed had recently assured the couple, she wrote, that *their* propaganda and activities rather than Roy's would soon be recognized "as official in India."[1] On the strength of that understanding, she, Chatto, and a colleague, Bhupendranath Dutta, plunged into creating a rival operation to Roy's, reaching out to associates, including Das and Ghose, who had not yet aligned themselves with Roy. By December 1921, they had founded the Indian News Service and Information Bureau as a base and cover for their revolutionary activities.[2]

The bureau consisted of three sections. The first was avowedly nonpolitical. At the nominal cost of one British pound per person, it helped any Indian in Germany, but particularly students, obtain a job and receive assistance with university studies or other concerns. Because the country's cost of living was low and its reputation for technical efficiency high, Germany attracted a large number of Indian students. As word spread that Chatto was helpful, trustworthy, and accessible, many young Indians began to pass through this part of the organization. However, the true purpose of this section was to aid the couple in identifying potential recruits, who were then approached—much as Har Dayal, a former associate of Chatto's, had done in the Bay Area during the summer of 1912—about participating in a second, secret piece of the bureau in which Agnes and Chatto conducted classes on subjects that ranged from their philosophy of revolutionary nationalism to the manufacture of explosives.[3]

A third part of the bureau promoted commercial enterprises, and it included a magazine and the Indo-German Trading Company, Ltd., a lucrative import-export business that turned 80 percent of its profits over to Indian nationalist work. It, too, had a covert purpose, which was to recruit Indian seamen who would transport revolutionary literature and armaments between Europe and India. This endeavor was run in collaboration with Ghose through the FFFI.

The Weimar Republic was generous in providing asylum to members of colonial freedom movements, and the German Foreign Office provided start-up funds and some shelter for the couple to carry out their work. Chatto anticipated greater assistance through an alliance with the German Communist Willi Muenzenberg, founder of the Communist Youth International, who would

The German Communist Willi Muenzenberg, 1921.

make his career working with people like Chatto who shared some but not all of the Communists' goals.[4]

In the months since the Comintern congress, when Muenzenberg had been appointed to the Comintern's executive committee, the former companion of Lenin had established the Berlin-based Workers International Aid (IAH). Ostensibly, it provided relief for victims of the Russian famine that winter, but it also existed to carry on illegal and subversive activities on behalf of the Comintern.[5] To assist Muenzenberg and others like him in performing their clandestine tasks, the Comintern had installed a man at the Russian Embassy in Berlin whose name was Jakob Mirov-Abramov. Officially, Mirov-Abramov served as its third secretary; in fact, he was the second-ranking member of the Comintern's Otdel Mezhdunarodnoi Svyazi (Department of International Liaison, or OMS), a vital albeit unpublicized branch of the executive committee responsible for technical issues of crucial importance to the Comintern—and to revolutionaries like Chatto. Arms smuggling, the distribution of propaganda, the courier service that moved people and money from one country to another, and secret telegraphic links between Moscow and other major cities in the world that allowed the Comintern to maintain confidential contact with its foreign sections and supply them with political direction all fell within the purview of the OMS—as did a number of espionage and covert action programs directed separately from mainstream Comintern activities. Muenzenberg's friend and colleague Mirov-Abramov oversaw these operations in Europe.[6]

The couple were so persuasive in convincing Indian students to embrace their politics that the British agent who tracked Agnes and Chatto's movements was soon lamenting that if he could only remove them from Berlin, "the whole of this organization would collapse," since no one else was sufficiently qualified to carry on their work.[7] Their life, financed largely on German currency, was difficult, but it was less grueling for them than it was for most citizens of the Weimar Republic.

With reparations payments to the Entente squeezed out of an economy already devastated by the war, the mark was being constantly devalued, creating an inflation that sent food prices climbing while wages increased only a few marks a week. People tried to compensate by working longer hours, occasionally until they fainted from exhaustion or turned to prostitution, Agnes wrote. But not everyone was hurting. Farmers with goods to sell and industrialists who drew credit from the Reichsbank made out nicely. The situation, Agnes wryly observed, had turned gambling on the mark into "the great indoor sport of the capitalists."[8]

Not everyone who criticized events in Germany was a leftist like Agnes. As the dual plagues of reparations and inflation continued apace, conservatives, too, raised objections. Avid to restore a more authoritarian state to power, they blamed the difficulties faced by Germany on the Weimar Republic itself, or on Jewish capitalists. Counterrevolutionary organizations were proliferating.

Agnes groused that since their return to Berlin, British authorities had pressured Weimar officials to harass them, pointing to a recent police raid on their home and their inability to renew their false passports as evidence. Forced into an underground existence, she wrote, their difficulties increased "by geometric progression." Throughout the closing months of 1921, she and Chatto would work until late in the evening, then find a cheap place to sleep. The stress caused by constant moving from hotel to hotel and house to house, not knowing where they would sleep from one night to the next, set off Agnes's neurasthenic heart ailment, but after undergoing treatment at a local hospital she resumed apace.

Pursued "night and day by British spies," as Agnes wrote, she feared for their lives, and there was some basis to her concern. That December, Chatto passed out after he drank some cocoa at a restaurant and became violently ill; the physician they consulted suspected arsenic poisoning. Agnes also claimed that two English agents with false keys attempted to break into their room. Her friend Josephine Bennett had given Agnes a handgun for her protection before she left New York, and she wrote that she found the instrument a comfort in her present life.

In the first flush of her romance with Chatto, many of Agnes's objections to matrimony dissipated. She spoke of a desire to wed, used Chatto's surname, and referred to him as her husband. She even discussed having children, but Chatto seemed uninterested in marrying *her*. Ashamed, Agnes would assert that he wished to but could not because he was already married to a devout Irish Catholic who refused to divorce him. In later retellings, the woman became "a nun in some hidden English convent."[9] In fact, Chatto had never married. Agnes also maintained that her lover was indifferent to women, although he was a womanizer who had lived with several European women before they met.

Agnes might tell herself and others that Chatto *could* not rather than *would* not marry her, but at some level, she always knew that her background was an impediment to her patrician partner, as the following letter reveals.

Once some well known Indian men and women came to Berlin and my husband was to go and meet them . . . This same night some American friends invited me to the theater. My husband was angry because I was going with these Americans although he had the appointment with the Indians. In defiance I went to the theater. But I could not enjoy myself, I felt so miserable that I had not come to an agreement with my husband. Then I got up and left the theater in the middle of the first act and decided to go to my husband and tell him I could not enjoy myself because of the difference of opinion between us. In happiness I rushed to that hotel where he was to meet the Indians. I went in through the doors and saw him in the midst of the Indians. I ran up to him, happy and smiling. But he was very much embarrassed and led me away and said: "You see, why have you come *here*? Do you not know that it makes my position impossible? I cannot introduce you to these people—they know my family. How then can I introduce *you* to them?" And I, stunned and shocked, asked, "Your family! But why should you not introduce me to people who know your family?" And he said, "Oh, it is impossible. You must go away." And he took me to the door and I went out on the street. I looked back and saw that all the Indians were staring after me. They thought I was some woman from the street, some prostitute or something, who had rushed into one of the men, and had been put out.

　...In the end, to get peace...I said: "You were right; you could not possibly have introduced me to Indians. They were such beautiful women, in silk Indian costumes, and I was badly dressed; and I am of the working class...I am sorry that I did not see clearly."[10]

The following March, Chatto's younger brother, Harindranath, arrived with his wife, Kamaladevi, for a visit, and the presence of his family exacerbated tensions. Kamaladevi treated Agnes with condescension, presenting her with a cheap string of beads on gold-filled wire that she tried to pass off as pearls.[11] Harindranath respected the ferocity with which Agnes watched over his brother, but he saw little else to recommend "the sickly, nervous proletarian woman," as he later recalled her. With obstinate defiance, Agnes punished the couple with fantastical tales of her life as a coal miner's daughter, but their judgments wounded her nonetheless.

In the spring of 1922, Chatto activated his mainstays into a new organization, the Indian Revolutionary Council. Kamaladevi would write that Chatto and his coterie of supporters seemed "pitiably placed and rather lost" in Berlin. However, the fact that the city was functioning once more as a center of Indian political activity was largely due to Chatto's industry, and when Soviet minister Chicherin passed through Berlin after attending the Genoa conference, Chatto met with him. Unaware that his behavior in Moscow the previous year had alienated the Russian diplomat, Chatto asked him to get the Comintern to reconsider its position. Chicherin reportedly replied that the only way he would consider promoting Chatto's council was on the condition that Chatto himself was excluded from it.[12]

When Roy arrived in April, his pockets brimming with Comintern gold, he claimed he had come to get in touch with developments in Bengal. However, he displayed more curiosity about the Bengalis in Berlin. By this time, the rising Comintern star, poised for membership on its executive committee, had little to fear from Chatto politically, but he appeared to be taking no chances. Soon he was at the center of a whispering campaign designed to discredit Chatto as a man. Through the young Bengali Suren Karr, stories were circulated about Agnes's sexual involvement with various Indians in New York including Lajpat Rai, Ghose, Das—and perhaps Roy himself.[13]

Agnes wrote that before they became lovers, Chatto had told her his revolution extended to women—that he believed the world could not advance without their freedom. She had even bragged to Florence that her "husband" was a social revolutionary who accepted as a matter of faith women's right to lead full lives before marriage. Agnes swore she had told Chatto before they "married" about her relations with other men so there might be no misunderstanding. Perhaps she had, but she had apparently neglected to mention that some of her lovers were Indians, let alone that one of them had been Roy.

The rumors of Agnes's indiscretions dealt Chatto, already laid low by the strain of his exile, a devastating blow. Not only did they wound his pride, they cost him the respect of his Bengali comrades, who expected their female partners to be virgins when they met. Chatto accused Agnes of having a weak character for having slept with other men, she wrote, and objected that he "got the leavings."[14] Hour by hour, she recalled, he put her under increasing "emotional pressure ... always accusing me because I had been married, because I had had another love affair. Always standing with a pointing finger at me. Always demanding that he read my letters ... always making subtle references to my 'sexual needs' that he could 'not satisfy' while 'others could.'"[15]

In truth, the couple had sexual as well as emotional difficulties. Chatto boasted of his knowledge and experience, but his upbringing had taught him to treat women sexually as "a convenient piece of bedroom furniture," Agnes wrote, and his formative encounters had been with prostitutes: a training she termed "as deadly as syphilis."[16] One consequence, she would confess, was that Chatto suffered from premature ejaculation, which left her in a constant state of "most awful nervous tension."[17]

Chronically short of funds, Agnes had acquired the habit of accepting financial gifts from more comfortably situated friends who admired her selfless devotion or hoped for more than friendship (a detail Agnes often conveniently ignored). Before the gossip started, Tarak Nath Das, who frequently demonstrated such ambiguous generosity with her, had agreed to send Agnes twenty-five thousand German marks. As Chatto grew suspicious of all her associates,

Agnes begged Florence to arrange for the funds to arrive through a neutral third
party to avoid his "insinuating references" and "vile remarks."

> I don't want anything whatever to come from any Indian directly. There is a
> dirty man here who has gossiped without any foundation, and it seems that
> every note I write to America is read by many people. I know the deep and
> sincere friendship of [Das] and I have a similar impersonal and sincere
> friendship to offer in return. But there are Indians who make it their business
> to gossip and make my life miserable . . . There are men here who . . . collect
> "news" from American fellows, and then . . . pervert it and circulate it broad-
> cast. There is no way of meeting a half lie or a rumor.[18]

Shortly thereafter, Agnes advised Florence to decline Das's money entirely.
The Indians in Berlin, Agnes wrote, harbored harsh prejudices against women
and foreigners. Inefficient in work, they were also "jealous of efficient persons."[19]

Chatto's envy often made him "beastly" toward Agnes, she wrote. After Roy's
mischief, she claimed, he "almost locked me up from the Indians, and refused
to let me go into the Indian work, and he said it was because the Indians would
learn of my sex life and ruin *him* because of it."[20] He also interfered with her
professional commitments. That March, Agnes had published an article in the
Indian press on Jodh Singh, a Sikh immigrant brought in as a witness in the San
Francisco trial, who had gone insane in prison after refusing to testify against his
countrymen. The story had attracted Agnes for some time, and the piece, strong
and impassioned, was picked up by the *Nation*.

> Jodh Singh was eventually brought into the marshal's office. He was . . . thin,
> emaciated, and weak. His black eyes, sunk deeply into his head, gave him a
> fearful appearance. His clothes were torn, and it was said that he — not the
> British secret service men — tore them. One Hindu, also a Sikh, spoke to him
> in his native tongue. Jodh Singh then ripped open the front of his torn shirt
> and forced up the sleeves of his coat. He bent down and touched his knees.
> On his breast and on his wrists were dark brown splotches — burned skin. The
> Hindu who was watching turned his head, and his face went white. He
> turned to talk and to question again. But Jodh Singh did not see him. His eyes
> had lost their gleam of intelligence, and it was only on occasion that they
> would revive it.[21]

It was Agnes's first publication in the magazine and a significant achievement, but Chatto resented her desire to write and told her, she wrote, that she
only pursued it to "show off." If she persisted in the face of his disapproval, she

claimed that he warned her, she was only to write what he told her. That way he could be sure it was correct. Agnes stopped writing.

In later years, she would say that when she had lived in New York and scoffed that love was something for "weaklings," Florence had tried to warn her that she protested too much—that when Agnes finally fell in love she was just the sort who would "simply be finished off!"[22] Florence was correct. As Agnes dropped the defenses she had built up over the years to protect her freedom, the relationship with Chatto, rather than freeing her, enslaved her. Chatto was the first man in Agnes's life with whom she was spiritually and physically intimate. In him she supposed she had found a partner who "was all that love means, all that comradeship seemed to mean in work and in life, all that friendship means; all that is gentle in the human heart," she later wrote. [23] His tyranny made her miserable.

Agnes was still a feminist, intellectually. If anyone dared suggest "that woman's intellect or capacity to build was inferior to that of man," Chatto's brother, Harindranath, observed, "she jumped up out of her seat like a wounded lioness and almost clawed him red in the face!"[24] But Chatto's distress at Agnes's failure to "lock up" her sex organs, as she put it, before she met him touched her in a vulnerable area. "I thought I really was vile and a prostitute which he called me," she wrote, "and that a man so brilliant, so vital, so powerful, so commanding and so intense in his love of his country could only be right and I be wrong. He is so compelling in his personality that I knew he must be right in all things."[25]

Unsure of Chatto's love, Agnes attempted to bind him to her as she had Sarah, by becoming physically and mentally ill. Her inability to achieve sexual release, she later acknowledged, contributed to her catalog of bodily afflictions. That May, Agnes entered a sanitorium in northern Germany with what she referred to as nervous trouble, but she remained unstable even after treatment. On her return to Berlin, her condition deteriorated further. In June she checked herself into a local hospital, "shot to pieces, nervously . . . My nervousness concentrates in my throat and causes nervous tenseness which comes in 'spells' and lasts for some 20 hours at a stretch. During this time," she wrote, "I am generally drugged else I would go pop."[26]

Agnes had originally planned to spend the summer of 1922 visiting southern Germany, where revolutionary syndicalists were organizing metal miners into a movement along the lines of the IWW. Like the Bolsheviks, revolutionary syndicalists were opposed to capitalism, but they rejected the Bolsheviks' insistence that they subordinate trade unions to the Communist Party. Mistrustful of political action and disdainful of the state, they emphasized class war, economic action, and large-scale organization. Their success in the early 1920s, particularly in Germany, was transforming anarchism from a tiny minority current into a cause with considerable mass support.

Berlin was the headquarters of the Revolutionary Syndicalists' International, and Agnes, who had already met its principal figures in Moscow, shared the movement's principles and spirit. In Berlin, she had socialized with Rudolph Rocker, its leading thinker, his wife, Millie, and their anarchist associates August Souchy, Senya Flechine, and Molly Steimer (whom Agnes had known in New York), but recurrent nervous attacks now kept her mostly confined to her bed. Agnes said that her need to conceal her problems from her acquaintances hindered her recovery, but when Goldman arrived and moved with Berkman into an apartment in the city's Charlotteburg district, Agnes sought her out as a role model, mentor, and mother surrogate.

By 1922, Goldman's articles in the *New York World* denouncing the Bolsheviks had earned her the enmity of most American radicals, but Agnes cared not a whit about a community an ocean away with whom she had never identified anyway. As she foundered in her life with Chatto, the older rebel showed an extraordinary understanding of Agnes and repeatedly proved herself a loving and intimate friend. Both women traveled in the same anarcho-syndicalist circles, and when Agnes was feeling up to it they socialized, explored the city, and discussed its political and cultural life. Agnes clung to Goldman's commitment to her well-being, for Goldman's conviction that the way in which people conducted their daily lives was their most important political statement encouraged Agnes to begin to examine her inner life without judging her present lack of active engagement a failing.

If Goldman romanticized the issue of sexual liberation by ignoring the ways in which men exploited women through it, "she went much further than most radicals of her era in grasping the politics of sex," her biographer observed.[27] Unlike mainstream feminists, who concerned themselves with women's suffrage and workplace issues, Goldman focused her theory of equality between the sexes on the more subjective, psychological aspects of emancipation. To her, the "internal tyrannies" of ethical and social convention were more damaging to women than the external ones. In Agnes's case she was dead on target.

Goldman recognized Agnes's conflict between the nineteenth-century female virtues of self-sacrifice and submission and more modern values like self-expression and independence. She also knew from her own experience how an assertive woman could become ensnared in a web "of deep, erotic dependence" and feel ambivalent about sex despite her contemporary views on love.[28] Her familiarity with the ways in which carnality both "releases our spirit and binds it with a thousand threads," as Goldman described it, made her extremely sensitive to Agnes's suffering.[29]

By the fall of 1922, authorities' harassment of the couple had eased, and Agnes felt better. She and Chatto had rented space in the home of an elderly widow, and Agnes, who now had a room to herself, wrote that it was so restful it felt "like a fresh bath."[30] Chatto was also treating her more respectfully, she reported. He had introduced her to a visiting friend as his wife and instructed his niece to address Agnes using the honorific "auntie." He also gave her a small job on the bureau magazine that she could do at home, and all of this pleased Agnes so well that she thought of writing for the Indian press again. However, their fragile accommodation dissolved in less than a month when a newly created Indian Independence Party, founded on Chatto's program of revolutionary nationalism and run by virtually all Chatto's colleagues with the exception of Chatto himself, won Chicherin's approval and Comintern funding.

Robbed of the role that should have been his, effectively banned from participating in the movement he had led for years, Chatto looked to the anarcho-syndicalist circles in which Agnes moved for support, collaborating with her on a plan to spread revolutionary syndicalist principles in India and accompanying her to one of their congresses, which she covered for the IWW paper.[31] His attempts to pass himself off as an anarchist were unconvincing. Goldman found Chatto clever and witty, but she later wrote that she never doubted for a moment that "it was Hindu nationalism to which he devoted himself entirely."[32] He vented his frustration on Agnes.

As recently as the previous spring, Agnes had blamed the Indian work for ruining her health. In Germany, she said, it was infinitely harder than it had been in the United States. By the end of 1922, she held Chatto alone responsible. It was not so much his jealousy as his domination, she explained. In their first year together, the imbalance between them had not been so extreme. However, as Chatto became more comfortable with her, he had grown increasingly controlling. Like a storm, she would write, Chatto "existed according to his nature, absorbing, influencing everything he touched."[33] Nearly two years into the relationship, everything about their life was of his choosing rather than hers and she felt as if she were suffocating.

As an adult, Chatto lacked the resources his family had known in India, but he still expected Agnes to replicate the lifestyle of his childhood. Much to her dismay, their small home had become a scaled-down version of the Chattopadhyaya household. "Moslems and Hindus of every caste streamed through as through a railway station or a hotel. Students came directly from their boats, carting all their bedding and cooking utensils," she later wrote.[34] For any given meal, Chatto would invite two or three other Indians to join them, and not all of them were revolutionaries, Agnes lamented. Some of the men Chatto met through the bureau had never helped another human being and had no interest in nationalist work.

Inept in the kitchen, Agnes hated to cook, but cook she did until "the very walls of our home seemed to be permeated with the odor of curry," she wrote.[35] Even so, she said that on occasion she still went without food herself because if there was not enough, Indian hospitality demanded that the male must eat. Then, she wrote, she would sit, hungry, while the men complained that European women were prostitutes. Chatto offered his services free to the Indians—he helped them search for rooms and shop and did nationalist work—but it was she who washed their clothing, ironed it, mended it, scrubbed the floors, and did the dishes. When Chatto acceded to the men's requests for money, she was the one left to meet telephone bills that ran into hundreds of marks or find the means to keep them going.

Agnes claimed that as Chatto's needs overwhelmed her, she did not speak against him. Small wonder. On the few occasions she tried to rebel or talk back, he choked or bit her, she wrote.[36] To maintain the peace, Agnes told a friend, she learned to say, "Yes, I am at fault; forgive me. I am sorry. I should not have done this or that. You were right. Forgive me and help me see what is the right thing to do in the future," even when she knew she had done nothing wrong.[37] But from the time Chatto physically abused her, she began to wilt and sink. The

Portrait in Berlin, mid-1920s.

paralyzing throat spasms she had experienced off and on since childhood
returned along with kidney trouble, insomnia, and nervous attacks she said
resembled epileptic fits, during which she fell to the floor and trembled.

As she shrank into herself, Agnes relinquished her remaining worldly obligations, and Chatto, she complained, showed little understanding of her state.
"He didn't think I was ill," she wrote. Accustomed perhaps to the quiet resignation with which his own mother bore her suffering, he told her she was feeble-
minded and lacked will, she said, and behaved the way she did just to disturb
him. In Greenwich Village, Agnes had looked down on those of Thorberg's
friends who sat around discussing their inability to overcome their complexes.
By the beginning of 1923, Agnes's despair drove her to consult a psychoanalyst
herself.

What Agnes had yet to acknowledge was that Chatto's attempts to control
her—even his abuse, troubling as it was—were not the sole cause of her
anguish. Equally disturbing was the fact that in their relationship, she had
become what she most dreaded and fought against: a domestic drudge, just like
her mother, who had lost her own identity in the name of love and become submerged in another. The battle Agnes waged to prevent such truths, or indeed
any painful memories, from reaching her consciousness was reducing her to a
bedridden invalid.

Agnes's analysis went poorly, in large part because she said she was unwilling
to address any aspect of her life that did not directly involve Chatto. Given her
resistance, all her analyst could do, Agnes wrote, was prescribe sleeping powders
for her insomnia and morphine for her nerves and "act as a prop now and then
when I need him. So when I am very bad I rush to him and we talk about things
in general. He hypnotised me to take away a part of my misery."[38] To try to lift
what Agnes later described as the "black curtain" that blocked her access to her
emotions, her analyst suggested that she write about her early experience, and
during bursts of relative health Agnes drafted three chapters of an autobiographical novel. Then, she said, her therapist committed an unexplained but "serious
blunder" of a personal nature that was perhaps sexual, and she put the project
aside.[39]

The chaos in Germany contributed to her distress. By 1923, the dual afflictions of Allied reparations claims and savage penalties on German trade that
sent the mark spiraling downward and prices upward had the country in an
untenable state. The Germans, who had come to understood the connection
between their inflation and the Entente's demands, hated their conquerors.
"There is no happiness here," Agnes wrote Florence. "I don't know when I've
heard a person laugh a really joyous laugh. The only time they laugh is when
they have beer before them, and then their laugh is heavy and deadly. I am

weary of Germany, just as one wearies of suffering, dullness and ugliness over a long period of time." [40]

At the start of the year, Chancellor Wilhelm Cuno had declared a moratorium on Allied reparations payments and delayed the delivery of raw materials in the hope of renegotiating more favorable terms. The French had responded with troops that occupied Germany's industrial center. Even then, the German government had refused to resume reparations payments. When the French blockaded the area and much of the occupied Rhineland, felling the tottering economy, mine and factory workers in the Ruhr were still waging a campaign of passive resistance.

The dams on inflation gave way in May 1923. As the paper mark plunged, real wages for salaried workers shriveled into meaninglessness. Families with savings lost everything. Trade and businesses were devastated; unemployment was rampant, but the government kept printing more currency. Soon all of Germany was frantic. Those with jobs would shop daily at the nearest store and buy whatever they could purchase, regardless of cost, to exchange for something else. A week's wages might buy a hundredweight of potatoes; six weeks' wages, a pair of boots.

Food became "a currency and an obsession," the artist George Grosz would recall. "At a breakfast of turnip coffee, mildewed bread and synthetic honey, one discussed lunch. At a lunch of turnip cutlets, muscle pudding and turnip coffee, one discussed a dinner of muscle wurst."[41] Worse than the lack of nourishment was the uncertainty, Agnes wrote. "Formerly a poor man knew that if he saved a mark for a week, it retained its purchasing power. Today, twelve milliards may buy a loaf of bread, but tomorrow it will only buy half a loaf, and next week it may not even buy one slice."[42]

The collapse of the currency affected Germans in a way that neither the war, the November 1918 revolution, nor the Treaty of Versailles had managed to do. A kind of insanity seized hold that undermined the foundations of German society, and Berlin—already crude and morally ambiguous—said the writer Stefan Zweig, became "the Babylon of the world."[43]

"Bars, amusement parks, honky-tonks sprang up like mushrooms . . . Along the entire Kurfurstendamm powdered and rouged young men sauntered and they were not all pros; every high school boy wanted to earn some money and in the dimly lit bars one might see government officials and men of the world of finance tenderly courting drunken sailors without any shame. Even the Rome of Suetonius had never known such orgies as the pervert balls of Berlin, where hundreds of men costumed as women and hundreds of women as men danced under the benevolent eye of the police."[44] Middle-class adolescent females boasted of their perversions; to be suspected of being a virgin, Zweig said, "would have been considered a disgrace in every school in Berlin."[45]

In Agnes's delicate state, the city under the inflation was more than she could bear. At eleven every morning and four in the afternoon, she wrote, her throat tightened and her head swam. She became dependent on the sleeping powders and morphine her analyst prescribed, and when the effects of her hypnosis wore off, she said, she suffered from nervous attacks that laid her out for days on end. Agnes wrote that she missed the Indians' company but avoided them and their gatherings, afraid of provoking Chatto's jealousy or the chance that someone like Roy would "take my misery and make a joke of it for every street corner."[46] With her poor command of German and marginal links to the culture, she felt terribly estranged and alone.

One saving grace was her budding friendship with the Danish writer Karin Michaelis. Michaelis was a venerated novelist known for her probing analysis of the inner lives of complex modern women like Agnes, and during the first half of 1923 the two women whiled away many afternoons in one another's company. Agnes said she was often so tired and ill she could not fathom why Michaelis found her interesting; she underestimated her appeal. Michaelis later recalled that meeting Agnes was "like love at first glance, this was friendship before any words had been said."[47] The laughter and warmth and depth of feeling that marked their encounters, Michaelis would say, permanently enriched her life. She believed that if Agnes had not found the Indian movement, her idealism and rebellious heart would have prompted her to invent a cause for which to fight.

> Agnes is one of the most uncompromising people I have met—and one of the most loving and self-sacrificing...a woman no one who has ever met her forgets...Though young in years, she has renounced everything: fame, personal happiness, comfort, safety, for one thing: complete dedication to a great cause. She would never consider becoming a member of any political party which laid down rules for her. She lives her life, and she fights her fight, as she finds fair and just. She is a lonely bird of tremendous wingspread, a bird that will never build a nest...
>
> And yet—with this obstinate defiance peculiar to her, which no one and nothing can make her give up—she is nevertheless the tenderest and most loving being...Watch her touch a flower, watch her pat a little child on the head, listen to her tell about her childhood...Her heart has shed...blood."[48]

Agnes continued to make little progress in her analysis, for some of the "insights" she gained in treatment only added to her confusion. In a letter she drafted to Michaelis shortly after she returned to Denmark, Agnes disparaged her "inappropriate" desire to be man's equal and define herself outside the sphere of marriage and motherhood. She blamed her behavior on her upbringing in the American West. When she was growing up, Agnes observed, "the woman who could win the respect of a man . . . was often the woman who could knock him down with her bare fists and sit on him until he yelled for help." [49] She had not liked it and had found it humiliating, she wrote, but she had nevertheless "tried to be a man. I shot, rode, jumped and took part in all the fights of the boys . . . because it was the proper thing to do . . . I forced myself into it, I scorned all weak, womanly things." [50]

Unless one had been a cowgirl—which Agnes was not—fighting, shooting, and riding were distinctly *not* the proper things to do in the rapidly industrializing west in which she came of age. Agnes had in fact been drawn to those activities precisely because they were not. She was so unsure of herself these days, however, that she recast her recalcitrant spirit as something forced on her from without and derided the "masterful" and "mannish" attitudes that hindered her ability to live peaceably with Chatto. [51]

As the spring of 1923 deepened, Agnes thought she was improving and returned to her home-based job on the bureau's magazine. Even so, she groused that since her analyst was only willing to "patch up places here and there," she lacked a proper understanding of her illness, and in June she abandoned treatment altogether, fearful that her doctor was getting too personal with her again. To escape her unhappiness and Germany's seemingly endless woes, Agnes fantasized about joining Michaelis and her actress friend Betty Nansen in Vienna. Only recently, Florence's suggestion that Agnes consult with Freud had seemed as improbable as her "drop[ping] into heaven and hav[ing] tea with God," she wrote. Now she boasted to Florence of perhaps making Freud's acquaintance socially since her new friends traveled "in a circle in which the great celebrities run." [52]

The women had invited Agnes to vacation with them in Denmark, where Michaelis had a summer home on the island of Thuro, and Agnes spoke wistfully of passing several weeks there rowing, writing, and relaxing, then spending a month in Copenhagen as Nansen's guest. She suspected Michaelis's invitation was an attempt to learn more about her early life for use in subsequent literary endeavors, but Michaelis had offered to pay Agnes's expenses and introduce her to Georg Brandes, the esteemed critic, who was her good friend and adviser. Agnes wrote that she was willing to let Michaelis pick her brain in exchange for the rest she craved.

By this time Agnes described her relationship with Chatto as equivalent to living on the edge of a volcano, but she was not ready to give him up. "I've married an artist," she explained to Florence, "a revolutionary in a dozen different ways, a man of truly 'fine frenzy'; nervous as a cat, *always* moving, never at rest, indefatigable energy, a hundred fold more than I ever had, a *thin* man with *much* hair, a tongue like a razor and a brain like hell on fire . . . I'm consumed into ashes. And he's always raking up the ashes and setting them on fire again. He doesn't believe in ashes; only in fire...and he is always smoldering."[53] Still, the diatribe with which she met a letter from Florence that said *she* was thinking of marrying displayed an irony and distance previously lacking.

> Beneath the skin of every man, it matters not who he is, lies the old Adam. Scratch him and you will find I am right. He is fine in theory, our modern man. But in practice he is a walking lie. He still judges woman by her vagina; in fact woman is nothing but a walking vagina to him, and he is the sole owner of it . . . If you ever get married, or contemplate it, look the man in the eye beforehand and say, "I have had many love affairs; so have you. I respect your own right. You must respect mine and keep your hands out of affairs which do not concern you and which have nothing to do with you" . . . Unless you do this, you are lost afterwards. Even then I will have no faith in the man. He will torture you throughout your life, in a thousand subtle ways. I hate all married men. I love those who are not married and who will not marry. They alone can be companions and friends of women. Marriage automatically crushes all the nobility in a man's soul. Not so in a woman's. She is often even more human than before marriage. But she throws herself to a wild beast when she marries.[54]

Agnes's reprieve from illness was only temporary. As the reality of her circumstances—that she was destitute and without a legal passport—sank in, and she had to relinquish her plan for a lighthearted jaunt abroad, her nervous collapses returned; she also wrote of "possible" damage to one of her lungs. When her physician suggested two months in the mountains as a restorative, Agnes initially said that after the way Chatto had treated her when he learned she "borrowed" money from Das, she was reluctant to accept funds she had not earned. However, by late June 1923 she was so desperate for a break and so frightened of her own instability that she overcame her reservations and took a "loan" from Das and another female friend and allowed Florence to "purchase" a few of her trinkets to subsidize a rest.[55] If that did not help, she wrote, she was at a loss as to what to do next.

When Goldman's niece Stella Cominsky stopped by the mountain resort of Bad Liebenstein to see Agnes that July, she found her in an agitated state. Agnes hoped her difficulty was the altitude and shifted to Oberbayern, high in the Bavarian Alps, where she said her brain was clearer. However, she remained depressed and unable to sleep. Convinced, as ever, that a change of locale might bring her peace of mind, she impetuously decided to pursue her interrupted journey to India and asked friends in London to help her secure a visa.[56]

The longer she participated in the Indian nationalist movement, it seemed, the further she got from the people and ideas that had inspired her. Worn down by the elitism, incompetence, and wrangling among the upper-caste Bengali intellectuals with whom she worked, Agnes longed for action, not analysis. In the Punjab, a mass movement of militant Sikhs known as the Akalis (the "Deathless") were waging a campaign that stirred her heart. Unlike activists elsewhere in India, the heroes of this revolt were humble village folk, persecuted beyond the limits of their endurance. These poverty-stricken, starving men were using their bare breasts as shields in their fight for India's freedom and their own, and Agnes found their proud martyrs' story compelling.[57] In the end, though, her imprisonment, her articles in the Indian press, and her association with Chatto all weighed against her. British India officials would let her sail to India, she wrote, but they would not let her in.

Unable to escape her torment in flight, Agnes grudgingly accepted that her condition was more entrenched than she thought. As her desire to understand why so many things "wrung her heart out," as she put it, acquired urgency, she crossed the Swiss border in search of work that would pay for psychoanalytic treatment with Freud or his assistant, Otto Rank.[58] By the time she called off her fruitless effort, she was not at all well. The least thing set her on edge for days, she wrote, and she slept only under strong sedation. In the vain hope, once again, that altitude rather than inner turmoil was causing her distress, she sought the lower elevation of Berchtesgaden, which is where Chatto found her.

He pleaded with her, she wrote, to return with him to Berlin. Seeing no other path open to her, she reluctantly consented. However, she set some conditions for her return. Whatever money remained from her vacation Agnes insisted be preserved for her to attend classes at Berlin University. Chatto was also to get her a passport in her real name so she might move about more freely, and she demanded to live alone. Confronted with the alternatives, which Agnes presented as either her "total destruction" or her departure, Agnes said, Chatto agreed to relinquish his claims on her attention and give her "perfect freedom in all things."[59] If, despite these precautions, her mental health continued to deteriorate in Berlin, she wrote Florence, she would consult Karl Abraham or Max Eitingon, two distinguished analysts at the city's Psychoanalytic Institute.[60]

Agnes returned to the city in September 1923. The apartment of her own and the legal passport never materialized, but she did get a room to herself with a door that locked. By the time Chatto came home from work, Agnes said, she had bolted herself in and gone to sleep. When he awoke, she was already at her typewriter. Their sexual relationship was temporarily at an end, but they still had dinner together on occasion. At such times, Agnes confided to Florence, she confined their conversation to impersonal subjects.

By "deadening her heart" to Chatto, as she put it, she managed to get through her days reasonably well. At night, though, his physical proximity aggravated her, and she wrote of being tormented by thoughts that she was wasting her life. Now thirty-one, she still felt like "an ignorant, uncultured, undeveloped animal" and saw no other paths open to herself.[61] She tried to distract herself by immersing herself in work for the bureau's magazine and articles for the Indian press, the French *Clarté*, and the *Nation*, but her dreams, she wrote, were riddled with nightmares—on those nights she could sleep at all.

In the fall of 1923, the inflation crisis approached its peak. "Month by month," Agnes later wrote, "I saw people die of slow hunger and watched funeral processions enter and leave the little church on my street. In the corner grocery I often observed gaunt workers pay out their week's wages, billions of paper marks, for a couple of loaves of bread, some potatoes, and margarine. Meat and fruit were beyond their reach. There was no sugar, only saccharine, and even this they could not afford. Families sought foreign boarders in order to get foreign currency, and decent foreigners were filled with shame."[62]

Shops were being looted throughout Berlin. There was unrest in most other cities and actual street fighting in many. A conservative, Gustav Stresemann, had replaced Cuno as chancellor. However, his government was expected to fall soon, and Agnes believed a fascist government, and civil war between the monarchists and Communists, would follow. For her part, she saw little difference between the two.[63] The divisive tactics of German Communist Party (KPD) members, who disrupted her syndicalist meetings with their shouting and whistling, and the "white-collared" elitism of its leaders had cost them Agnes's respect.[64] Their argument that establishing the republic had been a mistake offended her as deeply as the monarchists' claims, and she accused both of cynically manipulating people's misery to set themselves up in power.

On September 26, the Bavarian government declared a state of emergency, took over the Weimar Republic's army, and established its own right-wing dictatorship. To prevent the republic from dissolving, Stresemann's government proclaimed martial law. Two weeks later, the appointment of two KPD representatives to the cabinet of the socialist governments in Saxony and Thuringia led the Comintern to prod KPD leader Heinrich Brandler into ordering a Communist uprising to topple the government and the capitalist oppressors.

The uprising was a fiasco. The Weimar army easily suppressed the Communists' "revolution," along with the labor governments in both states. When Florence heard the news, she feared her hot-tempered friend had stormed the barricades and dared the government to shoot her. Agnes reassured Florence that she had not courted death in that way. The greatest threat to her life, then and now, she wrote, lay less in the reaction than with the Communists themselves. If *they* came to power, then she was at risk because the syndicalists and anarchists with whom she was associated topped the list of those the Communists hated, "even ahead of Hitler and his gang."[65]

The crisis of the German republic was not over. That November, while Munich authorities deliberated whether to make peace with Berlin or launch a military offensive against the Weimar Republic, Hitler's small band of National Socialists stormed a local tavern where the Bavarian dictator was speaking and proclaimed its own revolution. Once the Bavarian government decided to cooperate with the central government, it smoothly put down Hitler's Beer Hall Putsch and racist movement. However, by the time order was restored throughout the republic, the exchange rate was 1.3 trillion marks to the dollar. No real currency existed; everything had collapsed.

As the winter of 1923 loomed, Agnes sorely regretted her decision to return to Berlin. The Indian News Service and Information Bureau, like everything else in Germany, took a beating in the economic freefall, and Chatto was forced to suspend its operations, including the magazine on which Agnes worked. Even then, he accumulated so great a debt during this period that Agnes said she felt obliged to spend whatever money remained from her vacation trying to rescue him. Not only were her dreams of attending university on hold; the two were in such financial peril that Agnes had to prevail on their landlady for charity.

Agnes now entered a depression so dark she decided, "I either have to be analysed now or I die. I can not pass through another month of torture."[66] Over Chatto's strong objections, she secretly returned to therapy, this time with a female analyst, Elizabeth Naef, who was affiliated with the University of Berlin. Dr. Naef was not much older than Agnes, but she had studied with Freud in Vienna, and her reputation in the international psychoanalyst community was excellent, Agnes reassured friends—on a par with Otto Rank's.[67] The cost was a stiff two American dollars a day, money Agnes did not possess, but Florence offered to pay for half, and by this point Agnes said she was willing to lay down everything she had for some relief.

Dr. Naef was a woman of striking personality as well as ability, her colleague Ernest Jones remarked.[68] Although Agnes muttered that even her initial sessions were extremely depressing and left her cranky and melancholic, she trusted Dr. Naef in a way she never had her previous analyst. Her nervous and physical exhaustion, she wrote, compelled her to stay the course, but what seemed like a never-ending series of medical emergencies prevented Agnes from making any real progress.

First, according to Agnes, her landlady attempted to kill herself with an over-dose of Agnes's medications. Guilty and grateful for the woman's help, Agnes said, she nursed her back to health. Then her "brother-in-law" A.C.N. Nambiar caught pneumonia, and when his beautiful young wife, Suhasini, fainted in the face of his illness, Agnes felt obliged to step in. Then she came down with a fever herself. Just as the crisis passed, Chatto's older sister Sarojini's son fell ill with pneumonia, and Agnes assisted *his* nurse while simultaneously caring for an infant she said was dying of hunger.

To meet their expenses, Agnes wrote, she looked for work with an American firm and even considered a job with the American Consulate but could find nothing. By the end of 1923, although currency reform was stabilizing the mark and the national madness was ending, money was still tight, and jobs, even those with low wages and long hours, remained scarce. Agnes quit her therapy to stanch the demands on her limited funds; she was tired, she said, of being a drain on others. However, she had placed such faith in its ability to cure her that she found it hard to adjust to life without it, and she neglected to consider how the last few months had depleted her meager emotional reserves.

By this time, Dr. Naef had explained to Agnes that there was no organic basis to her kidney trouble and throat convulsions—that they were purely psychic in origin—but such knowledge did not prevent her symptoms from returning.[69] Within a week after leaving analysis, Agnes questioned her desire to live. "For whole days I remained in a coma," she recalled, "unable to move or speak, long-ing only for oblivion . . . More than death I feared insanity, and the terror of this possibility haunted my very dreams."[70] Sometimes Agnes blamed the endless dif-ficulties of her life in Germany for pushing her to the brink of madness; some-times she blamed Chatto. Mostly she blamed herself. Had she any ability, she wrote, she would not be in the situation in which she found herself.

"I would not have been crushed as I have been . . . All the analysis can not, in the long run, make up for intellectual deficiency . . . I'm sick of Europe and sick of my life here and sick of life in general. And I'm sick to death of the Indians and their eternal demands upon one. And I'm sick of Chatto . . . not sick so much as hate him—except when I see him in a gathering and see how damnably interesting and attractive he is, both mentally and physically—and how lovably naive, and a victim of any cunning person who comes along."[71]

On December 8, 1923, Agnes penned a desperate note to Florence.

I can not hold out. All my sleeplessness and my "insane spells" (impressions of life) have returned to torture me. How long I can last I do not know. I prefer death to these spells and to sleeplessness . . . The future is torture to me. You can never dream of what [these "insane spells"] mean to me, of the dread and

the fear with which I face them. The nights approach with their burden of
dread. Oh I wonder if it is worth it all . . . My subconscious mind seems to be a
nest of fear about death and when I lie down to sleep these terrible impressions leap out at me, sending me awake in one second, to sleep no more.

I tell you frankly that I do not know if I can last even until I hear from you
. . . You have done more than your share for me. I feel it an imposition to even
write this to you . . . Yet I have no one else.[72]

Days later she wrote again of the "insane spells" when her consciousness
became detached from her body and the rest of the material world. At such
times, she said, she felt "poised in space hundreds of miles away, watching
human beings and all events in a perspective. Everything seems so trivial, so
fleeting, so utterly useless."[73] To return herself to reality, she immersed herself in
quotidian pursuits—washing and ironing, singing, "beating" on the piano—and
worked on an article she hoped to place in Hearst's weekly. Try as she might, she
could not outrun her demons.

On December 28, 1923, Agnes suffered the worst attack she had yet experienced. During the episode, which lasted several days, she could not sleep, her
throat endlessly convulsed, and she hallucinated that Chatto had entered
through her locked door to murder her. In a hysterical note, Agnes begged Florence to let her return to New York and live with her. Chatto, she said, was trying to keep her in Germany by threatening to follow her to the United States,
where she knew British agents would arrest him. By this time, neither alcohol
nor drugs nor sleeping powders were providing her with any relief.

Three days later she struck "psychic bed-rock," as she put it. The cry of Job,
she later wrote, came closest to capturing her anguish, but this was worse. For
when she fell to her knees to plead for help, she appealed to a "power which my
mind told me did not exist. And my hopelessness was greater than that of Job's
because he had faith that God did exist, and it gave him strength," while she
lacked religious conviction.[74] Thrown back upon herself, she faced "a blank
wall. And it seemed that there is a point beyond which suffering cannot go in
sanity," she wrote.[75]

Telling herself that she needed some rest, Agnes took an overdose of her
sleeping powders. Luckily, she had succeeded only in injuring herself when her
landlady discovered her. The woman telephoned Dr. Naef, who convinced her
to return for at least another month of treatment, paying when she could. If
after that time she still could not stand her life in Germany, she told Florence,
she would slip away and return to America, telling Chatto nothing of her
whereabouts.

CHAPTER 6

Becoming a Writer

I am deeply convinced that from the lower strata of workers and peasants, from the workers, from various other organizations, from the universities, from the Red Army—a new writer will come. This writer will come from some backwoods area, from the provinces. This is the writer who is tied by his blood bonds and by his way of life to the worker and peasant...This writer will undoubtedly occupy a central position...We should orient our policy toward him and help him.

ALEKSANDR VORONSKY, MARXIST CRITIC, 1925

AGNES RETURNED to analysis in January 1924, her finances buoyed by a check from the *Nation* and a pledge from Florence of twenty-five American dollars a month toward her therapy and an additional two hundred dollars in charity. Agnes thanked her profusely for "a friendship such as seldom exists between two people. Some day," she promised, "I shall let you feel and know of my friendship for you as you have revealed yours to me...I love you. And...am conscious of...the priceless value of friendship such as yours."[1] Of her sudden windfall she told Chatto nothing. Having hit rock bottom, she hoped that in the future her analysis would keep her from "giving anything more to Indians," she wrote.[2]

Action came easily to Agnes; introspection was a struggle. She was determined to set her life on a more productive track, though, and with Dr. Naef's help she came to see how her pattern of "feel[ing] deeply, react[ing] violently and think[ing] little," as she put it, had contributed to her breakdown. As a professional woman and a socialist, Dr. Naef seemed to have a more flexible view of gender roles than Agnes's previous analyst, for under her care Agnes soon stopped blaming what she had described as "a deep castration complex" for her identification with traditionally masculine tastes, her energy, her contempt for women, or expectation of parity with men. It was not for want of a penis that she had been left a "half person," she wrote, and tried to compensate in other ways.

It was that she had vaulted through three generations of culture in thirty-one years and buried in the process every tendency that belonged to the life she had fled. Once Agnes opened for scrutiny the emotional tissue of her youth—the stormy relationships with her parents and the intense feelings of being unloved and an unwanted, misunderstood daughter—she began to acknowledge how traumatic it had been and the ways in which her "knots," as she described them, had contributed to her torment with Chatto. "Even my analyst says that she has known but two other persons who have passed through such a life as I," she wrote Florence. But they had moved on to create things, Agnes said, while she had "merely passed through it and then . . . collapsed."[3]

Agnes said Dr. Naef advised her patient that unburdening herself to friends would speed her healing, but Agnes was afraid to speak to Michaelis for fear she would use it in a novel, and she refused to discuss her childhood with Goldman and her anarcho-syndicalist friends. How could she? Having so embroidered its details to gain entree to her current circle, how could she bare her soul to them? The more Agnes transformed herself into a dirt-poor daughter of earth, the more difficult it had become to confront the ambivalence that lay beneath her self-created myths.

What sort of sympathy could she realistically expect, she must have wondered, if she confessed that her father was not one of the oppressed coal miners immortalized in the Ludlow Massacre but a detested deputy sheriff who beat and shot such men? Would her celebrated friends be as interested in the daughter of a snake oil salesman? Would they continue to seek her out if they knew she had once harbored the same prejudices as the rest of her family, or that periods of prosperity had banished the Smedleys from the very people from whom she claimed to spring? How could her accomplished friends understand that the cost of escaping her background made it too painful to embrace except as a pose?

Agnes could not resolve such basic issues as whether she was a journalist or an activist, an artist or an intellectual. Instead, she agonized over how little she had accomplished. The topic of what she would do with herself once she was again well figured prominently in her thoughts. Until she identified meaningful work in which to engross herself, she said that her days felt like a mere counting of time. Agnes wrote that she could not imagine a life in which she ignored "the vast sea which lives always in poverty and hunger, and the sea from which I came and in which my feet are planted," but she was unsure how to act on her feelings.[4]

Her inability to enter India, and the defeat that chased her efforts to work among the upper-caste Hindu exiles, made her view her future in the Indian independence movement as something of a puzzle. Restless and discontented, she turned to her newspaper work. In 1924, Agnes became a regular contributor to the *Deutsche Algemeine Zeitung,* Berlin's largest paper. As her depression lifted, she also submitted articles to the mainstream Swedish and Danish press along with the more radical French *Clarté,* the *Sinn Fein Weekly,* and the *Irish Independent.* Her struggle to overcome her inadequacies, real and imagined, made writing a challenge, and she often rewrote a single piece as many as eight times before she submitted it. Even then Agnes did not think she wrote particularly well, "but I write much. And muchness is essential to make money, unfortunately," she told Florence.[5]

Agnes said she would have preferred creating one thoughtful article a month to her present mode of production, which involved reworking the same few subjects for a variety of publications, but her reluctance to pursue a reporter's slot on the *New York World,* which, she wrote, friends had assured her was virtually hers for the asking, bespoke her lack of passion for a conventional journalistic career.[6] What Agnes really wanted, she was learning in therapy, was to become a creative writer. To achieve that fantasy, however, she would need to move beyond her impression that anything she read in books represented "the god-like" while anything in herself represented "the vile."[7] It was not that Agnes sought to abandon her political beliefs and become a detached literary aesthete. Rather, she longed for the freedom to delve deeply into her experience. By exploring her anger at a social system she believed had let her down along with others like her, Agnes hoped to produce a work of art of lasting value.

Her ultimate goal was a novel about her life, but Agnes began modestly enough with some prose poetry and two short autobiographical stories which she hoped to publish in the United States. Where to place them, though, was a mystery. The America of the Coolidge administration was a conservative, affluent place. By the mid-1920s, most rebellious American writers had lost interest in the working-class culture Agnes sought to portray. Those who remained politically committed were expected to subordinate their art to the class war and the Communist Party. The *Liberator,* which in earlier times was the obvious outlet for creative writing with radical implications, had been turned over to the CPUSA and become a purely political organ.

In Germany, however, the climate was different. Thanks in large part to American investment following the Dawes Plan, Germany, too, was enjoying a period of renewed prosperity. Unlike in the United States, however, in Germany—and particularly Berlin—there remained a talented pool of engaged revolutionary writers who were still creating imaginative literature, and a strong Russian presence in the city ensured an active cross-fertilization of their work.[8] In New York, Agnes had been too preoccupied with her need to earn a living to consider such ephemeral pursuits, but here in Berlin, the city's rich cultural life encouraged her to consider whether an artist's existence was within her reach.

While she pondered the idea, her aesthetic mentors, Michaelis and Goldman, kept her abreast of contemporary Russian literary movements and introduced her to Erwin Piscator's experiments with political theater, the dramas of Chekov, Shaw, and Ibsen, and the role of psychology in the work of John Galsworthy, Rebecca West, Somerset Maugham, and Evelyn Scott.

Early in 1924, the English Seminar program at Berlin University invited Agnes to lecture on Gandhi's ideas and methods. Chatto, who was evidently threatened by the idea that Agnes might succeed without him, expressed outrage at Agnes's "presumptuousness," she wrote, in speaking publicly on an Indian subject, but, she said, Dr. Naef recognized the importance of this opportunity and ordered him not to interfere. Chatto's disapproval made her sick with nervousness, Agnes wrote Florence. Still, she was so starved to do something ambitious she refused to allow herself any "shrinking." Even if she came up wanting, she wrote, the experience would have more significance than accomplishing something trivial.

With Goldman in the audience to give her courage, Agnes faced down the self-consciousness that had marred her previous attempts at public speaking and delivered her presentation to the thousand students who had assembled. It was so effective, she wrote, that even Chatto had nothing but praise. The lecture was a crucial event in Agnes's recovery. "For the first time in my life," she told Florence, "I have felt my strength."[9] From this time forward, her health steadily improved.

Inside India, the political landscape was bleak for those who desired India's freedom, but Comintern leaders like Zinoviev still wished the light of Communism to reach the hundreds of millions of Asians, particularly in India and China, and with Roy standing trial in India for conspiring to establish a Communist Party there, Chatto began to look more appealing to the Comintern. In February 1924, a German Communist "friend," as British intelligence described him (either Willi Muenzenberg or his friend and comrade-in-arms Leo Flieg, who handled the German Communists' covert activities with the Comintern's OMS), agreed to underwrite Chatto's Indian News Service and Information Bureau.[10] Agnes began receiving fifty dollars a month for her work on its magazine and in its office.[11]

The Russian famine of 1921–22 had long since ended, but the IAH, the "relief" organization Muenzenberg founded to aid it, had continued to grow—and his power along with it. In skillfully deploying charity as a vehicle for political action, Muenzenberg had come upon an impressive method for reaching beyond the Party faithful to thousands upon thousands of progressive idealists unwilling to march under the Communist banner. Their vigorous response to his appeals, which by 1924 had moved beyond Russia to embrace the world's proletariat, was enabling the organization to covertly influence a host of political activities outside the Soviet Union.

That March, Chatto moved with Agnes into a large, attractive apartment in a house outside the city. As her analysis progressed, she was increasingly confident of her ability as a journalist, but, she said, she had come to realize that if she were to support herself again and also find time for more creative endeavors, she simply could not cook, wash dishes, do laundry, mend, and iron as well as work for the bureau. "I am sick of doing servants' work and working on the magazine, too," Agnes announced just weeks after moving into their new home. "In fact, I refuse absolutely."[12]

To free up her time, Agnes said, she required a maid to help with the housework and a loan to pay for her analysis and the debts she had incurred during her illness. After several people turned her down, Agnes approached Margaret Sanger, with whom she had been out of touch since leaving the United States. Was Sanger willing to borrow a thousand American dollars from one of the wealthy women with whom she was in contact so Agnes could spend a year in relative peace while she tried to get back on her feet?[13] Between her future earnings and the profits from the bureau's reopened import-export business (which British agents suspected was currently smuggling guns into India), Agnes assured Sanger, she could repay it.

Perhaps it was the maternal neglect Agnes had experienced as a child, which had caused her to see herself as an orphaned waif, that fostered her assumption that the women in her life were somehow obliged to help her. Someone always seemed to respond. Sanger wrote back that as she had long been anxious about Agnes and desirous of assisting her, she wished to give her fifty dollars a month for a year—not as a loan but as a personal gift.[14] By May 1924, Agnes had sold six articles, including a tribute to the Akali movement for the *Nation*, which Sanger declared "splendid"—Agnes's best effort yet.[15]

> The [Akalis] realized [their] fate as [they] approached, but [they] w[ere] under a sacred pledge. In a calm and devotional manner, singing hymns, [they] advanced. The English commander gave a signal with a flag, and fire was opened. The Akalis...marched forward, with hands upraised...As their comrades fell about them they picked them up and marched on. Realizing that to stop them meant to kill the last man, cavalry surrounded them. Some thirty Sikh women in the procession, one whose baby was killed in her arms, attended the wounded. Upon their refusal to withdraw they were lashed and beaten...Since the Jaito massacre [2,500] more have...be[en] arrested. As they leave Amritsar...the streets and housetops are jammed with people.[16]

Heartened, Agnes asked Robert Morss Lovett, with whom she had worked at the FFFI, to secure a loan for her from the American Fund for Public Service, better known as the Garland Fund. The left-liberal foundation, whose board included Roger Baldwin, *Nation* editor Freda Kirchwey, Norman Thomas, Lewis Gannett, Scott Nearing, and Elizabeth Gurley Flynn, was particularly committed to pamphleteering and book publishing. Although for the moment, Agnes wrote Florence, she would use the money only to write what sold quickly, as soon as she escaped the "financial and mental purgatory" in which she currently existed, she would attempt something more creative.

Only Chatto appeared troubled by Agnes's recovery. Fearful that she would leave him once she was again self-supporting, he demanded that she terminate her therapy, she wrote, insistent that he was the only person capable of analyzing her. When she refused, he tormented her, according to Agnes. Then Chatto fell ill, just as she had earlier. At first, Agnes said, she took time from work to nurse him, but soon she suspected his malady was emotional in origin. Wary of his attempts to control her, she began to fend him off.

The maid never materialized, but Agnes's restored ability to care for herself altered the dynamic between them. By the spring of 1924, it was Chatto rather than Agnes who did the housework, she wrote, and while she was not yet ready to act on it, she expressed a desire to live on her own. Neurotic and destructive as the relationship was, though, she still loved Chatto, and even now she harbored hopes that their life together might yet work out. "I believe that a love such as my husband has for me, is not to be given up lightly," she wrote Michaelis. "There are many terrible things in that love, but I have also not dealt with our case in a sane manner, because I have been ill. I must first be well, and then if our situation does not improve, I will be justified in leaving him, and can do it without regret."[17]

In search of a more traditionally masculine freedom, Agnes assumed a more genderless persona. With her thin brown hair cropped short as a man's and a cigarette affixed to her lips, her appearance had more in common with the seamier side of Berlin cabaret than the coy rebellion of American flappers. Her anger at Chatto, however, made flexing her power over him tempting, particularly in the sexual arena. Agnes grumbled that she felt so old and drab and unappealing that she attracted only "middle-aged clerks in the post office. No young man tries…The only sign of life left in me is my swearing and cursing."[18] Even so, she began a dalliance with the professor who directed the English Seminar program at Berlin University.

Privately Agnes was contemptuous, but the connection was a useful one, and she enjoyed stringing him along. "He thinks I'm a Miss," she wrote Florence, "and I am! He is arranging for a course of English lessons in Berlin University.

So he, as a true German, invites me to lunch with him *every Tuesday at 1:30!* . . . And I know some day at 2:45 he'll take out his handkerchief, spread it on the floor, kneel on it in the proper attitude and ask me to *accept his hand!* Oh I know I'll yawn and tell him I'll let him know next week at 2:45."[19]

She also carried on a flirtation with the estranged husband of Karin Michaelis, although in the end she declined to pursue it. If she did, she reasoned, she would have to keep the relationship a secret from Chatto, and she did not wish to do that. Still, after years of professing indifference to sex, Agnes relished playing the role of coquette. She did not act on it, she boasted, but men responded to her "polygamous nature," and "any pair of pants going from the garbage man and up stops and tries his chances with me or wishes he could."[20] "Florence dear," she observed in another note, "men will love you through all eternity if you beat them . . . or . . . scorn them or turn on them a face filled with dislike or active anger!" Even Ernest, apparently. "Emotionally speaking . . . I'm more or less of a sadist," she declaimed; frail blond men like him were "abject slaves" in her hands.[21]

Agnes had not completely transformed into the heartless dominatrix she fancied herself. At night, her dreams frightened her so badly she could not remember them. The paralyzing cramps in her throat and body remained. But as Chatto grew suspicious of every man around him, she was thrilled. Chatto was not simply jealous, though; he was vulnerable. Despite enormous personal sacrifices and a quarter of a century in exile, his career was essentially sidelined. As his perception that Agnes might leave him gained strength, the awful isolation of his existence hit him with such force that he spiraled into mental illness. Terrified of being alone, he clung to her like a child, Agnes wrote, and Chatto's "baby dependence" only reinforced her desire to flee.

Hoping to tie her to him, perhaps, through the sheer drudgery required to keep them going, Chatto invited an Indian family to live with them. Agnes maintained that the husband, a devout Muslim, passed his days praying and eating opium, while his wife, whom Agnes described as just out of purdah and afflicted with gonorrhea contracted through her spouse's brothel visits, drove Agnes wild spying on the men through keyholes. In case she was not sufficiently chastened, Chatto then arranged for two Indian students, Bakar Ali Mirza and his younger brother, Mahdi, to share the couple's quarters.

Initially Agnes saw the pair simply as more bodies in need of cooking, scrubbing, and mending, but the young men, orphans who had been raised in asylums, adored her, she said. If she was kind, they affixed themselves to her side, shyly stroking her hand and vying with one another to assist her with chores. Before she knew it, Agnes was awash in maternal feelings—hardly what Chatto intended.

Agnes attributed her affection for Bakar and Mahdi to memories of her own two brothers, whom she had abandoned. Her relationship with the elder one, however, quickly became more complex. Bakar, who was eight years Agnes's junior, was melancholic, reserved, and beautiful— about as different from the overbearing Chatto as a man could be—and as Agnes strove to establish some distance from her companion, Bakar appealed to her not only as a son or nephew but as a romantic partner. Unlike Chatto, she wrote, Bakar was completely undemanding. Content to worship her from afar, he did not intrude on her life. He trusted her utterly, and he was still too young to be "vile," as she put it. By the time Bakar returned to Oxford in October 1924, Agnes said she loved him as deeply and "tenderly as I would a child in my arms, and yet savagely as a wild person protecting its young."[22]

Florence opined there was no man alive who could make her friend happy. Agnes did not disagree. "Yours is the only *permanent personal* love I have . . . ," she wrote. "My love for you is the one healthy spot in my life."[23] But Agnes's attachment to Bakar, a stray like the one she felt herself to be, gave her an opportunity to express the delicate feelings on which Chatto had trampled.

On the eve of Bakar's departure, the two proclaimed their love for one another. Then, in an extraordinary display of passive aggression, they informed Chatto and sought his advice. According to Agnes, she and Bakar refrained, by mutual consent, from consummating the relationship. For Agnes, who attributed her broken health to her departure from asceticism, the affair's innocence in the realm of action was a blessing. Unfettered by the vexing issue of physical intimacy, she could concentrate on what she referred to as the "spiritual" bond between them, with which she was more at ease.

Agnes said she was consumed by guilt and shame over her romance with Bakar, but in many ways she seemed quite pleased. The relationship allowed her to lord over Chatto that the walls of their "marriage" no longer contained her and to punish him for his ill-treatment without having to bear responsibility for an affair. Chatto tried to control his reaction for fear of alienating Agnes further. Not surprisingly, however, he found the attachment exceedingly hurtful, its lack of sexual content notwithstanding.

From England, Agnes said, Bakar wrote her letter after letter declaring his passion for her as if Chatto did not exist, often including information of interest to Chatto on the same pages. When Chatto soothed his ego with an affair of his own, Agnes, jealous, retreated briefly to her bed, but Chatto's gain was short-lived. In November 1924, after months of unproductive discussions, Agnes said, she told Chatto she was exhausted and warned him that if he did not enter analysis immediately she could remain only a few months longer. Under this scenario, Chatto agreed to enter treatment with the celebrated analyst Max Eitingon, who Agnes said was desirous of working with an Indian patient.[24]

In order to remain connected to Bakar in his absence, Agnes had sent him a letter of introduction to Sanger, who was in London that winter, and asked Goldman, who was also there, to take her "son" under her wing as a personal favor. "He studies our movement —and is one with us in spirit," Agnes wrote. "Therefore I send him to you with the request that you make it possible for him to study the movement in London. If you would do anything for me, do it instead for Bakar and feel assured that I appreciate your actions even more than if you did them for me personally... Please, as you love me, love Bakar whom I send to you."[25] As an older woman and a revolutionary, Goldman had the right combination of qualities, Agnes wrote, to attend to Bakar's upbringing.

That December, Agnes's German suitor offered her an appointment teaching English conversation and debate at Berlin University's English Seminar program, which she promptly accepted. Within two weeks of starting her job, she moved out of the house she shared with Chatto. Over his unalterable objections, she rented a room in the home of Mrs. Marshall Grabisch (sister of the American diplomat William C. Bullitt) and entered into what she described as a six-month trial separation while she arrived at a final decision about their "marriage."

Agnes was recovering. The strain of their estrangement sometimes made it hard for her to concentrate, and she was frequently sleepless and riddled with guilt, but she still contrived to teach her class and write. More than once, she wrote, university officials asked her to defend her unorthodox conduct, but her popularity with her female students protected her. To earn additional income, she worked in Mrs. Grabisch's literary agency.

The German professor made his move that same spring, clasping her in his "all too manly arms," Agnes wrote, and kissing her over her protests. Several of her left-wing colleagues also approached Agnes, now that she lived on her own, "but for the living life of me," she exclaimed, "I can't stick them and ask nothing better than that they keep a good safe distance from my fist."[26] By maintaining a rigid asceticism, Agnes intended to avoid getting mixed up in "some personal mess," as she put it, that existed on a less exalted plane than her attachment to Bakar. It was often "damned uncomfortable," she confessed, but she preferred to wait for a man who offered her both freedom and love rather than risk another bruising encounter.

Expunging sex from her life did not extinguish her ties to Chatto. The more time she spent on her own, the more certain Agnes became of her need to terminate their liaison. To Chatto, such a decision seemed tantamount to death. Every day, she wrote, he visited her room, his face dark with anguish. After berating her for ruining his life, he would beg her to return, telling her he felt too old to start anew and threatening to commit suicide if she did not.[27] The discussions tore Agnes apart. Whatever their personal differences, she explained, she still saw him as someone whose life remained a "standing example" to thousands of Indians, and she felt terrible for being the cause of such pain.

Knowing the esteem in which Chatto was held, Agnes said, she would regularly ask herself who she thought she was, in comparison with him, that she could leave despite his grave objections. In her opinion veteran revolutionaries including Goldman and Berkman all considered Chatto more valuable than herself, and Agnes tormented herself asking why she was so reluctant to sacrifice her personal happiness to the contribution Chatto could make if she remained with him. No matter how many times she turned the matter over in her head, she always arrived at the same conclusion: that while she was still "willing to work with him and . . . die for his ideas and his country," as she wrote, she could not live with him again, regardless of the outcome.[28]

Agnes explained to Michaelis that while she had indeed once loved Chatto, his domination and abuse had irreparably eroded her regard. She had let him behave as he pleased, she wrote; the result had left her so damaged that she would have died had she not been under treatment. That phase of her life was over.

> After four years of long illness which pointed to insanity, I am coming back to life. And I return with a heavy debt on my shoulders . . . Now I am very, very calm, and we look at each other across an impassable gulf. And he knows at last that he has lost the power to hurt me. That is a terrible thing to learn — that you can no longer hurt a person . . .
>
> . . . If I had many lives to live — as the Hindus believe they have — I could perhaps afford to experiment with this one and wait for my ideal love in another. But I do not believe in that. This is my only life, and it is the most precious of all possessions. I will not sacrifice it. And I have had enough suffering for many lives.[29]

Agnes did not know exactly what the future held, but she longed to escape the pressure of Chatto's demands. She thought again of visiting Michaelis in Denmark. She even considered returning to America. However, having come so close to killing herself, she took Chatto's threat of suicide seriously. In April she met with Dr. Eitingon to learn whether Chatto could survive her departure. According to Agnes, Dr. Eitingon said he would not be responsible for the outcome if she left, and urged her to remain in Berlin a few months longer. Agnes declared Chatto's fixation on her "a strange obsession," but she agreed to stay.[30]

Throughout the spring of 1925, Agnes was in regular contact with Sanger, advising her on the birth control movement in India and Germany and helping her ship thousands of illegal birth control devices to the United States.[31] She also struck up a friendship with Kaethe Kollwitz, the renowned German artist of the masses. Agnes told Goldman that before she met Kollwitz she had heard she was a Communist and for that reason had been predisposed against her.[32] Face-to-face, however, Agnes said she had found Kollwitz simple, kind, gentle, and "a real human being—a rare thing to say of anyone."[33] Kollwitz confided in her diary that she felt "very close to Smedley—have felt so since our first meeting."[34]

Agnes respected enormously Kollwitz's decision to live a spartan existence depicting the problems of the disinherited when she could have wrested a fortune from her talents, otherwise applied. She was also a fan of Kollwitz's strong, uncluttered style, which made her sketches, etchings, and wood-block prints accessible to the unlettered as well as the culturally initiated and expressed Kollwitz's political convictions while giving her creativity free reign. Agnes found Kollwitz's creations as "elemental as the sea," she wrote, and her heartrending themes of "fear, hatred, rebellion against injustice and the hunger for love, for happiness, for freedom that is the right of all" touched Agnes as the work of no other artist yet had.

The two women spent hours in rapt conversation on art, politics, and relationships between women and children, and women and men. Kollwitz also discussed with Agnes her experience with Chatto's financial backer, Willi Muenzenberg, with whom she had worked in 1921 and with whom, according to Agnes, Kollwitz refused to work again.

One of Muenzenberg's achievements at the IAH was his ability to draw internationally prominent writers, artists, and intellectuals into his campaigns for justice or against oppression; their attendance at his protest congresses and signatures on petitions and manifestos enhanced the value of IAH propaganda. Although they participated on the basis of moral sentiment, many were perhaps aware that the organization was hardly as nonpolitical as it claimed. Most likely they did not know, however, that their support of the IAH aided causes the Comintern supported, or that the organization covertly manipulated various affairs in foreign countries along lines that furthered Comintern interests.

Kollwitz warned her, Agnes wrote Goldman, about the German Communist's committees of "famous people" whose progressive sympathies he exploited. The Communists were "Jesuits," she said Kollwitz advised her; if one gave them a finger, they took the whole hand.[35] Agnes was no longer so sure. Over the last few years, the attempt by revolutionary syndicalists to provide European workers with an alternative to the Soviet model of Communism had faltered and lost momentum, and Agnes's confidence in their approach had flagged. She still shared Kollwitz's mistrust of more cerebral German Communists like Ruth Fischer and Arkady Maslow, but Communist advances elsewhere in the world were affecting Agnes's views.

After a century of plunder in the form of low import tariffs, most-favored-nation clauses, and extraterritorial jurisdiction that had brought China to its knees, Dr. Sun Yat-sen's Kuomintang (KMT), or Nationalist Party, had launched an extraordinary effort to free the country from the disunity brought on by provincial warlords and the foreign powers feeding on it. Motivated initially by simple nationalism, the father of the Chinese Republic had adopted more radical views. Under the aegis of Michael Borodin, the Soviet Union's emissary in China, Sun's government had formed an alliance with China's nascent Communist Party to develop a national, and hopefully social, revolutionary movement in south China. And the anti-imperialist, antifeudal drive Sun had fostered was heaving China against both the treaty powers and China's landlords.

By the spring of 1925, CCP organizers had enrolled eighteen thousand Chinese in KMT peasant unions; KMT membership had doubled. Newly trained, nationalistically inspired KMT army forces—organized, supplied, and led by the Soviets—were routing local warlord and militarist units seven times their size. People with a financial stake in China were growing uneasy, but Agnes was thrilled. In Moscow recently, Grigori Zinoviev, who was now the Comintern's dominant figure, had declared China the "central starting point for action in India." And the Comintern's argument, eloquently presented at this time in an international propaganda campaign directed by Willi Muenzenberg, appeared to have captured Agnes's imagination.

Muenzenberg had already organized several "Hands Off China" congresses over the last two years, which offered moral assistance in the form of appeals such as Kollwitz described and created a Chinese branch of the IAH that received nearly $250,000 from Russian trade unions. Neither effort had interested Agnes. This current project, done in collaboration with a London-based Comintern front organization known as the Chinese Information Bureau, which drafted the revolutionary propaganda, and the Comintern's OMS, which smuggled the material into China and India, evidently did.[36] Its message, that the enormous contingents of oppressed humanity living in the East were to emulate their Chinese brethren, found echoes in Agnes's work.

In articles for the IWW's *Industrial Pioneer* magazine, the liberal *Modern Review*, and the *Comrade*, a Communist publication in Delhi, Agnes, like the Comintern, looked to China for the first time. While she, too, spoke of a "united Asiatic bloc" whose goal was the destruction of "every vestige of British imperialism," she warned that the backlash of war was likely, since England and America would not willingly relinquish their hold on a continent in which they held three-quarters of the world's population in virtual serfdom to feed their industries and give their countrymen soft and easy lives.[37]

Agnes also drafted pieces that spring on Kollwitz, the position of Indian women, her famous "sister-in-law" Sarojini Naidu, her years in the Colorado mining camps, and the American Negro. Her byline began appearing in Germany's prestigious *Zeitschrift für Geopolitik*, Czechoslovakia's *Prager Tageblatt*, Switzerland's *Neue Zuricher Zeitung*, and Austria's *Neue Freie Presse*, and she hoped her good fortune in Europe might lead to better paying assignments with American magazines like the *Atlantic Monthly, Mercury, Century, Harper's*, and *Vanity Fair*.

"I will write as my ideals dictate, and my ideals are revolutionary," Agnes explained to Florence. "But I will sell anywhere... I am not a business woman, I know, but really, dear Florence, I can't always be a beggar and a pauper."[38] H. L. Mencken had recently recommended the literary agent Carl Brandt to her friend Emma Goldman, and Agnes asked him to represent her as well. Unfortunately, while Agnes's writing was lively and effective with an issue that emotionally engaged her, her attempts at objective reporting often led to less than inspired work. Moreover, her style and subject matter were out of temper with the times in the United States. The American editors she approached directly rejected her articles; Brandt turned her down. Soon enough, the journalistic opportunities available through some affiliation with Muenzenberg would prove an option Agnes could not afford to overlook.

The astounding financial success of the burgeoning Muenzenberg "Trust" (which by this time extended well beyond his original famine relief committees and aid organizations to a rapidly growing communications empire of publishing houses, newspapers, magazines, and distribution companies that were linked, in their turn, with banks, commercial firms, and other institutions) freed Muenzenberg considerably from the control of Party bureaucracy. He enjoyed a measure of autonomy unheard of elsewhere in the history of international Communism.[39] As Agnes had already observed in the case of Chatto, progressives of various stripes who found shelter under Muenzenberg's umbrella not only had access to money; those among them who wrote could avoid the pedantic, sectarian language of official Party publications and still reach a global audience.

In the mid-1920s, proletarian culture was a lively subject among literary radicals in Germany and the Soviet Union. Uninterested in the Lost Generation aesthetes who practiced art for art's sake and cared more about form than content, politically committed writers remained aggressive advocates of working-class literature, but they had moved away (like the visual artist Kaethe Kollwitz) from the stylistic conservatism, limited choice of subject matter, and revolutionary romanticism of the proletcult writers. Their books remained simply written; they still explored industrial conflicts and made the proletariat their hero, but they included workers' vices and weaknesses as well as their strengths.[40] For Agnes, who said she had never understood the optimism for the masses a writer like Maxim Gorky expressed, the more recent literary aesthetic suggested that a piece of class-conscious imaginative writing could also express more universal human truths.

That spring, Agnes returned again to the prose poem she had earlier attempted and worked on several short stories. At the suggestion of friends in the theater, she also began to draft an autobiographical play. Since her family (whom Agnes referred to as "an uncle in a penitentiary, a few women relatives who are prostitutes, and a father and a brother who are both day laborers") was not in a position to underwrite her artistic endeavors, she asked influential Village reformers who had helped her in the past to arrange a postponement on the repayment of her loan while she attempted something more expressive than the freelance journalism that paid her rent.[41]

Sanger responded promptly, covering the first two installments herself and offering Agnes praise and encouragement. "You can write *beautifully* and all you need is peace of mind...Creative work at writing and lecturing will restore your nerves in a short time...I am personally interested in your health, Agnes, and do wish you were here in New York where you would have the care you need and would not have to work so hard."[42] Roger Baldwin and Robert Morss Lovett secured the delay Agnes sought, and Dr. Naef agreed to waive her fees for the remainder of Agnes's treatment. However, in early summer, she conceded defeat.

The strain of remaining in Berlin for Chatto's sake had made her such "a mess, a wreck," she said, that she was too depressed and depleted to write. She had locked her drama in her desk drawer, and her articles likewise. "I just exist," she wrote Goldman, "hoping that maybe something will happen on the morrow which will give me back the illusion that life is worth while and that writing is worth while. In the meantime I drag on from day to day, a rag—nothing but a rag."[43]

Agnes knew that if she were to get on with her life, she had to break from Chatto completely. Convinced, as ever, that happiness lay where she was not, she looked in a desultory way into a position with Sanger's magazine or an American newspaper, but her heart was not in it. In the end, she arranged instead to spend a month in Czechoslovakia at the home of an actress friend, Lydia Busch, and another at Michaelis's island home off the Danish coast. There, she said, freed from financial worry, she hoped to get her drama in good enough shape to give to Goldman and Berkman's friend Eleanor "Fitzi" Fitzgerald, secretary, business manager, and den mother of the Provincetown Players, who was always on the lookout for experimental plays.[44] If nothing better presented itself by fall, Agnes said, she would return to her teaching job at that time.

As the heat of Berlin's summer bore down, she had her final scenes with Chatto. He handled the situation badly, compounding her already considerable distress by calling at all hours, she wrote, and "accusing me, accusing, accusing ... He threatened to kill himself; he was hysterical and sick, he said he was giving up his work and leaving Europe and would never return to India."[45] Still, when her classes ended on July 20, she returned to Chatto some money he had loaned her, turned over her room to the visiting Fitzi, and fled.

Agnes's melancholy, headaches, throat trouble, and insomnia all returned with a vengeance, and her fitful sleep was punctured by nightmares of Chatto and things creeping about trying to kill her. Beyond her anguish over the failed relationship, Agnes feared that away from Chatto she would lose her ties to the Indian movement, that people who in the past had tolerated her only as his companion might now refuse to work with her. Other vague, unnamed anxieties also gnawed at Agnes's heart.

Goldman understood her friend's distress. No matter how advanced a woman was, she remarked to Berkman, as a woman grew older she was likely to feel more acutely the absence of a husband, children, home, security, and companionship and to think "of getting on in age without anything worthwhile to make life warm and beautiful, without a purpose."[46] However much they fought against it, even emancipated women like herself and Agnes were too recently released from a society organized around marriage and motherhood to be impervious to its pressures. As middle age approached, nearly all the modern women she knew, Goldman wrote, seemed to feel that their lives were empty and that they had nothing to look forward to. They were no longer willing to be wives and mothers in their former sense, but they had yet to devise an alternative that allowed them to keep those roles while retaining their freedom.

Goldman knew well the high price Agnes would pay for her growth, but as she saw it, there was no other way. Despite her anguish, Agnes, like Goldman's other women friends, had no choice but to plunge ahead if she did not wish to remain "in the dull state of the cow," according to Goldman.[47] Having already decided that taking her life would not solve her dilemma, Agnes concurred, but she felt adrift and uprooted, unattached to anything and consumed by the sense that life was passing by without her having achieved anything to justify her rejection of all those things through which women traditionally found contentment.

It was in this state that Agnes reached Michaelis's home in August 1925.

In her analysis, Agnes had stared down the demons that contributed to her breakdown: her mother's failure to nurture her, her anguish as a working-class, racially mixed female, her anger at her father and its fallout on her relationships

Torelore, home of Danish novelist Karin Michaelis, where Agnes wrote *Daughter of Earth*. *Edgar Snow Collection, University of Missouri, Kansas City.*

with men, the defiant rebellion that had so far brought only pain and loss. But the insights she had gained were largely intellectual. To navigate this crossroads of her life, she needed to produce a creative rendering of her experience, and for that she relied on Michaelis.

Agnes had worried in the past that Michaelis, whose fiction depicted the inner lives of women like Agnes as they approached middle age, would steal her life story for a book, and indeed there were several parallels between Agnes and Michaelis's best-known protagonist, Elsie Lintner in *The Dangerous Age*. Haunted that she had nothing to show for her life after twenty-two years of marriage, Lintner had divorced her husband and retreated to an island like Thuro to keep her complacent life from slipping through her fingers. Lintner, too, had been infatuated with a younger man. But where Michaelis's fictive heroine could not expiate the melancholy hysteria that gripped her, Michaelis sought a better fate for her real-life friend.

Michaelis prevailed on Agnes to remain for three months instead of one to give herself sufficient time to complete an outline and draft in Michaelis's presence. To avail herself of the novelist's assistance Agnes shifted the play she had originally intended to the novel form. Out of consideration for particular persons Agnes would disguise some events, but she told Sanger she wanted it to be as true to her life as she could make it, written "in the baldest manner possible because my health is never a thing I can depend on, and my mind is so destroyed that I never know what I am capable of."[48]

Staying so long meant she could not teach her course at Berlin University and would have to forego the much-needed income. Even then, Agnes doubted she could produce a rough draft in so short a time, but she was so utterly unhappy and anxious to write that the risks seemed small in comparison. "I think if I write a book I may either feel better afterwards," she noted to Sanger, "or it will be finished anyway and I will have done what I could in this damned experience called life. It will be about all I have to give."[49]

Agnes longed to begin at once, but Michaelis, who had more experience in such matters, insisted that Agnes rest first, assisting with chores until she calmed down. Life on Thuro was primitive, and Michaelis must have hoped that Agnes would find the physical labor it required restorative. Even in summer, the island was cloudy and cold, with breezes so stiff they bent the trees, and wood for the fireplaces that warmed each room had to be chopped daily. All their water was pumped from a well. There was also a garden to be tended. Michaelis's small white house was set inside a vast flower and vegetable plot that ran straight to the sea, and after writing each morning Michaelis passed several hours digging, weeding, and planting in the broad beds interplanted with fruit trees.

In the beginning, Agnes, who described herself as a "sun child," found the climate too close a match for her own gray spirits to enjoy, but the atmosphere grew on her. Under the influence of Thuro, laboring alongside Michaelis, for whom living close to the land was a source of creative energy, Agnes began to recall her childhood in rural Missouri with a nostalgic sense of feeling securely rooted in its soil.

Life on the island was not all toil and sweat. The women's routine was basic and physical, but Michaelis was, after all, an established writer, and in the evenings accomplished artists, writers, and actresses occupied the big easy chairs and comfortable couches that lined her living room, attracted by her hospitality. Alexander Berkman was among her visitors that summer, and he and Agnes enjoyed teaching Michaelis's more highborn guests how to mop and wash dishes. However, of all who passed through Thuro, Agnes was fondest of Betty Nansen, who was then Denmark's leading actress and Europe's foremost interpreter of Ibsen. Their discussions on the playwright's themes of women's freedom and responsibility, on the artist's need to create, and on the necessity for one's art to remain part of one's life rather than existing for its own sake were close to Agnes's heart as she prepared to write.[50]

Agnes commenced work on her book in early September—an effort she later recalled as "akin to heavy physical and nervous labor."[51] "Before me stretches a

Danish sea, cold, gray, limitless," she began, drawing on the bleak surroundings of Thuro to establish her tone.

> There is no horizon. The sea and the gray sky blend and become one...
>
> For months I have been here, watching the sea—and writing this story of a human life. What I have written is not a work of beauty, created that someone may spend an hour pleasantly; not a symphony to lift up the spirit, to release it from the dreariness of reality. It is the story of a life, written in desperation, in unhappiness.
>
> I write of the earth on which we all, by some strange circumstance, happen to be living. I write of the joys and sorrows of the lowly. Of loneliness. Of pain. And of love...
>
> ...There have been days when it seemed that my path would better lead to the sea. But now I choose otherwise...
>
> To die would have been beautiful. But I belong to those who do not die for the sake of beauty. I belong to those who die from other causes— exhausted by poverty, victims of wealth and power, fighters in a great cause. A few of us die, desperate from the pain or disillusionment of love, but for most of us "the earthquake but discloseth new fountains." For we are of the earth and our struggle is the struggle of earth.[52]

Marie Rogers was her protagonist's name. "Marie" was Agnes's girlhood moniker; "Rogers," one she had used in New York in connection with her illicit activities. Though the family had been poor, Agnes wrote of her years in Missouri, the hateful class distinctions she later encountered were not apparent in their agricultural community, and she re-created her girlhood as a pastoral idyll spent playing "under a wide-spreading walnut tree down in the sun-flecked meadows" among farming families who "seemed to hover close to some tantalizing, communal racial memory."[53]

> All day the men worked in the fields or cut wood in the forests. The faint click of their axes came across the big sunny clearing. The forests were cool and the earth sweet; the trees were beginning to turn. Teams of horses drew high loads of cut wood and piled it in cords against the north side of our house and all along the drive. It was our firewood for winter, serving also as a shelter from the cold north winds.
>
> All day long the women peeled, sliced and canned fruit. By noon the sloping roof of the house was covered with a solid white mass of sliced apples drying in the sun, and by afternoon long rows of jars of jellies and preserves stood along the kitchen table...

Dinnertime came and the men returned to eat . . . Something seemed to stir in the blood of the men and women. Bonds of ownership were dropped or openly flouted. Men flirted with other men's wives. Women triumphantly marched off with other women's husbands to eat their dinner, and the men publicly announced their intentions of eloping . . .

Outside our house the men had constructed a huge square platform for dancing, over which they scattered candle shavings until it was smooth as glass . . .

"Now, folks, choose yer partners for a round dance!"

At his word the fiddler started and my mother and father led off. Around and around in an old-fashioned waltz, my mother bending back slightly, her ruffled skirts flying, and my father swinging her with a right good will. I was so excited that I ran about through the crowd, not knowing whither . . . This night was filled with moonlight and music.[54]

Displaying a fine ear for dialogue and a gift for physical description, she evoked people, places, and epochs middle-class readers rarely encountered, often drawing on rituals and images that had died out before she was born. Through this method, Agnes transformed her mother and older sister Nellie (Annie in the book) into prairie madonnas of the pioneer era, barefooted and dressed in loose-flowing calico dresses while they carried pails of water to their log cabin home. Her years in Colorado she also set twenty years in the past, "when the West was not yet industrialized, and when the cowboy was still alive," she confided to Goldman regarding passages like the following.[55]

There were . . . evenings when the weather was fine and the men would remain outside our kitchen door after supper, talking and singing, and when I hurried with the dishes to join them. One of the men would sing a song and the others would follow: songs of the West that are long since dead; songs with dozens of verses, all sung in the same tune, low and melancholy, unrolling stories of adventure, of the joys and sorrows of cattle men, of dying cowboys, of disaster, range songs and songs of love.

Sometimes one of the men would take out a "French harp" and begin to play. Another would get up and dance. Once it was a man, young and slender, with whom I was in love—but so secretly that no one but myself knew it. His blue shirt was open at the throat. He bent over and danced, swaying his body and arms; he stood in one spot on the hard earth and danced until the heels of his boots sounded like pistol shots on the hard, packed earth. He stood tall and straight, his hands on his hips, his face turned upwards to the moon, and the moonlight ran in little shining rivulets up and down the legs of his black boots.

At last the music ceased. There was silence, broken only by the wind rustling gently through the tree tops. The dancer wiped his forehead with a big red handkerchief. He drew his belt in another notch.[56]

The only hint of any darkness to come appeared in the descriptions of her relationship with her mother (Elly Garfield Rogers in her novel)."I remember my mother's thimble taps," she wrote, "and I remember a tough little switch that cut like a knife into the flesh. Why she whipped me so often I do not know...As the years of her unhappy married life increased, as more children arrived, she whipped me more and more."[57] A close reading exposes details like how the rich Missouri soil suddenly turns stony and "badly yielding" when Agnes recounts the decision of her father (John in the book) to uproot the family.[58] But it was, after all, a novel she was writing, and her psychological and social observations were searingly accurate.

Assuming her readers' familiarity with the notorious Ludlow Massacre, Agnes gave the earlier coal strike she had witnessed in Trinidad a prominent role in her story. When her desire to realistically depict working-class life clashed with her myths about the Smedley family history, the result more accurately reflected Agnes's rage at the social structure of class relations than the reality of their lives. Charles's stint as a patent medicine agent became his apprenticeship to an ophthalmologist, and she insisted that everyone from *her* side of the tracks hated the state militia called out to suppress the foreign miners.[59] In the same way, she wrote that the labor strife transformed her mother "from a poor farming woman to an unskilled proletarian with an instinctive and unhesitating sympathy for the miners. She hated rich or powerful people or institutions."[60]

To keep the family's image in accord with her political sympathies, her father's work as a deputy sheriff was absent from her text, and she argued that in Delagua, where Charles had employed twenty men and owned a dozen teams of horses and wagons, the immigrant miners accepted her as one of their own.[61] Surely Agnes grasped the correlation between the prosperity the Smedleys enjoyed there and Charles's standing with company officials, but she declared her father's good fortune "a mystery"—attributable, perhaps, to his colorful personality.[62]

If Agnes blurred the line between the Smedleys and the miners in her recounting of Delagua, in Tercio it became fuzzier still. Although Charles had had a lucrative contract with CF&I for which he hired several men, Agnes wrote that "to these miners, as to *us*, existence meant only working, sleeping, eating what or when you could, and breeding...Resentful everybody was but *we* bowed our heads and...*we* obeyed those who paid us our wages."[63]

Agnes's prostitute aunt Tillie (Helen in the book), who had married and set-

tled into a respectable middle age, remained alone in Agnes's tale as an indictment of the capitalist system, but her portrayal of the dysfunctional Smedley-
Rogers family life was as personal as it was political, and it brimmed with rage.
Still blind to the ways that her belated bond with her mother had coerced her
into collusion against Charles, Agnes depicted the father figure in her story as
the evil betrayer of her adolescence: a drunken, womanizing gambler responsible for her mother's unhappiness.

> My mother was standing with her hands in a tub of wet washing, her face . . .
> ashen . . . She seemed unable even to lift her hands out of the water. My father
> stood near her with a short, doubled-up rope in his hands . . .
> . . . I saw him standing there, broad shouldered, twice her size, the tobacco
> juice showing at the corners of his mouth. He was going to beat her . . . He
> had of late spoken admiringly of men who beat their wives . . . As I stood
> watching him I felt that I knew everything he had ever done or would do . . .
> And I hated him . . . hated him for his cowardice in attacking someone weaker
> than himself . . . hated him for attacking a woman because she was his wife
> and the law gave him the right . . . hated him so deeply, so elementally, that I
> wanted to kill.[64]

Ashamed of the mental instability that continued to afflict her, Agnes cast
her first neurasthenic collapse as a bout with starvation; her wrathful descriptions of her heroine's involvement with Ernest Brundin (Knut Larsen in the
book) suggested her more recent subjugation by Chatto.[65] The marriage was
Knut's idea, not hers, Agnes wrote; being called "Mrs. Larsen" had poisoned her
years in California.[66] She recalled herself not as the charismatic young woman
she had been but as someone so unseemly a teacher offered her money to "do
something to make myself look neater."

The most glaring piece of revisionism appeared in Agnes's retelling of her
emergence as an activist. Loath to admit her ambivalence about her working-
class roots while she labored to improve herself, and fearful of revealing her ties
to Har Dayal and the Ghadr Party, which might invite closer scrutiny, Agnes
credited the Wobblies with her introduction to political activism. Shifting the
date of the IWW Free Speech Fights to coincide with her time in San Diego, she
wrote as convincingly of her participation in the episode as if she had been there.

Agnes shrank from exploring her intense romantic friendship with Florence
(who remained Florence in the book), aware that it would label her a "lesbian,"
with its contemporary associations of illness and abnormality.[67] Privately, Agnes
would confess that her friend's recent decision to marry, like Agnes's continuing
attraction to other women, upset her deeply.[68] However, she was unwilling
to explore the shame such feelings engendered for public consumption, so she

dismissed Florence in the book as a superficial person who "had never worked for her living and did not know what it meant...a friend who loved, but did not understand me."[69]

The final section of her novel, which covered Agnes's involvement in the Indian independence movement, proved the most problematic, since much of the material was still too raw for her to work with imaginatively. Silent on the subject of the Ghadr Party, Agnes described her mentor as a moderate reformer along the lines of Lajpat Rai, but she slyly gave him a Sikh name, Sardar Ranjit Singh, and suggested they had met in California. Juan Diaz, a composite of Herambalal Gupta and M. N. Roy (who sported the same multicolored belt buckle she described Charles as having worn in her youth) was her villain.[70] Although she felt constrained about revealing much of her life with Chatto, she highlighted Roy's role in her imbroglio with Chatto by recounting her 1923 suicide attempt just after her 1917 liaison with Roy.

Agnes claimed that the character Anand Manvekar was a composite of Chatto and Bakar, but there seemed to be little of Bakar, beyond a certain gentleness, in the portrait.[71] Anand shared Chatto's jealousy and his manipulation of Agnes's worrisome attitude toward sex, but only her heroine's bitter feminism and violent objections to matrimony suggested Agnes's time in the world of weeping women, "enslaved by the institution of marriage and by their love for men," as she wrote. "Marry? No, I would not marry," Marie scoffs in one passage. "I have no desire to submit to the life that mot women live—darning socks, cooking, cleaning, depending upon a man for my living—in other words, just existing." In a subsequent section she revisits her position on maintaining her professional life.[72] When Chatto demanded that she omit her byline from her work or abandon writing altogether, the real-life Agnes responded by becoming ill; the fictive Marie insolently refuses. "What kind of work could I do if I gave this up...go back to taking down the thoughts of some man, then spend the day typing them? Should I have to sit at home, a wife, a housewife, doing nothing but the work I hated—a female at last?"[73]

Agnes completed the first draft of her book in November 1925, with Berkman and Michaelis looking over her shoulder. Michaelis's hand was evident in Agnes's selection of a first-person narrator, which lent a sense of immediacy to her tale, and the book's ruthless psychological analysis and introspection. Her unadorned style and industrial imagery drew on the literature of proletcult and its successor movements; the montage technique she employed was becoming popular in Germany. Her subject's feminist bias and desire for self-expression broke no new literary ground, and other leftist writers in Russia and Germany were exploring a darker, more realistic view of the working class, but the pained defiance of Agnes's angry, ambitious heroine fit no predetermined slot.

Marie's deep sense of isolation and alienation gave her a unique voice and personality that distinguished Agnes's work from her contemporaries on the left. She expressed a truth, previously unacknowledged, that was born of Agnes's own experience: that in the effort to rise beyond the class into which she was born, Marie's progress, like Agnes's, stood in apposition to her estrangement from her roots. While there was no going back, neither would she ever feel at home in the world she came to inhabit. The disaffection Agnes so ably depicted was not only her achievement as a writer. It went a long way toward explaining her ability as an actress—and her capacity to lead a double life.

To most people, she stressed the book's adherence to "my own life, from the coal fields of our dear dear John J. Rockefeller, through the years of endless struggle, the men in my life...my endless struggle for bread and the chance to study, my entrance into the Indian movement...and all that it meant to me."[74] In the years to come, Agnes, who often had difficulty recognizing the distinction between the truth and a good story, sometimes thought she had written a memoir instead of a novel. The fact that others would accept it as autobiography was a tribute to her narrative skill. To a trusted few, she confided that the book captured only part of her life.

"There are many things, of course, not there...And some is changed...In my book I have put in much of [my] private life—but left out the chief things that caused...trouble because of the effect on [Chatto]. One day long since I may write another book based largely on that. Just now it is too near to me. The reason the last part of my book is not good is because I did not tell the whole truth there, did not write out my heart on the paper. I could have done so—but there are public things to consider that are dear to all of us—dearer than a book."[75]

Berkman and Michaelis pronounced the manuscript eminently publishable, and since Berkman was so certain the subject matter could attract an American publisher, she asked her former attorney, Gilbert Roe, to aid her in identifying one. There were still revisions to be made, particularly on the final section, but Agnes wrote that Michaelis would try to place the manuscript with a Danish publisher and Goldman would look in Great Britain, despite the book's scalding anti-British tone. Agnes would find a German house herself. Unemployed, broke, in debt to Michaelis and others, all her worldly possessions crammed inside two suitcases, Agnes joked that *The Tramp* was a more fitting title than *An Outcast*, as Berkman proposed.[76]

Late that summer, Bakar had come to Thuro to discuss their future, but Agnes had put him off. Confused then, she was even less clear now. She said she dreaded the idea of returning to Berlin, where Chatto still lived and she faced a poverty that would force her to "live in a garret and cook over a spiritus lamp" while she completed her revisions. The meager compensation she received for her published work permitted nothing for the concerts, books, or theater she loved, but she hoped that once the book was published, which she anticipated to be the following spring or summer, her life would improve.

"This has been my one big attempt at doing something to build up my life anew," Agnes wrote Sanger as she prepared to depart. "I depend upon it almost completely...Then I will stand upon my own feet in every way, pay back all the terrible debts I have incurred, and go forward."[77]

On her way back, Agnes stopped in Copenhagen to interview Tit Jensen, a novelist and feminist who was active in Denmark's birth control movement, then proceeded directly to Berlin.

CHAPTER 7

Bend in the Road

There are only two choices left—to hang oneself or to change the world.

ERNST TOLLER

IF AGNES HAD WORRIED before she left that Chatto could not survive without her, she discovered on her return that her fears had been groundless. While she was gone, Chatto had found another partner, Lucie Hecht—an associate of Muenzenberg's who also did Agnes's German translations.[1] Agnes must have been taken aback at how quickly she had been replaced, but Chatto's affair allowed her to do what she had wanted for a long time, which was to continue her relationship with him but on a more "comradely" footing, as she described it. Agnes did not wish to live with him, but she still trusted Chatto's political judgment more than anyone else's, and she looked to him to interpret for her the revolutionary wave that was sweeping over China.

All hell had broken loose while Agnes was cloistered in Thuro. More than half a million Chinese workers had walked off their jobs in Shanghai to protest foreign imperialism, and the mood of revolt was spreading from the large coastal cities into rural south and central China. Fatal missteps by British authorities in China's foreign concessions had given the KMT a cause around which to rally mass support, and 500,000 Kwangtung peasants and 137,000 Hong Kong workers were now union members, organizers, or agitation or propaganda workers or had joined the KMT or CCP. In addition, an extremely successful blockade in British-owned Hong Kong had consolidated the power of Comintern adviser Michael Borodin, allowing him to reorganize the KMT with a distinctly left orientation.

A revolution of historic proportions appeared to be under way in China, and as "via revolutionary China to the Federal Republic of the United States of India" became the Comintern's fighting slogan, Chatto found himself with more opportunities for Soviet support than he had dreamed of since losing his battle for Comintern recognition to Roy. His rival still played a major role in determining Comintern policy and interpreting events in India. However, Roy's influence in his native country had declined considerably, and the Comintern's recent directive to expand direct contact with national movements of emancipation like the Indian National Congress increased the currency of Chatto's superior contacts among more moderate nationalist leaders like his sister Sarojini Naidu and family friend Jawaharlal Nehru.

On the understanding that the present upheaval in China would cause the "seismic tremors" in India predicted by Comintern leaders, Chatto had hitched his star to Muenzenberg's in Agnes's absence and joined the German Communist Party.[2] By the fall of 1925, he was awash in preparations for a new Muenzenberg organization designed to supplant his former ad hoc activities in the East. The League Against Colonial Cruelties and Oppression, directed by Chatto's companion Lucie Hecht and Muenzenberg lieutenant Louis Gibarti, would be one of the Comintern's chief means of attracting non-Communist support for the Chinese revolutionaries and influencing other Asian countries, particularly India.[3] Once the operation was up and running, Chatto would perform essentially the same functions he had at his bureau, maintaining contact with Indian students and professionals who passed through Berlin, drafting revolutionary propaganda, and generating popular opposition to British imperialism in India.

Agnes was doubtless intrigued, but until she completed her revisions she had no time for any active political involvement. The next several months were a period of retreat and of marshaling her energy for the years to come. Economically, she survived by coaching private students and lecturing occasionally on Indian subjects, but the book was her cynosure. "I eat and sleep, only," she explained to Goldman; "... that is sufficient for the time being."[4] By the spring of 1926, when she resumed her post at Berlin University, Agnes had gone over the entire manuscript twice. She had retitled it *The Struggle of Earth*; the choice seemed more in keeping with her decision to dedicate the novel to the working class, she wrote.

Agnes said an actress friend, Tilla Durieux, was concerned about how the book would be received in the United States, since it was so hostile toward mainstream American politics, but Gilbert Roe had assured her that the manuscript was so interesting and important he would have no trouble placing it. With the same bold naiveté that marked her political affairs, Agnes had also mailed a copy to the British playwright George Bernard Shaw with instructions to let her know, after reading it, whether the book was worth publishing.[5] Shaw's failure to respond to her unsolicited request created a permanent chip on Agnes's shoulder about the "Grand Old Man," as she referred to him henceforth.

"You are in my book—do you know that?" she wrote Florence, who of course had no idea how unflattering a portrait it was. When she toured Europe with her spouse on their honeymoon that spring, she invited Agnes to join them, but Agnes was evasive, saying she had been "such a useless piece of lumber so long" that all she wanted now was work on her book.[6] Sanger, who wrote asking Agnes to return to the United States to work on the *Birth Control Review* and help her prepare for her upcoming trip to India, met with a similar response.

"I know that unless I finish the book here in Europe I shall never have the opportunity. In America I should undoubtedly throw myself into some public work like yours and the possibility of working on such a book as I have tried to write would be lost... There is, you know, a very great difference between the atmosphere of Europe and that of New York. I do not get along very well, it is true, in Berlin, but I prefer all the disadvantages and struggles here to returning to New York... before I finish."[7]

Agnes had returned to Germany in reasonably good emotional health, but the pressure she put on herself to produce something of sufficient merit to compensate for all the time she felt she had wasted came at a cost. When Florence told her that Bakar, whom Agnes had asked her to meet in London, was rather young and their relationship, by implication, neurotic, Agnes took to her bed for several days, "watching a spot on my ceiling, and wondering what in the hell this life is about anyway." However, her despair was not long-lived. In April 1926, she returned again to Dr. Naef for treatment; this time, unencumbered by what Agnes referred to as her "hopeless" relationship with Chatto, she anticipated more satisfactory results. Even at her most despondent, she still believed that these days, she was "on the whole... much better than I was for the first three years of my married life. I see the light now and there is a future not altogether black—a new thing in my existence since I came to Europe."[8]

Throughout the spring and early summer of 1926, Florence implored Agnes to join them, but Agnes, citing her finances, her students, or the need to finish her book, repeatedly declined. An acquaintance of Tilla Durieux's at the *Frankfurter Zeitung*, she wrote most recently, had promised to look at the manuscript when she completed her revisions, and she had no intention of damaging her chances. "Can you imagine... what it will mean for me if the *Frankfurter Zeitung* takes my book?... It is the best newspaper in Europe, of a very high standard... It will mean money and the end of my misery."[9] She also confessed to feeling anxious that "you and I will have to start our friendship over for I am almost a new person now, and you may not find it agreeable. My picturesqueness that you mentioned is gone, I think."[10] She alluded as well to the anger and sense of betrayal Florence's marriage had stirred in her. But Florence was not to be put off, and a date was set for a visit.

Under the impression that Agnes was well connected in international Communist circles, Florence had asked Agnes to help her set up a visit to Russia, Agnes wrote, and inquired whether she knew Gerhart Eisler, the brother of German Party leader Ruth Fischer and a rising Communist star in his own right. Agnes had responded that while she had tremendous sympathy for the Party's working-class members, she had no connections with Russia and the name Eisler drew a blank. Eisler? "I know no chap named Eisler," Agnes wrote.[11] Chatto was in touch with leading Russian and German Communists, though, she observed, and as a personal favor to Agnes, she said, he agreed to facilitate their trip. A "trusted" German Communist in Berlin would recommend the newlyweds to a man in the local Russian Embassy, and through him the couple would get their visas for the Soviet Union in three or four days.[12]

As surely as the "trusted" German Communist to whom Chatto referred was Willi Muenzenberg, the man in the local Russian Embassy was Jakob Mirov-Abramov of the Comintern's OMS. Mirov-Abramov was the man to whom Muenzenberg turned when he needed to telegram Moscow, required a visa, or had other technical or organizational problems.[13] However, in the summer of 1926, Agnes still appeared personally unacquainted with them.

Florence arrived for their reunion while Agnes was in the final throes of her revisions. Not surprisingly, the encounter was a disaster. Agnes kept her real issues concerning their friendship unspoken, but she was openly contemptuous of Florence's lack of political consciousness and her pregnant state—which Florence had been too frightened to reveal before. The derision was a front, for Agnes loved children and would soon write of her desire to adopt "about six, if I have the money. Or at least two or three . . . out of curiosity and the desire for companionship and experimentation in education."[14] But she was jealous. According to Agnes, Florence, stung, retorted that Agnes was arrogant, intolerant, and "wasting" her time in the Indian movement and that it was neurotic to feel others' misery as intensely as she did.

Agnes labored to keep the visit pleasant, introducing Florence to her famous friends Tilla Durieux and Kaethe Kollwitz and her landlady Mrs. Grabisch (whom Florence mortified with irreverent references to constipation—evidently a lifelong problem), but she could not wait for Florence to leave. In a classic Freudian slip, she arrived at the train station to bid the couple farewell just as their train departed.

Agnes retyped her manuscript for the last time soon after. "I'm sick of the damned book," she declared. "Hope to never see it again when it is once out of my hands. Not even when it is published. Can't stick the damned thing."[15] Chatto had already arranged with the Russian ambassador to recommend the manuscript to publishers in Moscow, she wrote, but before she mailed it off, she gave the problematic final section to Mrs. Grabisch for one more round of comment. The prim woman was horrified, Agnes said, by her decision to expose her sexual life to public scrutiny and accused her of sensationalism and writing solely for financial gain. If she insisted on publishing it, she wrote, Mrs. Grabisch advised her to do so under another name.

Afterward Agnes would claim that the two women went out and got drunk. "Under the influence of the wine, I dropped my politeness and courtesy," she asserted, "... and ... told her ... that I did not give one God damn what people think of me; that I have lived with a dozen men and have only reached the age of thirty-four and have another thirty years ahead of me. That I may live with a dozen more—that is all my affair. And, to rub it in, that my mind is not yet quite made up on the matter! That just now I was living with no man, but that was a misfortune that was not my fault."[16] By the end of her harangue, Agnes boasted, she had reduced Mrs. Grabisch to tears. In truth the criticism so upset her she staggered off to get drunk alone.

The book out of her hands, Agnes accompanied Durieux to Salzburg as her paid companion and spent the next month mountain climbing and attending the city's storied festival plays, the ballet, concerts by the Vienna Philharmonic, and a Mozart festival. In the evenings, after Durieux (who was appearing in Frank Wedekind's *Franziska* and Shaw's *Caesar and Cleopatra*) had performed, Agnes sipped champagne in the company of acclaimed European writers and directors.

Agnes, who was capable of great warmth in her friendships, could also be quite heartless. Since she lacked understanding of her own worth, she could never really see why others cared deeply for her, and once she took up with Durieux, she casually dismissed Michaelis—so instrumental only the summer before in the writing of her book—as a "slave" of her estranged husband and undeserving of respect.[17] As Agnes outgrew her earlier need for Florence, the influential Durieux supplanted her dear friend almost as easily.

She attacked Florence in a letter for having accused her during Florence's visit of "wasting" her time on India. She did not criticize Florence for wasting her time having a baby, or her husband for studying music and playing the piano, Agnes wrote. "I love India; I love Indians even with all their weaknesses; I love the Indian movement with all its strength and all its imbecilities."[18] Oblivious to the hurt she inflicted, or Florence's many past kindnesses, she censured her for placing greater value on her personal happiness than on the class struggle to which Agnes devoted herself.

You are like a child that refuses to walk, and demands always to be carried. Otherwise you could look these terrible social things in the eye and study them without the negative emotions you have...

Here in this hotel I have seen things that have awakened many, many thoughts in me. There is an orchestra that plays the best there is in music, and in the evening we sit there and read or smoke or meet interesting people — and we always talk. There are children who come with their parents and sit there. Lovely, clean, well-dressed and well-fed children. I see them in the making — cleanliness, good taste, cultivated conversation about them, and the best there is in music. They will grow up the best and most cultured, and they will scorn the working class and say that the working class could have what it wanted if it only tried. Then I remember all the children we pass on the street: the only music they hear is the cheap trash they hear in the kino — for which they can pay ten pfennigs. Cleanliness to them is a bath once a month or once a year... Then I look about in the lobby and see slick, well fed, rich men smoking their cigars and ordering drinks and paying with a gesture that shows that money is nothing to them... I hear them talk about "anarchy" and the "danger of Bolshevism and Communism." As I sit and listen I doubt their humanity... And I long for the day to come when the working class will be sufficiently conscious to shake the earth to pieces and drown these people in a flood of their own blood...

Pardon if I judge you. I do not class you among the rich people of the world. I do not ask you to give up the little money you have to live on... But as I see it, your life, your very existence is not worth anything at all if you live passively in the very midst of injustice, and at the same time think only of protecting yourself and yours.... or bring others into existence, others who are protected from knowing what the great masses suffer, [if you] then think of protecting only them and yourself, you are a selfish, utterly selfish person...

You consider me neurotic that I feel misery so deeply. Then I wish to remain neurotic. If I thought my analysis would take me away from the class struggle, then I would never be analysed. If I thought love would blind my eyes to it, would make me think that me and mine were the only things worthwhile, or the chief things, then I would also stop the analysis. The class struggle I say, and mean the international struggle with which India is so intimately bound. It just happens that I have taken the Indian end to work with.[19]

Agnes left Durieux at the end of August to meet Bakar in Linz. "Certain problems," she said, had arisen between them. Bakar wanted an Islamic marriage for the sake of Indian society. Agnes said she would as soon be married by a Catholic priest and preferred death to accepting even the form of such "dead and primitive things" as Islam offered.[20] There was also the matter of where they would live. Although Agnes's various schemes to enter India had fallen through, she still very much wanted to go and saw nothing in the long term that could bind her to Europe. Bakar, however, remained attached to his life abroad. Their biggest challenge, Agnes grudgingly revealed, was that while she was chronologically eight years Bakar's senior, in experience she felt thirty years older. Her habits and outlook were formed, she said, while he was still a child. In the end, they agreed to defer a decision for another six months.

As September approached, Durieux proposed to underwrite Agnes's oft-deferred dream of attending Berlin University. Agnes wondered whether she could cope with the feelings of dependence such an arrangement might engender, but she protested too much. Virtually the only way for her to enter India legally was through some affiliation with an Indian university, and for that she needed a degree. Although she lacked the academic qualifications, Durieux believed two of her articles on Indian history, which the University of Munich was using as texts, could be used to illustrate her ability, and Karl Haushofer, a professor of Indian politics and history who later gained notoriety as a possible author of *Mein Kampf*, agreed to help. Years later, Agnes was still unclear whether her keen mind or her Asiatic connections had inspired him.[21]

Back in Berlin with time to reflect, Agnes realized how shabbily she had treated Florence and tried to repair the damage. Apologizing for her tendency to "go on the warpath" against her closest friends, she wrote that in another six months she would complete her analysis; then, she promised, she would be better. In the meantime, she urged Florence to visit her again in Berlin, dangling the city's fall cultural calendar as bait. All four municipal operas would be performing; they could attend any number of concerts and a popular lecture series run by the Psychoanalytic Association, which would be exploring such topics as the place of Marxism in psychoanalysis. But Agnes had pushed her friend too far. Florence returned to the United States without stopping again in Berlin.

The autumn of 1926 was an odd, uneasy time for Agnes. With the book off her hands, there was a hole in Agnes's life that had previously been filled by Chatto or her phantom love affair with Bakar. Having nothing in her personal life to replace her former concerns, she lost interest in her analysis and its intense scrutiny of her emotional state. Instead, she turned her attention to the world around her. The unfolding events in China were of particular interest, and to learn as much as she could, she embarked on a program of study guided, most likely, by the Chinese students Chatto encountered at the League Against Colonial Cruelties and Oppression or the recently opened KMT office in Berlin, where Kuomintang officials including General Liau Hanseng worked with Muenzenberg.[22]

The launching of the Northern Expedition in 1926 had inaugurated an extraordinary phase of the Chinese Revolution. As the National Revolutionary Army—its ranks swollen with Chinese Communists who held memberships in both the KMT and CCP—made its way to Peking, where it planned to wrest control from the ailing, ineffective government, it was capturing province after province. Millions of discontented peasants, incited by Communist political agents inside the KMT, hailed the soldiers as liberators and heroes. In Wuhan, one of two new KMT capitals, hundreds of thousands of newly enrolled trade union members were striking foreign-operated plants. Sporting red stars or hammer-and-sickle insignia, they greeted one another with clenched fist salutes, spouted slogans decrying imperialism, and declared the events in China inseparable from the world revolution. By the last quarter of 1926, to the astonishment of Chinese and foreign observers, the troops had taken half of China.

The movement was acquiring gravitas, and to maximize its impact on other colonial countries Muenzenberg was implementing another Comintern-sponsored campaign "to unite all subjected Asiatic people behind the Chinese revolution," as Agnes recalled.[23] Chatto had a leading role in the effort, which held great promise for India, but Ghadr Party activists including Agnes's friend Bhagwan Singh were also participating, organizing Sikh troops stationed in China into a "Union of Oppressed Peoples of the East," which had close ties to the KMT.[24] Agnes's own avowed interest in the Comintern's "Pan Asiatic movement for self defense" now drew her nearer to the orbit of Willi Muenzenberg, whom she likely met around this time.[25]

With his short, squat peasant's body and unpretentious manner, Muenzenberg exuded a working-class charisma Agnes would have found appealing. Although he was by now a Reichstag deputy, he was neither a narrow-minded party man nor a doctrinaire theoretician but an activist much like herself, with a freewheeling style that often found him out of favor with his comrades in the German Communist Party.[26] Muenzenberg, whose labors fell essentially within the framework of the Comintern, recognized the growing influence Soviet leaders exerted on the organization's goals. However, he still believed that the international Communist movement was the only one that was ready to fight with every available means for social progress and the emancipation of the world's oppressed. And Agnes was coming around.

Early that winter, she wrote an article for Lajpat Rai's paper, *The People*, on the Indonesian Communists leading a revolt against the Dutch in Java, in which she employed a striking new tone. While the *immediate* goal in Asia was "the national freedom of subjected lands," Agnes advised her Indian readers, such independence was only a "first and primary step" before other progress could be made. "Asiatics unite," she concluded with a paraphrase of the Communist Manifesto. "You have nothing to lose but your chains. And a world to gain."[27]

Shortly after the piece appeared, according to a Muenzenberg deputy, Louis Gibarti, Chatto introduced her to Muenzenberg's friend Mirov-Abramov, the stocky, bespectacled official in the Comintern's OMS.[28] Soon enough the "big man" in the OMS, as Muenzenberg's colleague later recalled him, was referring to Agnes as "a mutual friend" of theirs whom he held "in great esteem."[29]

Agnes began her graduate studies in November 1926. All her courses were in some way related to India, and for a brief moment, she said, she felt like she was walking in heaven. Before the first week was through, though, she began complaining. It was very difficult, she told Florence, to sit and listen while her professors expressed sympathy for the British Empire. The lectures were too intense and covered too much ground; other students had more professional experience while she lacked a foundation in science and math. Then there were language problems. In a very short time, her joy at arriving at a place where she described everything as "clean and cool and scientific" became a ringing attack.

Agnes would later blame her decision to abandon her university studies on financial pressures that required her to tutor private students when she needed to study, but that was not the case. In December, Chatto's youngest sister, Suhasini, arrived in Berlin and assumed Agnes's students, and Durieux covered Agnes's expenses so she did not lack for money. The truth—which she preferred not to reveal—was that she was up to her ears in preparations for Muenzenberg's upcoming congress, which would be held in Brussels a few months hence.[30]

The flourishing advance of China's National Revolutionary Army had globetrotting reporters scurrying off to Asia to cover the colonial fight for freedom. Influential middle class socialists and intellectuals in industrialized nations— Muenzenberg's core constituency—were monitoring its progress closely, lending the congress a historical significance that far exceeded organizers' expectations. During the last quarter of 1926, Agnes was actually working so hard she had little energy left for school.

Letters from her closest friends were not answered; all articles of a nonpolitical nature went unwritten. When Bakar arrived that December to spend the holidays with her, Agnes put him off, grumbling about a flulike cold and ugly cough. Convinced, like Chatto, that the events in China would soon extend to India, she did not intend to find herself stuck in a classroom, far from the center of action, while four hundred million Chinese carried out their revolution.

Both Chatto and Bakar attended the congress, so perhaps it was the discomfort of facing them together that discouraged Agnes. Given the ambiguity of her connection to Chatto, maybe she preferred to avoid the numerous members of the Chattopadhyaya family who were also participating. Perhaps it was simply passport problems. Two months earlier, the U.S. State Department had rejected

Agnes's passport application as suspect.[31] In any event, on February 10, 1927, when the First International Congress Against Colonial Oppression and Imperialism convened with great fanfare in the Palais Egmont, she was absent.

Several dozen Europeans and Americans, including Agnes's friend Roger Baldwin and the Communist economist Scott Nearing, were among the sea of delegates representing at least 134 organizations. The vast majority, however, were from colonies or territories oppressed by imperialism. Chatto had personally selected the Indian mission, and his family friend Jawaharlal Nehru, who represented the Indian National Congress, led the group. It was a great coup for Chatto after his years of eclipse by Roy. In fact, with his rival currently in China as part of the Comintern's delegation there, speculation was rife that Roy had been deliberately posted to China to ensure he created no trouble for Chatto in Brussels.[32]

The conference occurred at a most auspicious moment for the Chinese revolutionary nationalist armies. In January 1927, Chinese had reclaimed British concessions in Hankow and Kiukiang, and Great Britain was making no attempt to regain them. Peasant leader Mao Tse-tung described the events in his native province of Hunan as a colossal success and predicted that very shortly several hundred million peasants would rise up and trample all who stood in their path to emancipation. Foreign nationals, terrified of a "Red" takeover, were evacuating China's interior. But as the Kuomintang Party debated the course the revolution should take in the months to come, tensions mounted.

Foreign warships and troops were converging ominously on Shanghai. Moreover, the original Sino-Soviet collaboration to which Sun Yat-sen had agreed promised only a bourgeois nationalist revolution—not the social upheaval China was experiencing. Many KMT leaders had landlord connections and neither anticipated nor wanted the peasant liberation Mao foresaw. For the moment, though, China's revolution prevailed, and it occupied center stage at the congress. Chiang Kai-shek, the young commander of the military forces, sent a cable of support. So did Dr. Sun's widow, Madame Sun Yat-sen, and the provisional government of Wuhan. Nehru pledged the support of the Indian National Congress. Western luminaries including Upton Sinclair, Albert Einstein, and Maxim Gorky paid tribute to the Chinese struggle, which the latter described as the greatest hope for every nation oppressed by imperialism.

A permanent organization, the League Against Imperialism, was founded at the congress to replace the former League Against Colonial Cruelties and Oppression, and plans were laid to create branches in China and India. Headquarters would remain in Muenzenberg's Berlin office, which Chatto would run, in addition to overseeing propaganda into India.[33] The appointments of Reginald Bridgeman, a British Labour Party leader (and head of the Chinese

Information Bureau, who would later work for the OMS), as chair of the LAI's executive committee, of Nehru as a committee member, and of Madame Sun Yat-sen and Albert Einstein as honorary presidents suggested the organization's independence from any Communist party and its freedom from Comintern influence, but Party members and Comintern representatives were active behind the scenes, and the Comintern financed the conference.[34] Further, the selection of Muenzenberg as general secretary and his deputy Louis Gibarti as LAI secretary ensured that the final word would always be theirs.

The optimistic mood of the congress proved short-lived. Supported by puissant Shanghai financial interests and their Great Powers backers, Chiang Kai-shek soon repudiated the Soviet-dominated Wuhan government and established a new Nationalist government in Nanking under his control. Then, on April 12, 1927, he revealed himself as the leader of the KMT's right-wing opposition to a united front with the Communists. Severing relations with the Soviet Union, he embarked on a momentous campaign to eliminate all signs of radicalism throughout the country.

Open season was declared on Communists, labor leaders, and others out of favor with local militarists. Chinese Communist Party officials in Shanghai and Nanking were arrested and executed, along with thousands of workers. In city after city, union headquarters (usually synonymous with CCP headquarters) were closed down, and those in or near them were shot. Within days, China's radical movement was virtually liquidated—even in Canton, where the revolution had begun. Only Hunan, Hupeh, and Kiangsi provinces escaped the purge. To all but wistful dreamers, it was clear that the Wuhan government's days in power were numbered.

That May, the British government broke off diplomatic relations with the Soviet Union, and a skittish Soviet state began fiercely promoting the view that in less than a year Great Britain, acting in concert with the business leaders of capitalist nations, would extend what Agnes called its "holy war" against China's toiling masses into Soviet Russia, using India as its base. Agnes believed, however, that rather than defeat the world's first socialist state, the imminent cataclysm would launch the world revolution she awaited. Unable to conceive how the revolutionary working class could turn their guns against the Soviet Union, she thought that under pressure to choose, they would attack their real enemy— the capitalist system—in their native countries. This out-and-out class war would be fought without cease, as she saw it, until the capitalist order was destroyed, all of Asia freed, and the world's nations reorganized more equitably under a socialist system.[35]

By June 1927, the gravity of the Russian-British situation had thrown Agnes "completely into the arms of the Bolsheviks for all practical purposes," she informed Florence.[36] She still shared the revolutionary syndicalists' commitment to economic action and remained "non-political in so far as the Communist Party is concerned, and could never join it," she wrote,[37] but her exhilaration over China's revolution and her confidence that it would extend to India gave her a fresh appreciation of the Russian leaders' seeming willingness to defend Asia against the long arm of British imperialism. Convinced that such actions exemplified the Comintern's internationalist vision and its commitment to world revolution, Agnes entered the organization's Chinese work at this time on the basis of Chatto's recommendation.[38]

Agnes's only comment on the subject was her later acknowledgment that when the Chinese Revolution foundered "on the rocks of class warfare," and the Kuomintang, having broken the united front, declared war on the Communists, she became "involved."[39] Of what her involvement consisted she did not say, but she began simply enough as an advocacy journalist/propagandist for the Chinese Information Bureau, a Comintern front organization based in London, which established a Berlin branch around this time that was also known as the Chinese News Agency of Berlin.[40] Its director, Reginald Bridgeman, shared Agnes's dual focus on China and India and helped her in her work.[41]

Agnes's affiliation gave her access to Russian government documents as well as entrée to the middle-class Chinese revolutionaries (including Madame Sun Yat-sen) who began flooding into Berlin, to the French Communist and underground Comintern operative Paul Valliant-Couturier, and to the Comintern auxiliary the International Red Aid, whose journal now published one of her articles.[42] To mask her Comintern connections, Agnes never mentioned her association with the Red Aid, and she denied authorship of her pieces for the Chinese Information Bureau and Chinese News Agency of Berlin, claiming she merely "translated" the articles from German. However, as Agnes admitted to Sanger, her German, gleaned largely in conversation with her landladies, resulted in "very rough and often bad translations." Lucie Hecht did her translation work.

Only a few years earlier, Agnes had expressed contempt for the "white-collared" German Communists who her disrupted syndicalist meetings. Now she had nothing but praise for KPD leader Ernst Thalmann, whose "very sound knowledge, and . . . ability" she commended to readers, along with the "perfect discipline" of Germany's Red Front fighters.[43] Like Agnes herself, the troops, she wrote, were not necessarily Communist Party members, but they considered themselves Communists and accepted the Party's leadership.

Given her perception of its significance, the "war business," as she referred to Great Britain's impending attack on Russia, consumed her. Until recently, Agnes had enjoyed spending time with Durieux, who treated Agnes like royalty, sending a car to fetch her for dinner and introducing her to visiting celebrities including Maxim Gorky. Now she abruptly dropped the friendship, along with virtually all her university studies, to devote herself to her political life. Hampered now by her ignorance of Marxist theory, she also joined a study group Scott Nearing taught that spring in Berlin. She might lack Nearing's intellect, Agnes wrote, but she could at least learn his method of work.[44]

The purposefulness of her days invigorated her. Brushing the cobwebs of introspection from her mind, Agnes described her relief to be once again "working, child, working! . . . writing, writing, writing for the Indian press, counteracting British propaganda against Russia ...You cannot imagine how . . . Night and day I read, study, and write."[45] Had she consulted her anarcho-syndicalist friends, they might have warned her that many believed the Russians were just stirring up a war scare to serve their own purposes; knowing, perhaps, what their feelings would be, she scrupulously avoided such discussions, as she avoided Goldman and the rest of her former set.

Unaware that Soviet national interests rather than a commitment to world revolution increasingly guided Comintern policy, Agnes preferred to believe that that "fighting instrument," as she referred to the Third International, had declared all-out war on England's subjection of India and China. With that, she dismissed her former objections to Russian terror and barbarities as "enemy propaganda intended to thwart the freedom of oppressed nations."[46] Since the establishment of Soviet Russia, she now maintained, the country's actions had been governed by the noblest motives. Never would it interfere in the form of government the free nations of Asia wished to establish. The USSR, she wrote, sought only to destroy Great Britain's hold on other people's property.[47]

By summer, Agnes was acknowledging her work for the Chinese Information Bureau.[48] During this period, her major opus was a five-part series on England's war plans against Asia which appeared in Lajpat Rai's paper, *The People*. In her ardor to convince Indian readers that widespread, organized plans to provoke such a war existed "in British secret archives," Agnes failed to cite the Soviet government documents and journals she claimed as her source, but having crossed the line from reporter to propagandist, persuasion rather than accuracy was her chief concern.

Occasionally, Agnes objected that her workload was too heavy and she longed for a bit of rest. Her face, she said, had aged five years in the past few months, and she often wrote of being lonely. After the Brussels congress, she had spent considerable time with Roger Baldwin and her attachment to him brought home to her the acuteness of her isolation. "It was like meeting a brother I love," she observed, "and he awoke in my heart the bitter need of having friends like him whom I instinctively understand and who understand me.

When he left I lay awake all night trying to reconsider my life . . . surrounded by public work and thought but so lonely personally. You might think I fell in love with him—but I didn't. He showed me . . . without knowing it, the gulf between me and the Indians . . . With most Americans I feel a deeper gulf still."[49]

Agnes missed the kind of intimacy she had known with Chatto, but she had come to see the improbability of a future with Bakar. At thirty-five, having failed to achieve any lasting fulfillment in her relationships with men, she was beginning to reconcile herself to the idea that she was alone and likely to remain so. Even with all the analysis in the world, Agnes wrote, she would probably never be "all there" emotionally. The rigor of her political life allowed her to ignore the personal issues she could not resolve. Work would have to be her substitute for love, and in it she lost herself willingly. When Florence wrote of her baby, Agnes did not begrudge her friend her domestic contentment. "I am no longer hostile—but am just indifferent, and am so much more interested in other things," she replied.[50]

Several months previously, Agnes had submitted what was essentially a synopsis of her manuscript to the *Nation* for inclusion in its series "These Modern Women." Agnes wrote that *Nation* editor Oswald Garrison Villard said he found it one of the most extraordinary human documents he ever read but shrank from printing the piece, which apparently contained a discussion of her lesbian tendencies.[51] Advanced as the *Nation*'s readers were, Agnes remarked, even they had their limitations, and she groused that after an initial burst of excitement, H. L. Mencken at the *American Mercury* had also gotten cold feet.

Only *New Masses*, the radical American magazine on arts and politics, had promised to fight on the issue, she said. However, in August 1927, when the piece appeared anonymously, Agnes protested that both the word *lesbian* and a full paragraph on the subject had been deleted from her story.[52] With the world-weary air of a European sophisticate, she scoffed at America's backwardness in such matters, but she was not so bold as she made out. While her authorship must have been an open secret in Greenwich Village circles, she begged Florence not to reveal her identity for fear the Indians would use it against her.

Differences between the way Agnes described the Smedleys in the article and her manuscript were revealing. In southern Colorado, she wrote in *New Masses* with masterful obfuscation, she had been "a child worker" in one of the Rockefeller coal-mining towns—leading readers to assume she had actually worked in the mines. She still denied her father's allegiance to the coal companies and his stint as a deputy sheriff, but here she admitted his work for Trinidad's political bosses. In the article, she also reflected on her failure to champion her own class before moving to Europe—a matter on which she had been obdurately silent in her book—but having traveled as far from her origins as she had over the past decade and a half, she confessed to *New Masses* readers, she felt as estranged from its concerns as if she had "dropped from Mars" and doubted she could be of service.[53]

The fall of 1927 passed quietly. In the months since the Brussels congress, Nehru had grown close to Chatto, and the two consulted frequently on the political situation in India. Many observers, in fact, attributed Nehru's recent leftward shift to Chatto's influence, and when the Indian leader passed through Berlin en route to Moscow, he called on Chatto. Through him, Agnes got to meet Nehru, but her first impression was not favorable. Attracted to men like her father—aggressive men of action—she found Nehru's low-key, unassuming style too "female" for her taste. He was "so modest and reserved," she wrote, she found it hard to think of him as a political leader at all.[54]

That December, Margaret Sanger also visited Berlin. The birth control pioneer was on a European tour—her first attempt to make her movement international in scope—and Agnes arranged for her to address sympathetic audiences in the city. Despite the widespread availability of contraceptive devices, most unwanted pregnancies in Germany were still terminated by abortion, a statutory offense punishable by imprisonment, and Sanger was avid to establish a birth control clinic in the German capital.

Agnes was delighted to see her again and introduced Sanger to her friend Kaethe Kollwitz. However, while she enjoyed Sanger's lavish praise and the generous compensation for her labor, she resisted Sanger's request to serve as her personal representative on the project. She knew that Sanger still wanted her to commit herself fully to the cause, but Agnes considered herself too political, too dominated by "the whole class idea," as she put it, to be content with mere reform efforts.[55]

In a workers' state like Russia, she explained to Sanger, birth control was taken for granted. She said she did not intend to wait for a revolution to advocate contraception, but fighting for the overthrow of world capitalism seemed a more efficacious way of ensuring access to birth control for all who wished it. Besides, she protested, she knew little about founding a clinic. "I have no experience and it is not my line... My work has never been this, and I have had but a general though active interest," she wrote.[56] The reality, as she confessed elsewhere, was that she had begun making other plans, which she did not wish to be "worried and prevented from doing."[57]

By the end of 1927, the situation in China was quite grim from the revolutionaries' perspective. Chiang Kai-shek's right-wing forces had triumphed; the KMT united front with Chinese Communists sought by Moscow had proved a dismal failure. Frightened by Chiang Kai-shek's betrayal, many left-wing KMT leaders had turned against the Communists within their ranks; those who did not had fled the country, along with their Soviet advisers. It was at this point, when the repeated bloodlettings had reduced the CCP to impotence and Russian influence in China was all but annihilated, that Jakob Mirov-Abramov, Agnes's friend in the Comintern's OMS, sought her out.

As a report on the activities of her future collaborator Yakov Rudnik (better known as Hilaire Noulens) would explain, recent events had convinced the Comintern, and particularly the OMS, that it needed "a new *modus operandi*" in China, along with new methods and personnel, to reassert its presence in that country.[58] To do so, according to Muenzenberg deputy Louis Gibarti, who was close to his China activities, Mirov-Abramov advised Agnes that the OMS needed an American citizen like herself who, protected by the extraterritorial privileges of a U.S. passport, could help the Comintern establish new lines and methods of communication and explore "conditions on such territories where Russian agents would have been in danger."[59] Other requests would follow.

The question of whether such activities constituted espionage probably never arose. Certainly Agnes would be a spy in the sense that, in China, she would be keeping clandestine watch on various people and situations in order to obtain information. Her first posting, for example, would be in Harbin, a northern Chinese city near the Soviet border, where the Comintern viewed recent acts of Japanese aggression with the same wrath it had formerly reserved for the excesses of British imperialism.[60] In the broader sense of being employed to covertly pass classified information of strategic importance to a foreign government, she would not—at least for the moment.

From her base in Shanghai, Agnes would facilitate the carrying out of traditional OMS functions that included, but were not limited to, the distribution of propaganda, a courier service that moved people and money from one country to another, and illicit telegraphic links to Moscow.[61] Her analysis of conditions in China and work as an activist would place her in contact with CPUSA and Comintern officials including Alexander Trachtenberg on the Party's central committee, who oversaw the CPUSA publishing house; Earl Browder, future head of the CPUSA, who was then directing the Pan Pacific Trade Union Secretariat, subsidiary of the Comintern's trade union arm, the Profintern, which promoted Communist trade unions in China; and Harrison George, Browder's associate at the PPTUS, who also performed Comintern work. The activities she would perform in concert with them—which included doing favors for the Comintern, organizing workers and students, and writing journalistic reports— might fall in a gray zone legally, but they were not exactly espionage either.

Who would benefit from her activities, however, was another matter. As a friend of Mirov-Abramov's later wrote, Mirov-Abramov was the man through whom "all the threads of the conspiratorial activities of both the Narkomindel [Soviet Foreign Office] and the Comintern passed."[62] Although he encouraged the foreign non-Party radicals he recruited for the OMS to think they worked for the Comintern, on the understanding that they were more receptive to appeals from the Communist International than to a direct approach from the Soviets, that was not necessarily the case.[63]

Since Agnes would have more credibility as an independent, no one asked her to join a Communist party, in Germany or the United States, and there was no belonging to the Comintern, as it was not a membership organization. No money changed hands, either, at this time. Until better methods of communication were established, Agnes would transmit her reports for the OMS via Soviet boats that touched the Shanghai harbor.[64] The information would be conveyed to Vladivostok, site of the Comintern's Far East bureau. At a later date, accounts based on Agnes's material would be distributed from an unknown location on Soviet territory to the appropriate parties in Europe and America, who would either use it internally or arrange for its publication.[65]

Although by 1928 the Comintern's China policy served the needs of the Soviet state far better than it did the cause of Chinese Communism, Agnes was years from imagining how her unusual empathy for the people of the Far East might lead her into a situation from which she would recoil. For her, the Comintern was the single most critical weapon in the battle for the freedom of the world's oppressed nations. Wholeheartedly in favor of any method that ushered in a socialist society, she had no qualms about working covertly. Besides, the idea that Mirov-Abramov, a highly intelligent, devoted Communist and comrade-in-arms of the irrepressible Muenzenberg, wished to train *her* in conspiracy must have been immensely flattering.

The offer also appeared to be the only opportunity on Agnes's horizon with the potential to give her life the deeper meaning she urgently sought. Her early years had left her with a legacy of anger and a need for some ultimate justification of her life in order to feel worthy. Uninterested in further creative pursuits, anxious to put her years of introspection behind her, she no doubt hoped that in offering herself as a martyr to the Revolution, she might find in a career of political action what she could not attain in the personal realm. Agnes accepted the assignment despite the obvious dangers. Her chief interest remained India, but she reasoned that she could still pursue her Indian activities from China and in the not too distant future enter India from there.

In times to come, friends and acquaintances would contend that Agnes's instability and emotionalism made her a highly unlikely choice as a Comintern agent and that her lack of Communist "discipline" would have made it impossi-

ble for the Communists to use her in an organized fashion. They had no idea
how Agnes encouraged those impressions, exploiting her lack of any party affiliation to better hide her tracks. While she could not refrain from boasting to
Sanger about her new Russian connections, she never discussed with anyone,
ever, the purpose of her upcoming trip.[66]

Agnes spent Christmas Eve of 1927 with Bakar, but the affair was over.
Although she still cared for him in a maternal way, she was tired of pretending
that his companionship satisfied her. Citing her reluctance to spoil his career,
she sent him off; then, complaining of a cold and chronic appendicitis, she
retreated to her bed. She would never see Bakar again.

From her chamber, Agnes drafted articles on Sanger's trip to Berlin, the
Harlem Renaissance, and birth control in Russia; she also reviewed Sanger's
Happiness in Marriage and Herta Riese's *Sexual Distress of Our Time*. However,
by February 1928, the pain in her appendix had become intolerable. Sanger,
with whom Agnes regularly discussed her various maladies, had offered to pay
for an operation and postoperative treatment, and Agnes scheduled an appen-
dectomy. Fleetingly, she considered having herself sterilized at the same time.
However, when she heard that such women gained weight and wound up looking "like female eunuchs," as she put it, she decided against it.

Agnes entered the hospital in March 1928. Over the next two and a half
weeks Kollwitz was a frequent visitor, and her impressions of Agnes lying ill and

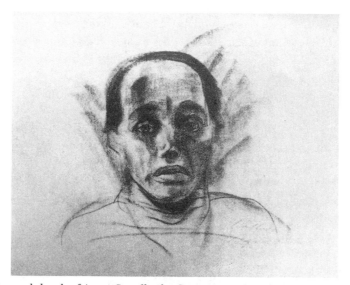

Charcoal sketch of Agnes Smedley by German artist Kaethe Kollwitz, 1928.
Artists Rights Society (ARS), New York/VG Bild-Kunst, Bonn.

troubled on her sickbed appear in a charcoal drawing and lithograph.[67] Josephine Bennett, a friend from the birth control movement, was constantly at her side, talking Agnes through her terror of sedation and generally caring for her. As Agnes often did with the women who nurtured or otherwise sustained her, she pronounced herself devoted to her current female benefactor. "I owe more to Jo than I can say," she wrote Sanger. "She has been unspeakably wonderful to me. She left me only to eat or to bring extra food or medicine for me. I love her beyond words for her silent love."[68]

Agnes recuperated slowly, something Sanger assured her was common among women of their temperament, but there was good news as well. Gilbert Roe had placed her novel with Coward-McCann, a start-up publishing house in New York City, and the book was slated to appear on the company's first list that fall, alongside works by Thornton Wilder, Alexander Woollcott, and Josephine Herbst.

After hobbling to and from her daily high-sun-ray treatments, Agnes would work until two or three in the morning revising and retyping her manuscript. Its publication, she hoped, would bring her a measure of the recognition she craved. "I need something to stand on, Margaret, and that will help some, I hope," she wrote.[69] She still fretted over her decision not to expose her private life with Chatto, which she feared marred the final section, but revisiting her haunted childhood had proved draining enough.

Earlier that winter, Agnes had been loath to help Sanger establish a clinic in Berlin. Once she was back on her feet, though, she began to meet with German physicians about the project, fussing all the while that she was already "beastly loaded with work" and could not manage it either in time or health.[70] Her myriad issues notwithstanding, Agnes was a first-rate organizer, and by April 1928 she had overseen the initial plan to open a clinic in Neukölln, a working-class, largely Communist district of the city; she was assisted by Helene Stoecker, editor of the influential *Neue Generation*, Adele Schreiber, a former Reichstag member, Helene Lange, mother of the German women's movement, and Kaethe Kollwitz.

Agnes stressed the clinic's nonpartisan nature in her correspondence, but of the committee who actually got the clinic off the ground, only two—Stoecker and Agnes—did not belong to the German Communist Party, and she had numerous objections to Stoecker's involvement.[71] Agnes lauded the Communist doctors' joint commitment to birth control and the working-class movement, which led them to promote birth control "on a Marxist rather than Malthusian basis," she observed in the *Birth Control Review*. They understood that only the destruction of the capitalist system—not simply birth control—could solve the global problem of poverty.[72]

These days, according to Agnes, the Communists were the only ones attempting anything "fundamental" in Germany. That did not keep her, however, from flexing her veto power when their views conflicted with hers.[73] Some of her Communist colleagues wanted Magnus Hirschfeld, a sexual reformer who combined birth control work with research on homosexuality, on the clinic committee, but Agnes refused, claiming it was bad for the birth control movement to have someone so widely known as a homosexual and a student of homosexuality associated with the project. "He can have his own clinic if he wishes and will do good work, perhaps," she informed Sanger. "But I'd like to see the clinic under the care of physicians, pure and simple, with no homosexuality or venereal diseases or tubercular appendages...I say nothing against him at all," she asserted, "except that B.C. and homosexuality are two different things and must not be confused in the minds of the public."[74]

Agnes did, however, have something against Hirschfeld and his ideas on homosexuality, and it was largely because she found them threatening that she resisted his involvement with the clinic. His position, that homosexuality was physical in origin and therefore "incurable," conflicted with Agnes's work in analysis, where she had been advised that her sexual proclivities were psychic in origin and therefore "curable." Birth control methods were "normal, healthy things used by normal, healthy persons," she wrote, while homosexuality, as she had come to understand it, was abnormal. She would not tolerate having birth control "mixed up...with any form of perversion" like Hirschfeld's, she wrote. [75]

The Berlin birth control clinic was modeled on Sanger's in New York City but adapted to German conditions. Although abortion was a crime in both countries, providing contraceptive information was not illegal in Germany, and Agnes pointed out to Sanger that their clinic would be competing with a number of "marriage advice" bureaus, which already discussed birth control in conjunction with other subjects. She also warned that their decision to use the words "birth control" instead of more ambiguous phrases like "marriage and sexual advice" might provoke a fight from Germany's growing reactionary movement, which was in the midst of a major drive to increase the nation's birth rate. Agnes's reservations notwithstanding, in April 1928 the committee began promoting the clinic in newspapers including Muenzenberg's popular tabloid, A.I.Z.

Sanger declared Agnes "a wonder" for getting the project off the ground, but she seemed indifferent. Her impending trip to China was foremost on her mind; the clinic was just a job. Outwardly Agnes approached her Comintern assignment in the same vagabond spirit in which she had earlier informed Goldman that the open road had always been more to her liking than "a carpeted room, a telephone and a beefsteak daily," but she was worried. After seven years abroad, Agnes was still living in Germany illegally, with documents that listed her under three different names and dates of birth. Unable to verify her American citizenship, the State Department refused to issue her a passport. Without one, she could not claim the extraterritorial privileges that would protect her in China.

The year before, when Sanger visited, Agnes had persuaded her to accompany her to the American Embassy in the hope that Sanger's illustrious name alone might suffice as documentation. In the end, though, U.S. officials had demanded proof, and Agnes had been forced to contact people in the States, many of whom had not heard from her in nearly a decade. Agnes's Missouri relatives, still angered by her desertion of her siblings, refused to help, but Gilbert Roe had tracked down her father in Oklahoma, where he was now a sheriff, along with the doctor who attended her birth. They had sent affidavits attesting to Agnes's American citizenship. So did Myrtle. Agnes found even this limited contact with her family burdensome. Despite her years of studied forgetfulness and her subsequent ones in analysis, she was hurt by her sister's failure to enclose a personal note along with the information Agnes had requested.

Ernest, by now remarried and the father of two children, had included a kind letter along with a copy of their divorce papers. The concern and admiration he expressed for the woman she said he only half jokingly suggested would one day die on the barricades prompted a melancholy response from her. "My life—yes I can say in passing that it has surpassed all the romances and detective novels. But what does that mean? It is romance only to those who see it from the outside. To me, who lived it, it has often meant unspeakable pain." On a personal level, Agnes wrote, she was "lonely and rather isolated...I write much. In India I am much better known than in Europe or America...It means nothing. The person who howls the loudest, even if that howl is empty, becomes well known. I have done nothing that will last longer than a week or a month. When I do more than that I won't have to write and tell you about it. You will learn of it."[76]

On May 10, 1928, Agnes again applied for a U.S. passport, good for travel and study in Germany, France, Austria, and Denmark only. This time, she succeeded. When it arrived the following month, Agnes (who knew she was leaving for China in the fall) disingenuously announced to Sanger that after seven years of underground life, she would finally be able to lead "more or less of a legal existence."[77]

Agnes would work for the Comintern in China, but it did not appear that the organization had agreed to support her there, and her personal finances were, as ever, in rather a mess. So perhaps there was a predatory element to the romantic friendship that now blossomed between her and Professor David Friday as she prepared to depart. Agnes professed to be very fond of Friday, a former chairman of the economics department at New York University who currently taught at the New School for Social Research, but they had hardly known one another a month before she wrote that he had loaned her enough money to maintain herself for a year in China.

The Berlin clinic opened in the summer of 1928, and the enthusiastic reception it received surprised Agnes as much as it did other committee members. She said positive articles appeared in nearly every leading Berlin paper; only a few extreme nationalist outlets disapproved. To the group's delight, the city soon assumed the clinic's operation, freeing sufficient funds for them to open a second clinic that conducted research and did statistical work. Agnes reported to Sanger that the outlook for birth control in Germany was quite promising.[78] The next time she visited, Agnes assured her, "the largest possible audiences" would attend her lectures.

Agnes left for Paris in August, telling friends that she needed to meet with a few people in the French labor movement before she could leave for China.[79] Not registering with the police, as required by law, she connected, most likely, with Gaston Monmosseau and "Herclet," the Pan Pacific Trade Union Secretariat representatives, respectively, of the Confederation du Travail and the Confederation du Travaile Unitaire, virtually the only trade unions in Europe with ties to the Comintern. Perhaps she also met with the French Communist writer Paul Valliant-Couturier, a favorite of Muenzenberg's, whose clandestine work would soon take him to China as well. That June, at the Chinese Communist Party's sixth congress (held simultaneously with the Comintern's in Moscow) the Comintern had directed the Chinese Party to pay special attention to the trade union movement, and the PPTUS was the organization it would use to conduct propaganda and other activities to influence China's floundering revolution.

In Paris, Agnes said, she completed her travel plans and met with her editor, Ernestine Evans, regarding final changes on her book. Now titled *Daughter of Earth*, it was scheduled for release in the spring of 1929, when it would lead the publisher's list. Anticipating its success, Coward-McCann planned to launch it with a publicity campaign that included full-page ads in the *New York Times*, the *Tribune*, and the *Saturday Review*. Agnes wrote that Evans had asked her, for legal reasons, to eliminate material on her two abortions, which had originally occupied an entire scene, and on the murder of her grandmother Rausey Ralls, since Mary Smedley was still alive and had never been accused of the crime. The story as it now stood was much changed from Agnes's original draft, but it was still true enough to her impressions of her girlhood that she did not want her family to see it. In a letter to Ernest she asked that, should he run into Myrtle, he not mention its publication to her.

Agnes counted on money from foreign editions to help her support herself in China. However, by the summer of 1928 she had failed to secure a German publisher, and Evans was of little assistance. At a loss, Agnes evidently reached out to the Muenzenberg apparatus, which steered her to Julian Gumperz, a respected figure in German Communist Party leadership circles and a key person in Muenzenberg's publishing empire.[80] Gumperz was the financial backer of the Malik Verlag, a lucrative enterprise that published Russian and other left wing fiction in Germany.[81] Agnes said that in exchange for 50 percent of the book's profits he offered to translate *Daughter of Earth* into German and release what she referred to as an "unexpurgated" edition. Agnes was leery at first, but she eventually agreed to turn over all translation and other rights to him. The two became lovers, friends, and collaborators not long after.

Emma Goldman, who now lived in the south of France, had hoped that Agnes would visit her there, but Agnes, who was familiar with Goldman's antipathy for the Soviet regime, had little interest in exposing herself through the sort of heart-to-heart talks the two women had previously enjoyed. Begging off on the flimsiest of excuses, she remained in Paris until late that summer, when she accompanied Gumperz to Frankfurt.

The business of establishing a network of contacts was much the same for a reporter as a covert agent, and Agnes said that in China she would also serve as the representative of an "Indian nationalist press agency"—most likely the one Muenzenberg deputy Louis Gibarti operated for the League Against Imperialism.[82] To function effectively, though, she also required some sort of legal cover that gave her shelter from which to operate and a visible means of support. Toward that end, she agreed to serve as Sanger's personal representative in China. Through Gumperz's intervention, she also received an offer from the *Frankfurter Zeitung* to become their special correspondent there.[83] Such was Muenzenberg's influence in the German publishing world that the prestigious Social Democratic daily also agreed to publish Agnes's novel, serially and in bound form, through its publishing house, the Frankfurter Societats-Druckeri. Given the nature of her assignment in China, she would be safer associated with the *Zeitung* than with the Communist-controlled Malik Verlag.

Agnes was not the first revolutionary to operate in Asia under cover of the *Frankfurter Zeitung*. In 1927, the Comintern agent Jur Herbert Mueller had been the paper's China correspondent. Six years hence, Agnes's partner in Soviet espionage, Richard Sorge, would work in Tokyo the same way. Affiliation with the eminently respectable publication helped allay suspicions that the correspondents' conduct inevitably aroused. Agnes made no bones about her lack of enthusiasm for her post. As her money would come from the *Zeitung*, she would give it half her time, she confided to Ellen Kennan, but the rest of her time and her true interests in China were "otherwise."[84]

French police called on Jo Bennett, in whose Paris apartment Agnes had stayed, days after her departure. On learning of their appearance, Agnes assumed it meant that Scotland Yard continued to track her movements; the dim view they took of her Indian activities was no secret to her. She did not anticipate, however, that a copy of its report, forwarded to the American Embassy in London, would find its way to the U.S. State Department, which would begin to monitor her activities.[85]

Much had changed within the Comintern during the months Agnes was away from Berlin. At its sixth world congress, held that August, the organization had abandoned its united front policy for one more in keeping with Stalin's new hard line. For the next seven years, bourgeois reformers who worked outside of Communist parties would not be tolerated. Communist Party members were instructed to infiltrate organizations that had mass memberships or that could influence public opinion, and win adherents or sympathizers. In the wake of the congress, some organizations came openly under Communist control and leadership. Others, including Muenzenberg's IAH and LAI, which depended on loose interpretations of Comintern policy for their relative autonomy, were ordered to form "party factions" and work behind the scenes through Communist "cells" that would secretly control them.

In the years to come, such institutions and others like them, which sprang up on an as-needed basis, would continue to appeal to the humanitarian sentiments of idealistic workers, intellectuals, and middle-class citizens, much as they had in the past. If these people chose to inquire, they would be told that the organizations and causes they aided were as nonpolitical and independent of Moscow as Muenzenberg's IAH had once been. However, it would be a lie, and no one knew this better than Muenzenberg himself.

Muenzenberg publicly lauded the decisions of the sixth Comintern congress; privately, he admitted that with the change in policy, he had lost control.[86] As the Comintern grew more centralized under Stalin's leadership, it would remain international in form only. In reality, it became a monopoly of power exercised by the Russian Communist Party, for whom Soviet example and guidance was paramount and whose directives would be applied without alteration to every other Communist Party in the world.

In this hard-line climate, Agnes's nonaligned status became problematic for

Officials of the League Against Imperialism, Berlin, 1930. Standing: Virendranath Chattopadhyaya (far left), Reginald Bridgeman (third from left), Willi Muenzenberg (fourth from left). Seated: General Liau Hanseng (second from right). *National Archives.*

the German Communist Party (KPD). Since her affiliation with the Comintern's OMS was a closely held secret, the increasingly sectarian KPD was suspicious of Agnes, and Gumperz would recall that the Party repeatedly warned its members to "exercise caution" in their dealings with her.[87] Agnes cared precious little what the KPD thought, for in her work with the OMS, she believed, she served a higher master.

Agnes received her visa for China that October; all that remained was to say her good-byes. She wrote asking Sanger to notify Gilbert Roe if the British arrested or detained her. Roe, who still acted as her pro bono attorney, was influential; if necessary, he could apply pressure in Washington to get her released, she explained. In November 1928, she boarded a train for Moscow, accompanied on the first leg of her journey by Chatto, whose activities were no longer supervised by Muenzenberg but by Georgi Dimitrov, incoming director of the Comintern's Berlin-based Western European bureau.[88]

Moscow in late 1928 was a different city from the one Agnes had visited seven years earlier. Then, she told Sanger, "Russia was prostrate after the terrible invasions. Not a wheel turned . . . — or but few." Since then the progress had been "tremendous . . . Now, instead of the miserable hovels, the workers have built huge apartment houses, with community kitchens and kindergartens, with electric light and baths . . . They are learning to read, they are building, they are standing against a world of wealth and privilege . . . If you could only come and see, and forget America, Margaret, with all its money and its ability to buy everything and everybody. Just see what these people are doing on nothing!"[89]

A few years later, Agnes would reputedly boast of meeting with Iosef Piatnitsky, Mirov-Abramov's superior in the OMS and chief of the department, but she never discussed her specific instructions.[90] Joseph Kornfeder, though, an American Communist who was attending the Comintern's International Lenin Institute in Moscow, would recall that a man named Johnson, whom Kornfeder described as "an important official in the Far East Section of Soviet intelligence" and who attempted to recruit Kornfeder that winter, mentioned Agnes as another American employed in the apparatus when he solicited Kornfeder.[91] Kornfeder recalled Agnes as working for Soviet intelligence rather than the Comintern, but he was not entirely incorrect. While it would be a few years before Comintern and purely Soviet intelligence officially merged, the distinction was rapidly becoming one without a difference—a fact well known to Mirov-Abramov, whose department was at the nexus of the merger.

During her month in Moscow, Agnes wangled an invitation for Sanger from the Ministry of Health; she also toured schools, hospitals, factories, and homes for the *bezprizorni*, attended the opera and theater, and visited some of the new collective farms that were being established near Moscow. Over the next few years, the policy would turn the nation's mighty state machine against millions of Russian peasants—uprooting and displacing them, stealing their land and everything else they had gained in the revolution. But in 1928, Agnes could not tolerate criticism of the world's first socialist state.

Goldman would later lament that her friend's conversion to Communism "killed all other feelings in her, as it does to everyone who is infected with that virus."[92] Does that explain why someone formerly so outspokenly resentful of oppression wherever she saw could now look the other way at abuses in the USSR, and counter criticism of the regime with questions about outsiders' silence regarding White Guard army atrocities against the Russian people and foreign invasions of the USSR?[93] Or had her position simply gone to her head? Most likely it was some of both, along with gratitude for Moscow's commitment to Asia's liberation. Over the next few years, though, as Agnes envisioned the USSR ushering in an egalitarian world order, she described Moscow, based on her impression, as her "own beloved city," and if she were ever to leave China, she wrote Ernest (which she doubted would be the case), it would only be for the Soviet Union, "the grandest, most inspiring place on earth."[94]

CHAPTER 8

Comintern Agent in China

No longer are you Karl Schmitt of Berlin...Anna Kyersk of Kazan...Peter
Savich of Moscow. You are without a name, without a mother, blank sheets
on which the Revolution will write its orders.

He who fights for Communism must be able to fight and to renounce
fighting, to say the truth and not to say the truth, to be helpful and unhelp-
ful, to keep a promise and to break a promise, to go into danger and to avoid
danger, to be known and to be unknown. He who fights for Communism
has of all virtues only one: that he fights for Communism.

DIE MASSNAHME, TRANSLATION BY ARTHUR KOESTLER

Traveling via Siberia, Agnes reached the Sino-Soviet border in the
closing days of 1928. She went through customs in Manchouli, then turned
to face a scene she later recalled as straight from the Middle Ages. "Chinese
coolies...clothed in rags, scrambling and shouting, threw themselves on our
bags and began fighting over each piece. Five or six fell upon my four suitcases
and two struggled for my small typewriter...Inside, six men crowded about me,
holding out their hands and shouting for money," she wrote.[1] Agnes said she
paid them handsomely to be rid of them, but the coolies sensed her discomfort
and lingered—shouting, threatening, and menacing her with their fists—until a
Chinese trainman literally kicked them off her train.

Only days before her arrival, Young Marshal Chang Hsueh-liang , the Mukden militarist who controlled the three northeastern provinces of Manchuria,
had accepted the formal sovereignty of the Nanking government. This act
would allow Generalissimo Chiang Kai-shek to claim that the KMT had established centralized control throughout the country. Agnes said she regretted having missed out on the action. In China, she wrote Ernest, there was "enough to
make you fight, and I certainly would have been in it."

With the Nationalist flag flying from southern Canton to northern Mukden,
Chiang had succeeded, nominally, in consolidating China's government—the
goal of the Northern Expedition undertaken two years earlier. However, Sun

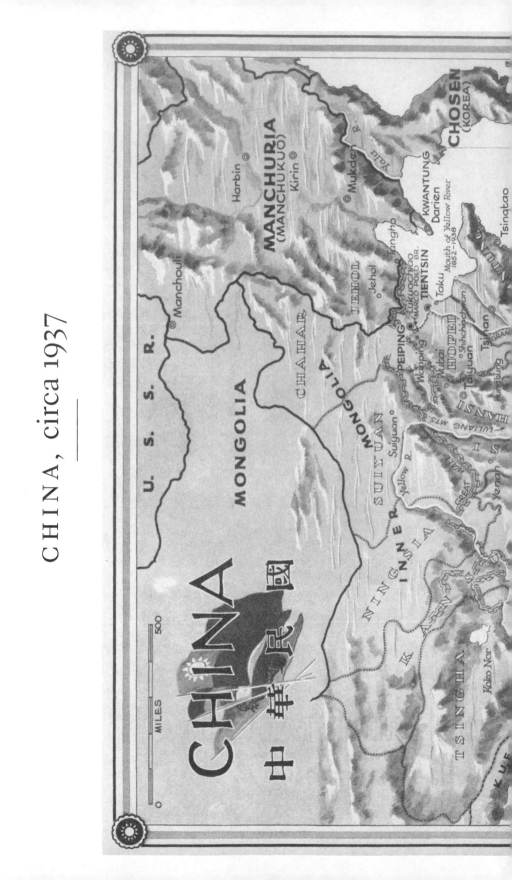

CHINA, circa 1937

CREDIT: Map by Vaughn Gray, from *Battle Hymn of China* by Agnes Smedley; copyright 1943 by Agnes Smedley; renewed 1971. Used by permission of Alfred A. Knopf, a division of Random House.

Yat-sen's dream of reunification was in many ways still a dream. The Young Marshal's cooperation in Manchuria brought great prestige to the Nationalist government, but most of the country remained controlled by troops loyal to generals other than Chiang. The regional militarists across China who had assisted in Chiang's ascent were loath to surrender the control on which they depended, or the semi-independent status they enjoyed in their home territories, and Chiang's intent to eliminate all armed opposition complicated the picture. In making the army the government's strongest component, equally pressing matters would also go unresolved or unaddressed.

At the Nationalists' capital in Nanking, KMT officials spoke of their desire for constitutional, representative rule. In practice, the country was run without elective or popular support. Chiang Kai-shek served as chair of the State Council (the ruling body that constituted the top level of the administration), ex-officio president of the Nationalist government, chair of the standing committee of the KMT central executive committee, and commander-in-chief of the Nationalist armies. To consolidate power in his hands, he played off factional divisions between the army and the civil bureaucracy. At the KMT's Central Political Institute and cadre training schools, personal loyalty to Chiang was as vital as the anti-Communism and anti-imperialist nationalism taught.

Extremely high debt payments and out-of-control military expenses made economic reconstruction a vital issue for the national government. However, while efforts were under way to create more modern monetary and banking systems, improve taxation, and encourage industry and commerce, a rise in customs revenues gained when the KMT won full tariff autonomy could not offset its failure to collect income taxes or land revenues. Since foreign corporations could not be taxed beyond a certain level, Chinese entrepreneurs bore the brunt of industrial taxes, and opium sales, prostitution, and organized crime were major sources of revenue.

In the large cities, Chiang's anti-Communist White Terror, which threatened opponents of the regime with constant arrest and execution, had decimated the Chinese Communist Party. Nearly a quarter of a million citizens, mostly left-wing workers and trade union activists, had been killed since Chiang turned on the Communists in April of 1927. The Comintern had ordered the CCP central committee, now driven underground in Shanghai, to reorganize the party, get new members, create new organizations, and organize workers in the country's industrial centers. However, at the start of 1929 only thirteen hundred workers in Shanghai still belonged to the CCP, and the state of affairs was equally dismal in other urban centers.

On university campuses, a governmental "control" bureau, working through the Ministry of Education, fostered a coercive atmosphere to discourage student unrest. Intellectual repression and attacks on Communists, however, failed to persuade students, intellectuals, or urban workers that the KMT was fulfilling its mission of reuniting the country and providing economic reform. In the countryside, increasingly desperate peasants were offering Communist forces significant support.

While urban CCP leaders complied with Moscow's request to focus on foreign imperialism and Japanese aggression, tyrannical, corrupt provincial administrators, conscription, heavy taxation, and a collapsing export market for commercial crops were eroding economic conditions in China's interior. In the absence of meaningful reforms by the KMT, infant mortality was high, life expectancy was low, education was virtually nonexistent, and such cruel customs as foot binding and arranged marriage still endured. Rural Communist leaders like Mao Tse-tung and Chu Teh were making inroads. Less forgiving than their urban counterparts of the Comintern's misadventures in China, they continued to see the peasants rather than the urban proletariat (as the Soviets envisioned) as the key to China's future, and they were less inclined to follow Moscow's orders. Their initial attempts at agrarian revolution and armed struggle against the KMT had failed, but at the moment the men's motley army of ten thousand, operating under the banner of peasant soviets in Hunan and south Kiangsi, was the only revolutionary force functioning in China.

Agnes reached her first OMS posting at Harbin in late December. A drought and famine that would ultimately claim the lives of twenty million Chinese was then ravaging nine of China's northern provinces, and on her arrival Agnes was beset by throngs of peasant women who had emigrated from their rural villages to escape starvation or avoid being sold into slavery. Their babies tucked inside their dirty jackets, they dropped to their knees before her, she wrote, and pleaded for alms. Once more, Agnes said, she gave generously in the hopes of clearing her path, only to find new crowds materialize from out of nowhere. Children, too, pursued her, beating their heads on the icy pavement as they begged. When she finally escaped into a rickshaw, she wrote, its puller refused to move until she paid off numerous people who clung to its sides.

"The certainty of finding influential friends anywhere in the world gives active Communists a wonderful sense of belonging to a great secret order," a contemporary of Agnes's observed.[2] Agnes found her passage through Manchuria smoothed by a number of student guides, nearly all of them urban CCP members driven underground since the disastrous turn of events in 1927. Trained by the Soviets to perform many of the tasks formerly undertaken by Russian agents, these young Chinese served as her translators, delivered her to the homes of sympathetic countrymen, and otherwise enabled her to perform her clandestine tasks.[3] Despite the dangerous times, Agnes's known Comintern ties encouraged personal interaction of a sort generally off limits to foreigners, and in the evenings after work they all socialized.[4] Her student guides, part of a new intelligentsia that had emerged at the end of the Ching dynasty barely a generation earlier, had been exposed to Western culture, and Agnes wrote with pleasure that they taught her "a lot" about modern dancing.[5]

Agnes's affection for her acquaintances was evident in her description of the northern Chinese as a "grand, grand people"—tall, strong, handsome, intelligent, and active—but there remained great tension in the air. In exchange for the Young Marshal's cooperation, Chiang Kai-shek had promised him autonomy in Manchuria—in open defiance of Japanese wishes. The arrangement and its possible consequences were of great concern to the Soviets, who feared possible Japanese aggression at their border and a potentially formidable alliance among the imperialist Great Powers, based on their shared hostility to the Russian and Chinese revolutions. Most vulnerable, from the Soviets' perspective, was the Chinese Eastern Railway, built in northern Manchuria during tsarist times with Russian funds and engineers and presently run as a joint Sino-Soviet enterprise.

In January 1929, Chinese authorities raided Soviet offices in Harbin, arresting several trade union officials whom they suspected to be Soviet agents and confirming Russian fears of an impending crisis.[6] During this time, Agnes met secretly and openly with Japanese Communists and factory workers, Chinese Eastern Railway officials, underground Chinese Communists ("Chinese patriots," Agnes called them), former KMT officials, military men, and students—assisted by the German consul general and her student guides and protected by her American passport and association with the *Frankfurter Zeitung*. The American consul found her keen interest in Chinese politics and deep understanding of the Manchurian-Mongolian problem so unnerving that he relayed concern about Agnes's presence in Harbin to the U.S. secretary of state.[7]

Agnes later claimed that a study she authored at this time on Japanese economic and political control over railways, government machinery, and industrial and real estate investments in Manchuria was written for the *Frankfurter Zeitung*. The paper, she would say, questioned her accuracy and did not run it until Japan invaded three years later. More likely this report, like several others Agnes drafted on Manchuria, was written for the OMS.[8] Most of her earliest pieces for the *Zeitung*, though, were feature stories, profiles like the one below.

She was a miserable-looking foot-bound woman refugee from the Shantung famine, begging in the streets. Hobbling along on her tiny feet over the frozen street, she slipped and fell, and landed sitting, sprawled out directly in the middle of the chief street of the city. A small bag of bread burst and scattered in every direction.

The street was filled with men who saw the accident. Not one came forward to help. Instead, they began to laugh, and the policeman on the corner watched and laughed with them. Three young beau brummels, dressed in expensive silk tunics, smart little black jackets and tight little black silk hats, joined the crowd. All laughed.

The peasant woman did not move a leg. But she braced herself with her hands and surveyed the crowd as a general might survey a battle-field. Then she began. She cursed the assembled men, all their ancestors back to the beginning of time, and all the brats they would send into the world in the future. What she said to them and the way she said it froze up the laughter on their faces—as if a sudden blast of Siberian weather had struck them. They began to hurry away, some half paralyzed from surprise and shock. And as they went the voice of the peasant woman followed them with her best wishes. New men turned the corner and, seeing her sitting there, began to laugh. But she turned her tongue on them, their laughter froze up, and they also hurried past as fast as their feet could carry them.

Then, with infinite trouble and misery, she managed to scramble onto her tiny, pin-like feet again. A child who had been standing by throughout helped her, gathered up the bread, and the two of them hobbled out of sight.[9]

Unaccustomed to Chinese ways, Agnes often approached her subjects with a candor that left them agape. In an interview with the president of Harbin's chamber of commerce, for example, an illicit opium dealer, she said she inquired how much a particular village smoked on a given week.

Dressed in his long blue fur-lined silk gown, he sat on the edge of his chair, his hands braced on his knees, and stared at me as a snake watches a bird. Recovering his composure, he graciously announced that it was an honor to meet a foreign lady who took an interest in Chinese affairs. My life must be bitter and I surely found the cold weather distressing...

"Did I enjoy good health, and did I like China?" he asked... "Had I seen the very old pagoda near the city?"...

He smiled pleasantly and assured me that it had been an honor to make my acquaintance and he hoped I would call again, although he felt certain my important work would make that impossible. He rose and with elaborate courtesy bowed me out of the building, down the walk and out of the gate![10]

It would take time and effort, Agnes wrote, before she learned to loosen recalcitrant Chinese tongues through seemingly endless hours of social interaction.

On January 11, 1929, Harbin consular officials received a confidential report from Mukden, which warned that Agnes might be "a Russian Communist travelling on an American passport."[11] As such, it advised, she needed to be watched closely. Within days, a Chinese comrade with a contact inside the American Consulate informed Agnes of the document's existence, she said. Since she had recently addressed a public gathering on the current unrest in India, she suspected the hand of the British and fired off letters of protest to Gilbert Roe and other well-placed American friends.

Although Agnes had, in fact, left Moscow in 1921 under the alias "Petroikas," she wrote that the name "Petrovsky," which appeared in the report, was "a mystery" to her. She maintained, somewhat disingenuously, that she had neither used nor heard the latter before; perhaps, she suggested, the "ever-busy British Secret Service" had confused her with the wife of M. N. Roy.[12] Since she had come to China under the impression that her American citizenship and passport afforded her protection, she hotly observed to Sanger, she wished her friend would lodge a complaint "with the American Embassy, or Legation, or whatever it is, in Peking."[13]

Having staked out her public posture, Agnes prepared to depart. Her comrade's source had warned her, she said, that she was about to be summoned before American authorities. Under the circumstances, little would be gained by pursuing the matter further. In early February 1929, Agnes joined the "great international brotherhood of people who 'ran away' in China," as she later put it.[14] In the future, she vowed to avoid Americans and American consulates in China "like the pest," restricting her contacts to Germans, who had a professional obligation to protect their correspondent, and sympathetic Chinese.

Agnes's next stop was Mukden, a medieval city with steel-studded gates that were shut from midnight to daybreak. Agnes's student guide had arranged for her to stay here with a Chinese family whose son belonged to the CCP. Like many of the households in which she resided, theirs was marked by conflict. During the first years of the Chinese Republic, educational reforms and the elimination of the examination system had enabled thousands of Chinese to study in Europe and the United States, where they were introduced to Western concepts of individual liberty and equality. This new class of intellectuals, who assumed important positions on their return to China, no longer accepted without question all aspects of Chinese culture and traditional ethics. Although they and the students they influenced exerted a modernizing force on Chinese society, disequilibrium currently reigned.

On a domestic level, Agnes wrote, fathers who wanted concubines or parents who expected their daughter-in-law to stand while they ate were clashing with once-dutiful offspring no longer willing to obey their parents' wishes or embrace their values. Agnes took copious notes on the men, but it was the women who really interested her—not just the hungry and wretched ones but the modern females with shingled hair, who smoked and had studied abroad, along with the young Communists she described in the composite sketch below.

Across the great historical stage on which the Chinese revolution is being played, appears and reappears the figure of a woman.

At first the figure looks delicate and the hands as frail as those of a child; but one sees more clearly, the slender body, of a little more than ordinary height, looks tough and wiry and the hands but thin from constant labor. The hair, smooth and black as a soft summer's night, is sometimes cropped close as a boy's, sometimes grown longer and clasped at the nape of the neck in a narrow brooch of green. At times the figure is clad in the uniform of a soldier, at other times in the faded cotton trousers and jacket of a woman of the masses; and at still other times in the elegant silk gown of a lady of the ruling classes.

This slight figure, now clad in a long silk gown that falls in an unbroken line from the throat to the ankles, turns her face to us. The face belies the costume. For here is none of the expressionless, doll-like beauty, or the cold passive indifference, or any of the calculating selfishness or cruelty that characterize the faces of women of the ruling classes. Instead, the face turned toward us is lit by some life that gives the eyes and entire countenance an expression of some living, burning conviction. It is a face of inspired intelligence. The eyes, black and shining, see everything, understand everything. In every action of the figure, in every word uttered on this vast historical stage, are expressed two forces: one love and passion; the other, a conviction that is hard and unyielding in its purpose.

The woman may speak for herself... It is best that [she] speak quickly, lest tragedy overtake her and silence her tongue forever. [15]

At Japanese-owned factories, mines, and schools for Chinese, Agnes said, she often heard Japanese express contempt for the Chinese but was reluctant to call attention to herself by kicking up a fuss until she heard from Roe. As it was, she was certain she was being watched by at least two secret services, and she believed that one of the British spies with which she said China was "lousy" had already paid a servant to poison her. Despite the danger, she had no intention of abandoning her journey.

From Mukden, Agnes traveled to Japanese-controlled Dairen, where, she later said, two Japanese kept her under constant surveillance. She would claim that the trip was too risky for a Chinese guide to join her, but a man Agnes later described as an Irish sea captain "friend" (who more likely worked with the Comintern) was there to help her; he also perhaps facilitated a meeting between her and departing PPTUS chief Earl Browder, who was in Dairen at the same time as Agnes, and at her subsequent stop in Tientsin as well.[16]

Peking, where Agnes alighted next, was the temporary headquarters of the PPTUS in China, and here she was a veritable whirlwind of activity. Most of her time, she reported, was spent interviewing Chinese Communist teachers, railroad workers, student organizers, and left-wing KMT and attending secret planning meetings for strikes and other protest activities. The reports she filed covered everything from China's system of contract labor to the government-sanctioned "Yellow" trade unions, along with the "brother" and "sister" societies that Communists were organizing to skirt the ban on "Red" trade union organizing, and the superstitions and regional issues that thwarted their efforts.[17] At the same time—to the consternation of British officials—she continued to speak in public on India's nationalist movement. She also met with Americans and Chinese who were interested in the possibility of birth control work in China. The major obstacle here, she wrote Sanger, was not convincing people of its need; they were already convinced. Rather, it lay in "the actual carrying out of the plan, with methods cheap enough and certain enough for China."[18]

In the years since she began taking pictures in San Diego, Agnes had become a good photographer, and in Peking she shot a great deal of film for what she described as a collection of photo essays on "toiling" China, in which Muenzenberg's people had expressed interest. At a local factory, she captured child workers who had been sold into slavery by their destitute parents. Now they worked twelve hours a day filling matchboxes in exchange for two meals of millet gruel and a nightly spot in barracks-like rooms that afforded them little protection from the elements.

One day while she was visiting Peking, Agnes lost her footing crossing a ditch. As she lay on the ground, unable to get up, she said, the curious stares of the gathering crowd—who never offered to help—made her suddenly realize how alone she was in China. She might not consider herself any different from the masses of ordinary Chinese, but she could see that she was just another wealthy foreigner to them: well dressed, well fed, "nothing but a source of money," as she put it.

During her stay in the city, Agnes trolled for contacts among a set of Chinese patricians—writers, activists, and feminists educated in America and England who were curious to learn the latest in Western thought. Of them, Agnes seemed fondest of Hsu Tze Mou, whom she described as being "as elegant and charming a lyric poet as ever left a trail of pining hearts around the globe."[19]

Cofounder of the influential literary journal *Crescent Moon*, Hsu was a romantic bohemian five years Agnes's junior who, according to Agnes, was a revolutionary in matters of love and sex, but wealthy and a social conservative. Normally Hsu's belief in art for art's sake would have repelled her, but she was lonely, and the two of them whiled away many hours in Peking's teahouses, restaurants, and theaters.

As a foreigner, no longer young or beautiful, and a woman who earned her own living and associated with men as their equal, Agnes had none of the attributes Hsu usually sought in a female companion, and she said he told her as much. It was the first time she had heard herself described as too old to be sexually desirable, and it shocked her. Although she had recently turned thirty-seven, she said she felt younger now than she had when she lived in New York. She was not ready for men to confide in her as if she were their mother. In many ways, she wrote, she still felt she was not a grown-up. "There is such an awful gap between my feelings and my age," she told Florence.[20] She handled the situation gracefully, however, and became Hsu's confidante, making a game of selecting women she thought he might find beautiful. She claimed that Hsu regretted she was not a man so he could introduce her to Peking's demimonde.

Agnes found the company of such cultured intellectuals diverting, but their teahouse philosophizing and passive despair at the confusion in contemporary Chinese life disturbed her. Since she never forgot that Chinese society rested on the backs of men and women not far removed from slavery, she resented what she felt was her new friends' acceptance of the government's inadequate political philosophy, Chiang's autocratic rule, and the deteriorating national economy. At a wine-sodden banquet they held in her honor before she left the city, Hsu bestowed Agnes with the Chinese name Shih Mei Di Li, a transliteration of her Western one. She repaid their hospitality with a full-throated rendition of "The Streets of Laredo." But as rickshaw coolies brought them home through the snowy streets, Agnes insisted that her acquaintances prove their earlier claim that there was no class system in China by decamping from their vehicles and pulling their coolies in them.[21]

Agnes reached Nanking, capital of Chiang Kai-shek's China, in early March 1929. She wrote that with leftist workers and intellectuals being dragged from their beds and tortured or beheaded in the streets, she dared not put any Chinese at risk by staying in their homes. Outwardly she even tolerated the official the KMT sent as her guide. She was not without resources of her own, though. Chen Han-seng, a salty-tongued agrarian research scholar who had been recruited by the Russians as a Comintern intelligence agent three years earlier, was already familiar with what he termed her "unusual connection" to the German Communists when he met her.[22] While Chen was sympathetic to China's revolutionary movement, he was not a known CCP member at this time, and his fluent English made him most useful to Agnes as she interviewed left-wing academics and underground Chinese Communists about the agricultural reforms that were then being touted by the Nanking government.

Although agriculture was China's major economic activity and source of revenue, the peasants who worked the soil (and comprised 85 percent of China's population) owned that land in theory only. In practice, fundamental problems in the system of land tenure forced them into tenant farming. They lived in debt to usurious landlords who demanded as much as 50 percent of their crops as rent and additional "presents" throughout the year; local officials, at the same time, taxed them at exorbitant rates. In Kansu province, for example, peasants were subjected to forty-four different taxes. "Even where the tax collector left something or the perennial warfare had missed some farmlands," one historian observed, "an ill-paid, hungry and unruly soldiery often extorted, looted and killed."[23]

Chen took Agnes to villages on the outskirts of Nanking so that she could see for herself the disorderly mud huts, fronted by open sewers, in which the peasants lived. Human feces were used as fertilizer, and almost every villager appeared to have a skin disease. The children, she would write, had scabby heads and boils.[24] Their poverty surpassed her comprehension.

In Nanking, Agnes began to receive her correspondence again. It was the first mail she had gotten since the secret report on her had surfaced three months earlier, and Agnes's responses registered her shock and outrage. She now understood, she wrote Roe, that basic principles of right and justice she had formerly considered inalienable were the result of centuries of the fiercest struggle. "We can be forced right down into the slime again, if men strong enough were in power," she remarked in an allusion to Chiang. China, she said, had opened her eyes to depths of suffering she had previously thought unimaginable, and always there was the Terror.

Those who spoke of a renaissance in China, she wrote Florence, were clearly uninformed. To her, the country's handling of political matters was more reminiscent of the Machiavellian period; its social conditions dated from the time of the Borgias. The chief problem facing officials, she remarked, was not "whether a man should be killed or not, but how wide and long the trench is in which the bodies are to be thrown."

Roe had advised Agnes to confront the American consul directly about the accusations that appeared in the report and her subsequent scrutiny by government officials. Unlike Roe, however, Agnes understood that her situation in China could not bear much scrutiny, and she demurred. "It is not that I fear anything at all, or fear the final outcome," she noted. "It is simply that the report in Manchuria showed so definitely that it came from the British Secret Service, and that the American Consul was cooperating with them in 'watching' me. I don't want to be watched, even when I am doing perfectly legitimate things as I am in China."[25] Still, the fact that the Americans might be observing her here on behalf of the British made her "so almighty angry," she wrote, that she was ready to blow up a consulate.

Had Agnes known the full story, she would have been angrier still. The previous month, an article in the Nationalist Chinese *Harbin Dawning* had reiterated the original charge—that Agnes was a Russian citizen traveling on an American passport—and accused her further of being a naturalized German citizen and Chatto's lawful wife. It was an ominous statement because, if it could be proven, it made Agnes liable to arrest by the British government of India as a political offender and imperiled her American citizenship. Ruth Shipley, the crusading anti-Communist who directed the State Department's passport division, was already investigating the case, and when she discovered Agnes's name in an old police file on New York radicals, she grew suspicious.[26]

Now that she was again receiving her mail, Agnes learned that *Daughter of Earth* had been released in the United States, Germany, and the Netherlands to overwhelmingly positive reviews. There had been some questions about whether the book was fiction or autobiography, and the lack of perspective in the second half had been commented on. But the *New York Times* had compared Agnes's Marie favorably to Thomas Hardy's Tess; the *New York Herald Tribune* would declare *Daughter of Earth* "one of the few great [stories] of an American woman"; and the *New Republic* pronounced it a "record of experience so authentic, so intense, that it burns itself indelibly into the mind of the reader, and leaves him with a sense of wonder at the enduring quality of the human fabric, and with a deep resentment at human cruelty and injustice."[27]

The serialized version was scheduled to appear in the *Frankfurter Zeitung* that fall, and additional translations were anticipated for China, the Soviet Union, and, eventually, a dozen other countries. Agnes still worried about its ability to reach beyond her former circle of Village radicals. In April 1929, she could not anticipate how the ranks of radicals would swell as the Wall Street crash in October and the world depression that followed would drive the political climate to the left. Even less could she imagine that a new American literary aesthetic, influenced by the Russian and German literary trends to which Agnes had already been exposed, would make her *the* female role model for America's left literary lions, hailed by one contemporary critic as the "mother of women's literary radicalism" in the United States and author of its "first truly proletarian novel."[28]

In an essay that ignited much debate, *New Masses* editor Mike Gold had called for the emergence of a different kind of "Red" writer: one with a firsthand knowledge of working-class life. His writing would be "no conscious straining after proletarian art, but the natural flower of his environment," Gold wrote, and he would speak with authority, however crudely, of his experience in America's tenements, factories, lumber camps, and steel mills.[29] Agnes was that man, or rather, that woman.

Before her book was even out, *New Masses* was recommending *Daughter of Earth* to its readers alongside Upton Sinclair's *King Coal* and John Dos Passos's *42nd Parallel*, describing her work as equal in stature to Sinclair's *The Jungle* and the best of Jack London. No other woman had written like that before, it proclaimed; no other novel was as "bitterly, beautifully drawn from the fibre of life."[30] Agnes's attempt to grapple with the issue of gender consciousness would soon enough pose problems for more orthodox Party theoreticians. For now, though, they saw her book as the first of what they hoped would be many great proletarian novels produced by American women from the working class.

Agnes left Nanking in late spring. Shanghai in summer would be viciously hot, but she had things to do in the coastal metropolis. Toward that end, she asked her friend Ellen Kennan (who, like Agnes, had recently exchanged her anarcho-syndicalist views for Communist ones) to send her the names and addresses of any trustworthy persons she knew there. If she needed a break from the heat, Agnes said, her friend Hsu Tze Mou had invited her to Peking, or she would visit Hankow, former site of the Wuhan government.

Agnes reached Shanghai in May 1929. It was a place where East met West but neither prevailed. Ornate skyscrapers traced the Bund, the waterfront's famous curve, and they housed grand foreign firms, banks, and department stores, but rickshaws still jousted with American luxury cars on its storied streets. And the Whanghoo River, a Yangtze tributary that formed the core and artery of the city, gave it a distinctive scent. Beyond the Bund lay the old walled Chinese city, its narrow lanes choked with beggars, fortune tellers, letter writers, elderly men airing pet birds in bamboo cages, dank specialty shops, brides in red-lacquer sedan chairs, noisy teahouses, fusty temples, and incense and spirit money peddlers.

By Chinese standards, Shanghai was a very young city, having come into its own only in the twentieth century. Its reputation for dissolution, rapacity, and squalor was rivaled only by inflationary-mad Berlin. Shanghai was also extraordinarily diverse. Nearly fifty thousand White Russians, British, French, Americans, Indians, Portuguese, Germans, and Japanese supplemented a core population of 2.5 million Chinese. The latter consisted of both native-born

Shanghai waterfront in the early 1930s. *From the collections of the Library of Congress.*

Shanghaiese and recent émigrés looking to escape the wars and natural disasters that were decimating the country's interior.

For the coolies and factory workers who labored in the city, Shanghai was an experience of unrelenting misery. For the Comintern, it remained the best spot to rekindle China's faltering revolution. The KMT-CCP split and subsequent rupture in diplomatic relations between China and the USSR had caused a massive breakdown in Comintern structure and activity, but Marxist theory demanded an industrial proletariat as a prerequisite for revolution, and Shanghai was the only city in China to have one of any consequence. Birthplace of the Chinese Communist Party, Shanghai had also been notably hospitable to revolutionaries during the first wave of the Chinese Revolution, when it was infiltrated by Communist workers and sheltered its heroes.

However, it was the city's treaty port status, which allowed Agnes and the handful of other Comintern operatives trickling back into China to enter without a passport or visa and operate beyond the reach of Chinese law, that was its greatest lure. Several wars and treaties had given a number of foreign powers a variety of unusual privileges for their nationals in China over the last seventy-five years. These included concession areas where nationals and subjects of the "treaty powers" could live or operate business enterprises while bound to the civil and criminal laws of their native countries.

One reason patriotic Chinese so bitterly opposed the "unequal treaties" was that only seven and a half of Shanghai's twenty square miles were under Chinese control. The rest was run by municipal authorities in the British-controlled International Settlement or in the French Concession. The existence of foreign troops on Chinese soil, foreign naval vessels on Chinese rivers, and ports that enforced treaty rights were examples of the foreign imperialism against which the KMT had rebelled under the direction of Soviet adviser Michael Borodin, but Communists still exploited the extraterritorial status that protected foreign radicals like Agnes in Shanghai. Even now, under the wholesale butcheries that marked the KMT's campaign of terror, patriots, rebels, and conspirators were as endemic to the city as gamblers and gangsters.

As she made her way from the station, Agnes watched in horror as a turbaned Sikh policeman beat a group of coolies straining to haul goods onto a handcart, in order to clear space for the limousine of a foreign official. Gertrude Binder, Scott Nearing's young American lover, met Agnes's train. Binder would recall that Agnes struck her on first impression as "slightly hysterical," but her plain-spoken humor soon won Binder over. "Who cares if I read all that trash?" she said Agnes boasted of her ignorance of classical Marxism. "I know who the enemy is, and that's enough."[31]

Binder lived in the French Concession, a slice of tree-lined avenues wedged between the International Settlement and the old Chinese city. The community was home to Du Yue-sheng, an immensely powerful gangster whose toughs had helped Chiang Kai-shek secure Shanghai in 1927; it also shielded a roaring opium trade, numerous conspirators, and the city's White Russian community. Lacking the protection of citizenship or extraterritorial status, the latter often pulled rickshaws, begged, or sold their bodies to survive.

During her first weeks in Shanghai, Agnes took hundreds of photographs for her picture book of "toiling" China. She also introduced herself to other foreign journalists, among them Edgar Snow, a compact, energetic twenty-three-year-old who was filling in at the English-language *China Weekly Review* while the paper's managing editor covered the hostilities that had recently erupted (as Agnes predicted) in Manchuria. As a way, most likely, to return to north China and see the events for herself without arousing further suspicion, Agnes asked Edgar Snow whether she might cover the famine for them there. Unlike other American correspondents in China, however, Agnes had never attended journalism school—and she was female. Snow proposed instead that she draft some book reviews for them, like the ones she wrote for the Indian *Modern Review*.

At the moment, the Comintern was more concerned with the threat to Soviet interests implicit in a Chinese takeover of the Chinese Eastern Railway, and the possibility of a war against the Soviet Union, than it was with China's revolution, but it had instructed the CCP to restore its urban proletariat base.

The Chinese youth who facilitated the work of the Party underground in Shanghai delivered Agnes to Ch'en Yun, the assistant to Chou En-lai, who was then directing its activities.[32] Unlike other operatives in Shanghai, who maintained connections with either the Comintern or the CCP, Agnes would work with both, and she began to assist the Chinese Party by serving as a channel for information from the USSR and by providing her room for use as a mail drop and liaison point.[33] According to Hsia Yan, who was then an organizer for the CCP, leaders of the Party's central committee treated Agnes as they would a privileged Party member, despite her lack of formal affiliation, since her Comintern affiliation was well known.[34]

In time, Agnes developed contacts not only in Shanghai but in Hankow and Canton. As instructed, she tracked those issues in China's larger cities and industrial centers of concern to the Comintern, transmitting her reports for the OMS to Soviet boats in the Shanghai harbor.[35] Police agents of various countries eyed Agnes warily; the Germans suspected she was organizing a Shanghai branch of the All China Labor Federation (Chinese affiliate of the PPTUS).[36] She quickly learned some tradecraft. According to one of the co-conspirators she trained, Agnes would scale the roof on one side of her apartment building, then

Near the time of Agnes's arrival in Shanghai. *Courtesy Agnes Smedley Collection, University Archives, Arizona State University.*

enter her apartment from a stairway that led down the other—always avoiding the elevator and exiting through a different hallway.[37] The skill with which Agnes carried out her tasks accorded her "a very high standing in the Secret Department of the Comintern," an associate of Muenzenberg's later reported.[38]

Between her photo project, her Comintern duties, and the assistance she rendered the CCP underground in Shanghai while it battled for survival under Chiang Kai-shek's White Terror, Agnes was too busy to fulfill her contractual obligations to the *Zeitung*, let alone establish a birth control clinic as Sanger wished. Her clandestine activities made her so anxious she suffered constant nervous headaches and gastric distress, and in the cities it must often have felt like a losing battle. Meanwhile, in the snow-covered mountains of Chingkan-shan, deep in China's interior, a few thousand starving, freezing, poorly equipped Red Army troops, comprised for the most part of dispossessed peas-ants, jobless farmers, mutinous soldiers, and local bandits, had accomplished a miraculous feat. Acting without the support—or sometimes the knowledge—of CCP leaders in Shanghai, partisan forces under the command of the guerrilla leaders Mao Tse-tung, Chu Teh, and P'eng Teh-huai had abandoned their for-mer base and established a central soviet district in a remote area of south Kiangsi.

Modeled on the 1905 Russian Revolution, when representatives from facto-ries had met and sought alliance with revolutionary political parties, peasants, and soldiers, the Kiangsi soviet was both a fighting organization and a primitive form of democratic government by the masses. It combined legislative and exec-utive powers in its administration, passing laws and carrying them out, and was backed by its own armed force. Through a radical program of land redistribu-tion, it was winning the support of local peasants, and other Red pockets were forming in numerous scattered, rural territories in China's interior. Accounts of the goings-on had begun to trickle into CCP headquarters in Shanghai.

As Agnes enthusiastically recounted soon after:

By the time 1928 passed and the early months of 1929 came, the Communists had extended their power until the peasants and workers in the valleys and even in the town of Lungkang to the east had turned on the White [KMT] troops ... and chased them from the land. Far and wide Partisan warfare flared up and peasants and workers fought with spears or knives or with cap-tured rifles. In the whole region along the big Kan river to the west, right to the gates of Kian city, there was ceaseless fighting between the peasants and Kuomingtang troops ...

... As the Red Army led by Chu Teh and Mao Tse-tung marched toward Tungku and Hsinkwo districts following their victory at Tapoteh, peasants in territory held by Kuomintang troops began to hold secret meetings. When the Red Army approached they would fall upon the White troops and fight; and when the Red Army finally marched in they would find towns or villages in the hands of peasants and workers and a few intellectuals—always with many dead and wounded. The living victors...had no mind for celebrations. All they asked was arms, arms, arms! They knew the Red Army could not remain with them long, and if the Whites dared return they must be ready to meet them.

The Red troops would give the few guns they could spare, instruct the peasants and workers in their use, and march onward.[39]

The desperate courage of these illiterate renegades, who battled enemy troops in unexpected guerrilla raids, using empty rifles, stones, and tree limbs when their ammunition gave out, along with the establishment of the Kiangsi soviet, were an inspiration to Agnes. The Nationalist government viewed the Red Army and its followers as criminals; even the CCP central committee was dubious. But for Agnes their stories, like the outlaw myths of Jesse James on which she had fed as a youth, suggested they were *good* badmen—men motivated by idealism rather than selfishness, men who preferred to die on their feet rather than live on their knees. From her perspective, these Chinese Robin Hoods broke the law in service to a higher cause, bespeaking freedom and independence in a country oppressed from within and without.

The men's defiant resistance to crippling conditions made more sense to Agnes than the intrigues of Shanghai's impotent leadership, and the hope they held out to the country's most sorely pressed citizens satisfied her yearning for a more moral world, one that extended social justice and liberty to all. If this rag-tag army succeeded in arousing in people a sufficient spirit of revolt, then the next wave of China's revolution would occur not in the cities but in the countryside, and among China's peasants rather than its working class. Moreover, it would demand military rather than political action—not at all what the Comintern envisioned. For the moment, however, Agnes's Comintern ties were to the CCP faction based in Shanghai, which hewed to Moscow's orders. Mao's group, geographically remote, remained off limits.

On the first of June 1929, the mortal remains of Sun Yat-sen were laid in their final resting place in the Western Hills outside Nanking, and Agnes acquired another useful contact. Sun's widow, the former Soong Ching-ling, was an outspoken opponent of Chiang Kai-shek, who was married to her younger sister. Madame Sun was also close to Muenzenberg and the Comintern's China activities.[40] According to Muenzenberg deputy Louis Gibarti, who had known Madame Sun since 1926, when he was organizing the founding conference of the League Against Imperialism, she was "for all practical purposes... a Communist." Although Mrs. Sun Yat-sen was not openly a Party member, he would explain, "she accept[ed] instructions from, and was under the discipline of the Chinese Communist Party."[41]

Agnes and Madame Sun had already met in Berlin two years previously, but they became reacquainted in Nanking when Madame Sun returned to China to attend her husband's memorial service. Agnes expressed reservations about the depth of Madame Sun's political understanding—since they were exactly the same age, Agnes felt free to judge the other woman as a peer—but she completely trusted her character and her integrity. By the time the two women returned to Shanghai a few days after the ceremony, they had embarked on what would prove—for a time—to be a very fruitful working relationship.

Madame Sun arranged for Chen Han-seng to begin tutoring Agnes on Chinese social, political, and economic conditions and advising her on the background of key Chinese. She also asked Kuo Mo-jo, whom Agnes described as China's foremost translator of socially conscious literature, to translate *Daughter of Earth* into Chinese and worked with Agnes to reestablish a China branch of the League Against Imperialism. By July, it was recruiting members and distributing propaganda.[42] In addition to providing the organization with written

Friend and colleague Madame Sun Yat-sen. *From the collections of the Library of Congress.*

reports, Agnes—working in concert with Chatto, with whom she remained in professional contact—also served as liaison to the LAI's Berlin headquarters, edited propaganda by local Indian revolutionists, and distributed to them money she received through the OMS courier system.[43] However, even as Agnes assumed her duties at the LAI, the organization was in eclipse.

That August, under the pretext of creating a less intellectual, more working-class organization, the Comintern purged the LAI's social democratic faction, including Nehru, and ordered it to join the International Red Aid. Agnes, in what was apparently an act of solidarity, published an article in the *Zeitung* on British attempts to suppress the organization's first annual "Anti-Imperialist War Day," so inflaming officials in the process that International Settlement police opened a file on her. In the months and years to come, the Moscow-based Comintern auxiliary, whose Russian leader lacked Muenzenberg's stature or ability, would assume responsibility for many of the China activities that the LAI had formerly controlled.

Several friends wrote that summer to tell Agnes they had enjoyed her book; she said that Nearing urged her to write another on her brother Johnnie. Not surprisingly, she also learned that her references to family transgressions had outraged relatives. To this day, she could not bring herself to write Ernest, but she apologized now to Florence for the "very bad job" she had done with her character. With *Daughter of Earth* soon to appear in Russian, and rumors that the Soviets planned to make it into a film, Agnes was rather full of herself. "So I'm in Zurich windows with Duse," she observed to Florence. "Oh well—maybe you should have said Duse was in the window with me!" In a review of Mike Gold's latest book, Agnes took the creator of America's proletarian literary aesthetic to task for being "strained and artificial" in his depictions of the masses, and when she contacted Upton Sinclair to inform him of arrangements she had made to have his books translated into Chinese, her tone made clear that she now saw herself on an equal footing with him.

Buoyed by her celebrity status, Agnes entered into a period of sexual promiscuity about which she was not at all secretive. "Out here," she wrote Florence, "I've had chances to sleep with all colours and shapes. One French gun-runner, short and round and bumpy; one fifty year old monarchist German who believes in the dominating role of the penis in influencing women; one high Chinese official whose actions I'm ashamed to describe, one round left-wing Kuomintang man who was soft and slobbery" and wore a fluttering white silk robe.[44] She also reportedly had an affair with Chen Han-seng and flirted with the writer Hu Shih.

Hu was married, but according to Agnes he had tremendous "BU"—Biological Urge, or sex drive—and a reputation as a serious ladies' man. "Between you and me," she confided to Sanger, "I'm capable of trying to break up his home."[45] Soon enough, though, she wrote that she had given him the "go-bye" and set her sights again on the poet Hsu Tze Mou—this time with more success. That's what men were for, Binder would recall her friend as saying, and if her preda- tory style rendered her partners impotent, Agnes laughingly derided them as "empty pants" and moved on.[46] Even as she boasted of her sexual conquests, she confessed that she was finding it hard these days to take much personal interest in anyone. Having lost faith in the private happiness she had formerly sought, she told Michaelis she was becoming acclimated to a life in which she lived "only for an idea . . . More and more I become political, intellectual, with emo- tions being crowded completely or nearly completely out of my life—I mean any emotions of personal love."[47]

By summer's end, Agnes wrote that she had observed rickshaw coolies fall dead in their shafts. She had seen poverty, disease, starvation, and physical and spiritual exhaustion of a depth she had previously thought unimaginable; she had learned of hundreds who were weekly being arrested, imprisoned, shot, and beheaded, their skulls paraded on poles in the streets under the KMT's reign of anti-Communist terror. Agnes claimed that by now she had grown accustomed to reading of young Communist students and workers caught by foreign authori- ties in Shanghai and turned over to Chinese officials who killed them "like dogs." The dividing line between life and death was very thin in China, she remarked to Sanger, "and you always stand observing it."

Her initial shock was fading. She was beginning to come through it, she said, "as one passes through a dark night of horror. Perhaps one loses much on the way and becomes hardened: I seem to have. But . . . I can look at all the beggars of China now and see beyond them to the thing that has made them like this. As such, I will waste no time on them. So many must die out here, you have only to choose which. There is no choice between life and death; there is only the choice between death and death."[48] By accepting the possibility of death—her own or others—as a reality of life in China, she said, she hoped to accomplish a great deal more than she had in her first few months. It was not despair, she wrote. It was simply accepting reality.

Only one issue still concerned her, and that was her fear that she might be forced out of China and returned to Europe or America. Agnes readily admitted that the country's poverty and misery were "deep as eternity" and that the hideousness of the White Terror was ghastly, but she had already come to love China and the Chinese people, she wrote, and felt more at home here than she ever had elsewhere. And at some point in the not too distant future, she was cer- tain another revolution was coming. Why was that? "Because the revolutionary movement out here is not a romantic idea or theory, but the grimmest of economic necessities. It is either rebel or die," she told Florence. Even if the present situation seemed more like "rebel *and* die," she added, she intended to stay—whether she went down with Asia or rose up with it.

Agnes was keenly aware, however, that her path had been selected by default. It was not one she recommended to others. When Florence mentioned that she had considered naming her second child after Agnes, she was mortified. That was no name to wish on a child, she said; her life was nothing a child should emulate. All she knew was that for her there was no other, and she hoped to die while still comparatively young. A woman of her kind, Agnes wrote, was "impossible when old. There is no place for us."

Despite their best efforts, by the fall of 1929 neither the American consul at Frankfurt-am-Main, the Berlin police, nor the British Passport Control Office had managed to prove that Agnes had forfeited her right to American citizenship by marrying an Indian or being naturalized as a German citizen, and Mrs. Shipley at the State Department's passport division reluctantly dropped her investigation. But British efforts to neutralize Agnes's impact in China, based on their long-standing hostility toward her, continued. Later that same fall, she wrote, they ordered their consul in Frankfurt to protest her articles for the *Zeitung* and demand that the paper censor her. When that failed, she said, they sent the police.[49] Agnes assumed the British would torment her next in Shanghai, but she had no intention of keeping still. Under Chen Han-seng's tutelage, she said, she was learning a great deal, and she used it in her investigations of a Japanese-run textile plant and other exploitative industries, as well as on several trips into China's interior.[50] Although little of this information appeared in her work for the *Zeitung*, her reports were no doubt helpful to the PPTUS. Agnes described her life at this time as inhumanly intense.

In the year since Agnes had arrived in China, Sanger had been sending her money in the hope that she would establish a clinic, but Agnes had made it plain that she could do little beyond some small-scale practical work: "a night clinic two or three nights a week, perhaps, in hospital rooms in a factory district in Shanghai, maybe something in Peking."[51] She was exhausted and overworked, she wrote, from her other activities. Moreover, she advised Sanger, unless the civil war that had recently broken out between a coalition of left-wing and military groups and the Nanking government turned into a real revolution, she considered birth control work among the masses unrealistic in the extreme.

Birth control required at least "a certain elementary knowledge and . . . standard of personal hygiene," Agnes observed. People here were so poor "that they cannot buy the water to wash their own faces once a day—so how in the deuce can [they] find water to douche? . . . There is a depth of destitution in China that has reduced human lives to conditions lower than animals. The workers in Shanghai live fourteen and fifteen in a room, the whole family sleeping on long boards for a bed. The earth is the floor and straw is the roof of their huts. A pessary, or chemicals for them—no, it is impossible. The thing is fantastic. They do not even have the money for food."[52] When China's first birth control clinic opened in Peking in December 1929, Agnes was not even there.

CHAPTER 9

Richard Sorge and the GRU

Long live the Soviets.
Down with the Kuomintang.
Long live the Red Army.
Down with the British Gang.

ADAPTED FROM THE CHINESE
BY LYDIA FILATOVA AND LANGSTON HUGHES

I N THE FALL OF 1929, the CCP had established a cultural committee whose
leader reported directly to the Party's central propaganda committee — a
move that signaled the CCP's recognition of the importance of dominating literary affairs. One of its earliest efforts was a campaign to win over China's preemi-
nent short story writer, Lu Hsun. For the past two years, a debate on the role and
value of radical literature had raged inside China, during which time Lu's insistence on remaining a bystander-critic and his disdain for rhetorical posturing
had made him a target of CCP attacks. Agnes herself accused him of being
"vacillating and critical" of China's social revolutionary writers.[1] Recently, however, Lu had become disillusioned with the Nanking government and come to
view himself as a Communist, at least in theory. His agreement to aid a Party
effort to promote Marxist literary theory and the practice of social realist literature brought Agnes to his doorstep.

As Lu Hsun recalled their first encounter, two young Chinese, Dong Chiu-si
and Cai Yun-shang ("man-wife teachers," according to Agnes, although others
recalled them as Comintern workers) delivered Agnes to Lu's home on Jing Yun
Road in the closing days of 1929 and reassured him of her intentions.[2] Short and
frail, with close-cropped hair that stood up "like a brush" and the most expressive face she had ever seen, Lu charmed her, she would write, with the "indefin-
able harmony . . . of [his] perfectly integrated personality."[3] He spoke no English,
so they conversed in halting German, with occasional words in other languages.

Over the next few months, the two writers planned the organization the CCP would use to wage a war of words against government authorities.

Because the lives of left-wing Chinese were in constant danger and radical literature was strictly proscribed, the pair's activities were fraught with risk; the CCP central committee provided security for their meetings. By March 1930, the League of Left Wing Writers, however, had been formally launched.[4] Agnes's covert channels were vital to the league's ability to move documents and information to and from Europe and the United States.[5] The organization also exploited her ability to galvanize well-known Western writers into active support—an effort in which she was aided, no doubt, by her ties to Muenzenberg.

"The White Terror is ghastly out here," she wrote Upton Sinclair that May. "Soon an organization of Chinese writers will issue an appeal to the writers of the world, and I hope you will give it publicity and write an article based upon the appeal. The jails are filled with May 1 victims [May 1 or May Day being the day on which labor unions and leftists traditionally honored workers] and we have news that eleven have been shot, after torture."[6]

When Agnes had information from the outside world to pass to the LLWW, she contacted Party organizer Hsia Yan through an intermediary. After they spoke, he would relay her information to members of the Party cell inside the

The writer Lu Hsun, another friend and colleague.
Museum of the Chinese Revolution, Beijing.

league.[7] In return, the Chinese Communists did what they could to help Agnes, providing her with entrée to Chinese and foreign Communists and giving her access to reports of the Party's central committee. Feng Da, a young leftist intellectual whom Agnes employed as her secretary, would translate them for her, making Agnes the only Western journalist in China at that time who was receiving information directly from CCP sources.

During the winter of 1929–30, three Russians attached to Soviet military intelligence (also known as the Fourth Bureau of the Red Army General Staff, and later as the GRU) arrived in Shanghai to replace a group whose task of establishing radio communication between Moscow and Shanghai had been accomplished. "Alex," their leader, handled technical liaison with Moscow. "Sober Weingarten" ran the group's wireless operations. The third man was Richard Sorge, the Russian-born offspring of a German father and a Russian mother, who served as their political collaborator.

In the five years since his friend and mentor, Iosef Piatnitsky, had switched Sorge's membership from the German to the Russian Communist Party (CCCP), Sorge had been working for the Comintern as an intelligence agent in

Soviet spy Richard Sorge. *National Archives, Washington, D.C.*

Europe, operating—like Agnes—through the OMS office run by Piatnitsky's subordinate Mirov-Abramov in Berlin.[8] However, before Sorge left for China (where he would pose as a special correspondent for the German *Soziologische Magazin*), he had requested that the type of information he preferred to collect, which involved economics, domestic, administrative, and foreign policy issues and, to some extent, military intelligence, be removed from the Comintern's jurisdiction and placed under the supervision of what he would describe as a "special arm" of the CCCP's central committee.

The move, he later explained, was in accordance with what he perceived as the "general shift in the center of gravity from the Comintern to the Russian Communist Party and the USSR itself."[9] Since by 1930 the Soviet Party so far overshadowed the Comintern in providing leadership for the Communist movement, he said, he had wanted to transfer "from party activities under the Communist International to . . . activities that promoted the welfare of the Soviet Union," as he put it.[10] However, he would remain in contact with Piatnitsky and the Comintern's OMS.[11]

Sorge was not a typical spy. Money did not motivate him; neither did professional advancement. Politics were his passion. At root, he was an activist like Agnes, but while he, too, loathed foreign imperialism in China and supported a world revolution, his goal was the protection of the motherland of Communism. If pressed, this included protecting the Soviet Union's own "special interests" in Manchuria.

Although Sorge was functioning in China not through the Russian Party's central committee, as he had sought, but the intelligence division of the Soviet Union's top military espionage agency, Piatnitsky, who had overseen Sorge's shift into purely Soviet work, harbored great hopes for his protégé. During Sorge's years in China, General Ian A. Berzin, director of the intelligence division of the Soviet Red Army's General Staff and Sorge's superior there, would give Sorge "a freer hand than any spy who had served the Soviet Union since 1917," one contemporary historian observed.[12]

Shortly after establishing himself at the foreign YMCA on Bubbling Well Road, Sorge (or "Johnson," as he identified himself in Shanghai) called on Agnes at her home in the French Concession with a letter of introduction from someone he referred to simply as a mutual acquaintance in Berlin.[13] In Moscow, Sorge would recall a decade later (after being captured and —according to some—tortured in Japan), he had been authorized to recruit personnel beyond the wireless contacts and radio men already in place; based on what he had heard of Agnes in Europe, he felt he could depend on her.[14] He said he sought Agnes's assistance in establishing an intelligence-gathering group in Shanghai soon after they met, and she agreed to help him.[15]

Sorge would later acknowledge that "money is a prerequisite to espionage work . . . [and] was essential" to his later operation in Japan, but he saw "no urgent need for it" in Shanghai since "indiscriminate spending might have led to detection," and people like Agnes were motivated "by strong ideological ties."[16] He would also recall that during the period she worked with him, from 1930 through the beginning of 1933, her job at the *Zeitung* was merely a legal cover for her clandestine activities.[17]

Under interrogation, Sorge would insist that he obtained Agnes's services "with her full understanding."[18] What he meant by this, however, is unclear. Perhaps Sorge was suggesting that in contrast to other ring members, who believed that in cooperating with him they would be pursuing the Comintern's agenda, Agnes knew that Sorge was in China to advance distinctly Soviet goals. Her only comment on the subject, however, was in a letter to Florence, in which Agnes mentioned that his method of communicating with his Russian superiors was far safer than hers.[19]

Many of the tasks Agnes would perform for Sorge over the next three years were essentially the same as those she already conducted for the OMS. She would act as a mail drop and liaison, offer her home for meetings, and gather information and write reports on matters of interest to Sorge, which he said initially included "the increasing importance of America's role in China and new American investments in Shanghai," and which he forwarded to Moscow.[20] Still, on whose behalf she conducted her intelligence gave her activities a qualitatively different flavor. It was one thing to succor world revolution via the Comintern. It was another to aid the military intelligence operations of Stalin's government.

Agnes's relationship with Mirov-Abramov compounded the ambiguity of her position. By 1930, the OMS had been detached from the diplomatic mission in Berlin. Mirov-Abramov was now back in Moscow, a ranking official in Russian intelligence as well as the OMS, and serving as the link between the Comintern and the Fourth Bureau for the coordination of espionage.[21] Agnes probably did not know that when she consented to work with Sorge. Most likely, she presumed — or Sorge told her — that she would be attending two bosses: the Comintern and the Soviet government.

A decade later, other ring members still considered the terms synonymous; Agnes had come to recognize significant distinctions between the two. However, it is unlikely she understood at the outset, as Sorge did, that the aims of the two institutions diverged.[22] The fact that her work for Russian military intelligence was in service to an ideal, or that aspects of how it would be used were far afield of Agnes's original purpose, does not mean, though, that it was not espionage. In her work with Sorge, Agnes would be acting on behalf of a foreign power. She would perform consciously and deliberately, under direct instructions, and "accept discipline." She would gather information secretly (though it was not necessarily secret information she gathered) and attend secret meetings at which secret information was passed. She would operate covertly: using safe houses, communicating through mail drops, assuming false names and identities, pay-ing agents, and acting as a courier—all of which are features of espionage. In the way that espionage suggests undermining your opponent, she would indulge in that s well. Her activities were not traitorous, in that she would not spy for the Russians *against* the United States. Spreading false information, creating panic, and promoting sabotage and inside agitation were also less features of espionage than the "direct action" tactics of anarcho-syndicalism and the Western radical-ism in which she came of age. But in keeping clandestine watch on the people and situations about which Sorge needed information to fulfill his assignment from Moscow, Agnes would not respect national boundaries.

At the beginning, Sorge was particularly interested in recruiting Chinese coworkers. Since he was under orders from Moscow to avoid any direct connec-tion with the Chinese Communist Party, Agnes introduced him to her circle of young Chinese friends. All of them had a history of working with foreigners on leftist causes; all were sympathetic to the revolutionary movement. Several even maintained some form of contact with the CCP, but none were known Party members. From among them, Sorge invited Chen Han-seng to join his group.[23]

Not long after Agnes began collaborating with Sorge (or "Sorgie," as she took to calling him), he became her lover as well as her comrade-in-arms.[24] Strikingly good-looking, with cold blue eyes, thick brown hair, and a sensuous mouth, Sorge was arrogant and hot tempered, and his appetite for high-powered motor-cycles, alcohol, and women seemed somewhat reckless for a person in his posi-tion, but his joie de vivre was quite rare in the Communist circles in which Agnes traveled, and she was enthralled.

Sorge did not make it a secret that the broad and generous "friendship" on which he insisted precluded such bourgeois sentiments as romance or monogamy. Agnes was so taken with her swashbuckling man of action that she tried to convince herself that she, too, had transcended such needs. "It is a rare husband that wears well . . . ," Agnes would write Sanger. "I never expect one to wear so well—that is perhaps because I myself do not." But a few months into her affair with Sorge, Agnes informed Florence that she had at long last found that "rare, rare person" who could give her everything she wanted and more. During the spring of 1930, she was frequently spotted on the back of Sorge's motorcycle, flying through the streets of Shanghai and feeling "grand and glori-ous," as she put it.

"I'm married, child, so to speak," she wrote Florence, "just sort of married, you know; but it's a he-man also and it's 50-50 all along the line and he helping me and I him and we working together in every way... I do not know how long it will last; that does not depend on us. I fear not long. But these days will be the best in my life. Never have I known such good days, never have I known such a healthy life, mentally, physically, psychically. I consider this completion, and when it is ended, I'll be lonelier than all the love in the magazines could never make me."[25]

That March, a Russian Communist named Yakov Rudnik (or Hilaire Noulens, as he was known in Shanghai) had returned to the city to direct OMS activities there.[26] With Rudnik, a career intelligence officer, overseeing the movement of all Comintern money and communications in Shanghai, Agnes could have diverted more attention to her affair with Sorge, but her political commitments still came first. "I have a duty heavier than... personal things," she explained to Michaelis, who was promoting *Daughter of Earth* in Europe. That overpowering sense of duty consumed all traces of her formerly rich inner life.

Agnes was working eighteen hours a day, but she said that even in her off-hours she could not rest. She could never forget, she explained, that beyond a few wealthy Chinese and foreigners, who were protected by multinational armed forces and enjoyed sheltered lives, most lived with horrific poverty, amidst an active network of spies, murderers, kidnappers, and criminals. Agnes found the stress so intense she said she often longed "for vacuum." Still, she refused to alter her schedule, which during the spring of 1930 involved several investigative trips with her Chinese associates to cities up the Yangtze in Kiangsu province, where Chiang Kai-shek had his power base, and other urban centers.[27]

After three years of usurious government taxes and landowners who either forced the peasants into tenancy or drove them off the land, people were again revolting. In half a dozen provinces across central and southern China, Agnes reported in the *Modern Review*, a social revolution had broken out in earnest, and though it was too soon to predict its outcome, huge changes were already under way. Mao's group of Communist military leaders had organized fifty thousand to sixty thousand hungry, illiterate peasants and defected government soldiers into more than a dozen openly Red armies. In the territories they conquered, Communist forces, assisted by masses of civilian peasants and a hundred thousand Red Guards, continued to confiscate property from large landowners and redistribute it to peasants. They had also begun to replace corrupt officials with local soviets where vice, gambling, and opium smoking were forbidden (along with temples, churches, and idol worship), to create schools, form clinics, reestablish peasant unions, and execute missionaries, land-rich peasants, gentry, and officials.

All the military advantages were on the side of Nanking. The bands of armed partisans fighting government forces were poorly equipped. Five to ten men commonly shared a single gun, and their ammunition was limited to what they captured in battle. However, Chiang Kai-shek was distracted at the moment by civil war against several provincial regimes that until recently had been part of the Nationalist coalition. With militarist rivalries splitting the KMT camp, men who preferred to die for their emancipation rather than starve often outmatched the Nationalist troops.

In Shanghai, CCP politburo leader Li Li-san recognized this opportunity for the Communists to regain the upper hand, but he was less interested than Mao's group in the agrarian revolutionary upsurge. Li Li-san preferred that the partisan forces in China's interior help the CCP capture a large urban base along the lines the Comintern had laid out. Canton, in southern Kwangtung province, was one of the large cities in which the Comintern had ordered Chinese Communists to step up military activities; it was also the one closest to Mao Tse-tung's rapidly expanding power base. Agnes and Sorge were both keen to see the progress of China's revolution and planned a trip to the area to observe political and agrarian conditions there. While she was in Canton, Agnes would also look into the ruined silk industry—a subject of particular interest to the PPTUS.

British authorities in Shanghai's International Settlement were not yet onto Sorge, but they were keeping their eyes on Agnes. So were American, German, French, and Nationalist Chinese officials. As she prepared to depart, Agnes wrote, a rumor that British political police considered her a representative of the Communist International came to her attention. The idea that *they* might accuse *her* of duplicity when *they* were violating people's most basic human rights outraged Agnes's personal sense of justice, and in a letter to Michaelis she vehemently, albeit ambiguously, denied the charge. She took it as "a great compliment," she wrote, that the British considered her sufficiently knowledgeable about Marxism and revolutionary tactics for the Comintern to honor her in that way, but they rated her "knowledge too high ... Such rumours are sinister things and are often forerunners of mean and terrible things. Out here Communists are shot and imprisoned. But I go on my way doing my work as ever, and it does not matter to me what they say. They are all dirty dogs, cut-throats and murderers ... I shall do my duty till I drop."[28]

Sorge left for Kwangtung province on May 9, 1930; Agnes followed him one week later. After stopping briefly in Amoy, she caught up with Sorge in Canton. Half a century later, Chen Han-seng, who accompanied them there, still kept their secrets. He maintained that the pair disappeared from Shanghai at this time "to celebrate their honeymoon in Hong Kong."[29]

Virtually all the Westerners who came to Canton stayed in the British Concession in Shameen, but Agnes appeared anxious to escape scrutiny. Neglecting to register with the consulate general, she rented a three-room apartment on the outskirts of Tungshan, on Chinese territory— an area favored by Russian Communist observers during the first wave of the Chinese Revolution. Its proportions were modest, she said, but it came furnished with a bed, a wardrobe, two tables with chairs, and sufficient space for her to set up a darkroom. The latter was an odd requirement for someone who did not develop her own film, but Sorge would need such a space to photograph documents, prepare microfilms, and establish the wireless station that was one mission of his trip. Although Sorge's predecessors had reestablished radio communications between Shanghai and Moscow by the late spring of 1930, they had yet to exist between Shanghai and Canton, and the need had become essential. As to who would utilize the extra table and chair—much less the darkroom—Agnes coyly noted to Michaelis, "You may think the two chairs express a hope—or a reality. Oh well—far be it from me to contradict a woman who knows so much about women as you do."[30]

That June, Sorge's superior returned to Moscow, leaving Sorge in charge of the group. Agnes was proud of their relationship, but she was discreet about revealing Sorge's identity, and in discussing him with friends she remarked only that he was a Westerner, Caucasian, better looking than any of her previous lovers—and that her association with him in Canton made her incoming mail secure enough for friends to converse with her freely. "No George and no Mary [Agnes's nickname for the British political police] will read what you write me," she assured Florence. "Not one line will reach anyone else." Her outgoing mail, she added, was equally secure, routed at present through Siberia.[31]

After her disastrous experience with Chatto, Agnes said she agreed with Sorge that monogamous relationships, as she had experienced them, were "senseless, dependent, and cruel," but Agnes was so attracted to Sorge that his philandering pained her. She papered over her desire for a more exclusive attachment with brash statements like "no man will ever get his hooks in me again," but her need for a deep and lasting love, she confessed in an unguarded moment, remained.

Agnes spent her days visiting factories and villages outside the city, where Chen Han-seng helped her interview workers and peasants. The *Zeitung* had recently renegotiated her contract, and in response to British pressure, it now contained terms that specifically forbade her from publishing in any Communist papers.[32] Mainstream journals like the *Herald Tribune* were not interested in the articles she sent them, though, while papers like the *Moscow News* were.[33] Recently the latter had approached her to become its China correspondent. Under the circumstances, perhaps she felt she had no choice; she said only that she hoped her study of Marxist economics helped her write less superficially and more "scientifically" about what she observed.

In Canton, Sorge acquired two radio operators who were already attached to the Fourth Bureau, but since he was still looking to recruit a few more trustworthy Chinese "helpers," Chen Han-seng introduced him to a "Mrs. Chui" (a Kwangtung native Sorge would recall as close to Agnes) and another Cantonese. They began providing Sorge, and indirectly Agnes, with military and political reports on the situation in south China.[34] Cantonese police were unaware of Sorge's activities, but that July Chinese authorities in Shanghai warned local officials to keep an eye on Agnes, who they said might be engaging in Communist propaganda.[35] A Cantonese censor was assigned to monitor her mail, but for the moment all was calm.

Accompanied by a guide from Lingnan Christian University whom Agnes loathed, she traveled south to Shuntak to study the three million "silk peasants" who labored in the declining industry. Nearly all the people Agnes met sold their cocoon crops in advance to buy food. After the harvest, as she wrote in the *Modern Review*, they found themselves in debt and were unable to get loans, or obtained them at usurious rates. Few owned their own mulberry trees. In the event of crop failures, which were increasingly common among the disease-plagued trees, families were sometimes reduced to selling their children. Workers' homes were huts with earthen floors; their beds were wooden boards, and a clay stove, narrow bench, table, and a few cooking utensils and cocoon frames were their only worldly possessions. Thousands of women, many of them Communists, worked in the filatures and weaving mills, and Agnes said she spoke with many of them. They told her their salaries were tiny, but they relished the independence it bought them, and they retained it by remaining single even though people accused them of being lesbians. Perhaps the PPTUS received a variant of the same report.

July 16, 1930, was the day CCP politburo leader Li Li-san had selected to kick off the massive worker demonstrations and rural uprisings by which the Soviets hoped to ignite the current warlords' war into a revolution. On that day, however, Agnes was nowhere to be found. The charge that she was legally married to Chattopadhyaya—and therefore needed to surrender her American passport or face prosecution for fraud—had resurfaced, and she had fled to Hong Kong to renew it; it was her best protection in China should any problems arise.[36] One might wonder what maneuvers Agnes pulled to enter, having remarked only the year before that as long as the island remained British territory, she had no more chance of visiting it than she did of visiting India.

To signal authorities that she had legal representation, should she need it, Agnes requested that American officials contact Gilbert Roe in the event of her death—despite the fact that he had died several months earlier. By the time Agnes returned to Canton, ostensibly to write up her report on the silk industry, Sorge had established radio communication between Moscow and Canton. Through that source, Soviet military intelligence would most likely be in at least occasional contact with the major soviet areas in south China.

Once Li Li-san's plans were in full swing, the police dogged Agnes's every move. "This is a warning for future letters," Agnes instructed Florence on July 19. "George and Mary, etc. are again hot on the trail of my letters. Refer no more to lovers and revolutions, etc."[37] By July 22, no uprisings had occurred but there were demonstrations in several cities, and the Red Army believed its positions, along with developments in the warlord war, provided favorable circumstances for Communist troops. Five days later, with KMT forces at a low ebb, the Fifth Red Army, led by P'eng Teh-huai, successfully occupied Changsha, capital of Hunan province, and proclaimed a soviet government. Li Li-san and his followers hoped that Wuhan would quickly follow and then all of China would soon erupt.

On July 30, 1930, a rather agitated Agnes called on Douglas Jenkins, the American consul general in Canton. Flashing her American passport, she protested her surveillance by Chinese police. Not only were they interfering with her journalistic endeavors; Jenkins reported her as saying she was afraid of being "shot in the back."[38] A heated exchange ensued, after which, Jenkins said, he assured Agnes that he would do everything he "properly" could to protect her as an American citizen. He noted that he did point out to her, however, that because south China was in a disturbed condition and Cantonese authorities were extremely uneasy about possible Communist uprisings, her failure to register with the consulate, like her conduct and place of residence, was suspicious for someone who was "only engaged in newspaper work and in no way interested in Communist or other propaganda."[39] As soon as Agnes left his office, Jenkins requested that the secretary of state ascertain at once whether she was indeed a Communist agent, as local authorities claimed.

With south China so unstable, authorities anticipated that the International Red Aid's second annual Anti-Imperialist War Day would inspire huge demonstrations that August 1. In the hope that they might catch Agnes out in some of its activities, they placed her under increased scrutiny.[40] At her next interaction with the American consul, following three days of further upheaval, she reported that her apartment had been invaded and rifled by armed police who had seized numerous papers in her possession. She refused to leave until Jenkins agreed to assist her.[41] He returned with Agnes to her apartment, where two armed police officers awaited her.

Jenkins wrote that he ordered them to leave at once, but the British representative who oversaw Cantonese police was reluctant to back off entirely. He explained to Jenkins that it was not that Cantonese authorities viewed Agnes as a Communist per se. Rather, they were simply worried that she might "unwittingly" be assisting Communists and others opposed to the Nationalist government by distributing Communist propaganda from Shanghai that she did not "understand."[42] What had happened, it seemed, was that the Chinese censor who surveilled Agnes's mail had come upon two parcels containing magazines — very likely the current issue of the League of Left Wing Writers journal — which pledged the organization's active participation in activities to promote the struggle toward soviet rule as the revolutionary masses prepared for what the magazine referred to as the "final war in the world revolution."[43] He urged that Jenkins demand Agnes leave the area at once to avoid being suspected of involvement in the widespread Communist movement in neighboring Kiangsi and Hunan.

On August 6, 1930, Agnes signed a sworn statement alleging that she was neither a Communist nor a member of the Communist nor any other political party. Neither was she in any way connected with the Communist International. She denied any involvement in Communist agitation, Bolshevik propaganda, or any subversive activity directed against the Nanking government and noted (with some truth) that she was not paid a dime, either by Russia or the Comintern, for her work. The packet of revolutionary literature from Shanghai, she asserted, was something she had neither asked for nor agreed to distribute. Any suggestion that her recent visit to Shuntak might be interpreted as Communist agitation "in connection with Communist cells" shocked her.[44]

The charge that she was not a journalist but a Communist originated with the British "secret service," she contended; they had long resented her Indian activities. They branded the least breath of liberalism Bolshevism, she complained, and though she had not fussed much about them in the past, "always comforting myself with the knowledge that were Jesus Christ living in China today, he would also be in the bad books of the British and other secret services," she refused to be treated as if she were guilty of anything. For that very reason, she maintained, she would not give up her apartment in Tungshan or provide the consul with the names of anyone she had seen during her stay, as he requested.

The next parry was a testament to the effective radio communication Sorge's group had recently established with Moscow. In an article for the official Russian paper *Izvestia*, Karl Radek, its principal commentator on international politics, *attacked* Agnes (whom he described as the bourgeois correspondent of an imperialist newspaper) for spreading erroneous stories about outrages China's

Red Armies perpetrated upon the country's poor in order to create sympathy for its landowners, usurers, merchants, and officials.[45] The disinformation was most useful in demonstrating Agnes's distance from the Soviet Union, but she was not out of danger yet.

Agnes returned to Hong Kong the second week of August, where she drafted a confidential letter to her editor-friend Ernestine Evans. Stressing her surprise at the charges leveled against her and her own clear conscience, Agnes wrote that "of course" she had not participated in the International Red Aid's demonstrations. Not only had the fact that August 1 was Anti-Imperialist War Day completely slipped her mind. When the Cantonese police had visited her apartment, she claimed she did not even know the Communists had taken Changsha! For days beforehand, Agnes wrote, she had been suffering from an eye inflammation, and the black eyeglasses she wore for the condition made reading or writing so challenging she had missed the entire event.[46]

Agnes did not try to hide that she was "of left opinions," but she swore she had nothing to do with the Comintern, did not belong to the Communist Party of any nation, and had not participated "in any way" in any Communist agitation. Was it her fault, she asked Evans, if "some group" in Shanghai gave her twelve copies of "some magazine" to distribute? She had not asked for it, and it had been "ridiculous for anyone to ever dream that I would or could distribute a liberal or radical magazine in Canton,"[47] but she was still grievously upset and did not know "what in hell . . . they are going to do with me." Since Roe's death, she confessed to Evans, she had no one to defend her in Washington; perhaps Evans could mention her predicament to Robert Morss Lovett, who was now at the ACLU. She was convinced that British authorities in Shanghai lay behind her current woes, wishing to force her out of China because she still wrote for the Indian press.

With every telling, her tale grew. Roger Baldwin heard that Chinese gendarmerie "armed to the teeth" had taken possession of Agnes's apartment and that she had never taken a step without being followed by armed men.[48] Only her American citizenship, she told him, had compelled American consular officials to save her life. Later, she would inform others that she had been arrested in Canton, or had lived for weeks under house arrest with armed gendarmes wandering in and out of her apartment at will.[49]

On August 11, 1930, the State Department advised Jenkins that it possessed no information indicating Agnes was a Communist agent. Though it no doubt vexed Cantonese authorities, the American consul concurred. Jenkins was clear eyed about what he described as Agnes's "decidedly revolutionary sympathies," particularly in regard to India, but he did not believe she was a Communist, that she was engaged in writing or distributing Communist propaganda, or that she was doing anything, in fact, against the interests of the present Chinese government.[50]

By mid-August, it had become evident that after the initial high point of the Chinese Communists' military campaign—the capture of Changsha—the attempt to spark a revolution in China, based on Russian advice and the Russian model, was failing. The First Army Corps under Chu Teh and Mao Tse-tung had attacked Nanchang, but they had been easily repulsed and forced to withdraw. Changsha, too, fell. The worker demonstrations that were supposed to precipitate urban uprisings had not materialized. No peasant revolts had inflamed the countryside, no troop rebellions paralyzed KMT forces. At this inauspicious moment, Agnes later claimed, she fell ill, but her Irish sea captain "friend" from Manchuria now resurfaced to rescue her.[51] On September 3, 1930 she was back in Shanghai.

CHAPTER 10

Cloak and Dagger in Shanghai

This class struggle plays hell with your poetry.

JOHN REED

O N HER RETURN to Shanghai, Agnes moved into an apartment on the Route de Grouchy. This time she registered immediately with the American Consulate. Hong Kong police soon shared their suspicions regarding Agnes's Canton activities with the Shanghai Municipal Police, but Agnes's allies were not idle either. At her urging, Robert Morss Lovett had notified Assistant Secretary of State Joseph Cotton that if British tactics in China resembled in any way the "highly discreditable" methods they had employed a decade earlier when he and Agnes had worked together at the FFFI, her complaints were probably justified, and the agency needed to protect her interests more vigilantly.[1] After examining the reports on Agnes from the Harbin and Canton consulates, Cotton was not so inclined. However, he did advise the American minister in Peking that powerful people in the United States were monitoring Agnes's situation in China closely.[2]

The last phase of the Russian-supported plan to rekindle China's faltering revolution was scheduled to be launched a few days after Agnes's return. On September 7, 1930, the Chinese Red Army was supposed to attack Changsha and Wuhan while Communist youth organizations led massive demonstrations against the KMT. Once again, though, the anticipated protests did not materialize, and a second Red Army attack on Changsha also failed. The revolutionary tide was ebbing, not rising, it appeared, and guerrilla leaders Mao Tse-tung and Chu Teh retreated to the mountains of southern Kiangsi in full defeat, along with a few thousand followers. Other Red Armies, which had been converging on Wuhan, were ordered to withdraw and seek shelter in smaller, rural soviet bases.

In the aftermath of the unrest, the KMT formally banned the League of Left Wing Writers and its journal, and sought the arrest of those responsible for the league's statement of support: part of a campaign to tighten control over the publication and distribution of left-wing literature. Nanking's order to shut down the LLWW drove the organization, and members including Lu Hsun, underground, but it did not silence them completely. Despite the risks, friends of Lu's inside and outside the CCP decided to flout the KMT by marking his fiftieth birthday with a party. Beyond the social value of allowing LLWW members to gather, the event would help the CCP, which controlled the league, to recruit members by gaining momentum for the organization around Lu Hsun.

One hundred artists and intellectuals representing the world of "dangerous thought," as Agnes described it, were invited by word of mouth and sworn to secrecy. On the evening of September 17, 1930, the event took place.[3] Agnes, who had booked the room at a Dutch restaurant in the French Concession, stood guard at the front door; sentries posted at the intersections that led to the restaurant also kept watch to protect prominent Communists in attendance. Speakers included the editor of *Shanghai Pao*, an underground Communist newspaper, a representative from the International Red Aid, and Ting Ling, an accomplished female writer (and later a great friend of Agnes's), who discussed the need for developing proletarian literature.

Since the publication of *Daughter of Earth*, Agnes received a good deal of fan mail. Though she professed little interest in hearing from people of means, she treasured correspondence from those of humbler backgrounds. As someone who identified herself as a person of color, Agnes was also keenly interested in the subject of race in America. When a young Langston Hughes sent her an inscribed copy of his novel *Not Without Laughter* to read after a reviewer noted parallels to hers, Agnes was already familiar with his sophisticated explorations of black life and culture. Indeed, she was such an admirer that she had already committed much of his first collection of poems, *Weary Blues*, to memory.

After staying up most of the night to read Hughes's gift, Agnes wrote him that she, too, was "astounded by the similarity" between their books—and by the two of them as well, assuming that his novel, like hers, had been drawn essentially from personal experience.[4] Watching Hughes embark on his own journey to the left, Agnes said he felt like her little brother, albeit one with "a much better use of the English language than I have, and—of course—you are essentially a poet."[5] She singled out for particular praise his recent "Call to Creation," which she claimed contained two lines on China that were better than anything other American poets or writers had produced.

Writer to writer, Agnes confided that she was so overwhelmed by her political commitments she doubted she would ever again be able to create work that required more than merely "throwing facts together. I have no leisure in which to coordinate my thoughts, least of all to express them in any form other than the harshness of daily life...I am stuffed full, up to the neck, with all that passes in...China; and...I am...not theoretical enough to take these things historically and to watch a great historical struggle from a distance."[6] In 1930, though, she was the better-known literary radical, and her recent foray into literary polemics emboldened Agnes to offer Hughes some "comradely" advice with a distinctly socialist cast.

In ending his novel happily, with its protagonist triumphant, she advised, Hughes had failed to depict the real fate of the Negro masses which "is not happy—but is beaten and debased by condition of beastly subjection." Why, she demanded, had he omitted any mention of the "Negro proletarians, or very poor farmers, on whose backs fall the full burden of class and race hatred and subjection, men who work and long—and are defeated until they organize and fight on a revolutionary basis"?[7] *Those* were the people about whom he should be writing, she instructed. Without them, his book was "individualistic—and therefore of passing value only," lacking intensity, depth, historic knowledge, and revolutionary consciousness. No technique, however superior, Agnes warned, could succeed without being wedded to the deepest class consciousness. Perhaps the fault lay in his petit bourgeois upbringing, which had not taught him sufficient suffering. To Hughes's credit, he took her criticism without comment.

By the fall of 1930, Agnes's reportage on China's peasant Red Armies had begun appearing in the United States in the *New Masses* and *New Republic*, as well the in the *Moscow News*, the *Frankfurter Zeitung*, and the *Modern Review*. Her good fortune attracted the attention of Shanghai authorities, but her position as the only foreign journalist with direct access to Chinese Communist sources appeared to be paying off.

That autumn she also made several friends, one of whom was Irene Wiedemeyer, a young German Jew with freckled skin, milk-blue eyes, and unmanageable red hair. While living in Berlin, Wiedemeyer had become involved with the Muenzenberg apparatus; after studying Asian revolutionary movements in Moscow, she had turned up in Shanghai, where she now operated a branch of the Zeitgeist Bookstore on the banks of Soochow Creek. The small shop, which stocked radical German, English, and French literature, was part of Muenzenberg's publishing syndicate and was used by the Comintern as a rendezvous and recruiting station; messages and information were conveyed to agents there on sheets of paper slipped between the pages of designated books.[8]

Ozaki Hotsumi, a Japanese journalist who was then a special correspondent for the *Osaka Asahi Shinbun*, was another new friend. A Zeitgeist regular, Ozaki was a non-Party Communist who assisted the CCP underground and handled League of Left Wing Writers propaganda for Japan. He had asked Wiedemeyer to introduce him to the "famous American authoress," he later recalled. Over the course of several earnest conversations either at Agnes's home in the French Concession or in the lobby of the Palace Hotel, according to Ozaki, she had mentioned her affiliation with a newly formed Chinese branch of the International Red Aid, on whose behalf she was attempting to instigate a worldwide protest movement against the White Terror; she also suggested that they exchange information on contemporary social issues.[9]

Initially, Ozaki would recall, they confined their discussions to health, labor, and agricultural problems, but they soon began to trade notes on more politically sensitive subjects including the inner workings of the KMT.[10] Ozaki said Agnes was so perceptive her questions sometimes frightened him, but he respected her as an activist, and by December 1930, when Chiang Kai-shek launched his first retaliatory measure against the Red Army's summer campaign—unleashing 350,000 Nationalist troops on the remaining soviet pockets in Kiangsi province—Ozaki was assisting Agnes with her extralegal activities for the International Red Aid in addition to his other work.

A third foreign friend Agnes made at this time was Sonja Kuczinski. A slim, dark-haired Berliner from a prominent leftist family, Sonja had worked in the past as an agitation and propaganda leader for the German Communist Party. Like Ozaki, Sonja, too, had been eager to meet Agnes, whom she considered "an important personality." She said she had greatly enjoyed reading *Daughter of Earth* while she still lived in Germany, but, she later confessed, she had also heard that Agnes was much further to the left politically than was publicly acknowledged.[11] And Sonja needed to talk.

Having come to Shanghai in the expectation that either the German or Russian Communist Party would put her to work helping the Chinese comrades, she had spent the last three months leading an outwardly bourgeois life with her architect husband; she was growing impatient, though. Since she was too inhibited to approach Agnes directly, Sonja would recall, she wangled an introduction through her boss at the Trans-Ocean Kuomin Telegraph Service—one of the legitimate businesses, perhaps, that the OMS had begun running in Shanghai to avoid the danger and difficulty of using couriers to finance Comintern work in China.[12]

On November 7, 1930, the anniversary of the Russian Revolution and a favored time for leftist gatherings, the two women met in the café of the Cathay

Hotel. Agnes was dressed simply for the occasion, Sonja later wrote. With her thin brown hair and broad forehead, she did not strike Sonja as in any way pretty, but she found Agnes intelligent and lively and said her sense of humor was infectious. Agnes spoke to Sonja for a while about how the British despised her for her earlier work in the Indian revolutionary movement; then Agnes grilled her.

Sonja later maintained that she did not know whether Agnes was a "comrade," but she trusted her nonetheless, and for the first time since arriving in Shanghai, Sonja spoke freely about her political views and her frustrating isolation.[13] Agnes invited Sonja to socialize with Chinese acquaintances, among them Lu Hsun and Chen Han-seng, and included her in invitations to restaurants and the theater. She also put Sonja to work writing for the League of Left Wing Writers' proscribed paper and translating Agnes's articles for the *Zeitung* into German. Sonja later recalled that she was initially somewhat puzzled as to why someone of Agnes's stature enjoyed her company as much as Agnes seemed to. At twenty-three, Sonja was fifteen years younger than Agnes, and though she was a Communist she had always been financially secure. Even here in Shanghai she lived a sheltered life. But Sonja was a nurturer, like the other women who grew close to Agnes, and as the American inevitably revealed her emotional fragility, Sonja sensed that her evenness and optimism were comforting. During Agnes's neurasthenic attacks of ill health, Sonja would hold her friend's hand. If Agnes felt alone, or called, depressed, at 3:00 A.M., Sonja would leave her husband to care for Agnes. By early 1931, Sonja thought of herself as Agnes's dearest friend.

The relationship had its rough edges. Early on, Agnes warned Sonja that while she was in solidarity with the KPD in opinion and activities, she found it difficult to submit to Party discipline. Sonja, who was a loyal Party member, often found Agnes's spontaneous, emotional reactions to political events upsetting, but Sonja quickly learned that if she tried too vehemently to argue her friend into the acceptable position, Agnes would storm off, enraged. A few hours later, though, Sonja would write, Agnes would telephone as if nothing had happened and resume their friendship.

"Perhaps she did not want to admit her membership in the Party even to me ... I think nevertheless she spoke the truth," Sonja later recalled.[14] Agnes did. She was more useful to the Communists outside the Party than in it, and her reluctance and/or inability to follow the Party line gave her credibility as an independent, even as she worked for the Comintern and Soviet military intelligence.

Sorge had also returned to Shanghai that fall, accompanied by his two wireless operators. The data he was currently gathering, on the economic and political policies of the Nanking government and its plans for the subjugation of warlords, frequently took him out of town; in the city, he relied for information on a circle of German merchants, scholars, military advisers to the Nanking government, and other officials who were linked to the German Consulate General. Much of his free time, however, he spent with Agnes—either alone or accompanied by his friend Gerhardt Eisler, the German Communist who had become the Comintern's chief representative in China. "Eisler? I know no chap named Eisler," Agnes had written in 1926. Now he was a personal friend.

By the winter of 1930, according to Sorge's later account, Agnes had become his principal confidante and assistant; she attended all meetings of direct ring members.[15] Women, Sorge would write a decade later, "are absolutely unfit for espionage work. They have no understanding of political or other affairs . . . and are . . . very poor sources of information." Agnes, however, was different. As a "wife," he later observed, "her value was nil," but she had a "brilliant mind and fit in well as a news reporter . . . In short, she was like a man."[16]

Not only was Agnes Sorge's chief recruiting agent, her home served as a site for his group's nocturnal gatherings, and she provided Sorge with data on American political and economic activities in China and the effect of the tense Sino-Japanese situation on Sino-American relations. Like other Communist writers, Agnes suspected that America's offer to mediate the Chinese Eastern Railway dispute the previous year had been a pretext for wresting control of the railway and getting U.S. money into Manchuria. She advised Sorge, who was under instructions to track the Nanking government's foreign policy, particularly with regard to America, England, Japan, and the Soviet Union, that American influence in Shanghai was growing "in striking contrast," as Sorge described it, to the Sino-Japanese conflict. She also informed him about efforts by Nanking to cement its ties with the United States and Great Britain, which were widening the rift between the Anglo-American bloc and Japan.[17] Sorge relayed this information to Moscow. In providing Sorge with such information, was Agnes acting against the interests of the United States, as her detractors would later allege? Perhaps. Perhaps not.

The material Agnes shared with Sorge was not classified. At least some of what she reported found its way into her published work. On the other hand, her participation in Sorge's intelligence group had drawn her incrementally beyond the line where political activism blurred into espionage. Her primary loyalty was to the workers of China and Russia—not the "masters of world imperialism," as she referred to the United States and Great Britain—and her need to be secretive about her work with Sorge well exceeded what was necessary to avoid government repression of her legal activities.

Agnes had recently introduced Sorge to a man who was probably Lu Hsun (Sorge later described him as the husband of the Cantonese "Chui" and a "serious tuberculosis case"). He began to work on problems peculiar to south China and maintained liaison between Canton and Shanghai. Agnes also introduced Sorge to a woman (perhaps the librarian wife of Chen Han-seng) who began procuring economic data and military information for Sorge.[18] Sorge believed that if he changed the venue of the ring's meetings from time to time and saw his people on crowded streets, weather permitting, or in foreigners' homes, members did not run much risk of detection. He was not wrong. Government agents remarked on the unusual number of Chinese going in and out of Agnes's apartment, but they did not act.[19]

Even so, Sorge was interested in acquiring additional foreign helpers to avoid having his Chinese recruits too closely observed. Agnes, who knew of Sonja's desire to be engaged in "active, useful" work, as Sonja would put it, introduced her friend to Sorge after obtaining Comintern approval.[20] Sonja later wrote that Sorge warned her at their first meeting of the risks she would run in assisting what she described as the Chinese Communists' revolutionary struggle, but he strongly hinted that her willingness to let "the comrades" use her home as a meeting place would be a welcome gesture of international solidarity. Happy for the opportunity to be of service, she recalled, she assented at once.[21]

At this time, Sorge was on the lookout for a suitable Japanese to bring him information on Japan's China policy and the internal situation in China. After conferring with Chen Han-seng (who relayed the request to knowledgeable Chinese and Japanese Communists), Agnes introduced Sorge to Ozaki Hotsumi. He was an excellent choice: intelligent, idealistic, a respected journalist, and fluent in English, German, Chinese, and Japanese. Ozaki later admitted that he never really believed the man who introduced himself as an American newspaperman named Johnson was either American or a journalist. When he first agreed to work with Sorge, Ozaki would write, he thought Sorge was affiliated with the International Red Aid, the same Comintern auxiliary for which Ozaki believed Agnes worked. However, soon after the three of them began meeting, in Agnes's apartment and restaurants around the city, Ozaki decided that Sorge more likely held an important post in what Ozaki referred to as the Comintern's "special espionage division" — the OMS — and that Agnes was his subordinate there. He was also aware, however, that Sorge would share his information with the Russian Party and the Soviet government.[22]

Unhappy with the Chinese Communists' failure in south China, the Comintern had banished Li Li-san to Moscow. In January 1931, the CCP elected a new politburo, several members of which were selected by Moscow because the Soviets trusted them unconditionally to follow the Comintern line. The move did not entirely quell the debate within the CCP over whether the urban insurrection favored by the Soviet Union or the rural uprisings urged by Chinese guerrilla leaders should direct the country's future revolutionary course. To ensure the matter would progress according to Comintern plans, Moscow evidently deemed further corrective action necessary.

On January 17, 1931, incoming CCP leader Wang Ming, a Moscow loyalist, informed the Shanghai Municipal Police that some of his dissenting comrades were conducting a secret meeting. As a result of his betrayal, twenty-four CCP members, including five young leaders of the League of Left Wing Writers, were arrested and turned over to KMT authorities. Had Agnes understood that one of her own was responsible for the treachery, perhaps she might not have left the city so soon thereafter, preferring to stay and fight, but it was decades before that information saw the light of day. Instead, after warning Lu Hsun that one of the men who had been arrested carried a document that implicated him, Agnes took off for the Nationalists' capital of Nanking, where Sorge, who had begun dividing the work of his agents according to their individual specialties, had asked her to go. A few days later, she and Ozaki proceeded to the Philippines, where a PPTUS conference, along with the founding congress of the Philippine Communist Party, was scheduled.

Publicly, Agnes maintained that she had gone to the Philippines to recuperate from the previous summer's events. Privately, however, she admitted that she "did nothing else but work." Her activities put her in contact with the American Communists Eugene Dennis (then the Comintern's representative to the Philippine Communist Party) and Earl Browder (now general secretary of the CPUSA) and the charismatic Philippine Communist leader Crisanto Evangelista.[23] The unfolding events in China's nearby Kiangsi province, where, she said, "the persecution of the revolutionary movement . . . especially of the peasant movement" had just begun, were the focus of her trip.[24] Rumor had it that she and Sorge hoped to visit the site of an upcoming congress of Chinese soviets.[25]

In February 1931, the KMT had unleashed a second extermination campaign against the Communists in Kiangsi. More than three hundred thousand government troops had descended on the province and massacred untold thousands of peasants during house-to-house village searches. In the mountainous battle areas, however, guerrilla tactics prevailed. Red Army rank and file, aided by an intelligence corps of local inhabitants who apprised them of Nationalist troop actions and a propaganda corps who scrawled mutinous messages on village walls, were beating back far better funded and equipped government forces.

On her return to Shanghai in early March 1931—exhausted rather than refreshed from her "vacation"—Agnes learned that the five League of Left Wing Writers activists arrested that January had been executed. Reportedly, they had been buried alive. All of those who died were CCP members—revolutionaries as much as writers. Nonetheless, Agnes and her left literary friends fastened on this extension of the KMT suppression campaign into the cultural arena to launch an international protest against the Chinese government.

Aided by the writer Mao Tun, Agnes and Lu Hsun drafted an English-language appeal and manifesto in memory of the Chinese writers "butchered" by the KMT, which appeared in the *New Masses* and the *New Republic*. The Muenzenberg network circulated Japanese, Russian, German, and French translations and distributed a protest by the Moscow-based International Union of Revolutionary Writers signed by several dozen distinguished authors including Henri Barbusse and Upton Sinclair.[26]

That April, Sonja, her husband, and their infant son, Mischa (named after *New Masses* editor Mike Gold), moved into a home in the French Concession, which she described as better suited for Sorge's meetings. She had become deeply involved in the group's work by this time, she said—hiding weapons for them, copying confidential documents, and acting as a liaison and messenger while Agnes worked on higher-level tasks. On her own initiative, Sonja had also begun to invite influential Germans to her home so that Sorge could eavesdrop on their conversations.

Sonja's inability to talk to her husband about the people who were closest to her or the work that formed the substance of her life took its toll on her marriage; a mutual attraction developed between her and Sorge. By the spring of 1931, it was Sonja who was seen on the back of Sorge's motorcycle, enjoying the high-speed rides that had thrilled Agnes the year before. When word of the affair reached Agnes, she took it badly. One of the ways she vented her distress was by disagreeing with Sonja on unrelated issues.

On June 15, 1931, Shanghai Municipal Police following the trail of a Comintern courier arrested the man known as Hilaire Noulens (or Paul Ruegg), along with a woman who posed as his wife. A key in Noulens's possession led police to an apartment where they seized numerous documents belonging to the Shanghai bureau of the PPTUS and the Comintern's Far East bureau (FEB), including several reports Agnes had most likely authored.[27] Luckily for her, by the time police caught up with Noulens, a secretary at the FEB had fled to Moscow with most of the organization's recent correspondence—and all the documents of the OMS.[28]

Under questioning, Noulens maintained that he was merely a Swiss trade union organizer who earned his living teaching French and German; police believed they had captured a Polish Comintern agent who oversaw PPTUS activities in Shanghai. In truth, Noulens was a Russian Communist named Yakov Rudnik, who ran the OMS operation there. Like his partner, Tatyana Moiseenko (better known in Shanghai as Gertrude Noulens), Rudnik was a career intelligence officer with many years' experience in Europe. In Shanghai, he was at the nexus of all Comintern communications and monetary networks.

After several passports and addresses were discovered among his possessions, Swiss authorities refused to exercise their jurisdiction in the case; the couple were remanded to Chinese military authorities. Soon police discovered that in the year since the FEB had been operating in Shanghai, "a sub-agency of the Communist International in Berlin" had disbursed close to half a million dollars in China—not just for "trade union" work but for the Red Army's open warfare against Chinese government forces.[29] The investigation unearthed nothing that directly implicated Agnes, but police were certain that she knew Noulens and that she was somehow connected to the FEB—if not as a staffer, than as a courier and liaison agent who provided funding to other Communist parties. On further analysis, they decided that her work was similar to Noulens's and entailed propagating Communist doctrine, organizing workers, and establishing Communist organizations.[30] Authorities were wrong about her affiliation but correct about her tasks. Still, they had no way to prove it, and Agnes never offered clarification.

A few years hence, Agnes would dismiss the incident as a British police raid on "a room with a chair in it" and derisively laugh off rumors that the seized documents proved that Communists had been plotting to overthrow the government or that she "had been sent out as the propaganda agent for the new regime."[31] At the time of the incident, though, the arrest of Noulens and the seizure of documents touched off a panic among Shanghai radicals—Agnes among them. Several Comintern agents fled to Moscow, while Agnes took off for Canton and Hong Kong to warn those who had not yet heard, leaving Shanghai in such haste that she carried no luggage with her.[32]

Sonja had been storing two suitcases for Sorge in her apartment: one filled with printed and handwritten material, the other with guns he had obtained from the German generals Chiang Kai-shek had hired to train Nationalist troops fighting the Communists. After emptying their contents onto her floor, Sorge advised Sonja to pack another suitcase for herself and her baby in case they needed to hide among the comrades in China's interior.[33] Within ten days of Noulens's arrest, the CCP underground organization was in ruins.

By the time Agnes returned to Shanghai on July 5, the Noulenses had had their first court hearing. During her absence, Sorge (whom the Shanghai Municipal Police now suspected of working with the PPTUS) had changed apartments. These days, he left his premises only rarely, fielding calls on a private phone extension he had installed in his ground-floor rooms. However, near the end of the summer the Comintern sent a person to Shanghai to reorganize the Far East bureau. Once life assumed some semblance of normalcy, Sorge's group began meeting again. Other Comintern activities also resumed in Shanghai, including the international protest campaign against Chiang Kai-shek's White Terror that Agnes had discussed with Osaki, which was run under the direction of the International Red Aid. Emboldened by the attention the "Incident of the Five Martyrs" had garnered a few months earlier, the Comintern now featured the captured OMS agents prominently in its project, and the plight of the "wrongfully imprisoned trade union officials," as Agnes would refer to Rudnik and Moiseenko, occupied much of Agnes's time and attention during the latter half of 1931.

Working closely, albeit covertly, with Muenzenberg and his deputy, Louis Gibarti, Agnes assembled sympathetic, non-Communist foreigners and Chinese into a "prisoner release" committee on which Madame Sun served as chairperson and Agnes as unofficial secretary. From Berlin, Muenzenberg and his associates bombarded the women with telegrams from internationally recognized writers, artists, and intellectuals—including Bertolt Brecht, Walter Gropius, Kaethe Kollwitz, Mies van der Rohe, Paul Klee, Theodore Dreiser, Sinclair Lewis, and John Dos Passos—who urged them to use their influence to seek clemency for the Noulenses.[34] Agnes then leaked the telegrams to Chinese authorities and the local press to great effect. Perhaps some of the signatories knew more than Muenzenberg told them. Most, however, did not even know Noulens' real name, let alone his true position.

Agnes took pains to conceal her role in the campaign, but she was too conspicuous a player to escape notice for long. In early September, a local British official wrote a three-part article for the *Shanghai Evening Post and Mercury* that accused Agnes of passing the cables and denounced her as a Communist and a member of the League Against Imperialism. (He was aware of her connection to Muenzenberg but unaware that the campaign was being run through the Red Aid.) Agnes, outraged, dismissed the charges as more British payback for her work in the Indian independence movement. Ten years later she was still fuming over what she called "a masterpiece of gutter journalism, attacking both my political and personal life." The Japanese *Nichi Nichi* went further, charging Agnes (with equal parts truth and hyperbole) of spying for Russian state security and sleeping with military men "to worm secrets from them," she later recalled. But the campaign against her had just begun.

As the Noulenses' trial got under way, a man who identified himself as a representative of the Red Aid appeared at Agnes's door. He claimed he had two letters for Agnes from Muenzenberg and requested that she help him conduct his "flood relief work" by introducing him to "suitable" Chinese.[35] (The Yangtze had flooded enormous areas of farmland that spring, killing two million and threatening millions more with dysentery, cholera, and famine.) Agnes was convinced he was a police agent, not an activist, and denied having anything to do with either the Red Aid or Muenzenberg. She was not even a member, let alone a functionary in that "Communist" organization, she would recall, and she said she chased him off with a leaded walking stick she kept for such purposes near her door. Two days later, she added, a second visitor met a similar fate.

Then the streetlight in front of her building went out and a dubious-looking "art" shop opened next door, leading Agnes to suspect that her apartment was under surveillance. When several Chinese whom Agnes believed belonged to the gangster Du Yue-sheng's villainous Green Gang started to patrol her neighborhood, she was terrified and asked two of her newest foreign friends—Harold Isaacs, a twenty-one-year-old Columbia University graduate only recently recruited to Communism, and Cecil Frank Glass, a South African correspondent for the Soviet news agency Tass—to move into her apartment and act as her bodyguards.

Since her residence was in the French Concession, Agnes also lodged a complaint with the French consul general, who sent a representative from the political department of the French Municipal Police to investigate. Agnes later described him as an effeminate man who dressed entirely "in white, with a blond waxed mustache and a dainty walking stick." She said he categorically denied any French involvement in the harassment, which she assumed meant the British were responsible, but she was not going down without a fight.

In mid-September, an editorial in the American-owned *China Weekly Review* blasted "local die-hards" for their underhanded persecution of Agnes.[36] Describing her as a respected writer for the *Zeitung*, the *New Republic*, the *Nation*, local Chinese papers, and the *Weekly Review*, the piece argued that while Agnes's views on Asian revolutionary movements were known to many European liberals connected with the LAI, she had received their telegrams in her capacity as the *Zeitung*'s China correspondent; she was neither a Communist nor a member of the organization. Besides, the article observed, the fact that the LAI might have Communists as members did not make it a "Communistic organization." Perhaps Agnes's sympathies were misguided, it argued, but passing cables to Chinese authorities and local papers was not a crime. Lest anyone forget, the piece concluded by pointing out that she was an American citizen who had registered with the local consulate general.

Agnes could not have said it better had she written it herself, which perhaps she had, but more pressing international developments soon overtook the

Noulens story. On the evening of September 18, 1931, without a declaration of war, Japanese troops blew up a stretch of railway in Manchuria. They captured Mukden, then swiftly occupied 1.3 million square kilometers in China's three northeastern provinces and declared them the Empire of Manchukuo. Inside China anti-Japanese feeling surged, but Chiang Kai-shek, who was in the middle of his third campaign to annihilate the Communist "bandits" in soviet Kiangsi, was more focused on political unification inside China than the risks posed by foreign aggression. He ordered a policy of nonresistance to the Japanese.

The Japanese conquest of Manchuria completely altered its position in the Far East. It also had great significance to the USSR, because the situation brought the Russians face-to-face with the Japanese in a vast border region that had formerly been largely neglected, from the standpoint of national defense. Responsibility for providing Russian military intelligence with information on the incident itself fell to an espionage group the Fourth Bureau had established in Harbin, but Sorge still needed to learn whether the event would develop into a Japanese military operation against the USSR. Since Ozaki was already stretched thin, Sorge asked him to find another trustworthy Japanese to investigate conditions in Manchuria and gather information about a possible Japanese military invasion of Soviet territory. Ozaki introduced him to Kawai Teikichi, a Japanese Communist trained by the Chinese LAI, who had several friends in north China and Manchuria. In the meantime, Muenzenberg organized an International China Aid Committee to mobilize pro-Soviet foreign support.

That October, Agnes moved to another apartment in the French Concession—this time on Avenue Joffre. Sonja's architect husband helped Agnes decorate and designed some furniture for her, but she had little time to enjoy it. For nearly a year, the *Zeitung* had refused to publish Agnes's work, based on complaints about her one-sided reporting. Now the paper received what Agnes described as a "long and lying report," which she claimed the British had purchased from White Russian agents, detailing at considerable length her purported Communist activities in China.[37]

As Agnes would recall the memo, after decrying her involvement with the Red Aid, it stated that she had attended the first All-China Congress of Chinese Soviets with a group of young Chinese Communists whom she caroused drunkenly with and offered herself sexually to each evening, and that, in addition, she had opened the congress by appearing "stark naked on the platform, wearing only a red hat, and had sung the Internationale."[38] The *Zeitung*, it appears, shared the information with Agnes just before it terminated her contract.[39]

In response, Agnes fired off a letter to Roger Baldwin in which she complained bitterly of her mistreatment. After failing to get the Chinese to kill her, she wrote, the British were alleging that she was the China representative of the

International Red Aid. How absurd! "This organization is branded as 'Red' in China, and its members, if caught, killed," she observed.[40] Why would she be so foolish as to involve herself in something that risky? Still, the harassment continued.

Although the Soviet Union had not had official relations with the Chinese Nationalist government since 1929, it revisited its position of implacable hostility toward Nanking in the aftermath of the Manchurian Incident, fearful of further Japanese aggression. Quietly at first, the Comintern began to encourage the Chinese Communists to consider a second united front with the KMT against the Japanese. Toward that end, Chatto, who by this time had become a member of the Comintern's Indian secretariat, wrote Agnes at her secret post office box requesting that she use her "good connections with certain Chinese circles" (i.e., with Shanghai's Moscow-leaning CCP leaders) to secure support for the move.[41] The Shanghai Municipal Police, which had been watching Agnes's box for months, now had the Chinese gendarmerie commander seize the correspondence as proof of her Communist ties.

When Agnes learned what had happened, she became hysterical. After lodging an official protest with the U.S. court in Shanghai, she wrote again to Baldwin, this time asking that he employ his Washington connections to call off the Britishers' persecution of her. No longer were they content merely to forward "dirty reports" about her activities to the Americans. Now, she said, they were planting "all sorts of incriminating Communist literature" in her post office box.[42] She also begged Madame Sun, Sanger, and Nehru to do something—at once—to save her. It was no longer a matter of preserving her citizenship, she said, but of protecting her life, for the British were after her "like ferocious dogs." As long as they acted in the strictest confidence, she said they could always reach her either through Chen Han-seng's secret post office box (whose number she provided) or through Madame Sun directly.

Nehru and Madame Sun promptly lodged protests with the Ministry of Foreign Affairs in Nanking. Sanger, too, pledged to do all she could. Baldwin advised the secretary of state that British officials and journalists, inflamed by Agnes's open championship of a Chinese nationalism that came at their expense, were having the Chinese police seize her mail illegally, and he demanded that the State Department pursue the matter promptly.[43] After reading the reports on Agnes's activities provided by the Shanghai consul general, the State Department once again refused to take any action on her behalf.[44]

By December, the campaign to free the Noulenses was as big an international cause célèbre as the Sacco-Vanzetti case, a historian familiar with the matter observes.[45] Muenzenberg had enlisted Albert Einstein to plead the Noulenses' case before the U.S. Senate Foreign Relations Committee and dispatched a delegation that included Theodore Dreiser, Clarence Darrow, Lewis Gannett, Norman Thomas, Thomas Dewey, and Roger Baldwin to lobby the Chinese Embassy in Washington.[46] Despite their efforts, though, the Noulenses remained behind bars, so Agnes, who was already handling publicity for the campaign in the United States, approached the American Civil Liberties Union to help rectify the matter.

On December 24, 1931, she drafted a letter to Baldwin in his capacity as head of the ACLU's International Committee on Political Prisoners. "I notice that the name of your Committee is 'International,'" Agnes remarked, as if coming on the information for the first time.[47] Did that mean he could he send a committee to China to investigate prisons that held political prisoners and obtain information on their numbers, treatment, places of confinement, and deaths from torture, cold, and contaminated food and water? If so, she noted, Madame Sun would be happy to join them. Even if the Nanking government refused Baldwin permission, its very refusal, she explained, would generate tremendous publicity against a regime that publicly boasted of its democracy and defense of freedom of speech, press, and assembly while quietly taking steps to ensure that "the two foreign political prisoners, Mr. and Mrs. Paul Ruegg [Noulens], were headed for a legal lynching."[48]

Baldwin did not reply. Even if he had, Agnes would have had to put the project to the side, for hardly more than a week after she wrote, Japanese troops invaded Shanghai. Her *Zeitung* post having been terminated, Agnes covered the story for the *Nation* and *International Literature*, the journal of the Moscow-based International Union of Revolutionary Writers. For thirty-four days, the fighting was so close to the edge of the protected foreign settlement that Agnes said she could view the action from the roof of her apartment building through field glasses. As the crisis intensified, the public clamored increasingly for a stronger policy against Japan, but Chiang Kai-shek did not even support his own troops at this time. Intent on destroying the Chinese Communists, whom he perceived as the greater threat, he was reluctant to squander resources on a war against the Japanese.

Initially, Sorge would later confess, he had relied on Agnes for information on "American activities in China, which consisted chiefly of large investments in Shanghai and investments in radio broadcasting and aviation enterprises" and were run by American businessmen and commercial attaches at the Shanghai consulate.[49] Recently, however, the United States had become diplomatically active "in connection with the problems of extraterritorial rights and the cessation of hostilities in Shanghai," Sorge explained.

As the Shanghai Incident further aggravated relations between China and Japan, and widened the rift between Japan and the United States and Great Britain, the Nanking government was "cementing its ties with the U.S. and Great Britain," Sorge would recall. With British activities in Asia "already receding," and the USSR "in a position where she had to give more consideration to diplomatic relations with the United States," Agnes began to provide Sorge with "sporadic" contributions on these complex problems.[50]

Sorge's superiors also needed to learn whether the attack was a single unrelated event or part of a larger Japanese plan to conquer all of China. If the latter were the case, the Soviet military desperately needed to learn whether Japan's next move would be farther south in China or toward Siberia in the north. For that reason, Sorge continued to meet with his ring members throughout the entire incident—even after the Comintern's Far East bureau shut down. The Chinese section of Shanghai had been reduced to rubble, and Japanese were unable to walk its streets in safety, so Sorge would meet Ozaki and Kawai in the dead of night, at the boundary of the Japanese Concession, and escort them by car to Agnes's home in the French Concession, where the four of them could converse freely.[51]

By 1932, Agnes's gift for identifying sympathetic young foreigners had created a broad circle of acquaintances whose friendship she exploited for the benefit of the Chinese Communists and the Comintern. Rewi Alley, a New Zealand activist, would recall being seduced by her burning eyes, bitter laugh, and passionate honesty of purpose. Others found inspiration in her indomitable spirit. Some confessed to being overwhelmed by her untiring indoctrination efforts. In the jungle that was then Shanghai, Alley later explained, Agnes rallied her troops with empathy, mischief, and "the glorious white charger of her imagination."[52]

Harold Isaacs, who had been Agnes's bodyguard after the Noulens arrest, would later disparage his friend's penchant for exaggeration, along with her tendency to view people "as puppets pulled by the strings of class forces, playing out a harsh morality play in which 'good' was pitted against 'wicked.'"[53] At the moment, though, he was managing to overlook her personal peccadilloes. Troubled by the Chinese press ban on coverage of subjects that displeased the KMT, he allowed her to press him into service.

After months of collaboration between Isaacs and Agnes, Madame Sun, the CCP central committee, the Comintern, and the CPUSA, Isaacs became the publisher and editor of the *China Forum*, an English-language weekly designed to inform local Chinese and influence international opinion on matters of importance to the Chinese Communists.[54] The paper exploited Isaacs's extraterritorial status by being printed in the French Concession but registered in the United States to avoid Chinese censors. The first issue appeared in Shanghai in January 1932. For the next eight months, *Forum* contributors—who included Agnes, Ozaki, Lu Hsun, Chen Han-seng, and China specialists inside the Chinese branch of the CPUSA as well as Isaacs—trumpeted the excesses of the White Terror to sympathetic audiences in China and abroad. Although it overplayed the extent of the Chinese Communists' successes and ignored problems in the Soviet Union, the Forum provided vital information on the kidnapping, extradition, imprisonment, and execution of tens of thousands of Chinese leftists and Communists by the KMT and gangster Du Yue-sheng's Green Gang, on the achievements of the Communist armies, the soviet government in Kiangsi, the Noulens case, and the Japanese attack on Shanghai.

That spring, Chiang Kai-shek renewed his offensive against the Kiangsi soviet, and Agnes found another opportunity to put her foreign friends to work. Encouraged by the success of the *China Forum*, the CCP wanted Agnes to write a book, to be published abroad, that would inform readers about the new soviet districts and describe Red Army resistance to Chiang's encirclement campaign. Toward that end, the Party underground began sending Red Army men, fresh from battle in the central soviet area, to speak with Agnes, accompanied by CCP representatives armed with maps. Rewi Alley, who spoke Chinese, translated for her and helped her assist the fugitive fighters by offering his home as an asylum and smuggling the men past police checkpoints in the official car that was a perquisite of his job on the Shanghai Municipal Council.[55] Agnes would later share the stories she heard with Otto Braun, the Comintern's military adviser to the CCP.

The timing for the project was auspicious. By the spring of 1932, Agnes had nearly completed *Chinese Destinies: Sketches of Present-Day China*, her volume of fictionalized Chinese tales—of a rickshaw coolie blinded by his freezing tears and hit by a car, then beaten by its owner; of timber workers who earned less than twenty Chinese cents a day, boys who refused to marry the girls their parents selected, youth lost to opium, and old-fashioned wives who bobbed their hair and danced on bound feet. The book described a world unknown to Western readers, and her colorful mosaic of daily life, which illustrated more vividly than any Marxist tract the debasement and oppression of millions of ordinary Chinese in a rapidly changing country, was under contract with the Fischer Verlag, a respected German firm that also published Herman Hesse, Thomas Mann, and Rainer Maria Rilke. Agnes's current project was the greater journalistic coup, however, for its publication would make her the first foreigner since the debacle in 1927 to report the inside scoop on the Chinese Communists. The story would benefit from a visit to the soviet areas, which would be a perilous feat, but by April she was already speaking of her desire to make the journey.[56]

Agnes's unwavering faith in direct action made it hard for her to labor quietly on peripheral jobs to advance the new society, however constructive they might be, her friend Rewi Alley observed, but Chiang Kai-shek's extermination campaigns, which forced the Communists into deepest secrecy, made her preference for more active involvement, such as providing shelter to hunted Chinese Communists, terribly risky. Agnes's extraterritorial status allowed her to evade government sanctions. Still, in a city where anyone could have an enemy killed simply by paying a sum to thugs, carrying a pistol in her handbag, as she did, was not sufficient protection.

Agnes believed that by carefully concealing her tracks, keeping her address confidential—even among friends—and ensuring that her work with Sorge remained a closely guarded secret, she was strictly observing the rules of conspiracy. However, she was followed routinely, and her journalistic endeavors earned her a place on the KMT's blacklist. In the years to come, Alley would grouse that she was oversuspicious on some occasions and not vigilant enough on others. Her detractors on the left would maintain that her flamboyant style

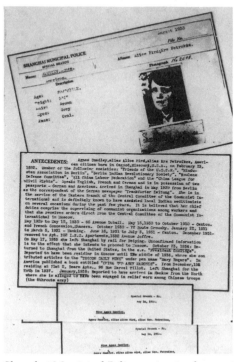

The Shanghai Municipal Police maintained extensive files on Agnes. *National Archives, Washington, D.C.*

attracted undue notice and accuse her of indiscretion. The most revealing comment Agnes herself made about her illicit activities at the time was a throwaway remark to Florence. "I may not be innocent," she wrote, "but I'm right."[57]

Agnes like to boast that in the three years she had lived in China, she had become "almost as hard and ferocious as many Chinese, filled with hatred, ready to fight at a moment's notice, without patience of any kind for the comfortably situated in life, intolerant of every doubting person."[58] In truth, she passed her days in a state of constant tension. A bit of good news might send her dancing around her apartment, singing along to her gramophone recordings of cowboy songs and ditties like "The Man on the Flying Trapeze." She was also well known for hosting parties where her vigor ensured no dull moments. But her cat-and-mouse game with authorities of several countries was playing havoc with her nerves, and after exhausting herself on the details of some covert plan gone awry, she often retreated to her bed. Friends tried to help by spending the night when she was most anxious, but even so, Agnes required a brief hospitalization in the spring of 1932.

Summer brought another KMT extermination campaign to the central soviet area, but the Communist movement in rural interior China continued to grow. Effective intelligence, good mobility in the mountains, carefully cultivated popular support, and successful guerrilla tactics would extend its influence beyond Kiangsi into the provinces of Hupeh, Hunan, Szechuan, and Shensi. A few years hence, a colleague of Agnes's would insist that her "very closeness to the Chinese Red Army . . . prevented her from visiting them."[59] In fact, Agnes spent the summer of 1932 in Kuling, a partisan area just outside the central soviet district in Kiangsi province, where the CCP central committee had arranged a bungalow for her, Sonja, and Sonja's baby.[60] Sonja later said she had asked Sorge whether Madame Sun could also join them there, but Sorge had been uneasy at the prospect of the three women being seen together and vetoed the idea.

In the mornings, Agnes conducted interviews on the Chinese soviets and their defender, the Chinese Red Army; in the afternoons, she and Sonja went hiking. The mountains were as overgrown as a jungle, and Sonja later recalled how much they admired the views of the Yangtze valley and the mountain chains of Hupeh, where the Red Army was camped. Relations between the two women, already strained in Shanghai, deteriorated further in Kuling. The women clashed repeatedly over the Noulenses' son, Dimitri (known in Shanghai as Jimmy). Sonja would complain that Agnes repeatedly demanded Sonja adopt him, which would have jeopardized her illegal work, and spoiled the child by overwhelming him with gifts.

Then the women learned that the Noulenses had begun a hunger strike. As they sat down to lunch that day, "Agnes suddenly said she could eat nothing," Sonja later wrote. "I replied—perhaps somewhat coolly—that that would not help the Noulenses. Agnes stood up and left the table. In the afternoon, I went for a walk by myself. When I returned, I found a letter: under these circumstances, she could not remain . . . I was too concerned with my personal happiness, my family life. Private affairs played too great a role for me. I was just not what one understands by 'revolutionary'."[61] Disgusted, Agnes returned to Shanghai five weeks early. Sonja said she attempted to discuss the women's split with Sorge, but he refused to mediate their dispute.

The Noulenses' trial concluded in August, and they were sentenced to death. While rumors flew through Shanghai that Muenzenberg, well known as a funnel for cash to and from the Comintern, had arrived on the scene, their sentence was commuted to life imprisonment. Officially, it was said that an amnesty law the Nanking government created two months previously had spared the couple's lives. People closer to the scene (including Agnes) credited Sorge, who reputedly received forty thousand dollars from an unnamed source to bribe a corrupt Chinese judge.[62]

Both the American consul general and the Nanking government were irate at the *China Forum*'s outspoken support for the Noulenses and its exhaustive trial coverage. Officials of the two countries wanted to suppress the paper as an embarrassment to the United States, and with the State Department's sanction, they succeeded that August. They then moved to withdraw Isaacs's extraterritorial protection (and by implication Agnes's). By establishing a precedent with the two of them, officials hoped to discourage the Comintern practice of running American radicals in Shanghai.[63]

Within weeks, Baldwin alerted the State Department that the Chinese government had "unofficially" requested Agnes's deportation; the argument continued throughout the fall of 1932. The State Department did not believe that either Isaacs or Agnes had broken any American laws, but it encouraged the Chinese government to find some way to banish the pair nonetheless. The American consul general in Shanghai did not care whether he snared Agnes for her work on the *Forum* or with the International Red Aid, her activities in Canton, or her relationship with Muenzenberg. He had had enough of her antics— whatever it was she was doing.

A desperate Agnes turned to Sanger for succor. "I am in the greatest difficulty," she wrote on September 20.[64] Chen Han-seng's post office box was under censorship, she said, and nothing sent there was reaching her. Agnes accused the British Shanghai Municipal Police of being behind her most recent problems and described the Chinese as their willing tools. Anticipating Sanger's likely response, Agnes noted that it was useless for her to protest to the consulate because the consul general in Shanghai was a "pro-British reactionary."

The reason for her concern, she said, was that she had recently sent a manuscript of short stories by China's censored revolutionary writers to her American publisher. Now, though, they could not reach her because she dared not trust them with her latest secret address. That, she explained, could only go to Baldwin, Mike Gold, and Scott Nearing. (For her correspondence with Philip Jaffe, the person through whom Agnes passed information regarding the Chinese Communists to the CPUSA and, according to Muenzenberg deputy Louis Gibarti, the PPTUS, she used other channels of communication she preferred not to discuss with Sanger.)[65]

Gilbert Roe's widow, Gwyneth, had been after Agnes for months to meet their twenty-five-year-old nephew, John King Fairbank, who was traveling through China after graduating from Harvard. In the decades to come, Fairbank would achieve prominence as America's foremost China scholar. During the autumn of 1932, he was a student at Peking's Tsing Hwa University, where he was learning to read Chinese before he visited the country's archives.

Until recently, Agnes had been loath to expend her energy on someone who sounded to her like just another "college boy from America"—in other words, someone who preferred drinking, loafing, and chasing women to studying China's revolution. Claiming that the people with whom she associated would be too hardened for Fairbank, she had discouraged any attempts at introduction. "You can tell your nephew that some of my friends have recently had their heads chopped off—actually, literally, in the streets," she had advised Mrs. Roe the previous spring.[66] Now that Japanese troops were pushing from occupied Manchukuo into north China and Jehol into Chahar, Agnes changed her mind.

With Ozaki no longer in China (under orders from the *Asahi Shinbun*, he had returned to Japan early in 1932) and Sorge soon to leave for Moscow, Agnes had begun to lay the groundwork for a Sino-Japanese intelligence operation in north China that she would run herself—assigning activities, receiving reports, and providing funding to her subordinates. Sorge later explained that by this time he had not only enlisted Agnes as a member of his ring, he had "made her a member of the Comintern headquarters staff."[67] He had been one of two sponsors, he said; "a member in Moscow" (most likely of the Russian Communist Party, perhaps one of the OMS officials: Mirov-Abramov or Piatnitsky), had "consented to be the other . . . on the strength of [his] recommendations and reports."[68]

Although Agnes was never a typical spy, her transformation was now complete. On this project, she would provide no information against the United

States—her enemy was strictly Japan—but the subsequent work she conducted, which involved gathering political, economic, and military information on the developing situation in north China and Manchuria, was initiated by her at the behest of Soviet military intelligence.[69] If the word spy perhaps fails to conjure the anticolonial, anti-imperialist, antifascist sentiments that fueled Agnes's conduct or the moral decency of her intentions, the fact that she performed this covert service on behalf of a foreign government rather than a political cause or a journalistic outlet still made it espionage in its essentials.

Agnes might have lacked her superiors' goals or loyalties when she decided to check out Fairbank on his visit to Shanghai that fall, but she appreciated his political innocence. He was ignorant of the revolution, but he was decidedly liberal in his views. Once he got past Agnes's profanity-laden conversation, like so many other young foreigners in China he found her incredibly warm and funny, and her outspoken rebellion against political tyranny was compelling. Her discourse was full of the people's struggle and its horrors, Fairbank would write, and she preached the Communist message: that the challenge of China's poverty was paralyzing unless one organized with others. He believed Agnes accepted Party "guidance" uncritically and might be a letter carrier for the CCP underground, but he doubted she was temperamentally capable of being an agent, either for the Comintern or any other part of the Communist Party apparatus.[70] That November, after he returned to Peking, when Agnes wrote to ask if she could stay with him and his bride for a few weeks' rest, he had no idea Agnes planned to use his home as a cover for her clandestine activities.[71]

Ozaki had remained in contact with Agnes since he left Shanghai the previous year. It was risky, he later admitted, but she was offended if he did not answer her letters detailing affairs in China, her work for the Red Aid, and the problems of the White Terror.[72] Recently, Agnes had requested that Ozaki meet her in Peking—to discuss "certain matters," he would say—and in late December 1932, Ozaki instructed Kawai Teikichi, the Japanese Communist who had already worked for Sorge in north China the previous year, to accompany him there. Kawai still had friends and connections in Manchuria and north China and, according to Ozaki, had expressed an interest in resuming his former activities. Agnes preferred to work with Ozaki, but he was only willing to consult with her and then leave.

Agnes fled Shanghai at the same time the men sailed from Kobe. She was under the impression that she was traveling incognito, but German police agents stationed in the city noted her departure. By the time Ozaki and Kawai reached Peking, Agnes was ensconced in the Fairbanks household. She seemed bent on converting the newlyweds. Every night over dinner, according to Fairbank, she conducted an unsolicited crash course on Communism, the missionary movement (which she detested), Soviet Russia, deteriorating conditions in Germany, American strikes, the mere bohemianism of the *New Masses*, and many other subjects about which the Fairbanks knew little or nothing.[73]

On one notable occasion, Agnes got the genteel couple drunk on port, then led them in the most unrestrained orgy of dancing and carrying-on Fairbank said he had known in China. She gave them literature on the world revolution. She introduced them, under false identities, to Communist luminaries who apparently included Richard Sorge, whom Agnes ironically referred to as "Valentino"—a "number one" man of action, as she described him, who knew considerable theory (and whose return path to Moscow placed him in north China at this time).[74] When Agnes asked Fairbank to serve as a letter drop for Valentino/Sorge, Fairbank naively agreed, enthralled by his colorful houseguest.

Not long after the Japanese conspirators reached Peking, Ozaki brought Kawai to a small cottage inside a Chinese home that Agnes (or "Mrs. Sung," as she was known in Peking) and her Comintern advisers and helpers were using as a safe house. A Chinese answered the door and ushered the two men into a room where Agnes, garbed in a black cotton Chinese dress, was seated along with a well-built, bespectacled Chinese whom Kawai knew as Aniki and a middle-aged German in a black suit (perhaps either Otto Braun, the Comintern's military adviser to the CCP, Arthur Ewert, the Comintern adviser who replaced Eisler and was a friend of Agnes, or "Paul," a pseudonym of Klaas Selman, alias Karl Rimm, who was Sorge's successor).[75]

Kawai said it was clear from the outset that Agnes would be directing this ring, under the supervision, he thought, of the OMS, which he described as the Comintern's special espionage division.[76] Her base, however, would remain in Shanghai until the spring of 1933, when she would report to Moscow.[77] Over the next several months, Kawai would be her key lieutenant, assisted by two Japanese friends who, Kawai assured Agnes, were "absolutely" trustworthy. The three men would operate out of Peking, Tientsin, and Dairen. Ozaki, having helped with the initial preparations, returned to Japan. By late January, the group had established a bookstore in Tientsin as a front for their espionage activities.

The Fairbanks were aware that various men were calling on Agnes. They believed the visits were part of her attempt to establish a Peking branch of the China League for Civil Rights. According to Agnes, the relatively new organization was designed to introduce into China "at least the fundamental liberties . . . some freedom of speech and press" and perhaps "halt the torture and secret slaughter of men or improve prison conditions."[78] Contemporary Chinese accounts acknowledge it as a front organization that provided a legitimate channel Nanking authorities could not shut down to agitate for the Noulenses (who remained incarcerated in a Chinese military prison) and for imperiled Party activists like the writer Ting Ling, who had been kidnapped.[79] Prominent liberals Hu Shih, Hsu Tze Mou, Lin Yutang, Yang Chien, and Tsai Yuan-pei had founded the organization. Its executive committee, however, included the far more radical Agnes, Harold Isaacs, Lu Hsun, and Madame Sun. Through them, the League for Civil Rights had connections to the CCP, the Comintern, and other international revolutionary groups—as the following story makes clear.

In January 1933, while Agnes was still in Peking, she announced that she had received an unsigned letter from a political prisoner, which had been smuggled out of a Chinese military jail. It described such barbarous abuse as placing burning incense beneath his nose until it bled violently, inserting a mix of petroleum and pepper inside his nostrils, piercing his fingernails with needles, and poking his genitals with a pig hair. Muenzenberg received the first copy, but Agnes also distributed the document to the China League for Civil Rights and the International Labor Defense, American branch of the International Red Aid.[80]

By the following month an English translation, along with an appeal from the China League for Civil Rights demanding the unconditional liberation of all the country's political prisoners, was receiving international attention, for what occurred in this prison, Agnes carefully explained, was common to all.[81] There was a problem, though, with her exposé. Hu Shih, who directed the Peking branch of the China League for Civil Rights, suspected it was a fake. After investigating the prison himself, he said the report did not match what he had seen. Although he impugned Agnes's Communist friends, rather than Agnes, for writing it to arouse anti-KMT feelings, he believed they had counted on her to publicize it, knowing her ferocious opposition to social injustice. With that Hu Shih resigned from the league.[82]

Although the extent of Agnes's involvement was never fully grasped, the suspicion that she had used the China League for Civil Rights to advance the cause of the Chinese Communists (no one suspected that it was actually the Comintern) damaged her credibility with Fairbank. He declined to deliver or receive any more letters for her, let alone work, as Agnes suggested, inside a "secret faction" of the league that met privately in advance of its general meetings to decide among themselves "the line of action to be carried through."[83] Agnes's vociferous protestations of wronged innocence notwithstanding, Fairbank had learned his lesson the hard way and would not repeat his youthful error.

"Thanks a thousand times for acting as my 'transmitting agency' with Valentino," Agnes wrote Fairbank in February 1933, when she was once again in Shanghai. ". . . Try to think of yourself as a friend whom I chose to trust when I could trust no one else. I could not trust a machine or a transmitting agency; nor even men who often proclaim themselves as revolutionaries. I had no way of reaching Valentino except through you and I knew no one whom I could trust except you. If ever in doubt, you could just imagine that I sent him a love letter. Is that a sufficient alibi?" [84]

The world to which Agnes returned in 1933 was a very different place from the one she had known only a short time previously. While the KPD was busy fighting social fascism in Germany, an angry, bitter populace had ushered the Nazis into power. Shanghai's German Communists were initially stunned by what had occurred "without a fight, without a fight!" as Arthur Ewert put it.[85] Within weeks, those who remained would be spouting Stalin's line—that Hitler's victory was but a brief interlude on the way to Communist power in Germany—but during this uneasy period the Zeitgeist bookstore closed, and Irene Wiedemeyer disappeared.

In Germany, Chatto's boss, Georgi Dimitrov, who directed the Comintern's Western European bureau in Berlin, had been taken into custody and charged with complicity in setting the Reichstag fire. Soon the once powerful KPD would be proscribed. Agnes said the Fischer Verlag canceled her contract after her name appeared on a list of banned authors. Muenzenberg, who realized the events in Germany signaled an end to his world as it he knew it, had joined the mass exodus of German leftist and Communist intellectuals bound for Paris, where he hoped to resume his activities. In the months before Hitler assumed power, however, he had been organizing a major anti-imperialist war congress, to be held in Shanghai that April. The event was still scheduled to take place.

Since the Japanese invasion of Manchuria, scores of celebrated antimilitarists had been mobilized into action. Conference participants included such internationally celebrated authors as Theodore Dreiser, Henri Barbusse, and George Bernard Shaw (who was also a member of the Noulens International Defense Committee as well as an honorary chairman of the LAI). Agnes advised Fairbank to consider attending, if he had not already heard the argument, but she confessed that she herself could not "work up much lather" about it.

The arrangements, it appeared, were soaking up time she could ill afford to spare, because her intelligence operation in north China was falling apart. For a few months after Agnes left Peking, Kawai had transmitted his reports to his Chinese contact, as instructed, although how useful the information was that Agnes had her Japanese associates gathering in Manchuria —descriptions of conditions, and interviews—is not known. Then, as the spring of 1933 approached, Kawai's assistant had a nervous breakdown. Kawai would later say that he subsequently failed to establish any connections of his own; Ozaki claimed Kawai simply lost touch with his Chinese contact. In the opinion of Sorge, Kawai had "personal difficulties" that compromised his effectiveness.[86] Another Japanese associate would complain of Kawai's perennial financial problems, scandalous personal life, and lack of political commitment.[87] Whether or not he was to blame, Agnes found herself cut off from her intelligence sources, and her ring in disarray, as Japanese troops penetrated the Great Wall and entered Hopei province in north China.

When Shaw arrived in Shanghai on April 17, Agnes was not in a mood to celebrate, and she said she anticipated nothing from Shaw except a few bad jokes. Several years had passed since the "Grand Old Man," as Agnes called him, had ignored her request to critique *Daughter of Earth*, but she had not forgiven the slight. She accompanied Madame Sun on the boat that stealthily retrieved Shaw from his ocean liner, and attended a luncheon that the China League for Civil Rights hosted for him at Sun's home on the Rue Moliere,[88] but Agnes thought that Shaw's questions on the Japanese invasion, the soviet districts, and the upcoming congress displayed an alarming lack of mental acuity.

Madame Sun suggested that they take him to see Chapei, the Chinese section of Shanghai. Agnes would recall that Shaw declined, saying all ruins looked

A visit by British playwright George Bernard Shaw, Shanghai, 1933. From left to right: Agnes, Shaw, Madame Sun, Cai Yuan-pei, Lu Hsun. (Two other participants, the American Harold Isaacs and the Chinese Lin Yutang, do not appear in this version of the photograph.) *Courtesy Agnes Smedley Collection, University Archives, Arizona State University.*

alike to him. He was interested in nothing, she said he asserted; he was merely a living corpse who had actually died long ago. It soon became clear to everyone involved that the seventy-seven-year-old playwright could not focus on the matter at hand. Before they parted, Agnes wrote, Shaw asked her if he hadn't met her before. When she reminded him that she had once sent him a manuscript, she said, Shaw chided her for her foolishness. If she had any good ideas, he would have stolen them from her.[89]

Early that May, Agnes asked Edgar Snow for letters of introduction to a missionary friend of his in Changli and to any leftist English-speaking Chinese professors or German-speaking journalists that he knew in Tientsin and Tangshan. She said she was planning to "make a general survey" of the area, but her Chinese would not take her very far.[90] From there, she wrote, she would be going to Denmark, where she hoped to write another book at the home of Karin Michaelis before returning to China in the fall.

"I do not want the whole thing known beyond you and Fairbank, because enemies will say I have gone to give reports to the Communist International or some other such institution," Agnes explained. In her absence, she beseeched Snow to continue sending information to the secret post office box she shared with Madame Sun in Shanghai. (Snow had begun by this time to work with the League for Civil Rights in Peking.) "Friends," she wrote, would use his information "and no breath of it will get out as to the source . . . I beg of you," she concluded, "to keep every hint of this from Isaacs," who had come to resent Communist interference with the *China Forum* and was drawing close to local Trotskyists. According to Agnes, "His gang here have connections with Japanese spies who find out *everything* they want to know."[91]

On May 17, 1933, Agnes boarded a train for Peking. There she would meet with Snow and seek to repair her network of informants before continuing on to Moscow. It was just as well. French Concession police claimed they had a copy of Agnes's correspondence with the Comintern, while British International Settlement police believed they had established a link between her and the Comintern executive committee.[92] The China League for Civil Rights would soon be in tatters—its chairman, Madame Sun, in hiding after receiving a letter with a bullet in it, and its secretary, Yang Chien, gunned down in broad daylight. For safety's sake, if nothing else, Agnes had to leave Shanghai for a time. She could accomplish nothing in the current political climate. Although she was scrupulously quiet about her destination, the Shanghai Municipal Police already knew where she was bound.

CHAPTER 11

A Fissure Opens

If you don't *feel* a thing, you will never guess its meaning.

EMMA GOLDMAN

AGNES RECEIVED a hero's welcome on her third visit to Moscow. During her visit to north China, she had been unable to reconstitute her ring, but if her performance there was less than stellar, she had achieved much in other areas. Wang Ming, now the CCP representative to the Comintern, had praised Agnes's work with the Chinese Communists at a recent Comintern plenum.[1] Sorge had also mentioned Agnes's "excellent work . . . gathering information to further his espionage activities in Shanghai" to his superior, General Berzin.[2] Even Agnes herself was later rumored to have boasted that the Soviets rewarded her efforts with a medal (perhaps the Order of the Red Banner, the highest honor the Soviet Union accorded foreigners, which her friend Sonja would receive).[3]

An enthusiastic response to the Russian translation of *Daughter of Earth* (Agnes claimed it had sold nearly a million copies) made Agnes a successful author in a country that placed tremendous value on writers like herself. Her payment was in rubles, which she could not use outside the country, but she was an official guest of the International Union of Revolutionary Writers, and a member of its advisory board. The organization placed a translator at her disposal, and Agnes went to work, arranging for the publication of the manuscript of censured stories she had smuggled out of China with her.[4] International Publishers, the American Communist Party's publishing house, would bring out the book in an English translation for which Agnes wrote an introduction. When she was not attending to the literary affairs of her Chinese colleagues, she toured the city.

The pace of Agnes's schedule allowed her only brief glimpses of Soviet life, but what she saw impressed her. "I passed through this country five years ago on my way to China," Agnes wrote Michaelis, "and I was here in 1921. Never have I dreamed there could be such a change, never have I dreamed that a new country could rise from the earth, that whole cities could be changed in five years, and new ones, with great modern apartment houses for workers, could spring up where nothing existed before. It is a gigantic country, simply filled with exultant enthusiasm and optimism."[5] The homeless children were all gone, she crowed, and had become skilled workers, technicians, university students, or soldiers.

Had Agnes been more skeptical, or spoken to someone unafraid to be candid, perhaps she might have learned that four people—sometimes families, often strangers—frequently shared a single room. The one-burner Primus stoves on which they cooked stank; so did their toilets. People's diets consisted primarily of black bread and cabbage soup; vegetables, lemons, meat, and milk were unavailable. Lines were necessary for everything. Unless you were a foreigner or a member of the Soviet security apparatus, it was impossible to procure such necessities as diapers, soap, or medicine, let alone good clothes or decent beds and linens. Hospitals, nurseries, and obstetric care were also in short supply. Compared to fully employed Russian workers in the socialist fatherland, one visitor would dourly observe, the German unemployed lived like kings, but Agnes did not seem to notice.[6]

During his recent visit to Moscow, Sorge had been ordered to assemble an espionage unit in Tokyo, and he was currently in Berlin acquiring the Nazi credentials that would help him infiltrate German diplomatic circles in Japan. Other Soviet operatives Agnes had known in China were around, though, among them Sorge's radio operator, Max Klausen, Irene Wiedemeyer, and Sonja Kuczinski. Since their blowup in Kuling, Agnes had kept the younger woman at arm's length. She did not know that Sonja had come to Moscow for six months' additional training. As Sonja explained it, "I felt that Agnes did not change the opinion of me she formed in Kuling and uncompromising as she was, she acted accordingly."[7] However, when they bumped into one another in the elevator of Agnes's hotel, the two women fell into one another's arms and Agnes resumed the friendship in Moscow as if nothing had occurred.

The institution to which Sonya (and evidently Klausen) had been sent was a special school the OMS operated undercover in the Moscow suburb of Podlipki. The Eighth International Sports Base, as it was known, was directed by Jakob Mirov-Abramov. According to Muenzenberg's companion, who was also a friend of Mirov-Abramov's:

The mysterious complex of buildings was protected by a double fence which was patrolled day and night by military guards with dogs. About eighty students of both sexes lived in modern surroundings; the teaching quarters had installations in every room for Morse code training and they were equipped with laboratories and workshops...

Candidates were nominated by Communist Party leaders from all countries and accepted by Mirov-Abramov after careful scrutiny. He proved an excellent psychologist. He invited the candidate into his office and asked whether he wished to make himself available for important cadre work in order to take part actively in the fight against Hitler and Fascism...After several meetings Mirov-Abramov asked the candidate to sign the written conditions for this training—which he almost always did—thereby totally committing himself to the Soviet espionage system. The trainees had to change their names and promise never to reveal their true identities, not even to their colleagues. During the training they had to break off all links with friends, were never allowed to leave the school alone, and were not permitted to take photographs or to talk to anyone about the school and their curriculum. The betrayal of secrets was punishable by death.

The candidates selected were young, unmarried, intelligent people with a special gift for languages or technical matters...Unsuitable candidates were eliminated by continual examinations. The curriculum was large and varied, it included languages, geography, history, Morse code and the decoding of messages. Trainees were taught to construct radio transmitters and receivers with simple materials, and learned to use them by contacts with radio amateurs all over the world...After completion of their studies some of the pupils, chosen by Mirov-Abramov personally, were given further arduous training at an army sports camp and finally sent to recuperate at a sanitarium in the Crimea. Then they were sent out into the world for the OMS.[8]

Sonja was being trained as a radio operator and was receiving instruction in radio construction, Morse code, and Russian. After completing her training, she would be dispatched to Mukden with a coworker to assume the reins of a newly constituted espionage ring in north China—a successor, perhaps, to the one that Agnes had failed to maintain—to work with "partisan groups," as Sonja would describe them, who were resisting the Japanese. Many years later, Sonja recalled that while "it was not usual for members of my school to meet...people outside of the collective, I did nothing behind their backs; they allowed me to see Smedley."[9] Of course, Agnes was a known quantity to the people who ran Sonja's school.

As a writer of considerable stature in the Soviet Union, Agnes had assumed that the Cooperative Publishing Society of Foreign Workers in the USSR, the country's foreign-language publishing house, would release her volume of sketches of Chinese life now that the Fischer Verlag had declined, but according to Sonja, the Soviets had "problems" with Agnes's manuscript. At issue were her accounts of Chiang Kai-shek's betrayal of the revolution. Although the Comintern still preached resistance to the Generalissimo as an integral part of resistance to Japanese imperialism, continued Japanese aggression in north China was moving the Soviet government along a contradictory path—toward a rapprochement with Chiang. In *Chinese Destinies*, Agnes depicted Chiang, his Nationalist government, and the ruling KMT Party as monsters of counterrevolution whose conflict with the Chinese Communists made them blood enemies.

Sonja later wrote that with the party line in the midst of change, Agnes's assessment of the Nationalists was too blunt and ruthless, and the Soviets considered it inadvisable to bring out the book.[10] If Moscow would not publish it, neither would International Publishers, the American Communist Party's publishing firm. Unlike Muenzenberg, whose savvy and ties to the formerly powerful German Communist Party had leveraged a modicum of autonomy for his writers, the CPUSA was weaker and more subservient to Moscow's views. In the end Agnes was forced to place her manuscript with the Vanguard Press—an American firm to which radical authors often turned when the Party questioned the political correctness of their views.

Although Agnes would insist, now and later, that the Soviet Union was to be "defended to the last stone," the rejection was a blow. As someone so well informed on the KMT-CCP conflict that she briefed the Comintern's own military advisers, she might well have raised the matter of Moscow's seeming indifference to China's revolution in a meeting she later boasted of conducting with Iosef Piatnitsky.[11] Recent Soviet decisions—to turn a blind eye toward Nationalist attempts to destroy Kiangsi's soviet government, and to mount a campaign that discredited the guerrilla tactics of peasant leader Mao Tse-tung—in pursuit of mutual recognition and an exchange of ambassadors did not sit well with Agnes, and their continuing predisposition toward a Soviet model of revolution, despite its record of failure in China, distressed her. Indeed, in two tales that Agnes slipped into her collection at the last moment, she had portrayed the guerrilla troops as the hope of China's future.

> Before the sun had hardly risen the mass meetings began, and when the night descended they had hardly ended. It seemed the people could not have enough of talking, once their tongues were loosed. Of course the men from the Red Army, especially the Political Department, started it all. For talking was one of their weapons, second only to their rifles. And how they could talk!

What they said sounded as if they were reaching tight down into the hearts of the peasants and demanding what they had always wanted—land, the abolition of debts and taxes, rice; why, even schools where the children and even the older people could learn to read and write! Then there would be unions of workers and peasants and armed Red Guards to defend them.

When they had talked, these Red Army men urged peasants to come up and say what was in their hearts...

In Shangpo in the days that followed there arose unions of peasants, apprentices, handworkers, arsenal workers, women fishermen, transportation workers, and many others, and there sprang to life the Young Guards, the Communist Youth League, the Pioneers, and the Communist Party. Red peasant guards took the place of the Min Tuan [militia], and were armed with their weapons. And from their delegates was elected the first Soviet government of Shangpo.

The city hummed with a new life. Red Army commanders were training the new Red Guards on the meadows beyond the walls. The arsenal workers bent their backs over the anvils and machines with new energy and enthusiasm. In the buildings that had once been the homes of the great families now moved crowds of men and women, for here were the headquarters of the people's organizations. The great clan house of Tsai was the headquarters of the Soviet government with a red flag floating over it. The buildings of three of the great families were turned into schools, and teachers came down from Hsinkou to the north, bringing new textbooks and new ideas. Then the doctors appeared and ancestral temples became hospitals, where the wounded from the long siege lay and where anyone could get free treatment and buy medicine for a few coppers at most.

In such a way did the Red Army reach into the hearts of the masses and start the long work of creating that which the peasants seemed to have always longed for. People would say to each other: "Now look! Didn't I tell you we must have a hospital there?" But [the people] had never told them at all—it only seemed that [they] had, for this was just what should be.[12]

Within a short time of her celebrated arrival, Agnes's attitude had earned her enough official displeasure that the Fourth Bureau denied her authorization to purchase food, clothing, and other daily necessities at the special store for foreigners —a perquisite someone of her stature should have easily procured. Klausen said Agnes sought his help to rectify the situation, but even he only "barely managed to get one for her," he would write, after appealing directly to Mirov-Abramov.[13]

Her nose out of joint, Agnes declined to write a book on children in the

Soviet Union that the Red Aid had proposed. Arguing that she lacked sufficient time and energy to take on another commitment, she suggested her friend Sonja write it instead.[14] She preferred to focus on selling her partially completed manuscript of Red Army tales and her collection of China photos, which, after considerable maneuvering, she placed with Moscow's foreign publishing house. Her advance, paid in rubles, was sufficient for two months' rest at a sanitorium in Kislovodsk, in the north Caucasus. There she planned to finish her book.

The attacks on her in Shanghai's foreign press and harassment by special agents had damaged her heart and nerves, Agnes later claimed, and the famed Narzan waters from Kislovodsk's mountain streams were said to cure neurasthenic sufferers like herself. Renowned in tsarist times as a watering place for Russian nobility, the town now offered its four-week treatment to more than ninety thousand Soviet citizens each year. Although these days bureaucrats and engineers outnumbered factory workers, and the best sanitorium, where wine and champagne flowed and patients dined on borscht and beef, belonged to the GPU (the Russian espionage service), the atmosphere remained healthfully upbeat. Louis Fischer, a German journalist close to Muenzenberg, met Agnes here at this time. He would write that he never forgot the woman he recalled as a "king of the spirit," who channeled a passionate temperament into politics.[15]

In Shanghai, Agnes had been so overworked and accustomed to having her mail opened that she had abandoned any attempts at personal correspondence. Here in Kislovodsk, she was able to reach out again to friends.

It is very wonderful in this town [she wrote Michaelis that July], where people with heart trouble come from all over the Soviet Union. In this one town there are forty-seven sanatoriums, and there are now about 45,000 workers here, either being cured for one thing or another, or for a general rest and to drink the Narzan waters . . . To the west, south, east, all along the Black Sea and the Caspian Sea, there are hundreds of rest homes for workers. Millions of workers are taking their month's rest in the mountains, at the seashore, or in one of these health resorts where I am. I have met here workers from every part of the Union, every kind of worker from engineer down to collective farmers; Chinese; Central Asiatic men and women of many nationalities. Here Red Army commanders and ordinary Red Army soldiers walk arm and arm with each other or with workers, talking. Everyone who comes on his vacation, comes with all expenses paid by his social insurance or the Commissariat of Health, and thereto his regular wages are paid.

. . . Artists from Leningrad and Moscow tour through the health and vacation resorts and we see the best there is. Last night I heard a soprano from the

Leningrad Opera sing Rigoletto, and I think it was the finest thing I have ever heard.

There are many workers' theaters on tour, and also the Moscow Art Theater. I have seen them here . . . In this one resort, I think every sanitarium must have its own small orchestra at least; then there are two big orchestras that play in the park in the forenoon, afternoon and evening.

. . . I wish you were here with me now. The mountains rear their heads all about me, and from my window I look at the mountains through giant poplars that rustle sadly in the wind.[16]

People's lives were easier here than in China, she later wrote. The Soviet economy had advanced more broadly and swiftly than China's. "China had developed a few of its roads and industries, but they were constantly staggered under the burden of self-seeking private interests. It had built primary schools, but the children of the poor could not afford to attend them. Within its armies the corruption was notorious. China was bound by a thousand chains both internal and foreign; the people of the Soviet Union labored under heavy burdens, but no one owned them, their land, or their industries. They were a proud, awakened people."[17] Still, she could not imagine not returning to China.

To live there, however, she needed a job that paid in a currency other than rubles and would serve as a cover for her political activities. Now that the Russians had purchased her Red Army manuscript, International Publishers would publish it, too, along with Vanguard. French and German translations were also in the offing. None paid well, though, and Agnes asked Michaelis if she knew any newspaper in Europe willing to make her its representative in China. She could commit to two or three articles a month, she wrote, but no more. The main reason she sought the post was that she needed the document publishers would provide authorizing her to act for them.[18]

For the moment, though, completing her book was Agnes's first priority. Agnes likened the situation confronting the Chinese Red Army in the winter of 1933-1934 to the trials the Russian Red Army faced between 1917 and 1922.

Foreign governments poured men and money into the equipment of the mercenary White Guard Armies against the Russian Revolution; as they have done in China, so did they in Russia attempt to set up wherever they conquered; and they filled the world press with lies and distortion. But still they could not stop the march of history.

. . . The Chinese Soviets and the Chinese Red Army will conquer in the end, for their aim and program are in harmony with the processes of historical progress. Because of this the iron battalions of China's Red Army are marching. Nothing can stop them.[19]

China's Red Army Marches (or *Red Flood over China*, as it was titled in the USSR) recounted the growth of the Chinese Red Army in Kiangsi from the first failed uprisings led by peasant leaders Mao Tse-tung, Ho Lung, and Chu Teh in the months that followed Chiang Kai-shek's 1927 anti-Communist coup to the proclamation of the Soviet Republic of China in November 1931. Where *Chinese Destinies* had hewed more closely to traditional journalism in dealing only with what Agnes had seen and her reactions to what she had witnessed (other than the two Red Army tales), *China's Red Army Marches* was more novelistic. It was based on real events, as Agnes described it, as opposed to actual reporting—an artistic rendering of information culled from interviews, secondhand tales, and her own imagination. To evoke legions of Chinese peasants increasingly fired by hope and struggle, she relied on her own passionate spirit and considerable descriptive powers. In these tales Agnes spoke of individuals' experiences, but she meant her readers to view the people about whom she wrote as representatives of a larger group who chose the mass actions linked to China's emerging Communist movement as an alternative to their despair.[20] Agnes's depictions of the country's revolutionary struggle would pioneer a new form of socially conscious art that considerably influenced leftist reportage in the 1930s.

The battle was ended and the red banners hung at rest. On the blood-stained mountain slope stood the lad, Yu-kung, silently looking down on the still face of the boy, Li-kwei. Where the head had buried itself in the snow was a pool of dark, frozen blood. The feet were wrapped in dried grass, bound by old rags...

Yu-kung drew a...breath and looked beyond. Down below, on the mountain path where the Red Army had met the White regiment coming from the north, lay other still bodies...still grasping their spears, knives, and bayonets ...Some lay outstretched over the rifles they had captured. Chu Teh and a group of members of the General Staff were passing among them, bending low, talking...

As Yu-kung stood looking down on the still face of his *Di-di* [younger brother]...there came the memory of Li-kwei's hand in his as the two of them had walked to the hovels they called home after twelve hours of work in the ore-sheds of Shuikoushan. Then came the mass meetings of miners, struggles, killings of workers. On January 4...came the Shuikoushan uprising ...followed [by] hard partisan fighting as the revolting miners fought their way to Leiyang. There both boys became buglers in the Red Army...

Yu-kung and Li-kwei had marched with Chu Teh and with two companies of peasant scouts...When Li-kwei had wearied, Chu Teh had swung him astride one of the ponies. There, sitting astride the cannons of the Revolution, Li-kwei played soft, wistful folk melodies on his bamboo flute...

Yu-kung recalled also the masses of Leiyang. Brave, heroic, filled with love for the Red Army...

The peasants had woven the broad bamboo or straw hats with conical crowns that hung down the back of each man — a protection against rain, snow, or the sun. The tailors had made a coarse sack for each man, and the Peasant Leagues filled these sacks with five or six *catties* [Chinese pound weights] of dry rice, two *catties* of salt, and a handful of dried vegetables... Each man had a hand towel, and some covering for the night...and a few of the older revolutionary soldiers carried flashlights for rare occasions...

...On the border of Hunan and Kiangsi Provinces...came Li-kwei's last battle...A regiment of Kuomintang troops had come from the north, down over a path hidden by shrubs and overhanging cliffs. The Red Army had met them suddenly and both sides were taken by surprise. Red Army scouts going in advance had fired three shots of warning. Knowing that this meant death anyway for them, they fired right into the ranks of the enemy, fighting until their last bullet was gone. Two of their stiffening bodies now lay below, clasping in a fierce embrace the bodies of two enemy soldiers...

It was in this battle that the boy bugler Li-kwei was hit by a flying enemy bullet...

Yu-kung watched his comrades lay his younger brother by the side of the men who had given their lives for the Revolution...

Then [he] turned from the mass grave where his brother lay. Down the path toward the east his tear-dimmed eyes caught the flash of the great red banner with the hammer and sickle now held high, unfolded in the wind. Grasping his bugle firmly and squaring his thin young shoulders, he looked about, ran to his unit, and began marching steadily forward.[21]

By September 1933, Agnes had still not completed a draft, but her first China book was about to be released, and she asked Michaelis to review it for the European press — and draft an article on China as well. For purposes of background information, Agnes enclosed a sixty-three-page document she said she had recently completed for Muenzenberg's Comite Contre la Guerre et le Fasisme (Committee Against War and Fascism). "It will appear *without* my name," Agnes noted, "and I must ask you never to mention my name in connection with it or what you write about China. You could always mention that you have information from the Anti-War and Anti-Fascist Association in Paris, moving figures in which are Romain Rolland and Henri Barbusse."[22] She importuned Michaelis, if she were to do the article, to worry less about the accuracy of her sources than about her ability to provide an impassioned "defense of the destitute Chinese workers and peasants fighting for the most elementary right to existence, with their naked bodies building up a new social system that allows them the first civilized, cultured existence they have ever known."[23] Michaelis apparently declined.

By September, Agnes wrote that her heart was a bit better but she remained very tired. Even so, she suddenly appeared in a great hurry to get back to Moscow. Originally, she had planned to stop at some of the much talked-about agricultural collectives, communes, and state farms on her return. If she had, she might have seen that while a combination of ruthlessness and economic measures had allowed Stalin to collectivize all the country's sown areas by the end of 1932, the fact that they were producing enough grain to feed everyone did not mean that everyone was allowed to eat it. In the very area where she was staying, a famine quite consciously encouraged by Stalin was starving millions of Ukranian-speaking peasants.[24] Instead, in her haste she decided to return directly to the capital, where she took an apartment in the same modern building as Fedor Gladkov, the acclaimed novelist of socialist realism.

Apparently, Comintern officials had sought her return after reviewing an alarming report from Madame Sun. In November 1933, Agnes now learned, Harold Isaacs, the American editor/publisher of the *China Forum*, had written a glowing tribute to the sixteenth anniversary of the Soviet Revolution that made no mention of Stalin. Told to recant, Isaacs refused, and CCP leaders in Shanghai had cut their ties to him, withdrawing all support, and their liaisons, from the *Forum*.[25] By January 1934, with Isaacs declining to cooperate in any way, the paper had folded, but the Chinese Communists still wanted an English language outlet in Shanghai that placed their views before an international readership. Since the creation of a successor publication required financial support from the American comrades in addition to U.S. registration, the CCP had asked Agnes to make a trip to the United States on their behalf.

Agnes evinced little interest in returning to the States, but she was always aware, as she told Michaelis, that her plans were "dependent *on other factors* than my desire.[26] On February 25, 1934, the OMS representative in Moscow who facilitated communication between Agnes and the CCP reported to China, via coded radiograph, that they had spoken with Agnes about the *Forum* and that she had agreed to leave for the United States within the next two months to enlist American support for the project.[27]

Sorge, Ozaki, Kawai, Klausen, Sonja, and Chen Han-seng—nearly all the other members of Sorge's Shanghai ring—would continue to work for Soviet military intelligence in China and Japan, but the Russians would not ask Agnes to perform any purely Soviet tasks again. She was too unruly. Operatives were not supposed to serve the Comintern, the Chinese Communists, and Russian military intelligence simultaneously. Neither were they supposed to handle legal, semilegal, and illegal work, as Agnes did. It was reckless behavior, from a conspiratorial point of view, and the Soviets feared the breach placed their covert operations at unnecessary risk.[28] Agnes was still useful to the Soviets, but she was no longer entirely trustworthy. That spring, the Comintern notified its agents in Shanghai that in the future Agnes was to assist them with front organizations only. Agents were advised to exercise "a lot of precaution" in their dealings with her "and...not have frequent appointments with Smedley...in order not to increase the risk of your failing."[29]

If Agnes was aware of what was transpiring, she seemed unfazed. A subsequent comment by Muenzenberg deputy Louis Gibarti suggests that by the spring of 1934 Agnes knew perfectly well that there was a difference between working for Russian military intelligence in China and "working on the party lines in China," as Gibarti put it, for the Comintern.[30] Convinced of the decisive role the Chinese peasantry played in the Chinese Revolution, she preferred to make China her primary focus, and with Chiang Kai-shek signing treaties that surrendered vast areas of Chinese territory to Japanese rule while Moscow looked the other way, she was disinclined to give Soviet interests priority.

According to Gibarti, Agnes would remain a "Far Eastern agent of the... Russian state organization Comintern."[31] Agnes, too, believed that on her upcoming trip and later, when she returned to Shanghai, she would serve the Comintern—as a kind of minister without portfolio, advising the CPUSA on its role in China's revolution. Regardless of what people in Moscow wished, she had no intention of abandoning her ties to the Chinese Communists. As the only American non-Party Communist who lived in Shanghai on a permanent basis, Agnes believed, she had created a significant position for herself in China's revolutionary upheaval. If the Chinese needed her help, she would serve their cause in whatever capacity she could.

Agnes wrote Florence of her impending return that March. "I'd really like to remain in America a few months. But my life is not my own and it is not always for me to decide...It may be that I wire you from Paris the name of the boat on which I am arriving and the date of arrival. But if I do, it would have to be with the absolute security that you would keep it strictly secret. I can't be eaten up by a thousand little things that prevent me from doing important ones."[32] Then she traveled to Leningrad, where Chatto currently lived.

These days, Chatto worked for local CCCP boss Sergei Kirov at the Institute of Ethnology in the Academy of Sciences, teaching young Russians the Indian dialects of the regions to which the GPU assigned them.[33] Agnes found the visit melancholy. "He was at last growing old," she later wrote, "his body thin and frail, his hair rapidly turning white. The desire to return to India obsessed him, but the British would trust him only if he were dust on a funeral pyre."[34]

She returned to Moscow the following month. While she awaited the final details of her assignment, she met with her Russian editor, cooked dinners for Sonja, and took Sunday breakfast at the home of Michael Borodin, formerly the Comintern's chief adviser in China, who now edited the *Moscow Daily News*.[35] In response to those who later asked how she could have missed the machinations inside the Soviet Union at this time, Agnes's public posture was defiant. "Certainly I had heard tales of political wrongdoing, but could my own country say that its politics were pure? Could one say it of French or English rule? No, not unless one chose to forget India, or to ignore the fact that the cruelties inflicted on the natives of French Indo-China were a byword in the Far East."[36]

Privately, however, her assessment of the Russians was darker, as she revealed a few years later. "The USSR tried to preserve Germany and Austria merely as an outer defense for itself, and they would not allow them to complete their revolution...In China I heard a thousand times the phrase, 'Sacrifice partial interests to the whole.' They talked of the whole world, the whole revolutionary movement, and I think the German and Austrian Communists conceived of themselves as 'partial interests' that had to be sacrificed for the whole. Then it was too late; their compromise led to their own destruction."[37] The German Social Democrats, she would say, were not the only ones to blame.

En route to Paris, Agnes stopped in Berlin to see for herself what she described as the "Fascist reaction...in full swing." There she learned that the Nazis had burned *Daughter of Earth* alongside novels by Theodore Dreiser, John Dos Passos, Upton Sinclair, and Jack London soon after Hitler assumed power, and that her former analyst, Dr. Naef, had committed suicide. "I saw my doctor's last note...," she later wrote Sinclair. "I recall the first sentence. 'Ich kann nicht mehr!' (I've had enough.)"[38] Agnes also spoke with a few German Communists in the city, who now lived an underground existence. "Haggard and bitter," as she described them, they attacked KPD leaders who were now in Paris for having left the country. They would have better served the movement, she said they told her, by remaining in Germany to work.

In Paris, where Muenzenberg had reestablished his headquarters, Julian Gumperz arranged for the Malik Verlag (which had relocated in Prague) to publish a German translation of Agnes's Red Army book. Gumperz was no longer connected with the firm, but his former partner, Wieland Herzfelde, still worked with Muenzenberg. In the future, Herzfelde would also act as Agnes's European agent.[39] Other Muenzenberg associates had her manuscript translated

into French. Soon it would be published by Muenzenberg's Editions du Car-
refour, along with several of her articles.[40] But Muenzenberg's office on the Rue
Mondetour did not exist for propaganda purposes alone. It also housed an illegal
bureau of Mirov-Abramov's espionage school, where his representatives handled
the technical aspects of Agnes's trip.[41]

On April 22, 1934, as her ship crossed the Atlantic, Moscow notified CPUSA
head Earl Browder that Agnes was on her way. "She will come to you," their
coded dispatch read. "Transmit [to] her [the] following message which we
received for her from China. Society should not be incorporated in USA. After
[her] arrival [in] Shanghai, Isaac will hand over immediately [the] printing office
through [the] American Consul."[42] Soon afterward, the Shanghai Municipal
Police learned that Agnes had left Moscow and was headed for the United States.

"Yes, I wonder sometimes —when I have time—of America and Americans,"
Agnes had written while still in Shanghai. "It has been thirteen years since I left.
It is far away—a strange country. It has changed much since I left. But perhaps I
have not—so much. It—America—remains the basis of my outlook, I fear. How
greatly our childhood dominates our existence!"[43] In 1934, as Agnes again
walked the streets of New York, she found America to be a "strange planet."

Agnes resumed her friendship with Sanger. She also visited Baldwin, whom
she asked to help an American Communist friend named Archie Phinney, who
had been detained in the Soviet Union with a suspicious passport problem.
However, her ties to Sanger and Baldwin were more professional than personal
connections—useful contacts that she needed to ensure her well-being in
Shanghai—and though Emma Goldman was in New York promoting her book
and most anxious to see Agnes, she left Goldman's letter unopened.

The actual friends of her youth fared even more poorly, and her reunion
with Florence was a disaster. "I thank the gods that I have . . . a friend whose
devotion has never failed . . . who gives and gives and gives without expecting
anything in return," Agnes had written her not so very long ago. "Wait until I am
able to return . . . I'll shower you with good things." Then, on her 1934 visit to
New York, Agnes learned that Florence had become a Trotskyite, and according
to Florence's later account, the friend she brought along to meet Agnes made
the mistake of arguing with her that it "was Stalin who had brought gangsterism
into the labor movement."[44]

Whatever reservations Agnes privately harbored about the Soviet leader, Florence's sympathy for Trotsky was still heresy to her. "You have introduced me to
a traitor," Florence later wrote that Agnes declared. She never spoke to Florence
again. Whether or not Agnes was a card-carrying Party member, Florence would

ruefully observe, she had indeed become a Communist. Eva Ginn, a Village acquaintance who kept the books at *New Masses*, appeared to be one of few people from days gone by of whom Agnes personally approved, but she fared better with her political tasks.

How did the Chinese Communists plan to promote their line among the English-speaking comrades until another publication replaced the *China Forum?* the Comintern had inquired back in February 1934. The answer, it appeared, was through *China Today*, journal of the American Friends of the Chinese People. A new front organization in New York City, the American Friends of the Chinese People was a branch of the larger Friends of China, which was controlled by Muenzenberg and, in turn, by the Comintern.[45]

For some time now, under the auspices of the CPUSA's Chinese bureau, the CCP underground in Shanghai had been sending information on soviet China, written on scraps of rice paper, to *China Today* Despite some errors and exaggerations, the magazine was a valuable source for data unavailable elsewhere. Its editorial board was a veritable who's who of international Communists active in Chinese affairs. Chi Ch'ao-ting, a Chinese Communist then attached to the American Party's Chinese bureau, was the magazine's political adviser. Far East specialist Thomas Arthur Bisson had been the CPUSA's bag man for the *China Forum*.[46] Frederick Vanderbilt Field, renegade scion of the Vanderbilt family, was a financial angel and ranking figure in the CPUSA's Chinese bureau. Philip Jaffe, Agnes's contact to the CPUSA and the brother-in-law of Chi, was *China Today*'s editor and the only non-Party member on its board. He was also executive secretary of the American Friends of the Chinese People and took his orders from Field.

Agnes, like the Russians, considered the American Party a more irritating than useful partner, but the Comintern had fostered a special relationship between the CPUSA and the CCP, based on the affluence and extraterritorial status of U.S. members. At the moment Agnes was one of the pivots on which that relationship turned.[47] For that reason, Agnes had requested in her last communication with Jaffe that he set up a meeting for her with "Comrade Ho," chairman of the CPUSA's China bureau, while she was in the city.[48] Jaffe later recalled that when he fetched Agnes (whom he had never personally met) at her hotel, she startled him by snapping, "How do I know it's you? Have you any I.D.?" Jaffe said he told her he was not carrying any identification on him and went outside to hail a cab. "How do I know where you're taking me?" he said she demanded when he opened the door for her. "Miss Smedley, this is New York, not Shanghai," Jaffe had responded rather sharply.[49]

Willi Muenzenberg and his deputy, Louis Gibarti, who handled the front organizations with which Agnes was associated, were also visiting New York City at the time, and Gibarti would recall speaking with Agnes there.[50] Although his activities "were more in the liberal sphere," Gibarti later explained, than "in the sphere of the American Communist Party," he was in frequent contact with Earl Browder during the spring and summer of 1934, as was Agnes.

Agnes's first impression of Browder, gleaned at the 1921 Comintern Congress, had not been favorable—in fact, she thought him "an idiot"—but in the intervening years Browder's work with the PPTUS had made him something of an expert on China, and though Agnes viewed their relationship as more one of equals than perhaps Browder preferred, she was prepared to get along on the basis of their shared interests, if for no other reason. Agnes briefed the general secretary of the CPUSA on the current work of the CCP. She also raised the need for a paper to replace the *China Forum*, as she had been instructed in Moscow. Her vision for the project included hiring Joseph Freeman, an ardent Marxist and talented editor, to help her run it.[51]

After they spoke, Browder called his secretary, Grace Granich, into his office and introduced her to Agnes. An ambitious Party functionary, Grace had an interest in China herself, acquired while working for the Shanghai representative of the PPTUS. Grace reminded Agnes that Chatto had already introduced them in Berlin in 1927, when Grace had been Scott Nearing's secretary.

Agnes had entertained Grace in Agnes's apartment, Grace later recalled, during which time their conversation had been "constantly interrupted by the telephone which [Agnes] answered with 'Smedley here.'" In between phone calls, according to Grace, Agnes had "railed against the USSR and the Communist party of the Soviet Union as well as Communist parties everywhere. With this as a background," Grace would observe, "I was naturally surprised to be meeting her again in the office of the General Secretary of the Communist Party, [and] to observe their relations were most cordial."[52]

Party members who watched Agnes operate in New York did not know what to make of her. One person familiar with the activities of the Chinese bureau of the CPUSA would claim that at this time Agnes was acting as a liaison agent between the CCP and the American Party's Chinese section.[53] Gibarti would insist that she was a "bonafide Soviet agent."[54] Editors at the *Daily Worker* later spoke of her as one of their most valued agents in China, although they were uncertain whether she worked for the CPUSA, the Comintern, or the USSR. Publicly, they said the paper treated her as an independent rather than a Communist.

Whittaker Chambers, who was then working in the Party underground, later recalled that "everyone knew Smedley was a Communist, even if she wasn't a member; officials believed her more valuable if her CP affiliations were not established."[55] Joseph Peters, a Hungarian Communist who then directed the CPUSA's underground section, was in close contact with Agnes during her visit, Chambers would remark. She "was always hanging around on the ninth floor of CP headquarters," he later claimed, near the offices of Party leaders.[56]

According to Chambers, John Sherman, a colleague in the Party underground, was anxious to meet Agnes before he left for Tokyo, where he was to work with Sorge.[57] Chambers later said that during Agnes's visit he received permission from Peters to broker a meeting between Sherman and Agnes in a Manhattan automat. Agnes was "somewhat cool" toward Sherman, Chambers later reported; she had arrived for the rendezvous under the impression that she would be meeting with Gerhardt Eisler, and was disappointed. Still, according to Chambers, Agnes urged Sherman not to go to Japan but to travel instead to China and write about the Chinese Communists.[58]

Agnes acknowledged in her correspondence that there were "things" she was arranging in New York to help her Chinese comrades. She kept busy in other ways, too, applying for a new passport and a Guggenheim fellowship and participating in the League of Struggle for Negro Rights, a front organization the CPUSA had created after numerous failed efforts to recruit African Americans into the Party. Agnes also attempted in New York to secure a foreign correspondent's slot at the *New York Post*—like the one, evidently, that had been arranged for Sherman. Given her reputation as the storm center of various international complications, no mainstream paper, of course, would have her.

The surging popularity of proletarian fiction, however, had secured Agnes's credentials as a celebrity of America's literary left. *Daughter of Earth*, an early success for Coward-McCann, had also done well for Grossett and Dunlap in an inexpensive reprint edition sold at newsstands, in drugstores, and in department stores. By 1934, the book had appeared in several languages and acquired the status of a cult classic, passed from hand to hand among leftist students and activists.[59] The favorable response to *Chinese Destinies* also made Agnes much sought after as a public speaker that spring.

The two Red Army tales she had inserted into the text had given Western readers their first glimpse of the Kiangsi soviet. The review in the *New York Times* by China scholar Owen Lattimore spoke admiringly of Agnes's "flaming sympathy for the workers, the peasants and the emancipated students of China," which gave the volume "a hot and passionate reality...For those who know little about China," he wrote, "*Chinese Destinies* will be a revelation; but it is the people who do know something about China who ought to find the book indispensable."[60] Lewis Gannett had lauded it in the *New York Herald Tribune* as "hot blooded and partisan and honest"—the story of the Communist movement

Dust jacket from the Grossett and Dunlap edition of *Daughter of Earth*.

in China as it had never been told before, better than any other book written in English on why the soviets had developed and endured in China's rural interior.[61] Several foreign translations were already under way.

New Republic editor Malcolm Cowley, who heard Agnes address a dinner meeting of Baldwin's International Committee for Political Prisoners, where she was the guest of honor, confessed to being puzzled as to how this "daughter of a coal miner," as he later described her, had managed to land in China as a correspondent for the *Frankfurter Zeitung*.[62] Still, he was impressed by Agnes and her relationship to Madame Sun Yat-sen and agreed to draft an introduction for a revised edition of *Daughter of Earth* (which omitted the final section on Agnes's Indian activities) that would appear the following year.

In it, Cowley observed that Agnes had "never acquired the qualities that comfortable people can afford to cultivate—tolerance...easy grace, discretion...The life she led is so much a part of her that she cannot look back on it laughingly or wistfully and obscure its outlines in a haze of sentiment."[63] The lessons she had learned —that poor people had to stand together, that they could not trust rich people or put their faith in churches or their government, that love and marriage were the gates to prison for a poor man's daughter, to be escaped at any price—had led her to a wider life to which she felt compelled to carry along "all the class of people to which her education had made her instinctively faithful." In the years since the ones described in *Daughter of Earth*, Cowley noted in conclusion, Agnes had "run more risks than any Hollywood professional daredevil, but ...they were always incidental to the purpose she had formed, that of fighting for and chronicling the lives of oppressed people everywhere."

That June, Agnes traveled upstate to visit Thorberg and Joseph Freeman, who wanted to understand more about the paper before he accepted the assignment. Just as she arrived in Kingston, though, Browder received a frantic cable from Moscow inquiring of her whereabouts. The Comintern needed her urgently. It advised her, if she was still in New York, not to leave until they sent her further instructions.[64] A follow-up message from Pavel Mif, who directed the Comintern's China policy, instructed Browder to inform her that a number of ranking Chinese Communists had been arrested in China.[65] Key Comintern operatives, including Agnes's friend Arthur Ewert and the American Communist Eugene Dennis, had fled following the arrests; Comintern operations in Shanghai were completely disrupted. Moreover, Mif reported, Isaacs refused to turn over the printing press to the Chinese Communists. Instead, as Agnes would learn, he had spitefully given it to his friend and fellow Trotskyist Frank Glass, who sold it and donated the proceeds to a Chinese Trotskyist group.

Agnes hurriedly returned to New York City, where the following cable from the Comintern was waiting for her in Browder's office:

> Due tense situation impossible at present to make connections between Smedley and Chinese Party or European comrades in Shanghai. Nevertheless paper must be started in the meantime. Smedley will work independently; regular assistance to paper by Chinese Bolsheviks cannot be expected. Therefore absolutely necessary find additional politically developed and legal with real passport American as her coworker or partner. Consult Smedley and let her incorporate publishing house in Shanghai as American undertaking. Inform Smedley printing press stolen and sold by Isaacs. Can Smedley take along Chinese Bolshevik about whom she has written for translation, etc. work to insure appearance particularly of paper in Chinese language? Whom you suggest for Smedley's coworker or partner? Is it possible for the indicated Chinese comrade to fill that position? Telegraph at once.[66]

Bisson convened a meeting of the Party faction of the American Friends of China to hear Agnes out on the debacle at the *China Forum*.[67] Evidently she said a mouthful, including a slanderous denunciation of Isaacs as a paid agent of the Japanese government that quickly filtered back to him in China. In the end, the Party gave her enough money to float the newspaper Agnes hoped would bring international publicity to the Chinese people's struggle against the KMT government for a year.[68] Grace Granich worked out a code for Agnes to use in China when she thought open communication was unsafe. With Browder's assurance that plans had been made to send Joseph Freeman to China to help her edit the paper, Agnes prepared to travel west, from whence she would sail to China at some as yet unspecified date.

"I . . . am in the turmoil of packing, securing railway and steamer passage, consulting a lawyer finally, and doing a thousand little final things that must be done before I leave," she wrote Gwyneth Roe that summer. "I will try to come in to see you before I go, but please forgive me if I do not succeed. I am burdened with a thousand little things . . . Thank you again for your true friendship. I shall not forget this at any time . . . I shall always be glad to hear from you if you wish to write, but I really do not know if you should write. For, if you do, you would eventually receive a call from some detective who would pose as my bosom friend . . . Anyway, I shall be glad to know that back here I have a friend who thinks of me."[69]

Agnes confessed to having "a dark feeling" about returning, but, thinking it was cowardice, she was determined to go anyway. "I will be hounded like a criminal when I return," she informed Michaelis. "There is the possibility that I will get a bullet in my back in the streets. Especially after my book . . . appears. But the Chinese face bullets and so can I . . . I never have wanted to die of a disease germ. But I hope to live on and on to help in the struggle . . . There will be one protection *only* for me when I return to China—the fact that I am not unknown to such people as you and your friends or colleagues. They hesitate to shoot white women whose friends may raise hell in foreign countries."[70]

Little did she know that on her return she would need as much protection from the Reds as she did from the Whites.

In Los Angeles, Agnes drafted a letter to Emma Goldman, whom she had been avoiding for months.

> I received your letter long ago but did not answer it for many reasons. Now, on the eve of my sailing for China, I will drop you this line.
>
> My main reason for not writing you or meeting your friends in New York is the fact that I have supported the Communists, especially in China. I spent the last year in the Soviet Union . . .
>
> I knew to meet your friends or you would lead to nothing whatever but bitterness. I do not want to think of you with bitterness, and I think you prefer not to think of me so. I face the possibility of death each day in China for my conviction, and I return to that possibility now. Since I was treated and regained

my mental and physical health in Germany I have studied and thought and experienced much; then finally chose the route I wished to travel.

I send you my greetings, and hopes for a long and happy life for you.[71]

Goldman was crushed, for she had never been willing to sacrifice her friendships at the altar of the revolution, as she put it.

> As you know, life has given me many blows [she wrote a friend several years later]. One such I received from a very old and dear friend of mine, Agnes Smedley. She came to New York while I was there. I wrote her a note saying how much I wanted to see her. Her reply was a note which she dropped in Stella's letter box to the effect that since she was Communist and was going back to China there was no use meeting again as we would only argue and she was not in a condition to do so. In other words, her Communism killed all other feelings in her, as it does to everyone who is infected by that virus. When I tell you that Agnes was as close to me as you for a period of years, you will understand how that hurt."[72]

On October 1, 1934, Agnes sailed from Los Angeles for Shanghai. It would be another five years before Agnes publicly aired her discomfort with the way that Soviet interests had come to dictate Comintern policy, but she seemed to think Ozaki Hotsumi might understand her misgivings, and had written him while she was still in the United States that she urgently wished to see him on her way to China. When her ship docked in Yokohama, she paid a visit to Ozaki's office at the *Ahasi Shinbun*.

Ozaki took her to dinner. Later, he would say that Agnes spoke candidly with him about her experience in Russia and the China problem. Afterward, she mentioned her intention to visit China's soviet district. When he remarked that it would not last long, Agnes flared up indignantly, he reported. No doubt his remark signaled to her an unpleasantly familiar willingness to "sacrifice partial interests to the whole" that she could no longer accept from the Soviet Union. It was at this point, according to Ozaki, that he told Agnes he had reestablished contact with Sorge in Japan. The information appeared completely new to Agnes, he would observe. In response, she informed him that she would no longer be connected with their former activities.[73]

In a vain attempt to win Ozaki over to the primacy of the Chinese Communists' cause, Agnes would send him nearly a dozen documents about the Comintern, including "articles criticizing fascism in the Comintern and stories on the Chinese Communists" from Shanghai, Ozaki subsequently asserted.[74] On the advice of Sorge, Ozaki did not acknowledge Agnes's correspondence. They never spoke again.

CHAPTER 12

An Unruly Agent

Truly, with Agnes on your team, you could self-destruct with
no need of enemies.

JOHN KING FAIRBANK

A GNES RETURNED to Shanghai October 23, 1934. Agents of Madame Sun
met her boat and spirited her away. To shake off possible pursuers, they
bore her through the streets for hours before concealing her in a hospital. Government authorities had not appreciated Agnes's impassioned tales of dynamic,
idealistic guerrilla forces triumphing over depraved, mercenary KMT troops.
More troubling still was her gift for making accessible what until then had been
considered strange and remote history, as revealed in the following story.

> The decorated beams, the sweep of the roof, the branch of the peach tree,
> confused him. He lifted himself on one elbow and gazed outward in the
> direction from which a flood of soft early morning light was pouring in upon
> him. Then full memory returned to his sleep-drugged brain and he realized
> that he was a Red soldier in the headquarters of the Red Army in Chintang,
> and that he was sleeping on the stage in the temple of the Li clan.
>
> On the stage lay other figures, some on the floor, others on long boards
> stretched between rough benches. As he looked, one of the figures stretched
> and yawned, and he saw the black moustache of Chu Teh, commander-in-
> chief of the Red Army, whom he had followed many thousands of *li* these
> past two years...
>
> A blast from three bugles rent the air, resounding in the cliffs beyond.
> ...It was five thirty in the morning. The Red Army had started its day.

Almost instantly the courtyard below the stage began to fill with men. They went to the stone jars filled with water and began washing themselves...

The temple, like other temples up and down the valley, hummed with excited talk. Beyond, on the Soviet borders, the Kuomintang militarists had become active and the Red troops guarding the borders were fighting. Each morning fresh radio messages were published on the wall newspaper of the battalions, and the troops read eagerly.

... Talk of fighting, of defense, filled the air. Soon the Army would finish its training and be on the march...

At the table where the General Staff ate there was much talk about the forthcoming Soviet Congress...

When the Red Army first marched into Chintang valley with its... banners of blood-red gleaming against the snow, the first Revolutionary Committee of the region had been organized. There had been a mass meeting of the Red soldiers with the population of the valley, and so many people came that it seemed the earth seethed with them. The Revolutionary Committee was elected freely from the audience... One month later... the masses... decided to found a Su-vai-ai—or Soviet Government...

... After[ward] ..., delegations of peasants would go to Mao Tse-tung, the Party Secretary, or to the chief of the political Department, and say...

"Now we are of humble intelligence and knowledge and we come to lay our problems at your feet. Enlighten our ignorance..."

... Mao... t[old] them of the experience of other Soviet districts in the year past...

The peasant delegation would talk still more, asking many questions of minute detail. Mao... would listen patiently and answer. Then the delegation would go away and decide to adapt the tactics that became famous in Kiangsi. Whole regions would retreat with the Red Army deeper into Soviet territory and there were often so many of them that it seemed a whole nation was on the march. They would retreat until the Red Army gave the command. Then the old and young, the sick and lame, and the women with bound feet would be put in the rear. The others, men and youth, women and girls, would then stand at command of the Red Army to do any manner of fighting within their power...

"Why?" asked the militarists in confused astonishment...

... the Red Army knew why, for it was the army of the masses, the army of the people, mingled with their body and their blood. The reveille that awoke them with the dawn awoke the masses with them to common labor and common struggle. With taps at night they all sank to rest, secure in each other's presence. So, when the Kuomintang politicians and the imperialists gazed at

one another in the fear of the future and asked their eternal, "Why?" the Red
Army, with the fierceness of consciousness, alone could answer:

"Because we are the people! We are the awakened masses! We are the
Army of Communism!"[1]

She was simple; she was direct. And her ability to capture Chinese peasants
in all their humanity enabled the Chinese Communists' message to reach an
ever widening audience. That made her dangerous. Before Agnes's ship even
reached port, Chinese censors had already seized and destroyed several dozen
advance copies of her most recent book. Despite official efforts to restrict access
to Agnes's writing, however, *Chinese Destinies* and *China's Red Army Marches*,
her first two volumes on China, were widely available, both in underground
English versions and in samizdat Chinese translations that were passed hand to
hand. Their publication made Agnes a legend in Shanghai—and the most
talked-about foreigner in China.

Unfortunately the books, extolled by one reviewer as "the Iliad and Odyssey of
the Chinese people," had the misfortune of hailing the dawn of soviet China just
as twilight descended on it, as Isaacs would aptly recall. During the summer of
1934, frustrated by the inability of their previous "bandit annihilation" campaigns
to crush the Chinese Red Army, the Nationalists had launched an all-out effort to
eliminate the central soviet districts of Kiangsi and Fukien provinces once and
for all. Utilizing aviation forces, artillery, tanks, and guns, half a million KMT
troops, advised by German generals Adolf Hitler loaned the Generalissimo, had
wrapped a cordon so tightly around the Communist soldiers that only 87,000 out
of nearly 150,000 managed to escape. Half of them had since been annihilated.
To avoid certain death at the hands of the Nationalist Army, the Red Army men
had set off for remote northwest China, where they hoped to establish another
base. Traveling by foot, they brought only the blankets, ammunition, and household goods they could carry with them. The epic Long March had begun.

Agnes's return was an open secret among her colleagues. Within a week, she
reestablished contact with fellow conspirators including Lu Hsun, who returned
to her a case filled with secret documents he had held on to during her months
abroad. Operating largely through the Pan Pacific Trade Union Secretariat,
Agnes began to organize workers in Japanese-owned textile factories. She also
helped Madame Sun run arms and ammunition to Red Army marchers, who
were skirmishing constantly with KMT troops along their path. Rewi Alley and
other idealistic young Westerners would transport the boxes, unaware of their
contents.[2] In the absence of word from Browder or the appearance of Joseph
Freeman, Agnes lost track of the plan for the paper and carried on with her
other doings.

"Almost any foreigner of a progressive nature sooner or later was drawn into the revolutionary current swirling around Agnes Smedley and her activities," George Hatem, a young American doctor she met at this time, later recalled. "She was able to light fires in the hearts of the people she met and mobilize them to do something for the revolution. She was a dynamo and spark that brought action."[3]

Agnes occasionally asked Hatem to turn the VD clinic he ran over to her so the comrades could make contact. "She told me on which days I should leave my clinic closed and give her the keys," he would write. "Some days she would teach me how to avoid the spies who were always at her door by going over the roofs of several buildings and then delivering letters to such and such a place."[4] Alex Camplin, an electrical engineer for the Shanghai Power Company and the roommate of Rewi Alley, installed a secret transmitter in their home so CCP leaders in Shanghai could receive progress reports from the Red Army during the Long March.[5] Nothing dismayed or frightened Agnes, Hatem said. She extended her protective services to Indian, Korean, and Japanese revolutionaries as well as their Chinese comrades.

All of Agnes's foreign helpers were committed progressives, but none of them belonged to any organized Communist Party—a great advantage in underground work. They did, however, participate in the same Marxist study group that Agnes, along with the Comintern and the CCP, used to identify potential recruits.[6] Agnes did not behave like the other operatives in Shanghai who utilized this resource and worked with either one or the other organization. She continued to work directly with both—in defiance of Moscow's orders. Those ties gave her wider access to a broader range of information on subjects that ranged from the firsthand accounts by Long Marchers to trade union opportunities in urban areas.

One manuscript in Agnes's possession, for example, contained an English translation of the experiences of a Long Marcher in Kwangsi on pages one through six; pages eleven through fifty-two of the same document went on to analyze labor conditions among Shanghai's cotton mill workers, waterfront laborers, rickshaw pullers, and tramway workers.[7]

There was no moon light [it began]. Nor was there any star. All the universe became a monotonous black.

Nor was the weather fine. It did not rain, but heavy mist began to set in.

Everybody was tired with the whole day's marching. Yet there was no suitable place to stop at. Of course we did not intend to find enough villages to live in, but even if we were to rest in the open, there was no space for bivouac.

At first I was carried on a stretcher. To shield myself against the cold, I pulled up the bedding so that I could lay my head under it. I felt the bedding was wet. Many times we crossed mountain streams, for I could hear the rapid murmuring, and then I knew these people who carried me were feeling the rocky beds with their feet, and the steps were not so steady. At places I helped them with flashlights...

Turning at a corner in the mountainside, there were six or seven fires...

"The Tuan-fee [bandits] are at it again," said the nurse.

"Yes, this is one of Chiang Kai-shek's important strategies. His plan, I understand, is firstly to follow closely in our footsteps, never to quit us, and then secondly to organize all the forces of the landlords and 'develop guerrilla warfare,' so to speak, to annoy us at the flanks and the rear...."

The document then shifts abruptly and continues.

The mills of Yangtsepoo, which were the older ones generally, had a greater proportion of native workers... The newer factories of Western Shanghai got a majority of their workers from North Kiangsi...

... Shen sin cotton mill Number 9... is the worst... Workers are all lodged in a dormitory, and not allowed to go out... A little girl of nine years old, named Yang Pa nei... work[ed] for us... and organized...

Shanghai waterfront workers are more gangsterlike...

Ricksha pullers are much more like peasants. These are still more difficult to organize...

... Tramway workers... understand much better how to organize... They are not always willing to distribute leaflets... Machine workers are the most firm and militant... Drivers are also militant... Ticket sellers are... not willing to strike. For they usually make a lot of money.[8]

No wonder that when the Fairbanks saw Agnes that November, she was already run-down and complained of heart problems and an incipient ulcer. The couple would claim that by now they had grown accustomed to the "atmosphere of conspiratorial paranoia and revolutionary zeal" Agnes carried with her. Wilma Fairbank's sister, who had just arrived in China fresh from Radcliffe, was not, and she was appalled.

Agnes's extrality afforded her protection from the political excesses of the Nanking government, but Chinese officials were still intent on limiting her influence. That December, they formally banned *China's Red Army Marches*— making it one of only three foreign publications so proscribed. They also had a hand, evidently, in a spate of articles that appeared in the Japanese and Chinese press near the end of 1934 accusing Agnes of being a "notorious international spy" for India in London and Paris during World War I.[9] During her previous sojourn in Shanghai, the pieces charged, she had worked for the League Against Imperialism in the employ of the Soviet Union. Now, they claimed, she worked with Madame Sun, the CCP, and two representatives of the Communist International "in connection with an international espionage organization."

Much of the information, of course, was true; Agnes suspected Harold Isaacs had provided the fodder for the attack. Since his conversion to Trotskyism, Isaacs had become intensely antagonistic. But during the early days of their collaboration, Agnes confessed to Edgar Snow, she had often confided in Isaacs. "Yes, Isaacs is an Isaacs-ist," she wrote. "Down here the Japanese secret anti-Communist service are glad to announce among themselves that they are now working with the Trotskyists through spies who pretend to be Trotskyists. They are — really, and the Trotskyist gang here hate me so much that they have told everything they know about me to them . . . Every Communist fears them more than active KMT spies."[10]

Particularly because the articles hit so close to home, Agnes was in no position to acknowledge anything publicly. "The only things in the report that were true," she maintained in an article for the *Nation*, "were my name and the statements that I was in Shanghai and that the police were watching me! Everything else was manufactured in the diseased brains of Japanese and Chinese spies and newspapermen."[11] In letters to the Shanghai consul general, her publisher James Henle at Vanguard Press, Baldwin, and Sanger, she also vehemently denied the charges.

She had it on good authority, she maintained, that the reports were an "ideological preparation" for a subsequent attempt on her life by the Blue Shirts, Chiang Kai-shek's secret police, and therefore she required additional diplomatic protection.[12] Well versed in the use of publicity to sway public opinion, Agnes stressed that her salvation lay in publicly exposing the charges against her as "lies." "Can you give any publicity to the main facts of it?" she inquired of Baldwin. "I ask it because, after discussion with Mrs. Sun Yat-sen, we are of the belief that nothing can stop these *s.o.b.'s* here except a press exposure . . . Mrs. Sun . . . says that the more publicity and noise you make against this libel, the better so that gangsters and their bosses will be afraid to play their dirty tricks on you."[13]

Agnes fired the first salvo in the counterattack herself. In a letter to the editor of the *Shanghai Evening Post and Mercury*, she defiantly protested the Chinese decision to proscribe *China's Red Army Marches.*

My book is banned because it is a book of fact, because it proves to all who might read it that tens of millions of Chinese workers and peasants and revo-

lutionary intellectuals are not the bandits that the KMT and the foreign imperialists wish the world to believe. My book shows the truth—millions of Chinese toilers lifting their heads from serfdom and slavery and waging the
greatest, the most tragic and yet one of the most inspiring liberation struggles
in human history . . .

   . . . It is my honor to have my book banned, to be a target of attack in the
press by running dogs of the ruling classes, to have atrocious lies manufactured and published against me in the official Japanese and Chinese press,
and now to have the Blue Shirts discussing my murder.[14]

Baldwin responded, with "warmest sympathy and admiration," that he had
notified Secretary of State Cordell Hull of her circumstances and was endeavor-
ing to publicize the matter in the United States.[15] Vanguard publisher James
Henle contacted Senator Robert Wagner regarding the danger in which Agnes
found herself.[16] Sanger raised with the Chinese ambassador "the very serious situation confronting a dear and personal friend of mine now living in China."
Agnes, Sanger wrote, was "an educated, refined, brilliant woman . . . [whose]
sympathies and interests lean toward the Indians, the Chinese and other Nationals who are fighting for freedom," but she was "in no sense of the word a Communist, nor is she receiving money from Moscow, nor from any other source,
but through her own efforts."[17]

The Muenzenberg propaganda machine was also activated on Agnes's
behalf. The American Friends of the Chinese People sent a telegram of protest
to the Chinese ministry in Washington, D.C., and recommended that similar
protests be sent to the Chinese government. The Chicago John Reed Club
cabled the Department of State to protest the threats against Agnes by the
Nanking regime. By March, Agnes's letter to her publisher at Vanguard Press
had been reprinted in *International Literature* and the *New Masses* (under the
headline "Agnes Smedley in Danger"), and *China Today* had run an editorial
on the subject.

The American consul general in Shanghai was utterly frustrated. Agnes, he
wrote Hull in April 1935, had "been complaining to her friends in the U.S. that
her life is in danger on the one hand, and deliberately attacking the Chinese
government on the other. Her call at the Consulate General last December, followed first by appeals to her friends in the U.S. and then activities that cannot
be but irritating to the Chinese officials, would indicate that she may be trying
to provoke some action against her in the hope of gaining publicity for her writings and the ideas she is interested in advancing."[18]

Consul General Cunningham advised the secretary of state that the chief of
the political branch of the Shanghai Municipal Police had told him Agnes was

well paid for her support of the Communist cause. What they said, at the moment, was true. When there was no money to be had, Agnes lived a hand-to-mouth existence and worked for the revolution for nothing, but she had no qualms about accepting payment when funds were available, and her current relationship with the CPUSA was a paid one.[19] Cunningham did not know the particulars of her financial situation, but it certainly seemed to him that Agnes was taking unfair advantage of her extraterritorial status to engage in political agitation against the Chinese government, and that she employed what he considered the most "provocative tactics" in doing so.

Of course, Agnes was not the only American taking advantage of her extrality in China. Any number were doing the same. American businessmen, for example, regularly violated Chinese commercial laws, and they were free to do so — as long as they did not violate any American laws. True, they were not writing Communist propaganda, conducting labor and political organizing drives, or providing assistance to Chinese fugitives, as Agnes was, but she had a legal right to do so. As long as Americans in Shanghai remained entitled to extraterritorial privileges, there was little Cunningham could do.

Agnes knew of the grumbling in official circles, but she expressed a withering contempt for those who sought to discourage her activities. She had no intention of giving the counterrevolution "a Roman holiday," as she described it. "Why should I?" she asked Fairbank. "Why should I do anything to please the gangsters, money-changers, slave dealers, opium traffickers, and salesmen of China? For the sake of the American people who read my writings, for the sake of the Chinese masses whom I defend, I have not the least intention of taking any action that could please the counter-revolution or its paymasters, Japanese and other foreign imperialists."[20]

Agnes's publicity campaign bought her additional freedom to pursue her clandestine activities. Other Shanghai operatives were not so fortunate. On May 5, 1935, the Shanghai Municipal Police arrested a man known to them as Joseph Walden (most likely the American Communist and Comintern operative Eugene Dennis). Variously described as director of the Comintern's Far East bureau or a key operative either in the Soviet Union's secret police or its military intelligence, he was charged with engaging in espionage on behalf of the Comintern.[21] Several other foreign Communists, along with nearly a dozen members of the CCP central committee, were arrested in a subsequent roundup. The arrests sparked a mass exodus of Comintern representatives from China.

With Comintern operations in a shambles, Browder proposed to Agnes that she return to the United States.[22] His suggestion enraged her. She had no intention of taking orders from *Browder*. How was he in a better position than she to assess the risk of her remaining in China? Besides, the American Party had no control over *her*. She was not even a *member*. According to Browder's secretary, Grace Granich, Agnes dashed off a belligerent note to the CPUSA chief that read, "Never, never will I leave China. I'll live like a Chinese coolie here, but I'll never come back to the U.S."[23]

The implications of "Walden's" arrest rippled far beyond Shanghai. Chen Han-seng, who, unlike Agnes, still worked with Sorge, had been waiting for Walden in Tokyo at the time of his arrest. When he failed to show up as planned, Chen said, he immediately knew something was amiss. He returned at once to Shanghai in search of Agnes, who hid him in Rewi Alley's house.[24] After making arrangements with the Soviet Consulate, Agnes had Alley deliver Chen to a Soviet ship on the Huangpu dock disguised as a wealthy Shanghaiese in white shorts, silk stockings, safari jacket, and pith helmet.

Without his spectacles, which might have revealed his identity, Chen squinted through the bouquet of red gladioli Agnes had given him to carry. She had told Chen to appear nonchalant, and Alley later wrote that, "The group of plainclothes detectives grouped around the bottom of the gangway . . . hardly bothered with more than a glance at what seemed one more of the obvious wealthy Shanghai types." After Agnes and Alley left the dock, Chen went inside and hid in the lavatory until his boat was safely at sea.

The arrest and subsequent imprisonment of so many members of the CCP central committee severely damaged its ability to function, and a decision was made to dissolve the Party outside those soviet regions that were still protected by the Red Army. Under these most difficult circumstances, Agnes was more useful to the Chinese Communists than ever. Her detractors in the CPUSA, however, would avow that the situation went to her head.

According to Browder's secretary, Agnes

had a small sum entrusted to her by a departing cadre to be given to certain trade union leaders as a subsidy for their work. Elaborate safeguards had been set up so that she would not meet or know the trade unionists who received the money. But one by one Agnes knocked down the intermediaries and was soon meeting the leaders directly. While she never told them she was a Communist representative, she would say, "when I was in Moscow, I talked with Piatnitsky and he said . . .", or, ". . . in New York discussing the work of the Chinese Party with Earl Browder he thought . . ." all the while denying her Communist affiliation. Inevitably everyone thought, of course, "She is a representative of the Communist International," and gave her opinions much weight. When she reinforced her advice with money to help the revolutionary cause, the conjectures became certainty.[25]

Whether the money Agnes gave CCP leaders actually came from a departing cadre, as Grace Granich later alleged, is not clear, but there is little question that the aid Agnes rendered the CCP, financial and otherwise, at this inauspicious moment in its history soon came to benefit her personally. In July 1935, when Red Army troops paused for virtually the first time since the previous autumn, the CCP sent Communist soldiers and their leaders to speak with her about their experiences on the Long March.

It would be a journalistic coup of the first order to break their historic story, as Agnes explained to Eva Ginn, a new correspondent.

"I am at work gathering material on another book, to continue my last one...," she wrote, "and it will include the great... march to the west. I am working with men during the hot summer months. Some have staggered back, sick with malaria, anaemia from long hunger, with heart trouble, with worms in the stomach and god knows what. But I request that you do not mention this to any soul. It is difficult to meet such men and work with them."[26] Shanghai in July and August was dreadfully hot, but Agnes worked uninterruptedly.

Throughout the summer of 1935, Agnes also apprised the CPUSA and the Comintern Secretariat on political conditions in Shanghai. In August, she reported to Browder that the climate for a successor paper to the *China Forum* had become more conducive.[27] The problem, though, was that after waiting more than a year for the CPUSA to send a seasoned editor to China to help her get such a publication going, Agnes had come to doubt it would ever happen. She decided to use some of the money she had gotten from the CPUSA for a newspaper to publish a book of wood-block prints by Kaethe Kollwitz instead.[28]

Lu Hsun had already introduced several other foreign artists to China, and he and Agnes had wanted to do a project on Kollwitz since 1931. Unlike other art forms, wood-block prints did not require much outlay for materials and could be cheaply reproduced, making it easy to propagandize among an illiterate audience. Unfortunately for Agnes, the unveiling of the Comintern's second united front policy in the summer of 1935 led Browder and the Comintern to recognize the value of a paper like the former *China Forum* in generating publicity for the new Comintern policy in China. They now made the project a priority.

On September 4, not long after Chiang Kai-shek spurned a CCP call for a national united front to fight continuing Japanese aggression, Browder shared his thoughts on the subject with Chatto's former boss Georgi Dimitrov, who had become the Comintern's general secretary:

The proposal to assist Agnes Smedley, now in Shanghai, to publish an English language anti-imperialist newspaper there, should be finally decided. She writes that conditions grow more favorable; such a paper would be of great influence. The CPUSA can provide her with helpers, politically and technically qualified. The Chinese comrades agree, with the provision that these comrades in Shanghai should not have connections with the Chinese Party which would endanger its work. The political value of the project is clear. It will require formal approval and provision of necessary funds. These . . . are our chief *undecided* problems. Quick decisions will help us work effectively.[29]

Browder and the Comintern were poised to move forward, with one caveat—that Agnes be made to realize that the days when she could wheel and deal independently in Shanghai were over. No longer could she be permitted to handle official Communist Party business without being accountable to any party. Henceforth, she would have to accept Party discipline if she wanted to work with the Communists. She was American, after all, and the Comintern was trying to run a professional operation in China.

Tired of waiting for a decision from the procrastinating Freeman, Browder asked Isador Schneider, another Communist writer, to consider running the paper.[30] When he declined, Browder, in evident frustration, asked his secretary, Grace Granich, whether she and her husband, Max (brother of *New Masses* editor Mike Gold), would accept the job, which now included ensuring that Agnes submitted to the CPUSA's authority regarding her China activities.[31] Neither of the Graniches was a writer, but Grace was a thoroughly trustworthy Party functionary, and Max was at least a Party member.

Unaware that plans for the paper were advancing, Agnes spent the fall of 1935 working on the Kollwitz book and immersing herself in China's reemergent student movement. With the Nationalists bent on continuing their war against the Communists, even as Japan occupied and conquered an economically and politically prostrate China, students were increasingly open to the Communists' argument—that Chiang Kai-shek abandon his civil war and declare one on Japan instead. At the start of 1935, Agnes had traveled to Peking, epicenter of their activities, to survey the situation. In October—by which time the student movement had become the key element of the revolutionaries' campaign—she headed there again.

Japan's growing control of China could be felt more directly in Peking, and Agnes reported that the Japanese were already ruling there "through puppets." Horrified by what she saw, she threw herself into full-time work with student leaders at Yenching and Tsing Hwa universities, "organizing, and . . . loads of things . . . through no invitation of my own," she told Ginn.[32] Many of her Chinese comrades had been arrested, Agnes wrote, and though she was giving their effort all her energy and attention, the class struggle split the students "into hostile camps. We are trying to unite them on a United Front program against imperialism, Japanese in particular, and for a struggle for democratic rights such as free speech, press, assembly, and organizing," but it was too early to predict the outcome.[33]

The first student demonstrations took place December 9. At this time, the Peking Students Union denounced the Nanking government and urged all citizens in north China to join them in opposing the Chinese "traitors" who openly supported the Japanese-inspired autonomy movement. Their counterparts from Tientsin soon joined them. At a second demonstration the following week, ten thousand teachers, professors, and newspapermen followed students into the streets and called for a united front of Chinese students and people who, regardless of class, party, or other affiliation, desired an end to China's civil war and the beginning of one against Japan. Sympathetic workers, intellectuals, writers, and artists formed the next wave of protesters, and the demonstrations continued for days, during which time Nationalist officials and generals were bombarded with thousands of declarations, manifestos, and circular telegrams.

In January 1936, the center of the student movement (and Agnes) shifted to Shanghai, where it became a critical component of the more broadly based National Salvation movement, which linked an ever increasing number of progressive organizations committed to Chinese resistance to Japan under the Communists' united front umbrella. Even though news of the startling developments received front-page coverage in the *New York Times*, Agnes's articles on the student movement did not appear in the United States. Wieland Herzfelde, her European agent, was placing her work in numerous German exile presses including *Die Neue Weltbuhne* and the *Pariser Tagezeitung*.[34] She was making banner headlines in Muenzenberg's hugely popular tabloid, *A.I.Z.*, and later in his *Die Volks-Illustrierte (VI)*, and page one of Moscow's *Komsomol Pravda*, but as a participant-observer in the events she covered, Agnes lacked the emotional distance of a traditional journalist, and *Harper's, Asia, Travel*, and *American Mercury* all rejected her work.

Eva Ginn, who had become Agnes's de facto literary agent in America, suggested "that in writing your articles for the purpose of submitting them to capitalist periodicals you try to tone down your attacks . . . It doesn't mean that you must necessarily cut out important data and information but that you must not show too much your hatred. If your articles are to be journalistic they should appear as coming from a disinterested onlooker . . . who is not supposed to inject his own feelings into his writing."[35] But Agnes was too invested in the outcome of what she reported to censor what she wrote.

Even if her intransigence limited her American outlets to Party-affiliated publications like *International Literature*, the *Negro Liberator*, and *China*

Today, she did little beyond lament to Ginn about her reputation as "a branded person." The *Nation*, which knew of Agnes's close relationship with Madame Sun Yat-sen, had suggested the two women collaborate on a series of articles for the magazine. But Madame Sun was extremely publicity averse, as it compromised her own covert work, and Agnes had turned them down.

By the spring of 1935, Agnes had turned forty-three. She had no personal life to speak of, no home or family to return to. She was probably not even paid for many of the political activities for which she placed her life at risk. Still, the magnitude of her purpose sustained her. "If we are to advance to a new society," she wrote Ginn, "and if we are to destroy the fearful system that is destroying us, we must be willing to give our lives." However, Agnes's commitment to China's revolution was about to be sorely tested.

Wang Ming, the Chinese Communist Party's representative to the Comintern, had approved Browder's request to create a second English-language newspaper in Shanghai—on the understanding that "the two comrades," Max and Grace Granich, oversee Agnes's activities and that Browder "categorically prohibit Smedley from maintaining connection with . . . individual Chinese

MOST SECRET.

No.:   3984/U.S.A.
Date.:   22nd October, 1935.

From: MOSCOW.
To: U.S.A.

No.:   359.
Date: 17th October, 1935.

EARL from VANMIN.

After organisation SHANGHAI of newspaper Anti-War, Anti-Fascist character as (1 group) anti-imperialist peoples United Front. For this purpose must be used money which has SMEDLEY.   Send for help SMEDLEY (1 group) comrades of which before spoke.   Categorically prohibit SMEDLEY from maintaining connection with (4 groups missing) individual Chinese Communists.   All instructions in connection with edition newspapers (The) will get through ZEALAND.

Decripted OMS radiogram concerning Agnes from Wang Ming, CCP delegate to the Comintern executive committee, to CPUSA General Secretary Earl Browder, 1935. *National Security Agency Archives.*

Communists."[36] It was not until December, when the electrifying climate gave the project urgency, that Browder informed Agnes that the Graniches were en route to Shanghai to start the paper.[37]

If Browder had indeed advised Agnes, as Wang Ming instructed, to stop working with the Chinese Communists, she had simply ignored him, but the news that the Graniches, rather than Freeman, would be her collaborators upset Agnes mightily. Freeman was a respected leftist writer and critic; the Graniches were Party functionaries. Besides, their impending arrival reminded Agnes that she would now have to account for the money with which the CPUSA had entrusted her, more than half of which had already been spent on the book of Kollwitz prints. The realization sent her into a tailspin.

On the advice of a friend, Agnes attempted to replace the money through currency speculation on the black market, but money management was never a strength of Agnes's, and she proceeded to lose even more. Distraught to the point of befuddlement, she penned a hostile note to Coward-McCann demanding payment for the revised edition of *Daughter of Earth* a second time. When that failed to produce results, she came down with what she described as "a desperate, distracting illness."

The Graniches arrived in January 1936. Agnes was ill disposed to meet them, but she seemed to hope that by charming the American apparatchniks, she might stall them for as long as she could. As Grace recalled the couple's first days in Shanghai:

> Eager to get started on our venture, we proceeded at once to find Agnes. She had given us an address of a couple of foreigners, one of whom was Rewi Alley, a New Zealander, the other Alex Camplin, an Englishman ... We called on them at once, and found them to be warm, friendly people. Agnes had told them we might be coming, and so they were ready to give us a warm welcome. A telephone call was made, and soon Agnes was there to greet us ...
>
> She was eager to get the magazine started, and we talked at length that first night about our plans. First, we had to find out about finances, and I had to ask her about the funds she was supposed to have for the magazine. She pushed this aside as a matter of no consequence, and began telling us tales of China, of the student uprising, the oppressions. She was a great story teller, and we had an exciting evening ...
>
> ... She immediately began making plans for us to meet everyone she knew in both the foreign and Chinese communities who could be of help to us. Day and night we were busy meeting people, at luncheons in Agnes's home, dinners in Chinese restaurants, in the homes of others, we met a succession of people. First of all and most important: we were taken to meet

Madame Sun Yat-sen, who graciously received us in her home in the French Concession.[38]

Agnes insisted that the couple visit Peking before embarking on any work in Shanghai, to better understand the task that awaited them; Madame Sun concurred. The two women sent the Graniches off with letters of introduction to several people they should meet in Peking, including the Snows and National Salvation movement leaders, but the trip only forestalled the inevitable. By February 1936, the Graniches had returned to Shanghai, and the four conspirators plunged into preparations for what Grace referred to from the start as *her* publication.

Sensing the direction in which the paper was headed, Agnes quickly made it clear, according to Grace, that she did not want her name on the masthead, nor did she wish to be involved with any of the actual editing or publishing. She would contribute one anonymous article per issue, but that would be the extent of her involvement. Grace would say that Agnes told them she sought anonymity for her work in order to avoid having the paper condemned as Red, but Max thought her reasons were otherwise. "We were unknowns," he later explained, "and added nothing prestigious" to the relationship.[39] Grace believed, in addition, that Agnes "resented the fact that we were the known and acknowledged editors and began to feel that her position as revolutionary China's only friend was being challenged."[40]

Still, they admitted that Agnes could be a lot of fun. That February, the three of them spent a good deal of time in one another's company. Besides her gifts as raconteur, Agnes was a wonderful drinking partner and, when it suited her, Grace later recalled, a generous and genial companion. "She taught us much about China and its revolutionary history, introduced us to her friends, and in general made life pleasant for us," Grace would acknowledge. But the Graniches had been ordered by Browder to bring Agnes into line, and their struggle to contain her "individualism" led to repeated clashes.

Agnes's neurotic dealings with her sexual partners also made them snigger. By the time she was in her forties, Agnes was rather hefty, and with her careworn face and her sensible sweaters and shoes, she was an unlikely temptress, but her choice and variety of bedmates remained a subject about which "the unsubtle Shanghai mind made heavy pleasantry," as one contemporary decorously put it.[41] The firsthand accounts Agnes shared with the Graniches were sometimes more than they could handle.

Late that month, they received a frantic late-night call from Agnes asking them to come to her apartment at once. Under the impression that she "was burning up or something," as Max described it, the couple rushed over, whereupon Agnes explained that an ex-lover had returned and tried to force his way into her room. When she wouldn't have him, they had argued for some time before he finally left. "Oh my God," Max said she told the Graniches, "he's back, he'll be at me every day." A second late-night call came the following day. The man had indeed returned, Agnes informed them, a hysterical edge to her voice. As he came up her stairway, she warned him that if he did not leave immediately she would beat him with the leaded walking stick she kept by her door. When he persisted, she had whacked him on the head until he fled. The next evening, in a third late-night call, Agnes said the man had arrived with his head shaven. He had done so, Max reported Agnes told him, so that she could beat him better.[42]

Despite the simmering tensions, the Graniches managed to put out the first issue of *Voice of China* without major incident. Agnes contributed an article on the student movement, and Madame Sun was so relieved the paper was at last in production that she organized an excursion to Hangchou to celebrate. In March, though, it all unraveled.

Ostensibly, the conflict began as an editorial issue. According to Grace, Browder had advised the couple before they left New York to "remember that their main enemy was Japanese imperialism, even though they would not like most of the things that the British and the U.S. were doing in China, and would be repelled by Chiang Kai-shek's dictatorship."[43] But in Agnes's article for the second issue, which dealt with Japan's takeover of north China, she had directed her vitriol against Chiang Kai-shek and his government instead of the Japanese—which violated the united front line. The Graniches pressed Agnes to edit it out and attempted to enforce their authority over her, but Agnes was very difficult, "very opinionated and stubborn," Max said, about the matter. From there things deteriorated rapidly.

Grace now demanded a full accounting of the money the Party had given Agnes for the paper. When she learned that less than half of it remained, she was furious. The power struggle between the two women quickly extended into the political arena. Grace (who never knew of Agnes's ties to the OMS) complained that in the same indirect way Agnes had earlier manipulated CCP figures, flaunting Comintern authority she did not actually have, she had enhanced her position among China's revolutionary cultural workers by frittering away funds entrusted to her to establish a "serious" newspaper on a frivolous art project. She saw no reason to encourage whatever goodwill the CPUSA and Comintern still bore Agnes.

Ruth Weiss, a young Austrian woman who ran errands for the paper, was selected to notify Browder of Agnes's transgressions. If she had it to do over again, Weiss tearfully confessed fifty years later, she would not have followed

Grace's orders, but at the time, she said, she did not feel she could refuse. She was much younger than the others, she explained, and just learning to be "progressive."[44] Her reluctance was compounded by the gratitude she bore Agnes for her intervention in an awkward situation.

Hans Shippe, political instructor of the Marxist study group to which many of Shanghai's foreign radicals belonged, had made what Weiss called "plush eyes" at her, then attacked Weiss for being "formalistic and petit bourgeois" after she rebuffed him. His comments had hugely insulted the budding revolutionary, and Agnes, who had her own objections to Shippe's smug, superior treatment of women, quickly surmised the reason for Weiss's upset.[45] After asking Weiss, "Did he try to make you? He tried to make me. He tries to make every woman he meets," Agnes had avenged Weiss's honor at the group's next meeting, striking the overweight Comintern agent with her walking stick and pushing him down the stairs.[46] Incidents like this had led foreign friends in Shanghai to nickname Agnes "Rusty Nails."

Shortly after Weiss contacted Browder, Agnes sent her a note saying that she could no longer be reached through the *Voice of China*. Weiss rushed over to Agnes's home, where she said she found her "pacing like a caged lion. 'I don't like Hitlers, especially if they're Communists,'" Agnes reportedly fumed.

Grace refused to discuss the incident, but later she wrote that she had had to blow the whistle on Agnes not only for her financial misconduct but because she was simply too "adventurous." Roaming the streets of Shanghai with a pistol to protect hunted Chinese Communists drew attention more than it helped, Grace warned. She claimed that Agnes's antics had placed a PPTUS representative in jeopardy.[47] In the future, Grace told Weiss, Agnes would do better to confine her activities to propagandizing, at which she excelled, and leave politics to the professionals.

Max, too, knew that Agnes was furious about the cable to Browder, but he felt that their criticism of her was warranted. "She was very difficult as far as Party affairs go, because she was so temperamental and unstable... She was too unstable to be... completely trustworthy," he later remarked.[48]

On March 31, 1936, Wang Ming responded to the Graniches' cable, word of which had reached him in Moscow. He ordered Browder to instruct Mike Pell, a PPTUS representative in Shanghai, "and also our Chinese comrades in the country that whoever goes to Shanghai must avoid connection with Smedley and Little Sister [probably Weiss] because police are following them and they are thus causing arrests of our comrades. We also have no confidence in Smedley and Little Sister. For instance, relatives of Little Sister are traitors."[49] Rudy Baker, who directed the organization's clandestine work in San Francisco, responded that the PPTUS was in no position either to condemn Agnes for her unauthorized behavior or to break off connections with her as instructed. The organization, he explained, was relying on her for information that made the work of their trade union apparatus in Shanghai possible in the absence of other connections.[50]

It would be a while before Weiss learned that she, too, was under attack by that "snake in the grass," as she came to call Grace Granich,[51] but word of Agnes's falling-out with the CPUSA traveled quickly through Shanghai's community of foreign activists. Most of them sided with the Graniches, for it was they, after all, who represented Party authorities. Agnes's vigor, Alley remarked, was often her downfall, and she could be pretty reckless. A better individual than collective worker, the line went, Agnes was somewhat jealous of her leadership of her little group and as a consequence made some "sizeable mistakes."[52]

Agnes grew increasingly agitated, but she truculently refused to bow to the CPUSA. "I'll never leave China!" she informed Grace, according to a later account by Max. "I'll wreck their god damned CP[USA], but they'll never get me out of here."[53] It was easier for Agnes to defy the American Party than it was to face down Comintern orders. The organization's second united front policy bespoke greater tolerance for a wider variety of views outside the USSR. Inside the Soviet Union, though, the reality was quite the reverse.

The purging of "slackers" and "saboteurs," which had taken place in the early 1930s, had already given way to eliminating both wings of Stalin's opposition by the time Agnes visited Moscow. In December 1934, the assassination of Leningrad Party leader Sergei Kirov had been used as the pretext to inaugurate a more frightening era; within a month of his death, tens of thousands of Soviet citizens were arrested and deported to Siberia, falsely accused of Kirov's murder. Although Stalin assured his subjects at home and his followers abroad that he and his party were devoted to human welfare and humanistic values above all else, the purges were increasing in an inverse ratio to the presence of internal opposition.

The Soviet leader's notorious lack of enthusiasm for the Comintern, and for foreign Communists, was causing the organization to hemorrhage. In the aftermath of the very congress that hailed the second united front era, Agnes's protecters in the OMS, Mirov-Abramov and Piatnitsky, had been removed from Comintern work. Over the next few months, as Agnes's crisis unfolded, both men would be arrested and then disappear in Stalin's first mass roundup of foreign Communists in Moscow. As the OMS was being dissolved, its functions assumed by the territorial sections of its ruling body, the agency, which Rudy Baker acknowledged had "previously had connections with [Smedley]," broke off with her completely.[54] Muenzenberg, whose Comintern defenders were identical to Agnes's, would also become imperiled and unable to help. Chatto, too, would disappear from Leningrad, never to be heard from again.

Agnes's dustup with the Graniches, and the political climate in the Soviet Union, cost her dearly with both the CPUSA and the Comintern. Her long-standing ties to the Chinese Communists, however, remained. If anything, they had become even stronger since the peasant leader Mao Tse-tung assumed leadership of the Chinese Party, and Soviet influence consequently declined. So when Fung Hsueh-fung, a Communist poet who had made the Long March, arrived in Shanghai in the spring of 1936 looking for a journalist to visit the Chinese Communists at their new base, where the twenty thousand surviving members of Mao Tse-tung's southern troops were recovering after a year of nearly continuous marching, Agnes assumed she had the inside track. His close association with Lu Hsun, and his willingness to share his experiences confirmed Agnes's impression.

> Every evening for weeks I sat with [Fung], taking notes of his conversation. Though calm and factual, his recital was filled with pictures of incredible suffering and perseverance. Speaking of the long wanderings in the snows of eastern Tibet, he would say:
>
> "Men grew so exhausted that when they squatted for natural functions, they were too weak to get up again. Thousands froze to death. For months we had only corn to eat, and many could not digest it. It passed through them. Others gathered it up, washed it, and ate it again—only to expel it once more...
>
> "When those of us who survived emerged at last on the plains of Kansu and saw our own native folk, we threw our arms about them, weeping and laughing. We were in rags or skins, or cloth primitively woven from sheep's wool. We were as gaunt as skeletons, and thousands of us were sick. The nights echoed with our coughing."[55]

Alley, who acted as Agnes's translator during the interviews, insisted that her account appeared in the Comintern's *International Press Correspondence* and that it was the first good report to appear on the Long March.[56] The article cannot be found, but there is little question that Agnes saw the story as hers. The Red Army was her subject; it had been for years. The manuscript on which she was at work was a sequel to *China's Red Army Marches*; the accounts it contained had been provided by CCP leaders. Moreover, given the recent unpleasantness in Shanghai, Agnes longed to flee to far-off Shensi.

But Agnes was not the only Western journalist who wished to describe the human drama behind the Red Army and its leaders. Edgar Snow also wanted to tell the story, and now the bad blood between Agnes and the Graniches returned to haunt her. Since the beginning of 1936, Snow, too, had been wrangling for an invitation to visit the Red Army at their new base. At the beginning of May, his request to visit the Chinese Communists still unanswered, he traveled from his home in Peking to press his case with Madame Sun in Shanghai. Since the CCP had essentially been dissolved there the year before, she was the Party's key contact person in the city, and Snow, who had been quietly collaborating with her over the past few years, knew her particular interest in influencing the media.[57]

She proved to be a willing listener. In years past, Agnes's liberated lifestyle had often offended the prim woman, as did her fondness for dropping Madame Sun's name in conversation and her references to herself as Madame Sun's "secretary." Moreover, Madame Sun had sided with the Graniches in their feud with Agnes, and loaned the couple money to keep the *Voice of China* afloat after the Graniches discovered the shortfall.[58] Fed on tales, perhaps told by Grace, who had become a close friend in adversity, Madame Sun spread stories among Shanghai progressives about how Agnes had used money entrusted to her for Party work "for herself—for her cook."[59]

Madame Sun's regard for Snow as a respected journalist with excellent media access no doubt also influenced her thinking. While Agnes was perhaps the more creative writer, she was well known to be quite Red in her sympathies—more propagandist than journalist. With Snow, it was the other way around. Like Agnes, Snow was sympathetic to the Chinese Communists. He also discreetly shared information and participated in the student movement. But Snow's reputation for objectivity gave him a credibility Agnes lacked. Unquestionably, he would be easier to get along with. After their brief, sensitive visit, Madame Sun recommended that the CCP select Snow as the person best suited to meet the Chinese Communists at their Shensi base.

Elated, Snow offered his editor at the *London Daily Herald* an exclusive contract for the rights to any articles he produced about his experience, which he hoped would include interviews with the Communist leaders Mao Tse-tung and Chu Teh. "If I succeed in seeing them, as I may," he wrote, "it will be a world scoop on a situation about which millions of words have been written, based only on hearsay and highly colored government reports."[60] Snow was a man of integrity. Before he set off, he felt obliged to break the news to Agnes directly.

As his wife later recalled their discussion, it was less a meeting than a battle. "She had been furious at my husband for wanting to go there and more so for having succeeded," Peg Snow would write, "as this defeated her dream of being the first journalist to go there and write about it."[61] Agnes was by turns enraged, heartbroken, and unbearably jealous. Fortune seemed to smile on the easygoing, good- natured Snow. Things came effortlessly to him. Although he had only recently become politically involved, his reports on China were appearing in the *New York Sun*, the *London Daily Herald,* and the *Saturday Evening Post*. He

was amply recompensed for his work. Agnes had devoted her life to China's revolutionary struggle, but she still struggled to earn a living as a China writer.

Moreover, according to foreign activists who knew Agnes in Shanghai, she
believed she deserved to go first and be in on any exclusive stories, based on all
she had done for the Chinese Communists. That was exactly the problem, one
of them later explained. "She felt she was first with the Chinese Revolution. She
was proprietary about it."[62] In typically histrionic fashion, Agnes appealed the
decision to Madame Sun Yat-sen, but according to a subsequent account,
Agnes's carrying-on so offended the dignified Madame Sun that she ordered
Agnes from her home.[63] One of Agnes's many flaws, a contemporary observed,
was that her personality lacked a middle range. "With her you were either perfect, or you were no damn good."[64] Agnes never forgave Madame Sun for what
she took as a personal betrayal. In the years to come, she either spoke of her with
tremendous bitterness or refused to discuss her at all.

The CCP central committee had sent Fung to Shanghai not only to identify a
suitable journalist but also to solicit desperately needed medical supplies for the
Red troops. Agnes, her affection for the soldiers undimmed by her setback,
agreed to raise money for the purchases and help smuggle the material to the
Red Army.[65] George Hatem, who would accompany Snow to the Communists'
base as a physician, said that before he left Shanghai in June 1936, Agnes gave
him "detailed instructions on how to behave as a doctor and a revolutionary.
She collected money and had me buy medicines to take with me. She even
bought dust glasses for Mao and Chu Teh and other army commanders and soldiers. She was concerned about their ability to direct battle and fight with dust
from the loess hills in their eyes."[66]

Agnes tried to remain focused on her own Red Army book even though
Snow would scoop her, but it was a struggle. Lonely and sick at heart, the Smedley family leitmotif—that "happiness is where I am not," as she wrote in *Daughter of Earth*—came to her often, and Agnes blamed the city of Shanghai for her
present despair.

> Shanghai is a fearful place [Agnes wrote a friend]. There is no cultural life
> here . . . My associates are confined to less than half a dozen . . . Yet when I . . .
> think of the Red Army on its long, ceaseless march, covering hundreds of
> miles in a short time, carrying and guarding hundreds of old, young, their
> wounded, fighting off attacks, hampered by lack of bullets and weapons, har-
> ried by airplanes, well, my life is a paradise indeed. Yet I would rather be with
> them than to be in Shanghai. I sometimes think life with them with all its

unspeakable hardships would cure my heart trouble and drive away my stomach ulcers. I think the sheer superhuman grandeur of their struggle would cure me of all things; and certainly I could die in peace if die one must. Death would then be worthwhile.[67]

Other news contributed to Agnes's morbid state. In May 1936, Lu Hsun, who suffered from tuberculosis, had been given six months to live, and Agnes took the news badly. "You ask how I am," she wrote Eva Ginn. "Serious difficulties with what is called 'the spirit.' I do not know what is wrong, but I seem unable to write... I'm just coming out of a two week period of depression which paralyzed me completely; I could do nothing but brood."[68]

By the summer of 1936, Agnes was no longer thinking clearly or behaving responsibly. According to PPTUS representative Rudy Baker, she had "pulled a revolver and threatened to commit suicide unless our friend Alec [Alex Camplin] agreed to do certain work for her. This incident supported by others indicates she is on the verge of a mental breakdown which only aggravates the dangers that she is creating with her activity. She has shamelessly accused two reliable comrades [the Graniches] of being Trotskyists and careerists. Numbers of letters that she wrote to these comrades clearly portray mental disintegration."[69]

Both Baker and Browder warned the Comintern that, despite the numerous complaints against her, Agnes persisted in meeting with PPTUS and Party comrades, as well as trade union and student groups, acting as a "self-appointed unofficial representative of the Comintern." The fact that she had earlier helped finance trade union and Party work for several months, they said, made it difficult to stop her. "It is necessary to liquidate this situation once and for all or else grave consequences will follow," the PPTUS warned.[70] "Recall her," Browder advised Moscow, "otherwise serious trouble."[71]

Agnes understood by now that she had committed some grievous tactical errors, and she was angry with herself for the way she had mishandled her dispute with the Graniches. "I know I'm no person to speak for or against the Party itself, for I've never been willing to join it," she wrote Eva Ginn. "However, I recognize that this is because I'm an individualist—and it's not because the Party is wrong."[72] She acknowledged that the pressure the CPUSA and Comintern were applying to isolate her in Shanghai was driving her nearly mad and that she was frequently suicidal.[73] But it was too late to take it back. All she could do was move forward.

By the summer of 1936, Chang Hsueh-liang, the former Manchurian warlord known as the Young Marshal, was commanding the provincial Tungpei army in Shensi. He had become a democrat, and his conviction that Chiang

Kai-shek needed to support a united front and counter Japanese aggression made him a formidable ally of the Chinese Communists. One way the Young Marshal expressed his convictions was by providing sanctuary to radicals under attack by the KMT government. This enabled Agnes's friend Liu Ding, a Red Army representative on Chang's staff, to arrange a visit by Agnes to a tourist resort in the area Chang controlled.

Initially, she would simply take a well-earned rest. When she was feeling better, she could repay the gesture by reporting on developments in north Shensi. It was as close to the Red Army as Agnes could get without an official invitation. Marshaling her nervous strength, she renewed her passport, packed her bags, and bought a railway ticket to northwest China.

"If I succeed in writing a decent book and if I succeed in living in the meantime, I will send the manuscript," Agnes wrote Ginn. "But if my money gives out and I find the book I'm writing is rotten, then you won't hear from me again, for I'm then going inland, where I intended to go in the first place . . . In that case, my writing career is ended. If I now collect money due me, I'll have enough money to last me six months . . . I send . . . pictures to . . . [*China Today* and] . . . to London, France, Prague and Moscow, and not one thinks of paying a cent. I could do it before, but not now."[74]

Agnes described her circumstances more candidly in a subsequent letter to Malcolm Cowley marked "Strictly Confidential. Please read and burn."

Six years ago I came into violent conflict with Grace and Max Granich (this is confidential) in Shanghai, because those thugs turned up suddenly, without my wish or permission, to be my "political commissars," in the publication of a magazine. I tried to work with them for months, in a situation that was in the midst of the white terror in which I carried fearful burdens. I had contacts with the Chinese Communists and, at times, many of their departments were destroyed and men slaughtered, so that but remnants remained. I picked up the remnants, the threads, and retained them in my hands until the Red Army reached the northwest and could send representatives to take over. It grated on Grace Granich that I, not even a Party member, should presume so much. I had no choice except to betray good men. I refused to do that. Under the white terror, with my own life in danger daily, doing the work of a dozen men, I then faced these two party representatives who tried to use me merely as a stooge. The Chinese trusted me, for the Chinese as a rule judge by actions, by experience. But when I refused to obey the orders of Mrs. Granich, I was marked for slaughter myself, in the political sense of the word. Mrs. Granich even told people that she would drive me out of China. It was a rotten thing for them that they could not expel me from the Party—for I had never belonged to the Party; so they could not expel me. That meant also that I could act as I considered best.[75]

On August 18, 1936, Agnes said she turned over her list of contacts to her "commissars," the Graniches, and took off—without their knowledge, and without telling them where she went. She was so anxious about what awaited her that she said she had a "heart attack" the day of her departure and fainted in a restaurant. But while she knew she had many weaknesses, she believed there was much she could still accomplish in China. The CPUSA and the Comintern could have the network which she had spent the past eight years building. They could not have her.

Agnes's attitude did not mean she was indifferent to the welfare of individual agents. On her way out of town, she asked Eva Ginn whether James Henle, the publisher of Vanguard Press, would "send a few free books to Mr. and Mrs. Paul Ruegg, First Kiangsu Prison, Nanking, China? Paul and Gertrude, the political prisoners, are in prison for life," Agnes wrote. "Paul is in perpetual solitary confinement. Both are intellectuals and Paul is extremely sensitive . . . Confinement of this sort is torture for him . . . I've collected . . . books from friends . . . ever since I returned to China." In her absence, Agnes feared, the couple would suffer without reading material.[76]

CHAPTER 13

Mutiny in Sian

Jesse James was a lad who killed many a man.
He robbed the Glendale train.
He stole from the rich and he gave to the poor,
He'd a hand and a heart and a brain.

TRADITIONAL

A GNES PASSED the fall of 1936 in Lintong, about fifteen miles from Sian in northwest China, where Liu Ding had procured a room for her. The former temple had originally been the pleasure palace of Yang Kwei-fei, the favored concubine of the ninth-century emperor Hsuan Tsung, but its charming architecture, gardens, ponds, and hot springs had recommended its current use. After spending two weeks in bed reading Chinese history, studying the language (a skill for which Agnes displayed little aptitude), and nursing her wounds, she began to take the waters. Daily treatment for her "heart trouble," as she called it, had a beneficial effect on her nerves.

Within a short time, Agnes resumed work on her collection of Long March tales, which she had tentatively titled *Chronicles of the Chinese Red Army*.[1] Ed Snow might have gotten to meet its leaders first, but she did not intend to cede him the subject, and Vanguard had the manuscript, which she described as "the history of an epoch," under contract. Snow, however, was financially secure while he collected data in nearby Pao'an. Agnes was strapped for cash, with 150 borrowed American dollars to her name.

Since her split with the CPUSA and the Comintern, funding from those sources had dried up. Agnes had asked Philip Jaffe and Frederick Field to bankroll her while she completed her project, but she knew her reputation made such aid unlikely.[2] Nor did she anticipate much luck with *Asia, New Republic, Harper's,* or *Pacific Affairs,* to whom she had mailed excerpts. *Partisan*

Review was the only American magazine that had recently bought her work of late; *China Today* and *New Masses* ran her articles, but neither of those outlets paid. International Publishers, which had already begun to advertise Agnes's book of China photographs when she fell from grace with the CPUSA, had abruptly canceled the project.[3] Moreover, the two China books she had done with Vanguard had been work-for-hire contracts, which meant she received no royalties from them.

Outside the U.S., the Indian *Modern Review* was using Agnes's pieces, but it, too, did not pay a great deal. Herzfelde continued to place her articles in the German exile press—prominent political journals of the anti-Nazi German left, along with others that were more frankly propagandistic—but none of them provided a livelihood.[4] Although Herzfelde's Malik Verlag had recently released German translations of her two China books in print runs of twenty thousand each, she had not received payment for them, either. Since it cost Agnes roughly thirty American dollars a month to live, she did not have much time before her need for paying work became paramount.

The only time she looked up from her manuscript, she said, was when friends came to visit. Although Agnes lacked the same access to top Red Army leaders that Snow now enjoyed, she was not far from the Chinese Communists' temporary headquarters in Pao'an, and her friend Liu Ding, who served as the Red Army representative in Sian in addition to his position on the Young Marshal's staff, sometimes stopped by with news. So did Wang Ping-nan, another trusted CCP member, who was doing double duty in the area as political secretary to General Yang Hu-ch'eng, a local warlord with radical inclinations. He often brought his German-born wife, Anna. When Edgar Snow resurfaced that November after five months with the new Communist leaders, Agnes attended a dinner party in his honor in Sian. She was still upset about Snow's scoop, but she was eager to hear his stories.

The event was hosted by Herbert Wunsch, a longtime Comintern helper who had established a dentist's office in Shensi's capital city earlier in 1936 to receive the medical supplies smuggled to the Red Army. Agnes's female writer friend Ting Ling, who had recently escaped captivity after being kidnapped by Chiang Kai-shek's Blue Shirts, also attended the event. While she waited to be ferreted into Red territory, Ting Ling was posing as Wunsch's cook.[5]

The reports Agnes heard from these sources were disturbing. Relations between Chiang Kai-shek and Chang Hsueh-liang's provincial Tungpei army, already strained by the summer of 1936, had deteriorated further that fall when the Japanese moved into Inner Mongolia and exerted diplomatic pressure on the central government to crack down on the Chinese Communists. But even as their geographical proximity drew the Young Marshal closer to the Chinese

The writer Ting Ling, a female friend and associate.
Museum of the Chinese Revolution, Beijing.

Communists in Shensi province, he remained first and foremost a nationalist, and he still hoped to persuade the Generalissimo that the Communists' desire to resist Japan was not a ruse to halt the civil war.

   With every passing month, though, Chang's hope dimmed. As the situation in Sian heated up, Agnes spent increasing time in the city, cementing her relationships with old contacts and making new ones. To political innocents like Michaelis, Agnes suggested that she had suffered some sort of relapse and needed to spend time in a hospital there, but in early December, when the temple where she was staying was evacuated to prepare for a visit by Chiang Kai-shek, who was coming to the area to launch his latest anti-Communist campaign, Agnes abandoned any pretense of retreat.[6] Putting her manuscript to the side, she secured a room in the Sian Guest House, the only modern hotel in the city.

   Over the next few days the hotel filled with high-level officers on Chiang's staff. During this time, hundreds of armed Blue Shirts established secret centers and a radio station in the city, giving Sian the flavor of an armed camp, Agnes would write. In addition to Chiang's men, Hsiao Li-tze, the governor of Shensi province and Chiang's private secretary, had his own armed guards and commanded the local police force. The Sian branch of the Kuomintang, she reported, was also heavily armed.

On December 9, Agnes was out in the streets taking pictures of a demonstration commemorating the anniversary of the previous year's anti-Japanese student action in Peking when one of Chiang's Blue Shirt police demanded to see her passport and residence visa and an explanation for her activities, she later wrote. After wrangling with city officials, he returned with Agnes to her hotel and warned the manager that if he did not throw Agnes out, Chiang's gendarme would do so himself and "settle the score with her once and for all," according to Agnes's account.[7]

Agnes sought the advice of her well-connected friends, who she said instructed her to stay put. If the Blue Shirts attacked her, she would write that they told her, "it will become an international incident and expose them as having attacked a foreign friend of China while refusing to fire a shot at the Japanese!" By that evening the atmosphere in Sian was ominous, but Agnes, like her friend Liu Ding, still believed that the danger lay in a Blue Shirt uprising facilitated by local police. It did not occur, either to Agnes or the Chinese Communists, that the Young Marshal might take matters into his own hands.

Two days later, on December 11, Chiang Kai-shek wrapped up his affairs in the northwest with a farewell dinner attended by top commanders of his own Central Army and the Young Marshal's Tungpei forces. The following day, Chiang planned to inaugurate his anti-Communist campaign and leave the area. Instead, at dawn on December 12, 120 Tungpei troops led by a young officer, Captain Sun, surrounded Agnes's former residence in Lintong, where Chiang was currently staying. Unable to persuade sentries to open the gate, they fought their way directly to Chiang Kai-shek's room, killing thirty of his bodyguards along their path including his nephew, Chiang Hsiao-hsien, leader of the Blue Shirt gendarmerie. The Tungpei men found Chiang Kai-shek's diary, some documents, and his false teeth, but no sign of the Generalissimo. On hearing the first shot at the gate, Chiang Kai-shek had slipped out the back door in his nightshirt and fled to a nearby mountain, where he hid in a cave behind a pile of stones.[8]

On the evening of December 11, Agnes had been unable to sleep. She was in her room at the Sian Guest House, observing the first streaks of dawn through her window, when she heard the bursts of machine-gun and rifle fire. Her first thought, she later wrote, was that Chiang Kai-shek's Blue Shirts were launching the fascist uprising she anticipated.

> My heart almost stopped beating when I heard the sound of running feet within the hotel, then hoarse shouts and excited voices. Rifle shots came from somewhere nearby and then above the ominous cries and the crashing of doors rose the sound of splintering glass. The sounds were all those of danger

and death. A woman screamed, men shouted, and automobile engines started up with a roar.

Rifle butts crashed against my door. Unwilling to help in my own murder, I backed into a corner just as three rifle shots splintered the wood and the glass panel crashed and scattered. I heard shouts of "Japanese!" and thought in terror: "God! They're going to kill me under the pretense that I'm a Japanese!"

A soldier's head appeared through the door panel and stared wildly about. I recalled enough Chinese to say: "I'm not Japanese. I'm an American."

Someone pushed him and he tumbled into the room. A crowd of gray-clad soldiers, rifles ready, poured after him and then milled around confusedly. Some dashed into the bathroom, others jerked open the door of the clothes closet, and then all but two streamed out and began beating on the manager's door, which was next to mine.

The two soldiers left in my room began moving about. One suddenly thrust his rifle barrel into my stomach and pushed me back against the wall, while the other dumped everything out of my dressing table. He filled his pockets with everything that struck his fancy—my eyeglasses, rolls of film, flashlight and batteries. He gathered up my woolen sweater and woolen underwear with particular exclamations of satisfaction.

The soldier pinning me to the wall reached out and flipped over the pillow on my bed. There lay my purse, with all my money. With cries of joy the two soldiers pounced upon it and divided up the money. One took my fountain pen and one my pencil, then each clipped his trophy into his breast pocket. Finally each dragged a woolen blanket from the bed and disappeared down the hall.[9]

Agnes had guessed wrong. The men who burst into her room on the morning of December 12 were not Chiang's Blue Shirts but local Hsipei troops under the command of General Yang Hu-ch'eng, who had entered into a secret alliance with Chang Hsueh-liang's Tungpei forces. While the Tungpei men kidnapped Chiang Kai-shek, Hsipei forces had occupied the hotel where Chiang's top officers and Nanking officials—and Agnes—were staying, and they were running amuck. None of Chiang's men escaped the Sian Guest House alive. The killing and shooting rampage also claimed Agnes's comrade-in-arms Herbert Wunsch, who went to the hotel at the height of the mayhem to keep an appointment with Agnes and was gunned down at the entrance.[10]

By the end of the day, the dust began to settle. Sian was in the hands of the Young Marshal and General Yang, who placed the city under martial law. The police station, KMT headquarters, and Blue Shirt secret centers had been captured, along with all the ammunition dumps prepared for use against the Red

Army and one hundred planes sent to fight them. Captain Sun located Chiang Kai-shek at nine o'clock that evening. According to Agnes, Chiang Kai-shek reminded Captain Sun that Chiang was his commander-in-chief. Captain Sun kowtowed, then replied, "You are also our prisoner."[11] Sun carried the Generalissimo down the hill on his own back (Chiang's feet had been bruised by the rocks) and delivered him to the Young Marshal and General Yang.

As some semblance of order was restored, young Manchurian officers took possession of Agnes's hotel and forced General Yang's marauding Hsipei soldiers to divest themselves of their booty. Other officers distributed news bulletins that explained the day's events and the demands of the Sian rebels. Since they had neither ousted nor replaced Chiang Kai-shek and they guaranteed his safety in captivity, what had transpired was technically not a coup. Nevertheless, they made it clear that they did not intend to release Chiang until he agreed to their demands: suspend China's civil war; reorganize the Nanking government to admit all parties; free all political prisoners, including detained National Salvation leaders, protect people's basic civil rights; allow the anti-Japanese movement to exist; build alliances with all countries that believed in China's independence, as Dr. Sun had wished; and convene a National Salvation conference at once.

The events caught the Chinese Communist Party—as they had Agnes—completely unawares. Initially, news of Chiang's capture seemed almost too good to be true. Some of the more radical CCP leaders wished to see the Generalissimo killed, and Mao went so far as to argue that Chiang Kai-shek be brought to Pao'an for a public trial since he owed the people of China "a blood debt as high as a mountain."[12] Agnes, too, was ready to see "that bastard," as she referred to China's leader, dead. Although she had tried to be a loyal soldier, the idea of a CCP-KMT united front had always been problematic for her, and she was no pacifist.

Beyond the sheer pleasure she took in Chiang Kai-shek's humiliation, Agnes understood more than any other Western observer "the reactionary nature of Chiang as a stubborn and deadly enemy of the Chinese people," Ting Ling later observed.[13] However, another group of CCP leaders, who included Chou En-lai, saw past the short-term gratification Chiang Kai-shek's death offered. They thought a peaceful solution, favorable to Chiang, would be more conducive to the Communists' long-term goals.

CCP leaders formulated the Party's response to Chiang's capture at a politburo meeting convened inside Mao's cave. Immediately, they would cable the Young Marshal praising his action and assuring him the CCP would follow his lead. Then a delegation led by Chou En-lai would fly to Sian. P'eng Teh-huai and other Red Army generals would move their troops from Pao'an to Yenan and the surrounding area and close ranks with friendly armies. Until Chou En-lai's party arrived, the CCP liaison office in Sian, where Agnes's friend Liu Ding worked, was to refrain from expressing any concrete views on the matter beyond resistance to Japan. Although it would be virtually the last occasion on which Stalin exerted great influence over the course of the Chinese Communist movement, Chou En-lai still preferred waiting to speak until he received the Soviet leader's blessing.[14] Moscow had lent its backing to resistance to Japan, but it had yet to explicitly express support for Chang Hsueh-liang and Yang Hu-ch'eng.

Over the next thirty-six hours, posters sprouted on city walls denouncing the Japanese aggressors and supporting a People's United Front, but Agnes, like all civilians in Sian, was confined to her premises. By the evening of December 13, she was wild with restive curiosity. As shuttered shops reopened and a new administration was established, Liu Ding sent her a military pass that allowed her to circumvent the restrictions of martial law by helping to care for the wounded.[15] With a red cross sign pinned to her arm and a medical kit in her hand, she began to roam the city.

The first mass demonstrations were already taking place. Thousands of students, workers, soldiers, and officers gathered on the streets, listening in on meetings conducted by the People's Anti-Japanese National Salvation Association and the Students' Union. The organizations, formerly banned, were now officially sanctioned. Manifestos that guaranteed people civil rights circulated. A specially trained political regiment of the Manchurian army dispatched units to outlying villages to arm and train peasants there. A National Salvation newspaper, two other dailies, and a student publication put out the news. Ting Ling would recall that Agnes was beside herself with excitement at having landed a ringside seat at this "tense and complicated political scene."[16] It went a long way toward easing her resentment over Snow's invitation to Pao'an.

Because press censorship was extremely tight and a blockade around the city prevented foreign reporters from entering, radio was the rebels' most effective means to counteract some of the wilder reports emanating from Nanking and communicate their own message to the outside world. Liu Ding now called on Agnes—the only American on the scene—to repay the kindness the Chinese Communists had shown her by handling English-language broadcasting at the radio station they had commandeered.[17] (Others would report in French, German, Russian, and Japanese.) The CCP had specifically instructed its liaison office in Sian to refrain from expressing any concrete views on the situation until Chou En-lai's party arrived. Agnes, however, did not feel bound by such constraints.

In her first dispatch for radio station XGOB, broadcast on December 14, Agnes reported that "Generalissimo Chiang Kai-shek, tottering dictator of

China, has been arrested as a traitor to his country... The arrest represents the cumulative effect of Chiang Kai-shek's ten-year traitorous betraying, counterrevolutionary policy towards China and his five years' exquisite betrayal of the Northeastern Army... Chiang became an obstacle in the path of anti-Japanese war; he had to be removed."[18]

Immediately there was a problem. In a telegram whose contents appeared in *Izvestia, Pravda,* and elsewhere abroad, Stalin put the CCP on notice that he viewed Chiang Kai-shek's kidnapping as a Japanese plot aimed at creating confusion and civil war in China. The USSR, he warned, would not be deceived into supporting the action, which it explicitly opposed.[19] In Stalin's opinion, what China needed was a united national front—which in his view the Young Marshal lacked the stature to direct. That left Chiang Kai-shek as probably the only person who could lead China in a war against the Japanese. For that reason, Stalin felt that the CCP should do its utmost to effect a peaceful settlement and secure Chiang's release.

Agnes was livid. How could Moscow not see that the Chinese Revolution had finally come? And if they did, how *dare* they betray China in this way? No, she decided, she would *not* be silent, she would *not* allow the Soviets to get away with this unchallenged. She could accommodate their concept of "sacrificing partial interests to the whole" no longer. Over the next few days, Agnes used her on-air platform to attack Moscow's position in blistering terms—oblivious, or indifferent, to the furor she might provoke in official Communist and Comintern circles.

The bitter accusations and condemnation Young Marshal Chang had drawn from such an unsuspected quarter, Agnes announced in her December 15 broadcast, showed the world that the Soviet Union was "only too eager to judge in advance, and to condemn, a movement that has an undeniable popular basis in the deepest aspirations of all classes. This hostile attitude, especially on the part of those who must—if they are better informed—sympathize with a popular movement that can only be compared with similar movements in Western countries for a united front against fascist aggression, is inexplicable and utterly unjustified."[20] In her broadcasts, and in printed versions of the same material that the Chinese rebels attempted to smuggle, with varying success, to a network of sympathetic reporters, Agnes defiantly insisted upon the continued incarceration of Chiang.

In the meantime, the United States, France, and England, who had been unable to bring their own reporters into Sian, accepted as true reports from Nanking claiming that the incident was an isolated act of violence by a disgruntled subordinate. Even as Chang Hsueh-liang struggled mightily to effect some compromise, the three nations lacked information that might have encouraged them to question Nationalist claims that Chang sought only to achieve personal power at China's expense — just as Chiang Kai-shek enacted his long-delayed plan for resistance to Japan.

On December 17, with government antiaircraft guns bristling and the matter threatening to career out of control, a six-day truce was declared while Chiang advisers T. V. Soong, W. H. Donald, and Madame Chiang Kai-shek arrived in the city, and the CCP delegation led by Chou En-lai flew to Sian in the Young Marshal's airplane. By this time both groups recognized that it was in their own best interest to negotiate a peaceful settlement, if only to forestall Nanking extremists from launching a full-scale civil war whose outcome neither side could predict.

Tungpei and Seventeenth Army troops greeted the Communist officers when they landed with cheers and slogans in support of the Red Army. "It was a historic moment," Agnes wrote. "I felt I was looking history in the face . . . I was never so happy in my whole life. It cured my heart in two days."[21] In her capacity as participant-observer, she met with several members of the CCP delegation, including Yeh Chien-ying and Chou En-lai.[22] When she learned that Chinese Communists were urging the Sian rebels neither to establish an independent government nor take stern measures against the Generalissimo, she was not at all happy about what an associate said Agnes considered an "about-face" from their initial position.[23]

Although she refrained from openly criticizing the CCP's decision, Agnes interpreted the Chinese Party's unexpected role as peacemaker as succumbing to Soviet pressure, selling out the Sian rebels to its own detriment as well as China's. The fact that the Chinese Communists had come not for vengeance but to pave the way for a "new era of unity," as Agnes later described it, frustrated her. Like other "ultraradicals" at the time, her friend Anna Wang later explained, Agnes was caught up in the moment's revolutionary potential and could not understand the Chinese Communists' support for Chiang.[24]

To ensure that she did not broadcast her dissatisfaction to listeners, Liu Ding found a project to absorb Agnes's energy. One of the first concessions Chiang made during the six-day truce was to release several hundred political prisoners. Among them were a few dozen captive Red Army soldiers, many of them sick with fever or infected wounds. Knowing Agnes's passion to meet the Red Army in the flesh, Liu Ding arranged for her to nurse the injured among them.[25] Agnes's first aid kit contained little more than bandages, lint, and a few bottles of cognac and iodine, but it gave her something to do. It also provided an outlet for her maternal instincts. Some of the men, Agnes wrote a reporter friend in Shanghai, had

untended old wounds that would soon kill them, some [had] wounds that festered along, some [had] leg ulcers, and many [had] the big, hard, bare feet of peasants — feet swollen and bloody from marching and fighting in the winter's snow. I washed the feet of these men, disinfected them, disinfected their wounds, bandaged them — and returned to the missionary hospital to ask for instructions about certain wounds . . . There were fifty-four women and forty little boys with the Red Army prisoners, and I went daily to take care of them also. Nearly all were poor peasants, and some had been slaves. I felt always that I was walking down one of the most tragic and terrible corridors in human history when I worked with them. The sight of poor peasants or slaves who had known nothing but brute labor all their lives, lying there with no covering, no bed, on stone floors, with untended and unhealed wounds, with big, hard, bloody feet — no, I shall never forget that, and shall carry that with me to my grave.[26]

The tenderness and concern with which Agnes ministered to the soldiers helped bridge the language barrier between them. Her favorite patients were the *hsiao kwei*, or "little devils," who served as messengers in the peasant armies. Entrusted with gathering information and carrying secret missives of importance, these boys, who ranged in age from ten to sixteen, had followed the Red Army from their native villages. Some still wore their black prison uniforms. Many had no families; others were the sons of landless laborers or poor peasants.

Although they were so young [a contemporary of Agnes's observed], they carried themselves and spoke like men: there was a steady look in their eyes that told its own tale of a childhood that had looked clear-eyed on suffering. They were an amazing little group and, of course, they won Agnes Smedley's heart . . .

. . . These were some of the "bandits" one had read so much about in the KMT press; in actual fighting, they were more dreaded than the regular Red Army men, for they were utterly reckless of life, and many Government troops who went over to the Reds confessed that their greatest fear had been of the "little devils" who knew none of the rules of polite fighting, and always shot to kill.[27]

Horrified by their shabby clothes and unheated quarters, Agnes insisted that Red Army officials provide the children with new uniforms and blankets at once. When they told her there was no money available for such things, she refused to take no for an answer. " 'What do you have all these committees for?' she demanded . . . 'These children need to be taken care of. I shall apply for a special grant from the Military Council.' "[28] The children got their blankets.

By December 23, negotiations for Chiang's release were well under way. A meeting the following day between Chou En-lai and the Chiang Kai-sheks produced a signed agreement. In exchange for his release and a guarantee of his safety, Chiang Kai-shek pledged to amend his former policies. He vowed to compromise in foreign affairs, end the civil war and oppression at home, and form an immediate united front of all parties in resistance to Japan. On Christmas Day 1936, the Generalissimo was released.

Chang Hsueh-liang accepted full responsibility for the incident, in the conviction that he was performing a lasting service to China, and insisted on accompanying Chiang Kai-shek back to Nanking. A naive but honorable man, the Young Marshal might have thought that Chiang's agreement was a successful outcome to the matter. But the leftist Tungpei and Hsipei officers, and the warlord General Yang, whose nominal command they were under, were not satisfied. Neither was Agnes, who was one of the rebels' most ardent supporters.

According to Ting Ling, Agnes was "quite confused when she heard that Chiang Kai-shek had been set free."[29] She was also angry and disappointed with the "middle group" in the CCP, she later told Cowley, whom she blamed for the decision. After her years maintaining Party "discipline" in deference to Comintern authorities, the genie was out of the bottle; the defiant spirit that had first gripped Agnes in Shanghai had become too overwhelming to suppress. In her December 27 broadcast, she remarked that she joined with all the mass organizations of the northwest in "seriously criticiz[ing] the release of Generalissimo Chiang Kai-shek before he had publicly pledged he would carry out the Sian agreement."[30]

CCP political leaders, who were actively struggling to make the rest of the Chinese Communists (and the Chinese people) believe that they could work with Chiang, did not appreciate Agnes's plainspoken denunciation of their position. Word that Agnes's activities in Sian were "causing the [CCP] much trouble" soon reached Shanghai, where the Graniches were only too happy to inform Browder that the time had come to "publicly repudiate Smedley."[31] American Communists needed to know that Agnes was not one of them, that she was officially out of favor with the American Party, regardless of her influence. Given her former ties to the Comintern, however, Browder first sought the approval of Wang Ming and the Comintern secretariat.

"I have had many disagreements with orthodox Chinese Communists," Agnes acknowledged several years hence, after returning to the United States. "Sometimes I hated them and they hated me ... But I always found other Communists who sided with me."[32] She did so now. In Chang's absence, General Yang, the Shensi general who had been the Young Marshal's chief collaborator, became Sian's unofficial commander-in-chief. As the Red Army threw its support behind Yang, Agnes took comfort in that.

Cipher telegram from CPUSA General Secretary Earl Browder seeking Comintern permission to publicly denounce Agnes, 1937. *Courtesy John Earl Haynes.*

Over the next few days, the town became a Communist mecca. Yang and his Red Army supporters made substantial efforts to arouse popular interest in the National Salvation program and began preparing the region for use as a base for operations against the Japanese in north China. During this time, a number of foreigners left the city. No newcomers entered, though, until December 28 when James Bertram, a young Rhodes scholar from New Zealand, managed to break through the blockade. Bertram was a friend of Snow's, sent to be his eyes and ears in Sian.

He put up at the Sian Guest House, as did Agnes, and on the first morning of his visit, he had a note delivered to her room. Agnes's response was soon forthcoming.

A woman something over forty came striding down the corridor, my card in her hand. She was short, strongly built, with a brown weather beaten face and short hair, and with extraordinarily wide-set, candid eyes.

"Mr. Bertram?" the voice was harsh and sounded hostile. She wore a red woolen jersey, brown skirt, and heavy brogues.

"Yes," I said. "You won't know me, but I've met some people you know in Shanghai." I gave the names.

"Indeed," said Agnes. "And what are you doing here?"

It was the question I had wanted to ask her. But I explained that I had come out of a natural curiosity to find out what was happening in Sian, and to do some writing about it. I had a connection, I added, with some English newspapers.

"What papers?" Agnes was relentless. I mentioned the [China] Daily Herald and—in a weak moment—the [London] Times.

"The London Times is no friend of China." Her mouth shut like a trap. "How did you get here? For all I know, you may be a British spy."

This was unpromising. "I came with a Tungpei man," I said. "Would you like to meet him? We're going out to Lintung with Sun-Ming chiu [General Sun]."

This name, which had been unknown three weeks ago, made a more favorable impression. Agnes Smedley was not unwilling, it seemed, to meet the man who had captured Chiang Kai-shek. But she was still a little suspicious about me. "Do you know anyone else in Sian?" she asked.

I . . . mentioned the young editor of Chang Hsueh-liang's Sian daily. Fortunately she had met him.

"Yes, I know him. Is he a friend of yours?"

"We used to live in the same room in Peking. He'll tell you I'm not a spy."

"Good," said Agnes decisively. "I'll ask him."[33]

Once Bertram had sufficiently distanced himself from the cause of world imperialism, he said, his acquaintance with Agnes developed rapidly. Bertram's Chinese was fluent (a skill that served him well in his subsequent post as press attaché for the British Embassy); he was also quite liberal in his political outlook, trustworthy, and sincere. The two began broadcasting together on December 29. As Bertram recalled it:

The Sian radio station was a compact little place, picturesquely situated behind an old palace in the heart of the city. It was always heavily guarded, for it was practically the only remaining link with the outside world. A military pass took us through the main gateway, past sandbags and machine guns trained on the square outside. Inside the courts there were always sentries on the prowl, and, until they had learned to recognize a visitor, their abrupt challenge from the darkness was apt to be disconcerting.

. . . Underneath the towering steel mast was a modern little studio, very gay inside, with blue cushions and Chinese carpets. We would slip through the heavily curtained doors with an eye on the clock, and a long-gowned servant would bring tea in an awed silence. Then Agnes would get to work with her elbows planted firmly in front of the microphone, while I usually sorted out uncompleted notes.

...There is a special kind of atmosphere about any broadcasting station, but Sian added the thrills of revolution and counter-revolution. I realized suddenly the vital importance of radio in any political movement. So long as Station XGOB continued to function, Nanking could not close down entirely on news from Sian.

...We tried very hard to be objective, and always satisfied ourselves that the facts we announced were accurate. But Agnes had a fine slashing style that was not always well suited to diplomatic statement, and an incurable fondness for the word "masses." In fact, the way she pronounced this word, with a broad "a" and a vigorous enunciation of the sibilants, would—I felt sure—identify her voice to anyone who had ever spoken to her for two minutes. By contrast, I tried to make my voice sound as unemotional as possible, modeling my delivery on the soothing accents of the BBC. In Sian, we thought we were doing pretty well.³⁴

Agnes also took Bertram to meet the freed Red Army prisoners. The "little devils" among them had been organized into a Children's Anti-Japanese Vanguard and were propagandizing at Sian's primary schools. She wished Bertram to see for himself the extraordinary children who had won her orphan's heart. Serious and unsmiling, they performed their revolutionary songs. "Was there

Young followers of the Red Army in northwest China. *From the collections of the Library of Congress.*

any other country in the world, I wondered as we came away, any other . . . movement, where children would do such work as this, would be shot or imprisoned for life as a menace to society? I began to understand Agnes Smedley's enthusiasm for the Red Army of China."[35]

After their nightly broadcasts, Bertram would join Agnes in her room for coffee, and they would sit and talk.

> All kinds of people drifted in during these evenings — journalists, students, officials, soldiers . . .
>
> I learned to know Agnes Smedley as a real person, in these long evenings of coffee fumes and tobacco smoke. I had imagined someone tremendously dynamic and dehumanized; Agnes was dynamic enough, but with it she was one of the most human and lovable people I had ever met. All her judgments were instinctive and emotional; she was the world's best hater, but she could be the most generous of friends. It was her misfortune to have the direct honesty that welcomes a fight in the open, but is peculiarly vulnerable to slander or attacks from the rear. And these, it seemed, she could never escape; for, when a woman writes her life history as Agnes Smedley had written it, all her cards are down.[36]

As the first week of January 1937 drew to a close, no word had filtered back yet from the Young Marshal, or the four aides who had joined him in Nanking. Sian, sensing something was amiss, grew restive. Under the aegis of radical Tungpei officers, a polyglot collection of students and radicals mobilized within the National Salvation movement. Wang Ping-nan organized a committee to guide the masses. With Sian placed on a war footing, the Great Powers now weighed in on the side of the Nanking government.

The situation in Sian, as they saw it, was worse than it had been at any time during Chiang's detention. General Yang had turned Red; his troops continued to loot. Red flags and Communist literature were widely available, and a number of Russian advisers had recently arrived in the city. Under the circumstances, a military clash between Central Government troops and Sian forces seemed inevitable. In light of the potential danger, particularly from airplane bombing, the Great Powers began to consider evacuating their foreign nationals.

Captain Scott, an assistant military attaché at the British Embassy in Peking, was the first Western official to investigate the area around Sian. Since most British nationals in the region were missionaries — a notoriously anti-Communist lot — they expressed to Captain Scott their fear of the Communist bandits. Interference from more powerful stations in Nanking and Hankow, who cut in on the same wavelength as the Sian Broadcasting Company with sirens, and from Agnes's own station manager, who was secretly a KMT member and diluted the strength of the station's transmission, made it difficult to hear Agnes's broadcasts clearly, even in Sian. But the missionaries told numerous tales, real and imagined, of Agnes's exploits since Chiang Kai-shek's kidnapping. To them Agnes had more than a bad reputation; she was the incarnation of the devil.

Not long after Captain Scott filed his report, unsurprisingly, the Shanghai Municipal Police resumed their interception of Agnes's mail. In doing so, they discovered two letters whose tone was considerably more authoritative than the one that Agnes adopted in her correspondence with journalistic colleagues. One was addressed to Emily Hahn, an American who served as a mail drop for Agnes in Shanghai.[37] Its contents, however, suggest it was intended for the Shanghai underground operatives with whom she still maintained contact.

> Up to the present [Agnes reported], Low En Lay [Chou En-lai] meets only success for the whole army of General Yang is on our side. The rest of the troops cannot be considered as being on our side but most of them are demoralized. The general situation in Shanghai is being watched as well as the propaganda which must begin in full with the opening of war actions. It is necessary, absolutely, to exercise an influence, by means of the propaganda, on English public opinion which is at present the main actor in obtaining the necessary means for further development of actions. With this regard I rely on the 'three G's' [Grace Granich, Max Granich, and unknown] and upon "B" [Browder].[38]

The second letter, routed through what she described as a "Central Research Bureau" in Shanghai, was addressed to David Berenberg, head of the American branch of the League Against Imperialism.

> Chu [sic] En-lai and myself had a long conference here with the Moscow delegation, and I confirm now my previous statement that Moscow will do nothing for the support of the Chinese Red Army. Stalin is playing here as well as in Spain—he will not support the foreign armies. Feldman [a Comintern agent] is here as a representative of the Habarovsk military authorities and last week Van Min [Wang Ming] arrived from Dmitrov [general secretary of the Comintern], who stated that military ammunition is expected soon via Ili and Hami. Besides that—the Urga depot promised a certain number of planes, but for the time being the Habarovsk authorities have postponed their forwarding.[39]

The correspondence, along with the reports on Agnes's activities in Sian, touched off a storm of criticism. On January 7, the American consul general in

Shanghai notified Nelson Johnson, the American
ambassador to China, and Secretary of State Cordell
Hull that Agnes was broadcasting "nightly in a pro-
Communist and anti-religious vein."[40] That same day,
an Associated Press dispatch detailing her role in Sian's
unrest made banner headlines from one coast of the
United States to the other. The article, which described
Agnes as a former schoolteacher "long associated with
radical movements in Asia," reported that she was "conducting radio propaganda to unite large disaffected military units in Shensi and Kansu Provinces under the Red
banner in defiance of the Nanking government" and
placed her at the forefront of the intensive campaign
then underway in Sian "to spread the Red gospel." [41] It
charged further that she was broadcasting English-language appeals for recruits for the Red uprising against
Nanking "every few hours." Missouri and West Coast
papers played up the story's local angle.

　The hand of the British could be detected in the
attention paid to Agnes's prior role in the Indian nationalist movement. "Miss Smedley Was Held for Agitating
on Behalf of India," read the headline of the sidebar
that accompanied the article in the *New York Times*.
Other papers acknowledged openly, if somewhat inac-
curately, that Agnes's propagandizing in Sian had provoked broad "opposition from British residents in the
interior provinces who recall her deportation from India
some years ago, where she was alleged to have con-
spired to provoke a nationalist uprising."[42]

　At a meeting with Ambassador Johnson in Nanking,
Dr. Hsu Mo, China's political vice minister for foreign
affairs, challenged her claim to American citizenship,
resurrecting the charge yet again that she was married
to an Indian and therefore a British subject.[43] The only
method Chinese and British authorities trusted to
silence her, evidently, was revoking her extraterritorial

Agnes's involvement in the Sian Incident made headlines
in the *New York Times*, January 7, 1937.

privileges. Dr. Hsu was dissatisfied with the outcome of the meeting, and he vented his frustration with Agnes to a reporter for the *New York Times*.

"A Chinese government spokesman declared today that the Nanking authorities were 'highly indignant' over the anti-government, pro-Communist broadcasts made almost daily from Sian by an American woman who, the authorities charge, is the well known author Agnes Smedley," the article stated, noting also that "the government broadcasting station in Nanking has been consistently attempting to drown out the woman's speeches."[44]

Socialist author Upton Sinclair rallied to Agnes's defense with a spirited article in the popular mass circulation weekly *Liberty*.

Newspaper dispatches bring up a strange tale from the province of Shensi in the remote northwestern part of China. An American woman, a schoolteacher... has become one of the leaders of the radicals of that disturbed and dangerous part of the world. She is organizing a "student propaganda corps" in Sian-fu; she is broadcasting several times a day to a million kindred spirits; when the American military attaché wishes to evacuate Americans from the fighting district, it is this middle-aged Middle Western schoolteacher who makes the arrangements for him.

Who is this Agnes Smedley, and what is she, and how did she get that way?... When I first met her, she was a young schoolteacher, very pretty, and happy over meeting an author to whose ideas she was sympathetic. If anyone had told me that twenty-one years later she would be leading an army of Celestial revolutionaries, I should have been much surprised.

No one can foretell how these mighty struggles of hungry and oppressed peoples will turn out. If George Washington had failed, you would have read of him, in British-printed history books, as a person something like Guy Fawkes, who plotted to blow up the House of Parliament. If Agnes Smedley's cause fails, she will be beheaded and forgotten, or perhaps written of as a sort of female Jesse James or Al Capone of China. On the other hand, if she wins, this school teacher from the American Far West will be remembered as we remember Lafayette and as the French remember Joan of Arc.[45]

By January 9, the threat of civil war hung palpably over the air in Sian. Central government troops were already positioned in Shensi. Red Army troops occupied districts only thirty-five miles to the north. That day, Sian staged the largest demonstration ever held in northwest China. More than a hundred thousand Chinese, both civilian and military, participated in the event. Agnes, perched in an ancient drum tower, watched awestruck as "endless lines of

America's Amazing Woman Rebel in China

Agnes Smedley. "If her cause fails she will be beheaded and forgotten."

Who Is This Little-Known Iowa Schoolteacher Who Has Leaped into Sudden Fame as a Fighting Leader? —Here, from One Who Knows Her Well, Are the Facts

by

UPTON SINCLAIR

READING TIME ● 8 MINUTES 20 SECONDS

NEWSPAPER dispatches bring up a strange tale from the province of Shensi in the remote northwestern part of China. An American woman, a schoolteacher said to be from Iowa, has become one of the leaders of the radicals of that disturbed and dangerous part of the world. She is organizing a "student propaganda corps" in Sian-fu; she is broadcasting several times a day to a million kindred spirits; when the American military attaché wishes to evacuate Americans from the fighting district, it is this middle-aged Middle-Western schoolteacher who makes the arrangements for him.

Who is this Agnes Smedley, and what is she, and how did she get that way? I answer these questions from personal acquaintance, from a correspondence extending over many years, and from the extraordinarily frank and revealing books which she has written. When I first met her, she was a young schoolteacher, very pretty, and happy over meeting an author to whose ideas she was sympathetic. If any one had told me that twenty-one years later she would be leading an army of Celestial revolutionaries, I should have been much surprised.

How does it happen that a child born of old American parentage, and living in Missouri, in Colorado, Iowa, California, New York, and in fact most of the states of the Union, becomes a partisan of races with skins darker than her own? Why does she take up the people first of India and then of China, making their cause her own, even to starvation, imprisonment, and the imminence of death? How does she win their confidence, so that they prefer her teaching to anything of their own?

She was born into a large family on a tenant farm in northern Missouri. Sex she saw early, and saw it as a hideous and brutal thing which brought unwanted babies into the world and riveted tighter chains upon a woman. Ideas of love and marriage were poisoned for Agnes Smedley in childhood, and the horror which she acquired affected her whole life.

The father took his family in a wagon to Colorado; and little Agnes saw the life of Trinidad, a mining town. The father, a miner, was cheated and abused, and hope died in him. Later there was a strike, with beatings and shootings of men and abuse of girls by the militia. At last the tent in which the family lived was swept away by a flood.

At sixteen Agnes was told that it was possible to earn a living teaching school. Because she could speak "a little Mexican" she got a chance to teach in a remote mountain cabin in New Mexico, her pupils being Mexicans, Indian half-breeds, and a few children of ranchers.

Upton Sinclair wrote admiringly of Agnes in *Liberty*, March 13, 1937.

marchers converg[ed] from every direction into a great throng that jammed the main boulevard," she later wrote, and strains of the Red Army's "Volunteer Marching Song," formerly banned, wafted through the city.[46] Local peasants toting guns and spears walked alongside representatives from proscribed worker and student organizations and middle-class supporters.

The following day, Agnes sent Edgar Snow several rolls of film from the demonstration, which she asked him to print and furnish to the press. Her storm with him had blown over, and she resumed the friendship as if nothing had transpired. She was too hurried to write a long letter, she explained, because she was "going in to see my family."[47] What she meant, of course, was the Red Army. On a recent visit to Sian, her friend Ting Ling, who now lived with the troops in north Shensi, had proffered a formal invitation, and Agnes had accepted at once.[48]

Bertram said he had anticipated her departure since the night a young man who served under P'eng Teh-huai had visited Agnes after work.

P'eng was Agnes Smedley's favorite Red leader; she knew every campaign he had fought. They settled down to discuss details of strategy five years old. The newcomer flushed with pleasure when he found that this foreigner knew the names of obscure villages in the South, once given a brief fame as the scene of fierce engagements...

Agnes lived every battle through the telling; though she would never admit it, it was the romance of the thing that caught her then—the desperate odds of rifles and hand grenades against bombs and heavy artillery; the struggle for survival of the little Kiangsi republic, islanded among its mountains, without salt, without a thousand things that the ingenuity of Berlin-trained engineers and scientists could only improvise from the roughest of materials ... It is the most dramatic story, perhaps, of modern times, and one of the least known...

...I could see Agnes making a private resolution that she would be at least the first foreign woman to enter the Red region in the northwest.[49]

On the evening of January 11, Bertram hosted a farewell party for Agnes at the Sian Guest House, although there was little in the way of provisions after the nearly monthlong economic blockade. Agnes, he said, wore a Red Cross armband. Officially, she would be traveling to the front to conduct first aid work there. "It was a transparent disguise," Bertram would observe, "but the recent headlines concerning Agnes's activities had suggested that the less foreigners knew about her movements, the better. He wrote:

There are many kinds of revolutionary . . . But Agnes Smedley fell into no easily recognizable category. A passionate individualist all her life, she had had
bred in her, by the sordid brutality of her childhood in America, a spirit of
revolt against the whole outside world . . .

. . . With a very imperfect knowledge of Chinese, she yet shared, in a way I
could hardly have believed possible for a foreigner, the revolutionary
instincts of the Chinese workers and peasants. She had the same resentment
that they felt against the class enemy—the landlord and the money lender;
against the ruling official bureaucracy; against the agents of finance capital
and foreign imperialism. She saw everything in black and white: there was a
revolution, and she was on one side of it—with the other side there could be
no compromise . . .

We had met by chance, and had little enough in common by background
and training. Agnes had an instinctive distrust of intellectuals; the detached
study of a subject was meaningless to her. But we shared—and this was perhaps the one thing that made her tolerate me—an unbounded admiration for
the common Chinese people: the mill worker in Shanghai, the girl at the silk
looms of Canton, the peasant who worked his fields (or another's) through
drought and flood and famine, with a patient persistence that is sub or superhuman. And, unlike those missionaries who call this "fortitude," and praise as
a heaven-sent virtue this quality of patience that might be better ascribed to a
necessitous fate, we felt, in this dumb ignominy of nearly a quarter of the
human race, a theme for tragedy and not for wonder.[50]

Agnes left the next morning, wearing her riding breeches and ubiquitous red
sweater and knowing, she later wrote, that if she were caught in the city,
Nanking authorities would be pitiless. After she had waited several hours, a
truck loaded with students and directed by a Red Army man pulled up. Agnes
clambered in and they drove off, past the Chou and Han tombs in the direction
of Sanyuan and the Red Army.

CHAPTER 14

Calamity Jane of the Chinese Revolution

I taught her the language of a cowboy's command,
To hold her six shooter in each little hand;
To hold a six shooter and never to run
As long as a bullet was left in her gun.

"THE COWGIRL," SONG

A GNES PASSED a deathly cold night in a mud hut inn. The following morning, her caravan headed for Tungli, an abandoned walled town that served as headquarters of the First Red Army Corps.

> After eight years of observing other Chinese armies [she wrote], my first encounter with the Red Army was a series of startling revelations. For there is a Red Army "type," a Red Army face. True, it is not universal, yet it distinguishes most of the Red Army men. On the whole, it is a young, strikingly vital face of astounding intelligence and consciousness. You could not call it a laughing or happy face, but it is a face that "lives." The dull, unconscious, depressed and hopeless face to be found in other Chinese armies is lacking here. I believe that, generally speaking, I could pick out a Red Army man almost anywhere in China.[1]

Speaking through an interpreter, she addressed two mass meetings. Then, accompanied by Ting Ling and representatives of a newly established Anti-Japanese Association, she proceeded by foot to the village base of Ho Lung, commander of the Second Red Army Corps.

Ho Lung was a former bandit from a peasant family in central China. He lacked the political training of other Red Army leaders, but his skill as a fighter was legendary, and to Agnes he appeared as graceful as a panther. In his fur hat, faded gray jacket, and black trousers, white socks peering from above blue cloth shoes, and green puttees wrapped from knees to ankles, Ho Lung looked to Agnes, she would write, like a figure in a Central Asiatic folk tale. He was illiterate but a gifted storyteller who spoke fluent German. According to Agnes, he had their group laughing constantly.

Ho Lung's men had only recently rejoined the main body of the Red Army, and Agnes said his forces seemed more heavily burdened than the first troops she met. They were undernourished and poorly clad. Many had hollow coughs she suspected were tubercular; their inflamed eyes suggested trachoma. Agnes also noted that when she and Ting Ling spoke at their meetings, the men did not always appear to understand what the two of them were saying.

From Ho Lung's headquarters, the women continued on to Sanyuan, a large village near the snow-covered mountain of Pei Wutienshan that functioned as the Red Army's field headquarters. On their arrival, they were greeted by cavalrymen dressed in long black coats and caps with red flaps and shining red stars. The men rode small, long-haired ponies they had captured in battle.

In Sanyuan, Agnes wrote, "we saw not only Red Army men but also peasant men and women going about their work as usual, transporting their cotton, driving carts, or standing in groups talking to Red Army men near villages . . . The scene was a usual one throughout the country—except for the Red Army men. We rode through the gates of a walled town, made our way through the crowded marketplace, and halted before a building before which stood two Red Army guards armed with automatic rifles. We passed through a succession of courtyards with ancient, decaying buildings on either side," until they reached the offices of P'eng Teh-huai, commander-in-chief of all the front-line Red Armies.[2]

Stocky and unattractive, P'eng Teh-huai had none of Ho Lung's grace or charm, but Agnes was no less enthralled. He was "ferocious," she wrote admiringly, "a real Bolshevik" whose whole being radiated "the image of an iron commander of a revolutionary army of people."[3] P'eng accepted no nonsense from his soldiers. He refused to entertain any personal talk; no women entered his life. But he was as hard on himself as he was on his men, she said, and lived just like the soldiers who served under him. His bedding consisted of a single padded quilt. Besides this, she wrote, "I could not find that he possessed any personal thing beyond the clothing he wore. I heard one commander speak longingly of soap, but P'eng Teh-huai ha[d] forgotten such a luxury, and d[id] not even possess his own towel."[4]

Agnes, who had grown up in a family that displayed little physical affection, perceived deep tenderness in the way P'eng clasped a child's hand and walked with him, engaged in talk, or grasped a soldier's shoulder, turning him around to question him earnestly, face-to-face, about his health and life. She expressed her regard for him in a similarly indirect fashion. P'eng had an ulcer but was too proud and austere to take care of himself, so Agnes, aware that Chinese etiquette dictated a host could not refuse a guest, plied him with her own medicines, soda crackers, and milk and ordered additional remedies for him from Sian. One fellow joked that P'eng had an ulcer because he refused to marry but thought about women all the time. Agnes retorted that he saved himself a lot of worry that way. "A stomach ulcer was less trouble than a wife, and certainly more desirable," she quipped.[5]

While Agnes visited with the Red Army leaders, the tense mood in Sian continued. In their broadcasts, the Communists were extremely careful not to criticize Chiang Kai-shek and beseeched the people to support his program of national unification and anti-Japanese policies. They did not halt their violent attacks on pro-Japanese elements in the Chinese government, however, and the Communists' increasing military and political hold over the area had led American and British officials to organize a rescue operation for their remaining nationals.

During this time, reports of Agnes collaborating with Mao Tse-tung and other Communist leaders, and conferring with the Russian advisers who had flown to Sian from Outer Mongolia, made further headlines abroad. In late January 1937, when *Life*, Henry Luce's phenomenally successful new picture magazine, ran its historic photo spread introducing mainstream America to the Chinese Communists for the first time, it included a shot of Agnes, who was described in an accompanying caption as "Mao's American ally" who specialized in agitating for equal rights for women.[6]

Agnes reached Yenan, the Communists' base and training camp, that February, just as the Sian Incident concluded. Yenan was a medieval fortress town protected by crenelated walls, defense towers, and the muddy Yen River, which served as a natural moat. Hundreds of years earlier, Central Asian cavalry troops had passed through this narrow, strategic valley on their way to conquer northwest China, and battlements still ringed nearby hilltops. Every surface in the town—from the pagoda and ancient burial mound to the tombs and stone tablets that lay everywhere—was covered with loess dust carried by the winds off the Gobi Desert.

She was assigned a room, sparsely furnished with a table, chair, and straw mats, in a labyrinthine compound that had formerly housed an extended landlord family. Other foreign visitors, a magazine operation, the Communists' organization and radio departments, and a handful of female Chinese occupied the remaining space. Just outside the complex was a flagstone "garden" with a few patches of dirt and two pitiful trees, where the *hsiao kwei* and bodyguards enjoyed their rare leisure.

Late in the evening on the first day of her visit, Agnes passed through a padded curtain and entered the dark cavern where Mao resided. She was most uneasy. Just a few days earlier—after the Comintern secretariat reassured Browder that Agnes's objections to the CCP's accommodation with Chiang Kai-shek "[do] not represent the Communists' attitude and [she] is not authorized to act in the name of them"—the CPUSA had publicly denounced her.[7] In a recent article in the *Daily Worker*, Browder had advised American Communists that Agnes was "a free lance journalist who has not in the past and does not now work under the direction of the Communist Party, or represent it in any way."[8] With Muenzenberg under siege, Mirov-Abramov under arrest, and no organization behind her, Agnes had reason to be apprehensive when she introduced herself to the Chinese Communist Party's chief political leader.

> Directly in the center of this darkness stood a tall candle on a roughhewn table. Its glow fell on piles of books and papers and touched the low earthen ceiling above. A man's figure was standing with one hand on the table; his face, turned toward the door, was in shadow. I saw a mass of dark clothing covered by a loose padded greatcoat. The section of earthen floor on which he stood was raised, accentuating his height, and the gloom of the cave, broken only by the solitary candle, lent a sinister beauty to the scene. It was like some ancient painting almost obliterated by time.
>
> The tall, forbidding figure lumbered toward us and a high pitched voice greeted us. Then two hands grasped mine; they were long and sensitive as a woman's. Without speaking, we stared at each other. His dark, inscrutable face was long, the forehead broad and high, the mouth feminine. Whatever else he might be, he was an aesthete. I was in fact repelled by the feminine in him and by the gloom of the setting. An instinctive hostility sprang up inside me.[9]

Mao was different from other Red Army men in additional ways that were not to Agnes's liking. A political rather than a military leader, he was an intellectual rather than a man of action—a thinker rather than a doer. Agnes would write that she was so preoccupied with her attempt to master her visceral aversion to Mao that she hardly heard a word he said during their first conversation, but probably it contained a rebuke of Agnes's role in the Sian affair.[10] She later confided to Malcolm Cowley the problems she encountered after being "caught out on a limb in China as a result of a switch" in the CCP line.[11]

As retribution for her lack of discipline, Mao informed Agnes that her book on the Long March had been scuttled; he ordered her to return the mass of historical documents, maps, and interview transcripts in her keeping. A "research committee" in Yenan, he informed her, would write the book instead. Agnes reluctantly agreed to terminate the project. "As for the Long Walk [March]," she wrote Snow soon after her encounter with Mao, "I can do nothing. There's a lot of that here but someone tells me its publication would hurt the good feelings of some people."[12]

Bad news also came from Agnes's American agent, Eva Ginn. Ginn had failed to place any of Agnes's articles on the Sian Incident, after trying to sell them to the United Press wire service, the *New Republic, Asia,* and the *New York Times Magazine.* Besides the ongoing problem of placing China stories in the United States, where they invariably took a backseat to coverage of the Spanish Civil War, Ginn explained, there was also the issue of Agnes's partisan style. "We know the reason," Ginn noted, for the latest round of rejections.

> It is because you show your definite bias and they pretend that their newspapers are unbiased. We know that is not true. They are biased in favor of the capitalists. How can you expect them to print articles that run down the capitalists? You must face the fact that if you throw in your lot with the workers you can depend only upon the workers . . . The *New Masses* was delighted to print your story. But when it came to paying for it they simply did not have the money . . .
>
> . . . If you want to write for the people that read the capitalist press you must write in a way that the people who run these papers will print . . . They simply won't take your material if you are so brutally antagonistic to the enemy.[13]

Agnes could accept that her political articles were too passionately subjective, but she also suspected her most recent work was not up to her usual standards; her stories, while remarkable, had perhaps been poorly written. "No human being can be an organizer of a thousand things, a sick person, and at the same time a decent writer. One thing or the other only can be done," she grudgingly confessed, while she had been trying to do it all.[14] In the future, she said, she would try harder.

Defeated and ashamed, Agnes spent the next several weeks in bed, isolated from the others and complaining variously of "heart failure," a stomach ailment, influenza, headaches, insomnia, and a cold in her lungs that blossomed into bronchitis. "Sometimes I did not want to live," she admitted to Snow, but "cowardice and curiosity and the fact that I was in this place and do not want to do anything to embarrass them, has once or twice prevented me from putting a bullet through my brain."[15] She refused to leave Yenan until her romantic fascination was sated. "I'm here for good so far as it rests with me," she announced in March 1937.[16]

By spring Agnes was up and about again, and what had drawn her to the Communists' base became clear. Yenan was chiefly an educational center. More than a thousand men and their commanders, most of them workers and peasants in from the front, were enrolled at a university for training in the united front principles that the Red Army now considered its foremost task. A separate Party school with another thousand students lay just beyond the base. Yet another thousand men attended an infantry school just west of Yenan. There were also schools for the guards and *hsiao kwei*, and a normal school where Agnes's friend Ting Ling taught Chinese literature.

In this overwhelmingly male environment (there were only a few dozen women in all of Yenan) Agnes—like that earlier western outlaw Calamity Jane—saw herself as a man among men. She embarked on a study of military tactics and strategy, took up rifle and pistol practice, and adopted the dark, baggy-trousered homespun uniform worn by the Red Army soldiers. It was a fitting costume for the born actress, and Agnes was particularly proud of her red-starred cap. "He who takes this takes my head with it," she shouted in earnest to someone who playfully tried to snatch it from her.[17]

Everyone was compelled to plant grain and vegetables for personal consumption in the bare brown military town. Even the Comintern adviser Otto Braun, who had accompanied the Red Army on the Long March, practiced his cavalry tricks here. After spending nearly a quarter of a century embroiled in internecine political warfare while living in large cities, Agnes found the straightforward country life appealingly familiar. Intuitively, she sensed that the Red Army men were kindred spirits—doers rather than thinkers—and they reminded her of the cowboys among whom she had come of age. Their willingness to renounce personal comfort, domestic happiness, and worldly success for the greater good, though, made them feel more like family, but this was one that lacked her mother's needs and subservience, and her father's shady ways.

When Charles Smedley (who had declared Agnes "dead" to him after the publication of *Daughter of Earth*) had died in the fall of 1936, Agnes maintained the distance she had put between herself and her family. With apocryphal flair, she later wrote that "on a hot summer's day in Oklahoma, he had won sixteen bottles of beer in a poker game, and drunk them all. Then he up and died." His passing was regrettable, she coolly observed—but not a national tragedy like the passing of her "true father," Lu Hsun, who died around the same time.[18]

In Yenan, where Agnes said she felt more at peace than she had at any time since her years in the Southwest, she determined to relive her western youth—this time with the Chinese Communist leaders as her "family." The joyous bond she established with them allowed her to experience an identification with the Chinese people's struggle to free themselves that justified all the years she had spent in Shanghai groping for some way to connect with the real China.

Agnes hit it off famously with Chu Teh, commander-in-chief of the Red Army, in contrast to her strained encounter with Mao. Chu's generous mouth "was…spread in a broad grin of…welcome and he stretched out both hands to me," Agnes later wrote of their introduction. Impulsively, she flung her arms around his neck and kissed him on both cheeks—in flagrant violation of the Chinese taboo against such public displays.[19]

Chu, a short, strong man with a kind, wrinkled face, was the son of Szechuanese tenant farmers. In 1927, he had led the famed Nanchang uprising that gave birth to the Communist-led forces. It was Chu who devised the guerrilla tactics that enabled the Red Army to repeatedly overcome the military encirclements of vastly more numerous, better-equipped KMT forces. Red Army men respected Mao but they loved Chu, and Agnes, too, felt an ease in his company she could never experience with an intellectual like Mao. At fifty, Chu was also something of a fatherly figure, and Agnes sensed a wistful melancholy about him that she said made her want to defend him against the world.

Since her book on the Long March had been canceled, she decided to spend her time in Yenan writing a biography of Chu. As she described it, the project

Agnes and Chu Teh, commander-in-chief of the Chinese Red Army, Yenan, 1937. *Courtesy of Lois Snow.*

would be "a history of revolutionary China as seen through the life of one man."[20] Since the great military leader was between battles, he was able to give her a fair amount of his time. Sometimes the two of them conversed in German; on other occasions Wu Kang-wei, a modern-thinking young actress from Peking, also known as Lily Wu, served as Agnes's secretary/interpreter.

"Every day, mostly in the evenings," one Yenan resident wrote, "Chu Teh would sit on the *k'ang* [wooden platform bed] in Agnes's cave and she would sit at a table with her typewriter, writing directly through an interpreter. Each session would produce a big stack of typewritten notes. Agnes would ask many questions, such as what was the weather like the day of that battle, or how did you feel on the day of marching all night. A lot of her effort came in trying to get Chu Teh to speak about himself and his development but he would return time and time again to telling the history of the revolution."[21]

Agnes soon developed a huge crush on the bearlike general.[22] "He's a grand fellow," she wrote Eva Ginn,

> a man of the utmost simplicity of character, utterly uncomplicated, direct, open, straightforward; a man without any false pride; tenacious; a brilliant military leader. A student at all times. Today I laughed to myself for an hour at his manner. He told how the Whites in Kiangsi once sent six companies against the Red Army, and kept four in reserve. A little Brigadier General led them, going out to wipe out the "remnant bandits." As Chu told me this story he was walking around my room with a fly swatter in his hand, diligently swatting any fly he could find. He was laughing a little low chuckle as he swatted and talked about that little general sending out six companies against him...I simply can't reproduce his little low laughter that tells more than all the words.[23]

In one of their early conversations, Agnes let it be known that she could ride, and to her great delight, Chu offered her one of the long-haired ponies Ho Lung's army had captured on the Long March.

> Chu Teh just gave me a beautiful little horse [she crowed to Snow]. The horse is a marvel. It is the fastest horse in the Army...It's a young thing, fiery and impatient. I went yesterday on him for the first time...I've a Mongolian saddle...and...the stirrups are so short that it's almost like sitting in a rocking chair...I thought I could ride until I saw our cavalry here...Some are Chinese, some Mongols. And they look as if they had whipped a dozen Japanese armies and can start on another...I was practically born riding a horse, but these fellows have ridden horses for many generations. So I've a long way to go to catch up.[24]

That spring, Agnes received permission to move into one of the private cave houses the Communists had built in the hills that surrounded the base, and she embarked on a domestic life here that she said made her happier and calmer than she had dreamed possible. On morning walks, she picked wildflowers for her room; she kept ducks and chickens for food and did most of her own cooking. Within a few months, she had also coaxed the soil outside her dwelling into producing an American garden replete with flowering vines, nasturtiums, eggplant, beans, squash, and cucumbers (whose seeds she planned to distribute to the peasants at the end of the season). Nowhere else on earth could she have lived as freely, she remarked.[25]

One of her bodyguards, a twenty-year-old Szechuanese who was one of the political prisoners released during the Sian Incident, was ill, and Agnes expended considerable energy nursing him. She also developed a fierce attachment to her *hsiao kwei*. The fact that these youth were orphans made it easier for her to express the tenderness of which she was capable. Like any proud parent, Agnes boasted to friends of her "children." "My current hsiao kwei is a character," she wrote a fellow journalist. "Until I made him build a chicken house, he kept the ducks and chickens under his bed at night . . . Each day he carries our two ducks down to the river and the three of them go swimming together. He collects tin cans, nails, string, boxes, and pictures galore from magazines I throw away, and just like little American boys, he has made himself a telephone with tin cans to which long strings are attached."[26]

Agnes also grew closer to several of the Communist leaders that spring. During one drunken evening with Chou En-lai, the vice chairman of the Revolutionary Military Council, who had been the CCP's chief representative during the negotiations in Sian, the two of them reportedly toasted every Communist country from Abyssinia to Zanzibar.[27] Though she still found Mao "as stubborn as a mule, with a steel rod of pride and determination running through him," she eventually convinced herself that the sinister quality she had initially detected was no more than spiritual isolation, and his "feminine" aspect merely sensitivity and intuition. Under that scenario, Agnes even professed to like him.[28]

Mao was "like a dear brother," she wrote Snow, "a damned lovable sort," who "possessed all the self-confidence and decisiveness of a pronouncedly masculine man."[29] He had more in common with Lenin than with Stalin, she thought — more political, less of an organizer — but even his archenemy here, the Comintern adviser Otto Braun, conceded Mao's genius at strategy.[30]

Agnes's relations with the wives of the leading cadres were another matter. Within the Red Army, leaders did not deny that men had sexual needs, but they expected military training and the numerous cultural activities that went on from reveille to taps to absorb the energies of the soldiers. Those who were sin-

Mao Tse-tung, Chu Teh, and Agnes, Yenan, 1937. *Museum of the Chinese Revolution, Beijing.*

gle were expected to remain celibate. Married couples, who were found almost exclusively among the leaders, were expected to be faithful to their spouses. Flirtations and romantic entanglements were strictly taboo. One American visitor likened the atmosphere in Yenan to Boy Scout camp.[31]

"It was not that Agnes...thought loosely about sexual matters," Snow later explained.[32] But she had, after all, come of sexual age in Greenwich Village, and was an outspoken champion of free love in the sense that she considered it fitting and healthful to pursue one's desire, and she was not above encouraging the addition of a little spice to what was for her a rather staid mix. Like her iconoclastic girlfriend Ting Ling, Agnes believed that the "undisciplined guerrilla warfare" practiced nightly in the bushes by the river bespoke the need for a more advanced sexual outlook in Yenan.[33] She had Sanger send her examination instruments and several hundred small-sized pessaries and, later, contraceptive foam for the troops.[34] (Agnes was not around when the Chinese opened the package. In water, the foam effervesced. Thinking it food, they drank it.)[35]

Among the leaders, though, only Mao seemed receptive to Agnes's emancipated views, as the following incident suggests. When a visiting Western journalist—a salty ex-Marine—inquired about Yenan's much-discussed position on sex—and was told that in this time of national crisis the army had no time for it, he had responded that the Communists could easily import five hundred women for this purpose. Clearly amused, Mao countered, deadpan, that the transportation would be too expensive.[36]

The spouses of Yenan's leaders had not endured the hardships they had known on the Long March so that their husbands could experiment with the young women who had begun streaming into the area as anti-Communist constraints loosened. These women might wear the same cropped hair and trousered uniforms as Agnes, but they did not share her desire for a more traditionally masculine freedom. Outwardly timid and submissive to their spouses, they controlled their partners indirectly, by withholding sex and refusing to end unhappy unions.[37]

Agnes disdained the mentality of these "feudal minded" females, as she called them. The most offensive of them, in her opinion, was Mao's wife, Ho Tzu-ch'en, a very subservient "domestic" type who had been Mao's secretary before they married and who Agnes felt lacked the necessary qualifications to be a revolutionary leader's wife.[38] But she scorned them all. Apart from those situations in which her interest in women's issues forced her into contact with the wives, she associated almost exclusively with the male leaders. When she was alone with them, she would chide them for being afraid of their partners. If the

Good friends Edgar Snow (left) and Evans Carlson. *Michael Blankfort Collection, Special Collections, Boston University.*

men could not free themselves from women's oppression, Agnes suggested only half jokingly, they probably could not liberate China.[39]

The wives, who were mostly from peasant backgrounds, had had little experience with Western women, let alone one as unconventional as Agnes. They were at a loss as to how to deal with her, but they were suspicious and resentful nonetheless. Some feared that Agnes's oft-aired denunciations of marriage and ringing endorsements of divorce veiled a misplaced interest in their husbands. None was more concerned than Chu Teh's wife, K'ang K'e-ching. Although nothing of a sexual nature evidently transpired between Agnes and Chu, Ka'ng K'e-ching did not like her husband spending such long periods of time alone with the female writer. K'ang found it strange that a foreign woman would spend so much time speaking with her spouse in her cave, and told Chu as much. According to Snow, when Chu laughingly apprised Agnes of the matter, her blue-gray eyes widened. "Isn't it bourgeois to think there is only one thing men and women talk about when they are together?" she disingenuously inquired.[40]

Chu had ordered his wife to stay out of his affairs, but Agnes began to complain that Yenan was the most puritanical, sexually repressed environment in which she had ever found herself. She particularly resented the lack of privacy regarding people's intimate affairs. Everybody "knows absolutely everything;" she wrote Snow, even "who has syphilis, etc."[41] In the meantime, the wives blamed Agnes for the atmosphere of defiance that was seeping into the town.

It was more her sympathy for the unloved and lonely that led Agnes to meddle in the unhappy marriage of Mao Tse-tung, Snow later observed, but Agnes's own unfortunate marital record also contributed to the zeal with which she abetted the demise of other unsatisfactory unions.[42] Now that she and Mao were getting along, he often visited her cave on his way to work in the evenings. (Mao was notorious for his nocturnal habits.) She would brew him coffee and while he drank it, dunking Agnes's soda crackers in his cup, they would talk, with her neighbor Lily Wu acting as their interpreter. Freed from battle, Mao was reading voraciously and writing political and philosophical essays and poetry. Though he had never been out of China, he was extremely interested in foreign ways, and since he and Agnes were the same age, he felt comfortable interrogating her on subjects that included her love life.

According to Agnes's confidant Edgar Snow, Mao had read Byron, Keats, and Shelley in translation, and he asked Agnes whether she herself had ever experienced the kind of romantic love of which those poets wrote. Agnes talked with him about her relationship with Chatto, and how the spiritual and physical had been linked. After further inquiries about how exactly their "love" expressed itself in their daily lives, Mao expressed puzzlement at how the two of them could then have argued and finally separated. Agnes, Snow reported, "was surprised at [Mao's] childish curiosity . . . He seemed to feel that somehow he had missed out on something."[43]

It was spring in Yenan, "with the young rice plants coloring the red earth with green, and apple blossoms coming into full bloom," Snow later wrote, and Mao was apparently reliving some of his youthful fantasies. There was a focus to his musings, though, and her name was Lily Wu. Elegant, refined, and beautiful, Lily Wu was a leading player in Yenan's theatrical productions when she was not interpreting for Agnes. She was also divorced, which was most unusual at the time.

Compared to the other women in Yenan, Snow would write that "Lily seemed a brilliant fairy tale princess . . . To the men . . . who had lived a long time among only peasants, Lily was more than a pretty face. She was comparable to Yang Guifei, the most beautiful woman in Chinese history."[44] Most of the single men, including Agnes's doctor friend George Hatem, had already proposed to her. Others sent presents and followed her around.

Lily was not someone Agnes would ordinarily have befriended, but she sensed the wives' resentment and allowed Lily to use her room when Lily had callers or needed a chaperone—a move that made the women of Yenan distrust Agnes all the more. It was soon apparent to Agnes that some of the romantic questions Mao was asking her were actually directed at Lily. During discussions, Mao would compose poems that she was in a better position to appreciate than Agnes. According to Snow, "Lily would respond poetically herself, using the same rhythm as Mao had in his poetry, and this pleased him. They discussed at length man-woman relationships in the new post-revolutionary liberated society where men and women would be equals. These thoughts were woven into their poetry, classical in form."[45] But they refrained from physical contact.

As Agnes settled into life in Yenan, she had had her record player and albums delivered from Shanghai. She had recently turned forty-four and her hair was beginning to gray, but she remained as energetic as a child, and while she knew that traditionally Chinese considered it suggestive and immoral for one body to touch another, she still liked to have fun. Late that March, she cajoled some of the Red Army leaders into a boisterous evening of square dancing, to the accompaniment of American cowboy tunes like "She'll Be Comin' Round the Mountain," "Red River Valley," and "On Top of Old Smokey."

"Chu Teh, who wished to learn everything on earth and never let pride prevent his trying," she wrote Snow, "joined me in opening the demonstration. Chou En-lai followed, but he was like a man working out a problem in mathematics. P'eng Teh-huai was willing to watch, but would not move a leg; he was married to the revolution. Ho Lung, who was the very embodiment of rhythm, could hardly contain himself until he was cavorting across the floor, which was made of wobbly bricks."[46] By the end of the evening, Agnes said, she felt as if a whole division of soldiers had stepped on her toes, but she had had the time of her life.

The episode earned her a bad reputation among the women of Yenan. A few had bound feet, so they might also have felt slighted. Agnes did not care. Invigorated by the experience, she moved on to social dancing. One afternoon later that spring, she taught Ho Lung to fox-trot at the cave of Comintern adviser Otto Braun, "and he can fox-trot, boy!" she told Snow. "He's filled with rhythm and music." Unfortunately, Braun's mistrustful Chinese wife had punched holes through their paper window to observe what was going on, and, as Agnes airily remarked, "I suppose a fine story got about."[47]

K'ang K'e-ching, who was already uncomfortable with Agnes's interest in her husband, had laid down the law about dancing after the square dance episode, but Chu showed up (along with several other leading cadres) for a subsequent dance class, which took place in Agnes's own cave, and he danced with her there. Chu, Agnes was pleased to report, "can dance well, having been in Berlin."[48] He was afraid of his wife, but he had defied her "like a true Red Army leader. It takes someone as strong as a commander-in-chief to defy some of these women here," Agnes wrote.[49]

By this time, Po Ku, a politburo member who had also attended the events, was becoming apprehensive about potential repercussions. He warned Agnes to keep the matter secret—which perhaps she did—but the next dance class, which occurred in Otto Braun's cave, was too well attended to keep under wraps for long. Lily Wu was the star of the evening, but it was Agnes and Chou En-lai who "showed the world how to dance," she bragged to Snow. "Chou's wife is outside in a temple as you perhaps know—else there might have been an interesting murder here . . . I haven't 'corrupted' Mao yet," Agnes reported, "but I shall do so soon. He says that if he ever goes abroad, he will go to study dancing and singing—that he wishes to learn the latest fox-trots! I think he should leave his wife here if he does."[50]

Po Ku warned Agnes again against letting word of the dancing get out, and she swore she said nothing to anyone. "But the stunt went on before a dozen," she commented, and by the end of April a scandal had erupted over the issue. Agnes considered it part of the feudal-mindedness she found so maddening that the women insisted on viewing social dancing as "a kind of public sexual intercourse," and she displayed little patience with them. "So far as I can see I've a reputation of corrupting the Army. It does not worry me at all. All the women are against it and all the men are for it. And my associates are all men. Mao says the women are against it because they can't dance," she jeered.[51] But the matter would not go away. Mrs. Mao and Mrs. Chu, who objected most strongly to the dancing, launched a campaign to proscribe it in Yenan. By the end of May, there were no more such events and many of the wives shunned Agnes, but it took another incident to put an end to her welcome.

According to Snow's subsequent account, one evening late that June after Agnes had gone to bed, she heard cloth-shod footsteps and Mao's Hunan accent outside her cave. Looking around, she noticed that the light was still on in Lily Wu's cave. Agnes heard Mao knock, and the door open and close as he entered. Just as Agnes drifted back to sleep, she discerned another set of footsteps approaching. Word of Mao's romance with Lily Wu had reached Ho Tzu-ch'en, and she was furious.

Flinging open the entrance, she reportedly shrieked at Mao, "You idiot! How dare you fool me and sneak into the home of this little bourgeois dance hall strumpet."

Agnes heard the fuss, threw on some clothes and went next door. There she found Mao's wife beating her husband with a long-handled flashlight. Mao, still in his uniform, sat on a stool. He made no attempt to stop her. Neither did his flummoxed guard. When Mao's wife had exhausted herself, Mao rose and ordered her to be quiet. "There's nothing shameful in the relationship between comrade Wu and myself. We were just talking," he said, according to Snow. "You are ruining yourself as a Communist and are doing something shameful. Hurry home before other Party members learn of this."

Outraged, Ho Tzu-ch'en turned on the terrified Lily. "Dance-hall bitch!" Snow said she screeched as she scratched Lily's face and pulled her hair. "'You'd probably take up with any man. You've even fooled the Chairman." The bleeding Lily hid behind Agnes, who became the next target of Ho Tzu-ch'en's rage.

"'Imperialist! You're the cause of all this," Ho shouted, and struck Agnes with her flashlight. Agnes responded with a blow that laid Mao's wife on the ground. Mortified, Ho demanded her husband explain what kind of person—Communist or otherwise—allowed a "foreign devil" to abuse his wife without rising to her defense, to which Mao responded that it was she who had provoked the attack, by "acting like a rich woman in a bad American movie." After further hysterics from Ho, Mao called for two additional guards, who lifted his wife, still resisting, and carried her home. The Chairman followed in silence.[52]

A crowd of curious Chinese who had been watching from their caves spilled into Lily's room. While Dr. Hatem cared for Lily's wounds, Agnes tried to defuse the situation by saying that the relationship between Mao and Lily was only platonic, but by the next morning Yenan was abuzz. Mao, who recognized the danger he was in, convened a meeting of the Party's central executive committee to explain himself, and an agreement was reached to have the case

treated in secret, but Ho Tzu-ch'en, still furious, urged the wives of other leaders to assist her in banishing Lily Wu for her carrying-on — and Agnes for her
role in the intrigue.[53] According to one Yenan resident, Ho even threatened to
have Agnes killed, a threat that Agnes, at least, took seriously.

The wives threw their support behind Mrs. Mao, adding salacious details to
the story as they passed it along. Animated debate on the pros and cons of
romantic love versus marriage raged in the streets. By the time a delegation of
American China specialists including Philip Jaffe, Owen Lattimore, and T. A.
Bisson, arrived in Yenan late that June to interview Mao and other Communist
leaders, debate on the Mao-Lily-Agnes affair was as lively as on the Stalin-Trot-
sky conflict.[54]

Agnes was among the large group awaiting the group's arrival. Recently, the
Daily Worker had printed a second denunciation of Agnes, warning readers of
her lack of formal ties to the CCP. Although it was signed by the CCP central
committee, Agnes was certain the CPUSA lay behind the attack, and she lost no
time castigating Jaffe for Browder's mistreatment of her, as well as the damage
sustained by Voice of China and China Today as a result of CPUSA control.[55]
Over the next few days, Jaffe also heard an earful from Agnes's critics, who
accused her of being a propagandist for women's emancipation, a go-between
for Lily Wu and Mao, a troublemaker, and a busybody — all of which had irri-
tated the CCP leadership.[56] Jaffe did not sense there was anything worse to
come from Chinese Party leaders until he and his wife visited the Party school
and its director requested that the CPUSA donate several scientific books to its
library. When Jaffe replied that he would send them in care of Agnes, as he was
accustomed to doing, he said the fellow looked quite alarmed. "No, no, please,
not to her, but direct to me," the man advised him.[57]

Jaffe left Yenan carrying the Long March materials Mao had reclaimed from
Agnes for Snow to use in *his* book.[58] Those who mocked Agnes's lack of discipline might well have noted that even after Snow's Red Star over China
appeared later that year to international acclaim, she never mentioned the matter to anyone. But she was heartsick at the havoc she had wrought. She had
never intended to be a disruptive force. Whatever damage she had done had
occurred because she felt she belonged there, where she had finally felt at
home. All she had meant to do was move her "family" a little further along on
their personal journey.

To prove to the Chinese leaders that she was not the individualistic rebel
they thought, Agnes impulsively decided to join the CCP. She would not be the
first American to join the Chinese Party; George Hatem was already a member.
When she laid her case before Mao, Chu Teh, and Chou En-lai, though, they

knew it would not work; it could not be enough for her to support many but not all of their goals.[59] For you to be in the Party, the Party had to be your life. Agnes would have to give up everything, including her personal autonomy. That she could not do, however much she wished to at this moment. The Communist leaders advised her that while she still had a contribution to make, it was better for all concerned if she continued to work outside the Party.[60] Anguished and enraged, Agnes went on a hunger strike and wept, for she knew their decision meant her family reunion was drawing to a close.

Mao met with the CCP executive committee a second time early that summer, at which time he sought their consent to his divorce in order to bring an end to the scandal. Before the committee reached a decision, China found itself at war. On the evening of July 7, 1937, Japanese troops, who had been maneuvering around Peking, demanded the right to search the walled town of nearby Wanping, on the pretext that one of their soldiers was missing. By the following morning, fighting had broken out at Wanping and the Marco Polo Bridge some fifteen miles southwest. As a thoroughly outnumbered Chinese provincial force offered valiant resistance, voices across the country importuned Chiang Kai-shek to provide military support. On July 18, 1937, the Generalissimo declared China at war with Japan.

The Nationalists hastily arranged for the Communist Red Army to be incorporated into central government forces. With the united front against the foreign invader about to become a reality, the CCP central committee quickly granted Mao his divorce. Ho Tzu-ch'en was reprimanded for behavior inappropriate to a Communist and revolutionary and exiled to a remote village, and later the Soviet Union, for continued political education. Lily Wu was also banished—ordered, along with Ting Ling and two dozen other cultural figures, to join a flying squadron of propagandists who would perform whenever the army halted, often deep into territory near enemy lines. Agnes was told to join her friends in the Front Service Unit on a team of dancers.[61]

The decision sounded alarmingly like a revenge invented by the wives, and Agnes, who was reluctant to leave Yenan altogether, found the idea preposterous. "Why put me among dancers?" she demanded in a baleful confrontation with Chu Teh. "Can we make revolution as dancers?"[62] If she were to travel to the front with the army, she insisted it be as a correspondent—not as a *dancer*, for goodness's sake. She was more than willing to go and write propaganda for China, she said, and had already discussed that possibility with Mao.[63] But Mao had evidently been playing her.

Her prospects inside the Soviet Union were similarly grim. At this time, as the unbridled mass terror and dramatic public "show trials" that characterized

the Great Purge approached their climax, the Comintern launched an investigation to unearth any compromising data on Agnes.[64] Recently, the head of the
Comintern's editing department had alerted the organization's executive committee that there were "objections" to the American author.[65] There would be
no reprieve from that quarter, should she be foolish enough to seek it.

The demand that she leave Yenan had already left Agnes too depressed to
write. When the rumor reached her soon afterward that the Nanking government
was once again urging American consular officials either to revoke her passport
entirely or refuse to renew it when her current one expired, Agnes found the additional pressure more than she could bear.[66] Snow's wife, Helen, or "Peg," who was
visiting Yenan that summer, said that Agnes was rational on some occasions; other
times she was entirely off kilter. She was hostile, nasty, suspicious, and quarrel-
some. She stole, hoarded food, and took money from Peg's purse, Peg said, to be
sure of having some. "The more I gave to her and the more I helped her," Peg
complained, "the more she demanded and the less thanks I got. Her feeling of
insecurity caused her to want to take everything she could get her hands on . . . She
took everything away from me that she could and hardly noticed it."[67]

One day during this period, Agnes decided to race several others on her fiery-
tempered Yunnan pony. Agnes boasted that her "Red Indian" blood made her
naturally at ease on a horse, but she was not particularly adept; Myrtle had been
the cowgirl in the family. During the contest, Agnes fell and injured her back.
As perhaps she had hoped, Chu Teh and other Communist leaders paid sympathetic visits to her sickbed, but they did not alter their views. Her friend Ting
Ling was in no position to help her, for she, too, was in trouble with Yenan leaders after complaining of sexism in the CCP.

By late August, Yenan had reorganized its troops under the central government, and divisions of the Communists' renamed Eighth Route Army began
leaving for northern Shansi, where they would engage in mobile warfare on the
enemy flank and rear lines. Agnes claimed she was too ill to depart Yenan with
Ting Ling and Lily Wu in the section of the Front Service Unit to which she
had been assigned. Instead, as torrential summer rains swept away fields and villages, Agnes remained on her *k'ang* bed penning a joint appeal with Mao to the
American and Canadian Communist parties requesting that they create a new
front organization to raise money for medical supplies, equipment, and a team
of doctors and surgeons treat wounded Communist soldiers.[68]

In the meantime, Comintern, American, and Chinese officials pursued their
discrete investigations into Agnes's activities. Following a veritable blizzard of
correspondence with State Department officials, Baldwin reassured her that, at
a minimum, her American extrality would remain intact until her passport
expired the following May. Comintern officials involved in the investigation of

Agnes noted darkly that she was not a Party member and accused her of having ties with unnamed "Trotskyists," but they had not discovered any more compromising data.[69]

By early September, Chu Teh, Agnes's sole defender, had left for the Wutaishan front, and Yenan's political leaders moved to put an end to Agnes's tenure. Agnes had already observed the iron will that lay beneath Mao's gentle manner. Still, the quiet fury with which he demanded she leave at once, bad back or not, rattled her.[70] After all she had done for the Chinese Communists, Agnes never forgave Mao for what she took as his callous rejection, but before she reverted to hating him again, she managed to wrest his consent to cover her march to the front with the Eighth Route Army as a correspondent—not a dancer. Chu Teh had already given her permission to join him in northern Shansi, where the Japanese had been conquering strategic cities and passes, and visit Eighth Route Army front headquarters.

Eva Ginn and Philip Jaffe would try to sell accounts of her journey with the troops to American and English magazines. Wieland Herzfelde at the Malik Verlag would represent her on the Continent and in the Soviet Union (or so she hoped).[71] Agnes was far from sanguine about the fate that awaited her, but she could no longer deny it was time to go. She notified friends in Shanghai that she would be traveling to the front as a war correspondent, taking on herself all risks and asking for American intervention only if captured by the Japanese. "I do not know where I shall be next May 1st when my passport expires—perhaps where passports are useless and everything is dust," she wrote Baldwin. "Never mind. I go to do my duty to the best traditions of American history and to the class I came from. Until I can learn the actual thing, I'll use my typewriter as a machine gun. But I'd love to use the real thing for a time at least." [72]

By this time, American women and children had been ordered to evacuate China. Fighting had broken out in Shanghai. Peking and Tientsin were already occupied. Railroads were being bombed and cut; ports were being closed. Edgar Snow had recently warned his wife, who remained closeted with Agnes in Yenan, that if she did not leave immediately, she would be unable to go for the rest of the year, but the rain delayed her departure. On September 6, 1937 the sun finally peeked through the clouds, and a Red Army group agreed to take Agnes with them to Sian, where they would deposit Peg. There Agnes could get her back X-rayed before continuing on to the front.

Agnes turned over her few treasures to Peg, along with instructions for their disposal. Peg also received Agnes's silk stockings, for there was no need for them where she was bound. The gramophone and records that had occasioned so much trouble she left behind. Agnes's sense of private property "tended toward confiscation," Peg wrote.

"Do you need that suitcase?" she wanted to know. "Let me have it."

Then and there she handed it graciously to her bodyguard, as a gift, while my bodyguard watched in astounded reproach . . .

"How much money do you have?" Agnes next demanded.

"Hardly any," I said. "Maybe a hundred dollars or so for my whole trip."

"Give it to me," she commanded. "You can borrow some here but I can't." . . .

I handed over my hundred dollars, feeling as guilty of riches as a fat bourgeoise on the way to the guillotine.[73]

On the morning of September 7, Agnes departed Yenan in high style, borne out on a bamboo stretcher carried by five bearers and accompanied by her personal bodyguard, her *hsiao kwei*, and thirty soldiers, along with Peg Snow and the wives of three Chinese leaders. That her career as an operative was over, there was no doubt, but if the Chinese Communist political leaders had washed their hands of Agnes, she was convinced that the outbreak of war ensured a place for her in its military.

CHAPTER 15

Selfless for the Cause

I'm not afraid of death, but I'd like to be in the fight a little longer.

JOE HILL

B Y STRETCHER and on horseback, on foot, men's backs, and occasionally via motor truck, Agnes made her way south. Exercise and removal of "psychosomatic problems of the Yenan variety," as Peg Snow put it, helped restore Agnes's equilibrium. Within a week, Peg said, Agnes's back acted up only when someone praised Chiang Kai-shek. Their group reached Sanyuan on September 17, just as the last detachment of the Eighth Route (Red) Army was beginning a night march to the Shansi front. The officers in Agnes's delegation scrambled to catch up with them; Agnes and the others set out for Sian the next morning.

X-rays revealed that her back injury was only muscular—painful but not dangerous. Once the doctors had strapped her up, Agnes went to work. By the fall of 1937, the CPUSA had established an organization to raise money to treat wounded Chinese Communist soldiers. The China Aid Council, as it was known, was an offshoot of the American League for Peace and Democracy, the CPUSA's largest and most influential front organization. Although it had already raised nearly fifteen thousand dollars, Agnes learned in Sian that Jaffe was having a hard time recruiting skilled practitioners for the medical mission she and Mao sought. The physicians that the Party had thus far approached "seem to think it means certain death and they do not want to make the sacrifice," Ginn wrote.[1] Agnes devoted some time attempting to resolve the matter with Jaffe, but she was impatient to catch up with the troops.

Throughout the summer the Japanese Imperial Army had been rolling over north China with very little resistance. However, on September 26, Commander Lin Piao's division of seasoned Communist fighters had scored China's first victory in the Sino-Japanese War, and in the spirit of the united front, Chinese government officials issued Agnes a special visa that allowed her to travel throughout northwest China undisturbed. She departed Sian that October, dressed in her army uniform, her leather satchel crammed with writing supplies, typewriter, camera, film, and first aid kit, and a gun hanging off each hip (or so she claimed). "If the Japanese finish me off," she told Sanger, "turn down an empty glass for me before your plate at least once a week. You have always been my true, unwavering friend, and I have always loved you."[2]

Agnes's experience in Yenan had taught her that there would always be a distance between her and the people about whom she wrote. The Chinese were *not* her family; she knew now that she could never truly share their lives. As Agnes and her Chinese traveling companions headed into the Wutai mountains, where Chu Teh and P'eng Teh-huai would receive her, Agnes wrote: "I remain a teller of tales, a writer of things through which I have not lived. The real story of China can be told only by the Chinese workers and peasants themselves."[3]

During the next three months, Agnes roamed the length and breadth of Shansi province outside the war zones with the Eighth Route troops, using its headquarters as her base. "We are moving through a region where not even ordinary rough paper can be bought," read one typical journal entry. "There are no nails, no oil or fat, no salt, no fuel for fire. I shall be writing in the dead of winter without a blaze to warm me. And (need I tell you?) without sufficient food... Today it was turnips, and yesterday it was turnips... Sugar is simply unheard of ...I...have my typewriter strapped to my back...I have less than 100 Chinese dollars with me...Almost all of it I use to buy corn for my horse and mule."[4]

Agnes recalled her time with the Eighth Route Army soldiers as an incredibly intense spiritual experience. Her stories about the men, however, were hastily written and lacked drama. *Asia, Current History, Harper's,* and the *Nation* rejected her pieces; *Pravda* declined her exclusive interview with P'eng Teh-huai.[5] In Europe, the *Rundschau über Politik, Wirtschaft und Arbeiterbewegung, V.I., Deutsche Volkzeitung,* and *Deutsches Volks-Echo* carried her dispatches from Shansi, but these German exile presses, run for the most part by Muenzenberg deputy Louis Gibarti, paid little or nothing, and Agnes counted on the sale of her journal to recoup the money she had borrowed for the journey.

On December 19, 1937, Agnes was sitting on a mud bank at Eighth Route headquarters, watching two army units play basketball, when Chu Teh approached with Captain Evans F. Carlson, an American naval officer who had come to study the Communists' techniques. Disdainful of U.S. officials, and apprehensive that he would treat her as other Americans in China did—like a kind of "glorified street walker...a camp follower...who lowered the prestige of the white race," as she described it—her welcome was less than forthcoming.[6] Captain Carlson heard the belligerent tone in Agnes's voice, but he said he was touched by her evident suffering. After studying her determined chin and intelligent eyes, he decided he liked what he saw. " 'No vanity about this lady,' I thought. Absolute honesty in thought, speech and action was written all over her."[7]

Once Agnes reassured herself that Carlson's air of utter simplicity was sincere, she began appearing at his doorstep every morning with coffee, honey, and Chinese flat bread. Starved for the company of someone who might understand her, Agnes went with him on long walks or rode with him into the country, during which time the two revealed themselves in hours of conversation. Thoughtful, competent, and handsome in a Lincolnesque way, Carlson was not particularly politically enlightened, but he was a deeply moral man, the son of a New England minister, and he shared Agnes's commitment to a selfless, ascetic life. Carlson looked to her to interpret the Red Army he was studying, and he wrote that he found Agnes "grand, attractive, alive, animated, wise, courageous, a wonderful companion"—albeit a little impetuous.[8] Many of Agnes's friends believed she longed for a more intimate connection with him.

To better understand the Communists' method of "ethical indoctrination," as Carlson called it, he had asked Chu Teh if he could observe the Communists' campaign in Wutaishan, where a new Japanese offensive was expected any day. Agnes requested to join him at the front. Chinese Army leaders warned her of the dangers women faced in a combat zone and argued that she was not strong enough. Agnes countered that she would not be the only one in danger and that she was stronger than some of the men and shot and rode as well as most. Still they refused. Chu Teh tried to soften the blow by telling her that the army wanted her "to live and work, and not go to Wutaishan and die," she later wrote.[9] Left unspoken was his discomfort with Agnes's desire to go with Carlson and visit further upheaval upon the Communists in the battlefield.

In late December, Chu Teh informed her that she would have to leave Eighth Route headquarters. With Nanking in the hands of the Japanese, he said, Agnes could serve the army best by moving to China's new capital in Hankow. The war was intensifying; the united front was coming together. Many Communist political leaders were also moving there, he argued. But there were other factors at play.

In the final week of 1937, the Comintern concluded its investigation of Agnes. Eugene Dennis had had good things to say about her work in Shanghai from 1931 to 1933; so had Comintern adviser Arthur Ewert and Madame Sun

Yat-sen.[10] Others had doubtless been less kind regarding the years thereafter. In Hankow, Agnes's contribution to the CCP would be restricted to relief efforts for partisan followers of the Red Army only. Any direct association, either with the Chinese Communist Party or the Chinese Communist Red Army, was henceforth off limits; any privileges formerly accorded her were officially at an end. Chu Teh promised it would be but a short time before she could return, but Agnes knew the truth was otherwise.

> I replied to them in words they did not understand. In different words, but with the same meaning, I said:
>
> Entreat me not to leave thee, or to return from following after thee; for whither thou goest I will go; and where thou lodgest I will lodge; thy people shall by my people and thy God my God.
>
> Where thou diest will I die, and there will I be buried...
>
> ...Hankow means spiritual death for me. I have lived in China for many years...I was always so filled with misery in [cities] that I was physically sick. But in your army I have recovered my health...These have been the only happy days of my whole life. Here alone I have found peace of mind and spirit...To leave you is to go to death, or the equivalent of death.
>
> I went out and walked across the fields of winter wheat. My mind threw up a veil between itself and reality so that I seemed to be passing through a dream. I kept thinking, "What a terrible dream this is. Soon I shall awake." I thought of Hankow or of other cities with horror.[11]

Agnes and Carlson celebrated Christmas Eve in Carlson's room; he would leave two days later. They made coffee and ate peanuts; Carlson played the harmonica and they sang. Chu Teh stopped by and performed a plaintive Szechuanese ballad; a staffer did a Chinese sword dance, but Agnes was disconsolate. On January 4, 1938, she departed Eighth Route headquarters on a Red Cross train. Four days later, she arrived in Hankow.

The next morning, still wearing her army uniform, ragged leggings, and a shabby, dirty overcoat, she called on the American ambassador, Nelson Johnson. Instead of the usual testy exchange, Johnson invited the military attaché, Admiral Harry Yarnell, to hear about Agnes's recent experiences. Although Johnson refused to challenge his superiors regarding America's sale of war materials to Japan, as she suggested, Agnes found him surprisingly curious about what she had to say. So, too, was the British ambassador, Sir Archibald Clark-Kerr, who invited her to lunch at the embassy. Foreign journalists had so many questions she held a press conference to field them all, for with China under siege and Nationalist and Communist political leaders demonstrating more unity of purpose than they had in more than a decade, Western observers recognized Agnes as an invaluable resource on Chinese Communist activities.

Delighted with her unexpected transformation from pariah to celebrity, Agnes never mentioned her recent experiences with the Chinese Communist leaders to her rapt audiences. Neither did she discuss the fact that she was jobless, destitute, and homeless, her myriad appeals for help from Jaffe and the CPUSA unanswered. Instead, she appealed to the Reverend Logan Roots, the liberal Episcopal Bishop of Hankow, to take her in. Before the month was out, Agnes had organized the Northwest Partisan Relief Committee to obtain food, clothing, and medical supplies for the Shansi peasant fighters.

Technically, the organization fell under the rubric of the China Aid Council; in reality it was her own personal scheme, which she ran in consultation with Chou En-lai, P'eng Teh-huai and Po Ku.[12] There was no one better than Agnes at describing the army's ill-fed, often barefoot peasant followers, who stalked Japanese troops through the snow-covered mountains with knives and clubs, oversaw the evacuation of entire communities with their food and other valuable supplies hours in advance of the foreign invader, poisoned wells, destroyed roads, set dynamite traps, menaced Japanese communication lines, attacked isolated outposts, and organized village resistance.

When the long-awaited Communist medical mission to China arrived that same month, Agnes met their plane in great excitement. Unfortunately, the team had not been screened before it left, and the American doctor on it was a drunkard with delirium tremens who had to be taken to the hospital. The Canadian physician on the team, Norman Bethune, was arrogant, temperamental, and unaccustomed to deprivation; his nurse, the daughter of a ranking Canadian Communist Party official, was defiantly apolitical.[13] Moreover, as payback for Agnes's insistence on running her own show in China, the China Aid Council refused to provide a cent for the group's upkeep in Hankow.[14] Agnes was terribly upset, but she supported the team with funds from her own organization until it left for Yenan. Eventually, Nehru (to whom Agnes had also appealed for assistance) authorized the Indian National Congress to dispatch a team of exceedingly competent Indian doctors, who replaced that "awful man," as Agnes referred to Bethune.[15]

By March 1938, Agnes's precarious finances were making her literally ill with worry. When Jaffe visited Yenan, she had given him hundreds of her photographs to sell, but he seemed to be sitting on them, and when some of her images finally appeared in *Fight*, a publication of the American League for Peace and Democracy, they did so without attribution or payment.[16] Wieland Herzfelde, who was living in Prague, had had Agnes's army diary translated into German, but conditions in Europe had become too chaotic for the Malik Verlag to bring it out, and the manuscript sat in Moscow gathering dust.[17]

The poor response had convinced Agnes that her work would never appear in the United States again, so when the British writers Christopher Isherwood and W. H. Auden stopped by her apartment in a former military building down the street from Eighth Route headquarters to pay their respects, she was in no mood for company. The two men, like dozens of other Western writers, radicals and diplomats pouring into the city during the first few months of 1938, saw Hankow as the next arena, after Spain, in the worldwide struggle against fascism and wished to report on the action. They had heard that Agnes was at its center.

> We found her in an upstairs bed-sitting room at Bishop Root's house, staring dejectedly into the fire. She is really not unlike Bismarck, with her close cropped grey hair, masculine jaw, deeply lined cheeks and bulging, luminous eyes. "Hullo," she greeted us listlessly: "What do you want?"
>
> We introduced ourselves, and she began to cross examine us, mocking us rather aggressively: "What's your background?" "Are you a leftist?" "Do you poetize?" Our answers seemed to amuse her. She shook a little, unsmiling, with the faintest kind of laughter; but all the time she held us, suspiciously, with her fearless, bitter grey eyes. We got a bad mark, I could see, when we admitted that we were staying at the British Consulate; and another when we told her that we had just been visiting the German military advisors. "What are they plotting now?" she asked. We protested that General von Falken-hausen was certainly quite above suspicion. "I don't trust any German!" exclaimed Miss Smedley, passionately.
>
> It is impossible not to like and respect her, so grim and sour and passion-ate; so mercilessly critical of every one, herself included—as she sits before the fire, huddled together, as if all the suffering, all the injustice of the world were torturing her bones like rheumatism.[18]

Agnes brought the men to the Communist leaders and helped the pair obtain permission to observe Communist troops in the northwest. When they returned to Hankow in April, Auden and Isherwood confessed surprise at finding Agnes cheerful and triumphant, dressed like "a spring vision," they would recall, in a girlish frock. Agnes informed the men that Vanguard Press would be pub-lishing her journal, releasing it that June to exploit the publicity generated by Snow's *Red Star over China*, and it looked as if Victor Gollancz would be pub-lishing it in England. Moreover, on the strength of Gollancz's recommendation, the *Manchester Guardian* had invited Agnes to become a special correspondent.

Isherwood and Auden found Agnes's single-minded focus on the Red Army distressing, but they were fascinated nonetheless, and along with Carlson, Chou En-lai, and Po Ku, the two writers were frequent visitors. Before they returned to

England, Auden asked Agnes for permission to photograph her. "If you weren't a leftist writer, I shouldn't let you do this," he reported that Agnes told him. "I hate my face."[19] The pictures did not come out, and Agnes thought *Journey to a War*, the men's subsequent book on their trip, silly and superficial. But she approved of Auden's poem "To a Chinese Soldier," which had been inspired by the visit.

Outside the city the war continued, and China was getting pulverized. By the spring of 1938, the Japanese had captured Shanghai. In June, after heavy fighting, they took Hsuchow and began moving toward Hankow. As the Chinese government prepared to withdraw to Chungking, Chinese armies took up positions in the mountain ranges surrounding Hankow and the other two cities of Wuhan. The mountains were the last natural barrier that protected central China, and the Communists moved with alacrity in an atmosphere electric with tension.

Agnes in Hankow, 1938. First row (from left): Po Ku, propaganda director of the Eighth Route Army liaison mission; Chou En-lai, the CCP's chief diplomacist; Wang Ming, who had recently returned from Moscow. Second row: U.S. consular official Robert Jarvis; Lo Jui-ch'ing, (second from left), chief of security forces during the Long March, who directed several security and intelligence divisions, unidentified man; Agnes (fifth from left, in necktie). *Museum of the Chinese Revolution, Beijing.*

Throughout the city, gaily hued posters summoned citizens to resist the enemy and suggested that Wuhan would become another Madrid. Educated youth read the Communists' publications, joined their organizations, and strengthened their "democratic people's movement." Reactionary forces weakened. "No one really thought that Hankow would be another Madrid," wrote John Patton Davies, a young American foreign service officer who was stationed in the city. "Still, in June and July many had not yet abandoned hope and there was an unreasoning exhilaration in crisis."[20]

As Westerners began leaving Hankow in anticipation of its fall, Davies's apartment became a gathering place for American diplomats, military observers, and journalists including Consul General Paul Josslyn, Lieutenant Colonel Joseph Stilwell, Captains Frank Dorn and Evans Carlson, *New York Times* correspondent Tillman Durdin, and Edgar Snow. Agnes mocked the care with which Davies selected flowers, food, and wine for his table, but she was no different from the others in finding an evening of his hospitality a much needed reprieve from the war.

The men, mostly liberal in their political outlook, generally supported the Chinese Communists and the Eighth Route Army at this time. They viewed the Communists' decision to transfer power to popularly elected regimes—reducing

Foreign correspondents, Hankow. Front row (from left): Agnes, unknown, Freda Utley. Second row: George Hogg, Mac Fisher, Tillman Durdin. *National Archives, Washington, D.C.*

rent, corruption, and domination by landowning gentry—as encouraging signs, and they applauded recent efforts to involve politically aware women and youth and educated nonlandlord classes, and create a new generation of leadership.[21] However, while they all shared a common sympathy for China and great affection for the Chinese people, Agnes was alone among them in believing that the Chinese masses—and all of mankind—could be emancipated in her lifetime and that oppression, want, and misery could be banished forever from the earth.

Outside this friendly circle, Agnes's critics complained that she was a Communist and a conscious Stalinist propagandist—even as the Communists condemned her as an unreconstructed liberal bourgeois idealist. In the years to come, she would also be accused of downplaying the ideology of CCP leaders to her fellow correspondents and military and diplomatic observers, suggesting that the Chinese Communists were nothing more than simple peasant reformers.[22] But to her Western friends in Hankow—many of whom would come to wield considerable influence on U.S. China policy—Agnes was the independent radical she had only claimed to be in years past, and to them she was "a heroic and tragic figure, doomed to destruction by her virtues, her compassion for human suffering, her integrity and her romanticism."[23]

When the British journalist Freda Utley encountered Agnes that July, she said, she had been expecting some sort of cross between Robespierre and the whore of Babylon.[24] Instead, she declared Agnes one of the few truly great people she had ever met. She found Agnes "putting into rickshaws and transporting to the hospital at her own expense some of the wretched wounded soldiers the sight of whom was so common in Hankow, but whom others never thought of helping." Agnes, Utley would write,

> had that burning sympathy for the misery and wrongs of mankind which some of the saints and some great revolutionaries have possessed . . . Unlike those doctrinaire revolutionaries who love the masses in the abstract but are cold to the sufferings of individuals, Agnes Smedley spent much of her time, energy, and scant earnings in helping a multitude of individuals . . .
>
> . . . Although she had lived so long in China . . . the *laissez-faire* atmosphere of China had made no impression whatsoever. She had retained to the full her splendid western American energy and a reforming spirit which drove her on to attempt the impossible, to set things right, to be everywhere and to remedy all abuses.[25]

There were those in the years to come who would wonder how these people could describe someone who had participated in Agnes's earlier activities as "an authentic American in the tradition of Tom Paine, the suffragettes and the Wobblies . . . curiously unconcerned with doctrine . . . too soft hearted and unruly to be a party member."[26] They did not know her during her months in Hankow, the most romantic in China's war.

That summer, *China Fights Back*, Agnes's diary of her travels with the Eighth Route Army, was released in the United States and Great Britain. *Herald Tribune* reviewer Lewis Gannett spoke admiringly of her readiness "to pay the last full price of her own convictions," noting that "of such stuff, in all ages, martyrs have been made."[27] Ironically, the book was not welcomed by the leftist press, which either attacked the tale for its failure "to place the Eighth Route Army in its proper perspective in a united China," or ignored it.[28] *China Fights Back* never achieved the success of Agnes's earlier China books.

"Communist tentacles extend through many publishing houses," she later wrote by way of explanation, "and Vanguard Press had a man who ran to the CP to 'report' on my book . . . Grace Granich . . . then wrote a letter to Madame Sun Yat-sen, declaring that I had written a new book in which all the Chinese National armies were branded as bandits . . . Madame Sun sent this letter to the Chinese CP headquarters . . . The American CP . . . put my . . . book on its 'index,' attacking it and refusing to sell it in its stores."[29] Agnes blamed its failure on Vanguard, which allowed Browder to read and censor her manuscript, she said, and on fellow activist Anna Louise Strong, who had helped with the revisions and whom Agnes accused of editing "everything vital from it."[30]

As the summer of 1938 wore on, neither the Communist guerrillas behind Japanese lines nor coordinated attacks by Nationalist and Communist forces could stem the Japanese advance. Air raids increased; it was only a matter of time before Hankow fell. "Every day and every moonlit night we would hear the dreadful wail of sirens," Agnes later wrote. "After each raid the city was full of the mangled bodies of victims; sometimes I worked in a Chinese railway hospital where hundreds lay on the floors bleeding to death. People died under our hands. I found myself growing coldly impersonal—selecting soldiers and workers who had only minor injuries and could be most quickly restored to fighting condition."[31]

Almost all the foreign wives and children, along with those of Chinese officials and the affluent, had been evacuated by September; the death and destruction was unremitting. During the next few crisis-ridden weeks, as KMT armies retreated in panic from seemingly endless waves of heavily armed Japanese, Agnes and her American friends developed an extraordinary camaraderie. After an air raid, or when too many wounded soldiers ground them down, "two or three of us would stand beneath the dark window of another friend of ours and clap," she wrote. "A sleepy head would be thrust out to ask: 'What's up?' And we would call: 'Conversation. Come down.' Our friend would wrap a bathrobe around him and come down to sit in a garden and talk of things that seemed portentous."[32]

It was Agnes, Utley said, who held their group together. "We might argue with her and tease her and attempt to shake the rock of her faith, but we all loved her and no one could refuse to do what she wanted."[33] One evening, Agnes talked them into singing to wounded Chinese soldiers at a local hospital. Few had good voices and none shared her theatrical zest, but she got them to join her on several old ballads and American wartime songs—to the astonishment of the patients. "It is hard to refuse anything to the pure in heart," Davies later explained.[34]

By the end of the month, even the "last ditchers" began to scatter. After much soul-searching, Carlson had resigned from the Marine Corps and was returning to the United States to warn Americans about the danger Japan posed and promote the Communist army's "ethical indoctrination" methods as a wartime weapon. Agnes wondered whether the time had come for her to return as well, but she could not bring herself to leave. At a farewell party for Utley, Agnes announced that she planned to slip out of town just before the Japanese entered Hankow and join New Fourth Army guerrillas in the war-torn Yangtze delta region. There thirty thousand former partisans, bandits, and Red Army men were sorely testing China's united front policy. It was the only story left about the Chinese Communists, she said, that hadn't been done to death by foreign journalists.

Her friends tried to discourage her. Some thought she was driven by a death wish—a charge that Agnes denied. Davies later wrote that he tried to warn her that she was giving herself to a revolution that was then on the upsurge. At this stage, it was idealistic; its leaders were resolute, bound by a fellowship inspired by dangerous enemies. But if their revolution succeeded and the Communists assumed power, then corruption would set in and Agnes would become disillusioned and betrayed. Why didn't she quit this kind of life and operate like other correspondents, Davies said he asked her.[35] Agnes wanted to know why people tried to question her faith when she saw no other way.

Everyone danced and drank, but the city's impending fall and the dispersal of their group cast a pall on the occasion. For Agnes, who would be leaving the first Americans with whom she had lived on friendly terms in nearly twenty years, the sense of loss was particularly acute. She had enjoyed her countrymen's company as a respite from her loneliness; she knew their life of home and love and lasting friendship would never be hers. But she was growing resigned to being a wanderer, no longer an American but not Chinese either.

Days before Hankow fell, Agnes departed in the company of Chinese Red

Cross Medical Corps director Dr. Robert Lim. That October, she began making
her way east, toward the active zone, in a New Fourth Army ambulance laden
with bales of towels, bolts of cloth, and cases of soap and quinine she had
begged or purchased with her own money. When she was not reporting on the
war for the *Manchester Guardian*, she would be investigating and publicizing
the plight of the Chinese wounded along the lower Yangtze, where the New
Fourth Army was the major military force.

On November 9, she reached New Fourth Army headquarters in Yunling
after floating down a Yangtze tributary on a bamboo raft. She was the first foreigner to reach the area. Her hosts replaced her summer dress with a leather
jacket, a sweater, and padded trousers and brought her to a loess house she
would use as a base. After unloading her typewriter, books, and manuscripts, she
filled a pot with wildflowers and went off to inspect the Rear Base Hospital for
the severely wounded.

One of the first modern hospital services in any Chinese army, the Rear Base
Hospital also functioned as the supply center for the entire New Fourth Army,
some of whose units were two or three weeks' marching distance further down
the Yangtze. It contained the army's only X-ray machine, along with micro-
scopes, autoclaves, a laboratory with an incubator and a pillmaking machine,
medical journals in several languages, and trained doctors and nurses. Like the

New Fourth Army welcomes Agnes, 1939. *Museum of the Chinese Revolution, Beijing.*

Eighth Route hospital in Yenan, the New Fourth unit in Anhwei province offered the local populace the only public medical service in the area. It treated civilians without cost while providing patients with a revolutionary education, courtesy of the army's political department.

The hospital, like the army itself, was the achievement of New Fourth Commander Yeh Ting, who had commanded the original Fourth Red Army during the 1927 Northern Expedition. But Yeh Ting, a convinced leader of the united front—then and now—was having problems. Although the effort was still officially working, it was straining at the seams, and Yeh Ting, a former Red Army officer who had resigned from the CCP but refused to join the KMT, was finding it exceedingly difficult to maneuver between the two.

The central government resented the New Fourth's rapid recruitment of local civilians. Fearful that the army was becoming too large and influential, Nationalists held Yeh Ting responsible for his troops but refused to equip or fund them. At the same time, the Communists were actively intriguing to prevent Yeh Ting from exercising control over the Communist-trained troops. At the time of Agnes's arrival, Yeh Ting's men were so disaffected that they refused to mention their leader by name; the vice commander, a Communist, attacked Yeh Ting openly.[36]

The New Fourth's medical service was an early target of the CCP's effort to wrest control of the army from Yeh Ting, and Agnes found herself mediating between CCP political leaders in Yenan, who demanded that the medical unit subordinate itself to the army's political department (which was headed by a Communist) and the non-Communist chief physician of the New Fourth's medical service, who sought to retain the unit's autonomy.[37] Not surprisingly, Agnes's attempts to steer a middle course made her unpopular with New Fourth Communist leaders.

Agnes claimed that it did not bother her. "I've been quite unpopular all my life and am used to it," she wrote.[38] In truth, the situation so disturbed her that she thought again of returning to the United States. In her letters to friends from Hankow, Agnes spoke nostalgically of the months when she had been popular and not living in the "emotional and human desert" she now inhabited. She mused about writing a play about her experience as a way to lift her spirits. In it, John Davies, with his bowls of beautiful flowers and fondness for Beethoven's Fifth Symphony and bourgeois culture, would be her protagonist, she wrote. Captain Carlson would be its tragic figure, reaching for but never touching the stars. Freda Utley would be "the flame, uncontrolled and forever attracting all, instinctively and unconsciously."[39]

By January 1939, the whole lower Yangtze River valley was fulminating. Agnes reported that the Japanese were driving two wedges into the area: one to her west, which the Fiftieth Chinese Army held, and another twenty miles east, near the mountain city of Nanling, which was under constant bombardment. Towns and villages were repeatedly changing hands. Thousands of civilians were fleeing to the rear, and seemingly endless numbers of the wounded were appearing at the Rear Base Hospital. By this time Bethune's nurse, Jean Ewen, had arrived to help out, bearing a gift for Agnes of foreign food, cigarettes, Scotch, and a sizable donation from the British ambassador. But the politicization of medical treatment in the New Fourth Army—and the larger issue of who controlled it—continued.

That February, while Agnes was away visiting a nearby central government force, she received a telegram from the New Fourth Army requesting that she return at once—the CCP push to take over the hospitals had prompted the resignation of Commander Yeh Ting. The central government refused to accept his resignation, but the furor had brought the Red Cross medical inspector and Chou En-lai to New Fourth headquarters to try to restore harmony.

According to Agnes's later account, the medical service emerged victorious. "Vice-Commander Hsiang issued an Army order in support of the modern Medical Service, its organization and practices. And at my request the Red Cross Medical Corps sent two mobile units to aid it. The first Army Medical Service of a Chinese Army was at last firmly established."[40] Ewen, who vehemently objected to the practice of mixing politics with sutures, as she put it, would recall a somewhat different story. She claimed that because Chou En-lai was not part of the Party's political bureau, there was little he could do "except to say the service would stand or fall on its merits as a functioning part of the Army," and the Army took over the hospitals.[41]

The question of who controlled aid to China's war victims, military and civilian, extended beyond the provision of medical services in the New Fourth Army. Progressive foreigners in China blamed the Nationalist government for the "mountainous accumulation of filth and reaction and incompetence and selfishness and hypocrisy," as Snow described it, that frustrated leftist relief efforts like the fledgling Industrial Cooperative movement and Madame Sun's China Defense League, and they disparaged Madame Sun's sister, Madame Chiang Kai-shek, for squandering money and supplies.[42] But they were unaware that despite the crying needs of Chinese soldiers and civilians, Madame Sun played politics, too—denigrating Dr. Lim, the nonaligned director of the Chinese Red Cross Medical Corps, and belittling Agnes's relief efforts, which competed with her own.[43]

Isolated and alone, Agnes expended enormous energy on obscure, thankless tasks, seeking out the impersonal love her courage and dedication inspired. She funded and oversaw construction of the first delousing, bathing, and scabies treatment station in the Chinese Army, traveled to other armies and battlefields as a gesture of American support, and paid attention to the refugee problem. She also wrote any number of letters, reports, and appeals for relief funds and medical supplies that made their way to Shanghai on bits of silk paper she sewed into travelers' jacket linings.[44] In early March, Japanese planes destroyed every hut in the village except the hospital operating room, and Agnes worked through the night nursing the wounded. When she could no longer stand upright, she said, she went to sleep on a table in her overcoat, using a volume of medical journals as her pillow. But other than work, her life did not exist, and she was terribly dispirited.

> I ... pine for the magic of Hankow [she wrote Utley, who had returned to London]. It was the bright spot in one decade of my life. There I met foreign men, some of them rotters, but most of them with the charm that belongs to many men of the western world. They themselves do not know how very different they are from the Chinese. Though I have never liked to be treated as bourgeois women are treated, still the foreign men ... have a deep and unconscious attitude of respect for women; a little feeling of protection for women; of helping a woman; and a kind of gentleness toward her. Often his kindness [is] blended a bit with tenderness or a breath of romance. It is difficult to explain, because it is there as an atmosphere. In the Chinese man this is totally lacking ... The foreign word "romance" ... in the Chinese language ... means promiscuous sexual relations. And "love" means sexual intercourse in its general use ... For a Chinese man to even touch a woman's arm or hand means something sexual and arouses shock.
>
> ... Shall I return to the western world, or shall I remain here? I fear I must remain in China ... and ... retain [Hankow] as a precious memory.[45]

Agnes was so caught up in her myriad tasks she was sending just one article a month to the *Manchester Guardian*, but, she said, she required considerable spiritual stimulus to do more creative work, and she did not have that here. Occasionally in the evenings, Agnes picked up musical programs from Europe or listened to international news on a short wave radio at the hospital. She would take down the information in shorthand and give it to an interpreter who translated it for the soldiers. But the system only functioned as long as the radio operated, they had batteries, and there were no typhoons.

Had Agnes not been so cut off from the outside world, she might have taken comfort when her photo essay on the New Fourth Army appeared in the July 1939 issue of *Life* and was viewed by millions of American readers.[46] Instead, she lay in a ditch while the Japanese bombed New Fourth headquarters and four surrounding villages. Up until late at night monitoring foreign broadcasts, too terrified by the intensity of the attacks to sleep during the day, Agnes was becoming as obsessive as any Christian martyr in her need to suffer with the people. It was perhaps inevitable in her unhappiness that she became restless for the road.

Late that summer, Agnes decided to cross the Yangtze between Japanese positions and enter the vast hinterland north of the river. It would be a journey of several months' duration, more dangerous than any she had previously undertaken. "Up to this time," Agnes later wrote, "I had been with armies which could retreat to the rear if forced to do so. This would no longer be possible."[47] Millions of Chinese still lived in the area, she reported, and they held all but the enemy fringes, but the area north of the river was surrounded on three sides by the enemy.

Agnes would travel with the first medical unit to service the northern guerrillas, in a group of one hundred trained military, political, and medical personnel. To prevent word from spreading that a foreigner would be passing through a battle zone, she would sit in a sedan chair, completely covered, whenever they passed through a village. The arrangement must have appealed to the actress in her.

Before their group set out on the evening of September 1, 1939, the officer directing their column instructed them, according to Agnes, that they could not talk, smoke, or use flashlights on the first leg of their journey. It would be dark until midnight, when the moon rose. If they heard fighting, they were to keep marching. Others would handle it. They would cross the Yangtze in junks.

> On the path there was no sound save the faint pad-pad of soft-clad feet mingled with the low creaking of bamboo poles over the shoulders of our carriers. Often I could see nothing. But sometimes the clouds above us shifted and then by the bright light of the stars I could make out the dim, moving shadows of two or three men in front of me . . .
>
> I heard the night birds, the wind through the trees . . . Once far away on our left I heard a faint call, like the bellow of a buffalo calf . . . Then, far to our right, I heard an answering call, and knew that guerrillas or civilians were giving us a signal—a signal that all was well.[48]

Agnes's group reached the Fourth Detachment of the New Fourth Army in mid-September. By the end of the month, they had abandoned the territory the New Fourth controlled for a more conservative area. Agnes spent the next five weeks at a field hospital in Lihwang, visiting various armies and filing reports on refugee relief and the needs of the wounded. The less politically enlightened military leaders and provincial officials she encountered disappointed her. So, too, did the areas they controlled.

> Along the highway I... found none of those slogans by which the Chinese express their hopes. No songs of conviction, no activity of the people. Sick and diseased people surrounded me everywhere, pleading for help—babies that had congenital syphilis—skin diseases, scabby heads—pus filled eyes— ulcerous legs...
>
> What destitution, dirt and disease!... I have used up half my medicine, but there is no end. Only a gigantic transformation could end this misery![49]

On foot and by horse, Agnes made her way through the enemy rear in her soldier's uniform, her pistol in her belt. Near Honan, she rode up to the door of an American missionary doctor, Casper Skinsnes, and asked him to put her up. A few days in Agnes's company convinced him that the kindly, sympathetic, generous-natured person he encountered would doubtless have remained a Christian, had she known a better home life in her youth.[50]

Agnes entered Hupeh province in December 1939 and was met by General Chung Yi, commander of the 173rd Division of the Kwangsi Army. Chung Yi, who came from a family of poor landowning scholars, had entered China's military academy when the national revolutionary movement had begun, but he was a progressive KMT and had refused to participate in the civil war. After the Japanese invasion, he left teaching and returned to active duty. Agnes later wrote that she liked him immediately. According to Agnes, Chung Yi liked her, too.[51]

He spoke admiringly of Agnes's bravery in coming to the front, she would write, and when he took her to observe the men's night maneuvers, the usual barriers of race and nationality were absent. Before she departed for a regiment nearer the battlefield, she reported, the two of them enjoyed a candlelit dinner and animated conversation about politics, writers, artists, and the theater. As Agnes described the encounter, the sexual tension between them was palpable, and Chung Yi pointedly asked her if a modern woman would wait as faithfully for her husband at the front as the famous woman in Sian had. Agnes awkwardly lobbed the question back to him.[52] On the morning of her departure, she would write, Chung Yi saw her off and gave her a small jade ring as a memento. Agnes promised that when he was ordered to the front, she would return and write about it. Given her tendency to exaggerate, it would be easy to dismiss Agnes's wartime story of near romance as a desire to improve her copy. Several years later, though, a character based on Chung Yi, and another on herself, appeared in a never published play she wrote.[53] Replete with details of their encounter, and questions about the problems an interracial couple would face, it suggests the poignant interlude was genuine.

By winter, a Chinese offensive was under way, and Agnes spent the next months among several Storm Guerrilla detachments of the New Fourth Army. The men skirmished constantly. Often they camped within a mile of the enemy, moving at night and sleeping by day, protected by armed civilians. Agnes traversed hundreds of miles through the snow with the men, mostly on foot. She lectured, addressed mass meetings, and worked with their wounded. She also filed some of the earliest stories to come out of China on Nationalist plans to wipe them out as the united front faltered.

Shen Kuo-hwa, a boy of ten or eleven (he was not sure which), was assigned to be her orderly.

> With that curious wisdom of China's children, he told me that he was small because he had never had enough to eat and had been sick so much when he was a "beggar boy." That was long ago, he explained, when he was "very little." Bandits had fallen upon his poor home in Honan, burning it to the ground, killing his father, and injuring his mother. His two elder brothers had both joined the Army to make a living, and after this disaster he had become a beggar boy to earn money to support himself and his mother... He had wanted to study, but found he could not because he was not "rich"... He had learned to write his name only after he had joined the guerrillas.[54]

Agnes deloused her *hsiao kwei's* uniform; she held him, combed his hair, and helped button his jacket. This embarrassed him a little, she would write, because no one had ever done anything like that for him before, and he said he was supposed to help her—not the other way around—but his affection for her was evident, as Agnes described it. When she decided to follow a platoon of troops joining a field regiment in the lake regions northwest of Hankow, she requested and received, permission to bring Kuo-hwa with her.

Her group was on a night march to the area when Agnes, who was traveling on horseback accompanied by a muleteer carrying her gear and by Kuo-hwa on foot, heard the rumbling of advancing motor trucks that signaled the approach of the Japanese.

> Immediately a wild whisper fled down the column ordering everyone to run and all nonfighters to get into the shelter of the hills. I saw the small figure of Kuo-hwa speeding across the highway ahead of me. In the darkness and con-

Agnes and the child she wished to adopt. *Museum of the Chinese Revolution, Beijing.*

fusion my horse dashed out to the end of a low, half-destroyed bridge, crouched and sprang. We landed on a road in the midst of figures scurrying in every direction. My muleteer grabbed the bit of my horse and ran toward the rice fields... [w]hispering fiercely: "Beat the horse! Beat the horse! The enemy is coming!"

We went over an embankment in one leap and out over the dark fields...

...I began to feel like a coward. We were abandoning our men, and I was the only one of our group that had even a small pistol!

Through [the horse's] hard breathing I heard the strange singing of the bullets...

I strained my ears for any human sound; when none came I went down the hill and said: "I'll give the guerrilla signal."...

...From far away a cautious signal answered...I grabbed my muleteer by the hand and my horse by the bridle and began to drag them in the direction of the signal...Soon we were very near...I drew out my pistol, released the safety catch, and waited.

Out of the darkness in front of us came three dark shadows. "Password!" they demanded harshly and we saw their rifles trained on us.

"Asses!" cried the muleteer in wild joy, and ran toward them and fell upon their necks.

The three guerrillas slung their rifles back over their shoulders and, laughing, gave me pats of joy that almost knocked me down.

"We got 'em! We got 'em!" they cried, and holding hands, we walked across the rice fields.[55]

Agnes's weeks with the Fourth Regiment of Storm Guerrillas were nightmarish. Kuomintang and Communist forces were actively vying for control of the area, and Agnes would write that the atmosphere was so strained it sometimes felt as if the Japanese threat were "a mere sideshow compared to this internal problem." The guerrillas were in desperate need of medical care and supplies, and millions of civilians suffered from dysentery, typhoid, cholera, and malaria—even in winter. Communications were terrible. Gasoline and other basic supplies hardly existed, she reported.

Agnes dispatched two guerrillas with reports on the situation through Japanese lines to her network in Hankow and abroad. They responded with quinine, disinfectants, and gauze, as well as a package that contained several magazines, a packet of American matches—and the first personal correspondence she had received in nearly a year. It was from Eva Ginn, who wrote of Stalin's nonaggression pact with Hitler and the disservice the CPUSA had done the American left by supporting it.

The matches impressed the guerrillas, but they were befuddled by the advertisements for cars, homes, and jewelry and the photographs of scantily dressed women that appeared in the magazines. Reading the *New Yorker*'s witty cartoons and book and theater reviews on her sampan in the lake, Agnes said she found the contrast between America and China unendurable.

As the spring of 1940 approached, the Chinese offensive faded out and the Japanese prepared for a counteroffensive. Agnes said the roar of artillery from the mountains to her west was constantly in her ears. Enemy trucks carrying supplies and troops regularly traveled the highways on the mountains encircling Hankow. In one week alone, she said, her guerrilla regiment fought three battles. "We slept in our clothing and almost every midnight a warning knock at our door would send us scrambling to our feet," she later wrote. "We would roll up our blankets and within five minutes be in small sampans out on the lakes."[56]

By this time, Agnes had developed malaria, a skin rash, and hives. Malnutrition was making her toenails fall off, wrecking her teeth, and inflaming her eyes. In her weakened state, she said, she was also susceptible to typhus. It was time to move on. Before she did, she requested permission from the commander of the Storm Guerrillas to legally adopt Shen Kuo-hwa.

Whether she thought through the idea is not clear. Agnes would later say she had given considerable thought to the difficulties of raising a Chinese child and to the lack of stability in her own life. In the end, the commander of the Storm Guerrillas was willing but Kuo-hwa was not. He would be sad to see her go, she said he told her, but he wanted to see China win the war. Perhaps, with exemplary Chinese indirection, he recognized a good excuse to escape the clutches of some very dubious foster-mom material.

Agnes arrived in Ichang on March 22, 1940, and promptly collapsed. After a three-week stint in a Scottish missionary hospital failed to restore her, she proceeded west to Chungking for X-rays. Huge changes had taken place in China since she had last been in contact with civilization, she reported. The government had turned this part of the country into a base of resistance and introduced a number of reforms and new institutions. Unfortunately, the changes had unleashed a conservative reaction. The united front was splintering.

Dr. Lim was under attack by right and left. There were witch hunts, as Agnes described them, at local educational institutions. Left-wingers, Communist activists, and intellectuals had fled or were fleeing to Hong Kong. In northwest China, central government troops kept the Eighth Route Army encircled, sporadically attacking both it and the New Fourth Army.

Agnes had problems of her own. The CPUSA's decision to support Stalin's accommodation with Hitler cost the Party the support of thousands of non-Communist American progressives, who abandoned the Communist-controlled Popular Front organizations in droves. The China Aid Council, through which Agnes had obtained relief money for China, was only one of front organizations thrown into disarray, and though it repeatedly denied accusations that it was Communist, contributions had dried up.[57]

To improve its image, the China Aid Council had broken from the discredited League for Peace and Democracy and installed another chairman and executive committee. In reality, though, the CPUSA now controlled the organization directly, and as a consequence the China Aid Council refused to mention Agnes by name, let alone work with her, relying instead on Madame Sun's China Defense League to distribute the funds the China Aid Council raised.

Agnes scoffed at her Communist detractors in the China Aid Council and the China Defense League. In her public appearances, she maintained that the only organization in the United States that was actually helping China's wounded was the distinctly non-Communist American Bureau for Medical Aid to China. She preferred to work for ABMAC.[58] Still, Agnes knew better than most that without American funds to distribute, she was of little use to the Chinese.

In May 1940, Agnes received a letter from Chung Yi. Dated early February, it said that his division would be on the Chunghsiang front and asked that she meet him there. Agnes later said she was not feeling well and did not respond. When she learned, not long after, that his division had been annihilated while trying to counterencircle enemy troops, and that Chung Yi had committed suicide to escape capture, she wished she had returned to be killed with him. Despite China's myriad internal conflicts, Agnes really believed it was fighting the battle for world democracy. The ignorance of the international community—and her inability to change it—enraged her and tore at her heart.

Late that June, while an air blitz attempted to reduce Chungking to ashes, Agnes moved southeast to Kweiyang, where the Chinese Red Cross Medical Corps headquarters had relocated. Dr. Lim gave Agnes a room in exchange for publicity work, and when she felt well enough she lectured and attempted to write up her experiences over the last eighteen months. Agnes said that in Chungking, Theodore White, a young reporter for *Life* and *Time*, had expressed interest in her photographs, and that the movie producer D. W. Griffith wanted to record some of her stories, but she wanted to save the material for a book of her own.[59] Most of the time, though, she could not summon the will to write.

Every week, Japanese naval planes arrived from the south to bomb the city, and Chinese Red Cross ambulances brought back the injured. On July 28, enemy planes detoured from their established route and bombed the Red Cross headquarters and medical center instead. Agnes escaped injury, but the attack destroyed the hospital for wounded soldiers and the orthopedic center and extensively damaged the medical training school. As soon as the planes had gone, Agnes dashed off an article and sent it, along with photographs, to the American press. The *New York Times* carried the story and wrote an editorial blasting the attack, but no amount of publicity could undo the damage.[60]

Dr. Lim made arrangements to decentralize the wards. At this time, Agnes sought his help to remain in China during the war. If he could get her to Hong Kong, she proposed to undertake a fund-raising effort for the Chinese Red Cross Medical Corps that would circumvent Madame Sun's China Defense League.[61] Then, under the auspices of the Chinese Red Cross Medical Corps, she would return to China and cover the Indo-China front, where heavy fighting had begun. The *Manchester Guardian* was still running her articles. That and the nine hundred dollars she had received from Vanguard Press for *China Fights Back* would allow her to live for a year.

In Hong Kong, Agnes intended to see a specialist about a chronic pain she had developed in her liver. She said she did not mind being killed at the front, but the prospect of surgery terrified her. A gun, she explained, "seems to absorb fear."[62]

In September 1940, Dr. Lim put her on a Red Cross truck bound for

Kweilin. There, a plane carrying banknotes from Hong Kong landed late one night. Agnes boarded, alone, for the return trip, flying over Japanese lines.

British officials were uneasy about having Agnes in Hong Kong, but Hilda Selwyn-Clarke, the wife of the island's director of medical services, vouched for her. On the condition that Agnes made no public speeches, published nothing inflammatory, or otherwise disturbed the peace of the colony, they let her enter. Selwyn-Clarke was secretary of Madame Sun's China Defense League and had been a go-between for Madame Sun and Agnes in Hankow. She had taken a room for Agnes at the posh Peninsula Hotel, but Agnes could not get comfortable. "It seemed a shame to dirty the spotless linens and the white bathroom," she later wrote, and the soft bed made sleep impossible. After breakfasting on ice cream, Agnes allowed Selwyn-Clarke to purchase a few items for her upcoming stay at the Queen Mary Hospital.

When the picaresque American writer Emily Hahn stopped by to visit, she found Agnes "looking most incongruous in a peach-colored satin nightgown."[63] Hahn, who had known Agnes in Shanghai, invited her to recuperate at her home, and Agnes was still there a week later when Hahn's lover showed up and asked for Emily. Charles Boxer was fifteen years Agnes's junior, but Agnes reportedly told Hahn she found him so cute she was tempted to invite him into bed with her.[64]

The police left Agnes more or less alone in Hong Kong, despite the ban on her participation in public life. Soon she was contributing articles, without attribution, to local English-language papers and lecturing at "private gatherings" in libraries and universities. Her relief activities also brought her into contact with Madame Sun. Agnes claimed that the older woman tried on several occasions to draw her into working with the China Defense League—perhaps by suggesting she deal not with Sun, but through Selwyn-Clarke, whom Agnes liked—for Agnes's reputation would add luster to the organization and might result in increased donations.

If Madame Sun was open to Agnes professionally, personally she remained as invested in their feud as Agnes. At the same time she apparently sent out feelers to Agnes, she quietly fueled CPUSA rancor by spreading stories to Grace Granich that Agnes's British publisher had paid her an eight-thousand-dollar advance for *China Fights Back*—more than ten times Agnes's usual fee—and claiming that Agnes "broadcast the fact that every cent of her money would be given to wounded soldiers . . . [when] for months her money ha[d] been lying in the bank with her full knowledge."[65]

Agnes wisely kept her distance. Feeling completely out of her element, she socialized with British progressives engaged in relief work for China, including Selwyn-Clarke, social worker Margaret Watson, Hong Kong University professor Norman France, and Bishop Ronald Hall, and avoided her American friends Snow and Carlson, who were also in Hong Kong but worked with Madame Sun in the league. Agnes was too disciplined to discuss the matter with such political innocents as Snow and Carlson, but privately she objected to the Communists' control of the China Defense League and their use of Madame Sun as a cover.[66] It was not that their work lacked value, she said, but she still had her memory, and she'd be damned if she allowed the Communists—American, Russian, *or* Chinese —to use her name and influence while they continued to blackball her.

"It is an embarrassment to them all," she wrote, "that I am the only foreigner that went to the front and the enemy rear, lived with the armies, worked with the armies, ever since the war began, and that I know more about the Chinese armies than any other foreign journalist . . . [or] Chinese intellectual—for those intellectuals seldom or never go to the front; and they never fight. If only the Communists could wipe out my record!"[67]

During this time, Agnes spent a sherry-soaked evening with Ai-ling Kung, the wife of China's finance minister and oldest of the three famous Soong sisters, which concluded in a rollicking Virginia reel. Afterward, Madame Kung agreed to sponsor a book of Agnes's stories to raise money for Dr. Lim's Emergency Medical Training schools.[68] She also introduced Agnes to her youngest sister, Mei-ling, the wife of Chiang Kai-shek. Agnes managed to put her partisan preju-dices to the side on this occasion.

Madame Chiang, Agnes later wrote, was "cultivated, tremendously clever, and possessed of charm and exquisite taste. She was groomed as only wealthy Chinese women can be groomed, with an elegant simplicity which, I suspect, must require a pile of money to sustain. Next to her I felt like one of Thurber's melancholy hounds. She was articulate, integrated, confident. As the years had made her other sister, Madame Sun Yat-sen, older and sadder, so had they increased Madame Chiang's assurance and power."[69] After their meeting, Agnes would send her several photographs she had taken in the war areas; she would also ghostwrite a chapter on the Chinese Red Cross Medical Relief Corps for a book by Madame Chiang.[70] Even here in neutral Hong Kong, though, the prob-lems of mainland China interposed.

After listening to several board members of the Chinese Red Cross repeat-edly attack Dr. Lim, to whom she was deeply attached, Agnes was furious at what she saw as their wish to force Lim from his position merely to advance their own power and prestige. For a time, she resisted the impulse to smash someone in the nose. Then, unable to stop herself, she provoked a confronta-tion so offensive it ruined her arrangement for getting back into China under the auspices of the Chinese Red Cross. Agnes always came to blows with the organizations with which she was connected, Hahn observed, usually on a point of principle; a "devil of discord" drove her.

Agnes's belated awareness that she had sabotaged herself precipitated a "heart attack" in late November, which left her lying in the street. A paralyzing depression followed, but it was too late to take it back. Friends urged Agnes to return to the United States until a more auspicious time. The Japanese had already occupied the coastal section of mainland China nearest to Hong Kong in preparation for an attack, and British women and children were evacuating the island. "To what?" Agnes retorted. "There's nothing I can do in the U.S.A."[71]

For several weeks, she lay ill in Selwyn-Clarke's home. Then Bishop Hall offered her his mountain cottage in Shatin, a part of Hong Kong which was on the mainland but still British territory. There she completed her collection of short stories on China's wounded and tried without success to work on her newest book. When Hsiao Hung, a thirty-year-old female novelist and former protégée of Lu Hsun's, joined her there, Agnes assumed a new role as patron. "Several years of marginal living, the war, and one emotional crisis after another had taken an irreversible toll on Hsiao Hung," her biographer wrote.[72] Hsiao Hung was talented but penniless; she was also dying of tuberculosis. In much the same way Michaelis sustained Agnes through the writing of *Daughter of Earth*, Agnes assumed the feeding and care of Hsiao Hung, who was racing to complete her third novel (posthumously published as *Tales of Hulan River*) before she died.

Occasionally Agnes came down to the city and mingled in the bars with the foreign correspondents. Erskine Caldwell, Margaret Bourke-White, and Ernest Hemingway passed through Hong Kong while Agnes lived there, and she met them all. Hemingway galled her. He would buy the other journalists drinks, she later wrote, and then boast of beating up a relative of Quisling at a barroom brawl in Idaho, or demonstrate sword and dagger tricks "by which, it seemed, a man's head could be cut off as easily as you could spit."[73] After what she had seen at the front, Hemingway seemed silly and soft, and unduly full of himself.

Agnes lingered in Hong Kong, hoping some fortuitous confluence of events would allow her to return to China, but the breaks did not go her way. In January 1941, any lingering illusions she nursed about the united front were shattered when Nationalist troops encircled the New Fourth Army in south Anhwei, killing four thousand and capturing two thousand more — including its commander, Yeh Ting. The increasing control asserted by government forces made it unlikely she could come back any time soon, but the German blitz raids over England, which destroyed the paper stores of the *Manchester Guardian*, sealed her fate. Although serious political observers in Hong Kong respected Agnes's analyses of contemporary Chinese affairs, the newspaper, forced to reduce its size, eliminated her correspondent's slot. The major source of her livelihood gone, she began making preparations to travel to America.

Someone asked Agnes whether after all her years in China she would be unhappy back in the United States "with all those foreigners," she later wrote. "He was quite right, yet I decided to return, hoping to be able to tell Americans about the way China lived and how they fought for freedom. I had become a part of the vast struggle of China . . . yet I remained American in many ways. I had, in truth, become one of those creatures who have no home anywhere."[74] With the greatest reluctance, Agnes wrote Upton Sinclair in April 1941 and sought his aid arranging lectures or other work through which she could earn enough money to retire for a year or two and write her book. "I know few people in America and have few connections, and I think I am known chiefly as a writer in England and on the Continent," she explained.[75] She would be returning to America unsuccessful, she said, but with her head unbowed, and she hoped that on the Pacific Coast they could resume the conversation they had begun in 1916. Sinclair did not respond.

Carlson lent her money for her fare, and on May 6, 1941, Rewi Alley saw her off on the freighter that would take her to the United States. It would take longer than the liners that stopped at Japanese ports, but Agnes said she was afraid to risk the latter because her name had recently appeared on a Japanese list of foreign journalists who would be treated as Chinese belligerents in the event of capture.[76]

"We stood on the main street, near the haughty banks" of the Hong Kong harbor, Alley wrote. "She looked at me a little queerly and said, 'Guess this is goodbye,' and we kissed and parted. And somehow the banks, and the bronze statue of Queen Victoria, looked insignificant beside her."[77]

Agnes's boat crept across the Pacific in an unbroken blackout. In late May, she entered the United States at San Pedro harbor, south of Los Angeles. After twenty years abroad, she was finally home.

CHAPTER 16

Back in the U.S.A.

I am a queer mixture of East and West, out of place everywhere, at home
nowhere: I cannot get rid of either that past inheritance or my recent acqui-
sitions. They are both part of me, and, though they help me in both the
East and the West, they also create in me a feeling of spiritual loneliness not
only in public activities but in life itself. I am a stranger and an alien in the
West. I cannot be of it . . . I have an exile's feelings.

JAWAHARLAL NEHRU

AGNES HAD remained in sporadic contact with Ernest Brundin during her
years abroad, and she stayed with him on her arrival. Ernest and his second wife, Eleanor, ran a hydroponic nursery outside Los Angeles. Over the next
few weeks, caring for their difficult houseguest was also a full-time job. Agnes
understood that her decision to leave China had brought the most important
chapter of her life to a close. Despite her bold public claim—that she had
returned to the United States because the Japanese had placed her name on an
official death list—she knew her reasons were otherwise, and her feelings about
what had happened to her in China were quite raw.

Looking around her, Agnes wondered for the first time whether her long-ago
decision to serve the Revolution had brought sufficient compensation. She was
lonely and regretted the absence of a great love in her life. In darker moments,
she even rued having ended her marriage to Ernest, for the years had been kind
to him in ways they had not been to her.[1] Since Shen Kuo-hwa had declined
her offer to adopt him, Agnes said she no longer wished to care for a child.
These days, she admitted it was unlikely she could. Still, she could not help but
compare the satisfaction Eleanor derived as a wife and mother to her own bitter
history.

Agnes was content, for the time being, to remain in Ernest's orbit, sleeping in
his office and taking her meals in their home, but she was as needy and
demanding as a child, oscillating between elation and despair, irrational at

times, and so anxious she insisted Eleanor accompany her to the doctor.[2] Southern California was also a dose of the new mass culture in the extreme. The commercialism that seemed to have overtaken American life appalled her. So did bridge-playing housewives who lived to shop and frequent the beauty parlor, the pervasive waste, and the cults and religious cranks that grew, Agnes wrote, "as scum forms on the surface of a stagnant pond," along with people's fascination with astrology and the scandals of Hollywood stars.

Thinking at first that her neighbors simply did not understand the crisis in the Far East, Agnes tried to enlighten them. Much to her distress, she wrote, "few were interested. Many thought me a subversive element. Businessmen attacked me as a threat to their Japanese trade . . . and most people shrank from every mention of the realities of war. Of other countries, they said in effect: 'Am I my brother's keeper?' and, like Pilate, they washed their hands of not only the rest of the world, but of the evils of our own society."[3] That the people Agnes buttonholed frequently did not know the difference between China and Japan, that they blandly insisted the Japanese would not *dare* attack the United States, that they resisted any stories about the war in China that were not entertaining or that required them to think beyond their own interests, made her fear for America's future. Sometimes, she confessed, she longed to shout at them, "Halt! Think! You ARE your brother's keeper!"

After competing with Agnes's image for the better part of two decades, Eleanor quickly wearied of Agnes in the flesh. Ernest took a little longer, but on an outing to a local dance hall, when Agnes loudly demanded that the band play an obscure radical song, then lost her temper when they told her they did not know it, she alienated him as well. After all these years, he realized, she still had the ability to mortify him.[4] In June, Agnes moved into her sister Myrtle's home in Chula Vista, south of San Diego near the Mexican border.

"I find no need to write to my relatives," Agnes had informed Michaelis back in 1930. "They play no part in my thought or emotions. They are nothing to me and I nothing to them. Amongst my comrades I have deeper and more lasting bonds than with my relatives."[5] The truth, of course, was more complicated. During her visit to southern California in the summer of 1934, Agnes had stayed with Myrtle and spent time with her brother Sam and sister-in-law Elizabeth, whose baby she adored. But while Agnes cared for her family members, she could not control her impulse to change them.

Despite admonishments from Myrtle that she had a life and opinions of her own, Agnes repeatedly harangued her sister to amend her political views, too, and Agnes arranged for Joseph Freeman to send her additional reading matter; she even offered to underwrite a visit by Myrtle to the Soviet Union. When Agnes returned to China, she had persisted, sending Myrtle $150 toward her trip to the USSR and prompting an indignant response; Myrtle returned the funds along with an icy observation that Agnes needed the money more than she did.[6] They had not spoken since.

On this subsequent visit, Agnes struggled to keep herself in check, but Myrtle, who by this time had become the principal of a local elementary school and something of a civic leader, was too successful for Agnes's jealous liking, while Sam, a professional gambler who lived nearby, was not successful enough.[7] Their conservative politics offended Agnes despite her best efforts to remain neutral, and her siblings, in their turn, found their older sister overbearing and intolerant. In truth, the distance between them was simply too great. It had been too long; they were too different. There would always be a place for Agnes in her siblings' hearts, but they could not have her in their homes. When a woman friend invited Agnes to share her one-room apartment in Hollywood, she accepted.

Vanguard Press had expressed interest in a book on her China experiences; Agnes pitched them four, including a narrative of her time at the front that depicted her "fierce struggles . . . against a few individual Communist leaders."[8] She feared she lacked the genius to write it as she believed it should be written, but she thought her material was in many ways the equivalent of what Tolstoy had drawn on for *War and Peace*. Hoping to buy the leisure to write, she repeatedly contacted Upton Sinclair, who lived nearby, about the possibility of paying lectures, but he brushed off the woman he had celebrated only recently as an American Joan of Arc with an autographed copy of his latest book.

Increasingly uneasy about her finances, Agnes looked up old China acquaintances including Auden and Utley, ignoring the latter's alarming isolationist tendencies, and appealed to others she had known in the birth control movement, or her China relief work, to help her find work. Having spent the war years at the front, she wrote, she had only recently learned that she had been the only one in China who was a volunteer. Certainly the men in the Chinese government were not, nor the merchants, nor the people in Hong Kong who directed the Chinese Red Cross, she observed. She was dismayed on looking back, she said, to discover that she had been "a kind of idiot running loose in China, actually believing in the sacred cause of the country."[9]

Agnes made her break with the CPUSA public soon after her arrival, using its support of the Hitler-Stalin pact as her pretext. She could not abide its antiwar position while war raged in China, and she denounced Party fronts like the American Peace Mobilization "as poisons drugging the American people and keeping them totally unprepared for the coming attack."[10] As time passed and her money began running out, though, she agreed to write for the *Clipper*, a publication of the Party-controlled League of American Writers, applied to join the league, and accepted a speaking engagement with the very organization she scorned.

Agnes's Faustian bargain brought her nothing but grief. Though she spoke at the Communists' meeting, she refused to spout the Party's antiwar line. Word of her latest transgressions soon enough reached the Graniches, who had the CPUSA distribute blizzards of pamphlets at her subsequent appearances resurrecting the charge that Agnes was untrustworthy, having "embezzled relief funds in China" vouchsafed to her by Madame Sun.[11] Agnes attempted to deflect the attack by insisting it was groundless—a "typical Communist smear campaign of the sort frequently directed against persons out of favor with the Party."[12] But the fact that she was in such obvious disrepute hurt her standing with the West Coast leftists who comprised most of her audiences, and her presence at Party gatherings and in Party publications attracted the attention of a local intelligence agency, which reported Agnes to the FBI.[13]

By July 1941, Hitler had invaded Russia, and the CPUSA amended its position to support the war. The American Party campaign against Agnes, however, continued. That month, after several more of her China photographs appeared without attribution or payment in *Friday* and *China Today* (edited these days by the Graniches), Agnes wondered whether a disparaging albeit truthful comment attached to her 1939 photoessay in *Life*—that she had been "snubbed" by the Eighth Route Army—had not also been the work of "some Communist" staffer she knew, perhaps the photographer Robert Capa.[14] Desirous that her peers on the non-Party left receive an alternative view, she contacted Malcolm Cowley, who had recently been subjected to a similar crusade.

In a letter marked "Strictly Confidential. Please read and burn," Agnes explained to Cowley that by so cravenly upholding Moscow's interests in supporting the pact two years earlier, the American party had isolated itself from the needs of its own people. Now "they lack[ed] the influence they might have had . . . riding in on the tail of the bourgeoisie two years too late instead of standing in the front line and extending their influence."[15] Playing up her position as an independent radical, she vowed that in any future lectures

> I will tell the truth . . . I consider the Chinese Communist Party as the main hope of China today. That viewpoint is going to infuriate the American Communist Party (or the Graniches and their followers) for they have the theory that once you refuse to follow their party line, you go right over into the ranks of the money-lenders. But I am what I always was—a real American democrat of the original brand of democrat, yet demanding that it be extended to eco-

nomic democracy... My mind may not be the right kind of mind, but it is all I have to go by, and I have not yet been convinced that it can be handed over to the Party to play with as they wish.[16]

Agnes admitted that the Party's difficulty dealing with her was not their fault alone—she was aware, she wrote, that she was not "a normal, balanced type of person"—but between what she described as the "Communist stunts" to isolate her and discredit her work, and the misgivings of mainstream publishers who still considered her too partisan to employ, she was sitting idle, and it tortured her that no one was taking advantage of her expertise. Cowley's response is not known, but Freda Utley claimed that during this period, Agnes said that her fellow correspondent Theodore White suggested, for a substantial sum, that he publish one of her articles in *Time* or *Life* under his byline, on the grounds that she "would help her beloved Chinese Communist soldiers more" in that way.[17] According to Utley, Agnes refused.

In frustration, she asked Vanguard publisher James Henle to set up a meeting between her and President Roosevelt so she could at least brief him on the Far East situation. Instead, Henle delivered a letter from Agnes to Eleanor Roosevelt, which the first lady turned over to Lauchlin Currie, the president's liaison on China. Currie advised the Roosevelts that while Agnes was an effective writer, who was looked on favorably by the British ambassador to China and Bishop Hall of Hong Kong, her past sympathy and association with the Chinese Communists had put her "somewhat out of favor with the Chinese Government." Should the Roosevelts wish to pursue her, Agnes would be more useful as a propagandist, to heighten interest and support for China, than a military intelligence source.[18]

By August, Agnes was down to her last sixty dollars. Vanguard had rejected her stories about the Chinese wounded, on which she had counted to raise quick cash, and had offered her only six hundred dollars for her "big" book on China, and six months in which to do it. Hard-pressed as she was, Agnes considered the advance, the time, and Vanguard's insistence that it be autobiographical unacceptable, and she told Henle as much.

I am dreadfully sorry, but I now feel that I must take my chances in the open market and try to find some publisher who is able to help me materially until I can produce a book that would seem to me worth while, and who could then place it before a very large number of readers. My health, my financial condition, and my whole life are now in such a condition that I must try to ignore any but business considerations regarding my writing. I feel badly about this ... Still the fact remains that I must try to get the best conditions from some publisher that would meet my needs. Perhaps I shall fail, perhaps I am not much of a muchness as a writer. But I have no choice but to try.[19]

In the meantime, Agnes's former comrade Julian Gumperz, who had left the German Communist Party and prospered as an investment counselor in New York, agreed to "loan" Agnes five hundred dollars to tide her over, and she persuaded the Feakins Lecture Bureau to book her for a series of college appearances and radio debates on the Far Eastern crisis. Her first major speech, at Philharmonic Hall in Los Angeles that September, was such a triumph that when Bishop Hall, who was visiting the area, could not make a subsequent engagement, Agnes brazenly donned some episcopal robes and took to the pulpit herself.[20] Before her appearances, Agnes, terrified, would ply herself with bourbon; strong receptions and the occasional standing ovation had her singing all the way home.

That fall there was more good news to celebrate. John Sanford, a leftist writer who had published a novel with Knopf, had sent Blanche Knopf an outline of Agnes's proposed China book, and she was interested. In response to Knopf's query, Lewis Gannett had advised her that while Agnes had "a confoundedly stiff conscience" and would be hard to handle, she had had a unique experience, which would produce, at a minimum, a good sequel to her other three China books, and—if she let her personality drive the narrative as she had in *Daughter of Earth*—perhaps a truly great one.[21] On that basis, Knopf offered Agnes a contract whose terms were good enough to keep her in food and shelter for a year.

Eva Ginn chided Agnes for being one of those writers, like James Farrell, who made her reputation at Vanguard and then abandoned them for a major publisher, but Agnes refused to feel guilty. *Daughter of Earth*, she reminded Ginn, had not been published by Vanguard, and it was, Agnes felt, a far more significant book than the three she had published with them.[22] Lacking the time and money to devote her full attention to her China books, she had not thought of them as literature. Now that she had an opportunity to write something of substance, she did not intend to let it slip by. However sympathetic Vanguard might be to her politics, for once in her life she wanted business to be business. Griping about her page limitation and Knopf's advice to draw on her personality and firsthand experience, along with liver pain, back pain, migraine headaches that left her prostrate, a duodenal ulcer that put her on a milk diet, and an earthquake and aftershocks that she said made her feel like she was at the front again, Agnes started the first section, peppering Gannett with a stream of nervous questions.

When the Japanese attacked Pearl Harbor that December, Agnes was one of few who were not surprised. "Our commanders and diplomats belong to the old world..., " she wrote. "Their 'expert' knowledge is based on the last world war. In Hawaii, they were perhaps all dancing, at ball games, or in whorehouses... We have a bunch of ignorant and pompous idiots commanding our armed forces... Our naval officers know nothing about warfare... All these assurances that 'the authorities have the situation well in hand' [are] bull, bull, lying bull."[23]

Agnes's contract with Knopf gave her cachet in Hollywood. Metro-Goldwyn-Mayer asked her for a screenplay on China even before the United States entered the combat. Once it did, any number of Hollywood leftists tried to exploit Agnes's understanding of America's new ally to advance their careers. One editor at Twentieth Century Fox sought material from Agnes for his picture on Japan and China; another requested slogans and a leitmotif for his, and a director at Warner Brothers met with her about a film on guerrilla warfare, which, Agnes said, he promised would draw heavily on *China Fights Back*.[24] While she considered all this, she learned that John Sanford was trying to sell a film script based on her lectures, using several stories she planned to use in her own forthcoming book.[25]

At first, Agnes said, she did not think there was anything terribly wrong about people who shared her politics appropriating her ideas. Taking her stories, though, was another matter, and when she discovered that all such transactions were commonly paid for, she became quite upset. Repulsed as much by her own naiveté as by what she called the "ghastly culture" of Hollywood, Agnes retreated to the country, moving into a small borrowed cottage in Ojai, a tiny community north of Los Angeles. There, without even a telephone to disturb her, she worked steadily.

Blanche Knopf had asked to see the first hundred pages when Agnes was done. Late in January 1942, she mailed them off, feeling, she wrote, "like a small boat in the middle of the Pacific." The response was not what she hoped. Knopf and Gannett, to whom Agnes had also sent a copy of her manuscript, criticized her overreliance on political generalizations and her absence from the text. They thought it vital that she engage her readers in herself as a human being, and they believed that having her experience drive the narrative would strengthen her message and allow the book to reach a larger audience.[26] In addition, they wanted an introductory section that covered her pre-China history. Agnes objected vehemently to every suggestion.

Having already published *Daughter of Earth*, she saw no reason whatsoever to detail her early years again, and she said that exposing her emotions about what had really happened to her in China, before time had softened them, made her feel as if she were being stripped naked. Then there were all the things she did not wish to tell. Hiding her fear behind a seemly show of Chinese modesty, she argued that inserting herself into her "walk through Chinese history" exploited China's suffering for her own glorification and would serve only to titillate jaded, sensation-seeking Americans. If Knopf really wanted her to produce a great book, she maintained, she would not write a single line of the one they were asking. Their suggestions filled her with shame, and she was certain, she added, that the result would ruin her in the minds of "really serious people"—and with all Chinese. Knopf was handling her roughly, she protested to Gannett, and the "contemptuousness" with which they dealt with her had brought her writing to a halt.[27]

Working herself into a froth, Agnes began to feel that the rural community to which she had retired was crowding her, and the sheer dottiness of her landscape chafed, as she indicated in this letter to Gannett.

> The neighbors all seem to come from Keokuk, Iowa. One of them has thirty cats. My landlady is a follower of Father Divine—there's a gang here. She believes also in horoscopes —many here do—and they all plant or cut their flowers by the stars. One woman nearby is a Communist and a Christian Scientist all in one and, in addition to Father Divine, my landlady has taken on the Communist Party. Krishna Murti lives near here and conducts a summer camp in the study of the soul . . . Sometimes when I look at southern California, I say: "Let the Japanese come!"[28]

John Sanford, who had heard something of the dispute with Knopf, now inserted himself into the fray. Although Sanford was only modestly acclaimed as a writer, he was enormously successful as a business agent for his wife, Marguerite Roberts, who was then one of MGM's best-paid contract screenwriters. That fact, and perhaps his status as one of Hollywood's ranking authors in the American Communist Party, encouraged Sanford to suggest to Agnes, unsolicited, that if the Knopfs had wanted theory about China, they could have "hailed it off the street like a taxicab."[29]

Anyone, he wrote, could string together the correct views on China, but only Agnes could write the book that would make Americans realize that China and its four hundred millions were America's strongest potential allies. For that reason, Sanford urged her to focus on helping China "kick the crap out of the Japanese" instead of worrying what her Chinese friends thought of her. If Agnes's current history of China "from Kubla-Khan to Chiang Kai-shek," as Sanford put it, would only reach dozens, while the story of Agnes Smedley in China had the potential to reach several thousands, then, he said, it was her *duty* to do the latter.

Perhaps it was a poor idea for Sanford to involve himself in the debate, but he may well have had Agnes's best interests at heart. Gannett and Knopf were evidently correct about Agnes manuscript. It did need more of her and less political theory, and if she refused to change it, she might lose the book contract altogether. But Sanford's "presumptuousness" in saying anything to her about China—a subject on which she felt she was the expert—enraged her, and the fact that he was the more established writer fueled her insecurities and made her dig her heels in.

In an irate epistle, Agnes refused even to discuss the content of her book with Sanford. He had not read a word of her manuscript and knew nothing about the subject, she fumed. She had granted permission to criticize her work to Lewis Gannett alone. Furthermore, Agnes wrote, she objected to the way Sanford addressed her in the "tone of a master to a hired boy" (as she heard it), since he had only met her three or four times. Maybe he had introduced her to Blanche Knopf. Even then, Agnes wrote, she refused to "eat dirt" from Sanford's hands. If that was the price for his help, she would have Knopf relieve her of that obligation by canceling her contract immediately.[30]

By April, Agnes had calmed down somewhat. As long as Gannett and Mrs. Knopf assured her that that "exquisite," as she referred to Sanford, would never see her manuscript, she would proceed. Political considerations, Agnes explained, lay behind her insistence. "He is a member of the American Communist Party and in the part which I am writing now there are some rather unhappy experiences with the Communists," she wrote. She was concerned that if Sanford had access to her manuscript, he would report on it to the Party, and Agnes said she did not want Browder to censor it as he had *China Fights Back*. The Communists "yelp about free press," she wrote, "but it is only a yelp."[31]

Promising to be a bridge to China and justify Gannett's faith in her, Agnes returned to work. For the next seven months, she labored like a demon. Her experience in China—minus the nettlesome details of her relationships with Muenzenberg, the Comintern, Sorge, and various Communist parties—became the core of her story, and she its central character. In a new voice, more mature and dispassionate, Agnes allowed her mastery of her subject to shine through.

Leaving Lihhwang, we moved westward through the towering Ta Pieg mountain range, ascending one summit only to find ourselves looking out on a sea of others...

From earth's grandeur we would descend into squalid valley villages where poverty bred sickness and suffering. Here was cause and effect in graphic simplicity: the villages arose in the shadows of the landlords' mansion—indeed, they were its shadows. High walls with watchtowers, pierced by loop-holes, protected the mansion. The landlords had fled, leaving agents behind to collect the rents.

Near one village I saw two peasant men, barefoot and in rags, hitched to a plow held upright by a barefoot, ragged woman. Behind them walked another woman carrying a small basket and dropping bits of dried manure into the furrow.

For many years before the Anti-Japanese War began, the border region of Anhwei, Hupeh, and Honan provinces had been Soviet territory guarded by Fourth Red Army Corps. Only after years of warfare had the Kuomintang armies been able to reduce it. How many people were killed no one will ever know, but the region was now sparsely populated, many villages were crumbling to dust, and old Red Army slogans on trees and wayside shrines were obliterated by whitewash.

The villages were so poor we could buy nothing to eat. One night we came into a large one and decided to sleep in an empty peasant hut. The floor was the usual packed earth, but the walls were crumbling and we could see the sky through the broken roof above. We bought two eggs, some rice and garlic, and after eating our meager meal we lay down on our piles of straw.

Only I was "rich" enough to afford a candle. When night fell, the people went to bed or sat in the darkness in front of their huts and talked in low voices. As I lay there thinking my painful thoughts, I suddenly heard voices singing in the night...I did not know the words, but I felt that into these old ballads the people had woven their hopes and sorrows...It went and on, a passion of desolation stretching back to time immemorial. [32]

Both Knopf and Gannett were well pleased with her subsequent sections.

Hard at work and completely isolated, Agnes appeared to miss the wire service story that May reporting that the Japanese Ministry of Justice had arrested Richard Sorge in Tokyo and charged him, along with his radio operator (Max Klausen) and two Japanese (Ozaki Hotsumi and Kawai Teikeichi) with Soviet espionage. [33] In Tokyo, it appeared, Sorge, who had been posing as a loyal Nazi, had become the confidant and adviser of the German ambassador, General Eugen Ott. Ozaki, who had replaced Agnes as Sorge's top associate, had secured a position in the Japanese cabinet that gave him access to secret documents and top-level decisions.

During the early years of World War II, it turned out, the ring Sorge assembled in Tokyo had provided Moscow with a great deal of useful intelligence. However, after Hitler attacked the USSR, information about Japanese policy had become so important to the Soviets that Sorge began using his transmitter too frequently. Eventually, Japanese counterintelligence discovered the radio station Klausen operated and broke Sorge's code. Sorge was arrested on the same October day in 1941 that he notified Moscow of Japan's preparations for war in the Pacific—a vital piece of information, two months before Pearl Harbor, that allowed the Soviet Union to shift urgently needed reinforcements from the Far East to stem the German advance toward Moscow. Klausen, Ozaki, and Kawai were apprehended soon after.

Although Sorge's Japanese interrogators were naturally more interested in the ring's Tokyo activities than in the earlier Shanghai phase, Sorge had spoken to them at length about Agnes's participation and drafted a written statement detailing her involvement. Agnes, he maintained, had not been sent from Moscow to work in Shanghai—which was technically true; she had been sent from Berlin. Sorge stressed her independence from the American Communist Party—which was also true but equally irrelevant, since Agnes's connection to the organized Communist movement was through Muenzenberg in the German KPD and Mirov-Abramov in Comintern intelligence—but he had acknowledged her as a valued member of his intelligence operation whom he had registered with Moscow, making her "a member of the Comintern Headquarters staff."[34]

None of this information, though, was known yet outside Tokyo, and the account that did appear in American newspapers—along with another item in August 1942 reporting, incorrectly, that Sorge had been sentenced to life in prison—seemed to escape Agnes's notice. For in October, when she completed her first draft, her mood was good.[35] Warner Brothers, she announced, had decided to wait until her current book was out to do their China film, and they had promised to hire her as a technical director when they produced it. Indeed, as Agnes made preparations to move to the East Coast, where she would do her revisions, she was of such excellent cheer that she claimed it was difficult to leave. Recently, she said, she had discovered so many nice things to do and people to meet in southern California. But leave she did.

En route to New York, Agnes stopped in Salt Lake City, Omaha, and Chicago, where she stayed with the family of Emily Hahn and caught up with several old lovers—so many, she joked, that she planned to tell them "to organize a union and join the C.I.O." She reached the city late in October.

After her months of solitude, Agnes reveled in her urban environment, quickly adapting to Manhattan's breakneck pace. She caught up with friends like Thorberg, explored old haunts in the Village, stayed out late carousing, and took in movies, shows, and museum exhibits. The city was expensive for someone of her limited means, and she groused that its residents were "filled with smart aleckness," but she loved the fuss her worldly and accomplished friends made over her, and though Agnes made a great show of not taking herself too seriously, she played her role of provincial western rube every bit as adroitly as her more urbane counterparts played theirs.

Not long after her arrival, Agnes attended a cocktail party at the home of Blanche Knopf. Sigrid Undset, the Nobel Prize–winning novelist, was there. So was Henry Luce, millionaire publisher of *Time, Life,* and *Fortune* and the head of United China Relief. Mrs. Knopf introduced them, and Luce sat beside Agnes and spoke with her at length about his own experiences in China. The son of Chinese missionaries, Luce had a long-standing interest in the country but rather conservative views, and Agnes said she sometimes had to laugh aloud at how thoroughly the Nationalists had snookered him.

After he left, murmuring that he hoped to see her again, Agnes said, Mrs. Knopf took her aside and told her "in a low, important voice" that "Harry came only to see you."[36] Wryly, Agnes wondered whether, if her book became a great financial success, she, too, might soon be calling Mrs. Knopf "Blanche" and Henry Luce "Harry." It was not that she wanted the money as an end in itself, but money, she could see, brought greater leisure and enhanced opportunities for a rich intellectual life, for which she yearned.

In New York, Agnes also met Pearl Buck, America's other famous female China writer, and hit it off famously with her. "She is the best that America has produced," Agnes declared, "intelligent, idealistic . . . uncomplicated in mind and attitude, and very, very frank." Two of her Chinese acquaintances were also in the city—Hu Shih of the "Biological Urge" (and the China League for Civil Rights) and the writer Lin Yutang—and Agnes got drunk with them. Hu Shih, who was presently China's ambassador to the United States, had taken to calling her "St. Agnes" for her fire-eating defense of China's poor.[37] Lin Yutang, she thought, was very much changed for the better. Since their early days together in Peking, she said, he had become "confident, smart, sophisticated, and a fierce patriot bitterly opposed to the limitation of the Atlantic Charter to white nations."

Agnes lunched with Lewis Gannett and exchanged information with ABMAC and various China relief officials. When the Overseas Press Club honored her at one of its functions, she caught up with the other Far Eastern correspondents and met several of their wives. "Goodness me!" Agnes wrote that one of them remarked in astonishment after being introduced. "I always expected to find you very ugly, but you're not so very." Joseph Barnes, a former Moscow correspondent who now directed the Office of War Information, hosted a dinner party for her at his home, and Agnes gleefully reported that he sent her off from the affair with "a big bundle of documents."[38]

An evening with Freda Utley was less successful. According to Agnes, Utley had become cynical and disillusioned in the years since she had left Hankow, and Agnes felt that because Utley had lost faith in everything, it bothered her that Agnes had not also discovered all civilization was rotten, all people motivated by the lowest objectives, and life itself degeneracy. Utley would recall their time together somewhat differently. She later wrote that Agnes's off-color jokes offended her, and she found it unseemly for a woman of fifty to be "boasting of her real and imagined conquests," as Agnes did. The experience left Utley wondering, as she wrote, whether Agnes was "trying to convince herself that her life had not been misspent in an abortive, self-sacrificing struggle for social justice, by demonstrating that she had also been a 'success' as a woman."[39]

Agnes did in fact have a new male companion: a poet and professor at New York University who was several years her junior. It was not a serious affair, though, and she still found politics vastly safer terrain. At a dinner celebrating India's declaration of independence, Agnes sat at the speaker's table with leading Indian activists and described it as old home week. There was not a man among them who did not know of her relationship with Chatto, and she was extremely flattered when they took possession of her as one of themselves, she reported. Roger Baldwin was toastmaster at the event, and he remained, Agnes reported,

> as handsome as the day. We stood in the big reception room and went through a regular rite which we have repeated in Germany, Moscow, China, and various cities in the U.S.A. He saw me, uttered a glad cry, held out his arms, and embraced and kissed me, then continued to hold on and chatter dear nothings. We finally separated and he introduced me to his watchful wife. I told her that Roger and I act like this on every continent, but immediately separate and forget each other until we meet again; then we repeat the process and say "good-bye," just like that.[40]

Her mood darkened as the winter of 1942–43 neared and the financial pressure on her mounted. The Theatre Guild had expressed interest in a play by her on China, Agnes wrote, but she could not work on anything substantial until she had finished revising her manuscript, and though Knopf was planning to send the final galleys to Warner Brothers and MGM, Agnes now realized that unless the book became a motion picture or a best seller, her fiscal prospects were only likely to worsen over time. She was already fifty; she would not be getting any younger. That November, as a money-saving measure, Agnes moved from her midtown hotel to a shabby residential facility on West Eighty-seventh Street where she had kitchen privileges. A bridge for her teeth and a winter coat set her back over two hundred dollars.

If worse came to worst, Agnes said, she would return to teaching when the book came out, but the idea of once again laboring at something she had so long ago rejected as insufficient depressed her. For the moment, she preferred to think that an article she was currently writing, on speculation, for the *New Yorker* about her 1933 encounter with George Bernard Shaw would generate some short term income. What Agnes would really have liked was to write a regular column on the Far East for a mainstream paper. However, she suspected that even if editors could get beyond her reputation as a radical, her confusion in the public mind with fellow leftist Anna Louise Strong, along with her gender, seriously damaged her case. An evening with Frances Gunther confirmed her latter concern.

Frances Gunther had been a correspondent in Europe and was a respected writer and speaker in her own right before she married John, she told Agnes, but she had received no credit for her years as her husband's assistant, and now that they were separated, only he was being hired as a commentator. Persuaded that Dorothy Thompson was the only woman at the moment who could beat out a man in this arena, Agnes, discouraged, put the idea to the side.

By January 1943, Agnes was borrowing money to get by. Her failure to "measure up," as she put it, humiliated her. During an evening out with Ernestine Evans, her editor on *Daughter of Earth*, Agnes vented her frustration, taking offense at Evans's claim of having discovered her, and misinterpreting Evans's offer of a cast-off suit as a suggestion that she "kow-tow" to Evans. She was not one of the "most worthy cases in New York City," Agnes said she haughtily informed her former editor.[41] In her correspondence with friends she enumerated the ways that putting her beliefs into practice, as Agnes described her career, made her superior. While Agnes had kicked up a row around the world, pursued by the police of several countries, Evans—along with Utley and Frances Gunther, Agnes added—was a self-important, dissatisfied woman who had never known what she wanted from life and lacked a central motivating passion like the one Agnes had known.

"We must weld the future with our efforts or there will be no future," Agnes advised her latest correspondent, a young hairdresser from southern California named Aino Taylor, who represented to Agnes the coming generation of women. "It is better ... to struggle and strive and fail, fail totally, rather than *not* to try ... Everything you do becomes new soil in which other things will grow." It was easier to drift with the tide, she knew, but she urged Aino to oppose the tendency to be mediocre or merely a "nice" woman. "We human beings live such a short time," she wistfully observed, "we must hurry and squeeze from life everything there is in it."

At the start of 1943, Agnes turned in her manuscript and found herself at loose ends. She was disgusted, she said, with loudmouthed, reactionary congressional representatives like Hamilton Fish and Martin Dies; sometimes she felt so alienated from American life it seemed as if she were living in a foreign country. Then that spring, while rereading Nehru's prison letters, Agnes discovered Thomas Jefferson. Enthralled with what she called his "universal genius," she declared him just the sort of American she wished to be considered: a militant democrat who fought the plutocracy to prevent corrupt, self-seeking men from exploiting the common people. Agnes loved *The Patriots*, a play about Jefferson's private life, and when she traveled to Washington to help China correspondent Betty Graham edit her book, Agnes visited Monticello and the new Jefferson Memorial and examined Jefferson's papers at the Library of Congress.

On her return to New York City, Agnes attended another of Blanche Knopf's cocktail parties, but by 1943 her interest in the celebrity party circuit was waning. She was too energetic and too broke, she said, to enjoy a pure life of the mind for any length of time. Recently, she wrote, Pearl Buck had mentioned that the reason she managed to get so much work done was that she lived in the country, so Agnes, swayed by Buck's logic, abruptly departed for upstate New York. Thorberg, who still lived a rather bohemian existence, was trying with mixed success to run a chicken farm in New Paltz, and over the next several months Agnes divided her time between Thorberg's home, New York City, and Washington, D.C., lecturing frequently on China.

Joseph Freeman was one of several prominent American progressives who came under her influence in this period. Freeman, who was so devastated by his recent break with the Party that he had contemplated suicide, saw Agnes as a model of how to remain true to one's youthful ideals and avoid the bitterness and cynicism that afflicted so many who left the Party, and often soured them on radicalism altogether. "You are a great, wonderful person," Freeman wrote after hearing her speak. "You make China live; you utter the most sublime hope of our times—and you are, miracle of miracles! Uncorrupted."[42]

Agnes was only too happy to help Freeman move beyond that "stooge organization rent with political racketeering" to which he had devoted the best years of his life, and she picked up the threads of their friendship on newly equal terms. The American Communist Party, she reminded him, was only part of the stream of American life; it was not *the* stream.[43] While she confessed to him that she had never been a member and was not privy to its inner workings, she said the CPUSA struck her as isolated nevertheless—both as a political party and from the American people. Today it might line up behind Mayor Hague of New Jersey; tomorrow it could support some "dog" like Congressman Dies. That was because the American Party was not rooted "in the necessities of American life, but only in the necessities of the Soviet Union." She still believed that the Soviet Union "must be defended to the last stone," she wrote, but she knew from her own experience how that country dealt with people who represented the

interests of other countries to the detriment of the Soviet Union, however justified their cause.[44]

The ostracism by Party members and their hostile attacks on Freeman's latest
book must be difficult, she wrote. She was quite familiar with the feelings, having lived through the same herself. It took a long time for those wounds to heal,
and she was still not over her own. She encouraged Freeman to seek solace, as
she did, in the broader spectrum of American life, and in the writings of
Thomas Jefferson and other exemplars of America's revolutionary tradition.
Their efforts to protect basic human liberties, Agnes wrote, still pointed the way
for people like themselves, and she took comfort in their example.

> Can't you feel that they are standing by your side, companions with you? Do
> you think they were not attacked and outcast as you, from men who were
> once their comrades? . . . My dear friend, do not waste energy and time on
> flagellation of your soul because you, a heretic, are outcast. Do not ever think
> of suicide. Get over these obsessions, for your mind is superior to the puerility
> that afflicts most of your former Party comrades. But do not—how dare I
> "advise you!"—allow personal suffering to blind you to the Communist prin-
> ciples of the new world. Let people persecute you, hound you. Pity them, "for
> they know not what they do."[45]

Sometimes, though, it was a Herculean task for Agnes to apply those profound sentiments to her own daily life. Haunted by the sense that old age was
creeping up on her, and that her lack of education limited her professional
prospects, she tried to keep her demons at bay by throwing herself into the
mindless absorption of physical labor on Thor's farm, candling eggs and gardening with a fury. Such efforts succeeded for a few months only. By June 1943,
Agnes was griping that the endless work had reinjured her back, that she lacked
time to write, that she was too weary to prepare any moneymaking lectures.
Thor, she said, was also impossible, quarreling endlessly with her husband and
resisting Agnes's efforts to put the farm in shape though saddling her with all the
responsibility.

Agnes appealed to Cowley and Gannett to help her get into Yaddo, a prestigious writers' colony in nearby Saratoga Springs where people were invited to
work for a few months without cost. There, freed from the need to earn her living, Agnes hoped to write, prepare her lectures, and try her hand at a drama. By
this time, Cowley had had his disagreements with Agnes and was uninterested
in pursuing a friendship. Agnes was ultimately a revolutionist, he later
explained, while he was ultimately a writer.[46] He was fond of her, though, and

wished her well in her literary endeavors. So did Gannett, who had played so vital a behind-the-scenes role in Agnes's upcoming book. Both men wrote in support of her application, ensuring her acceptance. Agnes arrived in Yaddo that July.

The seven-hundred-acre estate, set in the pine forests of the Adirondack Mountains, had originally been the private dwelling of the millionaire Trask family. These days, its forty-room mansion was occupied, in the evenings, by Agnes and a revolving set of artists and writers who spent their daylight hours cloistered in one of the dozens of private studios scattered across the property. With characteristic vigor, Agnes immediately embarked on a play, tentatively about a Chinese general who was troubled by his conscience. The form did not come easily to her, and by late afternoon she was ready to socialize. Cowley frequently stopped by for checkers, and Katherine Anne Porter, a dear friend of Thorberg's who lived nearby, befriended Agnes. Guests that summer included Margaret Walker, Carson McCullers, Jean Stafford, and Alfred Kantorowicz, along with two old friends of Agnes's: Karin Michaelis and Langston Hughes.

Yaddo guests, 1943. Seated: Isabella Howland, Margaret Walker, Jean Stafford, Harold Shapiro, Tomaras Kerr, Agnes Smedley, Karin Michaelis, Carson McCullers, Alfred Kantorowicz. Standing: Kappo Phelan, Elizabeth Ames, Rebecca Pitts, Paul Zucker, Hans Sahl, Langston Hughes. *Yaddo Papers, Manuscripts and Archives Division, The New York Public Library, Astor, Lenox and Tilden Foundations.*

Michaelis, now seventy-two and white-haired, was thrilled to see Agnes, whom she had never expected to meet again, and joined her regularly in town for cocktails or ice cream. Even in this distinguished company, Michaelis reported, Agnes remained the center of the crowd. Defiantly *not* urbane, she got drunk and bawdy at cocktail parties and performed or told stories of her life in China, her "fresh, irresistible laughter" echoing in the oversized rooms.[47] Coeds at nearby Skidmore College, where Agnes used the library, declared her "more vibrant than a 'Congress' thriller... and more intoxicating than a Worden beer."[48]

Agnes was fond of sneaking off with Hughes to the local black church, where they delivered political sermons and distributed tomatoes from the Yaddo garden. The freedom with which Agnes volunteered Hughes's time to edit high school poetry or chaperone visiting inner-city youth might well have distressed him, but Agnes compensated with openhearted gestures like her angry public refusal to join the international writers' association PEN because it did not admit African Americans as members—an act that apparently resulted in an invitation for Hughes to join its executive board.[49]

Except for the mosquitoes, Agnes's first few weeks at Yaddo were a perfect summer idyll of singing birds and chirping crickets, hard work, good times, and high expectations. *Battle Hymn of China,* Agnes's forthcoming memoir, went into its third printing even before its publication, and because interest in China was very strong, Agnes said, both MGM and Warner Brothers were seriously considering whether to develop *China Fights Back* as well as *Battle Hymn* into films. But all was not well for long with Agnes. It never was. On July 16, a Mr. Pettigrew from the FBI telephoned Thorberg and said he wanted to speak with Agnes the next time she came down to New York City.

All the bureau had on Agnes at this point was lists of the front organizations and publications with which she had been associated, and some clippings on her escapades in China provided by a miscellany of informants and private intelligence agencies. Most of the materials had already been made available to the Dies Committee, the Special House Committee for the Investigation of Un-American Activities. But Agnes did not know what their files contained, and she was apprehensive. Who was this Pettigrew? she asked Freeman and Baldwin. What department of the FBI did he represent? Was she within her legal rights to refuse to answer questions on political issues other than the Nazis or the Japanese? Could she be subject to arrest? Of course, she argued, she had no idea what the FBI's interest in her was, but she doubted it had anything to do with the Nazis or the Japanese.[50]

After receiving ample reassurances that she did not have to say anything that could potentially incriminate her, Agnes agreed to meet with the FBI in her publisher's office during a round of prepublication interviews. There, she later told a friend, she confined her statements to "certain Americans and Britons in the service of Japanese imperialism."[51] Any sense of security she gained from the exercise was false. In the spring of 1943, Agnes's name had appeared in a German newspaper article in connection with the Shanghai phase of Sorge's ring. On August 13, U.S. Army Intelligence opened a file on her in relation to the case.[52]

For the time being, though, life went on as usual. On the thirty-first, Agnes returned to Yaddo, where guests had a party waiting to celebrate her book's release. *Battle Hymn of China* appeared to rave reviews a week later. Critics agreed that while she had retained the same emotional loyalties she always had, Agnes had managed in this book to capture contemporary China in all its complexity.[53] They found her depiction of the country and the people's efforts to resist Japan—while their old society rotted away and a new one struggled to be born—as moving as anything yet written on China.

Battle Hymn was not just the best book on China, one correspondent commented—it was the "only" book on China, dwarfing all others in its authenticity.[54] He only hoped that the Chinese Communist leaders would not let their disagreements with Agnes, or the few cutting remarks she had made about them in her book, prevent them from recognizing her accomplishment in the international

Portrait circa 1943. *Courtesy Agnes Smedley Collection, University Archives, Arizona State University.*

battle against fascism, the place she had accorded the Chinese people in it, and the appreciation she inspired for those inside and outside China who attempt to move the world forward.

Agnes's "great and gallant" character also came in for praise. Reviewers admired her commitment to working for a better world, her trust in mankind's innate goodness, and her faith in the possibility of peace and justice on earth. Pointing to passages like the following, they suggested that Agnes's acceptance of the Chinese people's burdens as her own fell more within the tradition of Christian martyrs than within any Communist theory.

> As the light increased and the fog lifted we entered a market town on the shores of a great lake. Only three or four old men and women and a few children remained behind; all the rest of the population had rowed far out on the bosom of the lake. One of the old women took a huge brass gong, beat it, and bawled like a foghorn to the people on the lake: "Come back! Come back!"
>
> They came back and gathered about us in joy, but their excitement was greatest when they saw me . . . I heard men trying to decide whether I was a man or a woman, American, German, or English. One woman pulled back her little child in fear and declared: "She has eyes like a cat!"
>
> My little Kuo-hwa could not endure this. He stood up before them and cried: "She does *not* have eyes like a cat! She is a woman and our American friend! She helps our wounded! In Tingjiachun she found a wounded man and fed him and gave him a bath. She even helped him do all his business."
>
> The people turned their eyes on me in amazement. My "son" would not stop. "Look at her bandaged hand!" he demanded, taking my hand in his. "She got this when she picked up a pan of hot water while she was bathing a wounded soldier. She is both my father and my mother! If any of you are sick, she will cure you."[55]

In *Battle Hymn*, Agnes admitted aiding German espionage efforts during World War I, when she had collaborated with the Indian revolutionaries (who, she now also acknowledged, had received money from the German government), but such comments scarcely raised an eyebrow outside the FBI.[56] And with American Communists solidly behind the war, even Party stalwarts like Fred Field conceded that Agnes had written one of the most important books of her generation, albeit she was guilty of making "political howlers" and unqualified to speak on subjects like the CPUSA.[57]

The only passage that provoked controversy was the one in which Agnes described her relationship to the Communists: Russian, Chinese, and American. "For years I listened to the Communists with sympathy," she had written, "and in later years in China I gave them my active support, but I could never place my life and mind unquestioningly at the disposal of their leaders. I never believed that I was especially wise, but I could not become a mere instrument in the hands of men who believed that they held the one and only key to truth."[58]

Party followers like Jaffe, who had worked closely with Agnes for years, were shocked. He insisted that Agnes could not have written those lines because they employed "the language of critics of Lenin and Stalin"—which she was not. Anna Louise Strong, who, according to Agnes, had participated in the Party's proscription of *China Fights Back*, was not surprised; she lost no time informing Agnes that she was "rotten" for writing what she had and warned her that she "would come to no good end" as a result.[59] Harold Isaacs, who had experienced the duplicity of Agnes's statement firsthand, would resentfully observe that after telling and accepting as many lies as she had, Agnes "had many layers of sludge to dig through" before she could make such a claim.[60] Most readers accepted Agnes at her word—that she was neither a Communist nor a blind follower of the party line. Both were true enough, by this time.

The positive reception that greeted *Battle Hymn* brought Agnes additional opportunities. Already a gifted public speaker, she became a sought-after radio guest. NBC and the Canadian Broadcasting Network aired radio dramatizations of *Battle Hymn* and *China Fights Back* (even though one producer insisted on transforming Agnes into "Mr. Scott" before allowing her character to march with the Chinese guerrillas). When the politically progressive Book Find Club chose *Battle Hymn* as its fall selection, Agnes's speaking schedule became more crowded still. All this left little time for Agnes to pursue her literary life, but Yaddo was rather empty since America had entered the war, and manager Elizabeth Ames, grateful for Agnes's help nursing her dying sister, invited Agnes to stay on another year.

Despite her numerous outside engagements, Agnes managed to complete a draft of her drama. Its story line now revolved around a romance between a character modeled on her and a Chinese officer based on Chung Yi, whom Agnes called Major General Chou Tien-ying.[61] Several who read her first draft questioned whether an American audience would accept an intimate relationship between a Caucasian and a Chinese and suggested she bring in an "Evans Carlson figure" instead, but Agnes refused to alter the race of her heroine's love interest. She compromised by having her Chinese commander spurn his Western paramour instead, but even then Agnes knew the characters still needed work, and her script remained too "talky" to submit to the Theatre Guild any time soon.

Further revisions would have to wait, though, until she completed an extensive lecture tour through the South. She counted on its financial success, she wrote her old friend Ellen Kennan, to restore her sense of dignity. By late October, Agnes was instructing her "privileged Anglo Saxon audiences," as she described her listeners at universities and civic organizations throughout Georgia, Tennessee, Alabama, Louisiana, and Texas, that they were not God's chosen people. After the war was over, she warned them, a new civilization would emerge in Asia that was free of racial bias. In the new China, everyone would be equal.

The jarring poverty that was so commonplace in the segregated communities of the South caught Agnes unawares; the atmosphere struck her as being as menacing as any war zone. The prejudice, the name calling, the secret societies that murdered entire families of "uppity" Negroes in the dead of night reminded Agnes of the *Fememord* (or political murder) gangs that had preceded the rise of Hitler. If Jesus himself had traveled through the south, she declared, he would have been "run out of town or locked up in the hoosegow."[62]

The tour cleared Agnes's debts, but she told Hughes when she returned to Yaddo that what she had seen was so awful she felt guilty for not trying to stop it. She did, however, share her impressions in a fiery article for the Baltimore *Afro-American*, with which Hughes was affiliated.

On a visit to New York City that she made around this time, Agnes received two disturbing pieces of news. The first came from Chatto's nephew, who reported that the family had learned definitively that Chatto had been killed in the purges — information Agnes found so upsetting she insisted that it might still be only rumor, that his reputation in India had perhaps kept him alive. She insisted Ella Winter look into it the next time she went to Moscow. The second item was an article in the *New York Times* reporting that Richard Sorge had been sentenced to death in Tokyo for Soviet espionage, along with a Japanese member of the ring (Ozaki).[63] Jaffe, who later claimed he was with Agnes when she saw the piece, said she nearly fainted when she read it.

Already reeling as she headed out for the next leg of her lecture tour, Agnes was in no condition to cope with the accusation, aired during a debate at the Chicago Council on Foreign Relations, that she was a Communist who had tried to establish a "Communist empire" in Sian. The charge sounded suspiciously like the handiwork of a pugnacious new critic named Alfred Kohlberg. Although the U.S. was pouring vast sums of money and arms into China in order to win the war, General Joseph Stilwell, Chiang Kai-shek's American adviser and a friend of Agnes's from Hankow, was reporting increasing frustration with Nationalist armies sitting tight in defensive positions. Agnes, along with other progressive China experts inside and outside the State Department, complained that Chungking had largely suspended its war against the Japanese and was hoarding American contributions for eventual use against domestic opponents. She was also airing widespread reports that graft and corruption in

Chiang's regime might lead to the government's collapse. Kohlberg, a prosperous importer of Chinese embroideries, had returned from a trip to China convinced that such accusations were either unfounded or greatly exaggerated, and he felt duty bound to expose those who believed them as part of a "Communist conspiracy."[64]

By the time she got to Boston, Agnes was fretting about a heart attack, insomnia, an ulcer, gall bladder problems, low blood sugar, and her nerves. She completed most of her tour, but she was miserable. For the first time in her life, she objected to traveling. Sleeping in overheated Pullmans and rushing to catch trains or buses while dragging around luggage was no longer fun for her. On her return to Yaddo she promptly retreated to her bed.

In the spring of 1944, Agnes brought in the novelist Leonard Erlich to collaborate with her on her play. The project was not going well. In the years since she had written *Daughter of Earth*, Agnes had expended much of the creative fire that might have made her a great imaginative writer on more active involvements. Now she could not do it; she was in over her head. At summer's end, Agnes turned over everything she had written to Katherine Anne Porter to critique and instructed Ehrlich to complete it himself.[65] By fall, Agnes had returned to more familiar modes of self-expression.

The decision by Stalin, Roosevelt, and Churchill the previous winter to focus more on the Normandy invasion had reduced the significance of China in the war effort. During that time, the country's incipient civil war had intensified, unacknowledged, while a new Japanese offensive crushed the Chinese. Many in China were losing faith in Chiang's regime and its ability to resist the foreign invaders. Chungking officials, however, remained focused on the Nationalists' blockade of the Communist armies; they blamed Chiang's recent failures against Japan on Stilwell.

During the fall of 1944, skirmishing broke out between Communist and Nationalist forces. As the crisis in China mounted, Agnes's pungent analyses— of Chiang's scapegoating of Stilwell to divert attention from his own misrule, and America's role in bolstering the crumbling regime— appeared in the *New Republic*, the *Nation*, and *P.M.*, a fledgling progressive daily. Her reports on the Generalissimo's reluctance to end China's one-party dictatorship and establish the democratic coalition government Chinese Communists sought to advance long-promised national reconstruction restored Agnes to the good graces of CCP political leaders. They sent Agnes gifts, wrote her that "her past deeds [we]re all forgotten," according to Madame Sun, and invited her to visit them again.[66] Along with her higher profile, however, there were some negatives.

Kohlberg's objections to Agnes's "inadequate and distorted" versions of the tensions between the Kuomintang and the Chinese Communists and of political problems in China were no secret.[67] Weeks after her first round of articles appeared, KMT propagandists hired by Madame Chiang Kai-shek and other high Chinese officials on a recent visit seemed to pick up where Kohlberg left off. On October 25, 1944, as their campaign to induce conservative American Republicans, clergy, and newspapers—through various methods—to brand as "Red inspired" American reports that criticized the Chinese government and silence those who wrote them gained momentum, J. Edgar Hoover ordered the FBI's Albany field office to open an investigation of Agnes, "inasmuch as she has been for many years a notorious Communist expert on the Far East," he wrote.[68]

The agency did not plan to interview her directly, but it began to monitor her activities, collect articles by and on her, and cull information from government agencies and informants. Yaddo secretary Mary Townsend proved particularly helpful to them, providing drafts of Agnes's speeches, descriptions of her conversations with other guests, and the contents of her mail.[69] Muenzenberg was no longer alive (his "suicide" in 1940, after breaking with the Comintern, is widely suspected to be the handiwork of the NKVD), but Townsend reported that Agnes remained in contact with Muenzenberg's controversial former lieutenant, Otto Katz, along with other operatives and writers in and around the Muenzenberg stable including Egon Erwin Kisch, Bodo Uhse, Paul Merker, Anna Segher, and Ludwig Renn, who were sitting out the war in Mexico.[70]

During the 1944 election campaigns that fall, Agnes was active in the National Citizens Political Action Committee and appeared with Katherine Anne Porter at several Democratic rallies for Roosevelt in upstate New York. She also volunteered Porter's services for other political and charitable functions, including relief drives for China. Porter, like Hughes, did not seem to mind. "There is something so touchingly warm and good in Agnes, her heart is so tender and her thoughts so wild," Porter later wrote, that "it makes very little difference to me what she says or does politically: her feelings are right no matter how misled her acts, some of them."[71] Agnes found Porter similarly congenial, and the women ushered in 1945 with songs and a drunken ballet they performed in the Yaddo ballroom.

At the beginning of 1945, Porter left for Hollywood. Agnes sorely missed her, but she had little time to look back. These days her lectures provided her livelihood, and the first few months of the year were a blur of cities and engagements. America's views on Chiang Kai-shek and the CCP were crystallizing, and Agnes spoke frequently on the Chinese Communists' proposal to replace Chiang Kai-shek's one-person, one-party dictatorship with a program of democratic reform and have their joint military forces fight the Japanese. She was especially popular with college students and addressed audiences at Vassar, Harvard, Columbia, and elsewhere.

Her most colorful engagement during this period, however, was a debate with Lin Yutang and Representative Walter Judd for the radio program *Town Hall Meeting on the Air*. Not long ago, Lin had been critical of America's and Great Britain's Far East policy for being predicated on the West's domination of the East. Then Agnes had counted him a friend. Recently, though, Lin had returned to China for a trip through the area controlled by the KMT, and he came back to the United States an ardent supporter of Chiang. His change of heart made Agnes ready to fight him before the program even started.

On the air, she demanded to know why Lin did not simply tell the public flat out that he represented the Military Affairs Commission of the Chinese government and had received "a big fat check in American dollars from a Chinese government bank for his trip."[72] Lin turned pale, she said, and lunged at her while screaming he would sue her for libel. After the broadcast, Agnes continued the debate with Judd, but Lin, she said, was so angry he left the studio immediately after the program. Emily Hahn was also in the audience, but Agnes refused to speak to that "bitch," since she had announced her opposition to the CCP. All in all, though, Agnes reported, she had enjoyed herself immensely, and she said the producers assured her they had never had a more exciting meeting.

Agnes returned to Yaddo in April 1945. Worn down and in poor health, she vowed to put her lecturing days behind her forever. She had earned only a thousand dollars for her efforts. "Think of your weekly income!" she wrote Porter in Hollywood. For herself, though, Agnes wanted nothing further to do with the movie industry. Despite much talk by MGM and Warners the previous year about lucrative movie adaptations of *Battle Hymn* and *China Fights Back*, and gossip column reports that Bette Davis would produce the latter, in the end, according to Agnes, the studios had simply stolen whatever they wanted from her books for their China projects without paying her a penny.[73] They were all thieves, as far as she was concerned, who had sensed she was an easy mark and taken advantage of her. She advised Porter to hoard her current earnings from MGM and then get back to work on her book.

By this time, Elizabeth Ames had invited Agnes to make Yaddo her permanent home. She lived alone in an abandoned farmhouse on the property, where she hoped to resume her oft-interrupted biography of Chu Teh. Unlike some of the other guests, Agnes was not bothered by the lack of creature comforts. The arrangement also limited her contact with the odd and solitary Ames, whom Agnes said had begun to "press in on her." But if she had found playwriting difficult, biography proved even more daunting. Agnes had a clear enough vision of

Christmas postcard to Katherine Anne Porter, 1945. *Papers of Katherine Anne Porter, Special Collections, University of Maryland Libraries.*

what she wanted to accomplish, but the project brought out all her insecurities about her sketchy theoretical training and haphazard schooling.

That spring, Agnes heard from her sister Myrtle. She was dying of cancer and wanted Agnes to travel west so they could say good-bye. Instead, Agnes sent money and urged her sister to come to New York that winter to see Agnes's play performed onstage. Agnes explained to friends that the trip served no purpose since she could not save her sister, while she could serve millions by writing her book, but Myrtle's impending death was also an uncomfortable reminder that the differences that separated them would probably never be bridged and that Agnes was mortal herself. Hypochondriac that she was, Agnes reacted by fretting that she had cancer, too. When Myrtle died that May, Agnes maintained that she was too busy and broke to attend the funeral.

The war ended on August 14, but Agnes was uninterested in celebrating the Allied victory. She feared the war's aftermath would be worse than the war itself. As she saw it, the real fight against fascism had only just begun—and nowhere was this truer than in China. Looking back, Agnes believed she had been too soft on the Chinese Nationalists in *Battle Hymn* and perhaps concealed too many of the KMT's "most glaring evils." Now she wanted Americans to know that Chiang Kai-shek had been trying "to drown the peasant revolution in its own blood" for nearly twenty years and sought American support for his "vile purposes."[74]

Why, she asked in numerous articles, speeches, and letters to President Truman, was America supporting the Chungking government with massive assistance and American troops—even as Chiang's corrupt regime lost the support of the Chinese people? Why did her native land, with its own roots in revolution, need to serve "as the bulwark of world reaction" and try to strangle China's, backing a policy so dangerous it would plunge China into renewed civil war? The Chinese Communists did not represent only themselves, she argued; they represented every progressive element in China. Their call for a coalition government, the election of a national assembly, and the formation of a Joint High Command to which Communists and Nationalists alike would surrender their armies would merely complete the bourgeois democratic revolution Sun Yat-sen had started.

As opposition developed to America's China policy, Agnes pressed General Stilwell, who had been recalled from China, to join her in battle. He was reluctant to speak out. Once he retired, he told her, he planned to holler his head off.[75] For the moment, he remained in the U.S. military—unhappily, at a desk job in Washington, D.C. Besides, he told her, what she really needed was "a smoothie," and he did not qualify for that. "But I'll cheer for you," Stilwell wrote. "I respect front line soldiers, and the title fits you—keep your sense of humor and remember 'Illegitimus non Carburundum'—Don't let the bastards grind you down!"

Agnes's beloved friend Evans Carlson willingly entered the fray. After Pearl Harbor, he had returned to the U.S. Marine Corps, where he used the "gung ho" principles of ethical indoctrination he had learned in the Eighth Route Army to lead his Raider battalion to glory at Makin and Guadalcanal—before being relieved from command for his unorthodox ideas. Now a retired brigadier general, Carlson lent his name and reputation to the Committee for a Democratic Far Eastern Policy, a front organization established in the summer of 1945 to protest the continuation of America's wartime program of economic and military assistance to the Chinese Nationalist government and rally support for the Chinese Communists. Several progressive China hands including Edgar Snow were active in the organization, but Agnes, with her stormy relationship to the American Party, was not invited to join them.

By November 1945, negotiations between the Chinese Communists and Nationalists had collapsed. President Truman dispatched General George C. Marshall to stave off civil war, but Agnes did not think he could accomplish anything. When all was said and done, she gravely doubted America would resist the powerful interests that supported the KMT government, or that Chiang Kai-shek would surrender his position without a violent struggle.

CHAPTER 17

The Cold War

In the . . . prewar years of 1929–1939 . . . we are dealing . . . with a conspiratorial epoch in the history of modern China . . . Most of the old wheelhorses of the American Communist Party appear to have been operating in Shanghai, in one period or another, the "professionals" of the clandestine fraternity, as well as mere acolytes and dupes, who are flirting with the Red menace . . . in the bistros of the French Concession, in the furtive rendezvous of the Shanghai conspirators.

MAJOR GENERAL CHARLES A. WILLOUGHBY

B Y MARCH 1946, agents involved in the FBI investigation of Agnes had gathered information from over two hundred people and dozens of organizations and publications. They had discovered one of the books she published in the Soviet Union, several of her aliases, and a great deal regarding her 1918 arrest. Although Agnes had not violated any U.S. law, they had dogged every step of her lecture tours and vigorously pursued a claim that she was "armed at all times with a pistol of sufficient caliber to kill a human being."[1] More significantly, they had learned that in years past Agnes had written extensively for what agents termed the "propaganda branch of the Comintern" and that a "Communist organization," as they described it, had distributed some of her German-language work.[2] Despite the zeal with which the FBI pursued what was essentially a harassment campaign of Agnes for her political beliefs, agents did not realize that they had come upon Muenzenberg's network. Unaware of his significance in Agnes's life, they failed to follow up on the lead.

Whittaker Chambers, who had left the Comintern underground and broken with the CPUSA, had advised the agency that Agnes was a Communist even if she was not a Party member and that she had been "a common sight" on the ninth floor of Party headquarters during her 1934 U.S. visit, in close contact with the Comintern intelligence operative J. Peters.[3] After scrutinizing Agnes for more than a year, however, agents had turned up little suspect activity in her current life beyond her public championing of the Chinese Communists and the Soviet cause in Asia. Reduced to grumbling about her "mannish" appearance and "boyish" bob, the FBI downgraded its investigation to a "pending inactive" status.[4] Surveillance of Agnes would henceforth be limited to when she lectured or traveled.

The FBI did, however, pass on copies of its internal reports to Army Intelligence, which was proceeding with an investigation of its own. Before he was put to death, Sorge had made a confession that named Agnes as one of his main assistants in the Shanghai phase of his ring. After V-J Day, General MacArthur's Far East Command had obtained a copy of his statement. Since then, American occupation authorities and foreign newsmen stationed in Tokyo had been piecing together Agnes's role in Sorge's operations, relying on Japanese police interrogations, court records, and the confessions of captured ring members. The information they gathered was compelling.

In prison, Sorge had confessed that in China, Agnes had been his most valued assistant, that she had introduced him to many of the people he used in his ring and provided her home in the French Concession as a rendezvous for members. He said he had forwarded information Agnes had collected, including material on American activities in China and the effect of Sino-American relations on the tense Sino-Japanese situation, to Moscow, where he said he had "registered her with Comintern headquarters."[5]

Sorge's radio operator, Max Klausen, had also identified Agnes as a member of the Shanghai ring. Ozaki Hotsumi had described the Sino-Japanese intelligence group she had directed in north China, along with her work for the International Red Aid and on the Noulens case. Like Sorge, he recalled Agnes as a person of unusual ability: loyal to her principles, fervent in her convictions, and a selfless, zealous worker. A proponent of international Communism, Ozaki explained, Agnes had sought to serve the Comintern, the Russian Communist Party, and the Soviet government, "the three forming one composite whole."[6]

Nothing that linked Agnes to the Sorge ring had appeared yet in the American press, but surviving group members like Kawai, who had been released from prison at the end of the war, were beginning to tell their stories. As the Japanese considered whom to blame for their recent past, and whom to praise for fighting to prevent it, the suggestion made by Ozaki's attorney and Communist colleagues that Ozaki was a patriot, not a traitor, appealed to the national imagination.[7] On the first anniversary of Ozaki's death in the fall of 1945, Ozaki's friends honored him with a ceremony at which they called him a national martyr murdered by Japanese militarists and fascists. At the event, they mentioned that Ozaki had described Agnes as a "friend" in his prison letters to his wife.[8] Japanese newspapers, interested in the popular case, carried the item; a Tokyo acquaintance apprised Agnes.

Agnes must already have been quite worried, then, when Ozaki's friends approached her not long after to share her memories of Ozaki for inclusion in a collection of his prison letters they planned to publish.[9] Agnes declined. She was "involved in the Ozaki case in Japan," she noted vaguely to Colonel Raymond Robins, an American reformer and former diplomatic official with whom she had begun corresponding, and could say nothing until she understood just how much the police knew.[10] She expressed concern that America's "secret police" would use information obtained from Japanese files as evidence against her.

Agnes was confident that Ozaki had died without betraying any secrets, but what about the others? she wondered. What else about the ring was known? And by whom? Like other American leftists, whose recall of the nation's first Red Scare was still fresh, Agnes was concerned that at some point in the not too distant future "fascists" in the country would begin again to round up radicals and place them under arrest, and she was terrified that if U.S. authorities discovered her ties to Ozaki, she would be among the first they sought. Agnes told those who inquired into why she seemed so distressed that the hardships of her life in China had left her weary and dispirited. She attempted to burn off her anxiety in rigorous manual labor, but she quarreled with the other Yaddo writers, and neither the reissue of *Daughter of Earth* in Germany nor Malcolm Cowley's desire to write an article on the book's enduring appeal lifted her spirits.

Peg Snow was aware of Agnes's mounting unease, although she did not know its cause. She suggested that Agnes use her Quaker heritage as a shield against any future "reactionary attacks." Agnes had the Quaker conscience, Peg had told her, and like the Quakers refused to compromise even with herself. But Agnes resisted, for the moment, what she described as the "trick" of stepping out as one of the master race.

Throughout the spring of 1946, she continued to lecture on the Chinese Communists' burgeoning fight. She was disgusted with Stilwell's successor, General Patrick Hurley. He was an "ignorant, reactionary menace," in her opinion, who was making all the wrong decisions. With touching naiveté, she asked Robins to set up a meeting for her with his friend Senator Claude Pepper, through whom she hoped to wangle an introduction to President Truman. Truman needed someone like herself, she said, "to look him in the eye, and tell him what dangers we are running in China."[11]

That summer, Eastern Europe "went Red" under Soviet occupation. During this time, Chiang Kai-shek violated his agreement with General Marshall and ordered a general offensive against the Communist-controlled areas. As the civil war in China resumed, the U.S. Congress passed a bill that promised Chiang an additional loan of half a billion dollars in military assistance. Agnes was sickened by what she considered America's lost opportunity in China. The year

At the microphone. *Maud Russell Papers, Manuscripts and Archives Division, The New York Public Library, Astor, Lenox and Tilden Foundations.*

before, she wrote, when the Japanese had surrendered and the KMT government was weak, the United States had sent American troops and military supplies to prop up Chiang Kai-shek's "rotten and corrupt" dictatorship. It should have refused him aid until a coalition democratic government had been established. The decision was an infamous betrayal of the Chinese people, as she saw it. Well-intentioned Americans reading reports of government gangsterism and corruption in China might think General Marshall had been outwitted, or that the United States had miscalculated its postwar China policy, she wrote, but the Chinese people knew to their cost, she wrote for the *Nation*, "that our 'blundering' has all been in the direction of reaction."[12]

Now that China's Communist leaders had forgiven her, Agnes considered returning to that country, where, she said, she had known "spiritual exultation" and passed what she recalled as the best years of her life, but her memory of what had happened was not so poor that she was in a hurry to go. She was pleased enough when Chu Teh wrote to assure her that her wish to return could be realized "over time,"—that is, when the civil war concluded with the Communist victory he confidently predicted.[13] But when friends in Shanghai urged Agnes to come at once, she demurred, saying she doubted the State Department would give her a passport, or the Chinese Embassy issue her a visa.

Agnes spoke of her plan to rejoin the Chinese Communists when she finished her biography of Chu Teh. Then, like Penelope, she made sure she did not complete it. The book was under contract with Knopf, and Edgar Snow had agreed to edit it, but Agnes was vexed by the form, and she allowed her China activities to throw her endlessly off schedule.

In November 1946, Americans responded to Soviet aggression in Eastern Europe with fear and resistance, electing the first Republican Congress since the days of Herbert Hoover. As this postwar mood began to sweep the country, Agnes maintained that anyone with even liberal ideas was being called a fellow traveler, if not an outright Red. People like Henry Wallace and her dear friend Evans Carlson, who was running for the Senate in California, were trying to fight the reaction, she wrote, but they were too weak financially to compete with Luce's magazines or the conservative newspaper chains, and their inability to make a significant dent on public opinion left Americans swallowing "the most amazingly superficial propaganda."

She was not entirely wrong. Despite numerous accounts of Chinese Communist achievements in dismantling the country's feudal system—land reforms that freed people from crushing rents, taxes, and interest fees, and much-needed social, political, and economic improvements, along with better provisions for basic needs like food and clothing in areas the Communists controlled—most Americans continued to overestimate Chiang's popular support and ignore the weaknesses in his leadership. Accustomed to thinking of the Chinese as allies who welcomed American Christianity, medical aid, and political ideas, Americans underestimated the Chinese people's desire for serious change, and they considered China's revolution nearly done when it had only just started.

Newly elected congressional leaders announced their intention to insist on a Chinese government without the Chinese Communists. Pushing back, Agnes worked hard for the Committee for a Democratic Far Eastern Policy, drawing crowds at its rallies and contributing articles to its publication, but she said the fight to alter America's China policy was increasingly hard and bitter. These days, she wrote, the War and Naval departments, not the State Department, determined American foreign relations with China, and they were controlled— at the top—by "agents of the great banks and corporations." There was a serious storm brewing inside the United States, she opined, led by powerful reactionary forces; it would break within a year. In the meantime she chose to speak out. At her lectures, she would point to men in the audience whom she believed to be FBI agents and announce that she knew she was being "marked down for a concentration camp ... but that it was the duty of every American to fight up to the last moment, standing firmly on our Bill of Rights."[14]

In January 1947, Agnes left Yaddo for a series of lectures in New York, Chicago, and Boston. In Boston, she would also undergo tests for cancer at the Lahey Clinic. During a talk at Harvard, Agnes got into what she described as "a fierce and ugly fight" with Arthur Schlesinger, who accused her of whitewashing the actions of the Chinese Communists and ignoring their totalitarian goal. Agnes wrote that on this occasion her host, John Fairbank, who chaired Harvard's Chinese department, bailed her out. However, when an Army Intelligence agent confronted her after her lecture at the University of Chicago, she was on her own.

Agnes said she answered his questions, but the event worried her, and she confessed to Robins that she "rather expected" she would soon be ordered to appear before a revitalized House Committee on Un-American Activities, which after nearly a decade in existence was launching multiple investigations into Communist infiltration of various industries. Agnes boldly posited that she preferred prison to recognizing the "inquisition" that was replacing America's court system. Privately, though, she seemed panicked—seemingly to the point where she thought she might need to flee to the USSR. Resisting Robins's advice to seek legal counsel and ignoring his suggestions on how to behave if called, Agnes turned to the Soviet consul general, Jacob Lomakin.

On February 13, she wrote Robins that she had decided to "drop in and greet Mr. Lomakin" while she was in New York City.[15] In her breezy recounting, she "rolled into the Consulate around 12 and sent up a scrawled note." Lomakin invited her to come up. Later they went out for lunch and "sat talking until 3 p.m." Then he walked with her downtown, where she had an engagement. Agnes did not reveal to Robins the content of their conversation, but she noted that if her recent tests at the Lahey Clinic indicated cancer, Lomakin had invited her to "go to Moscow and be cured."[16] Shortly thereafter, Yaddo secretary Mary Townsend informed the FBI of various arrangements Agnes had made for Lomakin to visit her at Yaddo.

By the spring of 1947, the Chinese Communist armies (recently renamed the People's Liberation Armies) were winning victory after victory. Agnes's former collaborator Chen Han-seng, who was in the United States as Chou En-lai's liaison to the American Communist Party, telephoned her twice with exultant reports. The untimely death of Evans Carlson, who suffered a fatal heart attack during a discussion with presidential hopeful Henry Wallace, overshadowed the good news. Agnes, who had thought Carlson's heart condition was, like her own, not of physical "but of spiritual origin," as she put it, "rooted in sorrow and suffering," was shattered.

Carlson's associate Jimmy Roosevelt prodded the Marine Corps into giving Carlson a traditional military funeral and burial at Arlington Cemetery. Agnes returned from the ceremony out of sorts, convinced that Carlson had not been properly respected. She had sent flowers from herself and the Committee for a

Democratic Far Eastern Policy and wreaths in the names of Madame Sun, Chu Teh, and Edgar Snow, who lay hospitalized in Paris, but the Marine Corps had not publicized the funeral, Madame Sun was the only Chinese who sent condolences, and her and Carlson's mutual friend Sir Archibald Clark-Kerr, now Lord Inverchapel and the British ambassador in Washington, had avoided the event, explaining that he could not afford politically to be associated with Carlson. The behavior of CPUSA members in attendance also maddened her. They had not even waited for Carlson to be buried, Agnes protested, before asking his widow to let CPUSA officials use her name as they had her husband's.[17]

Something in Agnes seemed to die with Carlson. She could not come to terms with the loss. She kept recalling his visit to Yaddo the previous autumn, when he had wandered Agnes's hallway in his plum-colored bathrobe, speaking his languid drawl, laughing his slow laugh. Many responsible people, Agnes wrote Porter, had thought him "the only man on the political horizon who might capture the imagination of the American common people." Now he was gone. If anything happened to Snow, she warned him, then she wished to die, too. She had no desire "to be the last leaf of the tree."

Snow encouraged Agnes to proceed with the work the three of them had entered on in China. He wrote:

> You must get back to the biography, Agnes, which is more important than ever, and wherein you can write your own testament to Carlson and his work ... That too is part of our task, that the lessons life and friends teach us shall not be lost altogether.
>
> I am determined when I next come home to take an active part in politics, partly out of a sense of duty to Evans to help carry on a little of his interrupted efforts. You too must do the same. I don't agree with you that this is a time for people like us, to whom the world has given rare opportunities to learn far beyond [our] own capacity to assimilate and project—to view America pessimistically. I have a feeling that once we have had ... a shock (which is surely coming) we will draw upon all the knowledge and the best tradition in our past and provide the world with new hope and leadership. We must believe that.[18]

Agnes did not share Snow's optimism. Given the meager skills with which she had embarked on her life journey, she wrote, she was reasonably content with her accomplishments as a writer. Still, she felt that the time when her words could have much impact on her country had passed, and she viewed her biography of Chu as a burden. The world had changed so dramatically in the few years since World War II, she explained, and not for the better. Corporate profits were at an all-time high, but rapidly rising prices were forcing workers to spend their wartime savings, and anyone who was not an outright reactionary was being called a Communist—a technique, according to Agnes, that had already forced eight hundred men from the War Department.

Having lived in Weimar Germany in the years before Hitler assumed power, Agnes could not help but compare the situation there to the present political climate in America. Some progressives in the United States, she wrote, hoped that the anticipated passage of the most reactionary labor bill in the nation's history would disgust people enough to step forward and fight Congress, but she had heard that kind of talk before, and no resistance had emerged. Like John Brown, she observed, who had lit the flame of war in the antislavery movement by turning abolitionists' beliefs into actions, the American people had to *do* something to repel the rising reactionary tide. "Fascists . . . will not stop unless someone stops them," she advised. Most Americans, she feared, lacked the conviction to stop the "powerful gang of mad dogs running loose" in America.[19] And she was running out of steam.

In the summer of 1947, India achieved independence and Jawaharlal Nehru, once dismissed as a visionary and an idealist, became prime minister. Over the years, he had stayed in contact with Agnes, and he now invited her to come to India and serve as an adviser to his government.[20] She turned him down. While she hoped his voice and principles would be heard in the postwar world, she said, she preferred to return to China before America began imprisoning tens of thousands of leftists and liberals, including herself.

By this time, the FBI had discovered so little damaging information on Agnes that it closed her case.[21] General Douglas MacArthur, however, took a different view. While he shared J. Edgar Hoover's conservative politics, MacArthur's focus was on Asian affairs rather than contemporary domestic issues, and Agnes's views on China clashed with his ambition to develop Japan as war base from which to attack the Chinese Communists—if necessary. Moreover, the documents in his possession in Tokyo suggested to him that Agnes was a far more dangerous Soviet operative than the FBI investigation indicated. A ranking military leader, MacArthur was accustomed to having his orders obeyed. When he placed his investigation of Agnes in the hands of his intelligence chief and alter ego, Major General Charles A. Willoughby, MacArthur assumed the matter would be seen through to its proper conclusion.

On September 24, 1947, MacArthur's Far East Command sent Army Intelligence in Washington a three-page memo, based on Japanese records, that laid out with considerable accuracy Agnes's involvement in the espionage ring Richard Sorge had conducted for Soviet military intelligence during Agnes's early years in China. In January 1930, "under the direction of the 4th Bureau of the Red Army General Staff," it began, Sorge had gone to China with two other members of the bureau, posing as a special correspondent for the German *Soziologische Magazin*. In Shanghai, the report continued, the three men joined two other operatives, who were mentioned only by their code names. Within six months, it reported, Sorge was directing a unit in Shanghai that included five Japanese, three Germans, four Chinese, two operatives of unknown origin, and "Agnes Smedley, the well-known American Communist journalist who was acting as correspondent for the *Frankfurter Zeitung*."[22]

After introducing Sorge to Ozaki, the memo continued, she had asked Ozaki to supply her as well as Sorge with information, and until Ozaki left Shanghai in February 1932, he had met with Sorge and Agnes two or three times a month, providing them with intelligence on Japanese policies and troop movements, which Sorge had transmitted to Moscow. The memo also included Ozaki's impressions of the intelligence operation Agnes had run for the Soviets in north China during the winter of 1932–33, using Chinese and Japanese Communist agents. There was nothing on the later, more productive, Japanese phase of the ring. Agnes was the only American named.

For MacArthur's people in Tokyo, the fact that Agnes had provided information to the Soviet Union made her an intelligence agent and a spy—the two terms, to them, being interchangeable. If the material she offered Sorge was nonsecret, she had clearly operated secretly and attended meetings at which secret information was discussed. Having established to his satisfaction that Agnes had been unmasked as a Soviet agent, Willoughby followed up in October with a second memo. Somewhat broader in scope, it consisted in essence of lists of names—of Sorge ring members in Japan, of "helpers" who had acted without full knowledge of the implications of their deeds, of innocents suspected of complicity, of participants in another Soviet spy ring in China that had operated concurrently with the Tokyo phase of Sorge's operation, and of "Communists and Comintern agents," many Japanese in origin, whom a captured Sorge ring member had met in California. Other than California CPUSA official Sam Darcy, none were U.S. citizens. Agnes was relegated in this document to a single mention on a list of "known Soviet spies in China connected with Sorge during the China phase."[23]

Willoughby hoped the FBI would use his data "to trace the connection of Communist agents of American origin operating in the China phase."[24] The FBI obliged by launching a second investigation of Agnes—this time to determine whether she had engaged in any espionage activity on behalf of a foreign government since her return to the United States.[25] Without Agnes's colorful exploits, though, the information was not very sexy, from an American perspective, and the disclosures failed to generate much attention. That, a disappointed Willoughby confided to a colleague, had been one of the objectives of the document.

According to Willoughby, he had "furnished confirmatory data on espionage techniques and world wide ramification of Comintern i.e. Soviet agents," and he was frustrated that what he called his "leads" linking American Communists to the Tokyo apparatus were not being properly exploited. That December, Willoughby mailed a third, classified report on Sorge's espionage ring in the Far Fast to Army officials in Washington.[26] This report contained as much personal opinion as intelligence on Sorge's later success in Tokyo, and it gave Agnes—the only American citizen named as a direct member of Sorge's group—a far more prominent role.

It made no attempt to capture her heartfelt if misplaced intentions. MacArthur and his "little fascist" (as MacArthur affectionately referred to his intelligence chief) did not care. They recognized the potential propaganda value of their document in convincing Americans that "traitors" like Agnes were causing the country to lose the war against Communism in Asia. As Willoughby would explain, "The importance of the Sorge case, while discovered in Japan" was "its ancillary relation to Shanghai and the conspiracy to destroy Chiang Kai-shek and convert China into a Satellite Communist State."[27] Agnes was the bridge that allowed MacArthur's people to make their case. "The importance of Smedley," Willoughby maintained, "lies in her collateral activity in China." Copies of the document found their way into the hands of Tokyo correspondents for the *New York Daily News* and the *Washington Times-Herald*, who

Major General Charles A. Willoughby, Agnes's chief pursuer.
From the collections of the Library of Congress.

allegedly threw it in their wastebaskets.[28] However, the political climate in the United States did not favor such moderation much longer.

During the winter of 1947–48, Agnes addressed the National Council on American-Soviet Friendship, the Progressive Citizens of America, and the Committee for a Democratic Far Eastern Policy (which belatedly honored her as "the Matriarch of Far Eastern Writers"), but she curtailed her lecture schedule to meet her deadline on the Chu Teh biography. Dissatisfied with her progress, she grumbled that the current crop of Yaddo guests, who included Edward Maisel, Theodore Roethke, Arna Bontemps, Robert Lowell, and Marguerite Young, looked down on her for not spending her days "searching for the perfectly balanced sentence." They cared only about analyzing Kafka, Joyce, and Sartre, she wrote, and tossed "lesser mortals into the burning pit." Ill at ease among them, Agnes preferred to chat with tradespeople in Saratoga Springs, whom she lobbied on behalf of third-party presidential candidate Henry Wallace.

Doctors at the Lahey Clinic gave Agnes a clean bill of health. They warned her, though, that if she did not learn to live less intensely, her nervous heart condi-

At a rally for China, New York City, 1948. *Maud Russell Papers, Manuscripts and Archives Division, The New York Public Library, Astor, Lenox and Tilden Foundations.*

tion could prove as damaging to her in the long term as an organic heart ail-ment. "Hot chance!" was her reply, for even as she feared exposure, she had no intention of eliminating any of her risky but gratifying activities, which these days included feeding information to former secretary of the interior Harold Ickes on Americans who personally profited from the corruption and incompe-tence of Chiang's regime for his syndicated column.

Agnes was not the only one seeking to influence public opinion on China. With the Chinese Communists winning so quickly, conservative voices were also rising. Agnes complained to Katherine Anne Porter that the U.S. govern-ment was finding it desirable "to try and pump new life into Chiang Kai-shek and his gang," in the hope that under his leadership China would remain one of its most reliable allies in Asia—if only to discharge its accumulated obligations toward the American people, to whom China "owed" its freedom.[29] Republican critics of the Truman administration, working closely with the FBI, hired advo-cates of Chiang's government, and supporters of KMT China including its chief American propagandist, Alfred Kohlberg, had also developed a new line of attack—that the Chinese Communists depended on Moscow for support.

These people argued that Far East experts in the State Department (among them several friends of Agnes's from Hankow) who suggested that Chiang's gov-ernment would eventually collapse were part of a "Communist conspiracy" that required exposure. To his supporters, Chiang had become the personification of China's acceptance of American political and religious ideals. American China watchers who sympathized with the Chinese Communists' united front goals were outnumbered and outspent. Most Americans, to the extent that they fol-lowed China's civil war at all, failed to distinguish between Chinese and Soviet Communism. They were persuaded to support a foreign policy that halted *all* Communist expansion.

Around the time that Willoughby's classified report arrived in Washington, Kohlberg sent out a press release to a thousand sympathetic politicians, busi-nessmen, clergy, and journalists. In it, he announced that two American Com-munists (whom he left unnamed) had once been active in what Kohlberg referred to as "Stalin's great spy ring in Japan."[30] The *Chicago Tribune* was the first to mention Agnes by name. Citing Army Intelligence sources in Washing-ton, it reported that Agnes Smedley, who was presently "a principal apologist for the Chinese Communists," had formerly participated in the Soviet spy ring of Richard Sorge.[31]

The darkening in the atmosphere could be felt as far away as Yaddo. Mary Townsend and the writer Edward Maisel, disturbed by Agnes's seemingly perma-nent tenure, had complained to director Elizabeth Ames that Agnes's political activities reflected poorly on the writers' colony and that her influence over local coeds had outraged townspeople. Thus far Ames had defended Agnes's behavior on the grounds, she wrote, of "her being in that terrible spot . . . connected with finishing a book."[32] Then, in an unfortunate piece of timing, Agnes hosted a reception for CPUSA organizer Harold Klein just after the *Chicago Tribune* piece appeared. Afterward, Maisel and Townsend informed Ames (and the FBI) that Agnes had used the occasion to proselytize several Skidmore students. Ames felt forced to take a stand.[33]

Sources she trusted, Ames wrote Agnes, had charged that Agnes's radical activities were leading people to believe that Yaddo itself was "a source, or even a promoter, of such interests."[34] Until lately, Ames said, she had ignored rumors that Agnes cared more about her political commitments than her writing, but while Ames still wished Agnes "all good things," the time had come for her to choose. If she promised to work solely on her book, she could remain at Yaddo until autumn; if she persisted in combining her literary and political activities, she needed to leave immediately.

Agnes responded that her outside activities were far fewer than when she first came to Yaddo and were limited to talks on China. She claimed not to know which Skidmore girls Ames was talking about, and insisted the event in question was purely a social affair.[35] But even as she admonished Ames to look first at her own sins before attacking political radicalism, as practiced in the Soviet Union and elsewhere, Agnes felt she had no alternative but to leave at once if she wished to maintain her self-respect.

Porter, who knew nothing of Agnes's earlier history, was horrified by what she termed the whole "nasty business" at Yaddo. The influence that those "shameless flatterers and exploiters" Maisel and Townsend exerted over Ames froze her blood, she wrote.[36] She encouraged Agnes to stay with her China friend Mildred Price in New York City while she sorted things out. Porter thought Agnes would be happier and healthier once she was done with that "stupid, pretentious place," as Porter referred to Yaddo. She had no idea that being asked to move on, once again, at this point in her life made Agnes feel as though she had come to the end of the road.

On February 19, 1948, in a state of high agitation, Agnes returned to Ames a winter coat she had borrowed and a set of cocktail glasses she had used to entertain guests. Whatever happened next, she seemed to doubt it would involve anything resembling an ordinary social life. By the next day, she was gone.

Agnes passed the month of March in New York City, brooding and alone. The only thing she cared about was completing her book on Chu Teh, but she was too upset to work. When Josephine Bennett, an old friend from the birth control movement, invited her to live at the half-built vacation home she and her husband, Richard Brooks, were constructing in Sneden's Landing, New York, Agnes accepted. If she could concentrate over the noise of carpenters and other workmen, she could stay there rent free, have her own room and bath, and live virtually undisturbed.

The house, set inside the forests that traced the banks of the Hudson River, seemed much farther from the city than the hour's car ride it actually was. The only neighbors within shouting distance were the actresses Katharine Cornell and Gertrude Lawrence, the violinist Yascha Heifetz, and the mother of Katharine Hepburn. Even they could only hear her "if one hollers very loud and shouts and jumps in the air while doing so; and does it long enough," Agnes wrote, which was fine with her.

Agnes told Knopf that a gall bladder problem had left her run down and depressed, and she was granted additional time to deliver her manuscript. Then she set to work putting in a garden large enough for her, the Bennett-Brookses, and a dozen nearby families. She planned to edge the vegetable bed with flowers—mostly tulips—"if my dreams c[a]me true," she wrote, which, she ruefully acknowledged, was seldom the case. When she was not plowing up sod, Agnes scrubbed windows and woodwork. She continued to lend her name to petition drives and protest telegrams to Congress, but she doubted such things made much impression, and each time she did so, she wrote, she knew she was driving another nail in her coffin. But what did it matter, she asked, when she felt as if she were already living in one?[37]

In her vegetable garden, Sneden's Landing, New York, 1948. *Courtesy Ayako Ishigaki.*

Still, the house was warm and comfortable, and the Bennett-Brookses were kind and friendly on their weekend visits. By May 1948, Agnes was feeling well enough to return to her book. That same month, though, an article in Kohlberg's magazine, *Plain Talk*, destroyed her fragile composure. On a recent visit to Tokyo, Kohlberg wrote, where he had been the personal guest of MacArthur's intelligence chief, Charles A. Willoughby, he had been shown a copy of the still-classified spy report. In florid cold war rhetoric, Kohlberg repeated much of what MacArthur's Far East Command had already told Army higher-ups in Washington, D.C.

A close analysis of Japanese records had unearthed a Soviet spy ring in the Far East whose cardinal feature, as far as Americans were concerned, was that the nationally known writer Agnes Smedley, who for years had "championed in books and in American diplomatic and military quarters the cause of the Chinese Communists," had served "Stalin's secret service in the Far East," operating as a recruiting officer and courier for the Soviet spy Richard Sorge during the ring's early, Shanghai phase.[38] But that was not all.

"If the Communists could do this in Japan, where they were ruthlessly suppressed," Kohlberg concluded, "it staggers the imagination to try to figure out what they have probably succeeded in doing here in our country . . . If thirty of them could penetrate the intelligence service of the Japanese Army in China, how many must have been planted in the security branches of our defense establishments at home and abroad? How many Communist spies [we]re there in the U.S. Foreign Service and in the State Department?"[39]

No mainstream American newspaper carried Kohlberg's disclosure. Ironically, they seemed as suspicious of Kohlberg's political bias and factual accuracy as they were of Agnes's.[40] But as Chiang Kai-shek acknowledged serious losses in Manchuria, and it became increasingly evident to President Truman and Secretary of State Marshall that his government was a lost cause, no matter how much money the United States spent, anti-Communist hysteria blossomed, and Agnes—with her ties to the American, Soviet, and Chinese Communists— became an increasingly tempting target.

Soon after the article appeared in *Plain Talk*, the FBI entered Smedley's name and various aliases in its security index. In the event of any sudden difficulty with the Soviet Union, she would be a priority arrest.[41] At the same time, MacArthur's Tokyo headquarters began to exchange additional documents on the Sorge case with the FBI and Army officials in Washington. In them, Agnes was described not only as one of the most active workers for the Soviet cause in China but as a major proponent of the argument that the Chinese Communists were really not Communists at all but "local agrarian revolutionists."

The line, which had its roots in the CCP-KMT united front at the start of the

Sino-Japanese War, was really directed at the Far Eastern division of the State Department. Agnes had never claimed, either in her writings or in conversation, that the Chinese Communists were other than Communists. But Agnes was more vulnerable than her diplomatic friends at the Department of State, or other journalist and military friends from her Hankow days. A notorious radical, she lacked their institutional affiliation. She was also working class, single, and female, and her historically combative stance toward men in positions of authority sat poorly with powerful conservatives like MacArthur, Kohlberg, Henry Luce, former ambassador William Bullitt, Lieutenant Colonel Claire Chennault, and General Albert Wedemeyer. All that made it easier to blame Agnes for "duping" countless Americans, including high government officials, into a misguided sympathy for the Chinese Communists that minimized their threat and put America's safety at risk.

These men, who believed that China's revolutionary Communist movement was primarily as an expansion of Soviet power in the Far East, saw U.S. security as inextricably bound to the security of non-Communist China as a means of protecting America's Pacific defense positions. That June, their fears of world Communism intensified in the aftermath of a Soviet attempt to blockade Berlin. For them and others like them, devotion to Chiang's cause was becoming a test of one's Americanism, which made Agnes's breach of faith as damning as her collaboration with Sorge. As the pressure mounted, General Bedell Smith, the American ambassador to the Soviet Union, requested that the State Department declassify Willoughby's third report. Informed of the matter by Army officials in Washington, MacArthur cabled back that if his Far East Command would be held responsible, he declined.[42]

MacArthur had good reason to exercise restraint. The "case study in international espionage in the Far East" his intelligence chief had overseen provided a reasonably faithful rendering of the Sorge ring and of Agnes's "collateral" role in its Shanghai phase. However, it had some serious problems. The charge that Agnes had worked for Soviet military intelligence was true, as far as it went (although it failed to mention the ring she ran for the Soviets—without Sorge— in north China, or her connections to the Comintern). However, there was no supporting documentation, and its paranoid tone and inexplicable leap from Soviet espionage in the early 1930s to strident polemics on the current China policy debate and other contemporary but unrelated American issues, including Truman's Federal Employee Loyalty Program (intended to ensure that no one working for the U.S. government was or had ever been associated with the CPUSA), impugned its credibility.

Army officials demurred at the State Department request. They reassured MacArthur that any declassification action would take place in Washington—

meaning that in the event of the report's release to the press, Army officials in D.C., rather than MacArthur's Far East Command, would assume responsibility.[43] Throughout September 1948, as the crisis in China approached its climax, the Army insisted that as far as it was concerned, "the case was a closed one and . . . no publicity releases would be made on it" — even as General Willoughby pointed out *Reader's Digest's* interest in the story. However, by November, after Democrat Harry Truman won a stunning upset victory over Republican candidate Thomas Dewey and voters re-elected a Democratic majority to Congress, it became clear to embittered Republicans that there was too much political hay to be made with the Tokyo report to keep it under wraps much longer.

While President Truman and Secretary of State George Marshall pondered how much assistance the United States could offer China without becoming enmeshed in its civil war, the Truman administration had been avoiding any public commitment on the subject of more aid to China. But an unexpected visit by Madame Chiang Kai-shek, who personally appealed for "immediate and definite" U.S. aid, forced the issue, along with the release of Sorge spy report, into the open. Chiang's Washington allies estimated it would take five billion dollars to save his regime from a rout at the hands of the Communists. Dr. Sun Fo, the new premier of China's legislature, recommended that the United States send General MacArthur as America's chief military adviser to assure skeptics that the Nationalists would use the funds effectively.

MacArthur, "a sometime candidate for the Republican presidential nomination, was a great favorite with precisely those members of Congress most critical of the Truman administration's policy toward China. To many, he was the personification of the Asia First orientation of the nationalist wing of the Republican Party."[44] If Americans responded favorably to the report, it would not only be a public relations coup for MacArthur, it could influence China policy and the anti-Communist crusade in the United States.

Domestic events were moving in a direction that did not favor Agnes. On December 3, 1948, House Un-American Activities Committee agents seized microfilm copies of secret State, War, and Navy department documents from the late 1930s from a pumpkin on the Maryland farm of former CPUSA underground agent Whittaker Chambers. Karl Mundt, the HUAC chairman, announced that they were of "startling and significant importance . . . reveal[ing] . . . a vast network of Communist espionage . . . in the State Department that . . . far exceed[ed] anything yet brought before the committee in its ten-year history" and implicated Alger Hiss, a former State Department employee whom Chambers had accused of belonging to the Communist "apparatus" in Washington.

Until now, Truman had considered the probe "a red herring" and accused the lame-duck committee of headline grabbing. No longer. While Chambers and Hiss testified before a New York grand jury, HUAC released dozens of confidential State Department documents (which Chambers claimed that Hiss, now under indictment, and others had stolen, copied, and returned to the files)—including a 1938 report by General Stilwell that stated that only the Communists had a program to mobilize the masses in China. The publicity around the Stilwell report made it sound almost heretical, and the fact that Agnes had advised him did not go unnoticed. Meanwhile, Chiang Kai-shek, desperate to save his regime, trotted out every scare phrase known to cold war rhetoric. Presenting himself as a major figure in the battle for freedom and democracy, he traded on the idea that it was America's responsibility to "save" China.

In response to mounting documentary evidence of widespread Communist espionage, President Truman promised tighter anti-espionage legislation. That same December, the State Department again requested a copy of the Sorge spy report. This time, after eliciting the approval of the CIA and the FBI, the Army sent the still-classified document to the State Department for official and embassy use. At the same time that Mao launched his armies south of the Great Wall against the main force of the KMT, Secretary of Defense James Forrestal requested that the report be reviewed, declassified, and released to the press.

Throughout December 1948, debate on terms and conditions of the report's release raged back and forth across the Pacific, set against the backdrop of Soviet espionage in the U.S. government during the 1930s and the current China question. General MacArthur (whom the congressional "watchdog" Committee on Foreign Aid was supporting to direct Nationalist forces in China) remained concerned about the need to delete "certain names" from the report if the document were to be made public. The Army still objected to declassification on the grounds that it would reveal American awareness of Soviet intelligence techniques they might otherwise use again and because it wished to discourage the impression held by "certain foreign intelligence services that U.S. intelligence security is not dependable." (Most likely this meant that the report revealed that disbelieving American defense chiefs had neglected to share with U.S. commanders in the Pacific a warning Richard Sorge had sent Moscow—and Moscow had forwarded to the United States two months before Pearl Harbor: that a Japanese attack on the harbor was imminent).

Secretary of Defense Forrestal would not be put off. A leading advocate for the containment of Soviet Communism, he also dabbled—on his own—in foreign policy, and he was a vehement opponent of General Marshall's China policy. Forrestal prevailed on the Joint Chiefs of Staff to release the report, and on review they found no objection—from "a strictly military information viewpoint."[45] The FBI now weighed in in favor of release; the CIA and the Army remained opposed.

On December 21, 1948, the bureaucratic wrangling became public when Forrestal's desire to release the document naming "the American newspaper woman, Agnes Smedley" as a Soviet spy appeared in Drew Pearson's column in the *Washington Post*. On January 5, 1949, the Army officially agreed to declassify the report with the intention of releasing it to the press, provided "certain deletions" were made. Less than two weeks later, the agency forwarded an amended copy to its public information division.

By this time Tientsin and Peking had fallen to the Communists, shocking Americans who still believed that the struggle inside China favored the faction inclined toward the United States. Until now, it had seemed only fitting that a people Americans considered essentially democratic would maintain a pro-U.S. orientation, but as Americans belatedly confronted the possibility of a very different outcome in China, they viewed the matter less as an example of the limits of U.S. power than as proof of a domestic conspiracy.[46] Among those who had once seen "saving" China as America's task, Agnes joined the front ranks of those traitors who, in softening public opinion, had allowed the United States to "lose" China to the Reds.

If Agnes had needed convincing, the May 1948 article in *Plain Talk* served as proof that American "fascists" were indeed out to get her. Knowing as few others did how much truth there was beneath the overheated prose, Agnes had so far resisted the impulse to debate the charges. Biding her time, she stayed in seclusion at the Bennet-Brookses', working on her book and gardening. Although she toyed with the idea of fleeing the United States and establishing citizenship in the coming Chinese democratic republic, as she called it, mostly she seemed to hope that the story would simply go away.

Throughout January 1949, while an active, influential KMT lobby spent millions of dollars trying to convince American military and Republican leaders of the terrible danger a Communist victory posed to U.S. defense positions in the Pacific, Agnes assailed American support for Chiang Kai-shek. In a mimeographed newsletter she put out herself, she called for a Congressional investigation into American military, political, and economic aid to Chiang's regime including its recent activities in Formosa, General Claire Chennault's "civil" air transport in China, the extent of the KMT lobby in Washington, and private deposits by KMT officials and other powerful Chinese into American banks. Despite its best efforts, she warned, the United States was about to be "swept from the stage of Chinese history. America could not turn back the clock."[47]

On February 8, 1949, as the China issue was about to be debated on the floor of Congress, Agnes received a call from a wire service reporter. He told her he had just received a digest of the Sorge spy report, accompanied by a press release titled "Agnes Smedley, American Soviet Spy."

> This American, Miss Agnes Smedley [it began], has been one of the most energetic workers for the Soviet cause in China for the past twenty odd years. She was one of the early perpetrators, if not the originator, of the hoax that the Chinese Communists were not really Communist at all, but only local agrarian revolutionists innocent of any Soviet connections. This tall tale has had enormous effect in molding American opinion [o]n China, both private and official, and has bemused American writers for twenty years. Miss Smedley, in her five books and innumerable articles, other Communist writers, and numerous liberal innocents, have continued to spread this story until, today, high American Government officials find it difficult to believe any other. It should be noted also that Miss Smedley's writings are used as source material by most writers and commentators on China, many of whom think she might possibly be a Communist sympathizer, but, nonetheless, feel that she is one of the few writers on China who has plumbed the depths of truth because for so long she has lived with, and thrown in her lot with, the suffering Chinese. The harm has been done, but perhaps it could be mitigated if she is now exposed for what she is—a spy and agent of the Soviet Government.[48]

In two days' time, the reporter informed her, the U.S. Army planned to publicly denounce her as a Soviet spy.[49] Agnes geared up for battle. She hired a publicist and arranged to have her mail delivered to the home of a friend. She was certain that the FBI was watching her, which it was. Roger Baldwin's ACLU was no longer willing to defend her in these charged times, but she hired former assistant attorney general O. John Rogge, who had represented the Progressive Party during the Wallace campaign, as her counsel. Before the charges even saw the light of day, Rogge had notified Secretary of the Army Kenneth Royall what a shocking thing it was "that high army officials, with all the power and prestige of their office behind them, ha[d] seen fit irresponsibly to attempt to destroy the reputation and livelihood of an American citizen."[50] He demanded an immediate retraction of the "false, irresponsible charges" as well as a formal apology.

On February 9, Congressman Harold Lovre entered a copy of the report into the *Congressional Record*. The document listed as its author the "National Military Establishment." No one, it appeared, wanted his name on it. The bomb dropped the following day. At a press conference in Washington, Colonel George Eyster, deputy chief of the Army's public information division, released

the thirty-two-thousand-word report along with the press release even the FBI
deemed "flamboyant and bombastic."[51]

In potent language, the report opened:

> A powerful ring of Soviet spies was uncovered in Japan just before Pearl Har-
> bor. Probably never in history has there been a ring more bold or successful . . .
>
> Though the work of Dr. Richard Sorge and his companions belongs to
> history the lessons of their work should serve as a clear warning for today and
> the future. They concern not just the intelligence officer but every good citi-
> zen. Some of their implications are frightening. One begins to wonder whom
> one can trust, what innocent comrade or loyal friend may suddenly be discov-
> ered as the enemy. He may have any face.
>
> For nine productive years a daring and skillful band of spies worked . . . for
> their spiritual fatherland—Soviet Russia . . . Led by Dr. Richard Sorge, a Ger-
> man Communist posing convincingly as a loyal Nazi, this ring of spies almost
> succeeded in committing the perfect crime."[52]

The document covered the entire period of the ring's operation, from its creation in Shanghai in the early 1930s through its second, more significant phase
in Tokyo between 1934 and 1941. It credited Sorge with advising Moscow that
Japan had decided not to sign a pact with Germany against Russia and Britain,
paving the way for the 1939 Hitler-Stalin pact, and warning Moscow in May 1941
that Hitler planned to invade Russia on June 20—an attack that came two days
later. Sorge's subsequent intelligence—that Japan would push southward toward
French Indo-China instead of Siberia—was also disclosed. This information, it
acknowledged, had allowed the Russian Red Army to transfer sorely needed divisions to the European front in the decisive battle for Moscow later in the year.
No mention was made of ring members' early warnings of an imminent attack
on Pearl Harbor.

Momentous as they were, the achievements of the Tokyo ring were
recounted less passionately than those of Sorge's acknowledged "secondary mission" in Shanghai, along with Agnes's role in it, for while its contribution to
Russian intelligence was minor (at least as far as the report's authors knew), her
participation transformed a wartime story of espionage against America's enemy
into "proof" that the United States had been manipulated into a misplaced sympathy for the Chinese Communists. Understanding "the minds and motivations
of such spies and traitors" was as important as what the ring discovered, the
report argued; the issues "of what and how cannot well be separated from the
question of who."[53] In large part, the document consisted of biographical portraits of a dozen and a half participants: most of them Japanese, a few German

or Russian—and Agnes. Privately, Willoughby suspected that other Americans in addition to Agnes had cooperated with Sorge in China, but of the sixteen people he believed had participated in this phase, Agnes was the only one whose real name Willoughby said he knew.

"Shanghai was a free and easy place," the document stated; "all sorts of odd characters were drifting around. Sorge recruited and developed a ring of spies in China" [that included] "an American woman we know well...Agnes Smedley, American-Soviet spy." In the same words as the press release, Agnes was accused of laboring doggedly for the Soviets in China and of "hoodwinking" Americans for decades with the myth she had spread, if not created— that the Chinese Communists were merely local agrarian revolutionists, devoid of any Soviet connections.

Unaware of Mirov-Abramov and the ambiguous role he played somewhere between Comintern and Soviet intelligence, the report presumed Agnes had arrived in China as a Comintern agent, but it acknowledged that during the time she worked "closely with Dr. Sorge as a member of his ring from late 1930 until he left China," recruiting assistants for him, offering her home for meetings, and acting as his key deputy, it was not known "whether she had transferred to Red Army Intelligence, as had Sorge, or whether, by some special arrangement, she continued with the Comintern, and yet worked with Sorge. Based on Sorge's comments on the need to separate Soviet intelligence and Comintern-Communist intelligence, it concluded she had likely been transferred.

The report described in considerable detail Agnes's relationship with Ozaki and assumed that because Agnes recruited him, she had also "recruited other Soviet agents before and has recruited many others since." Yet it glossed over the intelligence ring Agnes had organized in north China "presumably to cover developments in Manchuria." Instead, it dwelled on the fact that she and Guenther Stein, a German-born journalist accused of assisting Sorge in Tokyo, were "still at large, posing as objective analysts of Chinese affairs, and still affecting the formation of American policy by the skill of their writings... The unhappy thought that a Soviet spy who had worked against the Japanese might later work against the United States had not occurred to many Americans."[54] Like other surviving ring members, it warned, she might still be "secretly busy with [her] trade at this very moment."

CHAPTER 18

Exile

We have been naught and we shall be all.

IWW

NOT ONLY DID the Sorge spy report use Agnes to stoke American fears of the Communist bogey just as they reached critical mass, it made her the first American to be blamed by name for the unexpected turn of events in China. Touching as it did upon so many controversial issues currently before the public, the story was front-page news across the country, with Agnes, "the American woman writer," receiving the lion's share of the headlines.

Tabloid coverage was particularly lurid. The *Journal-American*, the Hearst paper in New York City, reported:

> The Army warned today that remnants of a fabulous Russian spy ring ... may be at work in world capitals "at this very moment."
>
> There is that fleeting hint at a present day menace in the story of an espionage network so bold it slipped from the Japanese cabinet and German embassy in Tokyo secrets that helped change the course of the war ...
>
> The now-it-can-be-told parts of the report unfold an amazing tale centering around: Agnes Smedley, authoress, of Palisades, New York, accused of still being a Communist spy ...
>
> The report says [Sorge and Ozaki] were spies ... in China before shifting to Tokyo. It says Miss Smedley brought them together in Shanghai in 1930.
>
> It says she "is a spy and agent of the Soviet government" ... [in] An earlier and probably bigger ring ... in China ...

After occupation forces moved in, many of the minor figures in the ring were released as political prisoners. The new report indicates that wouldn't happen if the Americans had it to do over again.

At that time...few people had the idea that a Soviet spy who worked against the Japanese might later work against the United States.

Apparently the Army report was intended to warn this country to be on the lookout for spying here.

Beware, it says, of United States employees who even show sympathy with the Communist Party. It says that "party sympathy is enough to develop a high class agent and spy"...

NEW YORK

Herald Tribune — Late City Edition

FRIDAY, FEBRUARY 11, 1949 — FIVE CENTS

Army Says Soviet Spies Got Tokyo War Secrets; Accuses Woman Writer

Agnes Smedley Denies Charge Of Acting as a Spy for Soviets

Moscow Tipped Off Before Nazi Attack

Writer Says She Will Sue MacArthur for Libel if He Waives Immunity

Ring's Leaders Hanged, but Report Says Others May Be Still Operating

By Ralph Chapman

Branding as a "despicable lie" the charges in the intelligence report from General of the Army Douglas MacArthur's headquarters in Tokyo that she is "a Soviet spy and agent," Miss Agnes Smedley, author and former newspaper correspondent, last night challenged the general: "Waive your immunity and I will sue you for libel."

In a statement broadcast over the Mutual Broadcasting System, she said that the report, made public in Washington yesterday, proposes no action against her because General MacArthur knows that she is not guilty and that he is hiding behind a law which says that he "cannot be sued for falsehood." She charged further that she was chosen as "the victim" instead of others on his "secret personal blacklist" because she does not have the backing of any powerful newspaper or radio organization.

O. John Rogge, former Assistant

United States Attorney General and Miss Smedley's lawyer, concurred in her opinion that the report is an "outrageous libel." He said he has written Secretary of *(Continued on page 12, column 1)*

By James M. Minifie

WASHINGTON, Feb. 10.—Remnants of a spectacularly successful Soviet espionage ring which penetrated Japan's inmost councils may still be operating in the world's capitals, the Army Department warned today.

Before the ring was broken up in October, 1941, it had tipped off to Moscow the strength, timing and direction of the German attack on Russia in 1941 and the Japanese decision to turn south against Britain and the United States rather than north against Russia, the Army said.

The activities of the ring were described in a report drawn up by the intelligence section of General of the Army Douglas MacArthur's Far East Command Headquarters. The report did not reveal whether the Japanese decision to attack Pearl Harbor was also discovered and passed on to Moscow, but the Singapore objective was revealed. Sections of the 33,000-word report were taken out by the Army Department for "security reasons."

Committee Calls Officers

The implications of the report

Miss Agnes Smedley during an interview yesterday

Herald Tribune—Acme

Truman Calls Mindszenty Trial

The Army's charge that Agnes was a Soviet spy—and her indignant rebuttal—made front-page news.

It is a thriller of blinking lights, codes, hidden radios never set up in the
same spot twice. It involves fake passports, microfilms passed in cigarette
packs, money changing hands between shadowy figures in dark theaters ...

It was a network with "perfect sources" and almost got away with the "perfect crime."

By comparison, the Army sizes up the wartime Soviet spy network in
Canada as an "amateur show."[1]

"The reptile press of New York burned another witch at the stake with howls
of gloating," Agnes informed Harold Ickes. Carloads of reporters cruised the
streets of Sneden's Landing hoping to catch a glimpse of her. They harassed the
Bennett-Brookses by phone and in person, photographed the home from every
angle, asked to search it for secret radio transmission sets and interviewed carpenters about possible suspicious activities there.[2] One enterprising Missouri
journalist tracked down a relative of Agnes's in Osgood; he told the reporter that
as an admirer of General MacArthur he was "not inclined to take issue" with
the general's description of Agnes as an international spy. His wife recalled
Agnes as a nice girl who had "got in the wrong crowd."[3]

Ironically, for someone about whom the charge of being a Communist was
being bandied about so freely, Agnes received little help from the American
Communist Party in her moment of crisis. A single article appeared in the *Daily
Worker*; the CPUSA-controlled Committee for a Democratic Far Eastern Policy
was silent. When Edgar Snow pressed the organization to come forward on
Agnes's behalf, he was told that any comments by them would divert attention
from America's China policy.[4] The American Party, of course, had neither forgotten nor forgiven her history.

Agnes's frenzy affected her judgment. Under the foolhardy notion that a
good word from Mao Tse-tung or Chu Teh might somehow save her, she wrote
them notes begging them to come to her defense.[5] Wisely, they ignored her.

Edgar Snow, like many of Agnes's fellow China correspondents, was heartsick at this payoff for what he saw as her years of "unselfish service to others."
Snow had never fully grasped the extent of her Soviet connections, and he
believed that while Agnes was outspokenly pro-Chinese Communist, and had
cooperated with antifascists, antimilitarists, and anti-Japanese imperialists in
China, she had never been a spy—or at least had never engaged in anti-American espionage.[6] Certainly she had opposed American "pro-Fascist" elements, he
pointed out, but she did not trust the American Party, had never been a Communist Party member, and had reservations about Stalinism. And that, he
thought, explained everything.

Agnes confided to colleagues that she was taking the rap for storied *Herald*

Tribune correspondent Joseph Newman, the other American to whom Kohlberg alluded in his 1947 press release. Newman, who had been the newspaper's Tokyo bureau chief in 1940 and 1941, had indeed been named, along with Agnes, in the original report, but MacArthur's documentation was weak and the influence of the *Herald Tribune* strong, Agnes contended, while she was only a freelancer.[7] Still, she discouraged other China reporters from publishing an appeal on her behalf. The report "was trying to smoke out everyone who had written anything on China," as she perceived it, and she saw little value in making life any easier for authorities.

To raise funds for her legal expenses, fellow correspondents Jack Belden, Annalee Jacoby, Richard Lauterbach, and Edgar Snow formed a committee that garnered contributions from Sinophiles Pearl Buck, John Hersey, John Fairbank, and Harrison Salisbury—and several others who asked to remain anonymous.[8] Agnes then went on the offensive, returning fire with fire.

In a prepared statement, she declared it almost impossible to believe General MacArthur would rely on the files of the Japanese secret police, "the most discredited agency of that enemy government," to make his charge against her.[9] It was "a despicable lie." She was not now nor had she ever been a Soviet spy or agent of any foreign country. That her name appeared in their files was not surprising, she argued, since she had spoken out against Japanese aggression in China since 1930. Her name had even appeared on a Japanese death list during the Sino-Japanese War. She considered such a mention "a decoration." Why did MacArthur's staff attack her for it? The answer, she asserted, lay in the recent defeats of Chiang Kai-shek's government, which undermined the plans of American military authorities. Her statement was picked up by radio and newspapers throughout the United States and abroad.

The Army's public relations coup began to unravel within a day. Various papers, including the *New York Times*, questioned the appropriateness of the report's suggestions to strengthen the government's "loyalty" program and increase suspicion by and of individual U.S. citizens.[10] The idea that high American government officials had been "hoaxed" by Agnes's writings on the Chinese Communists, as well as the implication that U.S. policy toward the Chinese government had been influenced by these opinions, was also challenged, as were the report's lack of documentation, its paranoid, sensational style, and its reliance on opinion in making its charges.

The Army had also not counted on Agnes's influential supporters in the press corps. CBS correspondent Eric Sevareid recorded a sympathetic interview; muckraker I. F. Stone would publish four columns lambasting the reckless spirit in which the "amazing document" had been released and decrying the effect of a smear "by pure assertion, without presentation of evidence" on the nation's growing hysteria.[11] Theodore White wrote on behalf of "all of us all over the world who love you" that people were standing by ready to help.[12] Ickes devoted three syndicated columns to her case.

Ignoring the risk to his career, Edgar Snow published a defense of Agnes in the *Nation*, arguing that the entire charge against her was a nonstarter. Many of the facts in the case had already been published in Japan in 1945, he wrote. All the information had been available to the U.S. Army since the Occupation; parts of the document had already appeared. Why, he asked, was the report making banner headlines now? Could it be because MacArthur's program for a remilitarized Japan as an anti-Soviet bastion was being scrapped? Was it because the Bullitt-McCarran-Judd campaign to renew American intervention in China was on the front burner? Or did it merely reflect the "state of considerable confusion" that currently existed in the Army while America's wartime military establishment awaited reorganization?[13] That Agnes had "long been a sympathizer with colonial independence movements in general, and openly worked against Japan while she was a medical worker in both the Nationalist and Communist forces in China, is manifest from her own books and lectures," he tartly observed. On what basis did such sentiments and activities make her either a Soviet agent or a traitor?

In the meantime, Agnes kept up her demand for redress with a letter to President Truman, which her publicist widely leaked to the press.

> As an American citizen who has been viciously maligned by General MacArthur and members of his staff, I appeal to you as Commander in Chief to help me protect my reputation as a loyal American.
>
> Yesterday General MacArthur and his staff accused me of being a Soviet spy. Today in Tokyo MacArthur's Intelligence Officer in Tokyo, Major General Charles A. Willoughby, virtually admitted that I was but a pawn in the Army's propaganda war against Russia. My attorneys advise me that I am helpless, under the present laws of libel, to do anything about privileged smearing. I therefore appeal to you to either make General MacArthur apologize to me or else make him waive his immunity so that I can sue him for libel.[14]

Someone who knew her history might have remembered this was not the first time Agnes had threatened officials who accused her of Soviet espionage with a libel suit. Back in 1934, she had told Baldwin that if only there had been some decent court in Shanghai, she would have sued the Chinese Nationalists for libel.[15] Baldwin had delivered her threat to the U.S. secretary of state to good effect then. Perhaps it would work again now. But Agnes was more vulnerable than she seemed.

Anxious about prowling reporters and FBI agents, she avoided her room in

Sneden's Landing and stayed in a different place in New York City every evening. Even then, she could not sleep without sedation; under the tension, her nervous heart ailment returned. The uncertainty of her fate also terrified her. "We didn't know what was going to happen," Agnes wrote a friend, "and my lawyer said damned if he knew . . . He thought they might pounce upon me and haul me away and he gave me instructions about what to do and say. Three people had his office and home telephone numbers and the office and home telephone numbers of his partners in case I disappeared."[16]

Rivalries among the armed services and the looming reorganization of the military were factors in the response to the Tokyo report. In Washington, the pro-MacArthur House Committee on Un-American Activities endorsed MacArthur by attacking his superiors in the Army, accusing them of deleting certain portions of the report including the warning Moscow had conveyed to Washington prior to Pearl Harbor of Japan's war plans against the United States. As soon as February 12, Army officials in Washington signaled their support was wavering by publicly declining to express "actual agreement" with some of the statements in the report.[17] Sensing a shift in the wind, an FBI official close to the investigation warned his colleagues that "when this case begins to backfire on the Army be certain we are *not* drawn into 'pulling their coals' out of the fire. They brought this on themselves."[18]

Major General Willoughby refused to back down. In Tokyo, he told reporters that he would be "morally delighted to waive immunity" and assumed entire responsibility for the report.[19] Secretary of the Army Kenneth Royall, however, was nervous about his agency's legal liability. He ordered MacArthur to deliver a complete set of its documentation on Smedley's connection with the Sorge spy ring to Washington on the first available airplane and demanded that Willoughby promptly forward any additional evidence he could lay his hands on.[20]

Agnes returned to Sneden's Landing for some clean clothing that weekend. There she spoke with I. F. Stone in Washington, who warned her that when he phoned her, he had to speak first with local police.[21] Agnes wrote Colonel Robins that she felt as if she had aged ten years in the last few days. "Oh, my friend, why didn't I go to China and become a Chinese citizen months ago!" she asked him. "I could have worked in peace there . . . This country is no place for anyone who loves liberty." She also wrote Democratic Senator Glen H. Taylor requesting that he say a few words on her behalf to other congressional representatives and drafted a letter in her defense to the *Herald Tribune* (which she perhaps felt owed her something).

General MacArthur and his staff know very well that I am not a spy and agent of the Soviet Government. They also know that I have never had the journalistic capacity to corrupt all Far Eastern correspondents, State Department officials, radio commentators, and influence the course of history . . . The course of Chinese history was determined by the revolutionary Chinese people themselves. I merely reported what I saw of it. Other correspondents did likewise.

. . . I am convinced that this old spy report, in MacArthur's hands since V-J Day, is now dished up as propaganda for the sinister and dangerous policy now being pursued by our War Department; that is, to build up Japan as a war base against the new China and for a third world war. The American public has become very critical of our policy of propping up the corrupt and feudal Chiang Kai-shek regime. They are weary of shelling out billions of dollars to finance that regime. The only fruits of such a policy has been to blacken America's name with the Chinese people . . .

. . . The Tokyo Spy Report has much bigger game than myself in view. It is directed against every correspondent who may try to tell the truth about the Chinese civil war and our China policy, against many men in the State Department who might oppose a new military adventure in China, and against the freedom of expression of the American press.[22]

By Monday Agnes was feeling better; the Army was feeling worse. In response to Royall's demand, Willoughby sought further statements from judges, prosecutors, and other high-level Japanese investigators connected with the case—and another interview with Kawai. He also began trying to obtain the files that the British Shanghai Municipal Police had kept on Smedley and requested help from an "operator" who sounded a lot like Whittaker Chambers, the ex-Communist witness in the ongoing investigation of Alger Hiss. On February 16, however, Willoughby was forced to concede that he was having difficulty coming up with sufficient verifiable information to launch the counterattack on Smedley he said Secretary Royall wished.

Agnes's 1918 arrest for German espionage, Willoughby lamented, could not be used because she had been released for lack of evidence, and he could not show an "organic connection" between Agnes and the Committee for a Democratic Far Eastern Policy. He *could* prove that she had been on the 1933 staff of the International Union of Revolutionary Writers, and that she had at one time written for a magazine HUAC considered a "Communist dominated publication," but that was not enough, he realized, for "a solid press statement attacking Agnes Smedley through verified facts."[23]

On February 17, Royall announced that the report his public information division had issued the previous week did not represent Army policy.[24] At a press conference three days later, his public information officer, Colonel Eyster, explained that the Army had made what he referred to as a "faux pas" in releasing a "philosophical" report on Communist spying in Japan and China. He admitted that the agency had no proof to back up its charges and noted that it was not Army policy to "tar and feather people without proof."[25] Although he declined to state for publication the reason the "faux pas" had been made, he remarked that the "philosophy" had been added by U.S. intelligence agents in Japan and that strong orders had been issued to ensure that any future reports would be properly "edited" before they were made public.

Agnes issued a statement thanking the War Department for clearing her of the "outrageous and false" charge that she was a Soviet spy. Still, she observed, "the retraction rarely catches up with the lie." The experience had caused her irrevocable anguish as well as monetary loss and damage, she said, and though she hoped her victory marked an end to the policy of "smear first, investigate later," she wished a way could be found "to stop officials from slandering and libeling loyal citizens while cowardly hiding behind a law which says they cannot be sued for falsehood."[26]

Rogge assumed that the episode was at an end and that the Army had lost. Agnes was doubtful. As long as men like MacArthur and Kohlberg were ascendant, she said, the sword still hung over her head. "The hurricane has passed," she wrote late that February, back in her room along the Hudson, "but I do not know if it will yet have a tail that strikes back at me."[27] It would.

Between February 10 and February 18, when Agnes was "cleared," FBI investigators grilled Malcolm Cowley, Flannery O'Conner, Elizabeth Hardwick, Edward Maisel, and Robert Lowell about her. Apart from Cowley, none evinced any sympathy, political or otherwise. Lowell, however, took FBI suggestions of Communist infiltration of the writers' colony to another level. After conferring with other guests and Yaddo secretary Mary Townsend, he concluded that the institution had long been permeated "by moods or influences that were politically or morally committed to Communism" and that its director, Elizabeth Ames, had been "somehow deeply and mysteriously" involved in Agnes's political activities.[28]

Lowell's acrimonious charges and his subsequent attempt to have Ames ousted turned Yaddo into a battlefield. While Cowley maneuvered to keep the story out of the press, Lowell's supporters fed the FBI stories about Agnes's romance with the "great philanderer" Sorge and her friendships with other Communists. After the indecent way her "sweet Agnes" had been treated by MacArthur, Yaddo board member Katherine Anne Porter thought it contemptible that Lowell, whose behavior she found "vile beyond words in any situation at all" would drag Agnes's name through the mud again.[29] As Porter described it, "professional Communists" like Anna Louise Strong (whom Porter considered a "hysteric without either head or heart") and "sly fake refugees like Gerhardt Eisler" never suffered the consequences of their behavior. Unlike them, Agnes spent her own money on the causes in which she believed—and wound up in poverty with ulcers.

Not that she agreed with all her friend's choices. Much as Porter loved Agnes, when all was said and done, as Porter explained to a mutual friend, she considered Agnes to be "a lamentable dupe of the kind our generation and place produced in extraordinary numbers... Agnes had a painful childhood and a generally bad experience of life from the beginning—but given her beginnings where else could she have moved so freely, and have done better? It is true she has been censured a little here, but she must know that in every country she adores so, she would have been sent to a labor camp or put to death if a man corresponding in power to General MacArthur had accused her of treason."[30]

Agnes successfully fought off the spy charge, but she still suffered its effects. Over the next few months, she lost her audience for paying lectures. Newspapers refused to print even her letters to the editor. If she wanted to meet someone for a drink, she said, she felt obliged to warn him or her beforehand that authorities viewed her as a dangerous element. Agnes doubted the government had a "legal" case against her. If they did, she wrote, she was sure they would make it. Still she lived in fear that she might be unmasked at any moment.[31]

Officials were working on it. FBI director J. Edgar Hoover had come to believe that his failure to produce results embarrassed the agency, and he had agents scouring the country for Agnes's friends and relatives, interviewing former Party members and informants, poring over her tax records, surveilling her public appearances, and exchanging information with other government agencies. They were trying to create a coherent story from their conflicting reports. Since they did not reach anyone who knew of Agnes's link to Mirov-Abramov or to the Comintern's OMS, they remained puzzled as to how someone with her lack of Party affiliation and her erratic personality could be either a Soviet spy or a Comintern operative.

Willoughby was a true believer. His pride badly wounded by the repudiation of the report, he maintained that any errors in it were not ones of fact but of "handling."[32] Intent on gathering sufficient evidence against Agnes to restore his tarnished reputation. Willoughby and his subordinates enlisted the CIA to obtain her Shanghai police files, along with records of the German Gestapo. They analyzed Agnes's writings and press statements, her life, character, connection to the Sorge case, and her other Comintern ties in Shanghai. They spoke with the Tokyo police chief who had interrogated Sorge, and they obtained an affidavit from Kawai Teikichi, Agnes's key operative in north China. Kawai, who had recently recanted Communism, provided a full accounting of the ring Agnes had run for the Soviets independent of Sorge.[33] After receiving legal advice on how to avoid potentially libelous statements, Willoughby transmitted his findings to Washington in a series of numbered exhibits, which were now in the hands of the CIA, the FBI, and Army Intelligence.

By this time, Agnes had left Sneden's Landing for good and moved back to New York City. She said she was sick of the rumormongering by the American Legion, which claimed she was living in Sneden's Landing in order "to signal Russian ships coming up the Hudson," and of being a charity case.[34] After being turned down at several residential hotels in Manhattan, whose managers recognized her name and told her, she wrote, that they did not want trouble with the FBI, Agnes found one where no questions were asked. Unfortunately, when she turned in her manuscript that July, Knopf refused to accept it without substantial revisions. This meant that the remainder of her royalty advance, on which Agnes had counted to provide her livelihood, would not be available to her anytime soon.

Unable to remain financially afloat in New York while she reworked her book, Agnes decided to go to London, where her friend Hilda Selwyn-Clarke had a large apartment and the cost of living was lower. She hoped to continue on to China, where the Communists had seized control of the mainland, after finishing the revisions. She had lived a hard life, she said, and was weary unto death. Although she had never entirely forgiven CCP leaders, Agnes felt certain that someone like herself, who would always need a paying job to survive, would fare better in China than in the United States. She anticipated being able to teach at a Chinese university, or write a book on Chu Teh's experiences in a Communist society, when the new government formed. While there was no denying that the Communists had "bad tactics at times . . . this whole Cold War business," she wrote, was a menace in every way.[35]

In July 1949, President Truman authorized Secretary of State Dean Acheson to put out a China White Paper detailing American efforts to assist Chiang and the KMT failings that had made it impossible for the United States to do so, under the impression that even Chiang's most adamant congressional supporters could assess the situation more realistically by this time. Instead, the report inflamed Chiang's American supporters, anti-administration forces, and the "China Lobby," chief proponents of the argument that America was "losing" China due to a failure of support engineered by Communists inside the State Department, and heightened cold war tensions.

Agnes applied for a passport in August 1949. Ruth Shipley, the fiercely anti-Communist head of the State Department's passport division, was not inclined to oblige her. After handling Agnes's passport problems for nearly twenty years, Shipley was well acquainted with her political proclivities. As she would do with requests from hundreds of other leftists in the coming decade, Shipley promptly "mislaid" Agnes's application.[36]

By late September, Agnes was distraught. In a letter to Harold Ickes, she explained that she was the genuine article: a true American in the tradition of the country's revolutionary forefathers. Earlier, she had rejected Peg Snow's advice that she tout her ancestry as a means of deflecting attacks. Now it seemed more appealing, and Agnes wrote that while she preferred to remain a citizen of the country her forebears had helped found, if the government considered her so undesirable it could at least issue her a passport so she could leave and seek citizenship elsewhere. Ickes pleaded Agnes's case with Deputy Secretary of Defense Stephen Early, stressing her pre-Revolutionary American background, the lack of "even the shadow of Communism . . . upon her," and the absence of any legal basis for denying a citizen a passport because of her political views; he also threatened, in the mildest tones, to publicize the matter in his column.[37]

Agnes also tried to work her magic with Nehru. During the prime minister's U.S. visit that fall, she attempted repeatedly to ask that he, too, place her problem before State Department officials, but, Agnes claimed, the agency attached someone to Nehru's staff specifically to ensure that no one of whom it disapproved, let alone "an American citizen who had given all her adult life to supporting both the Indian and Chinese liberation movements," saw the prime minister while he was a state guest. This person, she said, erected numerous barriers that made it impossible for her to speak directly with Nehru.[38]

When the Chinese People's Republic was formally proclaimed in October 1949, its leaders officially invited Agnes to return and conveyed through Chen Han-seng two thousand dollars toward the cost of her journey.[39] Until she had a passport, of course, Agnes could not sail to England, much less China, and though she feared apprehension if she stayed in the U.S., she remained ambivalent about emigrating. In her distress, Agnes reverted to the faith of her forefathers and began attending Quaker services at a meetinghouse near her hotel. At least it was a free faith, she said, requiring no formal theology and granting all members full liberty of speech and thought.[40]

Near the close of the month, Shipley granted Agnes a passport—just as China announced its foreign policy of supporting the USSR and the United States withdrew its diplomats. Restricted to one year instead of the usual two, the document was valid for travel in France, Italy, and the British Isles only. Suspicious that Agnes might try to go from England to China, Shipley had also ordered the American Embassy in London to refer back to her any application Agnes made in England for additional passport facilities.

Agnes booked a one-way passage to England. Perhaps it was just as well. By this time HUAC had its own copy of the documentary exhibits Willoughby had sent to Washington, and the FBI planned to interview Agnes about her "Russian espionage activities in the Orient and in the U.S."[41] Edgar Snow hastily organized a drinking party for Agnes's fellow China hands; a handful of elderly friends from the birth control movement also bade her a tearful farewell.

On the fifteenth of November, 1949, Agnes arrived on the same docks from which she had sailed for Europe nearly thirty years before, accompanied by Chen Han-seng. Thorberg was waiting for Agnes in her cabin. She had heard from mutual acquaintances that Agnes was leaving the States, and after their many years of friendship, she was hurt that her former sister-in-law had not even called to say good-bye.

Agnes reached England in the third week of November, weighed down with pilfered foodstuffs for her friends. Margaret Watson Sloss, a friend from Hong Kong, had come down from Oxford to greet her, and she and Hilda Selwyn-Clarke spent the next few days catching Agnes up on the events of the last eight years. Agnes groused that she must have been the first American visitor required to register with British police, but she found the political atmosphere in London quite liberal and civilized in comparison with that in the United States. British trade unions might have fallen under the influence of American cold war labor leaders, she wrote, and even working-class British Communists displayed a vexing colonial consciousness, but no professors had been driven from their universities for belonging to the Communist Party, and the Labour government's attempt to provide medical care, food, and clothing to all who needed them was, she felt, at least a step in the right direction.

Agnes followed the debate on British recognition of the new Chinese regime from the sidelines, trying hard to be circumspect. She attended a number of events that were organized by British China activists and overseas Chinese students, but she was not looking to get into trouble. At one such meeting, Agnes ran into a U.S. Embassy official she had known in China. She said he was initially friendly but then avoided contact with her. Agnes took this to mean that the embassy regarded her as a spy.[42]

In London, she occasionally went sightseeing or to the movies and enjoyed the companionship of the economist Julian Friedman and Jack Chen, whose father, Eugene, had been a prime mover in the Wuhan government. During the day, when she had the apartment to herself, she preferred to rework her book—

though she made little progress. Given the current political climate in the United States, she doubted that Knopf would publish even a revised version. That, and the hostility with which the United States had greeted Communists' success, chipped away at her confidence. Once the novelty of her surroundings wore off and the reality of her political exile set in, she became depressed and combative.

Agnes's friend Hilda Selwyn-Clarke would later wonder — if she been wiser, more helpful, more understanding, or simply not working so hard at this time — whether she "might with long hours of discussion . . . [have] found out whether there was any other condition that was worrying [Agnes] beyond the constant torture of American policy, both internal and external, and the grinding worry of her book."[43] But as Agnes became increasingly remote, it was hard work comforting her. Agnes attributed her anguish to her friend's support of Britain's colonial policies, and though she vowed to leave it "to the great teacher, Time" to teach her Socialist friend the lessons of those "who try to maintain colonial beachheads in Asia or to hold down the African people," she quarreled frequently with Hilda, and the wit and generosity that had previously characterized their friendship diminished. That Christmas, Hilda's thirteen-year-old daughter, Mary, returned from boarding school for the holidays, and Agnes, who was ordinarily quite fond of children, complained that Mary and her friends' noisy coming and goings made it impossible for her to write.

In January 1950, Agnes had just begun feeling better when a most unwelcome letter arrived from Edgar Snow. Major General Willoughby, who continued his relentless search for some "corrective action," as he described it, had lobbied hard for a HUAC investigation of Agnes while Congressman Harold Lovre visited Japan. He had also asked Brigadier General Bonner Fellers, a friend and former subordinate of MacArthur's who was currently assistant to the chairman of the Republican National Committee, to use his influence to encourage HUAC to pursue "the Smedley affair," as Willoughby called it.[44] The House committee was largely Democratic, Willoughby noted, but surely there were some Republicans on it?

The story of Agnes's involvement in the Soviet spy ring of Richard Sorge, Willoughby argued, led straight into China and could be used to explain the disaster that had befallen that country. "While certain individuals emerge sharply in this story, they must be viewed against the sinister background of a world conspiracy," he advised HUAC's chairman in a subsequent note. "In its unimpeachable and devastating evidence, this case will tend to dispel false notions on the responsibilities for the China debacle and place this controversial subject into proper focus."[45]

The Shanghai Municipal Police files, which were now in his possession, shed great light not only on Agnes, as Willoughby saw it, but 180 other Americans including Earl Browder and Eugene Dennis: "all the old wheelhorses [*sic*] of the American Communist Party, not to mention the twilight zone fellow-travelers like [Owen] Lattimore and Edgar Snow," whom Willoughby held responsible for the "blueprint of the Communist conspiracy" that had achieved such striking success to date.[46] In light of the pressing situation in China, as well as the broader issue of Communist expansion in the Far East, Agnes's role in the Sorge case provided a "dramatic footnote" to the China story that HUAC could exploit.

The corrosive political climate in the United States favored Willoughby's campaign. In December 1949, the portion of Sorge's confession in which he discussed his relationship with Agnes appeared in Kohlberg's magazine, *Plain Talk*.[47] The following month, HUAC research director Benjamin Mandel requested Kohlberg's files on Smedley and sought his recommendation on potential witnesses.[48] After Kohlberg responded with names and additional suggestions, Mandel began communicating directly with Willoughby. Willoughby was soon so confident of HUAC's interest in Agnes that he boasted of it to the press.[49] It was this information Snow evidently relayed.

Snow's news hit Agnes hard. Arriving on the heels of what she considered the "shocking" guilty verdict at Hiss's second trial for perjury (his first trial, for allegedly passing classified State Department documents and, indirectly, spying against the United States for the Soviet Union, having resulted in a hung jury), Agnes took Snow to mean that "the bastards," as she referred to her cold war tormentors, did not intend to let up on her. If Hiss, that "Harvardian paragon of apparent rectitude" as one historian described him, had been convicted for perjury, Lord knew what she could expect at the hands of HUAC and men like Willoughby. To this day, she could not understand, even if all Willoughby's "so-called documents were true," she wrote, why it did not matter that the activities he described her engaging in had been directed against Japanese and Nazi imperialism—not the United States?[50]

With the months ticking away on her limited passport, Agnes realized what a terrible spot she would be in if she returned to the States, but she had yet to hear from Chen Han-seng or Madame Sun, both of whom were trying to secure a visa for her to Hong Kong, from whence she could slip into mainland China.[51] That March—feeling, she said, like a prisoner "momentarily at-large"—Agnes departed Selwyn-Clarke's in a huff for Margaret Sloss's home in Oxford.

Agnes's growing conviction that she would face life in prison if her case went to trial turned her objections to Willoughby quite personal—and sexually charged. He viewed her in similarly sexual terms. Henceforth Agnes referred to Willoughby as the "prissy General with a mincing Homo manner."[52] Willoughby fumed, in turn, that Agnes had forced him to draft "emasculated" statements and enjoyed a "baffling immunity" as a woman, exploiting "the complete matriarchy" of America's social structure.[53] He praised MacArthur's "potent" name and decried Agnes's hatred of man's dominant position, pointing to her dislike of marriage as proof of her contempt for things American.

On March 6, 1950, Willoughby mailed HUAC investigators an extract of his voluminous documentation against Agnes, along with the names of the 180 other Americans he had unearthed in the Shanghai police files.[54] The Tydings Committee investigation into Senator Joseph McCarthy's charge that fifty-seven State Department employees were CPUSA members opened two days later.

Two weeks into the Senate hearings, McCarthy hitched his star to Alfred Kohlberg and the China Lobby and denounced Owen Lattimore, a former adviser to Chiang Kai-shek who edited the journal of the Institute of Pacific Relations (an international think tank that fostered greater awareness of Asia and the Pacific), as the top Soviet spy in America. The connection between the State Department and Lattimore was tangential, but Lattimore and the Institute of Pacific Relations were bêtes noires of Kohlberg. With these charges, America's witch hunt was fully launched. Reports of Russian totalitarianism and the USSR's acquisition of the atom bomb (evidently through espionage), alongside the reality of active Communism in the United States, fed the deepening atmosphere of suspicion and fear.

Snow had Agnes as much as Lattimore in mind in April of 1950 when he remarked that the basic rights of "honest and loyal citizens" were being trampled. As he saw events in America, "scoundrels" like Willoughby, by exploiting their legal immunity, were turning the government into a laughingstock "to advance the career of a little two-bit, oath-violating lawyer scratching for power under the cover of a holy crusade against heretics and witches." He also criticized American journalists, who, by playing on people's fear of evil abroad, were "destroying the very virtues [they] would defend—fair play, justice, ordinary decency, human dignity."[55]

The following month, things really heated up for Agnes. On April 10, 1950, the *Journal-American* reported that she was scheduled to be subpoenaed by HUAC when she returned from abroad, as expected, within the next few weeks. The FBI, which now described Agnes's case as of "urgent and . . . great importance to the Bureau," expedited its review of the Sorge exhibits and advised its field agents throughout the United States to familiarize themselves with her background and activities and the allegations against her in preparation for her impending return. After Senator McCarthy had ex-Communists testify at Senate hearings, the FBI would grill them about Agnes.

Louis Budenz now recalled that *Daily Worker* foreign editor Harry Gannes had told him in the mid-1930s that Agnes was a Communist and "one of our most valued agents in China," although he could not say whether she had worked for the Comintern, the CPUSA, or the USSR. Gannes, Budenz said, knew that Agnes was sometimes irresponsible but had explained to Budenz that this irresponsibility sometimes helped her.[56] Elizabeth Bentley, a former Soviet spy, told the FBI that Joseph Eckhart, whom she described as a Soviet agent in China in the early 1930s, had described Agnes to Bentley in 1935 "as a Soviet intelligence agent in China," but he had been critical of her abilities, she advised, and considered her indiscreet. In a subsequent conversation with her espionage principal Jacob Golos, Bentley said, she learned that while Agnes "had once been a very important member of the Soviet intelligence setup," by 1941 she was considered a "has-been" or at least of waning importance—an impression Earl Browder confirmed for Bentley in a 1944 conversation.[57]

The report of Agnes's imminent return was news to Agnes, who still had six months before her passport expired, but when she received notice shortly after the article appeared that her ration book would not be renewed, she interpreted it to mean she was about to be ordered to terminate her stay in Great Britain. She might have been right. According to Willoughby, HUAC was indeed "applying pressure" at this time to compel Agnes's return to the United States so she could give testimony.[58]

Images of HUAC's power over her triggered a flare-up of Agnes's duodenal ulcer. Once the China Lobby had finished with Lattimore, she believed, she would be its next victim.[59] Several thousand marks were waiting for Agnes in an account in East Germany, where her books had been reissued, and her publisher there encouraged her to come and spend them,[60] but the terms of her passport forbade it, and she seemed too discouraged to take it on. Doctors at Oxford advised her that if she didn't listen to the radio, read the paper, discuss politics, or think about the United States, she could probably recover without medical intervention, but Agnes knew such a prospect was beyond her. Eager for relief, she scheduled surgery.

On April 28, 1950, Agnes advised Margaret Sloss that if she did not recover, the terms of her will stipulated that her niece, Mary Smedley, was to receive the fifteen hundred dollars Knopf owed her on acceptance of her manuscript. Except for Japanese rights to *Daughter of Earth* (which Agnes had already assigned Ozaki's widow toward the education of their child), all royalties from her books and her U.S. government bonds were to go to Chu Teh, to whom she asked that her ashes be sent for burial in China after the simplest possible funeral.[61] Her personal possessions—books, typewriter, camera, and clothing—were to go to the Chinese people to use as they saw fit. She was bitter, but very clear.

I have had but one loyalty, one faith, and that was to the liberation of the poor and oppressed; and, within that framework, to the Chinese revolution as it has now materialized . . . As my heart and spirit have found no rest in any land on earth except China, I wish my ashes to lie with the Chinese revolutionary dead.

Under no condition shall any American claim my body or any of my personal possessions, save the sum I leave to my small niece, and except for my executors, or the friends who are to receive my manuscript. Should I die, it will be with a curse on American Fascism, as represented by the American government, the American Congress, and all the armed forces and official representatives of America on my lips. Those are evil vicious forces, and any person, American or otherwise who serves such evil forces or is connected with them, is evil. For this reason I beg of you to keep all such persons from me even after I am dead.[62]

On May 2, 1950, Agnes entered the Acland Nursing Home, lonely and troubled in spirit. Two days later, she underwent a partial gastrectomy. On May 5, doctors reported that the surgery had gone well and their patient was recovering nicely. The following evening, however, Agnes grew wild and went into shock. Efforts to resuscitate her proved fruitless. By midnight, Agnes Smedley was dead.

Epilogue

One can imagine how Agnes Smedley would have reacted to the depreda-
tions of Chiang Ch'ing...during the...Cultural Revolution. My guess is
that her anti-establishment propensity would have made the air blue.

JOHN KING FAIRBANK

AGNES'S BRITISH FRIENDS, who knew the tabloids' fascination with her,
requested that the surgeon conduct a postmortem before issuing a death
certificate. Only after bronchopneumonia and acute cardiac failure following
surgery was determined as the cause of her demise did they notify the press.[1]
Now that Agnes was safely dead, Chinese Communist papers, including the official *Peking People's Daily*, bemoaned the "irretrievable loss of one of the best
daughters of the American people, and most staunch friends of the Chinese
people," whose contributions to their revolution would "stand forever a monu-
ment to true and lasting friendship between our two great people."[2] (They also
seized the occasion to blast MacArthur, already under fire for aiding and abet-
ting Japanese troops and pilots who the Chinese Communists feared were
secretly amassing in Taiwan to launch a war against them.)

Elsewhere in Asia and Europe, numerous obituaries either praised Agnes as a
visionary and heroine or denounced her as a Soviet spy. The American Communist Party press was conspicuously quiet. More mainstream journals recalled
her as a colorful, adventurous, controversial figure whose "peppery" character
had embroiled her with authorities in several countries and triggered two failed
charges of espionage.

On May 10, 1950, Agnes was cremated at the Oxford Crematorium, where
her ashes would remain until her executors could figure out a way to comply
with her request that she be interred in China. Her old friend Sonja Kuczinski,

who was living in a neighboring village, followed the story from a safe distance. She had known of Agnes's proximity since being posted to Oxford earlier that spring, she would write, but since Sonja still occupied what she described as a "critical position" in Soviet intelligence—running a string of agents for the GRU—she had avoided Agnes. Sonja would later say her heart was "heavy" about her decision, but she seemed unwilling to approach someone whose loyalty to Stalin was suspect, and claimed variously that it would have been irresponsible of her to endanger Agnes politically and that she had heard Agnes was embittered and shut herself off from others.[3]

A memorial service took place on May 18 at the Quaker meetinghouse in Manhattan that Agnes had attended. "We called the meeting of those she loved and admired, and who loved and admired her for her great heart, her integrity, and her unselfish devotion to the cause of the oppressed and the downtrodden throughout the world, and her faith in the attainability of human brotherhood. She had her faults," Edgar Snow, who organized the event, admitted, "but those qualities in her were rare and fine and gave off a glow before which we all warmed our hands."[4]

Madame Sun Yat-sen and Chen Han-seng, who remained in New York City, had been invited to speak but no Chinese, nor anyone connected with the Committee for a Democratic Far Eastern Policy, was among the six dozen admirers in attendance. Stilwell's widow, Lord Inverchapel, Harold Ickes, Prime Minister Nehru, Ella Winters, and a dozen others had sent cables, which were read, along with a Chinese message of condolence from *People's Daily*.[5] Snow was so distressed he could scarcely speak.

"Anyone who knew Agnes," he began,

> understood the cruelty and stupidity of the charge against her by MacArthur's headquarters that she was a spy against her country and an agent of the Comintern. Deeply as she sympathized with the Chinese Communists, even with them she could not bind herself to unqualified approval which party discipline would have demanded. She had to be free to speak against evil wherever she found it. She also had to be free to speak from her own heart and not as the party line dictated. In Asia she felt no fundamental contradiction between her convictions and those of the revolutionaries. In Europe and America she had too many doubts. As for Russia she knew little of it or of its leaders: she could never have pledged her soul to the service of a Communist Party which did not live up to her principles of decent behavior—and none did. She was therefore never a Communist—but she was a fighting revolutionary, through and through ...
>
> Agnes was a fanatic in righteous battle, that's true, but she was never a nar-

row bigot...Life was rich with beauty and value to her and it was just because she felt so keenly all its potential grandeur that she fiercely resented the society in which we live—the denial of those possibilities to the downtrodden and the underprivileged.[6]

Snow recalled with pleasure the charming, childlike quality that allowed Agnes to throw herself with equal verve into collecting money for wounded soldiers, pounding her typewriter, defending a friend, or mixing a salad. She was painfully aware of her limitations, he observed. "Though life had cheated her of opportunities in her childhood, she did not excuse herself for her failures. Before the criticism of someone she respected and trusted she was as humble as a child."

He noted that sympathy for suffering and a hatred of oppression—of her own sex, the poor, India, and other colonial countries—had been easier for her than the "intricacies of dialectical materialism" or revolution in Great Power countries. People's inability to resent injustice and inequality as deeply as she did had baffled her. Her firm belief in good and evil, he said, made her detest compromise, obfuscation, sham, hypocrisy, and dishonesty. Thoreau, Emerson, Whitman, and Jefferson represented her America.

In the exchange of letters that followed, a stunned and grief-stricken Hilda Selwyn-Clarke expressed "intense hurting regrets" for not having done more to succor Agnes during the last weeks of her visit. Katherine Anne Porter was surprised, she said, at how much she missed Agnes. She had found Agnes's life and personality very moving: "so much suffering and good faith and disappointment. I wish there were an afterlife in a pleasant place," Porter wrote, "'a place of light, rest and refreshment' as the Catholic burial service says, where she might meet Carlson again. They were two brave good soldiers if ever I saw any. She loved him so dearly I always hoped he loved her as well."[7]

Several of Agnes's friends believed Agnes had died because she no longer cared to live, and they castigated American officials for the inhuman treatment that had caused her despair. Jo Bennett Brooks thought that when Agnes, already greatly perturbed by the Lattimore case, had emerged from sedation and realized she would be forced to return to the United States, the shock had killed her. Snow was not so sure. Had she gotten back into China, he wrote, perhaps she would have lived longer. Now she was "in the Valhalla where she said she longed to be," he wrote, "and able to listen to the stories of warriors who died for the revolution."[8] For himself, Snow imagined Agnes would tire of that rather quickly. Then, he said, she would turn "to setting things right up there where the old guard and its ruling saints have been in power entirely too long." Soon she would have figured out "just what is at the root of the trouble with the whole system and what needs to be changed."

In view of Agnes's demise, the FBI discontinued its analysis of her books. It did not, however, close its investigation. MacArthur and his intelligence chief in Tokyo were also reluctant to give up their chase. While Agnes lay ill in England, the GOP had stepped up its attack on the State Department and accused Truman of coddling Communists in the government, losing the cold war in Asia, and allowing Communism to overrun China; Willoughby's attorney, J. Woodell Greene, had seized the occasion to notify their mutual friend Bonner Fellers at the Republican National Committee that MacArthur was "tremendously interested in seeing that the case came up before the Un-American Activities Committee."[9] Two weeks after Agnes's death, Willoughby appealed to Alfred Kohlberg directly, suggesting that since his "behind-the-scenes contribution to Senator McCarthy's abortive effort" to convict Lattimore was failing, he could now move instead to have Agnes's case "thrown into the breach."[10]

That June, Harold Velde, a Republican member of HUAC, made front-page news by demanding that Scotland Yard investigate whether Agnes had been "liquidated" by the Cominform (successor agency to the Comintern) on the eve of her proposed departure for the United States to prevent her from giving evidence to his committee. At the time of her demise, Velde informed the press, HUAC had been in the process of issuing her a subpoena. Agnes, he claimed, had been "ready to talk." As proof of her suspicious character, Velde pointed out that in the 1930s she had "put on slacks, had her hair cut like a man's, and worked as a war correspondent."[11] In response to acquaintances who argued that Agnes's health had apparently been good and her death unexpected, Katherine Anne Porter liked to point out that people "foully done away with" rarely died in nursing homes.[12]

Throughout 1950, views of Agnes coalesced along partisan lines, spurred by Truman's armed intervention of Korea, which brought American troops face-to-face with Communist Chinese forces—from opposing sides. Progressive voices, including Ickes's, pounded away at the injustice MacArthur had authorized and held up Agnes as a tragic victim.[13] However, when Agnes's will was filed for probate in December, reports that she had bequeathed a portion of her estate to the Chinese Communists, and her ashes to General Chu Teh (commander of the armies Americans were then fighting in Korea) for burial in China, persuaded Americans already primed to accept virtually any conspiracy theory that Agnes was a traitorous Red villainess who justified their most paranoid fears.

Late that December, Willoughby, frustrated by HUAC's seeming apathy, urged Kohlberg to investigate the high-level influence that was keeping his evidence from the American public.[14] Since Willoughby had nothing either on "that slippery snake in the grass," as he referred to Owen Lattimore, or the Institute of Pacific Relations, Kohlberg extended little help.[15] But in January 1951, the Senate established a rival committee to HUAC, the Senate Internal Security

Subcommittee, and when it convened its first investigation—into the activities and personnel of the IPR—Agnes (who had had nothing whatever to do with the organization) was included within the scope of its inquiry.[16]

General MacArthur was relieved of command soon afterward, but Truman's detractors fastened on the case against Agnes as a way to redeem the dishonored general. MacArthur had waited a long time to "pay off some of the creeps cluttering Washington," cold warrior Fulton Lewis Jr. wrote in his column in May 1951. Now MacArthur had a golden opportunity to get them back.

> He has all the answers ready for the Senate committee investigating the Truman-Acheson foreign policy in Asia, if somebody will just ask the questions...
>
> What the General latched onto was the Kremlin hotshot, Richard Sorge...
>
> One of Sorge's pets was Agnes Smedley, the American writer who was one of the busiest of the Chinese commy promoters. She was protected by the Pentagon after MacArthur had labeled her a pal of the Reds. Everybody but MacArthur got red faces later on when the Smedley woman died under mysterious circumstances in a British nursing hospital operated by the Communists. She willed her U.S. war bonds and other property to a Chinese Communist general, which didn't help Pentagon nerves very much.
>
> ... Smedley is going to be quite a figure in the General's tale of how the U.S. got betrayed in Asia.[17]

That same week, Chinese Communists held a memorial service for Agnes at the Youth Palace in Peking. Earlier that spring, a delegation of eight Chinese, Chen Han-seng among them, had transported her ashes from Great Britain for burial in accordance with Agnes's last wishes. Neither Chu Teh, Mao, nor Madame Sun attended, but eight hundred other Chinese—writers, journalists, personal friends, and a detachment of the People's Liberation Army—came to pay their respects. There was an exhibit with her books, typewriter, notebooks and photos, camera, radio, and correspondence with Chu Teh, and wreaths and scrolls from several organizations.

Beneath a large portrait of Agnes, the writers Mao Tun and Ting Ling, along with Chu Teh's wife and several of Agnes's foreign friends, spoke warmly of her work in and for China. Even on this day, however, her fall from official grace was noted. "A better individual than collective worker," Rewi Alley observed, "she often made sizeable mistakes."[18] Yang Kang, a journalist Agnes had known in the States, remarked that despite her great qualities, Agnes was "unable finally to rid herself of the individualism cherished by the old bourgeoisie" and resisted the "organization and discipline which would have given the sterling quality of her revolutionary heroism an opportunity for full development."[19]

Ting Ling attacked the "ruthless American reactionaries" whose persecution, she said, had prevented her friend from completing her biography of Chu Teh, but she avowed that Agnes's "frail constitution, aggravated by long years of intense work," rather than her rejection by Communist leaders, had forced her return to the United States. Deferring to the Party line, Ting Ling denied Agnes had anything to do with the Comintern or Soviet military intelligence and denounced MacArthur's attempt to implicate Agnes in a Far Eastern spy ring as "Red baiting."[20] She insisted his story of Agnes's close contact with the "two revolutionary martyrs" (Sorge and Ozaki) was a "fabrication," as was MacArthur's "slanderous" charge that the men had been Soviet spies.

George Hatem, now known as Ma Hai-te, provided the only confirmation of Agnes's clandestine life, obliquely noting that she had "participated in *every* type of revolutionary activity called for at that time," including "purchas[ing] an overcoat for a comrade about to undertake a dangerous assignment."[21] While Kawai had indeed reported in his initial interrogation that Agnes had Ozaki purchase an overcoat for Kawai before he left for Mukden in the winter of 1932 to gather information for Sorge, no investigator or reporter had so far divulged that detail.

After lunch, a rickety charcoal-burning truck carried mourners to Babaoshan, the cemetery for revolutionary martyrs on the western edge of the city. There Agnes's ashes were interred beneath a simple marble cenotaph inscribed "Agnes Smedley, revolutionary writer and friend of the Chinese people," and flowers placed on her grave.

Americans who had known Agnes in China were skeptical that such public displays accurately reflected Chinese feelings about her. "A friend of China is a foreigner who has been taken into the Chinese network of interpersonal relations and dutifully holds his end up," John Fairbank would write in the years to come. "He can be counted on...Westerners are notoriously likely to backslide in this relationship because they may put other considerations before the consistency of friendship."[22] But not Agnes, he observed; she had died at the right moment. Owen Lattimore concurred. "Had she lived long enough she would have been one of the first to be shot when the CCP took power," he noted. "She was more radical and idealistic than the members of the CCP: a fact which they recognized."[23]

On May 15, 1951, two footlockers containing the Shanghai Municipal Police files and Willoughby's index to them (in which he identified the 180 other suspicious Americans, including some from the State Department—he assured correspondents) arrived amidst great fanfare in Washington. Ten days later, Willoughby announced that he planned to leave Tokyo in order to help out his old chief, MacArthur, in D.C. Willoughby said he had a lot of unfinished business with the Pentagon, and a potentially lucrative movie deal riding on the outcome. With the press impatiently awaiting Willoughby's list of names, reports of Agnes's memorial service and burial in China created a furor. Kohlberg generated additional publicity with a press release that pointed out Agnes's influence over Generals Stilwell and Marshall and the high regard in which several of the State Department employees currently accused of harboring Communist sympathies had held her.

Maybe Smedley was dead, Kohlberg observed, but she had played an important role in bringing about the downfall of America's friends in China and the triumph of her enemies.[24] Freda Utley, now a vehement anti-Communist and an employee of Kohlberg's, accused Agnes of sowing the seeds of Nationalist China's destruction back in 1938, when she "tricked" gullible correspondents and military and diplomatic observers in Hankow into believing Chinese Communists were mere peasant reformers.[25]

On August 9, 1951, Willoughby appeared before the Senate Internal Security Subcommittee, which would eventually bring any number of Agnes's China friends and colleagues to the stand. At this time he produced the 1949 interrogation of Kawai Teikichi, which contained strong evidence of Agnes's work for Soviet military intelligence. But while Willoughby's supporters embraced his disclosures, the progressive press minimized or ridiculed them, and in his subsequent testimony at the belatedly conducted HUAC hearing, titled "American Aspects of the Sorge Spy Case," he produced no new leads against Agnes.

Meanwhile, the most damning evidence the FBI obtained went unpursued. Following up on a tip from Louis Budenz regarding Agnes's connection to the League Against Imperialism, the agency tracked down former Muenzenberg deputy Louis Gibarti, who had recanted and become an FBI informant.[26] In May 1951, agents hit pay dirt. According to their transcription, Gibarti advised them that Agnes had

gone to the Far East after getting in contact with Russian intelligence. She had been initiated into the China work when Borodin, the Comintern representative, and the Indian named Roy were staying in China in 1927 . . . Roy had selected Agnes Smedley for work in China in view of the recommendation of her husband [Chattopadhyaya]. The Russians wanted to use the protection of her American passport in exploring conditions on such territories where Russian agents would have been in danger.

She generally stayed in Shanghai from where she communicated thru the Russian boats touching the Shanghai harbor with Vladivostock, where, according to our knowledge, the Far Eastern center of the Russian intelligence was located during the 1920's and early 1930's.[27]

In his capacity as secretary of the League Against Imperialism, Gibarti, whom the FBI referred to as "Confidential Informant T-1," claimed he had received Agnes's reports, addressed to a place unknown to him on Russian soil, "by medium of Moscow." Mostly, he said, they depicted "the terroristic rule of Chiang Kai-shek after his arrival in Shanghai in 1927," but he acknowledged that they also included several on "Ruegg," the alleged Swiss trade union organizer arrested in Shanghai while working as a political agent for the Comintern in China.

"As a bona fide agent of the Soviet Union," Gibarti told the FBI, Agnes had been in "intimate contact" with CPUSA members Alexander Trachtenberg and Harrison George of the PPTUS, as well as with "pretty much everyone who had some position as a liberal in the U.S." Most tellingly, he reported that around 1927 Agnes "had a very high standing" in the Comintern's "Secret Department," particularly with such people as "Mironov," whom Gibarti described as "a big man of the Russian intelligence and also of the Secret Department of the Comintern." Gibarti had met Mironov "at a celebration of the anniversary of the Soviet revolution at the Soviet Embassy in Berlin," he reported. "At that reception Mironov mentioned Agnes Smedley as a mutual friend."[28]

Robert Morris, counsel for the Senate Internal Security Subcommittee, followed up with a personal visit to Gibarti in Paris. In a sworn deposition, Gibarti admitted his relationship with Agnes, whom he described as a "known and admitted Communist," and her work with the Chinese Communists, but Morris was focused on Owen Lattimore and did not press Gibarti for details.[29] For another two years the FBI pursued "outstanding leads" on two hundred of Agnes's associates—mostly China hands who had been critical of America's China policy and now fell under suspicion for harboring Communist sympathies. Then it closed her case.

In 1953, Agnes's *Daughter of Earth* and *Battle Hymn of China* were apparently among the titles burned in a "cleansing campaign" directed by Senator Joseph McCarthy at United States Information Agency libraries abroad.[30] Additional copies of those books—ironically, Agnes's least controversial—were removed from the shelves. Several months later an amended State Department policy allowed some books by "Communist authors" to be retained at USIA overseas libraries, but Agnes's were not among them.

First abroad and then in the United States, Agnes's books disappeared from libraries. Publishers allowed her books to go out of print. Knopf rejected her revised biography of Chu Teh, and Edgar Snow, to whom Agnes had assigned the thankless role of literary executor, found his attempts to place it elsewhere repeatedly frustrated. In 1955, a Japanese translation of the biography, edited by Snow, achieved a modest success. However, when the independent Marxist

Monthly Review Press published it in the United States the following year, it did poorly.

For the next fifteen years, the debate on Agnes continued in a minor way. A 1964 article in *Pravda*, which confirmed that Richard Sorge had been a Communist, an intelligence agent, and a Soviet hero, attracted the attention of conservatives, and Willoughby hoped the American press would now finally pursue his case against Agnes. But the *Pravda* piece, like a subsequent confession by Max Klausen, Sorge's radio operator, and a tribute to Sorge by Gerhardt Eisler in the East German press, went largely unreported in the United States. On the increasingly infrequent occasions when Agnes's name arose, Willoughby would rave about official attempts to "emasculate" the impact of his exposé, which left him and MacArthur prey to attacks by "crypto-communists." Snow, like other leftist liberals, would continue to depict her a martyr to the 1950s Red Scare. Both men died in 1972, their views of Agnes equally unbending.

With the demise of her most determined detractor as well as her staunchest supporter, Agnes might well have faded from view. But weeks after Snow's death, President Richard Nixon visited Peking. The historic event ushered in an era of diminished fear of Moscow that allowed for the normalization of relations with the People's Republic of China. Although there had been no place for Agnes's writings in the United States of the 1950s and 1960s, the civil rights struggle and the war in Vietnam gave a rising generation of Americans fresh insight into their society and the difficulties inherent in trying to build a better one. Resurgent interest in China and the growth of the modern women's movement made Agnes's passion and commitment once again seem impressive.

In 1973, the Feminist Press reprinted *Daughter of Earth*. Reviewers praised Agnes's depiction of the ways poverty crushed emotions and distorted relationships and perceptions—and described how little its victims understood the economic realities that damaged their lives. The battles and accomplishments of radical women were often edited out in the official remaking of history, novelist Marge Piercy remarked in the *New Republic*; Agnes's voice was a welcome counterforce that should be heard.[31]

The hard-won independence that had made Agnes an "unnatural" woman to her contemporaries made her a heroine to this next generation of women. By 1977, *Daughter of Earth* was in its fifth Feminist Press printing in the United States and available again in Europe and Asia. Since America was newly curious about the Chinese Revolution, publishers reprinted her China books. In the People's Republic of China, where Agnes had not been mentioned since 1960 (when Premier Chou En-lai launched a famous interview by Edgar Snow with a tribute to the memory of Agnes and Franklin Roosevelt), an article appeared that acknowledged her contributions to the revolutionary struggle.[32]

In 1984, U.S. Treasury officials finally allowed the monies Agnes had bequeathed Chu Teh three decades earlier to be transmitted to China. Under the auspices of the prestigious Academy of Social Sciences, Long March veterans—now high government officials—used the funds to establish an organization that would honor the three American journalists who had acquainted the world with the Chinese Revolution: Agnes Smedley, Edgar Snow, and Anna Louise Strong. At the inaugural meeting of the Smedley Snow-Strong Society the following year, Agnes was hailed as a "forerunner in promoting friendship and cooperation between the two countries."[33] No mention was made of her controversial activities.

In this more tolerant climate, Americans came to know Agnes from a liberal perspective—as the target of a brutal McCarthy era witch hunt. Throughout the 1980s, the prevailing view was that MacArthur's headquarters had charged an independent radical—and feminist—with complicity in a Soviet spy ring in the Far East. Although the accusation had been quickly withdrawn, the damage to Agnes's reputation had been permanent, the argument went. "Myths about Smedley's allegiance to the Communist Party . . . and a host of unsubstantiated

In 1985, China issued a commemorative stamp honoring Agnes for promoting "understanding and friendship between the people of China and other countries."

reports that she was a spy or traitor" had effectively wiped her from America's consciousness, German historian Gerd Alfred Petermann wrote.[34] In the *South Atlantic Quarterly*, David Duke argued that Agnes had been destroyed by scandalous Red-baiting after being scapegoated by Americans looking for excuses for their own failed cold war ventures.[35]

In 1988, a detailed biography of Smedley written by an American academic and his wife spent no time exploring the possible veracity of Willoughby's accusations and dismissed the charge that Agnes had worked for the Comintern in a single sentence.[36] In his review of the book for the English-language *China Daily*, Sinophile Hugh Deane dismissed as "absurd" the idea that Agnes had ever been a Soviet agent.[37] Orville Schell commented in the *Nation* that "it was not only supremely ironic but unjust that in 1949 she was accused of being a Communist spy and finally hounded from America by cold war extremism. Although there was never any evidence to link her to a Soviet espionage ring or the American Communist Party, she was found guilty by association."[38]

Further scraps of incriminating evidence fueled isolated attacks on Agnes from the right. After Sonja Kuczinski (who was living as Ruth Werner in East Germany) confessed her ties to Agnes and Sorge in a 1977 memoir, two British books charged that Roger Hollis, former chief of Great Britain's security agency, MI-5, was the elusive "fifth man" in the famous Soviet spy ring that had included Kim Philby, Guy Burgess, Donald Maclean, and Anthony Blunt and accused Agnes (or her friend Sonja) of recruiting Hollis in Shanghai in the 1930s.[39] The accusations, subsequently discredited, swayed few on the left against Smedley.

Today, Agnes is again obscure. The chill in Sino-U.S. relations has made her a less useful "friend" of the Chinese. The Smedley-Snow-Strong Society has been disbanded. On the fiftieth anniversary of Agnes's death in 2000, the Chinese Society for People's Friendship held only a small gathering for her in Beijing. Few of her books are currently in print. No motion pictures are planned.

But Agnes has left a legacy of enduring value nonetheless. In her six books and hundreds of articles, Smedley often blurred the line between propagandist and artist. Some might argue that her difficulty embracing the complexity of the world she observed and her tendency to polemicize prevent much of her work from sustaining the multiple layers of meaning that would make it literature. Regardless, her vibrant portraits for the *Frankfurter Zeitung* and books like *Chinese Destinies* and *China's Red Army Marches* offer a message of hope and optimism that still lifts our spirits in these cynical times. At her best, as in her novel, *Daughter of Earth*, and her memoir, *Battle Hymn of China*, she transformed brutality and suffering into gripping narratives of lasting power and beauty.

In the final analysis, though, it is Agnes herself rather than her writing that is most memorable. "She had more personality than is seen in her writing because her personality was restricted in print," Edgar Snow observed.[40] Her spirit was larger still. The overwhelming, intuitive forces that drove Smedley's life and art—her dogged insistence that human life have dignity and value, her willingness to die for her beliefs if it would relieve the suffering—were shaped by the experiences of her own young life, but her vision soon expanded to include millions of the earth's injured and oppressed. Those of us who respond with ardor to Smedley's message recognize that although we ourselves might be too complacent, too caught up in the complications of our modern lives—too happy, even—to join in perpetual combat with the forces Agnes Smedley took on, she was fighting many of the right battles: for herself, for us, and for history.

A NOTE ON SOURCES AND CITATIONS

A project of this range on someone like Agnes required reaching well beyond traditional sources. As a radical who lived through two Red Scares, Agnes had been leery of saving any personal papers. Her failure to attend an elite college, marry "up," or achieve distinction in a conventionally recognized field also made her unappealing for collection at traditional women's archives. Her peripatetic career required a global approach. In the end, diligent research turned up a treasure trove of correspondence along with recollections, written and verbal, from many who knew her, as well as a vast quantity of government files. However, like everything else in Agnes's complicated life, the sources I used to tell her story did not always fit the standard categories. This has made the task of "proper" citations challenging.

Some of my sources are no longer available. The conference proceedings of the S-S-S Society, published in an open period just before Tiananmen Square, provided a great deal of candid information that is no longer acknowledged. A few people I interviewed cannot be named, to protect their safety. Agnes's "personal" file from the Comintern did not make it to the Library of Congress. Unpublished oral histories and memoirs, passed hand to hand to those deemed trustworthy, arrived in difficult-to-read longhand drafts—in several versions, without pagination.

Some FBI records were deleted too extensively to cite. Far East Command documents on the Sorge case were organized under a variety of systems, with different pagination and translations; some versions were more comprehensive than others. Extensive government surveillance of Agnes also resulted in files from one agency containing documents from several others; those records sometimes had more data in one location than another. Finally, many of the materials I used originally appeared in languages other than English. Some differences in shading and interpretation are inevitable; hopefully, they are minor.

I have cited all sources as clearly as I can. For anyone with questions, my files are available.

ARCHIVES, LIBRARIES, AND PUBLIC DOCUMENTS

George Arents Library, Syracuse University
   Granville Hicks Papers
Hayden Library, Arizona State University, Tempe
   Agnes Smedley Papers: scattered correspondence with John Fairbank, Ernest Brundin, Randall Gould, Aino and Elviira Taylor, and between Edgar Snow and Harold Ickes; also records of Smedley's memorial service, drafts of Smedley's partially completed, unpublished play, lecture notes, an unpublished interview with George Bernard Shaw, photographs, and other ephemera
Beineke Rare Book and Manuscript Library, Yale University
   Langston Hughes Papers
Butler Library, Columbia University, New York City
   Indusco Papers
   American Bureau for Medical Aid to China Collection
California State Board of Health, Bureau of Vital Statistics
   Certificate of marriage
Carnegie Library, Trinidad, Colorado
   Oral history, Delagua
Emory University, Robert Woodruff Library for Advanced Studies
   Philip Jaffe Papers: International Labor Defense correspondence
Federal Archives and Records Center, Bayonne, New Jersey
   Records of the U.S. District Court for the Southern District of New York
Howard Gotlieb Archival Research Center, Boston University
   Michael Blankfort Papers
Maxim Gorky Institute for World Literature, Moscow
   Agnes Smedley Papers
Hoover Institution on War, Revolution, and Peace, Stanford University
   Norman Allman Papers
   Jack Belden Papers
   Joseph Freeman Papers
   Bonner F. Fellers Papers
   Alfred Kohlberg Papers: Benjamin Mandel file
   Freda Utley Papers
   Nym Wales [Helen Foster Snow] Papers: source material, Sian Incident; Smedley news dispatches, Sian; correspondence
   Charles A. Willoughby Papers
Houghton Library, Harvard University
   Lewis Gannett Papers: correspondence with Lewis Gannett, Blanche Knopf, Bernard Smith, and John Sanford
Huntington Library, San Marino, California
   Charles Erskine Scott Wood Papers
   Upton Sinclair Papers

Internationaal Instituut voor Sociale Geschiedenis, Amsterdam
 Emma Goldman, Alexander Berkman Papers
Kongelige Bibliotek, Copenhagen, Denmark
 Karin Michaelis Papers
Las Animas County Clerk's Office, Trinidad, Colorado
 Property Book Records
 Chattel Mortgage Records
Library of Congress, Washington, D.C., Main Reading Room
 State Commission for Safeguarding Public Order and the News Gathering Center of
  the Ministry of the Interior, "Betrifft: Durchsuchung der Raume der 'Liga gegen
  den Imperialismus,' 3 July, 1929–31 December, 1931"
Library of Congress, Washington, D.C., Manuscript Division
 Comintern Papers, correspondence of the secretariat (ECCI)
 CPUSA Papers
 Harold Ickes Papers
 Gilbert Roe Papers, in La Follette Collection; also contains correspondence from
  E. H. Van Shack
 Margaret Sanger Papers
Lilly Library, Indiana University, Bloomington
 Upton Sinclair Papers: includes "The Red Dragon: The Story of Agnes Smedley in
  America and China"
Douglas MacArthur Memorial Library and Archive, Norfolk, Virginia
 Charles A. Willoughby Papers
 National Archives, Washington, D.C.
 Record Group (RG) 46: Records of the U.S. Senate
  Senate Internal Security Subcommittee, name files, Institute of Pacific Relations
   Investigation
  Ralph Van Deman Papers
 RG 59: General Records of the Department of State
  Decimal File Records, 1910–49
  Records Related to the Internal Affairs of China
  Records of the Office of the Counselor (U-H Series)
 RG 60: General Records of the Department of Justice
  Classified Subject Files [193424]
 RG 65: Records of the Federal Bureau of Investigation
  Old German (OG) files
  Bureau Section (BS) files
 RG 75: Records of the Bureau of Indian Affairs
  Enrollment Records
 RG 118: Records of the U.S. Attorney
  Northern District of California, neutrality violation case files
 RG 123: Records of the U.S. Court of Claims
  Guion Miller Enrollment of Eastern Cherokees
 RG 165: Records of the War Department, General and Special Staffs.
  Military Intelligence Division (MID)
 RG 242: National Archives Collection of Foreign Records Seized 1941

Records of the German Foreign Ministry and the Reich Chancellery
RG 263: Records of the Central Intelligence Agency
Shanghai Municipal Police (SMP) files
RG 319: Records of the Army Staff
Office of the Assistant Chief of Staff, G-2, Intelligence, Intelligence Document
    (ID) files
National Archives of India, New Delhi
    Weekly Reports, Director, Intelligence Bureau, Simla, Home Political Deposits
    India Office, Whitehall, Home Political
National Security Agency Archives, Fort Meade, Maryland
    Government Code and Cypher School: Decrypts of Communist International
        (Comintern) Messages—Codename MASK
New York Public Library, Rare Books and Manuscripts Division
    Maud Russell Papers
    International Committee for Political Prisoners: includes correspondence with Roger
        Baldwin
Newberry Library, Chicago
    Malcolm Cowley Papers
Princeton University Library
    American Civil Liberties Union Archives: includes correspondence of Gilbert Roe
        and Walter Nelles
    Roger Baldwin Papers
Public Record Office, London
    British Foreign Office files
Revolutionary Museum, Beijing, China
    Correspondence with Chu Teh
Franklin D. Roosevelt Library, Hyde Park, New York
    Eleanor Roosevelt Papers
Russian Center for the Preservation and Study of Documents of Recent History
    (RTsKhIDNI), Moscow
    Records of the Communist International (now available at LC)
        Cipher telegrams of the Secretariat (ECCI) (495 series)
        Profintern (534) files
    Records of the Communist Party of the United States of America (now available at LC)
Schlesinger Library, Radcliffe College
    Adelaide Schulkind Papers
State of Colorado, Division of Archives and Personal Records, Denver
    Report of County Examination of Teachers, Las Animas County.
    County Superintendent's Annual Report, Las Animas County.
Swarthmore College Peace Collection
    Helene Stoecker Papers
Tamiment Library, New York University, New York City
    Socialist Party records
Harry S. Truman Library
    Harry S. Truman Papers
University of California, Berkeley
    Emma Goldman Project (Emma Goldman to Demi Coleman)

Tom Mooney Papers, Bancroft Library: correspondence with Roger Baldwin
Friends of Freedom for India Papers, South Asia Library: correspondence with Ed
    Gammons and Hindustan Ghadr Party
University Libraries, University of Maryland, College Park
    Katherine Anne Porter Papers
University of Missouri–Kansas City Archives
    Edgar Snow Papers
Yaddo, Saratoga Springs, New York
    Elizabeth Ames Papers (now at NYPL)
Wayne State University, Labor History and Urban Affairs Archives
    IWW Papers
Vanguard Press, New York City
    Eva Ginn Papers; also contains correspondence with Wieland Herzfelde
Wisconsin Historical Society, University of Wisconsin at Madison
    Raymond Robins Papers
    Gwyneth Roe Papers
Yale Library, Yale University
    Max Lerner Papers

Freedom of Information Act Requests

State Department Passport Division
Federal Bureau of Investigation
Army Intelligence (now available at National Archives)

Private Collections

Gertrude Binder: "Espionage," oral history
Joyce Brown: Ellen Kennan correspondence
Steve Finney: Smedley family photo album
Tom Grunfeld: Grace Granich oral history, Max Granich oral history (now at Tamiment
    Library, New York University)
Florence Becker Lennon: correspondence, memoirs (now at the University of Colorado,
    Boulder), correspondence with Tarak Nath Das
Paul Nichols: Smedley family juvenilia
Elizabeth Smedley: Smedley family photos
Lois Snow: correspondence, Long March materials (now at University of
    Missouri–Kansas City Archives)
Mamie McCullough Weston: correspondence
Toni Willison: correspondence with Katherine Anne Porter

Interviews/Correspondence

Betty Barnes, Nirode Barooah, Carolyn Beals, Abe Bernstein, Gertrude Binder, Meng
Bo, Eleanor Brundin, Esther Carroll, Harindranath Chattopadhyaya, Ram
Chattopadhyaya, Ellen Chessler, Oliver Clubb, Malcolm Cowley, Nellie Armstrong
Craig, Ranendranath Das, Hugh Deane, Peggy Dennis, Tillman Durdin, Israel Epstein,

Robert Farnsworth, Frederick Field, Jiang Feng, John Burt Foster, Maia Fox, Talitha Gerlach, Tom Grunfeld,Robert Haberman, Emily Hahn, Jack Hamilton, John Earl Haynes, Dorothy Healey, Baruch Hirson, Hu Chi-an, Huang Hua, Alfred Humphreys, Harold Isaacs, Ayako Ishigaki, Annie Joel, Harvey Klehr, Stephen Koch, Horst Krueger, Owen Lattimore, Herbert Leckie, Florence Becker Lennon, Lynn Lubkeman, A. B. McGill, Dean Mabry, Margaret Moe, Tapan Mukherjee, Tillie Olsen, Vladimir Pichugin, Francis Fox Piven, Billie Privett, Richard Popplewell, Elliot Porter, Arnold Rampersad, Barbara Ramusack, Jose Romero, Herbert Romerstein, Samaren Roy, Maud Russell, Harrison Salisbury, Harriet Sargeant, John Service, Judith Schwarz, Donald Sheckler, Jane Singh, Elizabeth Smedley, Helen Foster Snow, Elizabeth Glen Spector, I. F. Stone, Tracy Strong, Bernard Thomas, Wineva Todd, John Basil Utley, Ruth Weiss, Mamie McCullough Weston, Toni Willison, Ella Wolfe, Xia Yan, Lu Yi, Maochen Yu, Ida Zakula, Yassen Zassoursky, Peiyun Zhou

NOTES

Introduction

1. Agnes Smedley, *Daughter of Earth* (New York: Coward-McCann, 1929), 1–2.
2. Agnes Smedley to Edgar Snow, 19 April [1937], Edgar Snow Papers.
3. Ayahoo [Agnes Smedley] to Florence Becker Lennon, 8 December [1923], courtesy of Florence Becker Lennon.
4. Smedley to Lennon, 19 July [1930].
5. Agnes Smedley to John Fairbank, 24 August 1935, Agnes Smedley Papers.
6. I would like to acknowledge my indebtedness to Albert Camus's *The Rebel: An Essay on Man in Revolt* (1956; New York: Vintage International, 1991), tr. Anthony Bower.
7. Confidential Informant T-1 [identified by the author as Muenzenberg deputy Louis Gibarti], interview by FBI, 11 May 1951, FBI NY 100-68282. FBI documents refer to the League Against Imperialism as the "Anti-Imperialist League."
8. "Extracts from an Authenticated Translation of Foreign Affairs Yearbook, 1942," 232, in U.S. Army, Far East Command, Military Intelligence Section, *A Partial Documentation of the Sorge Espionage Case* (Tokyo: Toppan Printing, 1950), ID 923289, RG 319.

Chapter 1. Beginnings

1. For the Quaker background of the Smedley family, see Gilbert Cope, *Genealogy of the Smedley Family* (Lancaster, Pennsylvania: Wickersham Printing Co., 1901); Nancy Spears to author, 15 September 1987; Agnes Smedley to Raymond Robins, 12 April 1946. For the early roots of the Montgomery/Ralls family, see

Noel Currier-Briggs, *Virginia Settlers and English Adventurers*, volume 1, *Abstract of Wills, 1494-1798* (Baltimore: Genealogical Publishing, 1970), 102; Elizabeth Petty Bentley, compiler, *Genealogies of Virginia Families*, volume 3 (Baltimore: Genealogical Publishing, 1982), 112; Beverly Fleet, *Virginia Colonial Abstracts*, volume 3 (Baltimore: Genealogical Publishing Co., 1988), 417, 577. For the Montgomery/Ralls Revolutionary War service, see Richard Collins, *History of Kentucky*, volume 1 (Covington, Kentucky: Collins, 1882), 12, 354, 356; Goldena Roland Howard, *Ralls County, Missouri* (New London, Missouri: self-published, 1980), 410–12. For more on the Smedleys' contribution to the Revolutionary War, see Arthur Latham Perry, *Origins in Williamstown* (New York: Charles Scribner's Sons, 1896), 467–77, 523.

2. Agnes Smedley, *Battle Hymn of China* (New York: Alfred A. Knopf, 1943), 3.

3. Perry, *Origins in Williamstown*, 610.

4. For the Smedley Cherokee lineage, see Entry 1271, M[ary] J[ane] [Thompson] Smedley, Canadian District, Indian Territory, 1880, RG 75; Enrollment Number 7010 (Dawes Roll Number 16743), Jack Smedley, Canadian District, Indian Territory, 1902, RG 75; Application 37645, Jack Smedley, RG 123. Also Nellie Armstrong Craig, interview by author, Osgood, Missouri, 20 July 1987. Smedley also discusses her heritage in *Daughter of Earth* and *Battle Hymn*.

5. Agnes Smedley, *Daughter of Earth* (New York: Coward-McCann, 1929), 10. Wherever possible, I have attempted to verify the events referred to in Smedley's autobiographical novel from independent sources. I do, however, accept its essential emotional reality and apologize for any exaggerations that appear in this text as a result.

6. Robert E. Bieder, "Scientific Attitudes Toward Indian Mixed-Bloods in Early Nineteenth-Century America," *Journal of Ethnic Studies* 8, no. 2 (Summer 1980): 20–27; Billy Privett, interview by author, Osgood, Missouri, 13 July 1987.

7. Smedley, *Battle Hymn*, 4.

8. Privett, interview.

9. For the story of Rausey Privett Ralls, John Ralls, Jacob Armstrong, and Mary Smedley Armstrong Ralls, see Ruth Ralls Fisher, *This Small Town Osgood* (Milan, Missouri: Milan Standard, 1975), 28; Daughters of the American Revolution, General John Sullivan Chapter, *Cemetery Inscriptions of Sullivan County Missouri*, volume 1 (Milan, Missouri: privately printed, 1952), 1:1 and 2:93; Gladys Wells Crumpacker, *The Complete History of Sullivan County, Missouri*, volume 1, *1836–1900* (Milan, Missouri: History Publications, 1977), 673; Smedley, *Battle Hymn*, 3–4. Also Wineva Todd, correspondence with author, 14 September 1987; Privett, interview.

10. Privett, interview.

11. Smedley, *Daughter of Earth*, 3.

12. Ibid.

13. Enrollment Number 5864 (Dawes Roll Numbers 29517, 29518), Richard and William Smedley, Tahlequah District, Indian Territory, 1902, RG 75.

14. Smedley, *Daughter of Earth*, 7

15. Ibid., 19.

16. William A. Settle Jr., *Jesse James Was His Name* (Columbia: University of Missouri Press, 1966), 173. For more on James as an archtype of the "good badman,"

see Kent Ladd Steckmesser, *Western Outlaws: The 'Good Badman' in Fact, Film, and Folklore* (Claremont, California: Regina Books, 1983); Richard E. Meyer, "The Outlaw: A Distinctive American Folktype," *Journal of the Folklore Institute* 17 (May–December, 1980): 94–124.

17. Settle, *Jesse James*, 173.
18. Smedley, *Daughter of Earth*, 9–10.
19. Ibid., 7.
20. Ibid., 12.
21. Ibid., 24.
22. *Twelfth Census of the U.S.*, Farm Schedule 48, Bowman Township, Sullivan County, Missouri, 6 June 1900. In *Daughter of Earth*, Agnes refers to Charles's stint as a patent medicine agent as an apprenticeship to an eye doctor.
23. Smedley, *Daughter of Earth*, 29.
24. Despondent about her harelip, Eva Ralls swallowed carbolic acid after an argument with her mother in 1912; Bertha Ralls killed herself over a failed love affair in 1920. A. Frank Ralls hanged himself in 1940 although he was in no financial difficulty, and George Ralls committed suicide in 1969.
25. Elizabeth Smedley, interview by author, Chula Vista, California, 20 August 1984.
26. Smedley, *Daughter of Earth*, 5.
27. Ibid., 4–5.
28. Ibid., 4.
29. Ibid., 32.
30. Ibid., 25.
31. Privett, interview; Alfred Humphreys, interview by author, Osgood, Missouri, 13 July 1987. In Agnes's account, she refers to John Wolf by his real name.
32. Smedley, *Daughter of Earth*, 15.
33. George G. Suggs Jr., "The Colorado Coal Miners Strike, 1903–04," *Journal of the West* 12, no. 1 (January 1973): 36.
34. *Eighth Biennial Report (1901–1902) of the Bureau of Labor Statistics of the State of Colorado* (Denver: Smith-Brooks, 1902), 383.
35. Smedley, *Daughter of Earth*, 35.
36. Ibid., 42.
37. Robert A. Murray, *Las Animas, Huerfano, and Custer: Three Colorado Counties on a Cultural Frontier-A History of the Raton Basin* (Denver: Colorado State Office Bureau of Land Management, 1979), 89; Jose Romero, interview by author, Denver, 21 July 1985. For more, see Barron Beshoar, *Out of the Depths: The Story of John R. Lawson, a Labor Leader* (Denver: Colorado Labor Historical Committee of the Denver Trades and Labor Assembly, 1942), 1; "The Coal Project-III," *Rocky Mountain News*, 3 March 1985.
38. Dale Fetherling, *Mother Jones, the Miner's Angel: A Portrait* (Carbondale: Southern Illinois University Press, 1979), 60; Linda Atkinson, *Mother Jones: The Most Dangerous Woman in America* (New York: Crown, 1978), 137–39.
39. Suggs, "The Colorado Coal Miner's Strike," 41.
40. *Ninth Biennial Report of the Bureau of Labor Statistics of the State of Colorado, 1903–1904* (Denver: Smith-Brooks, 1904), 195; "Coal Men in Southern Fields Walk Out and Deputies Are Sworn In," *United Mine Workers Journal*, 12 November 1903.

41. Senate Document no. 122, 58th Congress, 3d Session, *A Report on Labor Disturbances in the State of Colorado from 1880 to 1904, Inclusive, with Correspondence Relating Thereto* (Washington: Government Printing Office, 1905), 341.

42. Smedley, *Daughter of Earth*, 97.

43. Ibid., 47, 50.

44. Ibid., 97.

45. Statement by Agnes Smedley, 2 January 1919, MID 9771-72/25, RG 165.

46. *Ninth Biennial Report*, 195–96.

47. Smedley, *Daughter of Earth*, 79–80.

48. Suggs, "The Colorado Coal Miners' Strike," 51.

49. In 1914, Colorado National Guardsmen were again called in to "keep order" in the southern Colorado coalfields. During this subsequent UMW strike, the militia opened fire on a strikers' camp in Ludlow, thirteen miles north of Trinidad, killing half a dozen strikers and destroying the camp. Thirteen women and children burned to death when the tent in which they were hiding caught fire and trapped them inside. Unlike the 1903–4 strike, the "Ludlow Massacre" became a national cause célèbre.

50. Agnes Smedley to Sam Smedley, 2 January 1909, courtesy of Paul Nichols; Agnes Smedley, "The Romance," *Tempe Normal Student*, 12 April 1912.

51. Anonymous [Agnes Smedley], "One Is Not Made of Wood: The True Story of a Life," *New Masses* 3, no. 4 (August 1927): 5.

52. In *Daughter of Earth*, Agnes claims that her parents quarreled bitterly over suffrage rather than Peabody's handling of the strike, but women had won the vote in Colorado more than ten years earlier. Given Charles's role in Peabody's campaign, Agnes had reason to obscure the issue.

53. J. Richard Snyder, "The Election of 1904: An Attempt at Reform," *Colorado Magazine* 45, no. 1 (Winter 1968): 25; George G. Suggs, *Colorado's War on Militant Unionism: James H. Peabody and the Western Federation of Miners* (Detroit: Wayne State University Press, 1972), 186–7.

54. Dean Mabry, interview by author, Trinidad, Colorado, 15 July 1985. In *Daughter of Earth*, Agnes refers to the mine operator by his real name, Charles F. Turner.

55. Grantee Index 6445, 22 June 1905, Property Book Records.

56. Smedley, *Daughter of Earth*, 96.

57. Ibid., 36.

58. Smedley, *Daughter of Earth*, 65; Mabry, interview; Romero, interview.

59. Smedley, *Daughter of Earth*, 38.

60. Ibid., 73.

61. Ibid.

62. Ibid., 60.

63. Submerged under water, Delagua no longer exists.

64. Smedley, *Daughter of Earth*, 81.

65. Mabry, interview.

66. Smedley, *Daughter of Earth*, 103.

67. Ibid., 140–41. According to family records, Buck's real name was either Sky Williams or Al Brown.

68. Ibid., 141.

69. Ibid., 85.

70. Ibid., 82, 96.
71. Barbara Hallas Lee, "Delagua," oral history, 6 February 1964.
72. "Personal Column," *Trinidad Chronicle News*, 17 April 1907; Romero, interview.
73. Smedley, *Daughter of Earth*, 78.
74. *Trinidad Chronicle News*, 17 April 1907.
75. Chattel Mortgage 74797, 3 April 3 1908; Smedley, *Daughter of Earth*, 91.
76. [Smedley], "One Is Not Made of Wood," 6; Smedley, *Daughter of Earth*, 91-92.
77. "Tercio," *Camp and Plant*, 6 February 1904.
78. Jose M. Romero, *El Valle de los Rancheros* (Jose M. Romero, 1987), 82; Romero, interview.
79. [Smedley], "One is Not Made of Wood," 5.
80. Smedley, *Battle Hymn*, 5.
81. *School Laws of the State of Colorado* (Denver: Smith-Brooks, 1909), 96.
82. Smedley, *Daughter of Earth*, 103; *Report of County Examination of Teachers*, Las Animas County, 18 March 1909.
83. *County Superintendent's Annual Report*, Las Animas County, 1909.
84. Smedley, *Daughter of Earth*, 103.
85. Ibid.
86. Ibid., 111.
87. Ibid., 112.
88. Agnes Smedley, "The Magazine Agent," *Tempe Normal Student*, 22 March 1912.
89. [Smedley], "One Is Not Made of Wood," 6.
90. Smedley, *Battle Hymn*, 6.
91. Smedley, *Daughter of Earth*, 101.
92. Smedley, *Battle Hymn*, 7.

CHAPTER 2. EMERGENCE AS A RADICAL

1. Smedley, *Daughter of Earth*, 103.
2. Agnes Smedley, "The Magazine Agent," *Tempe Normal Student*, 22 March 1912.
3. Smedley, *Daughter of Earth*, 129.
4. Ibid., 130.
5. Smedley, "The Magazine Agent."
6. Ibid.
7. Ibid. In her 2 January 1919 statement to the War Department (MID 9771-72/25, RG 165), Agnes acknowledged a breakdown. However, by 1925, when she wrote *Daughter of Earth*, she recalled the episode as a bout with starvation.
8. For more, see Charles W. Burr, "The Mimicry of Cardiac Affections by Neurasthenia," *International Medical Magazine* 12 (1903): 224–26; Burton E. Hamilton and Frank H. Lahey, "Differentiation of Hyperthyroidism and of Heart Disease from Neurasthenic States," *Journal of the American Medical Association* 78, no. 23 (1922) 1793–96; Howell T. Pershing, "Neurasthenia: An Increased Susceptibility to Emotion," *Journal of the American Medical Association* 61, no. 19 (1913): 1675–80. For a contemporary account, see F. G. Gosling, *Before Freud: Neurasthenia and the American Medical Community, 1870–1910* (Urbana: University of Illinois Press, 1987).

9. "Debate," *Tempe Normal Student,* 26 April 1912.
10. Smedley, *Daughter of Earth,* 42–45.
11. Ibid., 3.
12. Robert W. Young and William Morgan Sr., *The Navajo Language: A Grammar and Colloquial Dictionary* (Albuquerque: University of New Mexico Press, 1987), 138; Harold E. Driver, *Indians of North America* (Chicago: University of Chicago Press, 1969), 43. The Cherokee and Navajo languages have no cognates—they do not share a mother tongue.
13. "Recalls 'Red Empress' as Student at Tempe," *Phoenix Gazette,* 11 January 1937.
14. Smedley, *Daughter of Earth,* 151.
15. Ibid., 152–53.
16. Ibid., 152.
17. Ibid., 159.
18. Elinor Brundin, interview by author, Cerritos, California, 3 January 1987.
19. Agnes Smedley to Karin Michaelis, 1 April [1923], Karin Michaelis Papers.
20. Smedley, *Daughter of Earth,* 157.
21. Donald Sheckler, interview by author, Dulzura, California, 7 July 1985.
22. Smedley, *Daughter of Earth,* 159.
23. Ibid., 160; Statement by Agnes Smedley, 2 January 1919.
24. Smedley, *Daughter of Earth,* 161.
25. For more on Robert "Roberto" Haberman, a top adviser to Felipe Carillo during his socialist experiment on Mexico's Yucatan peninsula and a colleague of M. N. Roy, see MID 9140-665, RG 165; Carleton Beals, *Glass Houses: Ten Years of Free-lancing* (Philadelphia: J. B. Lippincott, 1938); Gregg Andrews, "Robert Haberman, Socialist Ideology, and the Politics of National Reconstruction in Mexico, 1920–1925," *Mexican Studies/Estudios Mexicanos* 6, no. 2 (Summer 1990):189–212; Diana K. Christopoulos, "American Radicals and the Mexican Revolution, 1900–1925," Ph.D. dissertation, SUNY, Binghamton, 1980.
26. Brundin, interview.
27. Smedley, *Daughter of Earth,* 93–94.
28. Anonymous [Agnes Smedley], "One Is Not Made of Wood: The True Story of a Life," *New Masses* 3, no. 4 (August 1927): 5.
29. Brundin, interview.
30. Office of Admissions and Records, University of California, Berkeley, to author, 10 February 1988. In *Daughter of Earth,* Agnes obscures the date of her enrollment to disguise her early involvement with the Ghadr Party.
31. A. Smedley-Brundin, "The Yellow Man," *Tempe Normal Student,* 28 February 1913.
32. Agnes Smedley to Tarak Nath Das, 2 December 1918, MID 9771-72/25-A, RG 165. Records of the Socialist Party at the Tamiment Institute do not list her as a member.
33. Smedley, *Daughter of Earth,* 165–66.
34. Emily Brown, *Har Dayal: Indian Revolutionary and Rationalist* (Tucson: University of Arizona Press, 1975), 8.
35. Ibid., 107–8.
36. "Plans for Revolution Revealed by Woman," *San Francisco Examiner,* 22 December 1917.

37. Special Agent Roy A. Mullen to A. R. Barr, 3 May 1929, State Department Passport (130) file, Agnes Smedley.

38. Statement by Agnes Smedley, 2 January 1919.

39. Joan M. Jensen, *Passage from India: Asian Indian Immigrants in North America* (New Haven: Yale University Press, 1988), 141. Also see Jeremiah Jenks, *The Immigration Problem: A Study of American Immigration Conditions and Needs* (New York: Funk and Wagnalls , 1917); Rajani Kanta Das, *Hindustani Workers on the Pacific Coast* (Berlin: Walter de Gruyter, 1923).

40. Brundin, interview.

41. Agnes Smedley to Florence Becker Lennon, 28 October [1924], courtesy of Florence Becker Lennon.

42. Ibid.

43. Brundin, interview; Certificate of Marriage.

44. Agnes to Dad, 6 September 1912, courtesy of Paul Nichols.

45. Statement by Agnes Smedley, 2 January 1919.

46. For more on the Ghadr Party, see Brown, *Har Dayal*; Harish K. Puri, *Ghadar Movement: Ideology, Organization, and Strategy* (Amritsar: Guru Nanak Dev University Press, 1983); Khushwant Singh, *Ghadr 1915* (New Delhi: R and K, 1966); Tilak Raj Sareen, *Indian Revolutionary Movement Abroad, 1905–1921* (New Delhi: Sterling, 1979); L. P. Mathur, *Indian Revolutionary Movement of the United States of America* (Delhi: S. Chand, 1970); Arun Coomer Bose, *Indian Revolutionaries Abroad, 1905–1922, in the Background of International Developments* (Patna: Bharati Bhawan, 1971); Anil Baran Ganguly, *Ghadr Revolution in America* (New Delhi: Metropolitan, 1980); Gurdev Singh Deol, *The Role of the Ghadar Party in the National Movement* (Delhi: Sterling, 1969).

47. Puri, *Ghadar Movement*, 110. For more, see Mark Naidis, "Propaganda of the Ghadr Party," *Pacific Historical Review* 20, no. 3 (August 1951): 255.

48. Statement by Agnes Smedley, 2 January 1919. Agnes says here only that she met an Indian "seditionist" in northwest California at this time who took her name and address and offered to send her something to read. But her concern about the "Eastern question," as she described it, and the anti-alien land laws fix the date of her initial interest in Asian issues at 1912–13, when Dayal was the only English-speaking Indian activist in the Bay Area who dealt with Caucasians.

49. [Smedley], "One Is Not Made of Wood," 5.

50. Ibid.

51. Smedley, *Daughter of Earth*, 166.

52. Statement by Agnes Smedley, 2 January 1919.

53. A search of the *Los Angeles Examiner* for the years 1912–16 turned up no articles under Agnes's byline.

54. [Smedley], "One Is Not Made of Wood," 6.

55. Smedley to Michaelis, 1 April [1923].

56. Smedley, *Daughter of Earth*, 171.

57. "Farewell Dinner at Lytton Apartments," *San Diego Normal Student*, 18 June 1914.

58. *San Diego Normal Student*, 13 May 1914; 9 December 1915; Sheckler, interview.

59. *San Diego Normal Student*, 9 March 1916.

60. Sheckler, interview; Myrtle Smedley photo album, courtesy of Steve Finney.

61. *San Diego Normal Student*, 17 February 1916, 16 March 1916.

62. "Former San Diego Normal School Student Fighting in China for U.S. Citizenship," *San Diego Union*, 24 May 1937.

63. "When Radicals Quarrel: Agnes Smedley's Reply," *China Weekly News*, 31 August 1935; Kamaladevi Chattopadhyaya, *Inner Recesses, Outer Spaces* (New Delhi: Navrang, 1986), 55.

64. Sheckler, interview.

65. Other American women who participated in what became known as the "Hindu-German Conspiracy" case include Frieda Hauswirth Das (a.k.a. Mrs. Warren), Ethel Dolson, Amy Dudley, G. F. Britton, Camille Gillingham (a.k.a. Mrs. Verne Smith), "Jean Fischer," "Sister Christine," and "Mrs. McCloud." See "Defense Admits German Plots Against India," *Chicago Tribune*, 20 October 1917; "Sought to Mix China in Indian Revolt," *New York Times*, 19 December 1917; "German-China Pact Sought in India Plot," *San Francisco Examiner*, 19 December 1917; "Plans for Revolution Revealed by Woman," *San Francisco Examiner*, 22 December 1917, "Woman's Aid Sought for Hindu Plot," *San Francisco Examiner*, 9 January 1918; "Ram Chandra Exposed by Aged Woman," *San Francisco Examiner*, 10 January 1918; "Missing Witness Located; Is Bride," *San Francisco Examiner*, 16 January 1918; "Berlin Plan to Stir Up Race Hatred Is Claimed," *San Francisco Examiner*, 19 January 1918; "Hindu in Plot Is Found Insane," *San Francisco Examiner*, 13 March 1918.

66. Office of Admissions and Records, University of California, Berkeley, to author, 10 February 1988.

67. Deol, *The Role of the Ghadr Party in the National Movement*, 128; Agnes Smedley to Roger Baldwin, 29 October [1927], Tom Mooney Papers; E. H. Van Shack to Agnes Smedley, 16 July [1919], Gilbert Roe Papers.

68. Gilbert Roe to Mr. O'Brien, 13 January 1919, File 193424/42, RG 60.

69. Statement by Agnes Smedley, 2 January 1919.

70. Smedley, *Daughter of Earth*, 180.

71. Upton Beall Sinclair, *Expect No Peace* (Girard, Kansas: Haldeman-Julius, 1939), 35.

72. *San Diego Normal Student*, 4 May 1916.

73. Smedley, *Daughter of Earth*, 202.

74. Ibid., 182.

75. Statement by Agnes Smedley, 2 January 1919.

76. "German Coin Paid Expense, Says Witness," *San Francisco Examiner*, 11 January 1918; "Hindu German Intrigue Letters Bared; Japanese Agents Figure in Conspiracy," *San Francisco Examiner*, 28 February 1918.

77. For a description of these tensions, see Singh, *Ghadr 1915*, 16–17; Bose, *Indian Revolutionaries Abroad*, 174–77; Jensen, *Passage from India*, 211.

78. Statement by Agnes Smedley, 2 January 1919.

79. Smedley, *Daughter of Earth*, 207.

80. Sheckler, interview.

CHAPTER 3. INDIAN ACTIVISM IN GREENWICH VILLAGE

1. For more on prewar Greenwich Village, see Albert Parry, *Garrets and Pretenders: A History of Bohemianism in America* (New York: Covici, Friede, 1933); Leslie Fishbein, *Rebels in Bohemia: The Radicals of the Masses, 1911–1917* (Chapel Hill:

University of North Carolina Press, 1982); Allen Churchill, *The Improper Bohemians: A Recreation of Greenwich Village in Its Heyday* (New York: Dutton, 1959); Edward Abrahams, *The Lyrical Left: Randolph Bourne, Alfred Steiglitz, and the Origins of Cultural Radicalism in America* (Charlottesville: University Press of Virginia, 1986).

2. *United States v. Sailendra Nath Ghose, Agnes Smedley and others*, Grand Jury Testimony, Henrietta Rodman, 17 April 1918, MID 9771-72, RG 165.

3. *United States v. Sailendra Nath Ghose, Agnes Smedley and others*, Grand Jury Testimony, Bayard Rodman, 17 April 1918, MID 9771-72, RG 165.

4. Agnes Smedley, *Daughter of Earth* (New York: Coward-McCann, 1929), 201.

5. Karin Michaelis, foreword, *Kun en Kvinde* ([Copenhagen]: Fremad, 1933), tr. H. B. Miller.

6. Ibid., 218.

7. Smedley, *Daughter of Earth*, 201.

8. Interview with Robert Haberman, 2 August 1921, MID 10058-0-91/1, RG 165; Confidential Memo, Office of Naval Intelligence, 21 December 1917, MID 9140-665/4, RG 165.

9. Other Civic Club members who would play a role in Agnes's life include Lajpat Rai, Henrietta Rodman, Roger Baldwin, Albert DeSilver, Ernestine Evans, Lewis Gannett, the Reverend John Hayes Holmes, Sailendra Nath Ghose, Ellen Kennan, Frieda Kirchway, Mary Knoblauch, Robert Morss Lovett, Robert Minor, Gertrude Nafe, Charles Recht, Gilbert Roe, Margaret Sanger, Truda Weil, Harry Weinberger, and Albert Rhys Williams.

10. In *Daughter of Earth*, the character Sardar Ranjit Singh is a composite figure, combining the qualities of Ghadr Party leaders Har Dayal and Bhagwan Singh, BIC leader Virendranath Chattopadhyaya, who would become her lover, and Lajpat Rai, head of the Home Rule League and the most moderate of the Indian nationalists who influenced her. Her choice of the Sikh surname "Singh" and her description of him as someone whose faith was built on the bodies of martyrs suggest the Ghadrite Bhagwan Singh as much as Lajpat Rai, as he is more commonly thought to be.

11. Alan Raucher, "American Anti-Imperialists and the Pro-India Movement, 1902–1932," *Pacific Historical Review* 43, no. 2 (February, 1974): 91–92. For more on Rai' s years in the United States, see "Indian Revolutionaries in the United States and Japan," in *Lajpat Rai: Autobiographical Writings*, ed. Vijaya Chandra Joshi (Delhi: University Publishers, 1965).

12. Statement by Agnes Smedley, 2 January 1919, MID 9771-72/25, RG 165; Grand Jury Testimony, Henrietta Rodman; *United States v. Sailendra Nath Ghose, Agnes Smedley, and others*, Grand Jury Testimony, Lajpat Rai, 17 April 1918, MID 9771-72, RG 165.

13. Smedley, *Daughter of Earth*, 221.

14. Rewi Alley, *Six Americans in China* (Beijing: International Culture, 1985), 120–21.

15. Agnes Smedley, *Battle Hymn of China* (New York: Alfred A. Knopf, 1943), 8. Agnes claims she came to share the revolutionists' views at this time in order to disguise her Ghadr Party ties.

16. "The Case of the Willie Letters: Report and Documents," 26 August 1918, MID 20541-722, RG 165.

17. Agnes Smedley to Florence Becker Lennon, 3 January [1924], courtesy of Florence Becker Lennon.

18. Florence Becker Lennon, "Memoirs," courtesy of Florence Becker Lennon; Tappan Mukerjee, interview by author, Washington, D.C., 12 January 1987.

19. *United States v. Sailendra Nath Ghose, Agnes Smedley, and others,* Grand Jury Testimony, Loretta Maguire, 17 April 1918, MID 9771-72, RG 165; Grand Jury Testimony, Bayard Rodman. In *Daughter of Earth,* the character Juan Diaz is a composite of Roy and another young Indian revolutionary named Herambalal Gupta, but it was Roy to whom she was attracted, and with whom she had a disastrous sexual encounter.

20. Abdul Qadir Khan, *Times* (London), 25 February 1930, in Gene D. Overstreet and Marshall Windmiller, *Communism in India* (Bombay: Perennial Press, 1960), 32.

21. Carleton Beals, *Glass Houses: Ten Years of Free-lancing* (Philadelphia: J. B. Lippincott, 1938), 42. For more on Roy, see M. N. Roy, *M. N. Roy's Memoirs* (Bombay: Allied Publishers, 1964); John Patrick Haithcox, *Communism and Nationalism in India: M. N. Roy and Comintern Policy, 1920–1939* (Princeton: Princeton University Press, 1971); Samaren Roy, *The Twice-Born Heretic: M. N. Roy and the Comintern* (Calcutta: Firma KLM, 1986).

22. Smedley, *Daughter of Earth,* 228.

23. Samaren Roy, correspondence with author, 6 December 1988.

24. Smedley, *Daughter of Earth,* 246.

25. Ibid., 250.

26. Roy, *Memoirs,* 487.

27. *United States v. Sailendra Nath Ghose, Agnes Smedley, and others,* Grand Jury Testimony, Thorberg Haberman, 17 April 1918, MID 9771-72, RG 165.

28. Margaret Sanger, *Margaret Sanger: An Autobiography* (New York: W. W. Norton, 1938), 252.

29. Joan Jensen, *Passage from India: Asian Immigrants in North America* (New Haven: Yale University Press, 1988), 214.

30. "India Rising a Berlin Plot: Chakraberty Admits Holding Conference in German Foreign Office," *New York Times,* 10 March 1917.

31. Friedrich Katz, *The Secret War in Mexico: Europe, the United States, and the Mexican Revolution* (Chicago: University of Chicago Press, 1981), 423–24.

32. Overstreet and Windmiller, *Communism in India,* 23.

33. Smedley, *Battle Hymn,* 8.

34. Smedley, *Daughter of Earth,* 242.

35. Grand Jury Testimony, Henrietta Rodman.

36. Roy, *Memoirs,* 488.

37. For Agnes's alibi, see Grand Jury Testimony, Thorberg Haberman; *United States v. Sailendra Nath Ghose, Agnes Smedley, and others,* Grand Jury Testimony, Lizzie Trayer, 18 April 1918, MID 9771-72, RG 165. For Agnes's willingness to accept German money, see U.S. Grand jury Testimony, Arthur U. Pope, 21 October 1918, MID 9771-72/4-23. For the Indians, see Bureau Section (BS) File 200600/1355, 5 July 1921, RG 60; E. B. Montgomery, 29 August 1921, File U-H 862.2-886, RG 59, courtesy of Elliot Porter.

38. For a synopsis of the plan, see "Indian Nationalist Party Case: Violation of the

Espionage Act," DOJ 193424/27, RG 60; Office of United States Attorney for the Northern District of California to the Attorney General, 26 June 1918, DOJ 193424/19, RG 60.

39. Smedley, *Battle Hymn*, 8–9; "The Case of the Willie Letters."

40. Roy, *Memoirs*, 488.

41. Ibid.; "Hindu Plot Defendants Fear Poison," *San Francisco Examiner*, 28 March 1918; "Find Enemy Aliens in Munition Plant, *New York Times*, 28 March 1918. In *Daughter of Earth* (283), Agnes also mentions Ghose's plan to poison Chakravarty.

42. "Hindu Plot Case to Go to Jury This Afternoon," *San Francisco Examiner*, 23 April 1918.

43. John Preston to the Attorney General, 3 September 1918, DOJ 193424/27, RG 60.

44. For this period of the Russian Revolution, see Edward Hallett Carr, *The Bolshevik Revolution: 1917–1923*, 3 volumes (New York: Macmillan, 1953); Richard Pipes, *The Russian Revolution* (New York: Alfred A. Knopf, 1990); Robert Service, *The Bolshevik Party in Revolution: A Study in Organizational Change, 1917–1923* (New York: Barnes and Noble Books, 1979); Sheila Fitzpatrick, *The Russian Revolution* (Oxford: Oxford University Press, 1982); Lewis Siegelbaun, *Soviet State and Society Between Revolutions, 1918–1929* (Cambridge: Cambridge University Press, 1992).

45. Irving Howe and Lewis Coser, *The American Communist Party: A Critical History, 1919–1957* (Boston: Beacon Press, 1957), 25–26.

46. For more on Chattopadhyaya's career at this time, see Nirode Barooah, "The Berlin Indians, the Bolshevik Revolution, and Indian Politics, 1917–1930," *My World: A Journal for Indians Living Abroad* (April 1978): 16–21; Nirode Barooah, "Virendranath Chattopadhyaya in Stockholm, 1917–1921," *Mainstream* 24, no. 26 (1 March 1986): 23–30; Nirode Barooah, "Virendranath Chattopadhyaya— II," *Mainstream* 24, no. 27 (8 March 1986): 15–20; Nirode Barooah, "Virendranath Chattopadhyaya—III," *Mainstream* 24, no. 28 (15 March 1986): 24–33; Orsen N. Nielsen to the Honorable Secretary of State, 21 October 1920, U-H 845.00/272, RG 59.

47. Annette Adams to the Attorney General, 26 June 1918, DOJ 193424/19, RG 60.

48. Agnes Smedley to H. Miter [Ghose], 27 February 1918, MID 10497-514/10 and MID 9771-72/124, RG 165. In exchange for his help, Chattopadhyaya sent Minor a letter of introduction to the mayor of Stockholm.

49. "The Case of the Willie Letters."

50. Grand Jury Testimony, Lizzie Trayer.

51. Office of MID to Chief, Military Intelligence Branch, Executive Division, 19 March 1918, MID 9771-72/3, RG 165; DOJ 193424/19, RG 60; U.S. District Court for the Southern District of New York Records, Docket C-11-359-360, Agnes Smedley alias Agnes Brundin, etc. Margaret Sanger later claimed that a few copies of her pamphlet on contraception were also found in Agnes's apartment and she was additionally charged with violating a local anti-birth-control ordinance. However, a search of municipal records could not confirm this.

52. Grand Jury Testimony, Bayard Rodman.

53. Grand Jury Testimony, Lizzie Trayer.

54. Cherie [Thorberg] Haberman to Robert Haberman, 20 March 1918, MID 9140-

665/41, RG 165; Cherie [Thorberg] Haberman to Robert Haberman, 27 March 1918, MID 9140-665/39, RG 165.

55. Smedley, *Daughter of Earth*, 239.
56. Cherie [Thorberg] Haberman to Robert Haberman, 20 March 1918.
57. "Hold American Girl as India Plotter," *New York Times*, 19 March 1918. Also see "Hindu Wanted by U.S. Taken with S.F. Girl," *San Francisco Examiner*, 19 March 1918.
58. Charles Sutton, *The New York Tombs: Its Secrets and Its Mysteries* (Montclair, New Jersey: Patterson Smith, 1973),vi.
59. Sailendra Nath Ghose to Tarak Nath Das, [1918], MID 9771-72/35, RG 165, Sailendra Nath Ghose to Tarak Nath Das, 18 April 1918, MID 9771-72/55, RG 165; Roy, *Memoirs*, 488.
60. "The Case of the Willie Letters."
61. Agnes Smedley Defense Fund to Mr. Sunderland, 16 April 1918, MID 9771-72, RG 165; Agnes Smedley Defense Fund to Friend, 24 May 1918, OG 216599, RG 65.
62. Willie [Purin Sinha] to Friend [M. N. Roy], 23 May 1918, in "The Case of the Willie Letters."
63. Agnes Smedley to Charles Erskine Scott Wood, [May 15, 1918], Charles Erskine Scott Wood Papers.
64. Ibid.
65. Gilbert Roe to Walter Nelles, 8 January 1919, Gilbert Roe Papers.
66. Interrogation of Mrs. Warbasse, 4 September 1918, MID 9771-72, RG 165.
67. Willie [Sinha] to Friend [Roy], 27 June 1918, in "The Case of the Willie Letters."
68. Willie [Sinha] to Mr. Bartellie [Roy], 12 July 1918, in "The Case of the Willie Letters."
69. Ibid.
70. Roy, *Memoirs*, 93.
71. Statement by P. N. Sinha, 3 August 1918, in "The Case of the Willie Letters."

CHAPTER 4. MOSCOW BECKONS

1. Agnes Smedley, "My Cell Mates, #2," *New York Call*, 22 February 1920.
2. Agnes Smedley, "My Cell Mates, #3," *New York Call*, 29 February 1920.
3. Transcript, Supreme Court of the United States, October Term, 1918, no. 741.
4. Agnes Smedley, "Dr. Helena Lange," *Modern Review* 41, no. 5 (May 1927): 571.
5. U.S. District Court for the Southern District of New York Records, Docket C-11-359-360. Although the New York indictment against Agnes and Ghose was dismissed in late 1918, the indictments against Tarak Nath Das and Bhagwan Singh were not dropped until June 1923.
6. Agnes Smedley to Tarak Nath Das, 20 December 1918, MID 9771-72/34, RG 165.
7. Agnes Smedley, *Battle Hymn of China* (New York: Alfred A. Knopf, 1943), 9-10.
8. Eleanor Brundin, interview by author, Cerritos, California, 3 January 1987.
9. Florence Becker Lennon, "Memoirs," courtesy of Florence Becker Lennon; Ella Wolfe to author, 12 June 1984.
10. Agnes Smedley, *Daughter of Earth* (New York: Coward-McCann, 1929), 287.
11. Nirode Barooah, "Virendranath Chattopadhyaya-III," *Mainstream* 24, no. 28 (15

March 1986): 29. Also see Tilak Raj Sareen, *Indian Revolutionary Movement Abroad, 1905–1921* (New Delhi: Sterling, 1979), 209.

12. Agnes Smedley to Tarak Nath Das, 24 April 1919, MID 9771-72, RG 165.

13. Julien Steinberg, ed., *Verdict of Three Decades: From the Literature of Individual Revolt Against Soviet Communism, 1917–1950* (New York: Duell, Sloan, and Pearce, 1950), 123.

14. Sareen, *Indian Revolutionary Movement Abroad*, 237.

15. Louis Budenz, interview by FBI, New York City, 28 April 1950, FBI NY 100-68282; FBI 61-6580-328.

16. Ellen Chesler, *Woman of Valor: Margaret Sanger and the Birth Control Movement in America* (New York: Simon and Schuster, 1992),169.

17. Surendra Karr to Jagat Singh, 2 May 1919, MID 9771-69, RG 165.

18. Robert Morss Lovett, preface, *China's Red Army Marches* (New York: Vanguard Press, 1934), v.

19. Chesler, *Woman of Valor*, 169.

20. Sir Cecil Kaye, *Communism in India: With Unpublished Documents from the National Archives of India, 1919–1924* (Calcutta: Editions India, 1971), 140, 143.

21. Gilbert Roe to Mr. O'Brien, 13 January 1919, DOJ 193424/42, RG 60.

22. Captain John B. Trevor to Director of Military Intelligence, 2 January 1919, MID 9771-72, RG 165.

23. Ibid.

24. Agnes Smedley to Mr. Pandit, 27 February 1919, OG 266726, RG 65.

25. Agnes Smedley to Tarak Nath Das, [January 1919], MID 9771-72, RG 165.

26. Smedley, *Daughter of Earth*, 292.

27. A. Mitchell Palmer to Gilbert Roe, 26 November 1919, DOJ 193424/74, RG 60.

28. Alex King to the Attorney General, 16 October 1919, DOJ 193424, RG 60.

29. Report of Betty Thompson, 20 November 1919, New York State Library, courtesy of Elliot Porter.

30. Florence Becker Lennon, interview by author, Boulder, Colorado, 23 August 1985.

31. Lennon, "Memoirs."

32. Agnes Smedley to Florence Becker Lennon, 29 June 1927, courtesy of Florence Becker Lennon.

33. For more, see Lillian Faderman, *Surpassing the Love of Men: Romantic Friendship Between Women from the Renaissance to the Present* (New York: Morrow, 1981).

34. Agnes Smedley to Friends, 1 March 1920; Agnes Smedley to Ed Gammons, 18 March 1920, Friends of Freedom for India Papers.

35. Lennon, "Memoirs."

36. Ibid.

37. Smedley, "Dr. Helena Lange."

38. See *New York Call*, 22 January–12 February 1920, for Gitlow trial coverage; 8 April–6 May 1920, Larkin trial coverage. (No byline.)

39. *New York Call*, 4 May 1920. Also see *Daughter of Earth*, 290-92.

40. Benjamin Gitlow, *I Confess: The Truth About American Communism* (New York: E. P. Dutton, 1940), 117; Elizabeth Gurley Flynn, *The Rebel Girl: An Autobiography, My First Life, 1906–1926*, rev. ed. (New York: International Publishers, 1973), 281.

41. Agnes Smedley to Hindustan Ghadr Party, 6 June 1920, Friends of Freedom for India Papers.

42. Carleton Beals, *Glass Houses: Ten Years of Free-lancing* (Philadelphia: J. B. Lippincott, 1938), 50. Robert Haberman was a founding member of this party.

43. Gene D. Overstreet and Marshall Windmiller, *Communism in India* (Bombay: Allied Publishers, 1964), 32.

44. Kaye, *Communism in India*, 142, 150–52.

45. Sareen, *Indian Revolutionary Movement Abroad*, 23740; Virendranath Chattopadhyaya, 18 March 1934, in Gangadhar Adhikari, ed., *Documents of the History of the Communist Party of India*, volume 1, 1917–1922 (New Delhi: People's Publishing House, 1971), 86.

46. Karin Michaelis, foreword, *Kun en Kvinde* ([Copenhagen]: Fremad, 1933), tr. H. B. Miller.

47. Internal Memo, 2 June 1921, BS 202600/795, RG 60. Also see MID 10058-863/3-5, 10058-863/12, MID 10058-974/1, RG 165.

48. Lennon, "Memoirs."

49. Smedley to Lennon, 17 January 1921.

50. Weekly Report, Director, Intelligence Bureau, Simla, 2 May 1921, Home Political, Deposit 55.

51. Smedley to Lennon, 17 January 1921.

52. Smedley, *Battle Hymn*, 12.

53. Smedley, *Daughter of Earth*, 317. According to Agnes, the character of Anand Manvekar, who utters these words, was a composite of Chatto and a subsequent lover, Bakar Ali Mirza. However, Agnes confirms Chatto's disdain for Gandhi in *Battle Hymn*, 24.

54. According to British intelligence expert Richard Popplewell, the character Chandra Lal in Maugham's "Giulia Lazzari" is based on Chattopadhyaya. Richard Popplewell, interview by author, Washington, D.C., 7 August 1987.

55. For more on Chattopadhyaya, see P. Unnikrishnan, "Indian Revolutionaries in the Soviet Union- I," *Link* 7, no. 3 (30 August 1964): 35-36; C. Sehanavis, "Pioneers Among Indian Revolutionaries in Germany," *Mainstream* 13, no. 6 (19 July 1975), 11–15; P. N. Chopra, ed., *Who's Who of Indian Martyrs*, volume 2 (New Delhi: Ministry of Education and Youth Services, Government of India, 1969–73), 60; Ilya Suchov, "New Light on Old Indian Revolutionary," *Soviet Land* 23, no. 2 (January 1970), 14–15.

56. Overstreet and Windmiller, *Communism in India*, 33.

57. In addition to Chatto and Agnes, Herambalal Gupta and B. N. Dutta were then in Berlin, along with representatives of the Egyptian, Persian, and Turkish committees. For more on the wrangling between Chatto's group and the Soviets, see Kaye, *Communism in India*, 2–6; Sareen, *Indian Revolutionary Movement Abroad*, 241–43; Tilak Raj Sareen, *Russian Revolution and India, 1917–1921* (New Delhi: Sterling, 1977), 72–74; Aaron Coomer Bose, *Indian Revolutionaries Abroad, 1905–1922, in the Background of International Developments* (Patna: Bharati Bhawan, 1971), 209-13.

58. Report, E. B. Montgomery, 27 June 1921–22 July, 1921, DOJ BS 200600/1355; Weekly Report, Director, Intelligence Bureau, Simla, 18 April 1921, Home Political, Deposit 54.

59. Kaye, *Communism in India*, 172–73; Weekly Report, 18 April 1921, Home Political, Deposit 54; Weekly Report, 2 May 1921, Home Political, Deposit 55.

60. Weekly Report, 18 April 1921, Home Political, Deposit 54.

61. Kaye, *Communism in India*, 169.

62. Besides Agnes and Chatto, the delegation included M.P.T. Acharya, Abdul Rab, Shafiq Ahmad, Amin Faruqui, Ahmad Mansur, Bhupendranath Dutta, P. S. Khankhoji, Gulam Lohani, Nalini Gupta, Das Gupta, Abdul Wahid, and Abdul Hafiz.

63. Smedley, *Battle Hymn*, 24–25.

64. Ibid., 25.

65. Ibid.

66. Ibid., 26.

67. Alice Bird [Agnes Smedley], "Enter the Woman Warrior," *Modern Review* 30, no. 5 (November 1921): 546.

68. Smedley, "The Parliament of Man," *Liberator* 4, no. 10 (October 1921): 13.

69. Roy, *Memoirs*, 93.

70. Ibid., 487.

71. Ibid., 489.

72. Ibid.

73. In addition to Roy's first-person account, see Kaye, *Communism in India*, 4–6; Agnes Smedley, "The Indian Revolutionary Movement Abroad: A Historical Sketch," *People* 5, no. 7 (18 August 1927): 31; Overstreet and Windmiller, *Communism in India*, 36–37; Adhikari, *Documents of the History of the Communist Party of India* 1:81–82, 87, 254; Unnikrishnan, "Indian Revolutionaries in the Soviet Union-I"; Nirode Barooah, "The Berlin Indians, the Bolshevik Revolution, and Indian Politics, 1917–1930," *My World: A Journal for Indians Living Abroad* (April 1978): 16-21. Bose's *Indian Revolutionaries Abroad* also mentions a first-person account by Chatto ally B. N. Dutta.

74. Barooah, "The Berlin Indians," 19.

75. Bose, *Indian Revolutionaries Abroad*, 210–11; Roy, *Memoirs*, 482–83.

76. Overstreet and Windmiller, *Communism in India*, 32–33.

77. Emma Goldman, *Living My Life* (New York: A. A. Knopf, 1931), 905. For more on Goldman and Berkman in Moscow, see Paul Avich, *Anarchist Portraits* (Princeton: Princeton University Press, 1988); Alice Wexler, *Emma Goldman in Exile: From the Russian Revolution to the Spanish Civil War* (Boston: Beacon Press, 1989); Alice Wexler, *Emma Goldman: An Intimate Life* (New York: Pantheon Books, 1984); Candace Falk, *Love, Anarchy, and Emma Goldman* (New York: Holt, Rinehart, and Winston, 1984); Richard Drinnon, *Rebel in Paradise: A Biography of Emma Goldman* (Chicago: University of Chicago Press, 1961).

78. Goldman, in *Rebel in Paradise*, 254.

79. Smedley, *Daughter of Earth*, 175–76.

80. Richard and Anna Maria Drinnan, eds., *Nowhere at Home: Letters from Exile of Emma Goldman and Alexander Berkman* (New York: Schocken Books, 1975), 22.

81. Goldman, *Living My Life*, 905.

82. Emma Goldman, "Travelling Salesmen of the Revolution," in *Verdict of Three Decades*, 123.

83. Christopher Andrew and Oleg Gordievsky, *KGB: The Inside Story of Its Foreign*

Operations from Lenin to Gorbachev (New York: HarperCollins, 1990), 64. For more, see Lennard D. Gerson, *The Secret Police in Lenin's Russia* (Philadelphia: Temple University Press, 1976); George Leggett, *The Cheka: Lenin's Political Police* (Oxford: Clarendon Press, 1981); Sergey Petrovich Melgounov, *The Red Terror in Russia* (London: J. M. Dent and Sons, 1926).

84. Agnes Smedley to Ellen Kennan, 11 November 1921, courtesy of Joyce Brown.
85. Smedley to Lennon, [June 1921].
86. Roy, *Memoirs*, 288.
87. Smedley to Lennon, [June 1921].
88. Ibid.
89. Roy, *Memoirs*, 490.
90. Overstreet and Windmiller, *Communism in India*, 37.
91. Adhikari, *Documents* 1:254–55; Tara Ali Baig, *Sarojini Naidu* (New Delhi: Publications Division, Ministry of Information and Broadcasting, 1974), 12–13; Roy, *Memoirs*, 482.
92. V. I. Lenin to Virendranath Chattopadhyaya, 8 July 1921, in Baig, *Sarojini Naidu*, 13. In his memoirs, Roy claims Chatto did see Lenin at this time, but that is not the case.
93. Barooah, "The Berlin Indians," 19. Also see Internal Memo, 12 September 1921, K142/ Ko15035, RG 242.
94. Roy, *Memoirs*, 487.
95. Ibid.
96. Ibid., 488.
97. Smedley to Lennon, 3 October [1924].
98. Ibid.
99. Ibid.
100. Kaye, *Communism in India*, 5.
101. Roger Baldwin to Agnes Smedley, 2 December 1921.
102. U-H 862.2-866, 29 August 1921, RG 59; Kaye, *Communism in India*, 6.
103. Smedley to Kennan, 11 November 1921.

CHAPTER 5. LOVE AND PAIN IN BERLIN

1. Agnes Smedley to Florence Becker Lennon, 31 December 1921, courtesy of Florence Becker Lennon.
2. Sir Cecil Kaye, *Communism in India: With Unpublished Documents from the National Archives of India, 1919–1924* (Calcutta: Editions India, 1971), 11, 32.
3. SIS Summary 766, 3 July 1922, British Foreign Office (FO) File 371/7572. For more on the Indian News and Information Bureau, see SIS Summary 946, 3 November 1922, British FO File 371/7300; Kaye, *Communism in India*, 11, 332; German FO File KI586, RG 242; India Office to Vincent, 18 October 1922, Home Political, Deposit 259/24, 1924.
4. British FO file 371/7300. Muenzenberg is identified here through his connection to the German Young Communist Party.
5. Babette Gross, *Willi Muenzenberg: A Political Biography* (East Lansing: Michigan State University Press, 1974), 130, 263; John Willett, *Art and Politics in the Weimar Period: The New Sobriety, 1917–1933* (New York: Pantheon Books, 1978), 71.

6. For more on the OMS, see Branko Lazitch, *Biographical Dictionary of the Comintern* (Stanford: Hoover Institution Press, 1986), xxix; Christopher Andrew and Oleg Gordievsky, *KGB: The Inside Story of Its Foreign Operations from Lenin to Gorbachev* (New York: HarperCollins, 1990), 81–82; Gross, *Willi Muenzenberg*, 130, 263; Edward Hallett Carr, *Socialism in One Country, 1924–1926*, volume 3, part 2 (New York: Macmillan, 1964), 909–10.
7. British FO File 371/7572.
8. Smedley to Lennon, 31 December 1921.
9. Agnes Smedley, *Battle Hymn of China* (New York: Alfred A. Knopf, 1943), 12; Horst Krueger to author, 24 June 1987. Also see Agnes Smedley to Margaret Sanger, 13 June 1929, Margaret Sanger Papers.
10. Agnes Smedley to Karin Michaelis, 21 February [1925], Karin Michaelis Papers.
11. Smedley to Lennon, 27 November [1923]; Smedley to Lennon, 16 February 1924.
12. Kaye, *Communism in India*, 57.
13. Smedley to Lennon, [April 1922].
14. Smedley to Michaelis, 21 February [1925].
15. Smedley to Lennon, "the 25th" [1925].
16. Smedley to Sanger, 3 January [1928].
17. Ibid. Also see Smedley to Sanger, "the 13th" [1928]; Agnes Smedley to Ellen Kennan, 25 April 1929, courtesy of Joyce Brown.
18. Smedley to Lennon, [April 1922].
19. Smedley to Lennon, 1 June 1922.
20. Smedley to Michaelis, 21 February [1925].
21. Agnes Smedley, "Jodh Singh," *Nation* 114, no. 2959 (22 March 1922): 342.
22. Agnes Smedley, *Daughter of Earth* (New York: Coward-McCann, 1929), 309. Here Florence is referred to by her real name.
23. Ibid., 321.
24. Harindranath Chattopadhyaya, *Life and Myself*, volume 1, *Dawn Approaching Noon* (Bombay: Nalanda Publications, 1948), 217.
25. Smedley to Lennon, "the 25th," [1925].
26. Smedley to Lennon, 8 August 1922.
27. Alice Wexler, *Emma Goldman: An Intimate Life* (New York: Pantheon, 1984), 277–78.
28. Ibid., 147.
29. Ibid., 279.
30. Smedley to Lennon, 11 November 1922.
31. Agnes Smedley, "Methods of Direct Action in the Revolutionary Class Struggle," 15 December 1922, IWW Papers; Smedley to Lennon, 1 June 1922.
32. Emma Goldman, *Living My Life* (New York: A. A. Knopf, 1931), 905.
33. Smedley, *Battle Hymn*, 15.
34. Ibid.
35. Ibid., 16.
36. Smedley to Michaelis, 21 February [1925]; Smedley to Lennon, "the 25th."
37. Smedley to Michaelis, 21 February [1925].
38. Smedley to Lennon, 8 May 1923.
39. Ibid.

40. Smedley to Lennon, 11 November 1922.
41. Otto Friedrich, *Before the Deluge: A Portrait of Berlin in the 1920s* (New York: Fromm, 1986), 125.
42. Agnes Smedley, "Starving Germany," *Nation* 117, no. 3047 (28 November 1923), 602.
43. Friedrich, *Before the Deluge*, 128.
44. Zweig, in Friedrich, *Before the Deluge*, 128–29.
45. Zweig, in Peter Gay, *Weimar Culture: The Outsider as Insider* (New York: Harper and Row, 1968), 130.
46. Smedley to Lennon, 19 January 1924.
47. Karin Michaelis, *Little Troll* (New York: Creative Age Press, 1946), 214.
48. Karin Michaelis, foreword, *Kun en Kvinde* ([Copenhagen]: Fremad, 1933), tr. H. B. Miller.
49. Smedley to Michaelis, 1 April [1923].
50. Ibid.
51. Smedley to Lennon, 27 November [1923].
52. Smedley to Lennon, 31 May 1923.
53. Smedley to Lennon, 4 June, [1923].
54. Smedley to Lennon, 8 May 1923.
55. Smedley to Lennon, 4 June [1923].
56. Smedley, *Battle Hymn*, 17. Most likely, Agnes refers either to Lila Singh, a female friend, or Chatto's brother-in-law A.C.N. Nambiar. Both were in London at this time.
57. Agnes Smedley, "The Akali Movement—An Heroic Epic," *Nation* 119, no. 3078 (2 July 1924), 15–17.
58. Smedley to Lennon, 17 July 1923
59. Smedley to Lennon, 11 August 1923.
60. Ibid. By this time, the Berlin Psychoanalytic Institute had begun to replace Vienna as the world center for psychoanalysis.
61. Smedley to Lennon, 8 October 1923.
62. Smedley, *Battle Hymn*, 20–21.
63. Smedley to Lennon, 11 August 1923; Smedley, "Starving Germany," 602.
64. Smedley to Kennan, 10 May [1923].
65. Smedley to Lennon, 16 February 1924.
66. Smedley to Lennon, [October 1923].
67. Smedley, *Battle Hymn*, 18; Agnes Smedley to Upton Sinclair, 4 June 1923, Upton Sinclair Papers, Lilly Library.
68. Edward Glover, ed., "Bulletin of the International Psychoanalytical Association: Report of the Thirteenth International Psychoanalytical Congress," *International Journal of Psychoanalysis* 15, part 4 (1934): 516.
69. Smedley to Lennon, 25 December 1923.
70. Smedley, *Battle Hymn*, 17–18.
71. Smedley to Lennon, 25 December 1923.
72. Smedley to Lennon, 8 December [1923].
73. Smedley to Lennon, 20 December [1923].
74. Smedley to Michaelis, 21 February [1925].
75. Ibid.

CHAPTER 6. BECOMING A WRITER

1. Agnes Smedley to Florence Becker Lennon, 3 January [1924], courtesy of Florence Becker Lennon.
2. Smedley to Lennon, 27 November, [1923].
3. Smedley to Lennon, 30 March 1924.
4. Ibid.
5. Smedley to Lennon, 16 February 1924.
6. Smedley to Lennon, 19 January [1924].
7. Ibid.
8. For more, see John Willett, *Art and Politics in the Weimar Period: The New Sobriety* (New York: Pantheon, 1978), 74–76, 97–98.
9. Smedley to Lennon, 16 February 1924.
10. Sir Cecil Kaye, *Communism in India: With Unpublished Documents from the National Archives of India, 1919–1924* (Calcutta: Editions India, 1971), 90; Sir David Petric, *Communism in India, 1924–1927* (Calcutta: Editions India, 1972), 53. Leo Flieg remained close to Muenzenberg and an important figure in the OMS until his death in Moscow in 1937.
11. Smedley to Lennon, 16 February 1924.
12. Smedley to Lennon, 17 March [1924].
13. Agnes Smedley to Margaret Sanger, 9 May 1924, Margaret Sanger Papers.
14. Sanger to Smedley, 4 June 1924.
15. Sanger to Smedley, 7 July 1924.
16. Agnes Smedley, "The Akali Movement—An Heroic Epic," *Nation* 119, no. 3078 (2 July 1924): 17
17. Smedley to Michaelis, 9 April [1924], Karin Michaelis Papers.
18. Smedley to Lennon, 17 June [1924].
19. Ibid.
20. Smedley to Lennon, 25 August 1924.
21. Smedley to Lennon, 28 October [1924].
22. Ibid.
23. Ibid.
24. Ibid.; Smedley to Lennon, 25 August 1924.
25. Agnes Smedley to Emma Goldman, [1924], Emma Goldman Papers.
26. Smedley to Goldman, 26 March 1925.
27. Smedley to Sanger, 12 February 1925.
28. Smedley to Michaelis, 2 February 1925.
29. Smedley to Michaelis, 21 February [1925].
30. Smedley to Goldman, [1925].
31. Sanger to Smedley, 8 January 1925; Smedley to Sanger, 22 April 1925 through June 1925, passim.
32. Smedley to Goldman, 26 March 1925.
33. Smedley to Goldman, [1925].
34. Kollwitz in Leonard Baskin, "Chinese Woodcuts, 1935–1949, with an essay by Agnes Smedley," *Massachusetts Review* 25, no. 4 (Winter 1984): 564.
35. Smedley to Goldman, [1925].
36. For more on the Chinese Information Bureau, see Petrie, *Communism in India*, 195–96, 199.

37. Agnes Smedley, "The Coming War Against Asia," *Industrial Pioneer* 3, no. 1 (May 1925): 5–6.

38. Smedley to Lennon, [July 1925].

39. R. N. Carew Hunt, "Willi Muenzenberg," St. Anthony's Papers, no. 9, *International Communism* (Carbondale: Southern Illinois University Press, 1960), 76. For more on Muenzenberg, see Helmut Gruber, "Willi Muenzenberg: Propagandist for and Against the Comintern," *International Review of Social History* 10, part 2 (1965): 188–210; Babette Gross, *Willi Muenzenberg: A Political Biography* (East Lansing: Michigan State University Press, 1974); Arthur Koestler, *The Invisible Writing: The Second Volume of an Autobiography, 1932–1940* (London: Hutchinson, 1954), 250–59; Jorgen Schleimann, "The Life and Work of Willi Muenzenberg," *Survey: A Journal of Soviet and East European Studies* 55 (April 1965): 64–91; Stephen Koch, *Double Lives: Spies and Writers in the Secret Soviet War of Ideas Against the West* (New York: Free Press, 1994).

40. For more, see Herman Ermolaev, *Soviet Literary Theories, 1917–1934: The Genesis of Social Realism* (New York: Octagon Books, 1977); Lynn Mally, *Culture of the Future: The Proletcult Movement in Revolutionary Russia* (Berkeley: University of California Press, 1990).

41. Smedley to Goldman [1925].

42. Sanger to Smedley, 28 February 1925.

43. Smedley to Goldman, [1925].

44. For more on Fitzi Fitzgerald, see Helen Deutsch and Stella Hanau, *The Provincetown: A Story of the Theatre* (New York: Farrar and Rinehart, 1931), 81, 134–36.

45. Smedley to Lennon, 27 July 1925.

46. Candace Falk, *Love, Anarchy, and Emma Goldman* (New York: Holt, Rinehart, and Winston, 1984), 340.

47. Ibid.

48. Smedley to Sanger, 5 September 1925.

49. Ibid.

50. Agnes Smedley, "Denmark's Creative Women II: Betty Nansen," *Modern Review* 40, no. 3 (September 1926): 266–67.

51. Smedley to Lennon, 12 November 1925.

52. Agnes Smedley, *Daughter of Earth* (New York: Coward-McCann, 1929), 1–2.

53. Ibid., 2, 18.

54. Ibid., 17–18.

55. Smedley to Goldman, [November 1925].

56. Smedley, *Daughter of Earth*, 99–100.

57. Ibid., 4.

58. Ibid., 25.

59. Ibid., 79–80.

60. Ibid., 97.

61. Ibid., 82.

62. Ibid., 83, 86.

63. Ibid., 96, 98.

64. Ibid., 91–92.

65. Ibid., 133–37. For the true nature of her illness, see Statement by Agnes Smedley, 2 January 1919, MID 9771-72/25, RG 165; Smedley, "The Magazine Agent," *Tempe Normal Student*, 22 March 1912.

66. Smedley, *Daughter of Earth*, 173–74.

67. For more, see Lillian Faderman, *Surpassing the Love of Men: Romantic Friendship Between Women from the Renaissance to the Present* (New York: Morrow, 1981).

68. Smedley to Michaelis, 27 June [1925].

69. Smedley, *Daughter of Earth*, 285.

70. Agnes's suggestion that Juan Diaz was a spy and responsible for her 1918 arrest could be attributed to either. Both also spent time in Mexico during World War I under assumed Hispanic names.

71. Smedley to Lennon, [July 1926].

72. Smedley, *Daughter of Earth*, 306.

73. Ibid., 332.

74. Smedley to Goldman, [November 1925].

75. Agnes Smedley to Ellen Kennan, 25 April 1929, courtesy of Joyce Brown.

76. Smedley to Goldman [November 1925].

77. Smedley to Sanger, 15 November 1925.

CHAPTER 7. BEND IN THE ROAD

1. Nirode K. Barooah, telephone interview by author, 15 October 1996. She is referred to as Lucie Peters in Babette Gross, *Willi Muenzenberg: A Political Biography* (East Lansing: Michigan State University Press, 1974), 182.

2. Ilya Suchkov, "New Light on Old Indian Revolutionary," *Soviet Land* 23, no. 2 (January 1970): 15; Gangadhar Adhikari, ed., *Documents of the History of the Communist Party of India*, volume 1, 1917–1922 (New Delhi: People's Publishing House, 1971), 82; Agnes Smedley, *Battle Hymn of China* (New York: Alfred A. Knopf, 1943), 14; Panchanan Saha, "Indian Revolutionary Movement and Germany—II," *Mainstream* 12, no. 7 (13 October 1973): 24.

3. Gross, *Willi Muenzenberg*, 182; Edward Hallett Carr, *Foundations of a Planned Economy*, 1926–1929, volume 3, part 1 (New York: Macmillan, 1976), 296.

4. Agnes Smedley to Emma Goldman, 19 [June 1926], Emma Goldman Papers.

5. Agnes Smedley, "Conversations with George Bernard Shaw," n.d., Agnes Smedley Papers.

6. Agnes Smedley to Florence Becker Lennon, 18 May [1926], courtesy of Florence Becker Lennon.

7. Agnes Smedley to Margaret Sanger, 6 April 1926, Margaret Sanger Papers.

8. Ibid.

9. Smedley to Lennon, [June 1926]. In Tilla Durieux, *Meine Ersten Neunzig Jahre* (Munich: F. A. Herbig Verlagsbuchhandlung, 1971), 316–17, Durieux places the event in 1927.

10. Smedley to Lennon, [June 1926].

11. Smedley to Lennon, [spring 1926].

12. Ibid. Also see Smedley to Lennon, [14 June 1926], [July 1927].

13. Gross, *Willi Muenzenberg*, 130.

14. Smedley to Lennon, 29 June [1927].

15. Smedley to Lennon, [July 1926].

16. Smedley to Lennon, [summer 1926].

17. Smedley to Goldman, 19 [June 1926].

18. Smedley to Lennon, [July 1926].

19. Smedley to Lennon, [August 1926].
20. Smedley to Lennon, [1926].
21. Smedley, *Battle Hymn*, 19.
22. Smedley to Lennon, 12 November [1926]; Smedley, *Battle Hymn*, 23; Gross, *Willi Muenzenberg*, 182.
23. Smedley, *Battle Hymn*, 23.
24. L. P. Mathur, *Indian Revolutionary Movement in the United States of America* (Delhi: S. Chand, 139; Sir David Petrie, *Communism in India, 1924–1927* (Calcutta: Editions India, 1972), 144, 148, 181–82, 208, 225.
25. Smedley to Lennon, 5 November [1926].
26. Arthur Koestler, *The Invisible Writing: The Second Volume of an Autobiography, 1932–1940* (London: Hutchinson, 1954), 251, 254; Jorgen Schleimann, "The Life and Work of Willi Muenzenberg," *Survey: A Journal of Soviet and East European Studies* 55 (April 1965): 74.
27. Agnes Smedley, "Indonesia's Struggle for Freedom—II," *The People* 4, no. 2 (9 January, 1927): 30.
28. Confidential Informant "T-1," interview by FBI, New York, 11 May 1951, FBI NY 100-68282. I have identified "T-1," described in the document as secretary of the Anti-Imperialist League in the late 1920s, as Louis Gibarti. In his subsequent testimony to the Senate Internal Security Subcommittee, the agency acknowledges him as an FBI informant. In the report, "T-1" refers to Mirov-Abramov as "Mironov," but Gibarti's references to "Mironov" as a "big man" in the "Secret Department" of the Comintern and Soviet intelligence and to his posting at the Soviet Embassy in Berlin in 1927 indicate it is Mirov-Abramov to whom Gibarti refers. "T-1" is also a generic term used by the FBI for information obtained through extralegal or illegal methods including unauthorized wiretaps; see Sanford J. Ungar, *FBI: An Uncensored Look Behind the Walls* (Boston: Atlantic Monthly Press, 1976).
29. Ibid.
30. Smedley, *Battle Hymn*, 23.
31. Marginalia, 10 May 1928 U.S. Passport Application, State Department Passport (130) File, Smedley, Agnes.
32. Gene D. Overstreet and Marshall Windmiller, *Communism in India* (Bombay: Allied Publishers, 1964), 96.
33. Saha, "Indian Revolutionary Movement and Germany—II," 24. For Bridgeman as an agent of the OMS, see Project MASK File 0820/U.K., 16 October 1934, and 120, 21 March 1934.
34. Gross, *Willi Muenzenberg*, 191.
35. Agnes Smedley, "England's War Plans Against Asia—I," *The People* 5, no. 8 (25 August 1927): 148; Agnes Smedley, "The Next War," *The People* 5, no. 12 (22 September 1927): 224.
36. Smedley to Lennon, 29 June [1927]. In their 1988 study of Smedley, Stephen and Janice MacKinnon omit this sentence when quoting the letter.
37. Ibid.
38. Confidential Informant T-1 [Gibarti], FBI NY 100-68282.
39. Smedley, *Battle Hymn*, 23.
40. See *Modern Review* 42, no. 1 (July 1927), 33; *The People* 4, no. 21 (29 May 1927):

426; *The People* 4, no. 26 (26 June 1927): 504. For more on the Chinese Information Bureau, see Petrie, *Communism in India*, 195–96, 199.

41. In the 1930s Bridgeman covered events in China and India for the Comintern newspaper, *Imprecor*.

42. For Agnes's access to Russian government documents, see *The People* 5, no. 7 (18 August 1927):137. For her interview with Madame Sun, see "The Chinese Woman Today: An Interview with Mrs. Sun Yat-sen of China," *Modern Review* 42, no. 7 (July 1927): 31–33. For her familiarity with Paul Vaillant-Couturier, see "German Workers Organize Against War," *Modern Review* 43, no. 1 (January 1928): 27. For her link to the International Red Aid, see Smedley, "Taina Zhod Singa," *Put' MOPRa* 3, no. 11 (June 1927): 8–9.

43. Smedley, "German Workers Organize Against War," 30, 32.

44. Smedley to Sanger, 30 January 1928.

45. Smedley to Lennon, 29 June [1927].

46. Smedley, "The Next War," 225.

47. Agnes Smedley, "India and the Next War, " *The People* 5, no. 15 (13 October 1927):280.

48. See "Who Is Putnam Weale?" *The People* 5, no. 7 (18 August 1927): 137.

49. Smedley to Lennon, 6 May [1927].

50. Ibid.

51. Smedley to Lennon, 29 June [1927].

52. [Agnes Smedley], "One Is Not Made of Wood: The True Story of A Life," *New Masses* 3, no. 4 (August 1927): 5–7.

53. Ibid., 7.

54. Smedley, *Battle Hymn*, 24.

55. Smedley to Sanger, 30 January 1928.

56. Smedley to Sanger, [early 1928].

57. Smedley to Sanger, [late 1927].

58. Frederick S. Litten, "The Noulens Affair," *China Quarterly* 138 (June 1994): 499.

59. Confidential Informant T-1 [Gibarti], FBI NY 100-68282.

60. Julian Gumperz, interview by FBI, 19 June 1945, FBI NY 100-68282.

61. See chapters 8 through 12.

62. Gross, *Willi Muenzenberg*, 130.

63. Christopher Andrew and Oleg Gordievsky, *KGB: The Inside Story of Its Foreign Operations from Lenin to Gorbachev* (New York: HarperCollins, 1990), 81.

64. Confidential Informant T-1 [Gibarti], FBI NY 100-68282.

65. Ibid.

66. Smedley to Sanger, [February 1928].

67. Leonard Baskin, "Chinese Woodcuts, 1935–1949, with an essay by Agnes Smedley," *Massachusetts Review* 25, no. 4 (Winter 1984): 564.

68. Smedley to Sanger, 18 March 1928.

69. Smedley to Sanger, 29 March 1928.

70. Smedley to Sanger, 23 April 1928.

71. Other participants were the physicians Richard Schminke, Martha Rubens-Wolf, Leo Friedlaender, and Max Hodann. For more on the clinic, see Smedley to Sanger, 23 April 1928; Agnes Smedley, "A Berlin Birth Control Clinic," *Birth Control Review* 12, no. 6 (June, 1928): 179.

72. Agnes Smedley, "Birth Control in Germany," *Birth Control Review* 13, no. 3 (March 1929): 77–78.
73. Smedley to Sanger, 12 October [1929].
74. Smedley to Sanger, 18 March 1928
75. Smedley to Sanger, 18 May 1928.
76. Agnes Smedley to Ernest Brundin, 22 March 1928, Agnes Smedley Papers.
77. Smedley to Sanger, 30 October 1928.
78. Smedley to Sanger, 7 July 1928.
79. Smedley to Sanger, 18 May 1928; Smedley to Goldman, August 1928.
80. Agnes Smedley to Karin Michaelis, 16 October 1928, Karin Michaelis Papers; Stephen Koch, *Double Lives: Spies and Writers in the Secret Soviet War of Ideas Against the West* (New York: Free Press, 1994), 158. For more on Gumperz's Comintern ties, see File K304/K105308, 12 November 1921, RG 242; Zentralkomitee der KPD to CPUSA, 27 February 1927, 515-1-1010, CPUSA Papers.
81. Wieland Herzfelde, "On Founding the Malik-Verlag," in *Malik-Verlag, 1916–1947: Berlin, Prague, New York—An Exhibition Organized by James Fraser and Steven Heller* (New York: Goethe House, 1984), 11.
82. Smedley to Michaelis, 16 October 1928; Agnes Smedley to Ellen Kennan, 25 April 1929, courtesy of Joyce Brown. Also see Petrie, *Communism in India*, 214.
83. Julian Gumperz, FBI NY 100-68282; Annie Joel, interview by author, New York City, 16 April 1987; Chen Hansheng [Han-seng], "Shi Mo Te Lai Zai Shanghai," in *Shi Mo Te Lai, Si Te Lang, Si Nuo Ji Qi Ta Zuo Ji You Ren Zai Shanghai: Tao Lun Hui Lun Wen Ji* (Shanghai: Three S Research Association, 1987), tr. courtesy of Robert Farnsworth.
84. Smedley to Kennan, 25 April 1929.
85. U.S. Embassy, London, 18 September 1928, File 845.00B/20, RG 59.
86. Gross, *Willi Muenzenberg*, 205.
87. Julian Gumperz, FBI NY 100-9125.
88. Suchkov, "New Light on Old Indian Revolutionary," 15; Adhikari, *Documents* 1:83; Chatto to Comrade, 30 March 1931, File 515-1-2267, CPUSA Papers.
89. Smedley to Sanger, 19 November 1928.
90. Grace Granich, Oral History, courtesy of Tom Grunfeld.
91. J. Z. Kornfeder, interview by FBI, 4 May 1950, FBI DE 105-279. In China the following year, when Agnes agreed to participate in the Soviet military intelligence ring led by Richard Sorge, he, too, was using the name "Johnson."
92. Emma Goldman to Demi Coleman, 24 February 1939, courtesy of Candace Falk.
93. Smedley, *Battle Hymn*, 26.
94. Smedley to Brundin, 24 December 1928.

Chapter 8. Comintern Agent in China

1. Agnes Smedley, *Battle Hymn of China* (New York: Alfred A. Knopf, 194), 31.
2. Hede Massing, *This Deception* (New York: Duell, Sloan, and Pearce, 1951), 105.
3. Smedley, *Battle Hymn*, 38; Shanghai Municipal Police (SMP) Report D4825, 2 May 1933, RG 263.
4. Jiang Feng, interview by author, Beijing, 15 June 1988.
5. Agnes Smedley to Ernest Brundin, 24 December 1928, Agnes Smedley Papers.

6. Richard Thornton, *The Comintern and the Chinese Communists, 1928–1931* (Seattle: University of Washington Press, 1969), 93.

7. G. C. Hanson to U.S. Secretary of State, 5 March 1929, 800.00B, Smedley, Agnes/1, RG 59.

8. Confidential Informant T-1 [Gibarti], FBI NY 100-68282.

9. Smedley, "Some Women of Mukden," in *Chinese Destinies: Sketches of Present-Day China* (New York: Vanguard, 1933), 202.

10. Smedley, *Battle Hymn*, 40–41.

11. Smedley to Lennon, 8 February 1929; Hanson to U.S. Secretary of State, 5 March, 1929, RG 59.

12. Agnes Smedley to Gilbert Roe, 14 January 1929, Margaret Sanger Papers.

13. Agnes Smedley to Margaret Sanger, 22 February 1929, Margaret Sanger Papers.

14. Smedley, *Battle Hymn*, 43.

15. Smedley, "The Dedicated," in *Chinese Destinies*, 68–69.

16. Smedley, *Battle Hymn*, 48–49, 93. For Browder's movements on his way out of China, see SMP D4805, 6 May 1933; SMP D4157, 30 September 1931; ZCS-638 [n.d.], RG 263. ZCS files, which are scattered among the Shanghai Police files, are official Gestapo records obtained by the CIA and shared with U.S. Army Intelligence after World War II.

17. Agnes Smedley, unpublished typescript, courtesy of Lois Snow.

18. Smedley to Sanger, 13 June 1929.

19. Agnes Smedley, "Tendencies in Modern Chinese Literature," *Modern Review* 47, no. 4 (April 1930): 433.

20. Smedley to Lennon, 6 May 1929.

21. Smedley, *Battle Hymn*, 57.

22. Jiang Feng, interview; Chen Hansheng [Han-seng], "Shi Mo Te Lai Zai Shanghai," in *Shi Mo Te Lai, Si Te Lang, Si Nuo Ji Qi Ta Zuo Ji You Ren Zai Shanghai: Tao Lun Hui Lun Wen Ji* (Shanghai: Three S Research Association, 1987), tr. courtesy Robert of Farnsworth. Also see Chen Hansheng [Han-sheng], *Sige Shidai De Wo* (Beijing: China Culture and History Press, 1988), 52. In this memoir, Chen refers to Agnes directly as a Comintern agent.

23. O. Edmund Clubb, *Twentieth-Century China* (New York: Columbia University Press, 1964), 187.

24. Smedley, *Battle Hymn*, 64.

25. Smedley to Roe, 12 April 1929, Gilbert Roe Papers.

26. R. B. Shipley to Bannerman, 24 April 1929; Shipley to American Consul General, Berlin, 24 April 1929, State Department Passport (130) File, Smedley, Agnes. For more on Shipley, who achieved notoriety during the early years of the cold war for illegally barring hundreds of American leftists (including Agnes) from traveling abroad, see David Caute, *The Great Fear: The Anti-Communist Purge Under Truman and Eisenhower* (New York: Simon and Schuster, 1978), 246.

27. "A Gallant Rebel," *New York Times*, 24 March 1929; Robert Morss Lovett, "The Frontier of Life," *New Republic* 58, no. 748 (3 April, 1929): 203; Lewis Gannett, "Books and Things," *New York Herald Tribune*, 30 September 1933.

28. Paula Rabinowitz, "Women and U.S. Literary Radicalism," in Charlotte Nekola and Paula Rabinowitz, eds., *Writing Red: An Anthology of American Women*

Writers, 1930–1940 (New York: Feminist Press of the City University of New York, 1987), 21, 28.

29. Michael Gold, "Go Left, Young Writers!," *New Masses* 4, no. 8 (January 1929): 1–2.
30. Walt Carmon, *New Masses* 5, no. 3 (August 1929): 17.
31. Gertrude Binder, "Espionage," courtesy of Gertrude Binder.
32. Jiang Feng, interview; Xia [Hsia] Yan, interview by author, Beijing, 20 June 1988.
33. Xia [Hsia] Yan, interview; Luo Ying, "Respected SSS, Shanghai People Remember You," *Voice of Friendship* 27 (February 1988): 6.
34. Xia [Hsia] Yan, interview.
35. Confidential Informant T-1 [Gibarti], FBI NY 100-68282.
36. ZCS-638 [n.d.]; ZCS-827, 7 March 1932; also see SMP D4718, 18 May 1933, RG 263.
37. Rewi Alley, *Six Americans in China* (Beijing: International Culture, 1985), 125; Telitha Gerlach, interview by author, Shanghai, 13 June 1988.
38. Confidential informant T-1, FBI NY 100-68282.
39. Smedley, "The Red Strongholds," in *Chinese Destinies*, 131–32.
40. Babette Gross, *Willi Muenzenberg: A Political Biography* (East Lansing: Michigan State University Press, 183; Project MASK File 1084/Ch, 9 November 1934, and 286/, 25 July 1934.
41. Louis Gibarti, Deposition, 28 August 1951, RG 46.
42. American Consul General, Batavia, to the Honorable Secretary of State, 25 September 1929, 893.00B/655, RG 59; 23 September 1929 Report, 800.00B-LAI/33; RG 59.
43. Ibid. Also SMP D7298, RG 263; State Commission for Safeguarding Public Order and the News Gathering Center of the Ministry of the Interior, "Betrifft: Durchsuchung der Raume der 'Liga gegen den Imperialismus,' 3 July 1929–31 December, 1931," Holding R 134. For Agnes's ongoing relationship with Chatto, see V. Chattopadhyaya to Agnes Smedley, 6 October 1931, 800.00B Smedley, Agnes/23, RG 59.
44. Smedley to Lennon, 19 July, [1930].
45. Smedley to Sanger, 10 August [1929].
46. Gertrude Binder, interview by author, Medford, New Jersey, 10 October 1987.
47. Smedley to Michaelis, 2 April 1930.
48. Smedley to Sanger, 13 June 1929.
49. Smedley to Sanger, 12 October [1929].
50. Chen Hansheng [Han-seng], "Shi Mo Te Lai Zai Shanghai"; Smedley, *Battle Hymn*, 64–69; Agnes Smedley, "Peasants and Lords in China," *New Republic* 64 (3 September 1930): 69–71. This article also appears in *Chinese Destinies*.
51. Smedley to Sanger, 12 October [1929].
52. Smedley to Sanger, 21 November 1929.

Chapter 9. Richard Sorge and the GRU

1. Agnes Smedley, "Through the Darkness of China: Peasant Armies Awaken New Cultural Activities," *Moscow News*, 22 December 1930.
2. Ling Yue-lin, "Wei Le Yi Ge Xin Di She Hui Er Sheng Huo He Gong Zhou—Si Mo Ti Lai, Yu Lu Xun You Yishu Ping," in *Shi Mo Te Lai, Si Te Lang, Si*

Nuo Ji Qi Ta Zuo Ji You Ren Zai Shanghai: Tao Lun Hui Lun Wen Ji (Shanghai: Three S Research Association, 1987), tr. courtesy of Robert Farnsworth; Jiang Feng, interview by author, Beijing, 15 June 1988.

3. Agnes Smedley, *Battle Hymn of China* (New York: Alfred A. Knopf, 1943), 78.

4. Xia [Hsia] Yan, interview by author, Beijing, 20 June 1988; Wang-chi Wong, *Politics and Literature in Shanghai: The Chinese League of Left-Wing Writers, 1930–1936* (Manchester: Manchester University Press, 1991), 45, 59.

5. Xia [Hsia] Yan, interview.

6. Agnes Smedley to Upton Sinclair, 3 May 1930, Upton Sinclair Papers, Lilly Library.

7. Xia [Hsia] Yan, interview. Also see Wong, *Politics and Literature in Shanghai*, 73, 75.

8. Richard Sorge, "Sorge's Own Story," 4, in U.S. Army, Far East Command, Military Intelligence Section, *A Partial Documentation of the Sorge Espionage Case* (Tokyo: Toppan Printing, 1950), ID 923289, RG 319.

9. Sorge, "Sorge's Own Story," 5–6.

10. Ibid., 12–13.

11. Christopher Andrew and Oleg Gordievsky, *KGB: The Inside Story of Its Foreign Operations from Lenin to Gorbachev* (New York: HarperCollins, 1990), 175.

12. Chalmers Johnson, *An Instance of Treason: Ozaki Hotsumi and the Sorge Spy Ring*, expanded ed. (Stanford: Stanford University Press, 1990), 12. Supreme Commander of the Allied Powers translations refer to Sorge's superior as "Beldin" rather than Berzin.

13. Police Interrogation, Richard Sorge, 24 July 1942, ID 923289, RG 319.

14. Preliminary Hearing, Richard Sorge, 15 December 1942, ID 923289, RG 319; Sorge, "Sorge's Own Story," 14.

15. Police Interrogation, Richard Sorge, 24 July 1942. Agnes's Comintern personal file (N 495/244/1533), obtained by the author from Moscow, contains several excisions and does not discuss her work in Shanghai before 1933. The files of Soviet military intelligence remain classified.

16. "Extracts from an Authenticated Translation of Foreign Affairs Yearbook, 1942," 195, in U.S. Army, Far East Command, Military Intelligence Section, *A Partial Documentation of the Sorge Espionage Case*.

17. "Foreign Affairs Yearbook, 1942," 191–92.

18. Police Interrogation, Richard Sorge, 24 July 1942.

19. Agnes Smedley to Florence Becker Lennon, 28 May 1930, courtesy of Florence Becker Lennon.

20. Police Interrogation, Richard Sorge, 24 July 1942.

21. Michael Parrish, *Soviet Security and Intelligence Organizations, 1917–1990: A Biographical Dictionary and Review of Literature in English* (New York: Greenwood Press, 1920), 284.

22. On this subject Sorge had the following to say. "At the beginning of my trial, I purposely used the general expression 'Moscow Center' for the question concerning the apparatus which gave me my commission. Thereby I intentionally left open the answer, as to whether by this I meant the Comintern or one of the chief apparatuses in Moscow. I did not want to throw directly into the discussion the very complicated problem of leadership, Communist leadership. In the

course of the particular discussions on my direct employer in Moscow, I first made the complicated but accurate statement that previously 'Moscow Center' had meant to me the Comintern and its apparatus . . . However, since 1929, a shift occurred for me, but also generally . . . and . . . the P.P. [presumably Communist Party] of the Soviet Union has been the 'Center.' The fact that, after my going over from the Comintern to other apparatuses in Moscow, I had meetings with Piatnitski, Manuilski, and Kuusinen, can be explained as follows: the leading members named of the Comintern are at the same time leading members of the Communist Party of the Soviet Union. Furthermore, they are old acquaintances and older friends of mine, who had assumed the responsibility for me and my trustworthiness in the new work. They are, further, internationally high learned personalities, who helped me with advice of organizational and political nature and followed with great interest my work in China and Japan. They never met with me, for Comintern problems, as employers, but as members of the Central Committee of the Communist Party of the Soviet Union" (Statement, Richard Sorge, May 1942, ID 923289, RG 319).

23. In his prison confession, Sorge refers to Chen as "Wang"; Sonja Kuczinski, a foreign "helper" of Sorge's, refers to Chen as "Professor Yang" or "Pete" [Ruth Werner, *Sonjas Rapport* (Berlin: Verlag Neues Leben, 1977), 63–68]. For more on Chen's work with Sorge, see Chen Hansheng [Han-seng], *Sige Shidai De Wo* (Beijing: China Culture and History Press, 1988).

24. Chen Hansheng [Han-seng], "Shi Mo Te Lai Zai Shanghai," in *Shi Mo Te Lai*, tr. courtesy of Robert Farnsworth; Smedley to Lennon, 28 May 1930.

25. Smedley to Lennon, 28 May 1930. Also see Smedley to Sanger, 12 October [1929].

26. For more on the Noulens affair, see chapter 10. Also see Frederick S. Litten, "The Noulens Affair," *China Quarterly* 138 (June 1994): 492–512.

27. Agnes Smedley to Karin Michaelis, 2 April 1930, Karin Michaelis Papers.

28. Smedley to Michaelis, 2 April 1930.

29. Chen Hansheng [Han-seng], "Shi Mo Te Lai Zai Shanghai."

30. Smedley to Michaelis, 23 July 1930.

31. Smedley to Lennon, 28 May 1930.

32. State Department Passport (130) File, Smedley, Agnes, 14 July 1930; Douglas Jenkins to he Honorable Secretary of State, 13 August 1930, 800.00B, Smedley, Agnes/9, RG 59.

33. Agnes Smedley, "The Social Revolutionary Struggle in China" and "The Revolutionary Peasant Movement in China," Lewis Gannett Papers. Agnes's articles for *Moscow News* began appearing in late 1930.

34. Mrs. Chui was perhaps Lu Hsun's wife, Xu Guangping (Hsu Kuang Han). Both Sorge and Kuczinski recall "Mrs. Chui" as a Guangdong native from an influential family who had a consumptive husband. See *Sorge's Own Story*, 5; Werner, *Sonjas Rapport*, 68.

35. Douglas Jenkins to the Honorable Secretary of State, 13 August 1930.

36. State Department Passport (130) File, Smedley, Agnes, 14 July 1930.

37. Smedley to Lennon, 19 July 1930.

38. Douglas Jenkins to the Honorable Secretary of State, 13 August 1930.

39. Ibid.

40. SMP D4718, 18 May 1933, RG 263.

41. Ibid.; Jenkins to the Honorable Secretary of State, 13 August 1930.
42. Ibid.
43. Agnes Smedley, "Through the Darkness of China: Peasant Armies Awaken New Cultural Activities," *Moscow News*, 22 December 1930; Wong, *Politics and Literature in Shanghai*, 95–96.
44. Agnes Smedley to the American Consul General, [August 1930], 800.00B Smedley, Agnes/10, RG 59.
45. "The Revolution in China, and the Menace of Imperialistic Intervention," *Izvestia* 216 (7 August 1930).
46. Agnes Smedley to E[rnestine Evans], [August 1930], 800.00B, Smedley, Agnes/11, RG 59.
47. Ibid.
48. Agnes Smedley to the International Committee for Political Prisoners, 25 October 1931, International Committee for Political Prisoners Papers.
49. Smedley, *Battle Hymn*, 93; Robert Morss Lovett, introduction to *China's Red Army Marches*, by Agnes Smedley (New York: Vanguard, 1934), vi.
50. U.S. Department of State to Douglas Jenkins, 11 August 1930, 800.00B, Smedley, Agnes/6, RG 59; Douglas Jenkins to the Honorable Secretary of State, 13 August 1930.

Chapter 10. Cloak and Dagger in Shanghai

1. Robert Morss Lovett to the Honorable Joseph P. Cotton, 22 September, 1930, 800.00B, Smedley, Agnes/11, RG 59.
2. J. P. Cotton to the Honorable Nelson T. Johnson, 30 September 1930, 800.00B, Smedley, Agnes/13, RG 59.
3. Wang-chi Wong, *Politics and Literature in Shanghai: The Chinese League of Left-Wing Writers, 1930–1936* (Manchester: Manchester University Press, 1991), 99; Agnes Smedley, *Battle Hymn of China* (New York: Alfred A. Knopf, 1943), 77.
4. Agnes Smedley to Langston Hughes, 14 March 1931, Langston Hughes Papers.
5. Ibid.
6. Agnes Smedley to Langston Hughes, 13 March 1931.
7. Ibid.
8. Stephen Koch, interview by author, New York City, 16 March 1990.
9. Police Interrogation, Ozaki Hotsumi, 5 March 1942, 21 July 1942, ID 923289, RG 319. For more on Ozaki and Smedley, see Chalmers Johnson, *An Instance of Treason: Ozaki Hotsumi and the Sorge Spy Ring* (Stanford: Stanford University Press, 1990).
10. Ibid.
11. Ruth Werner, *Sonjas Rapport* (Berlin: Verlag Neues Leben, 1977), 44.
12. Frederick Litten, "The Noulens Affair," *China Quarterly* 138 (June 1994): 500–501.
13. Werner, *Sonjas Rapport*, 44.
14. Ibid., 48.
15. Richard Sorge, "Sorge's Own Story," 15, 18–19, 22, in U.S. Army, Far East Command, Military Intelligence Section, *A Partial Documentation of the Sorge Espionage Case* (Tokyo: Toppan Printing, 1950); Police Interrogation, Richard Sorge,

22–23 July 1942; Preliminary Hearing, Richard Sorge, 15 December 1942; Police Interrogation, Ozaki Hotsumi, 5 March, 1942. All ID 923289, RG 319.

16. "Extracts from an Authenticated Translation of Foreign Affairs Yearbook, 1942," in U.S. Army, Far East Command, Military Intelligence Section, *A Partial Documentation of the Sorge Espionage Case.*

17. Police Interrogation, Richard Sorge, 24 July 1942.

18. Sorge, "Sorge's Own Story," 15–18; Werner, *Sonjas Rapport*, 46, 68.

19. Shanghai to Netherlands India Government, 24 February 1931, 29 June 1931, 893.OOB/803, RG 59.

20. Preliminary Hearing, Richard Sorge, 15 December 1942; Werner, *Sonjas Rapport*, 52.

21. Werner, *Sonjas Rapport*, 53.

22. Police Interrogation, Ozaki Hotsumi, 8 March 1942.

23. Agnes Smedley, " 'Politico' Used as Curse Word by Workers in Philippines," *Moscow News*, 19 May 1931; U.S. Treasury Attaché to Commissioner of Customs, 15 March 1931, FBI NY 100-68282; SMP D4718, 18 May 1933, RG 263.

24. Agnes Smedley to Gwyneth Roe, 30 April 1931, Gwyneth Roe Papers.

25. Jiang Feng, interview by author, Beijing, 15 June 1988.

26. Ling Yue-lin, "Wei Le Yi Ge Xin Di She Hui Er Sheng Huo He Gong Zhou You Yishu Ping—Smedley, Yu Lu Xun," in *Shi Mo Te Lai, Si Te Lang, Si Nuo Ji Qi Ta Zuo Ji You Ren Zai Shanghai: Tao Lun Hui Lun Wen Ji* (Shanghai: Three S Research Association, 1987), tr. courtesy of Robert Farnsworth; Wong, *Politics and Literature in Shanghai*, 106–7.

27. See Items 35 and 36, "Evidence, Court Testimony—Noulens," SMP D2527/43 [n.d.], RG 263. These descriptions of English-language reports addressed to "Alex," which detail the situation of textile workers in China, a strike by silk filature workers, and other industrial unrest in Shanghai between March and June of 1931, match reports by Agnes in the possession of Edgar Snow at the time of her death. For more on the Noulens case, see Litten, "The Noulens Affair," along with SMP D2527/41 and SMP D2527/45, RG 263. The former is an analysis by the CIA; the latter is a report by British intelligence.

28. Litten, "The Noulens Affair," 506.

29. Robert F. Kelley to Mr. Secretary, 12 July 1932, 800.00B, Communist International/110, RG 59.

30. SMP D4718, 18 May, 1933, RG 263.

31. Agnes Smedley, "Mosquitoes Turned Guerrilla Warriors," in *Chinese Destinies: Sketches of Present-Day China* (New York: Vanguard, 1933), 139–40.

32. Confidential Memo, U.S. Treasury Attaché, Shanghai, 10 August 1931, FBI NY 100-68282; K. S. Patton, American Consul General, to Netherland India Government, 12 January 1932, 893.00B/859, RG 59.

33. Werner, *Sonjas Rapport*, 76.

34. Babette Gross, *Willi Muenzenberg: A Political Biography* (East Lansing: Michigan State University Press, 1974), 220–21.

35. Smedley, *Battle Hymn*, 95. Also see Agnes Smedley to Roger Baldwin, 25 October 1931, International Committee for Political Prisoners Papers.

36. "Agnes Smedley and the Shanghai Die-Hards," *China Weekly Review*, 19 September 1931.

37. Smedley to Baldwin, 25 October 1931; Smedley to Baldwin, 18 November 1931, International Committee for political Prisoners papers.

38. Smedley, *Battle Hymn*, 97–98.

39. Agnes later blamed the Nazis for her dismissal from the *Zeitung*, but her last article for the paper was in November 1930, more than two years before they assumed power.

40. Smedley to Baldwin, 25 October 1931.

41. Virendranath Chattopadhyaya to Agnes Smedley, 6 October 1931, 800.00B Smedley, Agnes/23, RG 59.

42. Smedley to Baldwin, 18 November 1931.

43. Roger Baldwin to Secretary of State, 21 November 1931, 800.00B Smedley, Agnes/20, RG 59; Baldwin to Secretary of State, 24 November 1931, 800.00B Smedley, Agnes/22, RG 59.

44. Department of State, Division of Far Eastern Affairs internal memo, 9 January 1932, 800.00B Smedley, Agnes/23, RG 59.

45. Litten, "The Noulens Affair," 492.

46. Gross, *Willi Muenzenberg*, 220–21; *International Press Correspondence*, 12 November, 1931; Confidential Informant T-1 [Gibarti], FBI NY 100-68282 .

47. Smedley to Baldwin, 24 December 1931.

48. Ibid.

49. Statement, Richard Sorge, February 1942, ID 923289, RG 319.

50. Ibid.; Police Interrogation, Richard Sorge, 24 July 1942.

51. Sorge, "Sorge's Own Story," 15–16; Police Interrogation, Kawai Teikichi, 31 March 1949, 1 April 1949, ID 923289, RG 319.

52. Rewi Alley, *Six Americans in China* (Beijing: International Culture, 1985), 126.

53. Harold Isaacs, *Reencounters in China: Notes of a Journey in a Time Capsule* (Armonk, New York: M. E. Sharpe, 1985), 28, 62.

54. Harold Isaacs to T. A. Bisson, 5 October 1934, and Harold Isaacs to the Central Committee of the CCP, 20 May 1934, 811.5034, Searchlight Publishing/58, RG 59. Also see Luo Ying, "Respected SSS, Shanghai People Remember You," *Voice of Friendship* 27 (February 1988): 7; Israel Epstein, "Strong, Smedley, Snow and Their Links with Soong Ching Ling in Shanghai," in *Shi Mo Te Lai.*

55. Rewi Alley, "Some Shanghai Memories," in *Shi Mo Te Lai*; Rewi Alley, *At 90: Memoirs of My China Years—An Autobiography* (Beijing: New World Press, 1986), 77–79; Otto Braun, *A Comintern Agent in China, 1932–1939*, tr. Jeanne Moore (Stanford: Stanford University Press, 1982), 6. Braun recalls the book for which Agnes was gathering material as *China Fights Back*, but it was *China's Red Army Marches*.

56. Agnes Smedley to Margaret Sanger, 1 April 1932, Margaret Sanger Papers.

57. Agnes Smedley to Florence Becker Lennon, 4 April [1932], courtesy of Florence Becker Lennon.

58. Agnes Smedley to Gwyneth Roe, 30 April 1931.

59. Anna Louise Strong, introduction to *China Fights Back: An American Woman with the Eighth Route Army*, by Agnes Smedley (New York: Vanguard, 1938), xii.

60. Werner, *Sonjas Rapport*, 49,105; Police Interrogation, Nozawa Fusaji, 2 April 1949, 26 April 1949, ID 923289, RG 319.

61. Werner, *Sonjas Rapport*, 108–9.

62. Braun, A Comintern Agent in China, 2; Werner, Sonjas Rapport, 108; Agnes Smedley to John Fairbank, [February 1933], Agnes Smedley Papers. Also see Litten, "The Noulens Affair."

63. For more, see File 811.5034/ Searchlight Publishing, RG 59; SMP D2713, RG 263.

64. Smedley to Sanger, 20 September 1932.

65. Philip J. Jaffe, "Agnes Smedley: The Forgotten Defender of the Oppressed," Philip Jaffe Papers; Louis Gibarti, Deposition, 28 August 1951, RG 46.

66. Smedley to Gwyneth Roe, 30 April 1931.

67. Police Interrogation, Richard Sorge, 19 December 1941; "Extracts from an Authenticated Translation of Foreign Affairs Yearbook, 1942." This information does not appear in Agnes's Comintern files.

68. Ibid.

69. Police Interrogation, Kawai Teikichi, 9 November 1941, 31 March 1949, 1 April 1949; Police Interrogation, Ozaki Hotsumi, 27 July 1942.

70. John King Fairbank, Chinabound: A Fifty-Year Memory (New York: Harper and Row, 1982), 68.

71. In the spring of 1933, Agnes similarly attempted to help Comintern adviser Otto Braun "cover his tracks" in Peking, as he put it, by teaming him up with Edgar Snow, but Snow was extremely suspicious of Braun and refused to have anything to do with him. For more, see Braun, A Comintern Agent in China, 24; Agnes Smedley to Edgar Snow, 10 May 1933, Edgar Snow Papers.

72. Police Interrogation, Ozaki Hotsumi, 27 July 1942.

73. Fairbank, Chinabound, 68–69; Agnes Smedley to John Fairbank, [February 1933].

74. Smedley to Fairbank, [February 1933].

75. Police Interrogation, Kawai Teikichi, 31 March 1949, 1 April 1949. Agnes also wrote of introducing the Fairbanks to a man in Peking she called "Esperanto," and whom she described as a less beguiling figure than Valentino.

76. Police Interrogation, Kawai Teikichi, 31 March 1949, 1 April 1949.

77. Agnes Smedley to Comrade Weinstone, 11 January 1933, Comintern File N495/244/1533, private collection of the author; Smedley to Baldwin, 18 December 1932.

78. Smedley, Battle Hymn, 111.

79. Ling Yue-lin, "Wei Le Yi Ge Xin Di She Hui Er Sheng Huo He Gong Zhou You Yi Shu Ping—Smedley, Yu Lu Xun"; Lu Yi, "Shi Mo Te Lai Yu Zhongguo Min Quan Bao Zhang Tong Meng," in Shi Mo Te Lai.

80. The President [Muenzenberg] to Harold Isaacs, 20 January 1933, SMP D3956, RG 263; Agnes Smedley to International Labor Defense, 3 February, 1933, Philip Jaffe Papers; Smedley to Fairbank, [February 1933].

81. Agnes Smedley to International Labor Defense, 3 February 1933.

82. Fairbank, Chinabound, 69–73; Smedley to Fairbank, [February 1933].

83. Fairbank, Chinabound, 70–71.

84. Smedley to Fairbank, [February 1933].

85. Isaacs, Reencounters in China, 30.

86. Sorge, "Sorge's Own Story," 8.

87. Miyagi Yotoku, "The Sorge Spy Ring: A Case Study in International Espionage in the Far East," 81st Congress, 1st Session, volume 95, part 12, Appendix to the Congressional Record, A715.

88. Agnes Smedley, "Conversations with George Bernard Shaw," [1942], Agnes Smedley Papers.

89. Ibid.

90. Agnes Smedley to Edgar Snow, 10 May [1933].

91. Ibid.

92. 20 March 1933, SMP D3956, RG 263; 18 May 1933, 22 May 1933, SMP D4718, RG 263.

CHAPTER 11. A FISSURE OPENS

1. William O'Dell Nowell, interview by FBI, Detroit, 27 April 1950, FBI DE 105-279.

2. Statement, Ohashi Hideo, 16 April 1949, ID 923289, RG 319.

3. Confidential Informant, interview by FBI, [1949], New York, FBI NY 100-68282.

4. Short Stories from China, tr. Cze Ming-ting (New York: International Publishers, 1933).

5. Agnes Smedley to Karin Michaelis, 31 July 1933, Karin Michaelis Papers.

6. Hede Massing, This Deception (New York: Duell, Sloan, and Pearce, 1951), 92.

7. Ruth Werner, Sonjas Rapport (Berlin: Verlag Neues Leben, 1977), 110.

8. Babette Gross, Willi Muenzenberg: A Political Biography (East Lansing: Michigan State University Press, 1974), 264–65.

9. Werner, Sonjas Rapport, 131–32.

10. Ibid., 124.

11. Grace Granich, Oral History, courtesy of Tom Grunfeld.

12. Agnes Smedley, "The Fall of Shangpo," in Chinese Destinies: Sketches of Present-Day China (New York: Vanguard, 1933), 309–10.

13. "Extracts from an Authenticated Translation of Foreign Affairs Yearbook, 1942," in U.S. Army, Far East Command, Military Intelligence Section, A Partial Documentation of the Sorge Espionage Case (Tokyo: Toppan Printing, 1950), ID 923289, RG 319. Klausen, like Gibarti, refers to "Mironov." However, based on Klausen's description of "Mironov" as director of the OMS radio school in Moscow in 1934 and "Mironov's" familiarity with Agnes, Klausen seems to be speaking of Mirov-Abramov.

14. Werner, Sonjas Rapport, 131.

15. Louis Fischer, Men and Politics: An Autobiography (New York: Duell, Sloan, and Pearce, 1941), 200.

16. Smedley to Michaelis, 31 July 1933.

17. Agnes Smedley, Battle Hymn of China (New York: Alfred A. Knopf, 1943), 127–28.

18. Smedley to Michaelis, 12 July 1933.

19. Agnes Smedley, China's Red Army Marches (New York: Vanguard, 1934), xx–xxi.

20. Charlotte Nekola, "Worlds Unseen: Political Women Journalists and the 1930's," in C. Nekola and P. Rabinowitz, eds., Writing Red: An Anthology of American Women Writers, 1930–1940 (New York: Feminist Press at the City University of New York, 1987), 194.

21. Agnes Smedley, "The Death of Li-kwei," in China's Red Army Marches, 24–31.

22. Smedley to Michaelis, 22 October 1933. Perhaps the article Agnes wrote in 1935 for the Einheit der Weltbewegung gegen imperialistischen Krieg und Faschismus (vol. 1, no. 2) is taken from that document.

23. Smedley to Michaelis, 17 October 1933.
24. Robert Conquest, *The Great Terror: A Reassessment* (New York: Oxford University Press, 1990), 20.
25. Harold Isaacs, *Reencounters in China: Notes of a Journey in a Time Capsule* (Armonk, New York: M. E. Sharpe, 1985), 31.
26. Smedley to Michaelis, 7 September 1933.
27. File 0203, 6 July 1934, and 039, 25 February 1934, Project MASK. In a telephone conversation, Herbert Romerstein, author of a forthcoming book on Project MASK, confirmed to me that these documents are OMS communications to and from Moscow, sent by clandestine radios, which the British intercepted and decrypted.
28. File 0010, 7 June 1934, and 155, 26 May 1934, Project MASK. The advice in this radiograph is intended for "Milton," later identified by the FBI as Eugene Dennis, Browder's successor at the CPUSA, who worked for the Comintern in the Far East between 1931 and 1935.
29. File 0300, 20 July 1934, and 087, 22 April 1934; also File 0010, 7 June 1934, and 155, 26 May 1934, Project MASK.
30. Louis Gibarti, Deposition, 28 August 1951, RG 46.
31. Ibid.
32. Agnes Smedley to Florence Becker Lennon, 17 March 1934, courtesy of Florence Becker Lennon.
33. Ilya Suchkov, "New Light on Old Indian Revolutionary," *Soviet Land* 23, no. 2 (January 1970); 15; Gross, *Willi Muenzenberg*, 182–83.
34. Smedley, *Battle Hymn*, 23.
35. Werner, *Sonjas Rapport*, 128.
36. Smedley, *Battle Hymn*, 127.
37. Agnes Smedley to Joseph Freeman, 5 July [1943], Joseph Freeman Papers.
38. Agnes Smedley to Upton Sinclair, 4 June 1941, Upton Sinclair Papers, Lilly Library.
39. Agnes Smedley to J. Henle and Eva Ginn, 10 August [1937], Eva Ginn Papers.
40. Agnes Smedley to Comrade Ludkiewicz, 3 April 1934, Agnes Smedley Papers, Maxim Gorky Institute for World Literature. The first of these articles appeared in Muenzenberg's *A.I.Z.* 13, no. 15 (1934) and *Unsere Zeit* 7, no. 5 (1934).
41. Gross, *Willi Muenzenberg*, 242.
42. Comintern Cipher Telegram 495/184/24/76, 22 April 1934.
43. Agnes Smedley to Gwyneth Roe, 25 January 1933.
44. Florence Becker Lennon, "Memoirs," courtesy of Florence Becker Lennon.
45. For more on Friends of the Chinese People, see CPUSA File 515-1-3936.
46. Harold Isaacs to T. A. Bisson, 5 October 1934, 811.5034, Searchlight Publishing Co./58, RG 59.
47. T. Ryan [Eugene Dennis] to Comrades, 20 December 1937, Comintern File N495/244/1533, private collection of author.
48. Philip J. Jaffe, "Agnes Smedley: The Forgotten Defender of the Oppressed," in *The Odyssey of a Fellow Traveler*, Philip Jaffe Papers.
49. Ibid.
50. Conference with Louis Gibarti, 5 August 1952, RG 46.
51. Grace Granich, Oral History.

52. Ibid.
53. [Blacked out], interview by FBI, 17 November 1949, FBI NY 100-68282.
54. Confidential Informant T-1 [Gibarti], FBI NY 100-68282.
55. Whittaker Chambers, interview by FBI, 10 May 1945, FBI 61-6580-103.
56. Ibid.
57. Sam Tanenhaus, *Whittaker Chambers: A Biography* (New York: Random House, 1997), 100; Whittaker Chambers, interview by FBI, 31 December 1948, 16 March 1949, FBI NY 100-68282.
58. Whittaker Chambers, interview by FBI, 31 December 1948, 16 March 1949.
59. Betty Barnes, interview by author, New York City, September 1987.
60. Owen Lattimore, "A Long Way from the Whole Truth About China," *New York Times*, 10 December 1933.
61. Lewis Gannett, "Books and Things," *New York Herald Tribune*, 30 September 1933.
62. Malcolm Cowley, *The Dream of the Golden Mountains: Remembering the 1930s* (New York: Viking, 1980), 224–25.
63. Malcolm Cowley, introduction to *Daughter of Earth*, by Agnes Smedley (New York: Coward-McCann, 1935).
64. Comintern Cipher Telegram, 9 July 1934, 495/184/24/133.
65. Comintern Cipher telegram, Pavel Mif to Earl Browder, 14 July 1934, 495/184/24/147.
66. Comintern Cipher Telegram, 5 August 1934, 495/184/24/[illegible].
67. Isaacs to Bisson, 5 October 1934.
68. Grace Granich, Oral History.
69. Agnes Smedley to Gwyneth Roe [Summer 1934], Gwyneth Roe Papers.
70. Smedley to Michaelis, 2 November 1933.
71. Smedley to Goldman, 24 September 1934.
72. Emma Goldman to Demi Coleman, 24 February 1939, courtesy of Candace Falk.
73. Police Interrogation, Ozaki Hotsumi, 12 August 1942, ID 923289, RG 319.
74. Ibid.

CHAPTER 12. AN UNRULY AGENT

1. Agnes Smedley, "A Day Passes," in *China's Red Army Marches* (New York: Vanguard, 1934), 196–209.
2. " 'I'm No Red!' Broke, Ill, Agnes Smedley Lashes Accusers, Yearns for Missouri," *San Diego Sun*, 23 May 1937; Betford to Alexander, 8 May 1936, Profintern File 534-4-518; Rewi Alley, *At 90: Memoirs of My China Years* (Beijing: New World Press, 1986), 89; Ma Haide [George Hatem], "A Woman Made by History and Who Made History," *Beijing Review* 33, no. 19 (713 May 1990): 34.
3. Ma Haide, "A Woman Made by History," 35.
4. Ibid., 34.
5. Mei Da, "Rewi Alley's 55 Years in China," *China Reconstructs* 31, no. 7 (July 1982): 39; Ma Haide, " 'Go Northwest, Young Man' — Some of Rewi Alley's Revolutionary Activities," in *Shi Mo Te Lai, Si Te Lang, Si Nuo Ji Qi Ta Zuo Ji You Ren Zai Shanghai: Tao Lun Hui Lun Wen Ji* (Shanghai: Three S Research Association, 1987); Alley, *At 90*, 78, 80.

6. Rewi Alley, "Some Shanghai Memories," in *Shi Mo Te Lai*; Ruth Weiss, interview by author, Beijing, 20 June 1988.
7. Agnes Smedley, "A Dark Night," courtesy of Lois Snow.
8. Ibid.
9. *Central China Daily News*, 12 December 1935, 14 December 1935. Also see Agnes Smedley, "The Corrupt Press in China," *Nation* 141, no. 3652 (3 July 1935): 10.
10. Agnes Smedley to Edgar Snow, 7 January 1935, courtesy of Lois Snow.
11. Smedley, "The Corrupt Press in China," 10.
12. Agnes Smedley to Edwin Cunningham, 18 December 1934, 800.00B, Smedley, Agnes/35, RG 59; Agnes Smedley to Friend, 19 December 1934, 800.00B, Smedley, Agnes/32, RG 59; Agnes Smedley to Roger Baldwin, 19 December, 1934, ACLU Papers.
13. Smedley to Baldwin, 19 December 1934.
14. Agnes Smedley, Letter to the Editor, *Shanghai Evening Post and Mercury*, 5 January 1935.
15. Baldwin to Smedley, 18 January 1935, ACLU Papers.
16. James Henle to Senator Wagner, 16 January 1935, 800.00B, Smedley, Agnes/32, RG 59.
17. Margaret Sanger to Edwin Cunningham, 19 March 1935, 800.00B, Smedley, Agnes/46, RG 59; Margaret Sanger to Alfred Sze, 16 February 1935, 800.00B, Smedley, Agnes/46, RG 59 (also available in Sanger Papers).
18. Edwin Cunningham to Secretary of State, 27 April 1935, 800.00B, Smedley, Agnes/46, RG 59.
19. Grace Granich, Oral History, courtesy of Tom Grunfeld; Philip J. Jaffe, "Agnes Smedley: The Forgotten Defender of the Oppressed," 239, in *The Odyssey of a Fellow Traveler*, Philip Jaffe Papers.
20. Agnes Smedley to John Fairbank, 24 August 1935, Agnes Smedley Papers.
21. David Hornstein, *Arthur Ewert: A Life for the Comintern* (Lanham, Maryland: University Press of America, 1993), 159; Peggy Dennis, *The Autobiography of an American Communist: A Personal View of a Political Life, 1925–1975* (Berkeley, California: Creative Arts; Westport, Connecticut: Lawrence Hill, 1977), 13; Chapman Pincher, *Too Secret Too Long* (New York: St. Martin's Press, 1984), 35, 37.
22. Grace Granich, Oral History.
23. Ibid.
24. Chen Hansheng [Han-seng], "Shi Mo Te Lai Zai Shanghai," in *Shi Mo Te Lai*, tr. courtesy of Robert Farnsworth; Chen Hansheng [Han-seng], "We Owe Them a Deep Debt," in *Salute to Smedley, Strong, and Snow* (Beijing: Zhong Guo Xin Wen Chu Ban She [China Journalist Publisher], 1985), 120. Also see Rewi Alley, *Six Americans in China* (Beijing: International Culture, 1985), 128. In "Shi Mo Te Lai Zai Shanghai," Chen says that "Mrs. Hamburg" made the arrangements for Chen's wife. "Mrs. Hamburg" was most likely Agnes's friend Sonja Kuczinski, who had returned to China after her OMS training in Moscow and was known to the Shanghai Municipal Police under her husband's surname, Hamburger.
25. Grace Granich, Oral History.
26. Agnes Smedley to Eva Ginn, 12 July 1935, Eva Ginn Papers.

27. Earl Browder to ECCI, 14 August 1935, Comintern Cipher Telegram 495-184-34-164.

28. Tom Grunfeld, interview by author, New York City, 25 April 1987; Grace Granich, Oral History. The book of Kollwitz's wood-block prints was eventually published as *Kai Sui. Ke Le Hui Zhi Ban Hua Xuang Ji* (Shanghai: San Xian, 1936).

29. Earl Browder to Comrade Dimitrov, 2 September 1935. Comintern File 495-74-463.

30. Isador Schneider to Joseph Freeman, 17 January 1935, Joseph Freeman Papers. "It looks as if you and I are competing as to who is to hold off the trip to China longest," Schneider joked with Freeman.

31. Grace Granich, Oral History.

32. Smedley to Ginn, 1 January 1936.

33. Smedley to Ginn, 8 November [1935].

34. For more on the German exile presses, see Liselotte Maas, *Handbuch der deutschen Exilpresse, 1933–1945* (Munich: Carl Hanser Verlag, 1976).

35. Ginn to Smedley, 8 April 1935.

36. Wang Ming to Earl Browder, File 398A/USA, 22 October 1935, and 359, 27 October 1935, Project MASK.

37. Grace Granich, Oral History.

38. Ibid.

39. Max Granich, Oral History, courtesy of Tom Grunfeld.

40. Grace Granich, Oral History.

41. James Bertram, *First Act in China: The Story of the Sian Mutiny* (New York: Viking, 1938), 154.

42. Max Granich, Oral History.

43. Grace Granich, Oral History.

44. Weiss, interview.

45. Ibid.

46. Alley, *Six Americans*, 125; Rewi Alley, "Agnes Smedley: Champion of the Under-privileged," in *Salute to Smedley, Strong, and Snow*, 150.

47. Most likely, Grace referred to Maurice Appelman, known in Shanghai as Mike Pell and referred to as Young in Profintern File 534-4-518, Betford to Alexander, 8 May 1936. In a 1949 interview with the FBI, Appleman, who believed Agnes was an intermediary between the Russian and Chinese Communist parties in the mid-1930s, said that on his return to Shanghai after a trip to the Soviet Union, the CPUSA warned him not to contact Agnes again. Appleman thought this was either because Agnes was being used in a confidential capacity or because the Party no longer trusted her. He added that a Party functionary had also warned him that Smedley was "using poison ink and that a person would have to wear gloves when reading her letters to avoid poisoning." (Morris Appelman, interview by FBI, 17 November 1949, FBI NY 100-68282).

48. Max Granich, Oral History.

49. Wan[g] Min[g] to United States, File 131-132, 31 March 1936, and 5600-USA, 6 April 1936, Project MASK.

50. Betford to Alexander, 8 May 1936, Profintern File 534-4-518. For Betford as Rudy Baker see Harvey Klehr, John Earl Haynes, and Fridrikh Igorevich Firsov, *The Secret World of American Communism* (New Haven: Yale University Press, 1995), 59–60.

51. Weiss, interview.
52. Alley, *Six Americans*, 130.
53. Max Granich, Oral History.
54. Betford to Alexander, 20 October 1936, Profintern File 534-4-518.
55. Agnes Smedley, *Battle Hymn of China* (New York: Alfred A. Knopf, 1943), 133.
56. A search of *International Press Correspondence* from 1935 through 1937 did not turn up this article, but P. E. Skachkov, ed., *Bibliografiya Kitaia* (Moscow: Publishing House of Oriental Literature, 1960), 124, notes that a 1936 Russian translation of Agnes's China writing, *Geroi Sovetskogo Kitaia*, contains a section entitled "March to the West." Also see Ling Yue-lin, "Wei Le Yi Ge Xin Di She Hui Er Sheng Huo He Gong Zhou You Yi Shu Ping—Smedley, Yu Lu Xun," in *Shi Mo Te Lai*; Alley, *Six Americans*, 130, 138; Alley, *At 90*, 86.
57. Grace Granich, Oral History.
58. Robert Farnsworth, *From Vagabond to Journalist: Edgar Snow in Asia, 1928–1941* (Columbia: University of Missouri Press, 1996), 204.
59. Weiss, interview.
60. Farnsworth, *Edgar Snow in Asia*, 204.
61. Nym Wales [Helen Foster Snow], "Dispatches from Sian, 1936–1937," 122, Nym Wales Papers.
62. Israel Epstein, interview by author, Beijing, 17 June 1988.
63. Jaffe, "Agnes Smedley: The Forgotten Defender of the Oppressed," 241.
64. Epstein, interview.
65. Smedley, *Battle Hymn*, 133–34; Alley, *At 90*, 91–92.
66. Ma Haide, "A Woman Made by History," 35–36.
67. Agnes Smedley, "Shanghai in the Mid-1930s Described by Agnes Smedley," *China and Us* 8, no. 2 (March–May 1979): 14.
68. Smedley to Ginn, 3 June [1936].
69. Betford to Alexander, 20 October 1936, Profintern File 534-4-518.
70. Betford to Alexander, 20 July 1936, Profintern File 534-4-518.
71. Wan[g] Min[g] from Johnson Betford, 31 July 1936, Comintern Cipher Telegram 495-184-3.
72. Smedley to Ginn, 8 November 1935.
73. Smedley to Ginn, 6 August [1936].
74. Ibid.
75. Agnes Smedley to Malcolm Cowley, 24 July 1941, Malcolm Cowley Papers.
76. Smedley to Ginn, 6 August [1936].

Chapter 13. Mutiny in Sian

1. Agnes Smedley to Eva Ginn, 21 October 1936, Eva Ginn Papers.
2. Ginn to Smedley, 4 December 1936. Field is referred to here as Lawrence [Hearn], the name he used when writing for *China Today*; Jaffe is referred to by his alias, Phillips.
3. The book, *China—As It Really Is*, appeared on International Publishers' list for publication in 1935 but was never published.
4. For more on the German exile presses, see Liselotte Maas, *Handbuch der deutschen Exilpresse, 1933–1945* (Munich: Carl Hanser Verlag, 1976).

5. Ting Ling, interview by Tillie Olsen, 10 October 1981, courtesy of Tillie Olsen.
6. Agnes Smedley to Karin Michaelis, 19 November 1936, Karin Michaelis Papers.
7. Agnes Smedley, *Battle Hymn of China* (New York: Alfred A. Knopf, 1943), 140.
8. Tien-Wei Wu, *The Sian Incident: A Pivotal Point in Modern Chinese History* (Ann Arbor: Center for Chinese Studies, University of Michigan, 1976), 78; Smedley, *Battle Hymn*, 141.
9. Smedley, *Battle Hymn*, 141–42.
10. Rewi Alley, *Six Americans in China* (Beijing: International Publishing, 1985), 143; Peter Rand, *China Hands: The Adventures and Ordeals of the American Journalists Who Joined Forces with the Great Chinese Revolution* (New York: Simon and Schuster, 1995), 172.
11. Smedley, *Battle Hymn*, 141.
12. Wu, *The Sian Incident*, 101.
13. Ting Ling, "Agnes Smedley," *Masses and Mainstream* 4, no. 8 (August 1951): 84.
14. Wu, *Sian Incident*, 104.
15. Agnes Smedley to Randall Gould, 19 May 1937, Agnes Smedley Papers; Smedley, *Battle Hymn*, 145.
16. Ting Ling, "Agnes Smedley," 83–84.
17. Smedley, *Battle Hymn*, 147; Alley, *Six Americans*, 143.
18. Agnes Smedley, "Chiang Kai-shek's Arrest," 14 December [1936], Agnes Smedley News Dispatches, Nym Wales Papers.
19. Wu, *The Sian Incident*, 102.
20. Agnes Smedley, "Sianfu, 15 December 1936," Agnes Smedley News Dispatches. Also see Agnes Smedley, "How Chiang Was Captured," *Nation* 144, no. 7 (13 February 1937), 180–82.
21. Agnes Smedley to Helen Snow, 30 May 1937, Nym Wales Papers.
22. Smedley, *Battle Hymn*, 146–47.
23. Helen Snow, "Agnes Smedley's Comments on Sian," 191, Source Material, Sian Incident, Nym Wales Papers.
24. Anna Wang, *Ich Kämpfte für Mao* (Hamburg: Holsten Verlag Hamburg, 1973).
25. Rewi Alley, "Agnes Smedley: Champion of the Underprivileged," in *Salute to Smedley, Strong and Snow* (Beijing: Three S Research Association, 1985), 150.
26. Smedley to Gould, 19 May 1937.
27. James Bertram, *First Act in China: The Story of the Sian Mutiny* (New York: Viking, 1938), 172.
28. Ibid., 173.
29. Ting Ling, "Agnes Smedley," 84.
30. Agnes Smedley, "Sianfu, Shensi, 27 December 1936," Agnes Smedley News Dispatches.
31. Earl Browder to Wang Ming and Secretariat, 21 January 1937, Comintern Cipher Telegram 495-184-9.
32. Agnes Smedley, Lecture Notes, Agnes Smedley Papers.
33. Bertram, *First Act in China*, 156–57.
34. Ibid., 174–75.
35. Ibid., 173.
36. Ibid., 176–77.
37. Emily Hahn, interview by author, New York City, 23 September 1987.

38. Agnes Smedley to Emily Hahn, 25 January 1937, 800.00B, Smedley, Agnes/57, RG 59.

39. Agnes Smedley to David Berenberg, 25 January 1937, 800.00B, Smedley, Agnes/57, RG 59.

40. Clarence Gauss to Secretary of State, 7 January 1937, 800.00B, Smedley, Agnes/53, RG 59.

41. "American Woman Aids Chinese Rising," *New York Times*, 8 January 1937.

42. "U.S. Woman Aids Chinese Reds," *New York Sun*, 7 January 1937; "U.S. Girl Reported in China Revolt," *New York Post*, 7 January 1937.

43. Nelson Johnson to Secretary of State, 9 January 1937, 800.00B, Smedley, Agnes/55, RG 59.

44. "China Reproaches American Woman," *New York Times*, 10 January 1937.

45. Upton Sinclair, "America's Amazing Woman Rebel in China," *Liberty* 14, no. 11 (13 March 1937): 20. This story also appears as "The Story of Agnes Smedley," in *Expect No Peace* (Girard, Kansas: Haldeman-Julius, 1939), 34–37, and in manuscript form as "The Red Dragon: The Story of Agnes Smedley in America and China."

46. Smedley, *Battle Hymn*, 150.

47. Aritatino [Agnes Smedley] to Friend [Edgar Snow], 10 January 1937, Nym Wales Papers.

48. Bertram, *First Act in China*, 214.

49. Ibid., 176–78.

50. Ibid., 215–17.

CHAPTER 14. CALAMITY JANE OF THE CHINESE REVOLUTION

1. Agnes Smedley, "A Talk with P'eng Teh-hwei," Philip Jaffe Papers.

2. Ibid.

3. Agnes Smedley in Nym Wales [Helen Foster Snow], *My Yenan Notebooks* (Madison, Connecticut: Helen Foster Snow, 1961), 66.

4. Agnes Smedley, "A Talk with P'eng Teh-hwei."

5. Agnes Smedley to Edgar Snow, 19 April 1937, Edgar Snow Papers.

6. "First Pictures of China's Roving Communists," *Life* 1, no. 4 (25 January 1937): 9.

7. Secretariat to Browder, [1937], Comintern Cipher Telegram 495-184-17.

8. "A Warning Regarding News from China," *Daily Worker*, 29 January 1937.

9. Agnes Smedley, *Battle Hymn of China* (New York: Alfred A. Knopf, 1943), 168–69.

10. Ibid., 169.

11. Malcolm Cowley, interview by FBI, 27 May 1949, FBI NY 100-68282.

12. Smedley to Snow, 13 March 1937, in Wales, *My Yenan Notebooks*, 171.

13. Eva Ginn to Agnes Smedley, 15 February 1937, Eva Ginn Papers.

14. Smedley to Ginn and Henle, 10 March 1937, Eva Ginn Papers.

15. Smedley to Snow, 19 April 1937.

16. Smedley to Snow, 13 March 1937.

17. Rewi Alley, *Six Americans in China* (Beijing: International Culture, 1985), 145.

18. Smedley, *Battle Hymn*, 129; Elizabeth Smedley, interview by author, Chula Vista, California, 20 August 1984.

19. Smedley, *Battle Hymn*, 164.
20. Smedley to Snow, 19 April 1937.
21. Ma Haide, "A Woman Made by History and Who Made History," *Beijing Review* 33, no. 19 (7–13 May 1990): 36.
22. Malcolm Cowley, interview by FBI, 27 May 1949, FBI NY 100-68282; Toni Willison, interview by author, Ballston Spa, New York, 28 August 1984.
23. Smedley to Ginn, 2 July 1937.
24. Smedley to Ginn and Henle, 8 March 1937.
25. Agnes Smedley to Randall Gould, 21 July 1937, Agnes Smedley Papers.
26. Ibid.
27. Anna Wang, *Ich Kampfte fur Mao* (Hamburg: Holsten Verlag Hamburg, 1973).
28. Smedley, *Battle Hymn*, 169.
29. Smedley to Snow, 19 April 1937; Agnes Smedley, *The Great Road: The Life and Times of Chu Teh* (New York: Monthly Review Press, 1956), 226.
30. Wales, *My Yenan Notebooks*, 62.
31. Helen Foster Snow, *My China Years* (New York: William Morrow, Inc., 1984), 275–76.
32. Snow, "Mō Taku-tō no renai" (Mao's Love Affair: The Women of Yenan and Agnes Smedley), *Chou Koron* 69, no. 7 (July 1954), tr. courtesy of Robert Farnsworth.
33. Smedley, *Battle Hymn*, 163.
34. Smedley to Snow, 13 March 1937, in Wales, *My Yenan Notebooks*, 171.
35. Gertrude Binder, interview by author, Medford, New Jersey, 10 October 1987. Also Gertrude Binder, "Espionage," courtesy of Gertrude Binder.
36. Wales, *My Yenan Notebooks*, 64.
37. Snow, "Mō Taku-tō no renai."
38. Ibid.
39. Ibid.
40. Ibid.
41. Wales, *My Yenan Notebooks*, 64.
42. Snow, "Mō Taku-tō no renai."
43. Ibid.
44. Ibid.
45. Ibid.
46. Smedley, *Battle Hymn*, 171.
47. Smedley to Snow, 19 April, 1937.
48. Ibid.
49. Ibid. Also see Smedley, *Battle Hymn*, 170–71.
50. Smedley to Snow, 19 April 1937.
51. Ibid.
52. Snow, "Mō Taku-tō no renai."
53. Ibid.
54. Ibid.
55. "Smedley Is Not a Member of Chinese Party," *Daily Worker*, 4 May 1937.
56. Philip J. Jaffe, "Agnes Smedley: The Forgotten Defender of the Oppressed," in *The Odyssey of a Fellow Traveler*, 241, Philip Jaffe Papers; Philip Jaffe, interview by FBI, 28 April 1950, FBI NY 100-68282.

57. Jaffe, "Agnes Smedley: The Forgotten Defender of the Oppressed," 240.
58. Wales, *My Yenan Notebooks*, 164; Marginalia, Long March Materials, courtesy of Lois Snow.
59. Alley, *Six Americans*, 145; Ma, "A Woman Made by History," 36.
60. Haide, "A Woman Made by History," 36.
61. Su Fei Speech, November 1984, courtesy of Robert Farnsworth.
62. Ibid.
63. Wales, *My Yenan Notebooks*, 63.
64. Belov to Cadre Department, ECCI, 20 December 1937, Comintern File 495/244/1533, private collection of author.
65. Ianson to Comrades Marty, Van Min [Wang Ming], and Personnel Department, ECCI, 26 April 1937, Comintern File 495/244/1533.
66. Although an FBI search of Agnes's criminal record had uncovered nothing, and the State Department's division of Far Eastern affairs refused to pursue Agnes based on information obtained illegally by British police in Shanghai, Ruth Shipley had written a refusal on Agnes's passport record. Memo, 15 January 1937, State Department Passport Office (130) File, Smedley, Agnes.
67. Wales, *My Yenan Notebooks*, 172.
68. Smedley to Henle and Ginn, 10 August [1937]; Smedley, *Battle Hymn*, 186, 229; Jean Ewen, *China Nurse, 1932–1939* (Toronto: McClelland and Steward, 1981), 44–45; Agnes Smedley, *China Fights Back* (New York: Vanguard Press, 1938), 7.
69. Belov to Cadre Department, ECCI, 20 December 1937.
70. Helen Foster Snow to author, 26 July 1984.
71. Smedley to Henle and Ginn, 10 August [1937].
72. Smedley to Baldwin, 20 August [1937].
73. Snow, *My China Years*, 281.

CHAPTER 15. SELFLESS FOR THE CAUSE

1. Eva Ginn to Agnes Smedley, 25 October 1937, Eva Ginn Papers.
2. Agnes Smedley to Florence Rose and Margaret Sanger, 23 September 1937, Margaret Sanger Papers.
3. Agnes Smedley, *China Fights Back: An American Woman with the Eighth Route Army* (New York: Vanguard, 1938), 148.
4. Smedley to Ginn, in Agnes Smedley, *China Fights Back*, xv–xvi.
5. Agnes Smedley, "The Future of China's War," marginalia, Agnes Smedley Papers.
6. Agnes Smedley, *Battle Hymn of China* (New York: Alfred A. Knopf, 1943), 197.
7. Evans Fordyce Carlson, *Twin Stars of China: A Behind-the-Scenes Story of China's Valiant Struggle for Existence by a U.S. Marine who Lived and Moved with the People* (New York: Dodd, Mead, 1940), 69.
8. Michael Blankfort, *The Big Yankee* (Boston: Little, Brown, 1947), 206.
9. Smedley, *China Fights Back*, 250.
10. T[im] Ryan to Cadre Dept of ECCI, 20 December 1937, Comintern Cipher Telegram 495-244-1533. See Harvey Klehr, John Earl Haynes, and Fridrikh Igorevich Firsov, *The Secret World of American Communism* (New Haven: Yale University Press, 1995), 260, for Tim Ryan as Eugene Dennis.

11. Smedley, *China Fights Back*, 263–65.

12. Ilona Ralf Sues, *Shark's Fins and Millet* (Boston: Little, Brown, 1944), 216–18.

13. [James Bertram] to Edgar Snow, [spring 1938], Edgar Snow Papers; Jean Ewen, *China Nurse, 1932–1939* (Toronto: McClelland and Stewart, 1981), 50.

14. Jean Ewen to Edith Sawyer, 13 May 1939, Norman Bethune File, Indusco Papers.

15. Agnes Smedley to Jawaharlal Nehru, 23 November 1937, and Chu Teh to Jawaharlal Nehru, 26 November 1937, in Jawaharlal Nehru, *A Bunch of Old Letters* (New York: Asia Publishing House, 1960), 260–63; Smedley, *Battle Hymn*, 229. The Indian team, which included Dr. Dwarkaneth Kotnis and Dr. B. K. Basu, reached Yenan in February 1939. Bethune, a Canadian Communist Party member, died of septicemia soon after. He was canonized in death by the Chinese Communists. Kotnis remained in China as head of the first International Peace Hospital until his death in 1942. Basu worked in Yenan until 1943.

16. See *Fight*, August 1938, 5–9; *Fight*, September 1938, 13–15; *Fight*, January 1939, 10–s11.

17. Agnes Smedley, "Mein Kreig Stagebuch," Smedley Papers, Maxim Gorky Institute for World Literature.

18. W. H. Auden and Christopher Isherwood, *Journey to a War* (New York: Octagon Books, 1972), 50–51, 60.

19. Ibid., 171.

20. John Patton Davies Jr., *Dragon by the Tail: American, British, Japanese, and Russian Encounters with China and One Another* (New York: W. W. Norton, 1972), 195.

21. Edgar Snow, *Journey to the Beginning* (New York: Random House, 1958), 226–27.

22. See Freda Utley, *The China Story* (Chicago: Henry Regnery, 1951).

23. Freda Utley, *Odyssey of a Liberal: Memoirs* (Washington, D.C.: Washington National Press, 1970), 201.

24. Freda Utley, *China at War* (London: Faber and Faber, 1939), 215.

25. Ibid., 214–16.

26. Davies, *Dragon by the Tail*, 196.

27. Lewis Gannett, "Books and Things," review of *China Fights Back* by Agnes Smedley, *Washington Post*, 1 July 1938.

28. Nathaniel Weyl, "*China Fights Back*, by Agnes Smedley," review, *Amerasia* 2, no. 7 (September 1938): 362.

29. Agnes Smedley to Lewis Gannett, 15 April 1942, Lewis Gannett Papers. Also see Agnes Smedley to Freda Utley, [June 1939], in Utley, *Odyssey of a Liberal*, 207; Agnes Smedley to Malcolm Cowley, 24 July 1941, Malcolm Cowley Papers.

30. Agnes Smedley to Lewis Gannett, 15 April 1942; Edgar Snow to Peg Snow, 28 August 1938, Edgar Snow Papers.

31. Smedley, *Battle Hymn*, 227–28.

32. Ibid., 231–32.

33. Utley, *China at War*, 213.

34. Ibid., 214.

35. Davies, *Dragon by the Tail*, 196.

36. Ewen, *China Nurse*, 146.

37. Ibid., 144, 149; Agnes Smedley to [Hilda Selwyn-Clark], 16 November 1938 in Utley, *China at War*, 134.

38. Smedley to Utley, [n.d.], in Utley, *Odyssey of a Liberal*, 208.

39. Agnes Smedley to "Gang, " [n.d.], in Stephen R. MacKinnon and Oris Friesen, *China Reporting: An Oral History of American Journalism in the 1930s and 1940s* (Berkeley: University of California Press, 1987), 43.

40. Smedley, *Battle Hymn*, 258.

41. Ewen, *China Nurse*, 149–50.

42. Ed Snow to M, 3 March 1939, Edgar Snow Papers.

43. Janice R. MacKinnon and Stephen R. MacKinnon, *Agnes Smedley: The Life and Times of an American Radical* (Berkeley: University of California Press, 1988), 217.

44. Rewu Alley, *Six Americans in China* (Beijing: International Culture, 1985), 150.

45. Utley, *Odyssey of a Liberal*, 206–7.

46. Agnes Smedley, "China's Guerrilla Armies Stab Japan in the Back," *Life* 7, no. 1 (3 July 1939): 12–13.

47. Smedley, *Battle Hymn*, 301.

48. Ibid., 307–8.

49. Ibid., 379.

50. Casper C. Skinsnes, *Scalpel and Cross in Honan* (Minneapolis: Augsburg, 1952), 221.

51. Smedley, *Battle Hymn*, 411.

52. Ibid., 418.

53. Agnes Smedley, "A Play About China," volumes 31 and 33, Agnes Smedley Papers. The Chung Yi character is named Chou Tien-ying; Agnes is Lucy Stone, "an American woman writer . . . who does first aid at the front."

54. Smedley, *Battle Hymn*, 464–66.

55. Ibid., 470–72.

56. Ibid., 489.

57. Ida Pruitt to Ted Herman, 17 October 1939, Pruitt File, Indusco Papers.

58. Smedley, *Battle Hymn*, 504; Smedley to Ginn 28 July, 1940.

59. Smedley to Ginn and Henle, 4 May 1940.

60. "Red Cross Hospital Razed by Japanese," *New York Times*, 30 July 1940; "That Japanese 'Pride,'" [editorial], *New York Times*, 31 July 1940.

61. Smedley to Ginn, 28 July 1940.

62. Smedley, *Battle Hymn*, 505.

63. Emily Hahn, *China to Me: A Partial Autobiography* (Garden City, New York: Doubleday, Doran, 1944), 221.

64. Emily Hahn, interview by author, New York City, 23 September 1987.

65. Suzi [Madame Sun Yat-sen] to Grace Granich, 3 September 1939, FBI NY 100-88434-218, courtesy of Tom Grunfeld. In the correspondence, Agnes is referred to as Minnie (for Minnie Ha Ha, the Graniches' nickname for Agnes). Also see Smedley to Cowley, 24 July 1941.

66. Ibid.

67. Ibid.

68. Hahn, interview; Agnes Smedley, *Stories of the Wounded: An Appeal for Orthopedic Centres of the Chinese Red Cross* [pamphlet], (Hong Kong, 1941), 28.

69. Smedley, *Battle Hymn*, 523.

70. Robert S. Lim [Agnes Smedley], "The China Red Cross Medical Relief Corps

in Three Years of War," in May-ling Soong Chiang, *China Shall Rise Again* (New York: Harper and Brothers, 1941), 229–60.

71. Smedley to Ginn, 13 January 1941.
72. Howard Goldblatt, *Hsiao Hung* (Boston: Twayne, 1976), 112.
73. Smedley, *Battle Hymn*, 523.
74. Ibid., 525–26.
75. Agnes Smedley to Upton Sinclair, 21 April 1941, Upton Sinclair Papers, Lilly Library.
76. Smedley, *Battle Hymn*, 520.
77. Rewi Alley, *At 90: Memories of My China Years* (Beijing: New World Press, 985), 238.

CHAPTER 16. BACK IN THE U.S.A.

1. Tillman Durdin, interview by author, Beijing, 17 June 1988; Elizabeth Smedley, interview by author, Chula Vista, California, 20 August 1984.
2. Eleanor Brundin, interview by author, Cerritos, California, 3 January 1987.
3. "Yaddo Author Discusses 'New Force'—PAC," *Skidmore News*, 7 December 1944
4. Brundin, interview.
5. Agnes Smedley to Karin Michaelis, 23 July 1930, Karin Michaelis Papers.
6. Eva Ginn to Agnes Smedley, 14 June 1935, Eva Ginn Papers; Smedley, interview.
7. Smedley, interview.
8. Agnes Smedley to James Henle, 12 June 1941, Eva Ginn Papers.
9. Agnes Smedley to Co Tui, 15 June 1941, American Bureau for Medical Aid to China (ABMAC) Papers.
10. Agnes Smedley, *Battle Hymn of China* (New York: Alfred A. Knopf, 1943), 516.
11. Ralph Bates, interview by FBI, 4 May 1950, FBI NY 100-68282.
12. Ibid.
13. Item 11ND 4454, 13 June 1941, Smedley File, Norman Allman Papers; FBI SD 100-1541; File 100/541/5, 1941, RG 46. Major General Ralph Van Deman, who directed Army Intelligence during World War I, gathered most of the data on Agnes in southern California. Between 1929 and 1952, as a private citizen, Van Deman collected and exchanged information on 125,000 allegedly subversive persons and organizations with Army and Naval Intelligence, the FBI, and Senator Joseph McCarthy. These files are now in the National Archives.
14. In the article "Guerrilla Doctors of Shensi," by Edgar Snow (*Friday* 2, no. 23 [11 July 1941]: 15–17), Agnes's photographs are credited to the China Aid Council. For more on the subject, see Smedley to Co Tui, 20 July 1941, and Smedley to Board of Directors, 6 August 1941, ABMAC Papers. Also in Smedley to Cowley, 24 July 1941, Malcolm Cowley Papers.
15. Smedley to Cowley, 24 July 1941.
16. Ibid.
17. Freda Utley, *Odyssey of a Liberal: Memoirs* (Washington, D.C.: Washington National Press, 1970), 208.
18. Lauchlin Currie to Eleanor Roosevelt, 3 September 1941, Eleanor Roosevelt Papers.
19. Smedley to Henle, 2 September 1941.

20. Agnes Smedley to Lewis Gannett, 24 November 1941, Lewis Gannett Papers.
21. Gannett to Smedley, 23 October 1941.
22. Smedley to Ginn, 17 December [1941].
23. Smedley to Gannett, 8 December 1941.
24. Smedley to Ginn, 17 December [1941].
25. Smedley to Gannett, 22 February 1942.
26. Gannett to Smedley, 29 January 1942; Bernard Smith to Agnes Smedley, 2 February 1942, Lewis Gannett Papers.
27. Smedley to Gannett, 14 February 1942.
28. Smedley to Gannett, 4 February [1942].
29. Jack Sanford to Agnes Smedley, 17 February 1942, Lewis Gannett Papers.
30. Smedley to Sanford, 22 February 1942.
31. Smedley to Gannett, 15 April [1942].
32. Smedley, *Battle Hymn*, 372–74.
33. "German Spy for Moscow in Japan Reported Held," *New York Times*, 25 May 1942.
34. Police Investigation, Richard Sorge, 11 March 1942, ID 923289, RG 319.
35. "Japan's Military Has Supreme Rule," *New York Times*, 27 August 1942.
36. Agnes Smedley to Aino Taylor, 20 November 1942, Agnes Smedley Papers.
37. Earl H. Leaf, "The Post Reviews Far East Books," review of *Battle Hymn*, by Agnes Smedley, *Shanghai Evening Post and Mercury*, 24 September 1943.
38. Smedley to Taylor, 20 November 1942.
39. Utley, *Odyssey of a Liberal*, 209.
40. Smedley to Taylor, 20 November 1942, 27 January, 1943.
41. Smedley to Aino and Elviira Taylor, 27 January 1943.
42. Joseph Freeman to Agnes Smedley, 15 May 1943, Joseph Freeman Papers.
43. Smedley to Freeman, 13 July [1943].
44. Ibid.
45. Smedley to Freeman, 5 July [1943].
46. Malcolm Cowley, interview by author, Sherman, Connecticut, 24 September 1987.
47. Karin Michaelis, *Little Troll* (New York: Creative Age, 1946), 276.
48. "Agnes Smedley Will Present Unvarnished Truth About China," *Skidmore News*, 29 September 1943.
49. Charles H. Nichols, ed., *Arna Bontemps–Langston Hughes Letters, 1925–1967* (New York: Dodd, Mead, 1980), 143–44.
50. Smedley to Roger [Baldwin] or Joseph Freeman, 17 July [1943], Joseph Freeman papers.
51. Agnes Smedley to Harold Ickes, 22 September 1949, Harold Ickes Papers.
52. File 383.4 Germany, IRR X7158573 (Agnes Smedley), RG 319.
53. See John Chamberlain, "Books of the Times," *New York Times*, 18 September 1943; Malcolm Cowley, "Tell Your Countrymen," *New Republic*, 13 September 1943; Freda Utley, "The Book Shelf—With the Embattled People of China," *Asia*, October 1943; Evans Fordyce Carlson, "She Lived the War with China's Red Fighters: The Passionate Story of a Courageous American," *New York Herald Tribune Weekly Book Review*, 5 September 1943; Mark Gayn, "Thirteen Years in China," *Saturday Review*, 18 September 1943.
54. [Unknown] to Angus [Cameron], 30 September 1943, Agnes Smedley papers.

55. Smedley, *Battle Hymn*, 473–74.
56. Ibid., 9.
57. Frederick V. Field, "China Fights On," *New Masses*, 30 November 1943, 24, 25.
58. Smedley, *Battle Hymn*, 10.
59. Agnes Smedley to Aino Taylor, Elviira Taylor, and John, 6 November 1943.
60. Harold Isaacs to the Editor, *Survey*, 20 March 1965, Philip Jaffe Papers.
61. Agnes Smedley, "A Play on China," Agnes Smedley Papers. Also see Smedley, *Battle Hymn*, 410–18.
62. Agnes Smedley to Miss Stevens, 25 December 1943, ABMAC Papers.
63. "Japan Condemns German: Sentences News Writer Richard Sorge as Spy," *New York Times*, 30 September 1943.
64. David Caute, *The Great Fear: The Anti-Communist Purge Under Truman and Eisenhower* (New York: Simon and Schuster, 1978), 310; Ross Y. Koen, *The China Lobby in American Politics* (New York: Octagon Books, 1974), 134–35.
65. Agnes Smedley to Katherine Anne Porter, 10 March [1945], Katherine Anne Porter Papers.
66. Suzi [Madame Sun Yat-sen] to Grace Granich, 20 February 1945, FBI NY 100-88434, courtesy of Tom Grunfeld.
67. Alfred Kohlberg, Letter to the Editor, *New York Herald Tribune*, 11 April 1945.
68. John Edgar Hoover to Albany, 25 October 1944, FBI AL 100-9125; FBI 61-6580-2.
69. FBI AL 100-9125.
70. During the German offensive in May 1940, Muenzenberg was interned and assigned to a work company attached to a French regiment near Lyon. The regiment fled Valence in early June to escape rapidly advancing German armies, but discipline disintegrated during the forced march. While soldiers and internees fled to safety, Muenzenberg left his companions to search for an auto that would take him to Gurs, where his companion was interned. He was later found hanging from a tree. For Agnes's contact with Bodo Uhse, Egon Erwin Kisch, Ludwig Renn, Anna Segher, and Paul Merker, see 19 June 1945 Report, FBI AL 100-9125.
71. Katherine Anne [Porter] to George and Toni [Willison], 14 May 1949, courtesy of Toni Willison.
72. Smedley to Aino Taylor, 27 February [1945]. Also see Agnes Smedley to Katherine Anne Porter, 10 March [1945].
73. Wang Yung to Miss Smedley, 22 June 1944, Agnes Smedley Papers; Smedley to Henle, 28 June [1944].
74. Agnes Smedley to Raymond Robins, 16 August 1945, Raymond Robins Papers.
75. Joseph Stilwell to Agnes Smedley, 21 July [1945], Edgar Snow Papers.

CHAPTER 17. THE COLD WAR

1. 28 January 1946 Report, File 100-16688; SAC Albany to John Edgar Hoover, 15 February 1946; E. E. Conroy to Director, FBI, 6 March 1946; A. Cornelius to Director, FBI, 3 April 1946. In FBI 61-6580.
2. FBI NY 100-68282; FBI WFO 100-17302.
3. Whittaker Chambers, interview by FBI, 10 May 1945, FBI 61-6580-103.
4. 19 December 1946 Report, File 100-9125, FBI 61-6580-30.
5. "Extracts from an Authenticated Translation of Foreign Affairs Yearbook, 1942,"

192, in U.S. Army, Far East Command, Military Intelligence Section, *A Partial Documentation of the Sorge Espionage Case* (Tokyo: Toppan Printing, 1950), ID 923289, RG 319.

6. Police Interrogation, Ozaki Hotsumi, March 1942, ID 923289, RG 319.

7. Chalmers Johnson, *An Instance of Treason: Ozaki Hotsumi and the Sorge Espionage Case* (Stanford: Stanford University Press, 1980), 201.

8. Agnes Smedley to Raymond Robins, 8 February 1946, Raymond Robins Papers. In February 1946, some of Ozaki's prison letters to his wife appeared in *Jinmin Hyoron* (*People's Review*).

9. The book, *Aijo Wa Furu Hoshi No Gotoku,* or *Love Is Like a Falling Star,* did contain Agnes's name and was a best seller in Japan, although it was not translated into English.

10. Smedley to Robins, 8 February 1946.

11. Smedley to Robins, 12 April 1946 (includes Agnes's account of her exchange with Peg Snow about her Quaker heritage).

12. Agnes Smedley, "We're Building a Fascist China," *Nation* 163, no. 9 (31 August 1946): 237.

13. Chu Teh to Agnes Smedley, 1 July 1946, Agnes Smedley Papers, Revolutionary Museum.

14. Smedley to [Robins], 21 December 1946.

15. Smedley to Robins, 13 February 1947.

16. Ibid.

17. Agnes Smedley to Edgar Snow, 7 June 1947, Edgar Snow Papers.

18. Snow to Agnes, 13 June 1947. Also see Smedley to Snow, 2 July 1947, and Smedley to Porter, 11 June 1947.

19. Agnes Smedley to Anna Wang Martens, 24 July 1947, Edgar Snow Papers.

20. Ayako Ishigaki, "Agnes Smedley as I Knew Her," Edgar Snow Papers; Agnes Smedley to Harold Ickes, 29 October 1949, Harold Ickes Papers; Toni Willison, interview by author, Ballston Spa, New York, August 1984.

21. 13 May 1947 Report, FBI 61-6580-31.

22. "Summary of Information: Smedley, Agnes," 19 September 1947, ID 923289, RG 319.

23. "Summary of Information: The Members of the Sorge Ring," 16 October 1947, ID 923289, RG 319.

24. C. A. Willoughby to Director of Intelligence, Intelligence Division, General Staff, U.S. Army, 17 October 1947, ID 923289, RG 319.

25. D. M. Ladd to the Director, 14 May 1951, FBI 61-6580-328.

26. This report, published in the 15 December 1947 CIS Periodical Summary, remains classified. An edited version, "The Sorge Spy Ring: A Case Study in International Espionage in the Far East," was released in February 1949.

27. Annotation 3, "Soviet American Spy Prodigies," in U.S. Army, Far East Command, Military Intelligence Section, *A Partial Documentation of the Sorge Espionage Case.*

28. Alfred Kohlberg, "More on the Spy Prodigies," *Plain Talk* 3, no. 6 (March 1949): 32.

29. Agnes Smedley to Katherine Anne Porter, 21 December 1947, Katherine Anne Porter Papers.

30. "How High Up Are Stalin's Spies in the U.S. Government?" *Counterattack*, 9 January 1948.
31. "Bare Details of Slickest Red Spy Ring," *Chicago Daily Tribune*, 2 January 1948.
32. Elizabeth Ames to Katherine Anne [Porter], 8 January 1948, Yaddo Papers.
33. FBI NY 100-68282
34. Ames to Smedley, 19 February 1948, Yaddo Papers.
35. Smedley to Ames, 20 February, 1948.
36. Porter to Willison, 6 April 1948, courtesy of Toni Willison.
37. Ibid.
38. Alfred Kohlberg, "Soviet-American Spy Prodigies," *Plain Talk* 2, no. 8 (May 1948): 17.
39. Ibid., 21.
40. Kohlberg, "More on the Spy Prodigies," 32.
41. 8 May 1948 Report, FBI 100-356062-2.
42. Memorandum for Chief of Staff, 1 February 1957, IRR X7158573 (Agnes Smedley)
43. Ibid.
44. Warren Cohen, "Domestic Factors Affecting U.S. Policy Toward Asia, 1947–1950 and 19711973," Harvard University Asia Center, Triangular Relations Conference, http://www.fas.harvard.edu/~asiactr/archive/TR_Cohen.htm.
45. Ibid.
46. For more, see Eric Goldman, *The Crucial Decade—And After: America, 1945–1960* (New York: Vintage, 1960); Lewis McCarroll Purify, *Harry Truman's China Policy: McCarthyism and the Diplomacy of Hysteria, 1947–1951* (New York: New Viewpoints, 1976).
47. Agnes Smedley to Friend, 20 January 1949, Ickes Papers.
48. National Military Establishment, Department of the Army, For Release 10 February 1949, FBI 100-124002.
49. 1 February 1957 Memo, IRR X7158573 (Agnes Smedley).
50. Ibid.
51. Marginalia, FBI 61-6580-73.
52. National Military Establishment, "The Sorge Spy Ring: A Case Study in International Espionage in the Far East," 81st Congress, 1st Session, vol. 95, pt. 12, *Appendix to the Congressional Record*, A705.
53. Ibid.
54. Ibid., A723.

CHAPTER 18. EXILE

1. "MacArthur Bares Spy Ring. Says It May be Active Here. New Exposé Names Two New York Writers," *Journal-American*, 10 February 1949.
2. Agnes Smedley to Toni Willison, 26 February [1949], courtesy of Toni Willison.
3. "Cool to Miss Smedley: MacArthur Right as Far as Uncle Is Concerned," *Kansas City Star*, 12 February 1949.
4. Edgar Snow to Maud [Russell], 28 April 1949, Edgar Snow Papers.
5. [Unsigned, Army Intelligence] to Jack Neal, 4 April 1949, IRR X7158573 (Agnes Smedley).

6. Edgar Snow to Ayako Ishigaki, 9 January 1967, Edgar Snow Papers.
7. Smedley to Willison, 26 February [1949]; Agnes Smedley to Raymond Robins, 8 February [1946], Raymond Robins Papers.
8. Edgar Snow, [n.d.], courtesy of Lois Snow.
9. Agnes Smedley, "Text of Statement," Edgar Snow Papers. Also available in Harold Ickes Papers.
10. "Tokyo War Secrets Stolen by Soviet Spy Ring in 1941: Agents Led by Pseudo-Nazi Obtained Data Permitting Use of Troops in Siberia to Defend Moscow—2 Here Deny Role," New York Times, 11 February 1949.
11. "A Puzzling Report," New York Post, 11 February 1949.
12. Agnes Smedley to Harold Ickes, 6 March 1949, Harold Ickes Papers.
13. Edgar Snow, "General MacArthur's Fantasy: The Great 'Tokyo Spy Plot,' " Nation 168, no. 9 (19 February 1949): 202.
14. Agnes Smedley to President Harry Truman, 11 February 1949, Raymond Robins Papers.
15. Agnes Smedley to Friend, 19 December 1934, 800.00B, Smedley, Agnes/32, RG 59.
16. Smedley to Willison, 26 February 1949.
17. "Army Withholds Spy Data Backing: Declines to Give Its Support for All Charges Contained in Sorge Case Report," New York Times, 12 February 1949.
18. Marginalia, FBI 61-6580-73.
19. T. W. Hammond to Brigadier General V. T. Prichard, 12 February 1949, IRR X7158573 (Agnes Smedley) .
20. DA(CSGID) to CINCFE, 13 February 1949, IRR X7158573 (Agnes Smedley).
21. Smedley to Willison, 26 February [1949].
22. Agnes Smedley to Editor, New York Herald Tribune, 14 February 1949.
23. Colonel Bratton to General Willoughby, 15 February 1949, IRR X7158573 (Agnes Smedley).
24. "U.S. Army Embarrassed by Release of Spy Report," New York Times, 16 February 1949.
25. "Army Admits Spy Faux Pas; No Proof on Agnes Smedley," New York Times, 19 February 1949.
26. " 'Faux Pas' Inquiry on Spies Demanded: Two Ask Congress to Sift How the Army Accused Author Without Having Proof," New York Times, 20 February 1949.
27. Smedley to Willison, 26 February [1949].
28. Harvey Breit, John Cheever, Eleanor Clark, Alfred Kazin, and Kappo Phelan to Langston Hughes, 21 March 1949, Langston Hughes Papers; Ian Hamilton, Robert Lowell: A Biography (New York: Random House, 1982), 144–45.
29. Katherine Anne Porter to George and Toni Willison, 14 April 1949, Katherine Anne Porter Papers.
30. Porter to the Willisons, 14 May 1949.
31. Agnes Smedley to Chu Teh, [fall 1949], Agnes Smedley Papers, Revolutionary Museum.
32. General Willoughby to Colonel Bratton and General Dager, 7 March 1949, IRR X7158573 (Agnes Smedley).
33. Police Interrogation, Kawai Teikichi, 31 March and 1 April 1949, ID 923289, RG 319.
34. Smedley to Ickes, 6 September 1949.

35. Agnes Smedley to Mildred Price-Coy, December 1949, courtesy of Lois Snow.
36. Smedley to Ickes, 6 September 1949; Caute, *The Great Fear*, 246.
37. Ickes to Stephen Early, 19 October 1949; Smedley to Ickes, 30 September 1949.
38. Smedley to Ickes, 20 October 1949.
39. Jiang Feng, interview by author, Beijing, 15 June 1988; Chen Hansheng [Hanseng], "We Owe Them a Great Debt," in *Salute to Smedley, Strong and Snow* (Beijing: Three S Research Association, 1988), 119.
40. Smedley to Ickes, 6 September 1949.
41. 1 February 1957 Memo, IRR X7158573 (Agnes Smedley).
42. Smedley to Dearest Dears, 9 January 1950, courtesy of Lois Snow.
43. Hilda Selwyn-Clarke to Josephine Bennett Brooks, Mildred Price-Coy, and Edgar Snow, 9 May 1950, courtesy of Lois Snow.
44. Charles A. Willoughby to Brigadier General Bonner Fellers, 23 November 1949, Bonner Fellers Papers.
45. Charles A. Willoughby to Honorable W. E. Woods, 1 May 1950, ID 923289, RG 319.
46. Willoughby to Fellers, 23 November 1949.
47. Richard Sorge," Agnes Smedley and Gunther Stein," *Plain Talk* 4, no. 3 (December, 1949): 41–43.
48. Benjamin Mandel to Alfred Kohlberg, 2 December 1949, Alfred Kohlberg Papers.
49. Agnes Smedley to Edgar and Lois Snow 25 January, 1950; Agnes Smedley to Josephine Bennett Brooks, 27 January 1950, courtesy of Lois Snow.
50. Smedley to Snows, 25 January 1950, courtesy of Lois Snow.
51. Hu Chi-an, interview by author, Beijing, 18 June 1988; Rewi Alley, *Six Americans in China* (Beijing: International Culture, 1985), 164; Smedley to Snow, 30 November 1949; Smedley to Snows, 25 January 1950.
52. Smedley to Snows, 25 January 1950.
53. Charles A. Willoughby, "Preface: The Sorge Spy Ring, A Case Study in International Espionage in the Far East," footnote 24; G-2 Comment, Consecutive Exhibit #3, Documentary Appendices; both in U.S. Army, Far East Command, Military Intelligence Section, *A Partial Documentation of the Sorge Espionage Case* (Tokyo: Toppan Printing, 1950), ID 923289, RG 319.
54. William R. Grove Jr. to Director of Intelligence, General Staff, Department of the Army, 6 March 1950, ID 923289, RG 319; Frank S. Tavenner Jr. to General Willoughby, 20 February 1950, Charles A. Willoughby Papers, Hoover Institution.
55. Edgar Snow to Martin Sommers, 5 April 1950, Edgar Snow Papers.
56. Louis Budenz, interview by FBI, 25 and 28 April 1950, FBI 61-6580-205.
57. Elizabeth Bentley, interview by FBI, 25 April 1950, FBI NY 100-68282.
58. "The Kremlin: 1964 Confirms Accuracy of MacArthur's Intelligence: 1950," *Foreign Intelligence Digest*, September 1965.
59. "Miss Smedley Was Frightened," *London Daily Mail*, 16 June 1950.
60. Hilda [Selwyn-Clarke] to Josephine Bennett Brooks, Mildred Price-Coy and Edgar Snow, 9 May 1950, courtesy of Lois Snow; Gerd Alfred Petermann, afterword, in Agnes Smedley, *China Kämpft: Vom Werden des Neuen China* (Berlin: Oberbaumverlag, 1978).

61. Selwyn-Clarke to Bennett-Brooks and Snows, 9 May 1950.
62. Agnes Smedley to Margaret Watson Sloss, 28 April 1950, courtesy of Lois Snow.

EPILOGUE

1. Duncan J. Sloss to Consul General for U.S., 7 May 1950, FBI 61-6580-295; American Foreign Service Report of Death of American Citizen, 14 June 1950, State Department Passport (130) File, Smedley, Agnes; Medical Report on the Late Miss Agnes Smedley, 30 May 1950, courtesy of Lois Snow.
2. *New China News Agency*, 15 May 1950; "Loss of a Friend," *China Weekly Review*, 20 May 1950.
3. Ruth Werner, *Sonjas Rapport* (Berlin: Verlag Neues Leben, 1977), 137.
4. Edgar Snow to Harold Ickes, 12 May 1950, courtesy of Lois Snow.
5. Edgar Snow to Hilda Selwyn-Clarke, 22 May 1950, courtesy of Lois Snow; *New China News Agency*, 15 May 1950.
6. Edgar Snow, "Remarks," Agnes Smedley Papers.
7. Katherine Anne Porter to Toni Willison, 15 November 1950, Katherine Anne Porter Papers.
8. Snow to Selwyn-Clarke, 22 May 1950.
9. J. Woodall Greene to Brigadier General Bonner Fellers, 1 May 1950, Bonner Fellers Papers.
10. Charles A. Willoughby to Alfred Kohlberg, 16 May 1950, Charles A. Willoughby Papers, MacArthur Archives (also available in Senate Internal Security Subcommittee Files, Institute of Pacific Relations Investigation, RG 46); Greene to Fellers, 22 May 1950.
11. "Probe Woman Author's Death," *London Daily Express*, 13 June 1950.
12. Porter to Willison, 15 November 1950.
13. Harold Ickes to Mary Knoblauch, 24 July 1950; Harold Ickes to Katherine Dreier, 26 July 1950; Harold Ickes to the Editor, *Newsweek*, 13 July 1950, Harold Ickes Papers.
14. Charles A. Willoughby to Alfred Kohlberg, 27 December 1950, Willoughby Papers, MacArthur Archives.
15. Willoughby to Kohlberg, 28 January 1951, Willoughby Papers, MacArthur Archives.
16. Benjamin Mandel to Alfred Kohlberg, 24 February 1951, Alfred Kohlberg Papers.
17. "Washington Report," *Washington Times Herald*, 11 May 1951.
18. Rewi Alley, "Memorial Speech," courtesy of Tom Grunfeld.
19. Yang Kang, "Agnes Smedley, Friend of the Chinese People," *People's China* 3, no. 10 (16 May 1951): 13–14.
20. Ting Ling, "Agnes Smedley," *Masses and Mainstream* 4, no. 8 (August 1951): 85.
21. *Kuang Ming Daily*, 6 May 1951.
22. John King Fairbank, *Chinabound: A Fifty-Year Memory* (New York: Harper and Row, 1982), 436.
23. Kenneth Shewmaker, *Americans and Chinese Communists, 1927–1945: A Persuading Encounter* (Ithaca: Cornell University Press, 1971), 282.
24. Press Release, American China Policy Association, 28 May 1951; Kohlberg to Senator Wayne Morse, 11 June 1951, Alfred Kohlberg Papers.

25. See Freda Utley, *The China Story* (Chicago: Henry Regnery, 1951).

26. Robert Morris to Eva Adams, 21 January 1952; Frank Shroeder to Richard Arens, 21 July 1952, Louis Gibarti File, RG 46.

27. Confidential Informant T-1 [Gibarti], 11 May 1951, FBI NY 100-68282. FBI documents refer to the League Against Imperialism as the "Anti-Imperialist League."

28. Ibid.

29. Deposition, Louis Gibarti, 28 August 1951, Gibarti File, RG 46.

30. Although the State Department refused to formally identify the titles or authors of the burned books, Agnes's name appeared on the first list the agency released of Americans whose books had been banned at USIA libraries abroad. For more, see Robert L. Johnson to Donald B. Lourie, 15 July 1952, State Department Decimal File 511.0021/7-1553, RG 59. Also see "Replies Refused by Dr. Weltfish: Miss Utley, Ex-Red, Testifies U.S. Libraries Abroad Had 'Shocking' Communist Books," *New York Times*, 2 April 1953; "Books of 40 Authors Banned by U.S. in Overseas Libraries," *New York Times*, 22 June 1953; "State Department Denounces Book Burnings as 'Wicked Act,' " *New York Times*, 9 July 1953.

31. Marge Piercy, "Reconsideration of Agnes Smedley: Dirt Poor Daughter of Earth," *New Republic* 171, no. 24 (14 December 1974): 19.

32. Li Ling, "Agnes Smedley: An American Who Loved China," *China Reconstructs* 29, no. 5 (May 1980): 18–21.

33. "Tribute to U.S. Writer," *China Daily*, 8 May 1985.

34. Gerd Alfred Petermann, afterword, in Agnes Smedley, *China Kampft: Vom Werden des Neuen China* (Berlin: Oberbaumverlag, 1978).

35. David Duke, "Spy Scares, Scapegoats, and the Cold War," *South Atlantic Quarterly* 79, no. 3 (1980): 245–56.

36. Janice MacKinnon and Stephen MacKinnon, *Agnes Smedley: The Life and Times of an American Radical* (Berkeley: University of California Press, 1988).

37. "Smedley: Life and Times of An American Radical," *China Daily*, 31 March 1989.

38. Orville Schell, review of *Agnes Smedley: Life and Times of An American Radical*, by Stephen and Janice MacKinnon, *Nation* 245, no. 21, (19 December 1987): 762.

39. Chapman Pincher, *Too Secret Too Long* (New York: St. Martin's Press, 1984); Peter Wright, *SpyCatcher: The Candid Autobiography of a Senior Intelligence Officer* (New York: Viking, 1987). Contending that such insider information would not only damage national security but cost Great Britain the confidence of other intelligence services, the government of Great Britain banned the latter from publication there. In 1991, John Cairncross, a former British intelligence agent, acknowledged being the "fifth man" in the ring.

40. Snow, "Mō Taku-tō no renai" (Mao's Love Affair: The Women of Yenan and Agnes Smedley), *Chou Koron* 69, no. 7 (July 1954), tr. courtesy of Robert Farnsworth.

INDEX

DATE DUE

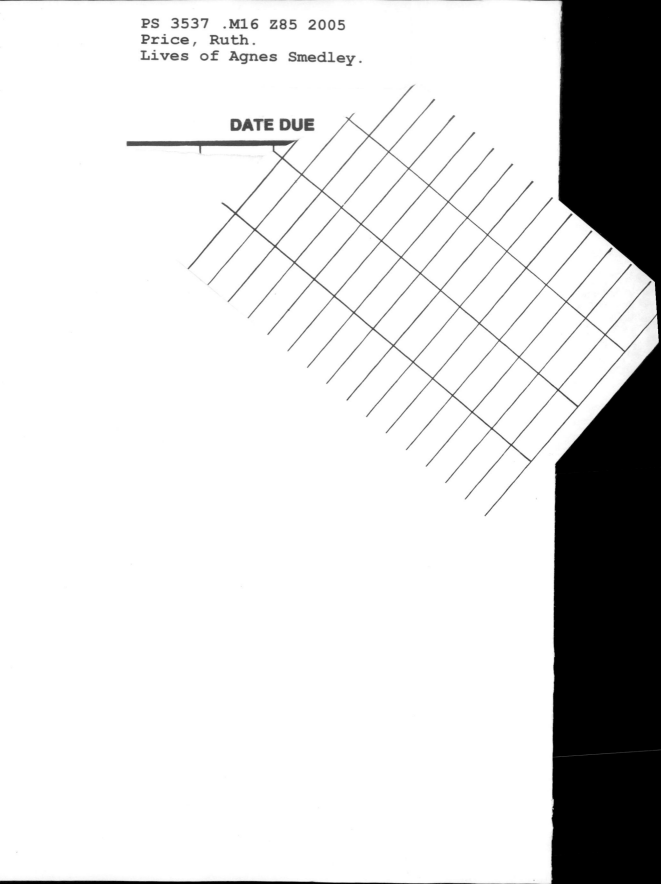

DATE D

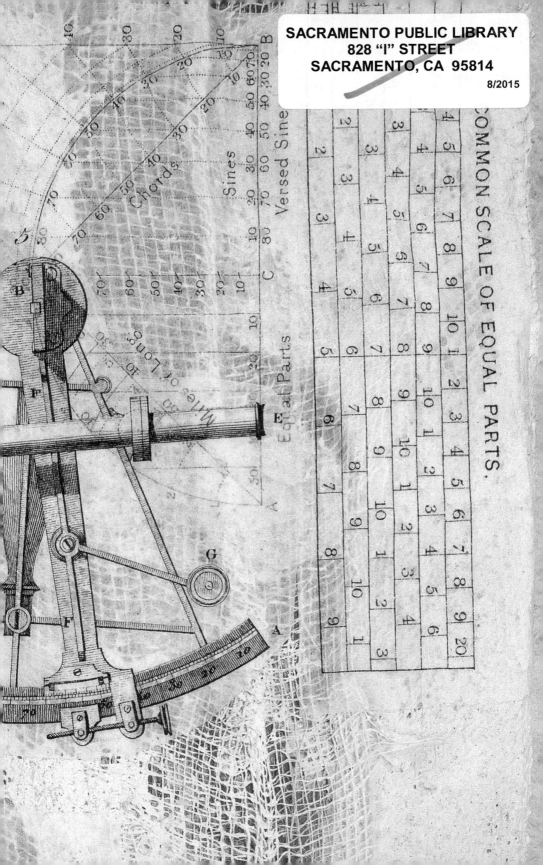